DECISION THEORY WITH IMPERFECT INFORMATION

DECISION THEORY WITH IMPERFECT INFORMATION

Rafik A Aliev
Oleg H Huseynov
Azerbaijan State Oil Academy, Azerbaijan

World Scientific
NEW JERSEY • LONDON • SINGAPORE • BEIJING • SHANGHAI • HONG KONG • TAIPEI • CHENNAI

Published by

World Scientific Publishing Co. Pte. Ltd.
5 Toh Tuck Link, Singapore 596224
USA office: 27 Warren Street, Suite 401-402, Hackensack, NJ 07601
UK office: 57 Shelton Street, Covent Garden, London WC2H 9HE

Library of Congress Cataloging-in-Publication Data
Aliev, R. A. (Rafik Aziz ogly), author.
Decision theory with imperfect information / Rafik A. Aliev & Oleg H. Huseynov (Azerbaijan State Oil Academy, Azerbaijan).
pages cm
Includes bibliographical references and index.
ISBN 978-9814611039 (hardcover : alk. paper)
1. Fuzzy decision making. 2. Decision making--Mathematical models. I. Huseynov, Oleg H., author. II. Title.
QA279.6.A45 2014
003'.56--dc23

2014022702

British Library Cataloguing-in-Publication Data
A catalogue record for this book is available from the British Library.

Printed in Singapore

Dedication

Dedicated to the memory of my wife Aida Alieva

RAFIK ALIEV

To my parents and grandparents

OLEG HUSEYNOV

Foreword

Professor Aliev's magnum opus, Decision Theory with Imperfect Information (with a Foreword by Prof. Lotfi Zadeh), or DTII for short, is a path-breaking contribution to a better understanding of how to make decisions in an environment of imperfect information—information which is uncertain, imprecise, incomplete or partially true. In real-world settings, such information is the norm rather than exception. Professor Aliev's work builds on existing theories of decision-making, but leaves them far behind.

Decision theory as we know it today, is rooted in the pioneering work of von Neumann and Morgenstern, Theory of Games and Economic Behavior, 1944. von Neumann and Morgenstern's brilliant work spawned a huge literature. A notable development in the evolution of decision theory was the development of Prospect Theory by Kahneman and Tversky in 1979—a theory for which they were awarded the Nobel Prize in economics in 2002.Prospect theory was an important step in the direction of enhancing the capability of decision theory to deal with real-world problems. Professor Aliev's magnum opus contains a very insightful and very detailed critical analysis of existing theories of decision-making. Existing theories contain much that is deep, rigorous and elegant. However, there is a basic problem. Existing theories are based on the classical, Aristotelian, bivalent logic. Bivalent logic is intolerant of imprecision and partiality of truth. Fundamentally, bivalent logic is not the right logic to deal with the pervasive imprecision of the real world. Professor Aliev's work shifts the foundation of decision theory from bivalent logic to fuzzy logic. Informally, fuzzy logic is a system of reasoning and computation in which the objects of reasoning and computation are classes with unsharp (fuzzy) boundaries. In the real world, such classes are the norm rather than exception. It is important to note that almost all words in a natural language are labels of classes with unsharp boundaries. Examples. Tall, cheap, fast, usually, most, likely, etc. Representation of the meaning of such words as probability distributions, is not effective. In the realm of decision theory, what is of particular importance is representation of imprecise probabilities and imprecise rewards as fuzzy probabilities and fuzzy rewards, respectively. In Professor Aliev's work these and other concepts are allowed to be described in a natural language. One of the major contributions of Professor Aliev's work is the development of a conceptual framework for decision-making and computation with information which is described in a natural language.

A concept which plays an important role in computation with natural language is that of precisiation of meaning. Informally, if p is a proposition drawn from a natural language, then its meaning is precisiated by representing it in a mathematically well-defined form. More concretely, p may be viewed as a carrier of information about a variable, X, which in general is implicit in p. Information about X may be viewed as a restriction on the values which X is allowed to take. There are many kinds of restrictions. Principally, restrictions are possibilistic, probabilistic and bimodal. A bimodal restriction is a mixture of possibilistic and probabilistic restrictions. Example. It is likely that X is small, is a bimodal restriction. In large measure, a natural language is predominantly a collection of possibilistic and bimodal restrictions. This is why the concept of a restriction plays an important role in Professor Aliev's work.

In existing theories of decision-making and economic behavior, imperfect information is dealt with through the use of probability theory—and only probability theory. The conventional wisdom is that probability theory is all that is needed to deal with any kind of uncertainty. This is the core of the Bayesian doctrine. The insufficienists, including Professor Aliev and myself, do not share this view. More concretely, there are three principal types of uncertainty. Type 1 uncertainty relates to randomness. Type 2 uncertainty relates to incompleteness of information. Type 3 uncertainty relates to unsharpness (fuzziness) of class boundaries. Probability theory is rooted in uncertainty of Type 1.However, over the years, probability theory moved in the direction of enlarging its domain to accommodate uncertainty of Type 2. Bayesianism is a manifestation of this move. A controversial issue is: Is probability theory the right theory to deal with uncertainty of Type 3? My position is: No, it is not. What is needed for dealing with uncertainty of Type 3 is fuzzy logic and its important constituent, possibility theory. Probability theory and possibility theory are distinct theories with distinct agendas.

Fuzzy logic plays a minor role in existing theories of decision-making and economic behavior. In sharp contrast, fuzzy logic plays a pivotal role in DTII.

To understand Professor Aliev's work, familiarity with fuzzy logic is a necessity. DTII includes a very readable and authoritative exposition of fuzzy logic. What is very impressive is that in DTII what is employed is not merely the basic machinery of fuzzy logic, but the most advanced concepts and techniques. Specifically, one finds in DTII applications of extended fuzzy logic, fuzzy geometry and the calculus of Z-numbers. A Z-number is expressed as (value of a variable, certainty of value). Typically, the components of a Z-number are described in natural language. Example. (High reward, likely). What is important about Z-numbers is that in real-world settings much of uncertainty involves variables whose values are Z-numbers.

Professor Aliev's work brims with new concepts, new methods and new ideas. For me, it is hard to find adequate words to describe the fundamental importance of the theory which Professor Aliev has constructed—a theory which is likely to find wide-ranging applications in real-world settings. Professor Aliev's preface speaks for itself.

Professor Aliev and his publisher, World Scientific Publisher, deserve a very loud applause for producing a path-breaking volume which opens the door to profound changes in the methodology of decision theory and modeling of economic behavior. Professor Aliev's magnum opus is not easy reading. It deserves careful study and analysis. Understanding of the deep theory which Professor Aliev has developed requires a significant expenditure of time and effort—an expenditure which is justified by the wealth, importance and originality of Professor Aliev's ideas.

Lotfi A. Zadeh
Berkeley, CA
February 20, 2014

Preface

Decision making is one of the key parts of human activity. It is especially important for human-centric systems, in particular, economic, political, military and other systems. There exist a large spectrum of theories of decision making starting from von Neumann-Morgenstern Expected Utility up to multiple priors-based theories and Prospect theory. The most famous and main representatives of this spectrum are von Neumann-Morgenstern Expected Utility, Savage's subjective Expected Utility, Maximin Expected utility, Choquet Expected Utility, Prospect theory. These theories yielded good results. However, they are created to deal with precise, perfectly known decision-relevant information which is intrinsic for thought experiments and laboratory examples. In contrast, every day decision making and decision making in complex human-centric systems are characterized by imperfect decision-relevant information. Imperfect information, as Prof. Lotfi Zadeh states, is information which in one or more respects is imprecise, uncertain, incomplete, unreliable, vague or partially true. Main sources of imperfect information is uncertainty of future, impossibility to exactly predict values of the variables of interest and ambiguity related to mental condition of a decision maker (DM) as a principal mental condition inspired by behavioral determinants. Due to this, preferences of a DM in the real world are vague. The principal problems with the existing decision theories consist in that they do not have capability to deal with situations in which probabilities and events are imprecise as they are in the most of realistic settings. As a result, the existing theories employ unrealistic decision models. More concretely, these methods are developed to deal with precise (numerical) probabilities or a crisp set of probability distributions, ideal description of states of nature, precise outcomes and perfect, that is, binary logic-based formulation of preferences. In the present decision theories a small transition to dealing with imprecise, non-numerical information takes place. Mainly, this transition is only related to information on probabilities and is represented by the use of non-additive measures, sets of probability distributions, second-order probabilities. Transition to imprecise probabilities is a form of generalization as a coercive measure to provide the decision theories an ability of modeling experimentally observed evidence of humans' decision making. However, this generalization is, in our opinion, not sufficient. We need new theory with imperfect information described in natural language (NL) on all the elements of a decision problem. This is often the only information with which people reason in real-world decision problems. Being not developed for dealing with such information, the existing methods are not adequate to apply to real world decision problems. Development of such a theory is now possible as we are in possession over vast resources of new mathematical concepts (as fuzzy logic, Z-restriction), methods and theories for addressing problems and issues in economics, decision making and related fields.

Humans have outstanding ability to make proper decisions under imperfect information. A new decision theory should to some extent model this outstanding ability of humans. This means that the language of a new decision theory falls within the class of fuzzy mathematics and computation with NL-based information, but not within the class of concepts and techniques drawn from traditional mathematics including probability theory. Enlargement of a role of NL in decision analysis is a generalization which helps constructing models which are more flexible to deal with imperfect information and, as a result, allow yielding more realistic (not more exact!) results and conclusions. This opens doors to modeling phenomena of decision making which are impossible to analyze by using the existing approaches. For example, experimental evidence show that parametrical modeling of a DM's behavior, on which such a famous behavioral decision theory as Cumulative Prospect theory is based, often cannot describe human choices. From the other side, as we can observe in real life, NL is often used as an intuitive description of a rather complicated behavior.

Operating over NL-described information requires formal representation of meaning of words. The only theory developed for mathematical description of linguistic information is the fuzzy set theory. Recently, we conducted research with University of California at Berkeley (USA), Berkeley Initiative in Soft Computing, under a leadership of Prof. L. Zadeh on a new theory of decision making with imperfect information. The theory allows to model vague preferences naturally arising in real decision activity.

A lot of books were published in the realm of decision making under uncertainty, but they are mainly devoted to multicriteria decision problems. Up to day there is no book in the realm of decision making that embraces a decision problem under vague preferences, imprecise probabilities, not purely defined states of nature, and imperfectly described behavior of a DM. In the theory suggested in this book we tried to sufficiently overcome this gap between real-world decisions and their formal analysis.

The book is organized into 12 chapters. The first chapter is devoted to an explanation of the main existing decision theories, their underlying motivations and features. A common description of a decision making problem including alternatives, states of nature, outcomes and preferences is explained. The key decision theories based on the use of utility function and the relations between these theories are explained. Disadvantages of these theories which consist in incapability to deal with imperfect relevant information are widely discussed.

For the present book to be self-containing, foundations of fuzzy sets theory, fuzzy logic and fuzzy mathematics which are used as the formal basis of the suggested decision theory with imperfect information are given in Chapter 2. We would like to mention that this chapter contains a material on a spectrum of computations with uncertain and imprecise information including the basics of interval arithmetic, fuzzy arithmetic, operations over type-2 fuzzy sets, and, for the first time, the foundations of the arithmetic of discrete Z-numbers. The suggested arithmetic of discrete Z-numbers includes basic arithmetic operations as addition, standard subtraction, multiplication, standard division, determination of Hukuhara difference, algebraic operations as the square and the square root of a Z-number, and comparison of Z-numbers.

Motivating examples and the existing approaches for modeling uncertain (vague) preferences including fuzzy preference relations, linguistic preference relations, probabilistic approaches to modeling uncertain preferences, and incomplete preferences are explained in Chapter 3. Chapter 4 provides motivation to deal with imperfect information. Various kinds of imperfect information as naturally present in real-world problems are discussed and a need to use the fuzzy set theory for modeling imperfect information is grounded.

Chapter 5 provides a comparative analysis of the existing numerical measures of uncertainty including probability measures and non-additive measures and motivation to use fuzzy-valued measures in decision analysis.

In Chapter 6 we suggest a generalized theory of decision making with NL-based information on the base of the use of formalisms of type-1 and type-2 fuzzy sets. The main part of the theory is based on a fuzzy utility function describing vague preferences under a mix of fuzzy and probabilistic uncertainties. For the first time we provide representation theorems on the fuzzy utility function described as a fuzzy Choquet integral with fuzzy-valued integrand and fuzzy-valued fuzzy measure. Further we provide an introduction to the basics of type-2 fuzzy decision modeling as a more adequate formalism to deal with high imprecision and vagueness of real decision-relevant information.

Decision making under imperfect information on the base of hierarchical models is a subject of Chapter 7. We consider fuzzy decision making in a two-level multi-agent system and decision making on the base of a two-level interval probability model for an individual decision making under ambiguity.

Chapter 8 deals with a theory of decision making under imperfect information without utility function. The motivation of the suggested theory is that humans often try to conduct direct comparison of alternatives as vectors of attributes' values. Basic scientific concept underlying such comparison is the Pareto optimal set based on a counterintuitive assumption that all alternatives are considered equally optimal. In this chapter we suggest a Fuzzy Pareto optimality based approach to decision making with linguistic information. As compared to the existing approaches, the suggested approach has fundamental capability of a direct comparison of NL-described alternatives by using linguistic preference degrees. The latter are obtained by soft constraining of a Pareto optimal set of alternatives on the base of their degrees of optimality.

A new approach to behavioral decision analysis under imperfect information is suggested in Chapter 9. For modeling a human behavior we introduce a concept of *a state of a DM* as a principal mental condition conditioned by behavioral determinants. The basis of decision analysis in the suggested approach is a Cartesian product of states of nature and states of DM. This allows considering objective and subjective conditions of decisions at the same fundamental level. The element of the considered Cartesian product is entitled *a combined state* as a pair of state of nature and a state of a DM. As human behavior naturally depends on objective conditions, each combined state is assigned a joint linguistic probability measuring imprecise estimation of this dependence. In contrast to the basics of the existing behavioral decision theories, this allows for a more fundamental and transparent analysis of behavioral decision making. In order to more adequately describe uncertain relationships between a mental condition of an economic agent (state of a DM) and his behavioral determinants, two approaches based on fuzzy and Dempster-Shafer theories are considered.

Chapter 10 is devoted to decision making when relevant information is too vague to be precisiated (described) by fuzzy sets but stays at a level of image perceptions. Modeling of outstanding capability of humans to make decisions based on unprecisiated visual perceptions is a motivation of the research suggested in this chapter. Unprecisiated visual images are considered as information granules described by 2D convex sets. The length of a set is measured along the first dimension and represents an imprecision of perception-based information on a value of interest considered. The variable width of the set is measured along the second dimension and represents a distribution of truth degrees along the imprecise value. Additionally, the third dimension expressed by color shading along the second dimension to represent an imprecise truth degree can be used. These information granules are considered as geometric primitives for dealing with which new fuzzy geometry and the extended fuzzy logic suggested by Zadeh are used. An approach to decision making with outcomes and probabilities described by geometrical primitives is developed on the base of reasoning with fuzzy geometrical IF-THEN rules.

Chapter 11 is devoted to a new general theory of decisions. This theory implements Prof. L. Zadeh's idea to develop of a general theory of decision making. Prof. L. Zadeh mentions that real problems in economics and other humanistic fields are characterized by imprecise and partially reliable information on probabilities, events, gains, losses and behavioral determinants. The suggested general theory of decisions is based on a formalism of Z-restrictions suggested by L. Zadeh as the most adequate framework to capture and process imprecise and partially reliable information described in NL. The second main advantage of the theory is joint consideration of objective and subjective conditions of decisions which was proposed in Chapter 9 and is further developed in this chapter. These two main aspects bring the suggested theory on a principally new level of decision analysis beyond the existing achievements. The theory uses a unified decision model based on a utility function represented as a Z-valued Choquet like integration with respect to bi-capacity. The use of bi-capacity allows to more adequately model interaction of gains and losses under imperfect information. We show that the existing decision theories including Expected Utility, Choquet Expected Utility and Prospect Theory are special cases of the suggested general theory of decisions.

Chapter 12 presents applications of the suggested theory to benchmark and real-world decision problems with imperfect information in economics, business, production, medicine and other areas. The obtained results prove validity of the suggested theory.

We consider that the main contribution of this book is to shift the foundation of decision analysis and economic behavior from the realm bivalent logic to the realm fuzzy logic and Z-restriction, from external modeling of behavioral decisions to the framework of combined states. These two principles allowed to create a new general theory of decisions. This book is intended for researchers and practitioners and will be useful for anyone who is interested in solving real-world decision problems with imperfect information. The reason is that the book is self containing and includes detailed advices of application of the suggested theory. At the same time, it represents in a systematic way the suggested decision theory with imperfect information into the educational systems. The book will be helpful for teachers and students of universities and colleges, for managers and specialists from various fields of business and economics, production and social sphere.

We would like to express our thanks to Professor Lotfi Zadeh, the founder of the fuzzy set and Soft Computing theories and a creator of the idea to develop a general decision making theory, for his permanent support, invaluable ideas and advices for our research.

R.A. Aliev
O.H. Huseynov

Contents

Chapter 1

Theories of Decision Making under Uncertainty

1.1 What is Decision Making? A General Framework of a Decision Making Problem

What is decision making? We permanently make decisions in our life–we decide what to have for a dinner, what university to go to, what job to choose, how to develop business etc. When deciding what university to enter, we consider the universities available in a scope of our future profession. When deciding how to develop our business we may consider whether to extend it, improve quality, or open a new direction. In its sense, decision making implies making a choice among appropriate alternatives. Some decisions, which are to be done in simple or quite familiar situations, can be made simply on the base of intuitive judgments. However, in general, making choices encounters the fact that the result of our choice depends on objective conditions of future, which are uncertain and out of our control. This means that making sound decisions requires to consistently take into account influence of various factors under uncertainty. Such analysis is not compatible with highly constrained computational ability of a human brain. Thus, decision making needs to be based on the use of mathematical methods as a strong language of reasoning. This requires at first to formally define the problem of decision making. Depending on the decision relevant information on future, various routine decision making problems are used. However, all kinds of decision making problems have a common stem which is represented by the main elements of any decision making problem.

The first element is a set $\mathcal{A}$ of alternatives (sometimes called alternative actions, actions, acts, strategies etc) to choose from:

$$\mathcal{A} = \{f_1,...,f_n\}, n \geq 2$$

where $n \geq 2$ means that decision making may take place when at least two alternatives exist. In the problem of business development, f_1 may denote "to extend business", f_2 – "to improve quality of services", f_3 – "to open a new direction".

The next element of decision making problem is used to model objective conditions on which the results of any alternative action depend. This element is called *a set of states of nature*: $\mathcal{S} = \{S_1,...,S_m\}$. A state of nature S_i is one possible objective condition. $\mathcal{S}$ is considered as a "*a space of **mutually exclusive** and **exhaustive** states*", according to a formulation suggested by L. Savage [360]. This means that all the possible objective conditions (possible conditions of future) are known and only one of them S_i, $i = 1,...,m$ will take place. The main problem is that it is not known for sure, which S_i will take place. For example, in the problem of business development, the set of states of nature may be considered as $\mathcal{S} = \{S_1, S_2, S_3, S_4\}$, where S_1 denotes "high demand and low competition", S_2–"high demand and medium competition" S_3 – "medium demand and low competition", S_4 – "medium demand and high competition".

The set $\mathcal{S}$ may also be infinite. For example, when considering inflation rate, $\mathcal{S}$ can be used as a continuous range.

The third element is results of actions in various states of nature. These results are called outcomes or consequences. Any action result in an outcome (lead to some consequence) in any state of nature. For example, if someone extends his business and high demand occurs then the profit will be high. If a low demand occurs, then extension results in a low profit, or even, in a loss. The outcomes may be of any type – quantitative or qualitative, monetary or non-monetary. A set of outcomes is commonly denoted $\mathcal{X}$. As an outcome $X \in \mathcal{X}$ is a result of an action f taken at a state of nature S, it is formalized as $X = f(S)$. So, an action f is formally a function whose domain is a set of states of nature $\mathcal{S}$ and the range is the set of outcomes $\mathcal{X}$: $f:\mathcal{S}\to\mathcal{X}$. In order to formally compare actions $f\in\mathcal{A}$, it is needed to formally measure all their outcomes $X\in\mathcal{X}$, especially when the latter are qualitative. For this purpose a numeric function $u:\mathcal{X}\to R$ is used to measure an outcome $X\in\mathcal{X}$ in terms of its *utility* for a decision maker (DM). Utility $u(X)$ of an outcome $X\in\mathcal{X}$ represents to what extent $X\in\mathcal{X}$ is good, useful, or desirable for a DM. $u:\mathcal{X}\to R$ is used to take into account various factors like reputation, health, mentality, psychology[266] and others.

The fourth component is preferences of a DM. Given a set of alternatives $\mathcal{A}$, the fact that a DM prefers an alternative $f\in\mathcal{A}$ to an alternative $g\in\mathcal{A}$ is denoted $f\succ g$. Indifference among f and g is denoted $f\sim g$. The fact that f is at least as good as g is denoted $f\succsim g$. Preferences are described as a binary relation $\succsim\in\mathcal{A}\times\mathcal{A}$.

In general, a decision making problem is formulated as follows:

Given

the set of alternatives $\mathcal{A}$,

the set of states of nature $\mathcal{S}$,

the set of outcomes $\mathcal{X}$

Determine an action $f^*\in\mathcal{A}$ such that $f^*\succsim f$ for all $f\in\mathcal{A}$.

In some models they formulate decision problem in a framework of outcomes and their probabilities only and don't use such concept as a set of states of nature. In this framework an alternative is described as a collection of its outcomes with the associated probabilities and is termed as lottery: $f=(X_1,P_1;...;X_n,P_n)$.

The main issue here is to impose some reasonable assumptions on properties of DM's preferences. The latter critically depend on a type and an amount of information on $\mathcal{S}$. Several typical cases exist with respect to this. In the idealized case, when it is known which state of nature will take place, we deal with *decision making under certainty*. In the case when objective (actual) probability of occurrence of each state of nature is known we deal with *decision making under risk*. In the situations when we find difficulties in assessment of unique precise probabilities to states of nature we deal with *decision making under ambiguity* (in the existing theories this is also referred to as *decision making under incomplete information, decision making under ignorance*). In the situations when there is no information on probabilities of states of nature we deal with *decision making under uncertainty* (in the existing theories this is also referred to as *decision making under complete ignorance*). It is needed to mention that these four typical cases are rigorous descriptions of real-life decision situations. In general, real decision situations are more complex, diverse and ambiguous. In real-life, decisions are made under imperfect information on all elements of a decision problem. As Prof. L. Zadeh states, imperfect information is information which is in one or more respects is imprecise, uncertain, incomplete, unreliable, vague or partially true [452]. For simplicity, imperfect information may be degenerated to one of the four typical cases described above.

From the other side, DM's preferences are determined by psychological, cognitive and other factors.

The solution of a decision making problem depends both on information and preference frameworks and consist in determination of the best action in terms of a DM's preferences. However, it is difficult to determine the best action by direct treatment of the preferences as a binary relation. For this purpose, a quantification of preferences is used. One approach to quantify preferences is to use a *utility function*[360,397]. Utility function is a function $U:\mathcal{A}\to R$ that for all $f,g\in\mathcal{A}$ satisfies $U(f)\geq U(g)$ iff $f\succsim g$. Generally, any utility function is some aggregation $U(f)=\int_S u(f(S))dS$. The utility models differ on the type of aggregation $\int_S$. However, any utility function is a function existence of which is proven given the assumptions on properties of preferences. The use of utility function is more practical approach than direct treatment of preferences. However, the use of this approach leads to loss of information as any utility function transforms functions to numbers. From the other side, there exists some type of preferences for which a utility function does not exist.

In this chapter we will consider main categories of decision models suggested in the existing literature. Some of them are quite simple being based on idealistic assumptions on relevant information and preferences. Those which are based on more realistic assumptions are distinguished by an increased complexity.

Within the realm of decision making problems, there is another principal direction. In this direction an alternative is described by performance indices, called criteria. For example, a car may be characterized by its cost, velocity, reliability, comfort. This direction is of a huge number of approaches.

1.2 Expected Utility Theory of von Neumann and Morgenstern

Utility theory is one of the main parts of decision analysis and economics. The idea of a utility function consists in construction of a function that represents an individual's preferences defined over the set of possible alternatives [76,246,299,362,397,398]. Formally speaking, a utility function $U(\cdot)$ is such a real-valued function that for any two possible alternatives f and g an inequality $U(f) \geq U(g)$ holds if and only if f is preferred or indifferent to g. For decision making under risk the first axiomatic foundation of the utility paradigm was the expected utility (EU) theory of von Neumann and Morgenstern [397]. This model compares finite-outcome lotteries (alternatives) on the base of their utility values under conditions of exactly known utilities and probabilities of outcomes. Formally, let $\mathcal{X}$ be a set of outcomes without any additional structure imposed on it. The set of lotteries in the expected utility theory is the set of probability distributions over $\mathcal{X}$ with finite supports [170]:

$$\mathcal{L} = \left\{P : \mathcal{X} \to [0,1] \middle| \sum_{X \in \mathcal{X}} P(X) = 1\right\}.$$

Each probability distribution represents objective probabilities of possible outcomes. The EU model, as initially suggested, is not based on a general decision problem framework which includes the concept of a set of states of nature. However, it can easily be applied in this framework also, once we consider an action f as a lottery $f = \left\{P : f(S) \to [0,1] \middle| \sum_{S \in \mathcal{S}} P(f(S)) = 1\right\}$ as $f(\mathcal{S}) \subset \mathcal{X}$. Important issue to consider may be more complicated cases when various lotteries $\mathcal{L}$ can be faced with various probabilities. Such case is referred to as a compound, or a two-stage lottery, that is, a lottery which compose several lotteries as its possible results. To model this within $\mathcal{L}$ a convex combination is defined which reduces a compound lottery to a lottery in $\mathcal{L}$ as follows: for any $P,Q \in \mathcal{L}$ and any $\alpha \in [0,1]$ $\alpha P + (1-\alpha)Q = R \in \mathcal{L}$, where $R(X) = \alpha P(X) + (1-\alpha)Q(X)$. The axioms stating the assumptions on preference which underlie EU model are the following:

(i) **Weak-order:**

(a) Completeness. Any two alternatives are comparable with respect to $\succsim$: for all f and g in $\mathcal{A}$ one has $f \succsim g$ or $g \succsim f$.

(b) Transitivity. For all f,g and h in $\mathcal{A}$ If $f \succsim g$ and $g \succsim h$ then $f \succsim h$.

(ii) **Continuity:** For all f,g and h in $\mathcal{A}$, if $f \succ g$ and $g \succ h$ then there are α and β in $\alpha,\beta \in (0,1)$ such that $\alpha f + (1-\alpha)h \succ \ \succ g \succ \beta f + (1-\beta)h$.

(iii) **Independence:** For all acts f,g and h in $\mathcal{A}$, if $f \succsim g$ then $\alpha f + (1-\alpha)h \succsim \alpha g + (1-\alpha)h$ for all $\alpha \in (0,1)$.

The completeness property implies that despite the fact that each alternative f or g has its advantages and disadvantages with respect to the other one, a DM supposed to be always able to compare two actions f and g on the base of his/her preferences: either f is preferred to g or g is preferred to f, or f and g are considered equivalent. The problem when f and g are absolutely not comparable should be resolved before the set of alternatives is completely determined. This problem may be solved by obtaining additional information to eliminate "ignorance" of preferences with respect to f and g. Alternatively, one of the alternatives should be disregarded.

In order to explain the intuitive interpretation of the axioms let us provide real-life examples.

Example 1. (Completeness). Bob feels that he have got a cold, but in two days he will have a trip abroad. He considers two alternatives: f – to have a hot tea with raspberry jam and g – to take medicine. Bob cannot exactly know state of his organism. In general f is not so strong tool to get better as g, but as opposed to g, f is harmless for his stomach. Moreover, why to use medicine if the organism is able to recover in two days without it? From the other side, the trip is a too important for him to risk by not taking medicine. So, at first he is not sure what to do and decides to take his temperature. If his temperature is below 37°C then he will have tea with raspberry jam, otherwise he definitely will take the medicine to be surer that he will recover in two days.

So, even having non-comparable alternatives, Bob finds a way to define his preference among them by obtaining the additional information as his temperature value.

Example 2. (Completeness). Assume that John would like to go for a walk if it is not cold. John has three alternatives to choose from: f – to go for a walk and to take on a coat, g – to go for a walk and not to take on a coat, h – not to go for a walk. Based on the weather forecast, he considers that one of the two possible weather conditions may take place: *warm* and *cool*. Then John clearly prefer both f and g to h. Concerning his preferences among alternatives f and g he decides that it would be better to take a coat (f). The reason is that even if it is *warm* and not *cool* he can just take a coat off and bring it by hands. Thus, John completely determines his preferences as follows: $f \succ g$, $f \succ h$, $g \succ h$.

Example 3. (Transitivity). Assume f guarantees *small gain*, g - neither gain nor loss, h – *very large loss*. You are likely to prefer f to g and g to h: $f \succ g$, $g \succ h$. Assume that you are at initial welfare having g and your emotional condition is normal. However, sometimes later it becomes apparent that you will very likely to have h, that is, your welfare is very likely to be much below g. As a result, you feel upset much, that is, your emotional condition negative and is worse than it was when you had g. Assume now, that the danger is past, you have your welfare defined by g and are not upset any more. Suppose now that they say you: "you are likely to have f !" – therefore, you would rejoice and your emotional condition would rise and become notably better than it was when you had g. So, with respect to g your emotional condition of having f is good and of having h is bad. This means that, as compared to g, the alternative f is better for you than h: $f \succ h$. We can conclude that given preference $f \succ g$ and $g \succ h$ we can consider g as a reference point, or, in other words, as a nexus to derive that $f \succ h$. Transitivity axiom can also be explained on Example 2.

Example 4. (Independence). Assume f guarantees *medium gain*, g - neither gain nor loss, h – *high loss*. Consider several choice situations within this example. 1) Suppose you need to make a choice between f and g and you choose f. 2) Assume that the choice situation 1) will be met only as one of the two possible states of nature, probability of which is α, and with probability $1-\alpha$ you will face with the other state of nature at which the *high loss* is inevitable. So, you can choose f refusing g only after time passes and if the corresponding state of nature takes place. It is reasonable to consider that introduction of h as a possible event does not change your preference between f and g because occurrence of h and choice situation with f and g are mutually exclusive events. This means that after nature comes to its first state you should choose f for your preferences to be dynamically consistent. We can argue that the first and the second situations are the same in the sense that the preferences between f and g are identical. Now consider the third situation. 3) You are asked to choose among two alternative strategies: in the first the nature with probability α will give you f and with probability $1-\alpha$ you will have h (that is, you have $\alpha f+(1-\alpha)h$ lottery); the second is the same as the first one except f is substituted for g (you have $\alpha g+(1-\alpha)h$ lottery). This third situation differs from the second only in timing of your decision. That is, in the second you can make your choice only after the corresponding state of nature occurs, in the third one you make your choice and then wait for a state of nature to occur. The likelihood of the state of nature producing h does not depend on what you prefer – f or g. Consequently, if you prefer f to g you should prefer choice strategy where f may occur to that where g may occur (with the same probability) because h is equally likely to occur regardless of what strategy is chosen. This means that from $f \succsim g$ it should follow $\alpha f+(1-\alpha)h \succsim \alpha g+(1-\alpha)h$, that is your preference $f \succsim g$ direction is independent of introduction of h –

you should not change your preference $f \succsim g$ if h may also occur.

Example 5. (Independence). Suppose that you are planning to go to a small shop just near your house where they sell fruits and prefer buying apples to buying pears. If we denote buying apples by f and buying pears by g, then your preferences are $f \succ g$. Suppose now that there is also another shop located at the other side of the street you live in, where the same apples and pears are sold at the lower prices. So, you can save your expenses going to the shop at the other side of the street, but then buying fruits for you will be connected with a danger to become a victim of a road accident. Let us denote the danger by h. This means that after deciding to go to the shop located at the other side of the street you will no more have 'pure' alternatives f and g, but instead of them you will have $\alpha f + (1-\alpha)h$ and $\alpha g + (1-\alpha)h$ respectively, where $1-\alpha$ is the probability of h. However, it would be strange to suppose that after crossing the street, you will prefer to buy pears instead of apples. It is reasonable to suppose that you will buy apples and not pears after crossing the street. The reason is that crossing the street is just related to saving expenses and in no way is connected with your preferences with respect to apples and pears. So, your preferences should be $\alpha f + (1-\alpha)h \succ \alpha g + (1-\alpha)h$.

Example 4 can also be used to explain **continuity** axiom. At first, given $f \succ g$ and $g \succ h$ consider the case $\alpha f + (1-\alpha)h \succ g$. This means that if you even to a small extent prefer f to h then you will be willing to refuse g and to risk having a *high loss* with probability $1-\alpha$ in order to get f if, of course, α is sufficiently high. In other words, there are such a high probability α of f that you would consider it reasonable to risk to have the *high loss* to play the game $(\alpha, f; (1-\alpha), h)$ refusing g because f is naturally expected to occur, whereas h is really unlikely.

From the other side, the likelihood $1-\beta$ of the loss could be too high for even a large degree of your preference $f \succ h$ to risk for f. This is the case when it is really better to have neither loss nor gain than to face with a real danger of having the high loss. This means that in this case $1-\beta$ prevails as a reason for your choice and drives your preference to the opposite direction to $g \succ \beta f + (1-\beta)h$.

Example 6. (Continuity). Assume f guarantees saving \$20; g will generate -\$20; h is a current rush. It is clear that $f \succ g \succ h$. Suppose now that in afternoon your wall outlet is failed and you consider whether to repair it yourself or to call an electrician: f – to repair your wall outlet yourself and save \$20, g – to call an electrician who will repair the wall outlet and pay him \$20. You may decide to choose f if you have past experience and all necessary tools for repairing, despite that there is some probability of current rush h. That is, when probability of current rush is sufficiently small you will prefer to repair your wall outlet yourself instead of calling an electrician: $\alpha f + (1-\alpha)h \succ g$, where $1-\alpha$ is probability of current rush. Suppose now that the wall outlet failed as a result of fault in the evening. Then you are likely to be afraid to repair the wall outlet yourself because, in a lack of illumination, a probability $1-\beta$ of accidently touch a bare resulting in current rush is rather high. So you will prefer paying \$20 to an electrician to preserve your health and, maybe, your life: $g \succ \beta f + (1-\beta)h$.

Let us now present the utility representation of the von Neumann and Morgenstern's (vNM's) axioms (i)-(iii). The vNM's EU representation theorem is given below:

Theorem 1.1 [397]. *$\succsim \subset \mathcal{L} \times \mathcal{L}$ satisfies (i)-(iii) if and only if there exists $u : \mathcal{X} \to \mathcal{R}$ such that for every P and Q in $\mathcal{L}$:*

$$P \succsim Q \text{ iff } \sum_{X \in \mathcal{X}} P(X)u(X) \geq \sum_{X \in \mathcal{X}} Q(X)u(X).$$

Moreover, in this case, u is unique up to a positive linear transformation.

Thus, a value $U(P)$ of utility function for a finite-outcome lottery $P = (X_1, P(X_1);...;X_n, P(X_n))$ is defined as $U(P) = \sum_{i=1}^{n} u(X_i)P(X_i)$.

The problem of decision making is to find such P^* that $U(P^*) = \max_{P \in \mathcal{A}} U(P)$.

1.3 Subjective Expected Utility Theory of Savage

The assumptions of von Neumann and Morgenstern expected utility model stating that objective probabilities of events are known makes this model unsuitable for majority of real-world applications. For example, what is an actual probability that a country will meet an economic crisis during a year? What is an actual probability that sales of a new product will bring profit next year? What is an actual probability that I will not get the flu upcoming winter? In any of these examples we deal either with the completely new phenomena, or phenomena which notably differs from the previous events, or phenomena that depends on uncertain or unforeseen factors. This means we have no representative experimental data or complete knowledge to determine objective probabilities. For such cases, L. Savage suggested a theory able to compare alternative actions on the base of a DM's experience or vision [360]. Savage's theory is based on a concept of subjective probability suggested by Ramsey [86] and de Finetti [125]. Subjective probability is DM's probabilistic belief concerning occurrence of an event and is assumed to be used by humans when no information on objective (actual) probabilities of outcomes is known. Savage's theory is called subjective expected utility (SEU) as it is based on the use of subjective probabilities in the expected utility paradigm of von Neumann and Morgenstern instead of objective probabilities. SEU became a base of almost all the utility models for decision making under uncertainty. The preferences in SEU model is formulated over acts as functions from $\mathcal{S}$ to $\mathcal{X}$ in terms of seven axioms. Here we discuss two of them, which are most critical. The one is called "sure thing principle", according to which the preference between two actions depends only on those states at which these actions differ. The axiom uses a concept called an event as the subset $E \subset \mathcal{S}$; an event occurs if any $S \in E$ takes place. This axiom is given below.

Axiom. Sure thing principle. *Let* f, g, f', g' *be actions and* E *an event. Assume*

$$f(S) = f'(S),\ g(S) = g'(S),\ S \in E$$

and

$$f(S) = g(S),\ f'(S) = g'(S),\ S \notin E$$

then

$$f \succsim g \Leftrightarrow f' \succsim g'.$$

In order to better understand what this implies, let us consider the following example with four states of nature (Table 1.1).

In this example we have two events: $E = \{S_1, S_2\}$ and its complement denoted $E^c = \{S_3, S_4\} = S \setminus E$. Consider $f \succsim g \Rightarrow f' \succsim g'$. Actions f and g differ if $E = \{S_1, S_2\}$ occurs and coincide otherwise. Actions f' and g' can be considered as "obtained" from f and g by changing their equal outcomes from $f(S_3) = g(S_3) = \$8$ and $f(S_4) = g(S_4) = \$4$ to \$3 and \$2 respectively. According to the "sure thing principle", if you prefer f to g, then you should necessarily prefer f' to g'. This is justified as follows. If $E = \{S_1, S_2\}$ occurs, the "obtained" actions f' and g' coincide with f and g respectively. If E^c occurs, f' coincide with g' (as well as f and g do). The logic of $f' \succsim g' \Rightarrow f \succsim g$ is analogous. So, $f \succsim g \Leftrightarrow f' \succsim g'$.

Table 1.1. For the sure thing principle

	E		E^c	
	S_1	S_2	S_3	S_4
f	\$10	\$2	\$8	\$4
g	-\$5	\$7	\$8	\$4
f'	\$10	\$2	\$3	\$2
g'	-\$5	\$7	\$3	\$2

The other important assumption is that beliefs in occurrence of events do not depend on the consequences these events may result in. Suppose you prefer *be healthy if an event B occurs and to get a cold otherwise* to *be healthy if event C occurs and to get a cold otherwise.* Then you should also prefer *receiving \$100 if event B occurs and 0 otherwise* to *receiving*

\$100 if event C occurs and 0 otherwise. The logic is that the first preference implies you believe in occurrence of B more than in occurrence of C.

These are the two core assumptions of SEU model, and for the extensive description of all the seven axioms one may refer to [360]. The Savage's utility representation is as follows: provided that $\succsim$ satisfies all the axioms, there exists a unique probability measure μ on $\mathcal{S}$ and a function $u:\mathcal{X}\to\mathcal{R}$ such that

$$f \succsim g \text{ iff } \int_{\mathcal{S}} u(f(S))d\mu \geq \int_{\mathcal{S}} u(g(S))d\mu.$$

The problem of decision making consists in determination of an action $f^* \in \mathcal{A}$ such that

$$U(f^*) = \max_{f\in\mathcal{A}} \int_{\mathcal{S}} u(f(S))d\mu\,.$$

In quantitative sense, SEU model coincide with vNM's model – we again have expectation with respect to a probability measure. However, qualitatively, these theories differ. In vNM's model it is supposed that actual probabilities of outcomes are known. For example if to consider an ideal coin, then probabilities of the outcomes are equal to 0.5. SEU model is developed for more realistic tasks – when actual probabilities are not known. For example, an actual probability of whether it will rain on 15th of October in the next year, is unknown. For such cases, in SEU it is suggested to use a DM's subjectively determined probabilities.

The main implications of SEU model are the following: 1) beliefs of a DM are probabilistic; 2) the beliefs are to be used linearly in utility representation of an alternative.

1.4 Prospect Theory and Rank-Dependent Utility Models

In von Neumann-Morgenstern and Savage theories it is assumed that individuals tend to maximize expected utility being motivated by material incentives (self-interest) [3] and make decisions in a rational way. In turn rationality means that individuals update their beliefs about probability of outcomes correctly (following Bayes' law[69]) and that they can assign consistent subjective probabilities to each outcome. These theories are well-composed and have strong analytical power. However, they define human behavior as "ideal", i.e. inanimate. Experimental evidence has repeatedly shown that people violate the axioms of von Neumann-Morgenstern-Savage preferences in a systematic way. Indeed, these models are based on assumptions that people behave as 'computational machines' functioning according to predefined mathematical algorithms. Of course, these don't correspond to the computational abilities of humans. From the other side, these models are developed for a perfect information framework, e.g. humans either know actual probabilities or they can assign subjective probabilities to each outcome. Really, actual probabilities are very seldom known in real life, and the use of subjective probabilities is very often questionable or not compatible with human choices.

Humans' decision activity is conditioned by psychological issues, mental, social and other aspects. These insights inspired a novel direction of studying how people actually behave when making decisions. This direction is called *behavioral economics* and takes it start in the Prospect Theory (PT) [222] of D.Kahneman and A. Tversky. PT [222,387] is the one of the most famous theories in the new view on a utility concept. This theory has a good success because it includes psychological aspects that form human behavior. Kahneman and Tversky uncovered a series of features of human behavior in decision making and used them to construct their utility model. The first feature is that people make decisions considering deviations from their initial wealth, i.e. gains and losses, rather than final wealth. An alternative in their model is a lottery in which an outcome is considered as a change from a DM's current wealth called *reference point*, but not as a final wealth. They call such a lottery a prospect.

Furthermore, a so-called gain-loss asymmetry was observed: influence of losses on human choices dominates influence of gains. Humans' attitudes to risk depend on whether they deal with gains or losses. In one experiment conducted by Kahneman and Tversky, they suggested people to make a choice given the following alternatives:

To get additional $3.000

To get additional $4.000 with probability 0.8 and nothing with probability 0.2

80% of people chose the first alternative despite that the second one has the larger expected value: $3.200. So, they did not wish to risk playing the second game, i.e. they are risk averse. Then they were suggested to choose among the above games with gains replaced by losses:

To loss $3.000

To loss $4.000 with probability 0.8 and loss nothing with probability 0.2

In this case the choice of the majority of people was the opposite. 92% of people chose the second alternative despite that its expected value $3.200 of loss was larger than $3.000 of certain loss. So, people wish to risk in order to escape the sure loss, i.e. they are risk seeking dealing with losses. Based on the above mentioned evidence, Kahneman and Tversky concluded that the main factor that influences human choices in such experiments is loss aversion. People consider losses as a more important issue than gains.

For representing the features of perception of gains and losses, Kahneman and Tversky use value function $v()$ to model DM's tastes over monetary outcomes X (as changes from the current wealth), instead of a utility function (which is used in, for example, SEU, to represent tastes over net wealth). Value function, as based on the experimental evidence on attitudes to gains and losses, has the following properties: 1) it is steeper in domain of gains than in domain of losses; 2) it is concave for gains and is convex for losses; 3) it is steepest in the reference point. Schematic view of the value function is given in Fig. 1.1.

The second main insight observed from experimental evidence is distorted perception of probabilities. In making decisions, people perceive the values of probabilities not exactly as they are but overestimate or underestimate them. This comes from the fact that the change of

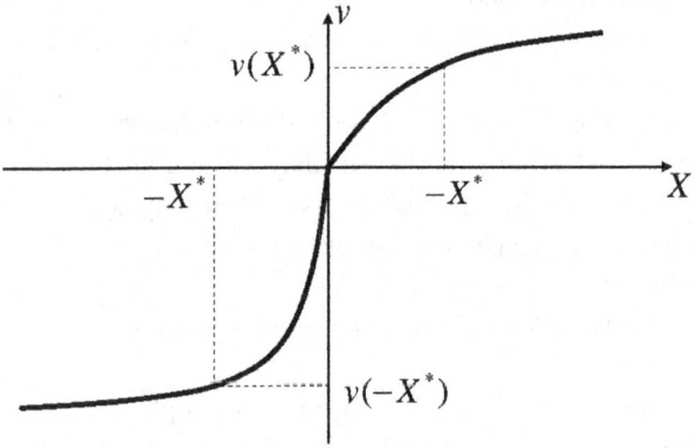

Fig. 1.1. Value function

probability from, for example, 0 to 0.1 or from 0.9 to 1 is considered by people as notably more sufficient than the change from 0.3 to 0.4. The reason was explained as follows: in the first case the situation changes qualitatively – from an impossible outcome to some chance, in the second case the situation also change qualitatively – from very probable outcome to the certain one. In other words, appearance of a chance or appearance of a guaranteed outcome is perceived more important than just the change of probability value. As a result, people overestimate low and underestimate high probabilities. In order to model this evidence Kahneman and Tversky replace probabilities P with weights $w(P)$ as the values of so-called weighting function $w:[0,1]\to[0,1]$. This function non-linearly transforms an actual probability to represent distorted perception of the latter. Schematic view of the weighting function $w()$ is given in fig. 1.2:

In Prospect theory, Kahneman and Tversky suggested a new model of choice among prospects $(X_1, P(X_1);...;X_n, P(X_n))$. In this model, a value

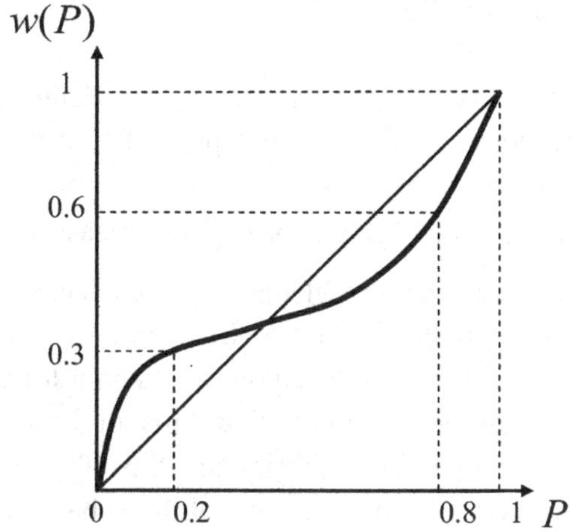

Fig. 1.2. Weighting function

function $v()$ is used instead of utility function $u(X)$ and a weighting function $w()$ is used instead of probability measure in a standard expectation operation. However, this model was formulated by Kahneman and Tversky in [222] for at most two non-zero outcomes. The model has the following form (compare with the expected utility):

$$U((X_1,P(X_1);...;X_n,P(X_n))=\sum_{i=1}^{n}v(X_i)w(P(X_i)).$$

There are various forms of a value function $v()$ and a weighting function $w()$ suggested by various authors. Many of them are listed in [329]. However, any weighting function must satisfy the following: $w()$ is non-decreasing with $w(0)=0$, $w(1)=1$. Commonly, $w()$ is nonadditive, that is, $w(P+Q)\neq w(P)+w(Q), P+Q\leq 1$.

Prospect theory is a successful theory for decision making under risk and explains such phenomena as Allais paradox [36], certainty effect and framing effects [222].

1.5 Choquet Expected Utility

Choquet Expected Utility (CEU) was suggested by Schmeidler [362] as a model with a new view on belief and representation of preferences in contrast to SEU model. In SEU model an overall utility is described as $U(f)=\int_S u(f(S))d\mu$ where μ is a probability measure. However, uncertainty as a vagueness of knowledge on occurrence of events may result in a non-additive belief for $S \in \mathcal{S}$. Schmeidler considered a simple motivating example for this. Suppose you have a coin for which you find out, by tossing it very many times, that falls of heads and tails are equiprobable, that is, their probabilities are 0.5. Therefore, it will be reasonable for your beliefs to be these probabilities based on frequencies. Suppose now you will consider a coin which is in a pocket of another person; you did not tossed it at all and don't know whether it is ideal. You may assume that the probabilities of heads and tails for this coin are equal to 0.5. This is quantitatively the same beliefs as those for your own coin. However, the basics are different. The first beliefs are based on real evidence, whereas the second beliefs are assumptions (though they may seem reasonable) – certainly, there is a reason to trust the first beliefs much more than the second ones. For the second coin, heads and tails may seem for you symmetric in terms of information on their occurrence, i.e. – you may think that there is no reason to believe in occurrence of one concrete result to the other one. So, it is questionable to subjectively assess some probabilities to the heads and tails. However, it is reasonable for you to think that some of the results of tossing is more likely than the other. Then your belief may be, for example, $v(heads)=v(tails)=0.3$. But, at the same time, $v(heads\ or\ tails)=1$. So, $v(heads\ or\ tails) \neq v(heads)+v(tails)$ – your belief is non-additive.

Motivated by evidences like the above mentioned, in CEU a belief is described by a capacity [109] – not necessarily additive measure η satisfying the following conditions [362]:

1. $\eta(\varnothing)=0$
2. $\forall A,B \subset \mathcal{S}$, $A \subset B$ implies $\eta(A) \leq \eta(B)$
3. $\eta(\mathcal{S})=1$

Capacity is a model of a belief used for the cases when it is impossible to definitely separate states of nature by using probabilities of their occurrence. In CEU η is referred to as nonadditive probability.

The use of a capacity is not an only advantage of the CEU. The only use of a capacity instead of an additive measure in Riemann integration (Riemann integration is adopted in SEU) is not proper. Riemann integration of acts with respect to a capacity arises several unavoidable problems. Particularly, it depends on the way the act is written. For example, consider an act f expressed in two alternative forms: $(\$1,S_1;\,\$1,S_2;\,\$0,S_3)$ and $(\$1,\{S_1,S_2\};\,\$0,S_3)$. Riemann integration will give different results for these expressions as, in general, $\eta(\{S_1,S_2\})\neq\eta(\{S_1\})+\eta(\{S_2\})$. The other problems such as violation of continuity and monotonicity are well explained in [170]. CEU is based on the use of Choquet integral which is a generalization of Lebesgue integral. This generalization is obtained when a capacity is used instead of an additive measure in Lebesgue integral. The use of Lebesgue integration removes the problems related to Riemann integration.

CEU is axiomatically developed for the Anscombe-Aumann framework [362], in which acts are functions from states to lotteries, i.e. to probabilistic outcomes [40]. The main difference in the assumptions on preferences in CEU from those in the expected utility models is a relaxation of the independence axiom. The independence property in this model is assumed only for comonotonic actions. Two acts f and g in $\mathcal{A}$ are said to be comonotonic if for no S and S' in $\mathcal{S}$, $f(S)\succ f(S')$ and $g(S')\succ g(S)$ hold. This means that f and g behave analogously. Motivation of a departure from the independence axiom may be shown in the following example. Consider a box containing balls of the same color. The only information is that the color is either white or black. Assume the two acts which can be chosen prior to open the box: the first gives \$10 if the color is white and 0 if it is black, the second gives \$0 if the color is white and \$10 if is black. These acts can be written as functions f and g: $f(white)=10$, $f(black)=0$, $g(white)=0$, $g(black)=10$. As information on white and black is symmetric, we suppose $\tilde{f}\sim\tilde{g}$. Consider now the following mixes of these acts with act $h=g$:

$f_h = \frac{1}{2}f + \frac{1}{2}h$ and $g_h = \frac{1}{2}g + \frac{1}{2}h$. This will produce $f_h(white) = 5$, $f_h(black) = 5$ and $g_h(white) = g(white) = 0$, $g_h(black) = g(black) = 10$. Whereas f and g are qualitatively similar, f_h and g_h – not. In the first pair we have uncertain acts. In the second we have a certain act and an uncertain act: f_h gives a certain outcome \$5 whether g is uncertain to give \$10 or \$0. These acts differ qualitatively and one may prefer certain \$5 (reliable result) to \$10 about which it is not known whether it will occur (not reliable result): $f_h = \frac{1}{2}f + \frac{1}{2}h \succ g_h = \frac{1}{2}g + \frac{1}{2}h$. Hence, the independence is violated: $\tilde{f} \sim \tilde{g}$ and $f_h = \frac{1}{2}f + \frac{1}{2}h \succ g_h = \frac{1}{2}g + \frac{1}{2}h$. In this example, uncertainty of the results disappears when mixing f with $h = g$. The effect when uncertainty or risk decreases (or disappears as in the considered example) is called hedging effect [171]. The latter may result in violation of the independence. Due to this, in CEU independence is assumed only for comonotonic acts, as for such acts hedging is impossible [170]. The axiom assuming such independence is called comonotonic independence and is the following:

Comonotonic Independence. *For all pairwise comonotonic acts* f, g *and* h *in* $\mathcal{A}$ *if* $f \succsim g$, *then* $\alpha f + (1-\alpha)h \succsim \alpha g + (1-\alpha)h$ *for all* $\alpha \in (0,1)$.

The other axioms of the CEU model are quite trivial. The utility representation in this model is $U(f) = \int_S u(f(S))d\eta$, where η is a non-additive probability (capacity) and u is nonconstant and is unique up to a positive linear transformation. For finite S, i.e. for $S = \{S_1, ..., S_n\}$ CEU representation is as follows:

$$U(f) = \sum_{i=1}^{n} (u(f(S_{(i)})) - u(f(S_{(i+1)})))\eta(\{S_{(1)}, ..., S_{(i)}\}),$$

where (i) in the index of the states S implies that they are permuted such that $u(f(S_{(i)})) \geq u(f(S_{(i+1)}))$, and $u(f(S_{(n+1)})) = 0$ by convention. Sometimes they use an equivalent expression for CEU representation:

$$U(f)=\sum_{i=1}^{n}u(f(S_{(i)}))(\eta(\{S_{(1)},...,S_{(i)}\})-\eta(\{S_{(1)},...,S_{(i-1)}\}))$$

with $\{S_{(1)},...,S_{(i-1)}\}=\varnothing$ for $i=1$.

One can see that SEU model is a special case of CEU model when η is additive. The disadvantages of CEU relates to difficulties of satisfactory interpretation of η. The typical cases are when η is taken as a lower envelope of a set of probability distributions possible for a considered problem (when a single distribution is unknown). Lower envelope is the measure that assigns minimal probability to an event among all the probabilities for this event , each determined on the base of one possible probability distribution. This requires solving optimization problems which increases complexity of computations. In general, non-additive measure construction is difficult both from intuitive and computational points of view.

1.6 Cumulative Prospect Theory

Cumulative Prospect Theory (CPT) [387] was suggested by Kahnemann and Tversky as a development of PT. PT was originally presented as a model for comparison of prospects with at most two non-zero outcomes. However, even for such primitive cases, the use of a non-additive weighting function in PT arises at least one difficulty. Consider different descriptions denoted f and g of the same prospect h:

$$f=(\$10,P_1;\$10,P_2;\$0;P_3) \text{ and } g=(\$10,P_1+P_2;\$0,P_3).$$

As, in essence, f and g are the same prospect, they should have the same overall utilities: $U(f)=U(g)$. However, this cannot be achieved in PT due to non-additivity of $w()$. Indeed,

$$U(f)=v(\$10)w(P_1)+v(\$10)w(P_2)=v(\$10)(w(P_1)+w(P_2)),$$

$$U(g)=v(\$10)w(P_1+P_2),$$

and as $w(P_1+P_2)\neq w(P_1)+w(P_2)$, then $U(f)\neq U(g)$.

In order to overcome this difficulty, Quiggin [341] and Yaari [424] suggested to use non-linear transformation of not a probability $P(X)$ of an outcome $X = A$, but of a cumulative probability $P(X \geq A)$ that an outcome X is not less than a predefined value A. Consider a prospect $f = (X_1, P(X_1); ...; X_n, P(X_n))$ with non-negative outcomes, such that $X_1 \geq ... \geq X_n$ (this ordering does not lead to loss of generality, as this can always be achieved by permutation of indexes). EU of this prospect will be

$$U(f) = \sum_{i=1}^{n} p(X_i) u(X_i)$$

that can be rewritten as

$$U(f) = \sum_{i=1}^{n} \left(\sum_{j=1}^{i} p(X_j) \right) (u(X_i) - u(X_{i+1}))$$

where $u(X_{n+1}) = 0$ by convention. $\sum_{j=1}^{i} P(X_j)$ is a cumulative probability that an outcome of f is not less than X_i. By applying non-linear transformation w to $\sum_{j=1}^{i} P(X_j)$, one will have:

$$U(f) = \sum_{i=1}^{n} w \left(\sum_{j=1}^{i} P(X_j) \right) (u(X_i) - u(X_{i+1}))$$

that can be rewritten

$$U(f) = \sum_{i=1}^{n} \left(w \left(\sum_{j=1}^{i} P(X_j) \right) - w \left(\sum_{j=1}^{i-1} P(X_j) \right) \right) u(X_i).$$

As one has

$$\left(w \left(\sum_{j=1}^{i} P(X_j) \right) - w \left(\sum_{j=1}^{i-1} P(X_j) \right) \right) \in [0,1]$$

and

$$\sum_{i=1}^{n}\left(w\left(\sum_{j=1}^{i}P(X_j)\right)-w\left(\sum_{j=1}^{i-1}P(X_j)\right)\right)=w\left(\sum_{j=1}^{n}P(X_j)\right)=w(1)=1,$$

one can consider $q_i=\left(w\left(\sum_{j=1}^{i}P(X_j)\right)-w\left(\sum_{j=1}^{i-1}P(X_j)\right)\right)$ as a probability. However, Q_i depends on ranking of outcomes X_i – for various prospects value of Q_i will be various. For this reason, such representation is called rank-dependent expected utility (RDEU). For the case of many outcomes, PT is based on the use of RDEU model with a value function:

$$U(f)=\sum_{i=1}^{n}w\left(\sum_{j=1}^{i}P(X_j)\right)(v(X_i)-v(X_{i+1})).$$

The representation of RDEU is a special case of that of CEU. Considering $w\left(\sum_{j=1}^{i}P(X_j)\right)$ as a value of a non-additive measure, one arrives at CEU representation [170]. CEU is more general than RDEU: RDEU requires that the probabilities are known, whereas CEU – not. The second problem with PT is that it does not in general satisfy first-order stochastic dominance [170].

Kahneman and Tversky, the authors of PT, suggested CPT as a more advanced theory which is free of the PT's above mentioned drawbacks. CPT can be applied, in contrast to PT, both for decisions under risk and uncertainty. In CPT, gains and losses (measured by a value function) aggregated separately by Choquet integrals with different capacities and the results of aggregations are summed. The representation of CPT is:

$$U(f)=\int_S v(f^+(S))d\eta^+ + \int_S v(f^-(S))d\eta^-,$$

where $f^+(S)=\max(f(S),0)$ and $f^-(S)=\min(f(S),0)$, $\int_S$ is Choquet integral, v is a value function (the same as in PT), and η^+,η^- are capacities. For the case with risky prospects, i.e. with known probabilities of states of nature it uses two weighting functions. Consider, without loss of generality, a risky prospect $f=(f(S_1),\ p(S_1);...;f(S_n),\ p(S_n))$ with $f(S_1)\geq,...,\geq f(S_k)\geq 0>f(S_{k+1})\geq,...,\geq f(S_n)$. The CPT representation for f is the following:

$$U(f)=\sum_{i=1}^{k}\left(w^{+}\left(\sum_{j=1}^{i}p(S_j)\right)-w^{+}\left(\sum_{j=1}^{i-1}p(S_j)\right)\right)v(f(S_i))$$
$$+\sum_{i=k+1}^{n}\left(w^{-}\left(\sum_{j=i}^{n}p(S_j)\right)-w^{-}\left(\sum_{j=i+1}^{n}p(S_j)\right)\right)v(f(S_i)).$$

The use of different weighting functions w^{+} and w^{-} for probabilities of gains and losses comes from an experimental observation that people differently weight the same probability p depending on whether it is associated with a gain or a loss; however the same experimental evidence showed that both w^{+} and w^{-} are S-shaped [387]. w^{+} and w^{-} obtained by Kahneman and Tversky from the experimental data have the same form with different curvatures:

$$w^{+}(P)=\frac{P^{\gamma}}{(P^{\gamma}+(1-P)^{\gamma})^{1/\gamma}},\quad w^{-}(P)=\frac{P^{\delta}}{(P^{\delta}+(1-P)^{\delta})^{1/\delta}}$$

$\gamma=0.61$, $\delta=0.69$. As a result, w^{+} is more curved.

The dependence of beliefs on the sign of outcomes is referred to as sign-dependence. Sign-dependence for the case of decisions under uncertainty is modeled by using two different capacities η^{+},η^{-}. When $w^{+}(P)=1-w^{-}(1-P)$ or $\eta^{+}(A)=1-\eta^{-}(S\setminus A), A\subset S$, the sign-dependence disappears and CPT is reduced to RDEU or CEU respectively.

CPT is one of the most successful theories – it encompasses reference-dependence, rank-dependence and sign-dependence. It combines advantages of both PT and CEU: describing asymmetry of gains and losses and modeling non-additive beliefs under uncertainty. As opposed to PT, CPT satisfies first-order stochastic dominance.

However, CPT suffers from a series of notable disadvantages. One main disadvantage of CPT is that gains and losses are aggregated separately, and in this sense the model is additive. Drawbacks and violations of such additivity were empirically and experimentally shown in [77,78,250,421]. The other main disadvantage is that CPT, as it is shown in [315], may be good for laboratory works but not sufficiently suitable for real applications. The research in [315] shows that this is related to the fact that CPT is highly conditioned by the combination of parameters' values used in value and weighting functions. Roughly speaking, the same combination works well in one choice problem but badly in another. For example, such problems with parameterization is assumed as a possible reason of the experiments reported in [49], where it was illustrated that CPT fails to capture the choice between mixed gambles with moderate and equal probabilities.

1.7 Multiple Priors Models

One of the underlying motivations of the CEU is that a DM's beliefs may not be probabilistic in choice problems under uncertainty, i.e. they may be incompatible with a unique probability measure. In CEU, this evidence is accounted for by using a non-additive probability. Another way to describe non-probabilistic beliefs is to model them not by one probability distribution but by a set of probability distributions (priors), which led to development of a large class of various utility models. This class is referred to as multiple priors models. The use of multiple priors allows describing the fact that in situations with insufficient information or vague knowledge, a DM can not have a precise (single) probabilistic belief on an event's occurrence, but have to allow for a range of values of probabilities, i.e. to have an imprecise belief. Indeed, various priors from a considered set will in general assign various probabilities to an event. From the other side, imprecise probabilistic beliefs imply existence of a set of priors.

The first two known examples showing incompatibility of a single probability measure with human choices were suggested by Daniel Ellsberg in 1961 [144]. These examples uncovered choices under uncertainty in which human intuition does not follow the sure thing principle. One example is called Ellsberg two-urn paradox. In this experiment they present a DM two urns each containing 100 balls. A DM is allowed to see that urn I contains 50 white and 50 black balls, whereas no information is provided on a ratio of white and black balls in urn II. A DM is suggested to choose from bets on a color of a ball drawn at random: on a white color and on a black color. Each bet produces a prize of \$100. After bet is chosen, a DM needs to choose the urn to play. Majority of people were indifferent whether to bet on white or on black. However, whatever bet was chosen, most of people strictly preferred to choose urn I to play – they prefer betting on an outcome with known probability 0.5 to betting on an outcome with probability that may take any value from [0,1]. This choice is inconsistent with any probabilistic belief on a color of a ball taken at random from urn II. Indeed, betting on white and then choosing urn I means that a DM believes on the number of white balls in urn II being smaller than in urn I, whereas betting on black and then choosing urn I means that a DM believes on the number of black balls in urn II being smaller than in urn I. No single probabilistic belief on colors for urn II may simultaneously explain these two choices – the probabilities of a white and a black balls drawn at random from urn II cannot be simultaneously smaller than 0.5.

The second example is called Ellsberg single-urn paradox. In this example a DM is offered to choose among bets on colors of balls in one urn. This urn contains 90 balls among which 30 are red and the other 60 are blue and yellow in an unknown proportion. The following bets on a color of a ball taken at random are suggested (Table 1.2).

Table 1.2. Ellsberg single-urn decision problem

	Red	Blue	Yellow
f	\$100	0	0
g	0	\$100	0
f'	\$100	0	\$100
g'	0	\$100	\$100

For example, f yields \$100 if a ball drawn is red and 0 otherwise whereas f' yields \$100 whether a ball drawn is red or yellow and 0 otherwise. Majority of subjects prefer f to g (i.e. they prefer an outcome with known probability 1/3 to an outcome with unknown probability being somewhere between 0 and 2/3). At the same time, majority prefer g' to f' (i.e. they prefer an outcome with known probability 2/3 to an outcome with unknown probability being somewhere between 1/3 and 1). These two choices cannot be explained by beliefs described by a single probability distribution. Indeed, if to suppose that the beliefs are probabilistic, then the first choice implies that subjects think that a red ball is more probable to be drawn than a blue ball: $P(red) > P(blue)$. The second choice implies subjects thinking that a blue or yellow ball drawn is more probable than a red or yellow ball drawn – $P(blue) + P(yellow) > P(red) + P(yellow)$ which means that $P(blue) > P(red)$. This contradicts the beliefs underlying the first choice. Indeed, information on occurrence of complementary events *blue* and *yellow* represented only by probability of their union cannot be uniquely separated into probabilities of *blue* and *yellow*.

The observed choices contradict the sure thing principle, according to which $f \succ g$ should imply $f' \succ g'$. Indeed, f' and g' can be obtained from f and g respectively by changing from 0 to \$100 the equal outcomes of f and g produced for yellow ball. However, the evidence shows: $f \succ g$ and $g' \succ f'$. Violation of the sure thing principle also takes place in the Ellsberg two-urns experiment. The intuition behind the real choices in these experiments is that people tend to prefer probabilistic outcomes to uncertain ones. This phenomenon is referred to as uncertainty aversion, or ambiguity aversion. Term ambiguity was suggested by Daniel Ellsberg and defined as follows: "a quality depending on the amount, type, reliability and 'unanimity' of information, and giving rise to one's 'degree of confidence' in an estimate of relative likelihoods" [144]. Mainly, ambiguity is understood as uncertainty with respect to probabilities [91].

The principle of uncertainty aversion was formalized in form of an axiom by Gilboa and Schmeidler [171]. To understand formal description of uncertainty aversion, let us recall the Ellsberg two-urn example. Suppose an act f yielding \$100 for a white ball drawn from an unknown urn and an act g yielding \$100 for a black ball drawn from an unknown urn. It is reasonable to consider these acts equivalent: $f \sim g$. Now mix these acts as $\frac{1}{2}f + \frac{1}{2}g$, obtaining an act which yields a lottery of getting \$100 with probability ½ and 0 with probability ½ no matter what ball is drawn. That is, by mixing two uncertain bets we got a risky bet – the hedging effect takes place. The obtained act is equivalent to a bet on any color, say white, for a known urn that provides the same lottery. But as this bet is preferred to f and g, we may state that $\frac{1}{2}f + \frac{1}{2}g \succsim f$. The uncertainty aversion axiom is a generalization of this and it states that for equivalent acts f and g, their mix is weakly preferred to each of them: $\alpha f + (1-\alpha)g \succsim f$. This axiom is one of the axioms underlying a famous utility model called Maximin Expected Utility (MMEU) [171]. According to the axiomatic basis of this model, there exist a unique closed and convex set C of priors (probability measures) P over states of nature, such that

$$f \succsim g \Leftrightarrow \min_{P\in C} \int_S u(f(S))dP \geq \min_{P\in C} \int_S u(g(S))dP,$$

where u is unique up to a positive linear transformation. In simple words, an overall utility of an act is a minimum among all its expected utilities each obtained for one prior $P \in C$. The consideration of C as convex does not affect generality. Applying MMEU to both Ellsberg paradoxes, one can easily arrive at the observed preferences of most people.

Ghirardato, Maccheroni and Marinacci suggested a generalization of MMEU [168] consisting in using all its underlying axioms except uncertainty aversion axiom. The obtained model is referred to as $\alpha-$MMEU and states that $f \succsim g$ iff

$$\alpha \min_{P\in C} \int_S u(f(S))dP + (1-\alpha)\max_{P\in C} \int_S u(f(S))dP$$
$$\geq \alpha \min_{P\in C} \int_S u(g(S))dP + (1-\alpha)\max_{P\in C} \int_S u(g(S))dP.$$

$\alpha \in [0,1]$ is referred to as a degree of ambiguity aversion, or an ambiguity attitude. The higher α is, the more ambiguity averse a DM is; when $\alpha = 1$ we get MMEU. When $\alpha = 0$, the model describes *ambiguity seeking*, i.e. a DM relies on ambiguity because it includes the best possible realization of priors. The values $\alpha \in (0,1)$ describe balance between ambiguity aversion and ambiguity seeking to reflect the fact that a person may not have extreme attitudes to ambiguity.

The important issue is the relation between CEU and MMEU. One can easily find that the Ellsberg single-urn paradox may be explained by CEU under the capacity η satisfying the following:

$$\eta(\{S_r\}) = \eta(\{S_r, S_b\}) = \eta(\{S_r, S_y\}) = \frac{1}{3},$$

$$\eta(\{S_b\}) = \eta(\{S_y\}) = 0,$$

$$\eta(\{S_b, S_y\}) = \frac{2}{3},$$

where S_r, S_b, S_y denote states of nature being extractions of a red, a blue and a yellow balls respectively. Schmeidler showed that an ambiguity aversion is modeled by CEU if and only if a capacity satisfies $\eta(H \cup G) + \eta(H \cap G) \geq \eta(H) + \eta(G)$. Such η is called a convex capacity. Schmeidler proved that under assumption of ambiguity aversion, CEU is the special case of the MMEU:

$$(Ch)\int_S u(f(S))d\eta = \min_{P \in C} \int_S u(f(S))dP$$

where $(Ch)\int_S$ denotes Choquet integral, η is a convex capacity, and C is a set of probability measures defined as $C = \{P | P(H) \geq \eta(H), \forall H \subset S\}$. Such C is called a core of a convex capacity η. The capacity given above that expresses Ellsberg paradox, is a capacity whose value for each event is equal to a minimum among all the possible probabilities for this event, and therefore, satisfies $\eta(H) \leq P(H), \forall H \subset S$. Given a set of priors C, a convex capacity η satisfying $\eta(H)=\min_{P\in C} P(H)$ is called a lower envelope of C.

However, MMEU is not always a generalization of CEU. If η is not convex, there is no C for which CEU and MMEU coincide. Indeed, CEU does not presuppose an ambiguity aversion. For example, if you use concave η, CEU will model ambiguity seeking behavior [170]. Also, a capacity may not have a core.

If to compare CEU and MMEU, the latter has important advantages. Choquet integration and a non-additive measure are concepts that are not well-known and use of them requires specific mathematical knowledge. From the other side, there exist difficulties related to interpretation and construction of a capacity. Capacity, as a belief, may be too subjective. In contrast, a set of priors is straightforward and clear as a possible 'range' for unknown probability distribution. The idea to compute minimal EU is very intuitive and accepted easily. At the same time, it often requires to solve well-known optimization problems like those of linear programming. However, determination of a set of priors as the problem of strict constraining a range of possible probabilities is influenced by insufficient knowledge on reality. In such cases, the use of a non-additive belief obtained from experience-based knowledge may be a good alternative.

The main disadvantages of the MMEU are that in real problems it is difficult to strictly constrain the set of priors and various priors should not be considered equally relevant to a problem at hand. From the other side, in MMEU each act is evaluated on the base of only one prior. In order to cope with these problems Klibanoff et al. suggested a smooth ambiguity model as a more general way to formalize decision making under ambiguity than MMEU [239]. In this model an assessment of a DM's subjective probabilistic beliefs to various probability distributions is used to represent important additional knowledge which differentiates priors in terms of their relevance to a decision situation considered. In this approach the authors use the following representation:

$$U(f)=\int_C \phi\left(\int_S u(f(S))dP\right)dv.$$

Here $P \in C$ is a possible prior from a set of priors C, v is a probabilistic belief over C, ϕ is a nonlinear function reflecting extent of ambiguity aversion. ϕ rules out reduction of a second-order probability model to a first-order probability model. An introduction of a subjective second-order probability measure defined over multiple priors was also suggested in[107,364,366] and others.

In [99] they suggested a model in which an overall utility for an action is obtained as $U(f) = \min_{\rho \in \mathcal{L}_\beta} \frac{1}{\varphi(\rho)} \int_S u(f(S)) d\rho$. Here φ is a confidence function whose value $\varphi(\rho) \in [0,1]$ relevance of the distribution ρ to the decision problem and $\mathcal{L}_\beta = \{\rho : \varphi(\rho) \geq \beta\}, \beta \in (0,1]$ is a set of distributions considered by a DM.

A wide class of multiple priors models is referred to as variational preferences models suggested in [270,406], robust control idea-based model suggested in [192], ε-contamination model suggested in [139]. The generalized representation for these models is the following:

$$U(f) = \min_{\rho \in \Delta(S)} \left[\int_S u(f(S)) d\rho + c(\rho) \right]$$

where c is a "cost function" whose value $c(\rho)$ is higher for less relevant distribution ρ, and $\Delta(S)$ is the set of all the distributions over $\mathcal{S}$.

1.8 Hierarchical Uncertainty Models

We tried to cover main famous theories for decisions under ambiguity, that is, for decisions under imprecise probability-relevant information. Although the mentioned theories are of the most advantageous utility models, they are missing an important aspect: real-world imprecise probability relevant information falls into a framework of a second-order uncertainty. This framework is characterized by a hierarchy of two levels. The first level supports imprecise information on probabilities represented by ranges for probabilities of states of nature. The second level supports imprecise beliefs of a DM to the assigned ranges. In other words, one deals with uncertainty (imprecise beliefs) about uncertainty (imprecise probabilities). Indeed, a DM or an expert cannot actually express a precise belief on relevance of a prior to a decision problem under consideration (as it is suggested in some of the above mentioned models) but will be rather imprecisely confident in imprecise probabilities. Such framework is more intuitive and likely for perceptions relevant to real decision activity. In this section we consider the structure of hierarchical uncertainty models representing second-order imprecise probability information for decision making.

In these models it is suggested not to confine by the imprecise information to probabilities itself, but to include some measure to represent a belief to this information. This involves two levels of uncertainty: the first level is represented by imprecise probabilities of a variable of interest (e.g. state of nature), whereas the second level is used to support beliefs to these imprecise probabilities. The beliefs at the second level represent important additional information reflecting degrees of confidence of experts' opinions or other sources of imprecise information on probabilities [35]. The general scheme of information structure of such models is shown in Fig. 1.3.

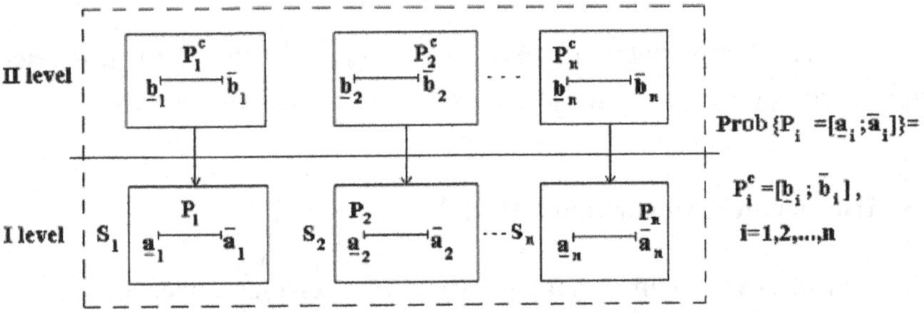

Fig.1.3. Information structure for the second-order imprecise hierarchical model

In this scheme $S=\{S_1,S_2,...,S_n\}$ denotes a set of states of nature while an imprecise probability distribution $P(S_i)=P_i$ expressed over states of nature S_i is represented by interval probabilities $P_i=[\underline{a}_i;\overline{a}_i]$, $i=1,2\ ,...,n$: $P_1=[\underline{a}_1;\overline{a}_1]$, $P_2=[\underline{a}_2;\overline{a}_2],...,P_n=[\underline{a}_n;\overline{a}_n]$. As an expert opinion on probability assessments is usually imprecise, an expert confidence $\text{Prob}\{P_i=[\underline{a}_i;\overline{a}_i]\}=P_i^c$ in assessment of probabilities P_i of states of nature S_i is also described by intervals:

$$\text{Prob}\{P_1=[\underline{a}_1;\overline{a}_1]\}=P_1^c=[\underline{b}_1;\overline{b}_1],\ \text{Prob}\{P_2=[\underline{a}_2;\overline{a}_2]\}=P_2^c=[\underline{b}_2;\overline{b}_2],\ldots,$$
$$\text{Prob}\{P_n=[\underline{a}_n;\overline{a}_n]\}=P_n^c=[\underline{b}_n;\overline{b}_n].$$

The intervals $[\underline{b}_i;\overline{b}_i]$ represent the second-order uncertainty, i.e. uncertainty of confidence about uncertainty expressed by interval probabilities at the first level.

From the point of view of multiple priors, a second-order imprecise hierarchical probability model may be described as it is schematically shown in Fig. 1.4. The intervals $[\underline{a}_i;\overline{a}_i]$ at the first level represent the set M of the distributions over $\mathcal{S}$. The intervals $[\underline{b}_i;\overline{b}_i]$ used at the second level sort out (constrain) a set $N\subset M$. Thus confidence to an expert's opinion, represented by $[\underline{b}_i;\overline{b}_i]\ i=1,2,\ldots,n$, restricts a set M to its part N as an only set to consider.

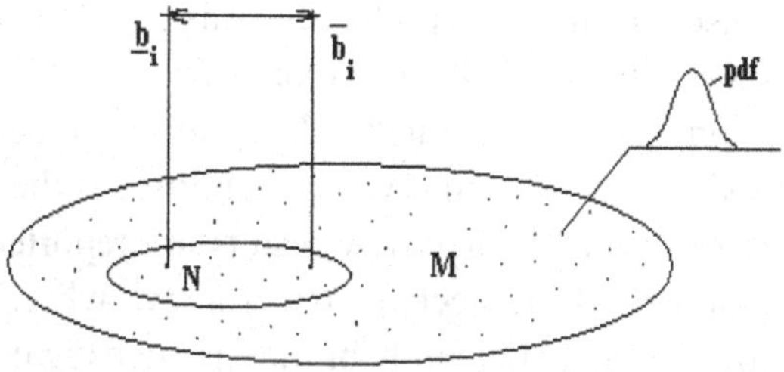

Fig. 1.4. Second-order imprecise hierarchical probability model as constrained multiple priors

Hierarchical models were first suggested in [174]. One of the well-known second-order imprecise hierarchical models is suggested in [123], in which imprecision at its second level is represented by means of lower probabilities. Author shows that no matter whether the first level of this model is precise or imprecise, the model has the same implications for decision analysis and decision reasoning. The suggested hierarchical model is a generalization of imprecise probabilities, Bayesian models and fuzzy probabilities. However, one should mention that this model doesn't deal with probability distributions (multiple priors) which are more general and human-like description of incomplete probability relevant information than lower probabilities [402]. Indeed, lower probability can be obtained as a lower envelope of multiple priors. From the other side, this model is too complicated for decision making. In studies reported in [45] the unified behavioral theory of lower prevision and some open problems in the theory are discussed. In [45,59] the problem of practical representation of combination of experts' beliefs represented by imprecise probabilities is considered. The possibilistic imprecise second-order probability model is considered in [401]. Modeling of linguistic uncertainty in terms of upper probabilities, which are given in behavioral interpretation, is considered in [403].

A large class of models is Bayesian hierarchical models [69,174], which are based on an assumption of existence of second-order precise probabilities reflecting quality of experts judgments. A wide research on hierarchical models conducted in [123,124] advances arguments for Bayesian hierarchical models as the most general models.

The main shortcoming of the mentioned hierarchical models is that they require the use of an exact probability distribution at the second level. This limits a practical use of these models.

Further developments of a hierarchical model are related to creation of hierarchical models that have interval probabilities at the second level. A comprehensive review and some new results are reported in [390]. A quasi-Bayesian model of subjective uncertainty where beliefs are represented by lower and upper probabilities is investigated in [71]. A universal and commonly discussed framework for interval probabilities processing is based on the Walley's theory of imprecise probabilities and the underlying principle of natural extension [399]. This theory is more scientifically grounded among the above mentioned theories on modeling uncertainty and incompleteness of information. Main drawback of this approach, however, is impossibility to use it when experts' beliefs are contradictory. Another drawback of the approach is related to a large number of resulting optimization problems. The use of this theory is also related to strong requirements on consistency of a given class midvalues. The main approach that can be considered to avoid strong restriction on consistency in information structure of decision making problem is the use of the second-order imprecise probability hierarchical model with interval probabilities at the second level. Such hierarchical imprecise models were suggested in [178, 383, 390]. An analysis of such models is conducted in [390]. We have to mention, however, that the decision making procedures presented in [390] were applied to simple classical decision making problems. In [125] a method of specific interval choice is given, introducing the concept of the ignorance function. Some types of hierarchical models are considered in [69]. In [178, 383, 388,389, 390, 392] generalized models are suggested which are imprecise at the second level and allow to deal with complete ignorance at both the levels.

Hierarchical models are effective tools for decision analysis under imprecise and contradictory expert judgments. They have natural structure that allows taking into account important additional information to consider imprecise probabilities not 'as is' but to an extent of a confidence of experts' opinions. The reason for this is that in real problems, in contrast to examples like Ellsberg paradoxes, sources of information are too imperfect for describing probabilities only at the level of their intervals. However, power of hierarchical uncertainty models results in a high computational complexity that makes difficulties in practical use and tractability of these models.

1.9 Analyses of the Existing Decision Theories

Analyzing the above mentioned decision theories on the base of preference frameworks and types of decision relevant information on alternatives, states of nature, probabilities and outcomes, we arrived at conclusion that these theories are developed for a well-described environment of thought experiments and laboratory examples. Such environment defines mainly three simplified directions of decision making theory: decision making under uncertainty, decision making under risk and decision making under ambiguity. We will try to discuss main advantages and disadvantages of the existing theories which belong to these directions.

The decision making methods developed for situations of uncertainty includes Laplace insufficient reason criterion, Savage minimax regret criterion, Hurwitz criterion, Wald maximin solution rule [393] etc.

Maximin solution rule models extreme pessimism in decision making, whereas its generalization, Hurwitz criterion uses linear combination of pessimistic and optimistic solutions. The main shortcoming of these methods is that most of them are not developed to deal with any information on probabilities of states of nature, whereas in real-life decision making DM's almost always have some amount of such information.

The main methods of decision making under risk are von Neumann and Morgenstern EU, Hodges-Lehmann criterion [204] and Prospect theory. The EU theories have strong scientific foundations together with simplicity of the utility models. But, unfortunately, they are based on idealized preference and information frameworks. A decision maker is considered fully rational and relying on coarsely computational, inanimate reasoning. Decision relevant information is based on assumption that future may be perfectly described by means of states of nature like extraction of a white or a black ball. Likelihood of states of nature is described by objective probabilities. However, due to absence of sufficient information, they are commonly unknown. On the other hand, even if objective probabilities are known, beliefs of a DM do not coincide with them due to psychological aspects. Subjective probabilities are slightly more realistic, but are incapable to describe choices under uncertainty even in thought experiments.

Reconsideration of preferences framework underlying EU resulted in development of various advanced preferences frameworks as generalizations of the former. These generalizations can be divided into two types: rank-dependence generalization and sign-dependence generalization [100]. Advanced preference frameworks include various reconsiderations and weakening of independence axiom [147, 167, 171, 362], human attitudes to risk and uncertainty (rank-dependent generalization), gains and losses [222, 387] etc.

PT is suggested for decision making under risk and models such important psychological aspects as asymmetry of gains and losses and distorted evaluation of probabilities. However, this theory requires probabilities and outcomes to be exactly known which sufficiently restricts its application in real-world problems. From the other side, the psychological biases are precisely described in this theory, whereas extents of psychological distortion of decision-relevant information (probabilities and outcomes) are rather imprecisely known.

A large number of studies is devoted to decision making under ambiguity [61,91,106,141,146,147,158,165,166,168,170,180,208,229]. Ambiguity is commonly referred to the cases when probabilities are not known but are supposed to vary within some ranges. The terms 'uncertainty' and 'ambiguity' are not always clearly distinguished and defined but, in general, are related to non-probabilistic uncertainty. In turn, decision making under uncertainty often is considered as an extreme non-probabilistic case – when no information on probabilities is available. From the other side, this case is also termed as decision making under complete ignorance. At the same time, sometimes, this is considered as ambiguity represented by simultaneous consideration of all the probability distributions. The studies on decision making under ambiguity are conducted in two directions – a development of models based on multiple probability distributions, called multiple priors models [171,172,406], and a formation of approaches based on non-additive measures[391,399,400,403,406,409] such as CEU. Mainly, these models consider so-called ambiguity aversion as a property of human behavior to generally prefer outcomes related to non-ambiguous events to those related to ambiguous ones.

CEU is a nice model as describing common inconsistency of the independence assumption with human decision reasoning and non-additivity of beliefs. Non-additivity is an actual property of beliefs conditioned by scarce relevant information on likelihood of events or by psychological distortion of probabilities. This property allows CEU to describe the famous Ellsberg and Allais paradoxes. CEU is a one of the most successful utility models, it is used as a criterion of decision making under ambiguity and decision making under risk. However, non-additive measure used in CEU is precise (numerical) the use of which is questionable for real-world problems where probabilities are not as perfectly (precisely) constrained as in Ellsberg paradoxes. From the other side, CEU is developed for precise utility-based measuring of outcomes that also is not adequate when the latter are imprecisely known and uncertain being related to future.

CPT encompasses PT and CEU basics, and as a result, is both rank-dependent and sign-dependent generalization of EU. Nowadays, CPT is one of the most successful theories and allows to take into account both asymmetry of gains and losses and ambiguity attitudes. However, no interaction of these behavioral factors is taken into account. It is naive to assume that these factors don't exhibit some mix in their influence on choices, as a human being can hardly consider them independently due to psychological issues and restricted computational abilities. From the other side, CPT, as well as PT and CEU, is developed for perfectly described information and well-defined preferences of a DM (this also restricts its ability to adequately model human choices affected by ensemble of behavioral factors).

Multiple priors models were suggested for situations when objective probabilities are not known and a DM cannot assign precise probabilistic beliefs to events but has imprecise beliefs. Indeed, in real world, due to incompleteness of information or knowledge rather a range of probabilities but not a single probability is used describing likelihood of an event. This requires to use a set of probability distributions instead of a unique prior. Within such a set all distributions are considered equally relevant. In general, it is much more adequate but still poor formulation of probability-relevant information available for a DM – in real-life problems a DM usually has some information that allows determining which priors are more and which are less relevant. Without doubt, a DM has different degrees of belief to different relevant probability distributions. In real-world problems, the values of probabilities are imprecise but cannot be sharply constrained as in Ellsberg paradoxes, which are specially designed problems. For addressing this issue, models with second-order probabilities were suggested [61,107,239,364]. For example, in the smooth ambiguity model [239] Klibanoff et al. suggested using a subjective probability measure to reflect a DM's belief on whether a considered subset of multiple priors contains a 'true' prior. The use of this second-order probability allows to depart from extreme evaluation of acts by their minimal or/and maximal expected utilities, and to take into account influence of each relevant prior to acts' overall utilities. However, for a human being an assessment of a precise subjective probability to each prior becomes almost impossible when the number of priors is large. Such a hard procedure does not correspond to extremely limited computational capability of humans. If probabilistic beliefs over states of nature often fail, why should they often work over a more complicated structure – a set of priors?

Second-order precise probability model is a non-realistic description of human beliefs characterized by imprecision and associated with some psychological aspects that need to be considered as well. The other disadvantage of the belief representation suggested in [239] is that the problem of investigation of consistency of subjective probability-relevant information is not discussed – consistent multiple priors are supposed to be given in advance. However, a verification of consistency of beliefs becomes a very important problem. An extensive investigation of this issue is covered in [399].

The other existing multiple priors models like the model based on confidence function and the variational preferences models considered in [270,406] also use complicated techniques to account for a relevance of a prior to a considered problem. From the other side, in these models each decision is evaluated only on one prior and the pessimistic evaluation (min operator) is used.

We mentioned only main existing models for decision making under ambiguity in this chapter. Let us note that the mentioned and other existing utility models for decision under ambiguity are based on rather complicated techniques and may be too subtle to be applied under vagueness of real-life decision-relevant information. In real life, amount, type, reliability and 'unanimity' of information, considered in Ellsberg's formulation of ambiguity, are not perfectly known that presents some difficulties in application of the existing models and decreases trust to the obtained results.

Hierarchical models improve modeling of probability relevant information by introducing the degree of belief to the source of this information (e.g. expert opinion). These models generalize models with precise second-order probabilities and, in contrast to the latter, describe human-like description of information related to states of nature and probabilities. For example, the belief representation in the smooth ambiguity model of Klibanoff et al.[239] based on subjective probability distribution over a set of priors can be considered as a special case of an imprecise hierarchical model. However, most of the works devoted to hierarchical models are related to a huge amount of optimization problems. From the other side, hierarchical models, like multiple priors models and all the other main theories, don't account for vagueness of objective conditions and impreciseness of outcomes, but rely on rigorous framework.

Generalizing the above mentioned drawbacks of the existing theories, we may conclude that the existing decision models yielded good results, but nowadays there is a need in generation of more realistic decision models. The main reason for this is that the existing decision theories are in general developed for thought experiments characterized by precise, perfect decision relevant information. The paradigm of construction of 'elegant' models does not match imperfect nature of decision making and relevant information supported by perceptions. Indeed, even the most advanced utility models are motivated by behavioral phenomena that were observed in thought experiments with simplified conditions. However, as David Schmeidler states, "*Real life is not about balls and urns*" [170]. The existing decision theories cannot be sufficiently accurate because in real-world decision situations human preferences are vague and decision-relevant information on environment and a DM's behavior is imperfect as perception-based. In contrast, humans are able to make proper decisions in such imperfect conditions. Modeling of this outstanding capability of humans, even to some extent, is a difficult but a promising study which stands for a motivation of the research suggested in this book. Economy is a human-centric system and this means that the languages of new decision models should be not languages based on binary logic and probability theory, but human-centric computational schemes for dealing with perception-based information. In our opinion, such languages are natural language (NL), in particular, precisiated NL (PNL) [449], and a geometric visual language (GVL) [8,179] or a geometric description language (GDL) [8,179]. New theories should be based on a more general and adequate view on imperfect perception-based information about environment and a DM's behavior. The main purpose of such a generalization is to construct models that are sufficiently flexible to deal with imperfect nature of decision-relevant information. Such flexibility would allow taking into account more relevant information and could yield more realistic (not more precise!) results and conclusions.

The other main disadvantage of the existing decision theories relates to modeling of behavioral factors underlying decision making like risk attitude, ambiguity attitude, altruism etc. The most of the existing theories are based on precise parametrical modeling which is too coarse and "inanimate" approach to model human activity conditioned by emotions, perceptions, mental factors etc. The existing non-parametric approaches are more adequate, but, they also are based on perfect and precise description of human decision activity. There is a need for a fundamental approach to modeling behavioral decision making.

In real-world decision making imperfect information is supported by perceptions and is expressed in NL or in framework of visual images. In this book we suggest new approaches to decision making under imperfect information on decision environment and a DM's behavior.

In the present book we suggest a theory of decision making under NL-described imperfect information on states of nature, probabilities and outcomes. For formalization of NL-described information the fuzzy set theory as a mathematical formalism for describing partial truth, imprecision and vagueness is used. Decision analysis in this theory is based on a fuzzy-valued Choquet integral-based utility function able to model natural vagueness of preferences under NL-described information.

The suggested theory of decision making with imperfect information is then extended for behavioral decision analysis. In this theory, a DM's behavior, i.e. subjective conditions, is taken into a consideration at the same level of abstraction as objective conditions. We model a DM's behavior by a set of his/her states each representing one principal behavior or, in other words, one principal subjective behavioral condition a DM may exhibit. In line with states of nature, states of a DM constitute in the suggested theory a common basis for decision analysis. Such framework is more general than behavioral basics of the existing theories like CPT and allows for a transparent analysis. Analytical and experimental investigation show that such theories as EU, CEU and CPT are special cases of the suggested theory of behavioral decision making under imperfect information.

The suggested two theories of decision making under imperfect information is that they are based on the use of a utility function. In turn, the use of a utility function consists in an evaluation of a vector-valued alternative by means of a scalar-valued quantity. This transformation is counterintuitive and leads to loss of information. The latter is related to restrictive assumptions on preferences underlying utility models like independence, completeness, transitivity etc. Relaxation of these assumptions results into more adequate but less tractable models. In contrast, humans conduct direct comparison of alternatives as vectors of attributes' values and don't use artificial scalar values. From the other side, sometimes construction of utility function is not practical or even is impossible. For such cases we suggest approach to decision making with NL-described information based on the Fuzzy Pareto optimality (FPO) principle[152]. The FPO is free of the counterintuitive assumption of Pareto optimality principle's according to which all alternatives within a Pareto optimal set are considered equally optimal. In contrast, FPO concept allows to differentiate "more optimal" solutions from "less optimal" solutions. This is intuitive, especially when dealing with imperfect information.

In real-life decision making there are cases when perceptions supporting imperfect decision-relevant information are too vague to have their reliable analytical precisiation, i.e. by means of membership and/or probability density functions. Such information is supported by perceptions in form of cloud visual images. For these cases we suggest a new formalism for decision analysis which is based on a new fuzzy geometry and the extended fuzzy logic suggested by Prof. Lotfi Zadeh. In this formalism we describe unprecisiated perception-based information by means of fuzzy geometrical objects. The decision model in this approach is represented by fuzzy if-then rules and a new fuzzy geometric reasoning to reason from the unprecisiated information to end-up comparison of alternatives.

The approaches suggested in the present book utilize synthesis of the fuzzy sets theory as a mathematical tool for description and reasoning with perception-based information and probability theory.

Chapter 2

Fuzzy Logic and Approximate Reasoning

2.1 Fuzzy Sets

Fuzzy sets, introduced by Zadeh in 1965, provide us a new mathematical tool to deal with uncertainty of information. In this chapter, we will review basic concepts of fuzzy sets, fuzzy relations, fuzzy numbers, linguistic variables, and approximate reasoning which will be used in the rest chapters of the book.

2.1.1 *Types of fuzzy sets*

Definition 2.1. Type-1 fuzzy sets. Let X be a classical set of objects, called the universe, whose generic elements are denoted x. Membership in a classical subset A of X is often viewed as a characteristic function μ_A from [0,1] to $\{0,1\}$ such that

$$\mu_A(x) = \begin{cases} 1 \ \textit{iff} \ x \in A \\ 0 \ \textit{iff} \ x \notin A \end{cases}$$

where $\{0,1\}$ is called a valuation set; 1 indicates membership while 0 - non-membership. If the valuation set is allowed to be in the real interval $[0,1]$, then A is called a Type-1 fuzzy set $\tilde{A}$ [11,20,29,240,242, 243, 435, 470]. $\mu_{\tilde{A}}(x)$ is the grade of membership of x in $\tilde{A}$

$$\mu_{\tilde{A}} : X \to [0,1].$$

As closer the value of $\mu_{\tilde{A}}(x)$ is to 1, so much x belongs to $\tilde{A}$. $\mu: X \rightarrow [0,1]$ is refered to as a membership function (MF).

$\tilde{A}$ is completely characterized by the set of pairs:

$$\tilde{A} = \{(x, \mu_{\tilde{A}}(x)),\ x \in X\}$$

Example The representation of temperature within a range $[T_1, T_2]$ by Type-1 fuzzy and crisp sets is shown in Fig. 2.1a, and 2.1b, respectively. In the first case we use membership function $\mu:[T_1,T_2] \rightarrow [0,1]$ for describing linguistic concepts *"cold"*, *"normal"*, *"warm"*. In the second case right-open intervals are used for describing of traditional variable by crisp sets.

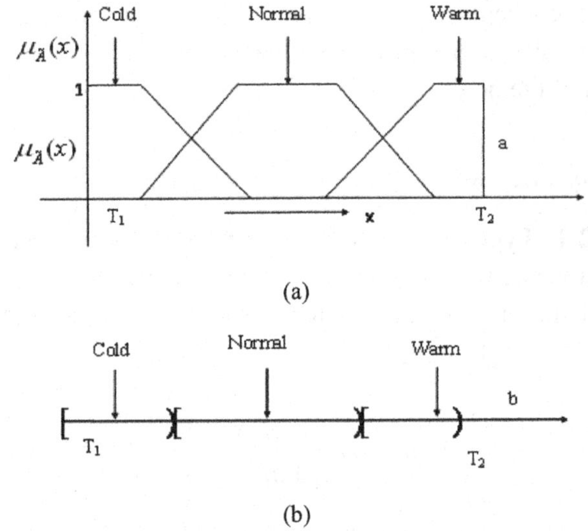

Fig. 2.1. Representation of temperature by (a) Type-1 fuzzy and (b) crisp sets

Fuzzy sets with crisply defined membership functions are called ordinary fuzzy sets or Type-1 fuzzy sets.

Fuzzy Type-2 sets possess more expressive power to create models adequately describing uncertainty. The three-dimensional membership functions of Type-2 fuzzy sets provide additional degrees of freedom that make it possible to directly and more effectively model uncertainties.

Definition 2.2. Type-2 fuzzy set [95,230,231,291,293,294,358,463]. Type-2 fuzzy set (T2 FS) in the universe of discourse X can be represented as follows:

$$\tilde{\tilde{A}}=\{((x,u),\mu_{\tilde{\tilde{A}}}(x,u))|\forall x\in X,\forall u\in J_x\subseteq[0,1]\} \tag{2.1}$$

where $0\leq\mu_{\tilde{\tilde{A}}}(x,u)\leq 1$. The Type-2 fuzzy set $\tilde{\tilde{A}}$ also can be represented as follows:

$$\begin{aligned}\tilde{\tilde{A}}&=\int_{x\in X}\int_{u\in J_x}\mu_{\tilde{\tilde{A}}}(x,u)/(x,u)\\&=\int_{x\in X}[\int_{u\in J_x}\mu_{\tilde{\tilde{A}}}(x,u)/u]/x\end{aligned} \tag{2.2}$$

where x is the primary variable, $J_x\subseteq[0,1]$ is the primary membership of x, u is the secondary variable. $f(x)=\int_{u\in J_x}\mu_{\tilde{\tilde{A}}}(x,u)/u$ is the secondary membership function at x. $\iint$ denotes the union over all admissible x and u.

If X is a discrete set with elements $x_1,...,x_n$ then Type-2 fuzzy set $\tilde{\tilde{A}}$ can be as follows:

$$\tilde{\tilde{A}}=\sum_{x\in X}\left[\sum_{u\in J_x}f_x(u)/u\right]/x=\sum_{i=1}^{n}\sum_{u\in J_x}[f_x(u)/u]/x_i. \tag{2.3}$$

Several examples of Type-2 membership functions are given in Fig. 2.2.

The shaded area referred to as footprint of uncertainty (FOU) and implies that there is a distribution that indicates the third dimension of Type-2 fuzzy sets.

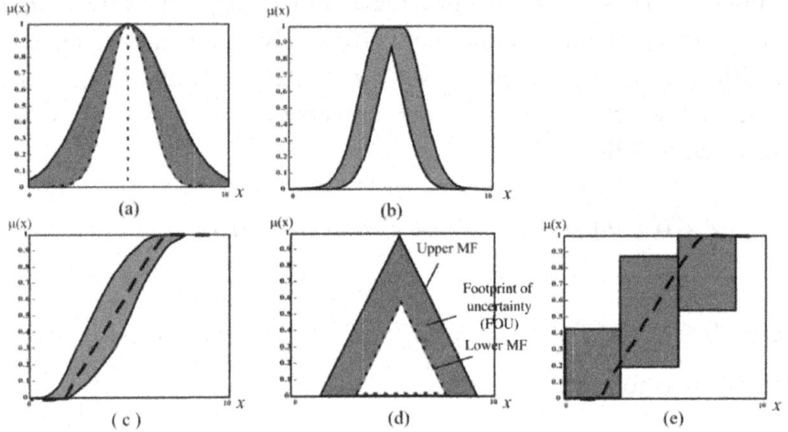

Fig 2.2. Examples of MFs and FOUs: (a) Gaussian MF with uncertain standard deviation; (b) Gaussian MF with uncertain mean; (c) Sigmoidal MF with inflection uncertainties; (d) Triangle type-2 MF; (e) Granulated sigmoidal MF with granulation uncertainties

Example.

Fuzzy set of Type-2 is shown in Fig. 2.3.

If $x=x_1$ four numbers α_1, α_2, α_3, α_4 are produced, by which the ordinary fuzzy set defined with trapezoidal membership function assigned to x_1 is determined.

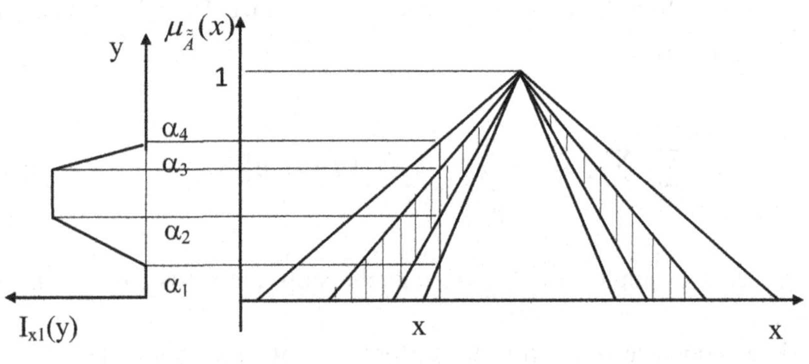

Fig. 2.3. Fuzzy set of Type-2

Definition 2.3. Interval Type-2 Fuzzy set. As special case of a general Type-2 Fuzzy set (T2 FS), Interval Type-2 fuzzy sets uses a subinterval of [0,1] as its membership value. Interval Type-2 fuzzy sets (IT2 FSs) in comparison with general T2 FSs are more effective from computational point of view. This fact made IT2 FSs a widely used framework for design of fuzzy systems.

When all $\mu_{\tilde{\tilde{A}}}(x,u)=1$ in (2.2) then $\tilde{\tilde{A}}$ is an interval Type-2 fuzzy set (IT2 FS).

Consequently IT2 FS can be expressed as

$$\tilde{\tilde{A}} = \int_{x \in X} \int_{u \in J_X} 1/(x,u),\ J_x \subseteq [0,1]. \tag{2.4}$$

Graphical representation of Interval Type-2 Fuzzy set is given in Fig. 2.4 [11].

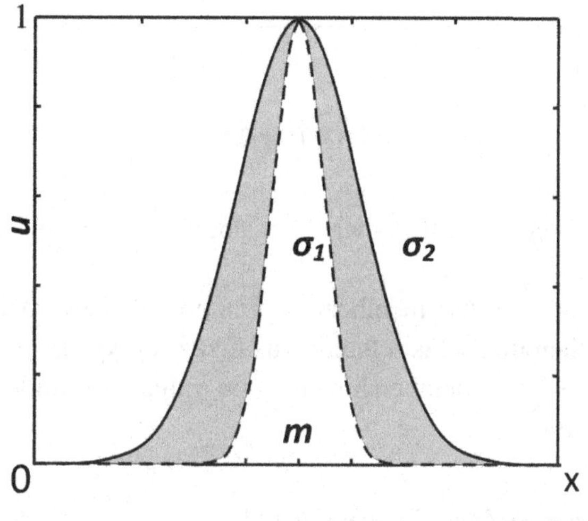

Fig. 2.4. Interval Type-2 Fuzzy set

Example.

$$\tilde{\tilde{A}} = \mu_{\tilde{\tilde{A}}}(x_1^{\alpha_1}, x_1^{\alpha_2})/x_1 + \ldots + \mu_{\tilde{\tilde{A}}}(x_n^{\alpha_1}, x_n^{\alpha_2})/x_n.$$

Membership function of interval-valued fuzzy set $\tilde{\tilde{A}}$ [1,11,89] is given in Fig. 2.5.

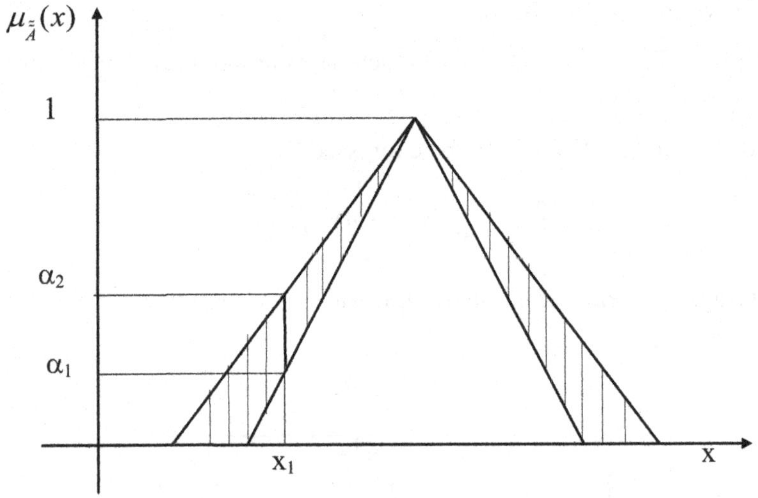

Fig. 2.5. Interval Type-2 fuzzy set $\tilde{\tilde{A}}$

The fuzzy sets of still higher types could be obtained recursively in similar way.

If fuzzy set in X has membership function as Type m-1, m>1 fuzzy set on [0,1], then that set is refered to as fuzzy set type m.

Fuzzy set whose membership function value is a random variable is called probabilistic set.

2.1.2 *Properties of Type-1 fuzzy sets [11]*

Definition 2.4. Equality of fuzzy sets. Two fuzzy sets $\tilde{A}$ and $\tilde{B}$ are said to be equal denoted $\tilde{A} = \tilde{B}$ if and only if

$$\forall x \in X, \quad \mu_{\tilde{A}}(x) = \mu_{\tilde{B}}(x).$$

Definition 2.5. The support and the crossover point of a fuzzy set. The singleton. The support of a fuzzy set $\tilde{A}$ is the ordinary subset of X

that has nonzero membership in $\tilde{A}$:

$$\text{supp}(\tilde{A}) = A^{+0} = \{x \in X, \mu_{\tilde{A}}(x) > 0\}$$

The elements of x such as $\mu_{\tilde{A}}(x) = 1/2$ are the crossover points of $\tilde{A}$.

A fuzzy set that has only one point in X with $\mu_{\tilde{A}} = 1$ as its support is called a singleton.

Definition 2.6. The height of a fuzzy set. Normal and subnormal sets. The height of $\tilde{A}$ is

$$hgt(\tilde{A}) = \sup_{x \in X} \mu_{\tilde{A}}(X)$$

i.e. the least upper bound of $\mu_{\tilde{A}}(x)$.

A is said to be normalized iff $\exists x \in X, \mu_{\tilde{A}}(x) = 1$. This implies $hgt(\tilde{A}) = 1$. Otherwise $\tilde{A}$ is called subnormal fuzzy set.

The empty set $\varnothing$ is defined as

$$x \in X, \mu_{\varnothing}(x) = 0.$$

The univesre of discourse X is defined as

$$\forall x \in X, \mu_X(x) = 1.$$

Definition 2.7. α-level fuzzy sets. One of important ways of representation of fuzzy sets is α-cut method. Such type of representation allows us to use properties of crisp sets and operations on crisp sets in fuzzy set theory.

The (crisp) set of elements that belongs to the fuzzy set $\tilde{A}$ at least to the degree α is called the α-level set:

$$A^{\alpha} = \{x \in X, \mu_{\tilde{A}}(x) \geq \alpha\}.$$

$A^{\alpha} = \{x \in X, \mu_{\tilde{A}}(x) \geq \alpha\}$ is called "strong α-level set" or "strong α-cut".

Now we introduce fuzzy set $\tilde{A}_\alpha$, defined as

$$\tilde{A}_\alpha(x) = \alpha A^\alpha(x). \tag{2.5}$$

The fuzzy set $\tilde{A}$ may be defined in terms of its α-cut as $\tilde{A} = \bigcup_{\alpha \in [0,1]} \tilde{A}_\alpha$, where $\bigcup$ denotes union of classical sets.

Definition 2.8. Convexity of fuzzy sets. A fuzzy set $\tilde{A}$ is convex iff

$$\mu_{\tilde{A}}(\lambda x_1 + (1-\lambda)x_2) > \min(\mu_{\tilde{A}}(x_1), \mu_{\tilde{A}}(x_2)) \tag{2.6}$$

for all $x_1, x_2 \in R$, $\lambda \in [0,1]$, min denotes the minimum operator.

Alternatively, a fuzzy set $\tilde{A}$ on $\mathcal{R}$ is convex iff all its α-level sets are convex in the classical sense.

Definition 2.9. The cardinality of a fuzzy set. When X is a finite set, the scalar cardinality $|\tilde{A}|$ of a fuzzy set $\tilde{A}$ on X is defined as

$$|\tilde{A}| = \sum_{x \in A} \mu_{\tilde{A}}(x).$$

Sometimes $|\tilde{A}|$ is called the power of $\tilde{A}$. $\|\tilde{A}\| = |\tilde{A}|/|X|$ is the relative cardinality. When X is infinite, $|\tilde{A}|$ is defined as

$$|\tilde{A}| = \int_X \mu_{\tilde{A}}(x)\,dx.$$

Definition 2.10. Fuzzy set inclusion. Given fuzzy sets $\tilde{A}, \tilde{B}$ $\tilde{A}$ is said to be included in $\tilde{B}$ $\left(\tilde{A} \subseteq \tilde{B}\right)$ or $\tilde{A}$ is a subset of $\tilde{B}$ if $\forall x \in X$, $\mu_{\tilde{A}}(x) \le \mu_{\tilde{B}}(x)$.

When the inequality is strict, the inclusion is said to be strict and is denoted as $\tilde{A} \subset \tilde{B}$.

2.1.3 *Representations and constructing of Type-1 fuzzy sets*

It was mentioned above that each fuzzy set is uniquely defined by a membership function. In the literature one can find different ways in which membership functions are represented.

List representation. If universal set $X = \{x_1, x_2, \ldots, x_n\}$ is a finite set, membership function of a fuzzy set $\tilde{A}$ on X $\mu_{\tilde{A}}(x)$ can be represented as table. Such table lists all elements in the universe X and the corresponding membership grades as shown below

$$\tilde{A} = \mu_{\tilde{A}}(x_1)/x_1 + \ldots + \mu_{\tilde{A}}(x_n)/x_n = \sum_{i=1}^{n} \mu_{\tilde{A}}(x_i)/x_i.$$

Here symbol / (slash) does not denote division, it is used for correspondence between an element in the universe X (after slash) and its membership grade in the fuzzy set $\tilde{A}$ (before slash). The symbol + connects the elements (does not denote summation).

If X is a finite set then

$$\tilde{A} = \int_X \mu_{\tilde{A}}(x)/x.$$

Here symbol $\int_X$ is used for denoting a union of elements of set X.

Graphical representation. Graphical description of a fuzzy set $\tilde{A}$ on the universe X is suitable in case when X is one or two-dimensional Euclidean space. Simple typical shapes of membership functions are usually used in fuzzy set theory and practice (Table 2.1).

Fuzzy n cube representation. All fuzzy sets on universe X with n elements can be represented by points in the n-dimensional unit cube $-n$-cube.

Table 2.1. Typical membership functions of $\tilde{A}$

Type of Membership Function	Graphical Representation	Analytical Representation
triangular MF	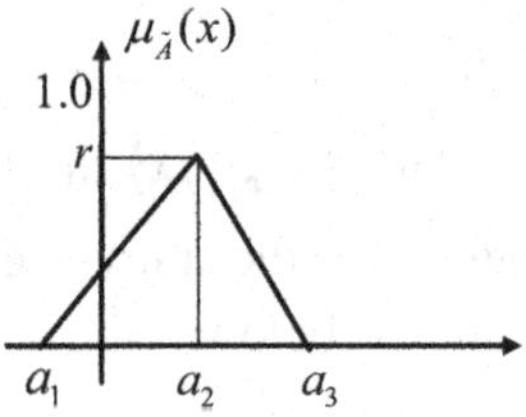	$\mu_{\tilde{A}}(x) = \left\{ \begin{array}{l} \frac{x-a}{a_2-a_1} r, if\ a_1 \le x \le a_2, \\ \frac{a_3-x}{a_3-a_2} r, if\ a_2 \le x \le a_3, \\ 0, otherwise \end{array} \right\}$
trapezoidal MF	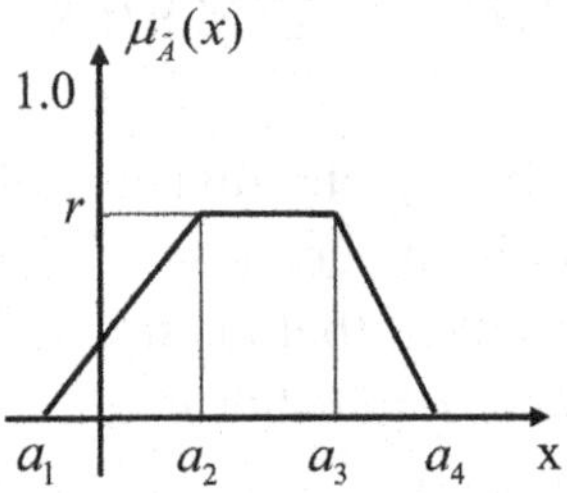	$\mu_{\tilde{A}}(x) = \left\{ \begin{array}{l} \frac{x-a}{a_2-a_1} r, if\ a_1 \le x \le a_2, \\ r, if\ a_2 \le x \le a_3 \\ \frac{a_4-x}{a_4-a_3} r, if\ a_3 \le x \le a_4, \\ 0, otherwise \end{array} \right\}$
S - shaped MF	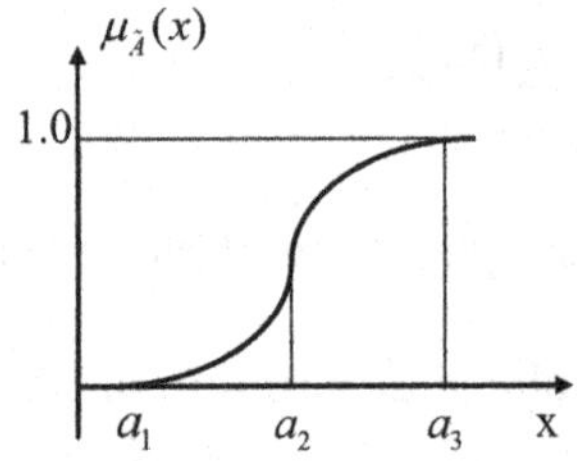	$\mu_{\tilde{A}}(x) = \left\{ \begin{array}{l} 0, if\ x \le a_1 \\ 2\left(\frac{x-a_1}{a_3-a_2}\right)^2, if\ a_1 < x < a_2, \\ 1-2\left(\frac{x-a_1}{a_3-a_1}\right), if\ a_2 \le x \le a_3, \\ 1, if\ a_3 \le x \end{array} \right\}$
Gaussian MF	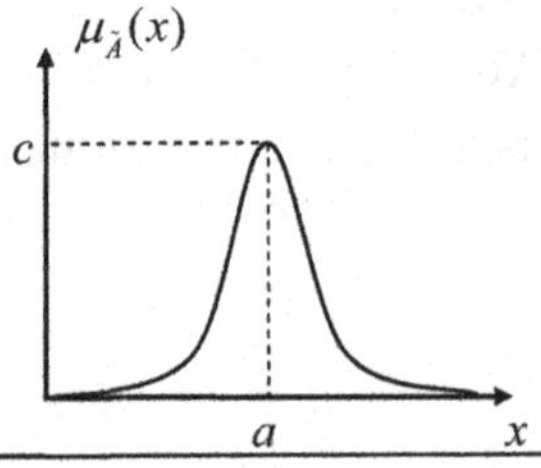	$\mu_{\tilde{A}}(x) = c \exp\left(-\frac{(x-a)^2}{b}\right)$

Assume that universe X contains n elements $X = \{x_1, x_2, ..., x_n\}$. Each element x_i, $i = \overline{1,n}$ can be viewed as a coordinate in the n dimensional Euclidean space. A subset of this space for which values of each coordinate are restricted in $[0,1]$ is called n-cube. Vertices of the cube, i.e. bit list $(0,1,...,0)$ represent crisp sets. The points inside the cube define fuzzy subsets.

Analytical representation. In case if universe X is infinite, it is not effective to use the above considered methods for representation of membership functions of a fuzzy sets. In this case it is suitable to represent fuzzy sets in an analytical form, which describes the shape of membership functions.

There are some typical formulas describing frequently used membership functions in fuzzy set theory and practice.

For example, bell-shaped membership functions often are used for representation of fuzzy sets. These functions are described by the formula:

$$\mu_{\tilde{A}}(x) = c \exp\left(-\frac{(x-a)^2}{b} \right)$$

which is defined by three parameters, *a, b* and *c*.

In general it is effective to represent the important typical membership functions by a parametrized family of functions.The following are formulas for describing the 6 families of membership functions

$$\mu_{\tilde{A}}(x, c_1) = [1 + c_1(x-a)^2]^{-1} \tag{2.7}$$

$$\mu_{\tilde{A}}(x, c_2) = \left[1 + c_2 |x-a|\right]^{-1} \tag{2.8}$$

$$\mu_{\tilde{A}}(x, c_3, d) = \left[1 + c_3 |x-a|^d\right]^{-1} \tag{2.9}$$

$$\mu_{\tilde{A}}(x, c_4, d) = \exp\left[-c_4 |x-a|^d\right] \quad (2.10)$$

$$\mu_{\tilde{A}}(x, c_5) = \max\left\{0, \left[1 - c_5 |x-a|\right]\right\} \quad (2.11)$$

$$\mu_{\tilde{A}}(x, c_6) = c_6 \exp\left[-\frac{(x-a)^2}{b}\right]. \quad (2.12)$$

Here $c_i > 0$, $i = \overline{1,6}$, $d > 1$ are parameters, a denotes the elements of corresponding fuzzy sets with the membership grade equal to unity.

The problem of constructing membership functions is problem of knowledge engineering.

There are many methods for estimation of membership functions. They can be classified as follows:

1. Membership functions based on heuristics.
2. Membership functions based on reliability concepts with respect to the particular problem.
3. Membership functions based on more theoretical demand.
4. Membership functions as a model for human concepts.
5. Neural networks [11] based construction of membership functions.

The estimation methods of membership functions based on more theoretical demand use axioms, probability density functions and so on.

2.1.4 *Operations on Type-1 fuzzy sets*

There exist three standard fuzzy operations: fuzzy intersection, union and complement which are generalization of the corresponding classical set operations.

Let $\tilde{A}$ and $\tilde{B}$ be two fuzzy sets in X with the membership functions $\mu_{\tilde{A}}$ and $\mu_{\tilde{B}}$ respectively. Then the operations of intersection, union and complement are defined as given below.

Definition 2.11. Fuzzy standard intersection and union. The intersection ($\cap$) and union ($\cup$) of fuzzy sets $\tilde{A}$ and $\tilde{B}$ can be calculated by the following formulas:

$$\forall x \in X \quad \mu_{\tilde{A}\cap\tilde{B}}(x) = \min\ (\mu_{\tilde{A}}(x), \mu_{\tilde{B}}(x)),$$

$$\forall x \in X \quad \mu_{\tilde{A}\cup\tilde{B}}(x) = \max\ (\mu_{\tilde{A}}(x), \mu_{\tilde{B}}(x)),$$

where $\mu_{\tilde{A}\cap\tilde{B}}(x)$ and $\mu_{\tilde{A}\cup\tilde{B}}(x)$ are the membership functions of $\tilde{A}\cap\tilde{B}$ and $\tilde{A}\cup\tilde{B}$, respectively.

Definition 2.12. Standard fuzzy complement. The complement $\tilde{A}^c$ of $\tilde{A}$ is defined by the membership function:

$$\forall x \in X \quad \mu_{\tilde{A}^c}(x) = 1 - \mu_{\tilde{A}}(x)$$

As already mentioned, $\mu_{\tilde{A}}(x)$ is interpreted as the degree to which x belongs to $\tilde{A}$. Then by the definition $\mu_{\tilde{A}^c}(x)$ can be interpreted as the degree to which x does not belong to $\tilde{A}$.

The standard fuzzy operations do not satisfy the law of excluded middle $\tilde{A}\cup\tilde{A}^c = X$ and the law of contradiction $\tilde{A}\cap\tilde{A}^c = \varnothing$ of classical set theory. But commutativity, associativity, idempotency, distributivity, and De Morgan laws are held for standard fuzzy operations.

For fuzzy union, intersection and complement operations there exist a broad class of functions. Functions that qualify as fuzzy intersections and fuzzy unions are defined as T-norms and T-conorms[135].

Definition 2.13. T-norms. T-norm is a binary operation in [0,1], i.e. a binary function T from [0,1] into [0,1] that satisfies the following axioms

$$T\left(\mu_{\tilde{A}}(x), 1\right) = \mu_{\tilde{A}}(x) \tag{2.13}$$

if $\mu_{\tilde{A}}(x) \le \mu_{\tilde{C}}(x)$ and $\mu_{\tilde{B}}(x) \le \mu_{\tilde{D}}(x)$ then

$$T(\mu_{\tilde{A}}(x), \mu_{\tilde{B}}(x)) \le T(\mu_{\tilde{C}}(x), \mu_{\tilde{D}}(x)) \tag{2.14}$$

$$T(\mu_{\tilde{A}}(x), \mu_{\tilde{B}}(x)) = T(\mu_{\tilde{B}}(x), \mu_{\tilde{A}}(x)) \tag{2.15}$$

$$T(\mu_{\tilde{A}}(x), T(\mu_{\tilde{B}}(x), \mu_{\tilde{C}}(x))) = T(T(\mu_{\tilde{A}}(x), \mu_{\tilde{B}}(x)), \mu_{\tilde{C}}(x)). \tag{2.16}$$

Here (2.13) is boundary condition, (2.14)-(2.16) are conditions of monotonicity, commutativity and associativity, respectively.

The function T takes as its arguments the pair consisting of the element membership grades in set $\tilde{A}$ and in set $\tilde{B}$, and yields membership grades of the element in the $\tilde{A} \cap \tilde{B}$

$$(\tilde{A} \cap \tilde{B})(x) = T[A(x), B(x)] \quad \forall x \in X.$$

The following are frequently used T-norm-based fuzzy intersection operations:

Standard intersection

$$T_0(\mu_{\tilde{A}}(x), \mu_{\tilde{B}}(x)) = \min\{\mu_{\tilde{A}}(x), \mu_{\tilde{B}}(x)\} \tag{2.17}$$

Algebraic product

$$T_1(\mu_{\tilde{A}}(x), \mu_{\tilde{B}}(x)) = \mu_{\tilde{A}}(x) \cdot \mu_{\tilde{B}}(x) \tag{2.18}$$

Bounded difference

$$T_2(\mu_{\tilde{A}}(x), \mu_{\tilde{B}}(x)) = \mu_{\tilde{A} \cap \tilde{B}}(x) = \max\{0, \mu_{\tilde{A}}(x) + \mu_{\tilde{B}}(x) - 1\} \tag{2.19}$$

Drastic intersection

$$T_3(\mu_{\tilde{A}}(x), \mu_{\tilde{B}}(x)) = \begin{cases} \min\{\mu_{\tilde{A}}(x), \mu_{\tilde{B}}(x)\}, & \text{if } \mu_{\tilde{A}}(x) = 1 \\ & \text{or } \mu_{\tilde{B}}(x) = 1 \\ 0, & \text{otherwise} \end{cases} \tag{2.20}$$

For four fuzzy intersections the following is true

$$T_3(\mu_{\tilde{A}}(x), \mu_{\tilde{B}}(x)) \le T_2(\mu_{\tilde{A}}(x), \mu_{\tilde{B}}(x)) \le T_1(\mu_{\tilde{A}}(x), \mu_{\tilde{B}}(x)) \le T_0(\mu_{\tilde{A}}(x), \mu_{\tilde{B}}(x)) \tag{2.21}$$

Definition 2.14. T-conorms. T-conorm is a binary operation in $[0,1]$, i.e. a binary function $S:[0,1] \times [0,1] \to [0,1]$ that satisfies the following axioms

$$S\left(\mu_{\tilde{A}}(x),0\right)=\mu_{\tilde{A}}(x)\text{ ; (boundary condition)} \tag{2.22}$$

if $\mu_{\tilde{A}}(x)\le\mu_{\tilde{C}}(x)$ and $\mu_{\tilde{B}}(x)\le\mu_{\tilde{D}}(x)$ then

$$S(\mu_{\tilde{A}}(x),\mu_{\tilde{B}}(x))\le S(\mu_{\tilde{C}}(x),\mu_{\tilde{D}}(x))\text{ ; (monotonicity)} \tag{2.23}$$

$$S(\mu_{\tilde{A}}(x),\mu_{\tilde{B}}(x))=S(\mu_{\tilde{B}}(x),\mu_{\tilde{A}}(x))\text{ ; (commutativity)} \tag{2.24}$$

$$S(\mu_{\tilde{A}}(x),S(\mu_{\tilde{B}}(x),\mu_{\tilde{C}}(x)))=S(S(\mu_{\tilde{A}}(x),\mu_{\tilde{B}}(x)),\mu_{\tilde{C}}(x))\text{ ; (associativity).} \tag{2.25}$$

The function S yields membership grade of the element in the set $\tilde{A}\cup\tilde{B}$ on the argument which is pair consisting of the same elements membership grades in set $\tilde{A}$ and $\tilde{B}$

$$(\tilde{A}\cup\tilde{B})(X)=S[\tilde{A}(x),\tilde{B}(x)]. \tag{2.26}$$

The following are frequently used T-conorm based fuzzy union operations.

Standard union

$$S_0(\mu_{\tilde{A}}(x),\mu_{\tilde{B}}(x))=\max\{\mu_{\tilde{A}}(x),\mu_{\tilde{B}}(x)\} \tag{2.27}$$

Algebraic sum

$$S_1(\mu_{\tilde{A}}(x),\mu_{\tilde{B}}(x))=\mu_{\tilde{A}}(x)+\mu_{\tilde{B}}(x)-\mu_{\tilde{A}}(x)\cdot\mu_{\tilde{B}}(x) \tag{2.28}$$

Drastic union

$$S_3(\mu_{\tilde{A}}(x),\mu_{\tilde{B}}(x))=\begin{cases}\max\{\mu_{\tilde{A}}(x),\mu_{\tilde{B}}(x)\}, & \text{if } \mu_{\tilde{A}}(x)=0 \\ & \text{or } \mu_{\tilde{B}}(x)=0 \\ 1, & \text{otherwise}\end{cases} \tag{2.29}$$

For four fuzzy union operations the following is true:

$$S_0(\mu_{\tilde{A}}(x),\mu_{\tilde{B}}(x)) \le S_1(\mu_{\tilde{A}}(x),\mu_{\tilde{B}}(x)) \\ \le S_2(\mu_{\tilde{A}}(x),\mu_{\tilde{B}}(x)) \le S_3(\mu_{\tilde{A}}(x),\mu_{\tilde{B}}(x)). \tag{2.30}$$

Definition 2.15. Cartesian product of fuzzy sets. The Cartesian product of fuzzy sets $\tilde{A}_1,\tilde{A}_2,\dots,\tilde{A}_n$ on universes $X_1,X_2,\dots,X_n$ respectively is a fuzzy set in the space $X_1 \times X_2 \times \ldots \times X_n$ with the membership function $\mu_{\tilde{A}_1\times\tilde{A}_2\times\ldots\times\tilde{A}_n}(x)=\min\left\{\mu_{\tilde{A}_i}(x_i)\,|\,x=(x_1,x_2\ldots,x_n),x_i\in X_i\right\}$.

Definition 2.16. Power of fuzzy sets. m-th power of a fuzzy set $\tilde{A}^m$ is defined as

$$\mu_{\tilde{A}^m}(x)=[\mu_{\tilde{A}}(x)]^m \ , \ \forall \mathrm{x}\in \mathrm{X},\ \forall \mathrm{m}\in \mathrm{R}^+ \tag{2.31}$$

where R^+ is positively defined set of real numbers.

Definition 2.17. Concentration and dilation of fuzzy sets.

Let $\tilde{A}$ be fuzzy set on the universe:

$$\tilde{A}=\left\{x,\mu_{\tilde{A}}(x)/x\in X\right\}$$

Then the operator $Con_m\tilde{A}=\{(x,[\mu_{\tilde{A}}(x)]^m)/\mathrm{x}\in\mathrm{X}\}$ is called concentration of $\tilde{A}$ and the operator $Dil_n\tilde{A}=\{(x,\sqrt{\mu_{\tilde{A}}(x)}\ )/\mathrm{x}\in\mathrm{X}\}$ is called dilation of $\tilde{A}$.

Definition 2.18. Difference of fuzzy sets. Difference of fuzzy sets is defined by the formula:

$$\forall x\in X,\quad \mu_{\tilde{A}|-|\tilde{B}}(x)=\max\{0,\mu_{\tilde{A}}(x)-\mu_{\tilde{B}}(x))\}. \tag{2.32}$$

$\tilde{A}|-|\tilde{B}$ is the fuzzy set of elements that belong to $\tilde{A}$ more than to $\tilde{\mathrm{B}}$.

Symmetrical difference of fuzzy sets $\tilde{A}$ and $\tilde{\mathrm{B}}$ is the fuzzy set $\tilde{\mathrm{A}}\nabla\tilde{\mathrm{B}}$ of elements that belong more to $\tilde{A}$ than to $\tilde{\mathrm{B}}$:

$$\forall x\in X\quad \mu_{\tilde{\mathrm{A}}\nabla\tilde{\mathrm{B}}}(x)=\left|\mu_{\tilde{A}}(x)-\mu_{\tilde{B}}(x)\right|. \tag{2.33}$$

Let us mention that fuzziness is essentially different from randomness. In view of this, let us consider the following concept.

Assume that $P(X)$ is a power set of the universe X. The mapping $\Pi : P(X) \rightarrow [0,1]$ with the following properties:

1. $\Pi(\varnothing) = 0, \Pi(X) = 1$;
2. $A \subseteq B \rightarrow \Pi(A) \leq \Pi(B)$;
3. $\Pi(\bigcup_{i \in I} A_i) = \sup_{i \in I} \Pi(A_i)$,

is called possibility measure. Here I is index set.

In possibility theory every possibility measure is uniquely determined by the possibility distribution function.

Given a possibility measure Π on power set $P(X)$ of X, function $r : X \rightarrow [0,1]$ such that

$$r(x) = \Pi(\{x\})$$

for all $x \in X$, is called a possibility distribution function of Π.

We can write that

$$\Pi(A) = \max_{x \in A} r(x)$$

for each $A \in P(X)$.

For

$$\forall A, B \subseteq P(X),\ \Pi(A \cup B) = \max(\Pi(A), \Pi(B)),$$

whereas for probability measure, one has

$$\forall A, B \subseteq P(X),\ P(A \cup B) = P(A) + P(B) - P(A \cap B).$$

For detailed comparison of probability and possibility measures one can refer to Chapter 5.

When X is not finite then

$$\Pi(A) = \sup_{x \in A} r(x).$$

2.1.5 *Interval and fuzzy numbers, generalized fuzzy numbers*

Let's first consider Type-1 fuzzy number [11].

Definition 2.19. Type-1 Fuzzy number. A fuzzy number is a fuzzy set $\tilde{A}$ on R which possesses the following properties: a) $\tilde{A}$ is a normal fuzzy set; b) $\tilde{A}$ is a convex fuzzy set; c) α-cut of $\tilde{A}$ A^{α} is a closed interval for every $\alpha \in (0,1]$; d) the support of $\tilde{A}$ A^{+0} is bounded.

Intervals are special cases of fuzzy numbers. Interval analysis is frequently used in decision theories, in decision making with imprecise probabilites. Because of this first we will consider operations over intervals of real line.It is easy to see that a result of operations over closed intervals is also a closed interval. Due to this fact, the bounds of the resulting closed interval are to be expressed by means of the bounds of the given intervals.

Below we introduce the basic operations over closed intervals. Assume that the following intervals of the real line $\mathcal{R}$ are given:

$$A=[a_1,a_2];B=[b_1,b_2].$$

Addition. If

$$x\in[a_1,a_2] \text{ and } y\in[b_1,b_2] \tag{2.34}$$

Then

$$x+y\in[a_1+b_1,\ a_2+b_2]. \tag{2.35}$$

This can symbolically be expressed as

$$A+B=[a_1,\ a_2]+[b_1,\ b_2]=[a_1+b_1,\ a_2+b_2]. \tag{2.36}$$

The image of A. If $\mathrm{x}\in[\mathrm{a}_1,\mathrm{a}_2]$ then $-x\in[-a_2,-a_1]$. This is symbolically expressed as

$$-A=[-a_2,-a_1].$$

Let us consider the result of $A+(-A)$. According to the operations given above, we can write:

$$A+(-A)=[a_1,a_2]+[-a_2,-a_1]=[a_1-a_2,\ a_2-a_1].$$

Note that $A+(-A)\neq 0$

Subtraction. If $x\in[a_1,a_2]$ and $y\in[b_1,b_2]$, then

$$x-y\in[a_1-b_2,a_2-b_1] \tag{2.37}$$

$$A-B=[a_1,a_2]-[b_1,b_2]=[a_1-b_2,a_2-b_1]. \tag{2.38}$$

Multiplication. The production of intervals $A,B\subset\mathcal{R}$ is defined as follows:

$$A\cdot B=[\min(a_1\cdot b_1,a_1\cdot b_2,a_2\cdot b_1,a_2\cdot b_2),\ \max(a_1\cdot b_1,a_1\cdot b_1,a_2\cdot b_1,a_2\cdot b_2)] \tag{2.39}$$

For the case $A,B\subset\mathcal{R}_+$ the result is obtained easily as

$$A\cdot B=[a_1,a_2]\cdot[b_1,b_2]=[a_1\cdot b_1,a_2\cdot b_2]. \tag{2.40}$$

The multiplication of an interval A by a real number $k\in\mathcal{R}$ is defined as follows:

$$\text{if } k>0 \text{ then } k\cdot A=k\cdot[a_1,a_2]=[ka_1,ka_2],$$

$$\text{if } k<0 \text{ then } k\cdot A=k\cdot[a_1,a_2]=[ka_2,ka_1].$$

Division. Under assumption that the dividing interval does not contain 0 and $A,B\subset\mathcal{R}_+$ one has

$$A:B=[a_1,a_2]\ :\ [b_1,b_2]=[a_1/b_2,\ a_2/b_1]. \tag{2.41}$$

Based on (2.41), the inverse of A can be defined as follows:
If $x\in[a_1,\ a_2]$ then

$$\frac{1}{x}\in\left[\frac{1}{a_2},\frac{1}{a_1}\right]$$

and

$$A^{-1} = [a_1, a_2]^{-1} = [1/a_2, 1/a_1]. \quad (2.42)$$

In general case the ratio of A and B can be done as follows

$$[a_1, a_2]:[b_1, b_2] = [a_1, a_2]\cdot[1/b_2, 1/b_1]$$

$$= [\min\{a_1/b_1, a_1/b_2, a_2/b_1, a_2/b_2\}, \max\{a_1/b_1, a_1/b_2, a_2/b_1, a_2/b_2\}]. \quad (2.43)$$

Note that,

$$A\cdot A^{-1} = [a_1/a_2, a_2/a_1] \neq 1.$$

The division by a number $k > 0$ is equivalent to multiplication by a number $1/k$.

Now we consider arithmetic operation on fuzzy numbers. There are different methods for developing fuzzy arithmetic[102,435]. In this section we present three methods.

Method based on the extension principle [11,435]. By this method basic arith-metic operations on real numbers are extended to operations on fuzzy numbers. Let $\tilde{A}$ and $\tilde{B}$ be two fuzzy numbers and $*$ denote any of four arithmetic operations $\{+, -, \cdot, :\}$.

A fuzzy set $\tilde{A} * \tilde{B}$ on $\mathcal{R}$ can be defined by the equation

$$\forall z \in R, \quad \mu_{(\tilde{A}*\tilde{B})}(z) = \sup_{z=x*y} \min\{\mu_{\tilde{A}}(x), \mu_{\tilde{B}}(y)\}. \quad (2.44)$$

It is shown in [240] that $\tilde{A} * \tilde{B}$ is a fuzzy number and the following theorem has been formulated and proved.

Let us mention that a fuzzy number with continuous membership function is referred to as a continuous fuzzy number.

Theorem 2.1. Let $* \in \{+, -, \cdot, :\}$, and let $\tilde{A}$, $\tilde{B}$ denote continuous fuzzy numbers. Then, the fuzzy set $\tilde{A} * \tilde{B}$ defined by (2.44) is a continuous fuzzy number.

Then for four basic arithmetic operations on fuzzy numbers we can write

$$\mu_{(\tilde{A}+\tilde{B})}(z) = \sup_{z=x+y} \min[\mu_{\tilde{A}}(x), \mu_{\tilde{B}}(y)] \tag{2.45}$$

$$\mu_{(\tilde{A}-\tilde{B})}(z) = \sup_{z=x-y} \min[\mu_{\tilde{A}}(x), \mu_{\tilde{B}}(y)] \tag{2.46}$$

$$\mu_{(\tilde{A}\cdot\tilde{B})}(z) = \sup_{z=x\cdot y} \min[\mu_{\tilde{A}}(x), \mu_{\tilde{B}}(y)] \tag{2.47}$$

$$\mu_{(\tilde{A}:\tilde{B})}(z) = \sup_{z=x:y} \min[\mu_{\tilde{A}}(x), \mu_{\tilde{B}}(y)]. \tag{2.48}$$

Method based on interval arithmetic and α-cuts. This method is based on representation of arbitrary fuzzy numbers by their α-cuts and use interval arithmetic to the α-cuts. Let $\tilde{A}, \tilde{B} \subset \mathcal{R}$ be fuzzy numbers and $*$ denote any of four operations. For each $\alpha \in (0,1]$, the α-cut of $\tilde{A} * \tilde{B}$ is expressed as

$$(\tilde{A} * \tilde{B})^{\alpha} = A^{\alpha} * B^{\alpha}. \tag{2.49}$$

For $*$ we assume $0 \notin \mathrm{supp}(\tilde{B})$.

The resulting fuzzy number $\tilde{A} * \tilde{B}$ can be defined as (see section 2.1)

$$\tilde{A} * \tilde{B} = \bigcup_{\alpha\in[0,1]} \alpha(A * B)^{\alpha}. \tag{2.50}$$

Next using (2.49), (2.50) we illustrate four arithmetic operations on fuzzy numbers.

Addition. Let $\tilde{A}$ and $\tilde{B}$ be two fuzzy numbers and A^{α} and B^{α} be their α-cuts

$$A^{\alpha} = [a_1^{\alpha}, a_2^{\alpha}]; B^{\alpha} = [b_1^{\alpha}, b_2^{\alpha}]. \tag{2.51}$$

Then we can write

$$A^\alpha + B^\alpha = [a_1^\alpha, a_2^\alpha] + [b_1^\alpha, b_2^\alpha] = [a_1^\alpha + b_1^\alpha, a_2^\alpha + b_2^\alpha], \forall \alpha \in [0,1] \qquad (2.52)$$

here

$$A^\alpha = \{x / \mu_{\tilde{A}}(x) \geq \alpha\}; B^\alpha = \{x / \mu_{\tilde{B}}(x) \geq \alpha\}. \qquad (2.53)$$

Subtraction. Subtraction of given fuzzy numbers $\tilde{A}$ and $\tilde{B}$ can be defined as

$$(\tilde{A} - \tilde{B})^\alpha = A^\alpha - B^\alpha = [a_1^\alpha - b_2^\alpha, a_2^\alpha - b_1^\alpha], \forall \alpha \in [0,1]. \qquad (2.54)$$

We can determine (2.54) by addition of the image $\tilde{B}^-$ to $\tilde{A}$

$$\forall \alpha \in [0,1], B^{\alpha^-} = [-b_2^\alpha, -b_1^\alpha]. \qquad (2.55)$$

Multiplication. Let two fuzzy numbers $\tilde{A}$ and $\tilde{B}$ be given. Multiplication $\tilde{A} \cdot \tilde{B}$ is defined as

$$(\tilde{A} \cdot \tilde{B})^\alpha = A^\alpha \cdot B^\alpha = [a_1^\alpha, a_2^\alpha] \cdot [b_1^\alpha, b_2^\alpha] \quad \forall \alpha \in [0,1]. \qquad (2.56)$$

Multiplication of fuzzy number $\tilde{A}$ in $\mathcal{R}$ by ordinary numbers $k \in \mathcal{R}_+$ is performed as follows

$$\forall \tilde{A} \subset \mathcal{R} \quad kA^\alpha = [ka_1^\alpha, ka_2^\alpha], \forall \alpha \in [0,1]. \qquad (2.57)$$

Division. Division of two fuzzy numbers $\tilde{A}$ and $\tilde{B}$ is defined by

$$A^\alpha : B^\alpha = [a_1^\alpha, a_2^\alpha] : [b_1^\alpha, b_2^\alpha] \ \forall \alpha \in [0,1]. \qquad (2.58)$$

Definition 2.20. Absolute value of a fuzzy number. Absolute value of fuzzy number is defined as:

$$abs(\tilde{A}) = \begin{cases} \max(\mu_{\tilde{A}}(x), \mu_{-\tilde{A}}(x)), & \text{for } \mathcal{R}_+ \\ 0, & \text{for } \mathcal{R}_- . \end{cases} \qquad (2.59)$$

To date we have considered arithmetic operations on the traditional Type-1 fuzzy numbers. In [57] it is pointed out that in many real life problems it is not possible to restrict the membership function to the normal form and further considered Generalized Fuzzy Number (GFN) concept.

Now will consider arithmetic operations on GFN. In practice usually generalized fuzzy numbers are converted into normal fuzzy numbers through normalization process. Although, this procedure is mathematically correct but it decreases the amount of information that is available in the original data, that is, it results in loss of information.

Definition 2.21. Generalized fuzzy number [57]. A fuzzy set $\tilde{A}$, defined on the universal set of real numbers $\mathcal{R}$, is said to be generalized fuzzy number if its membership function has the following characteristics:

(i) $\mu_{\tilde{A}} : \mathcal{R} \to [0,1]$ is continuous.

(ii) $\mu_{\tilde{A}}(x) = 0$ for all $x \in (-\infty, a] \cup [d, \infty)$.

(iii) $\mu_{\tilde{A}}(x)$ is strictly increasing on $[a,b]$ and strictly decreasing on $[c,d]$.

(iv) $\mu_{\tilde{A}}(x) = w,$ for all $x \in [b,c]$, where $0 < w \leq 1$.

A generalized fuzzy number $\tilde{A} = (a,b,c,d,w)$ is said to be a generalized trapezoidal fuzzy number if its membership function is given by [57,381]

$$\mu_{\tilde{A}}(x) = \begin{cases} \dfrac{w(x-a)}{(b-a)}, & a \leq x \leq b \\ w & ,b \leq x \leq c \\ \dfrac{w(x-d)}{(c-d)}, & c \leq x \leq d \\ 0, & otherwise. \end{cases}$$

Meaning of GFN here is that if data is collected from on expert and on the basis of collected data decision maker is $w \times 100\%$ in favor that for example demand will be greater than or equal to b units and less than or equal to c units.

Now we consider arithmetic operations on trapezoidal GFN [57].

Two trapezodal GFN $\tilde{A}_1$ and $\tilde{A}_2$ are given.

$$\tilde{A}_1 = (a_1, b_1, c_1, d_1; w_1) \text{ and } \tilde{A}_2 = (a_2, b_2, c_2, d_2; w_2).$$

Addition

$$\tilde{A}_1 \oplus \tilde{A}_2 = (a_1 + a_2, b_1 + b_2, c_1 + c_2, d_1 + d_2; \text{minimum}(w_1, w_2))$$

Subtraction

$$\tilde{A}_1 \Theta \tilde{A}_2 = (a_1 - d_2, b_1 - c_2, c_1 - b_2, d_1 - a_2; \text{minimum}(w_1, w_2))$$

Multiplication

$$\tilde{A}_1 \otimes \tilde{A}_2 = (a', b', c', d'; \text{minimum}(w_1, w_2)),$$

$$\text{where } a' = \text{minimum}(\text{a}_1 a_2, \text{a}_1 d_2, \text{a}_2 d_1, d_1 d_2)$$

$$b' = \text{minimum}(\text{b}_1 b_2, b_1 c_2, c_1 b_2, c_1 c_2),$$

$$c' = \text{maximum}(\text{b}_1 b_2, b_1 c_2, c_1 b_2, c_1 c_2),$$

$$d' = \text{maximum}(\text{a}_1 a_2, \text{a}_1 d_2, \text{a}_2 d_1, d_1 d_2)$$

Scalar Multiplication

$$\lambda \tilde{A}_1 = \begin{cases} (\lambda a_1, \lambda b_1, \lambda c_1, \lambda d_1; w_1), \lambda > 0 \\ \lambda d_1, \lambda c_1, \lambda b_1, \lambda a_1; w_1), \lambda < 0 \end{cases}$$

2.1.6 *Operations on Type-2 fuzzy sets and numbers*

First we consider some properties of Type-2 fuzzy sets. To indicate second order uncertainty one can use the concept of the footprint of uncertainty.

Definition 2.22. Footprint of Type-2 fuzzy set. The footprint of uncertainty (FOU) of a Type-2 fuzzy set $\tilde{\tilde{A}}$ is a region with boundaries covering all the primary membership points of elements x, and is defined as follows [94-96,213,284-289,291]:

$$\mathrm{FOU}(\tilde{\tilde{A}}) = \bigcup_{x \in X} J_x \tag{2.60}$$

Definition 2.23. Embedded fuzzy sets. The embedded Type-2 fuzzy set of Type-2 fuzzy set $\tilde{\tilde{A}}$ is defined as follows [293]:

$$\tilde{\tilde{A}}_0 = \int_{x \in X} [f_x(\theta)/\theta]/x, \tag{2.61}$$

where θ is the element, which can be chosen from each interval J_x. For discrete case, $\tilde{\tilde{A}}_0$ is defined as follows:

$$\tilde{\tilde{A}}_0 = \sum_{i=1}^{R} [f_{x_i}(\theta_i)/\theta_i]/x_i. \tag{2.62}$$

Set-theoretic operations on Type-2 fuzzy sets

Two Type-2 fuzzy sets $\tilde{\tilde{A}}$ and $\tilde{\tilde{B}}$ in a universe X with membership functions $\mu_{\tilde{\tilde{A}}}(x)$ and $\mu_{\tilde{\tilde{B}}}(x)$ are given: $\mu_{\tilde{\tilde{A}}}(x) = \int_u f_x(u)/u$ and $\mu_{\tilde{\tilde{B}}}(x) = \int_w g_x(w)/w$, where $u, w \subseteq J_x$ indicate the primary memberships of x and $f_x(u), g_x(w) \in [0,1]$ indicate the secondary memberships (grades) of x. Using Zadeh's Extension Principle, the membership grades for union, intersection and complement of Type-2 fuzzy sets $\tilde{\tilde{A}}$ and $\tilde{\tilde{B}}$ can be defined as follows [230]:

Union:

$$\tilde{\tilde{A}} \cup \tilde{\tilde{B}} \Leftrightarrow \mu_{\tilde{\tilde{A}} \cup \tilde{\tilde{B}}}(x) = \mu_{\tilde{\tilde{A}}}(x) \sqcup \mu_{\tilde{\tilde{B}}}(x)$$
$$= \int_u \int_w (f_x(u) * g_x(w)) / (u \vee w), \tag{2.63}$$

Intersection:

$$\tilde{\tilde{A}} \cap \tilde{\tilde{B}} \Leftrightarrow \mu_{\tilde{\tilde{A}} \cap \tilde{\tilde{B}}}(x) = \mu_{\tilde{\tilde{A}}}(x) \sqcap \mu_{\tilde{\tilde{B}}}(x) = \int_u \int_w (f_x(u) * g_x(w)) / (u * w), \tag{2.64}$$

Complement:

$$\tilde{\tilde{A}} \Leftrightarrow \mu_{\tilde{\tilde{A}}}(x) = \neg \mu_{\tilde{\tilde{A}}}(x) = \int_u f_x(u) / (1-u). \tag{2.65}$$

Here $\sqcap$ and $\sqcup$ are intersection/meet and union/join operations on two membership function Type-2 fuzzy sets, * indicates the chosen T-norm.

T-norm and T-conorm

A T-norm can be extended to be a conjunction in Type-2 logic and an intersection in Type-2 fuzzy set theory, such as a Minimum T-norm and a Product T-norm [335].

A T-conorm of operation can be used to stand for a disjunction in Type-2 fuzzy logic and a union in Type-2 fuzzy set theory, such as maximum T-conorm.

Type reduction

To defuzzify Type-2 fuzzy sets one can use type reduction procedure. By this procedure, we can transform a Type-2 fuzzy set into a Type-1 fuzzy set. The centroid of a Type-2 set, whose domain is discretized into points, can be defined as follows [231]:

$$C_{\tilde{\tilde{A}}} = \int_{\theta_1} \cdots \int_{\theta_N} \left[\mu_{D_1}(\theta_1) * \cdots * \mu_{D_N}(\theta_N) \right] / \frac{\sum_{i=1}^{N} x_i \theta_i}{\sum_{i=1}^{N} \theta_i} \tag{2.66}$$

where $D_i = \mu_{\tilde{\tilde{A}}}(x_i), \theta_i \in D_i$.

Definition 2.24. Type-2 fuzzy number. Let $\tilde{\tilde{A}}$ be a Type-2 fuzzy set defined in the universe of discourse R. If $\tilde{\tilde{A}}$ is normal, $\tilde{\tilde{A}}$ is a convex set, and the support of $\tilde{\tilde{A}}$ is closed and bounded, then $\tilde{\tilde{A}}$ is a Type-2 fuzzy number.

We concentrate on triangular Type-2 fuzzy numbers.

Type-2 triangular fuzzy number $\tilde{\tilde{A}} = (\tilde{A}_1, \tilde{A}_2, \tilde{A}_3)$ on R is given by $\tilde{\tilde{A}} = \{(x, (\mu_A^1(x), \mu_A^2(x), \mu_A^3(x)); x \in R\}$ and $\mu_A^1(x) \le \mu_A^2(x) \le \mu_A^3(x)$, for all $x \in R$. Here $\tilde{A}_1 = (A_1^L, A_1^N, A_1^U)$, $\tilde{A}_2 = (A_2^L, A_2^N, A_2^U)$ and $\tilde{A}_3 = (A_3^L, A_3^N, A_3^U)$.

Let consider arithmetic operations on Type-2 triangular fuzzy numbers [131].

Two Type-2 triangular fuzzy numbers

$$\tilde{\tilde{a}} = (\tilde{a}_1, \tilde{a}_2, \tilde{a}_3) = ((a_1^L, a_1^N, a_1^U), (a_2^L, a_2^N, a_2^U), (a_3^L, a_3^N, a_3^U)) \text{ and}$$

$$\tilde{\tilde{b}} = (\tilde{b}_1, \tilde{b}_2, \tilde{b}_3) = ((b_1^L, b_1^N, b_1^U), (b_2^L, b_2^N, b_2^U), (b_3^L, b_3^N, b_3^U))$$

are given.

Addition of $\tilde{\tilde{a}}$ and $\tilde{\tilde{b}}$ is determined as

$$\tilde{\tilde{a}} + \tilde{\tilde{b}} = ((a_1^L + b_1^L, a_1^N + b_1^N, a_1^U + b_1^U), (a_2^L + b_2^L, a_2^N + b_2^N, a_2^U + b_2^U), (a_3^L + b_3^L, a_3^N + b_3^N, a_3^U + b_3^U)).$$

Subtraction of $\tilde{\tilde{a}}$ and $\tilde{\tilde{b}}$ can be defined as

$$\tilde{\tilde{a}} - \tilde{\tilde{b}} = ((a_1^L - b_3^U, a_1^N - b_3^N, a_1^U - b_3^L), (a_2^L - b_2^L, a_2^N - b_2^N, a_2^U - b_2^U), (a_3^L - b_1^U, a_3^N - b_1^N, a_3^U - b_1^L)).$$

Scalar multiplication of $\tilde{\tilde{a}}$ is defined as

If $k \ge 0$ and $k \in R$ then

$k\tilde{\tilde{a}} = ((ka_1^L, ka_1^N, ka_1^U), (ka_2^L, ka_2^N, ka_2^U), (ka_3^L, ka_3^N, ka_3^U))$ and if $k < 0$ and $k \in R$ then

$k\tilde{\tilde{a}} = ((ka_3^U, ka_3^N, ka_3^L), (ka_2^U, ka_2^N, ka_2^L), (ka_1^U, ka_1^N, ka_1^L)).$

Multiplication of $\tilde{\tilde{a}}$ and $\tilde{\tilde{b}}$ is determined as follows:
Define $\sigma b = b_1^L + b_1^N + b_1^U + b_2^L + b_2^N + b_2^U + b_3^L + b_3^N + b_3^U$.
If $\sigma b \geq 0$, then

$$\tilde{\tilde{a}} \times \tilde{\tilde{b}} = \left(\left(\frac{a_1^L \sigma b}{9}, \frac{a_1^N \sigma b}{9}, \frac{a_1^U \sigma b}{9} \right), \left(\frac{a_2^L \sigma b}{9}, \frac{a_2^N \sigma b}{9}, \frac{a_2^U \sigma b}{9} \right), \left(\frac{a_3^L \sigma b}{9}, \frac{a_3^N \sigma b}{9}, \frac{a_3^U \sigma b}{9} \right) \right).$$

If $\sigma b < 0$, then

$$\tilde{\tilde{a}} \times \tilde{\tilde{b}} = \left(\left(\frac{a_3^U \sigma b}{9}, \frac{a_3^N \sigma b}{9}, \frac{a_3^L \sigma b}{9} \right), \left(\frac{a_2^U \sigma b}{9}, \frac{a_2^N \sigma b}{9}, \frac{a_2^L \sigma b}{9} \right), \left(\frac{a_1^U \sigma b}{9}, \frac{a_1^N \sigma b}{9}, \frac{a_1^L \sigma b}{9} \right) \right).$$

Division of $\tilde{\tilde{a}}$ and $\tilde{\tilde{b}}$ may be calculated as follows:
whenever $\sigma b \neq 0$ we define division as follows:
If $\sigma b > 0$, then

$$\frac{\tilde{\tilde{a}}}{\tilde{\tilde{b}}} = \left(\left(\frac{9a_1^L}{\sigma b}, \frac{9a_1^N}{\sigma b}, \frac{9a_1^U}{\sigma b} \right), \left(\frac{9a_2^L}{\sigma b}, \frac{9a_2^N}{\sigma b}, \frac{9a_2^U}{\sigma b} \right), \left(\frac{9a_3^L}{\sigma b}, \frac{9a_3^N}{\sigma b}, \frac{9a_3^U}{\sigma b} \right) \right).$$

If $\sigma b < 0$, then

$$\frac{\tilde{\tilde{a}}}{\tilde{\tilde{b}}} = \left(\left(\frac{9a_3^U}{\sigma b}, \frac{9a_3^N}{\sigma b}, \frac{9a_3^L}{\sigma b} \right), \left(\frac{9a_2^U}{\sigma b}, \frac{9a_2^N}{\sigma b}, \frac{9a_2^L}{\sigma b} \right), \left(\frac{9a_1^U}{\sigma b}, \frac{9a_1^N}{\sigma b}, \frac{9a_1^L}{\sigma b} \right) \right).$$

Inverse of Type-2 triangular fuzzy number $\tilde{\tilde{a}}$ is determined as $\tilde{\tilde{a}}^{-1} = \frac{1}{\tilde{\tilde{a}}},\ \tilde{a} \neq 0.$

Definition 2.25. A Type-2 triangular fuzzy number matrix (T2TFM) [131]. T2TFM of order $m \times n$ is defined as $A = (\tilde{\tilde{a}}_{ij})_{m \times n}$ where the *ij*th element $\tilde{\tilde{a}}_{ij}$ of A is the Type-2 triangular fuzzy number.

Let us briefly consider operations on Type-2 triangular fuzzy matrixes. Let $A = (\tilde{\tilde{a}}_{ij})$ and $B = (\tilde{\tilde{b}}_{ij})$ be two fuzzy matrixes of same order. The operations on them are as follows:

Addition

$A+B=(\tilde{\tilde{a}}_{ij}+\tilde{\tilde{b}}_{ij})$

Subtraction

$A-B=(\tilde{\tilde{a}}_{ij}-\tilde{\tilde{b}}_{ij})$

Multiplication

For $A=(\tilde{\tilde{a}}_{ij})_{m\times n}$ and $B=(\tilde{\tilde{b}}_{ij})_{n\times k}$, $AB=(\tilde{\tilde{c}}_{ij})_{m\times k}$ where $\tilde{\tilde{c}}_{ij}=\sum_{p=1}^{n}\tilde{\tilde{a}}_{ip}\cdot\tilde{\tilde{b}}_{pj}$, $i=1,2,\ldots,m$ and $j=1,2,\ldots,k$

Transpose

$A^T=(\tilde{\tilde{a}}_{ji})$

Interval Type-2 fuzzy sets

To date computational complexity of using a general Type-2 fuzzy sets is with some extent high. To simplify computation with Type-2 fuzzy sets we usually use interval Type-2 fuzzy sets.

As it was mentioned above a general Type-2 fuzzy set is expressed as

$$\tilde{\tilde{A}}=\int_{x\in X}\int_{u\in J_X}\mu_{\tilde{\tilde{A}}}(x,u)/(x,u)\quad J_X\subseteq[0,1] \tag{2.67}$$

where $\iint$ denotes union over all admissible x and u. For discrete universes of discourse, $\int$ is replaced by $\sum$.

As it is mentioned above when all $\mu_{\tilde{\tilde{A}}}(x,u)=1$ then $\tilde{\tilde{A}}$ is an interval Type-2 fuzzy set (IT2FS).

Consequently İT2 FS can be expressed as

$$\tilde{\tilde{A}}=\int_{x\in X}\int_{u\in J_X}1/(x,u),\quad J_X\subseteq[0,1]. \tag{2.68}$$

At each value of x, say $x=x'$, in (2.67) the 2-D plane whose axes are u and $\mu_{\tilde{\tilde{A}}}(x',u)$ is called a vertical slice of $\mu_{\tilde{\tilde{A}}}(x,u)$.

Based on the concept of secondary sets, we can reinterpret an IT2 FS as the union of all secondary sets, and we can reexpress $\tilde{\tilde{A}}$ in a vertical-slice manner, as [294]

$$\tilde{\tilde{A}} = \{(x, \mu_{\tilde{\tilde{A}}}(x)) \mid \forall x \in X\}$$

or, alternatively, as

$$\tilde{\tilde{A}} = \int_{x \in X} \mu_{\tilde{\tilde{A}}}(x)/x = \int_{x \in X} \left[\int_{u \in J_x} 1/u\right]/x, \quad J_x \subseteq [0,1].$$

IT2 FS footprint of uncertainty can be described as

$$\mathrm{FOU}(\tilde{\tilde{A}}) = \bigcup_{x \in X} J_x. \tag{2.69}$$

In accordance with Mendel-John representation theorem for an IT2 FS $\tilde{\tilde{A}}$ is the union of all of its embedded IT2 FSs.

Assume that $X = \{x_1, x_2, \ldots, x_n\}$ is discrete or discretisized primary variable, $U_i^j \in \{\underline{\mu}_{\tilde{\tilde{A}}}(x_i), \ldots, \overline{\mu}_{\tilde{\tilde{A}}}(x_i)\}$ is sampled secondary variables. In accordance with Mendel-Jonh representation Interval Type-2 fuzzy sets (IT2FS) can be expressed as follows:

$$\tilde{\tilde{A}} = 1/FOU(\tilde{\tilde{A}}) = 1/U_{j=1}^{n_A} A_e^j \text{ where } A_e^j = \sum_{i-1}^{n} U_i^j / x_i \tag{2.70}$$

$$\tilde{\tilde{A}} = \sum_{j=1}^{n_A} \tilde{\tilde{A}}_e^j$$

where $j = 1, \ldots, n_A$

$$\tilde{\tilde{A}}_e^j = \sum_{i=1}^{N} [1/u_i^j]/x_i \ , \ u_i^j \in J_{x_i} \subseteq U = [0,1]$$

and

$$n_A = \prod_{i=1}^{N} M_i$$

in which M_i denotes the discretization levels of secondary variable u_i^j at each of the N x_i.

Operations on IT2 FS. In [294] theorems on union, intersection and complement has been proved.

Let consider the set-theoretic operations of union, intersection, and complement and the arithmetic operations of addition and multiplication on IT2FS [294].

IT2FS $\tilde{\tilde{A}}$ and $\tilde{\tilde{B}}$ are given.

$$\tilde{\tilde{A}} = \int_X [\int_{J_x^u} 1/u]/x$$

$$\tilde{\tilde{B}} = \int_X [\int_{J_x^w} 1/w]/x$$

Union/join

$$\mu_{\tilde{\tilde{A}} \cup \tilde{\tilde{B}}}(x) = [\underline{\mu}_{\tilde{\tilde{A}}}(x) \vee \underline{\mu}_{\tilde{\tilde{B}}}(x), \overline{\mu}_{\tilde{\tilde{A}}}(x) \vee \overline{\mu}_{\tilde{\tilde{B}}}(x)] \quad \forall x \in X \tag{2.71}$$

Intersection/meet

$$\mu_{\tilde{\tilde{A}} \cap \tilde{\tilde{B}}}(x) = [\underline{\mu}_{\tilde{\tilde{A}}}(x) \wedge \underline{\mu}_{\tilde{\tilde{B}}}(x), \overline{\mu}_{\tilde{\tilde{A}}}(x) \wedge \overline{\mu}_{\tilde{\tilde{B}}}(x)] \quad \forall x \in X \tag{2.72}$$

Complement/negation

$$\overline{\mu}_{\tilde{\tilde{A}}}(x) = [1 - \overline{\mu}_{\tilde{\tilde{A}}}(x), 1 - \underline{\mu}_{\tilde{\tilde{A}}}(x)] \quad \forall x \in X \tag{2.73}$$

Addition

$$F + G = [\underline{\mu}_F S \underline{\mu}_G, \overline{\mu}_F S \overline{\mu}_G] \tag{2.74}$$

Multiplication

$$F \times G = [\underline{\mu}_F T \underline{\mu}_G, \overline{\mu}_F T \overline{\mu}_G] \tag{2.75}$$

Here $\bar{\mu}_{\tilde{\tilde{A}}}(x)$ and $\underline{\mu}_{\tilde{\tilde{A}}}(x)$ are the upper and lower membership functions (UMF and LMF) respectively and can be determined as

$$\bar{\mu}_{\tilde{\tilde{A}}}(x) \equiv \overline{\mathrm{FOU}(\tilde{\tilde{A}})} \quad \forall x \in X$$

$$\underline{\mu}_{\tilde{\tilde{A}}}(x) \equiv \underline{\mathrm{FOU}(\tilde{\tilde{A}})} \quad \forall x \in X.$$

Arithmetic operations on IT2 Fuzzy Numbers.

Type-2 fuzzy number (T2FN) is very frequently used in Type-2 fuzzy decision making and control. We consentrate on triangular Type-2 fuzzy number (TIT2FN).

The TIT2FN can be determined as follows:

$$\tilde{\tilde{a}}_i = \left(\tilde{a}_i^l, \tilde{a}_i^u\right) = \left([a_{i1}^l, a_{i2}^l], [a_{i1}^u, a_{i2}^u]; \tilde{s}_i^l, \tilde{s}_i^u\right),$$

where $\tilde{a}_i^l$ and $\tilde{a}_i^u$ are Type-1 fuzzy sets, $a_{i1}^l, a_{i2}^l, a_{i1}^u, a_{i2}^u$ are the reference points of the interval Type-2 fuzzy set $\tilde{\tilde{a}}_i, \tilde{s}_i^l$ is the upper membership function and $\tilde{s}_i^u$ is the lower membership function, $\tilde{s}_i^l \in [0,1]$ and $\tilde{s}_i^u \in [0,1]$ and $1 \le i \le n$.

Let us consider arithmetic operations on TIT2FN [461].

Addition

Two TIT2FN are given

$$\tilde{\tilde{a}}_1 = \left(\tilde{a}_1^l, a_1^u\right) = \left([a_{11}^l, a_{12}^l], [a_{11}^u, a_{12}^u]; \tilde{s}_1^l, \tilde{s}_1^u\right)$$

$$\tilde{\tilde{b}}_2 = \left(\tilde{b}_2^l, b_2^u\right) = \left([b_{21}^l, b_{22}^l], [b_{21}^u, b_{22}^u]; \tilde{s}_2^l, \tilde{s}_2^u\right)$$

The addition of $\tilde{\tilde{a}}_1$ and $\tilde{\tilde{b}}_2$ is defined as:

$$\tilde{\tilde{a}}_1 + \tilde{\tilde{b}}_2 = \left(\tilde{a}_1^l, \tilde{a}_1^u\right) + \left(\tilde{b}_2^l, \tilde{b}_2^u\right) = \begin{bmatrix} \left(a_{11}^l + b_{21}^l, a_{12}^l + b_{22}^l; \min\left(\tilde{s}_1^l, \tilde{s}_2^l\right)\right), \\ \left(a_{11}^u + b_{21}^u, a_{12}^u + b_{22}^u; \min\left(\tilde{s}_1^u, \tilde{s}_2^u\right)\right) \end{bmatrix}$$

Subtraction

The subtraction of $\tilde{\tilde{a}}_1$ and $\tilde{\tilde{b}}_2$ is defined as:

$$\tilde{\tilde{a}}_1 - \tilde{\tilde{b}}_2 = \left(\tilde{a}_1^l, \tilde{a}_1^u\right) - \left(\tilde{b}_2^l, \tilde{b}_2^u\right) = \begin{bmatrix} \left(a_{11}^l - b_{21}^l, a_{12}^l - b_{22}^l; \min\left(\tilde{s}_1^l, \tilde{s}_2^l\right)\right), \\ \left(a_{11}^u - b_{21}^u, a_{12}^u - b_{22}^u; \min\left(\tilde{s}_1^u, \tilde{s}_2^u\right)\right) \end{bmatrix}$$

Multiplication

The multiplication of $\tilde{\tilde{a}}_1$ and $\tilde{\tilde{b}}_2$ is defined as:

$$\tilde{\tilde{a}}_1 \times \tilde{\tilde{b}}_2 = \left(\tilde{a}_1^l, \tilde{a}_1^u\right) \times \left(\tilde{b}_2^l, \tilde{b}_2^u\right) = \begin{bmatrix} \left(a_{11}^l \times b_{21}^l, a_{12}^l \times b_{22}^l; \min\left(\tilde{s}_1^l, \tilde{s}_2^l\right)\right), \\ \left(a_{11}^u \times b_{21}^u, a_{12}^u \times b_{22}^u; \min\left(\tilde{s}_1^u, \tilde{s}_2^u\right)\right) \end{bmatrix}$$

Division

The division of $\tilde{a}_1$ and $\tilde{b}_2$ is defined as:

$$\tilde{\tilde{a}}_1 \div \tilde{\tilde{b}}_2 = \left(\tilde{a}_1^l, \tilde{a}_1^u\right) \div \left(\tilde{b}_2^l, \tilde{b}_2^u\right) = \begin{bmatrix} \left(a_{11}^l \div b_{21}^l, a_{12}^l \div b_{22}^l; \min\left(\tilde{s}_1^l, \tilde{s}_2^l\right)\right), \\ \left(a_{11}^u \div b_{21}^u, a_{12}^u \div b_{22}^u; \min\left(\tilde{s}_1^u, \tilde{s}_2^u\right)\right) \end{bmatrix}$$

2.1.7 *A Z-number and operations on Z-numbers*

Decisions are based on decision-relevant information which must be reliable. Basically, the concept of a Z-number relates to the issue of reliability of information. A Z-number, Z, has two components, $Z=(\tilde{A},\tilde{B})$ [455]. The first component, $\tilde{A}$, is a restriction (constraint) on the values which a real-valued uncertain variable, X, is allowed to take. The second component, $\tilde{B}$, is a measure of reliability (confidence) of the first component. Typically, $\tilde{A}$ and $\tilde{B}$ are described in a natural language.

The concept of a Z-number has a potential for many applications, especially in the realms of economics and decision analysis.

Much of the information on which decisions are based is uncertain.

Humans have a remarkable capability to make rational decisions based on information which is uncertain, imprecise and or incomplete. Formalization of this capability, at least to some degree motivates the concepts Z-number [454].

The ordered triple $(X, \tilde{A}, \tilde{B})$ is referred to as a Z-valuation. A Z-valuation is equivalent to an assignment statement, X is $(\tilde{A}, \tilde{B})$. X is an uncertain random variable. For convenience, $\tilde{A}$ is referred to as a value of X, with the understanding that, $\tilde{A}$ is not a value of X but a restriction on the values which X can take. The second component, $\tilde{B}$, is referred to as confidence (certainty). When X is a random variable, certainty may be equated to probability. Typically, $\tilde{A}$ and $\tilde{B}$ are perception-based and are described in NL. A collection of Z-valuations is referred to as Z-information. It should be noted that much of everyday reasoning and decision-making is based on Z-information. For purposes of computation, when $\tilde{A}$ and $\tilde{B}$ are described in NL, the meaning of $\tilde{A}$ and $\tilde{B}$ is precisiated through association with membership functions, $\mu_{\tilde{A}}$ and $\mu_{\tilde{B}}$, respectively. Simple examples of Z-valuations are:

(snowing hard in the middle of January, likely);

(World population will reach approximately 9.6 billions by 2050, very likely).

Nowadays there is no general and computationally effective approach to computations with Z-numbers. There is a need in development of a universal approach to computations with information described by Z-numbers which can be relatively easily applied for solving a wide spectrum of real-world problems as control, decision analysis, optimization etc. In turn, this requires to define operations over Z-numbers including addition, multiplication and others. In the existing works a small attention is paid to theoretical basics of operations over Z-numbers and, as a result, the basic principles of arithmetic of Z-numbers were not suggested. In the present study we concentrate on discrete Z-numbers, that is, Z-numbers whose components are discrete fuzzy numbers. We suggest theoretical basics of the arithmetic of discrete Z-numbers. The motivation to use discrete Z-numbers is based on three main aspects. The first is that due to highly constrained computational ability of a human brain, a human being uses linguistic description of real-world information. In turn, linguistic information, as a rule, is represented on the base of a discrete set of linguistic terms. The second aspect is the fact that computation with discrete fuzzy numbers [345,365] and discrete probability distributions are characterized by a significantly lower computational complexity than that with continuous fuzzy numbers [11,240] and density functions. The third aspect is the universality of uncertainty modeling. Indeed, in discrete case one does not need to assume a type of probability distributions that will constrain modeling ability, but can consider a general case. Below we present necessary prerequisite material underlying the suggested arithmetic of discrete Z-numbers.

Definition 2.26. A discrete fuzzy number [365]. A fuzzy subset $\tilde{A}$ of the real line $\mathcal{R}$ with membership function $\mu_{\tilde{A}}:\mathcal{R}\to[0,1]$ is a fuzzy discrete number if its support is finite, i.e. there exist $x_1,...,x_n\in\mathcal{R}$ with $x_1<x_2<...<x_n$, such that $\text{supp}(\tilde{A})=\{x_1,...,x_n\}$ and there exist natural numbers s,t with $1\le s\le t\le n$ fulfilling:

1. $\mu_{\tilde{A}}(x_i)=1$ for any natural number i with $s\le i\le t$
2. $\mu_{\tilde{A}}(x_i)\le\mu_{\tilde{A}}(x_j)$ for each natural numbers i,j with $1\le i\le j\le s$
3. $\mu_{\tilde{A}}(x_i)\ge\mu_{\tilde{A}}(x_j)$ for each natural numbers i,j with $t\le i\le j\le n$

Let $\mathcal{D}^n$ be the space of all discrete fuzzy subsets of $\mathcal{R}^n$. Then denote by $\mathcal{D}^1_{[a,b]}$ the corresponding space of fuzzy sets of $[a,b]\subset\mathcal{R}$.

Definition 2.27. A discrete random variable and a discrete probability distribution [98]. A discrete random variable is a variable which takes only a countable number of distinct values.

Consider a random variable X with outcomes space $\{x_1,...,x_n\}$. Let $p(x_i)$ denote the probability of an outcome $X=x_i$, where $p(x_i)\in[0,1]$ and $\sum_{i=1}^{n}p(x_i)=1$. A function p is called a discrete probability distribution or a probability mass function.

Definition 2.28. A convolution of discrete probability distributions [98]. Let X_1 and X_2 be two discrete random variables with the corresponding outcome spaces $\{x_{11},...,x_{1i},...,x_{1n_1}\}$ and $\{x_{21},...,x_{2i},...,x_{2n_2}\}$ and the corresponding discrete probability distributions p_1 and p_2. The probability distribution of $X_1 * X_2$, $*\in\{+,-,\cdot,/\}$, is the convolution $p_{12}=p_1\circ p_2$ of p_1 and p_2 which is determined as follows:

$$p_{12}(x)=\sum_{x=x_{1i}*x_{2j}} p_1(x_{1i})p_2(x_{2j}).$$

Definition 2.29. Probability measure of a discrete fuzzy number [436]. Let $\tilde{A}$ be a discrete fuzzy number. A probability measure of $\tilde{A}$ denoted $P(\tilde{A})$ is defined as

$$P(\tilde{A})=\sum_{i=1}^{n}\mu_{\tilde{A}}(x_i)p(x_i).$$

Definition 2.30. Addition of discrete fuzzy numbers [365]. For discrete fuzzy numbers $\tilde{A}_1,\tilde{A}_2$ their addition $\tilde{A}_{12}=\tilde{A}_1+\tilde{A}_2$ is the discrete fuzzy number whose α-cut is defined as

$$A_{12}^{\alpha}=\{x\in\{\text{supp}(\tilde{A}_1)+\text{supp}(\tilde{A}_2)\}\mid \min\{A_1^{\alpha}+A_2^{\alpha}\}\le x\le \max\{A_1^{\alpha}+A_2^{\alpha}\}\}$$

where

$$\text{supp}(\tilde{A}_1)+\text{supp}(\tilde{A}_2)=\{x_1+x_2\mid x_j\in\text{supp}(\tilde{A}_j), j=1,2\},$$
$$\min(A_1^{\alpha}+A_2^{\alpha})=\min\{x_1+x_2\mid x_j\in A_j^{\alpha}), j=1,2\},$$
$$\max(A_1^{\alpha}+A_2^{\alpha})=\max\{x_1+x_2\mid x_j\in A_j^{\alpha}, j=1,2\},$$

and the membership function is defined as

$$\mu_{\tilde{A}_1+\tilde{A}_2}(x)=\sup\{\alpha\in[0,1]\mid x\in(A_1^{\alpha}+A_2^{\alpha})\}.$$

Definition 2.31. Standard subtraction of discrete fuzzy numbers. For discrete fuzzy numbers $\tilde{A}_1,\tilde{A}_2$ their standard subtraction $\tilde{A}_{12}=\tilde{A}_1-\tilde{A}_2$ is the discrete fuzzy number whose α-cut is defined as

$$A_{12}^{\alpha}=\{x\in(\text{supp}(\tilde{A}_1)-\text{supp}(\tilde{A}_2))\mid \min(A_1^{\alpha}-A_2^{\alpha})\le x\le \max(A_1^{\alpha}-A_2^{\alpha})\}$$

where

$$\text{supp}(\tilde{A}_1) - \text{supp}(\tilde{A}_2) = \{x_1 - x_2 \mid x_j \in \text{supp}(\tilde{A}_j), j = 1,2\},$$

$$\min(A_1^\alpha - A_2^\alpha) = \min\{x_1 - x_2 \mid x_j \in A_j^\alpha, j = 1,2\},$$

$$\max(A_1^\alpha - A_2^\alpha) = \max\{x_1 - x_2 \mid x_j \in A_j^\alpha, j = 1,2\},$$

and the membership function is defined as

$$\mu_{\tilde{A}_1 - \tilde{A}_2}(x) = \sup\{\alpha \in (0,1] \mid x \in (A_1^\alpha - A_2^\alpha)\}.$$

As it is known, for the standard subtraction the following holds:

$$\tilde{A}_2 + (\tilde{A}_1 - \tilde{A}_2) \neq \tilde{A}_1.$$

Definition 2.32. Multiplication of discrete fuzzy numbers. For discrete fuzzy numbers $\tilde{A}_1, \tilde{A}_2$ their multiplication $\tilde{A}_{12} = \tilde{A}_1 \cdot \tilde{A}_2$ is the discrete fuzzy number whose α-cut is defined as

$$A_{12}^\alpha = \{x \in (\text{supp}(\tilde{A}_1) \cdot \text{supp}(\tilde{A}_2)) \mid \min(A_1^\alpha \cdot A_2^\alpha) \leq x \leq \max(A_1^\alpha \cdot A_2^\alpha)\}$$

where

$$\text{supp}(\tilde{A}_1) \cdot \text{supp}(\tilde{A}_2) = \{x_1 \cdot x_2 \mid x_j \in \text{supp}(\tilde{A}_j), j = 1,2\},$$

$$\min(A_1^\alpha \cdot A_2^\alpha) = \min\{x_1 \cdot x_2 \mid x_j \in A_j^\alpha, j = 1,2\},$$

$$\max(A_1^\alpha \cdot A_2^\alpha) = \max\{x_1 \cdot x_2 \mid x_j \in A_j^\alpha, j = 1,2\},$$

and the membership function is defined as

$$\mu_{\tilde{A}_1 \cdot \tilde{A}_2}(x) = \sup\{\alpha \in [0,1] \mid x \in (A_1^\alpha \cdot A_2^\alpha)\}.$$

Definition 2.33. A scalar multiplication of a discrete fuzzy number. For a discrete fuzzy number $\tilde{A}$ its scalar multiplication $\tilde{A}_1 = \lambda \tilde{A}$, $\lambda \in \mathcal{R}$, is the discrete fuzzy number whose α-cut is defined as

$$A_1^\alpha = \{x \in \lambda \cdot \text{supp}(\tilde{A}) \mid \min(\lambda A^\alpha) \leq x \leq \max(\lambda A^\alpha)\}$$

where

$$\lambda \cdot \mathrm{supp}(\tilde{A}) = \{\lambda x \mid x \in \mathrm{supp}(\tilde{A})\},$$

$$\min(\lambda A^{\alpha}) = \min\{\lambda x \mid x \in A^{\alpha}\},\ \ \max(\lambda A^{\alpha}) = \max\{\lambda x \mid x \in A^{\alpha}\},$$

and the membership function is defined as

$$\mu_{\lambda\tilde{A}}(x) = \sup\{\alpha \in [0,1] \mid x \in (\lambda A^{\alpha})\}.$$

Definition 2.34. Standard division of discrete fuzzy numbers. For discrete fuzzy numbers $\tilde{A}_1, \tilde{A}_2$ $(0 \notin \mathrm{supp}(\tilde{A}_2))$ their standard division $\tilde{A}_{12} = \tilde{A}_1 / \tilde{A}_2$ is the discrete fuzzy number whose α-cut is defined as

$$A_{12}^{\alpha} = \{x \in (\mathrm{supp}(\tilde{A}_1)/\mathrm{supp}(\tilde{A}_2)) \mid \min(A_1^{\alpha}/A_2^{\alpha}) \le x \le \max(A_1^{\alpha}/A_2^{\alpha})\}$$

where

$$\mathrm{supp}(\tilde{A}_1)/\mathrm{supp}(\tilde{A}_2) = \{x_1/x_2 \mid x_j \in \mathrm{supp}(\tilde{A}_j), j = 1,2\},$$

$$\min(A_1^{\alpha}/A_2^{\alpha}) = \min\{x_1/x_2 \mid x_j \in A_j^{\alpha}, j = 1,2\},$$

$$\max(A_1^{\alpha}/A_2^{\alpha}) = \max\{x_1/x_2 \mid x_j \in \mathrm{supp}(\tilde{A}_j), j = 1,2\},$$

and the membership function is defined as

$$\mu_{\tilde{A}_1/\tilde{A}_2}(x) = \sup\{\alpha \in [0,1] \mid x \in (A_1^{\alpha}/A_2^{\alpha})\}.$$

As it is known, for the standard division the following holds:

$$\tilde{A}_2 \cdot (\tilde{A}_1/\tilde{A}_2) \neq \tilde{A}_1.$$

Definition 2.35. Hukuhara difference of discrete fuzzy numbers. For discrete fuzzy numbers $\tilde{A}_1, \tilde{A}_2$ their Hukuhara difference denoted $\tilde{A}_1 -_h \tilde{A}_2$ is the discrete fuzzy number $\tilde{A}_{12}$ such that

$$\tilde{A}_1 = \tilde{A}_{12} + \tilde{A}_2.$$

Hukuhara difference exists only if $n \geq m$. Denote $\text{supp}(\tilde{A}_1) = \{x_{11}, ..., x_{1n}\}$, $A_1^\alpha = \{x_1^\alpha{}_{1_\alpha}, ..., x_1^\alpha{}_{n_\alpha}\}$, $1_\alpha, n_\alpha \in \{1, ..., n\}$ and $\text{supp}(\tilde{A}_2) = \{x_{21}, ..., x_{2m}\}$, $A_2^\alpha = \{x_2^\alpha{}_{1_\alpha}, ..., x_2^\alpha{}_{m_\alpha}\}$, $1_\alpha, m_\alpha \in \{1, ..., m\}$. Hukuhara difference $\tilde{A}_{12}$, where $\text{supp}(\tilde{A}_{12}) = \{x_1, ..., x_k\}$, $A_{12}^\alpha = \{x_{l_\alpha}, ..., x_{r_\alpha}\}$, $l_\alpha, r_\alpha \in \{1, ..., k\}$ exists if and only if cardinality of A_1^α is not lower than that of A_2^α for any $\alpha \in (0,1]$, and the following is satisfied:

$$A_1^\alpha = \bigcup_{i=1}^{r_\alpha - l_\alpha + 1} A_{1,i}^\alpha,$$

where $A_{1,i}^\alpha = \{x_1^\alpha{}_{i1}, ..., x_1^\alpha{}_{im}\}$, $x_1^\alpha{}_{i(j+1)} - x_1^\alpha{}_{ij} = x_{2(j+1)}^\alpha - x_{2j}^\alpha$, $j = 1, ..., m$; $\alpha \in (0,1]$.

Definition 2.36. A square of a discrete fuzzy number. For a discrete fuzzy number $\tilde{A}$ its square $\tilde{A}^2$ is the discrete fuzzy number whose α-cut is defined as

$$\left[\tilde{A}^2\right]^\alpha = \{y \in \text{supp}(\tilde{A}^2) \mid \min((A^\alpha)^2) \leq y \leq \max((A^\alpha)^2)\}$$

where

$$\text{supp}(\tilde{A}^2) = \{y \mid y = x^2, x \in \text{supp}(\tilde{A})\},$$

$$\min(A^\alpha)^2 = \min\{y \mid y = x^2, x \in A^\alpha\},$$

$$\max(A^\alpha)^2 = \max\{y \mid y = x^2, x \in A^\alpha\}.$$

Thus, $\left[\tilde{A}^2\right]^\alpha = \left(\tilde{A}^\alpha\right)^2$. The membership function of $\tilde{A}^2$ is defined as

$$\mu_{\tilde{A}^2}(y) = \sup\{\alpha \in [0,1] \mid y \in \left[\tilde{A}^2\right]^\alpha\}.$$

Definition 2.37. A square root of a discrete fuzzy number. For a discrete fuzzy number $\tilde{A}$. where $\text{supp}(\tilde{A}) \subset [0, \infty)$, its square root $\sqrt{\tilde{A}}$ is the discrete fuzzy number whose α -cut is defined as

$$\left[\sqrt{\tilde{A}}\right]^{\alpha} = \{y \in \text{supp}(\sqrt{\tilde{A}}) \mid \min\sqrt{A^{\alpha}} \le y \le \max\sqrt{A^{\alpha}}\}$$

where

$$\text{supp}(\sqrt{\tilde{A}}) = \{y \mid y = \sqrt{x}, x \in \text{supp}(\tilde{A})\},$$

$$\min\sqrt{A^{\alpha}} = \min\{y \mid y = \sqrt{x}, x \in A^{\alpha}\},$$

$$\max\sqrt{A^{\alpha}} = \max\{y \mid y = \sqrt{x}, x \in A^{\alpha}\}.$$

Thus, $\left[\sqrt{\tilde{A}}\right]^{\alpha} = \sqrt{A^{\alpha}}$. The membership function of $\sqrt{\tilde{A}}$ is defined as

$$\mu_{\sqrt{\tilde{A}}}(y) = \sup\{\alpha \in [0,1] \mid y \in \left[\sqrt{\tilde{A}}\right]^{\alpha}\}.$$

Definition 2.38. A discrete Z-number. A discrete Z-number is an ordered pair $Z = (\tilde{A}, \tilde{B})$ where $\tilde{A}$ is a discrete fuzzy number playing a role of a fuzzy constraint on values that a random variable X may take:

$$X \text{ is } \tilde{A}$$

and $\tilde{B}$ is a discrete fuzzy number with a membership function $\mu_{\tilde{B}} : \{b_1, ..., b_n\} \to [0,1]$, $\{b_1, ..., b_n\} \subset [0,1]$, playing a role of a fuzzy constraint on the probability measure of $\tilde{A}$:

$$P(\tilde{A}) \text{ is } \tilde{B}.$$

A concept of a discrete Z^+ -number is closely related to the concept of a discrete Z-number. Given a discrete Z-number, $Z = (\tilde{A}, \tilde{B})$, Z^+ -number Z^+ is a pair consisting of a fuzzy number, $\tilde{A}$, and a random number R:

$$Z^+ = (\tilde{A}, R),$$

where $\tilde{A}$ plays the same role as it does in a discrete Z-number $Z=(\tilde{A},\tilde{B})$ and R plays the role of the probability distribution p, such that

$$P(\tilde{A})=\sum_{i=1}^{n}\mu_{\tilde{A}}(x_i)p(x_i),\ P(\tilde{A})\in \operatorname{supp}(\tilde{B}).$$

Now let us consider the suggested arithmetic operations over discrete Z-numbers.

A general framework of arithmetic operations over discrete Z-numbers. At first we provide general framework for arithmetic operations. Let $Z_1=(\tilde{A}_1,\tilde{B}_1)$ and $Z_2=(\tilde{A}_2,\tilde{B}_2)$ be discrete Z-numbers. Consider computation of $Z_{12}=Z_1 * Z_2,\ *\in\{+,-,\cdot,/\}$. First, $Z_{12}^{+}=Z_1^{+} * Z_2^{+}$ is determined:

$$Z_1^{+} * Z_2^{+}=(\tilde{A}_1 * \tilde{A}_2, R_1 * R_2)$$

where R_1 and R_2 are represented by discrete probability distributions:

$$p_{R_1}=p_{R_1}(x_{11})\backslash x_{11}+p_{R_1}(x_{12})\backslash x_{12}+...+p_{R_1}(x_{1n})\backslash x_{1n},$$

$$p_{R_2}=p_{R_2}(x_{21})\backslash x_{21}+p_{R_2}(x_{22})\backslash x_{22}+...+p_{R_2}(x_{2n})\backslash x_{2n},$$

for which one necessarily has

$$\sum_{k=1}^{n}p_{R_1}(x_{1k})=1, \tag{2.76}$$

$$\sum_{k=1}^{n}p_{R_2}(x_{2k})=1, \tag{2.77}$$

and also may consider compatibility conditions

$$\sum_{k=1}^{n} x_{1k} p_{R_1}(x_{1k}) = \frac{\sum_{k=1}^{n} x_{1k} \mu_{\tilde{A}_1}(x_{1k})}{\sum_{k=1}^{n} \mu_{\tilde{A}_1}(x_{1k})}, \tag{2.78}$$

$$\sum_{k=1}^{n} x_{2k} p_{R_2}(x_{2k}) = \frac{\sum_{k=1}^{n} x_{2k} \mu_{\tilde{A}_2}(x_{2k})}{\sum_{k=1}^{n} \mu_{\tilde{A}_2}(x_{2k})} \tag{2.79}$$

and $\tilde{A}_{12} = \tilde{A}_1 * \tilde{A}_2$, $* \in \{+,-,\cdot,/\}$, is defined on the base of Definitions 2.30, 2.31, 2.32 or 2.34 and $R_1 * R_2$ is the convolution $p_{12} = p_1 \circ p_2$ determined for $* \in \{+,-,\cdot,/\}$ on the base of Definition 2.28.

Next we realize that in $Z_1 = (\tilde{A}_1, \tilde{B}_1)$ and $Z_2 = (\tilde{A}_2, \tilde{B}_2)$ the 'true' probability distributions p_{R_1} and p_{R_2} are not exactly known. In contrast, the information available is represented by the fuzzy restrictions:

$$\sum_{k=1}^{n} \mu_{\tilde{A}_1}(x_{1k}) p_{R_1}(x_{1k}) \ is \ \tilde{B}_1, \quad \sum_{k=1}^{n} \mu_{\tilde{A}_2}(x_{2k}) p_{R_2}(x_{2k}) \ is \ \tilde{B}_2$$

which are represented in terms of membership functions as

$$\mu_{\tilde{B}_1}\left(\sum_{k=1}^{n} \mu_{\tilde{A}_1}(x_{1k}) p_{R_1}(x_{1k})\right), \mu_{\tilde{B}_2}\left(\sum_{k=1}^{n} \mu_{\tilde{A}_2}(x_{2k}) p_{R_2}(x_{2k})\right).$$

This imply that one has the fuzzy sets of probability distributions of p_{R_1} and p_{R_2} with the membership functions defined as

$$\mu_{p_{R_1}}(p_{R_1}) = \mu_{\tilde{B}_1}\left(\sum_{k=1}^{n} \mu_{\tilde{A}_1}(x_{1k}) p_{R_1}(x_{1k})\right),$$

$$\mu_{p_{R_2}}(p_{R_2}) = \mu_{\tilde{B}_2}\left(\sum_{k=1}^{n} \mu_{\tilde{A}_2}(x_{2k}) p_{R_2}(x_{2k})\right).$$

Now, as $\tilde{B}_1$ and $\tilde{B}_2$ are discrete, the values of $\mu_{\tilde{B}_j}(b_{jl})$, $b_{jl} \in \operatorname{supp} \tilde{B}_j$, $j = 1,2; l = 1,...,n$ will be found by solving a series of goal linear programming problems:

$$\sum_{k=1}^{n} \mu_{\tilde{A}_j}(x_k) p_j(x_k) \to b_{jl}, \tag{2.80}$$

subject to

$$\left. \begin{array}{l} \sum_{k=1}^{n_j} p_j(x_{jk}) = 1 \\ p_j(x_{jk}) \geq 0 \end{array} \right\}. \tag{2.81}$$

Having obtained the solution p_j of the problem for each $l = 1,...,n$ denote $p_{jl} = p_j$ and calculate a degree

$$\mu_{p_j}(p_j) = \mu_{\tilde{B}_j}\left(\sum_{k=1}^{n} \mu_{\tilde{A}_j}(u_k) p_j(u_k) \right), j = 1,2.$$

The fuzzy sets of probability distributions p_{1l} and p_{2l} induce the fuzzy set of convolutions p_{12s}, $s = 1,...,l^2$, with the membership function defined as

$$\mu_{p_{12}}(p_{12}) = \max_{p_1, p_2} [\mu_{p_1}(p_1) \wedge \mu_{p_2}(p_2)] \tag{2.82}$$

$$\text{subject to } p_{12} = p_1 \circ p_2 \tag{2.83}$$

where $\wedge$ is *min* operation.

At the next step we should compute probability measure of $A_{12} = A_1 * A_2$:

$$P(\tilde{A}_{12}) = \sum_{w} p_{12}(w) \mu_{\tilde{A}_{12}}(w).$$

Thus, $P(\tilde{A}_{12})$ is a number $P(\tilde{A}_{12}) = b_{12}$ when p_{12} is known. However, what is only known is a fuzzy restriction on p_{12} described by the membership function $\mu_{p_{12}}$. Therefore, $P(\tilde{A}_{12})$ will be a fuzzy set $\tilde{B}_{12}$ with the membership function $\mu_{\tilde{B}_{12}}$:

$$\mu_{\tilde{B}_{12}}(b_{12s}) = \sup(\mu_{p_{12s}}(p_{12s})) \tag{2.84}$$

subject to

$$b_{12s} = \sum_k p_{12s}(x_k)\mu_{\tilde{A}_{12}}(x_k). \tag{2.85}$$

As a result, $Z_{12} = Z_1 * Z_2$, $* \in \{+,-,\cdot,/\}$ is obtained as $Z_{12} = (\tilde{A}_{12}, \tilde{B}_{12})$. Let us consider four basic arithmetic operations in details.

Addition of discrete Z-numbers. In this case $A_1 * A_2$ is a sum $\tilde{A}_1 + \tilde{A}_2$ defined on base of Definition 2.30 and $R_1 * R_2$ is a convolution defined on the base of Definition 2.28 as

$$p_{12}(x) = \sum_{x=x_1+x_2} p_{R_1}(x_1)p_{R_2}(x_2).$$

So, we will have Z_{12}^+ as

$$Z_{12}^+ = (\tilde{A}_1 + \tilde{A}_2, p_{12}(x)).$$

Next, performing successive computations of membership functions of $\tilde{B}_1$ and $\tilde{B}_2$ based on (2.80)-(2.81), membership function of a fuzzy set of convolutions $p_{12s}, s = 1,\ldots,l^2$, based on (2.82)-(2.83), and the membership function $\mu_{\tilde{B}_{12}}$ of a fuzzy set $\tilde{B}_{12}$ based on (2.84)-(2.85), we arrive at the resulting Z-number:

$$Z_{12} = (\tilde{A}_1 + \tilde{A}_2, \tilde{B}_{12}).$$

Subtraction of discrete Z-numbers. $A_1 * A_2$ is defined as $\tilde{A}_1 - \tilde{A}_2$ on base of Definition 2.31 and $R_1 * R_2$ is a convolution defined on the base of Definition 2.28 as

$$p_{12}(x)=\sum_{x=x_1-x_2} p_{R_1}(x_1)p_{R_2}(x_2).$$

So, we will have Z_{12}^+ as

$$Z_{12}^+=(\tilde{A}_1-\tilde{A}_2,p_{12}(x)).$$

Next, performing successive computations of membership functions based on (2.80)-(2.85), the resulting Z-number is found:

$$Z_{12}=(\tilde{A}_1-\tilde{A}_2,\tilde{B}_{12}).$$

Multiplication of discrete Z-numbers. $A_1 * A_2$ is defined as $\tilde{A}_1\cdot\tilde{A}_2$ on base of Definition 2.32 and $R_1 * R_2$ is a convolution defined on the base of Definition 2.28 defined as

$$p_{12}(x)=\sum_{x=x_1\cdot x_2} p_{R_1}(x_1)p_{R_2}(x_2).$$

So, we will have Z_{12}^+ as

$$Z_{12}^+=(\tilde{A}_1\cdot\tilde{A}_2,p_{12}(x)).$$

Next, performing successive computations of membership functions based on (2.80)-(2.85), the resulting Z-number is found:

$$Z_{12}=(\tilde{A}_1\cdot\tilde{A}_2,\tilde{B}_{12}).$$

Standard division of discrete Z-numbers. $A_1 * A_2$ is defined as $\tilde{A}_1/\tilde{A}_2$ on base of Definition 2.34 and $R_1 * R_2$ is a convolution defined on the base of Definition 2.28 defined as

$$p_{12}(x)=\sum_{x=x_1/x_2} p_{R_1}(x_1)p_{R_2}(x_2).$$

So, we will have Z_{12}^+ as

$$Z_{12}^{+} = (\tilde{A}_1/\tilde{A}_2, p_{12}(x)).$$

Next, performing successive computations of membership functions based on (2.80)-(2.85), the resulting Z-number is found:

$$Z_{12} = (\tilde{A}_1/\tilde{A}_2, \tilde{B}_{12}).$$

Let us consider computation of a scalar multiplication of a Z-number $Z_Y = \lambda \cdot Z_X$, $\lambda \in \mathcal{R}$. Let $Z_X^+ = (\tilde{A}_X, R_X)$ where R_X is represented as

$$p_X = p_X(x_1)\backslash x_1 + p_X(x_2)\backslash x_2 + ... + p_X(x_n)\backslash x_n.$$

Then the discrete Z^+-number Z_Y^+ is determined as follows:

$$Z_Y^+ = (\tilde{A}_Y, R_Y)$$

where $\tilde{A}_Y = \lambda \tilde{A}_X$ is determined on the base of Definition 2.33 and R_Y is represented by a discrete probability distribution

$$p_Y = p_Y(y_1)\backslash y_1 + p_Y(y_2)\backslash y_2 + ... + p_Y(y_n)\backslash y_n \tag{2.86}$$

such that

$$y_k = \lambda x_k \text{ and } p_Y(y_k) = p_X(x_k). \tag{2.87}$$

Next we compute $\mu_{p_X}(p_{X,l}) = \mu_{\tilde{B}_X}\left(\sum_{k=1}^{n} \mu_{\tilde{A}_X}(x_k) p_{X,l}(x_k)\right)$ by solving linear programming problem analogous to (2.80)-(2.81).

Now recalling (2.86)-(2.87), we realize that the fuzzy set of probability distributions p_X with membership function $\mu_{p_X}(p_{X,l})$ naturally induces the fuzzy set of probability distributions $p_{Y,l}$ with the membership function defined as

$$\mu_{p_Y}(p_{Y,l}) = \mu_{p_X}(p_{X,l}),$$

taking into account (2.86)-(2.87).

Next we should compute probability measure of $\tilde{A}_Y$ given p_Y on the base of Definition 2.29. Given a fuzzy restriction on p_Y described by the membership function μ_{p_Y} we construct a fuzzy set $\tilde{B}_Y$ with the membership function $\mu_{\tilde{B}_Y}$ defined as follows:

$$\mu_{\tilde{B}_Y}(b_{Y,l}) = \sup(\mu_{p_Y}(p_{Y,l}))$$

subject to

$$b_{Y,l} = \sum_k p_{Y,l}(x_k)\mu_{\tilde{A}_Y}(x_k).$$

As a result, $Z_Y = \lambda \cdot Z_X$ is obtained as $Z_Y = (\tilde{A}_Y, \tilde{B}_Y)$. Let us mention that as $p_{Y,l}(y_k) = p_{X,l}(x_k)$, $\mu_{p_Y}(p_{Y,l}) = \mu_{p_X}(p_{X,l})$ and $\mu_{\tilde{A}_Y}(y_k) = \mu_{\tilde{A}_X}(x_k)$ with $y_k = \lambda x_k$, one has

$$b_{Y,l} = b_{X,l} \text{ and } \mu_{\tilde{B}_Y}(b_{Y,l}) = \mu_{\tilde{B}_X}(b_{X,l}),$$

which means $\tilde{B}_Y = \tilde{B}_X$. Therefore, it is not needed to carry out computation of $\tilde{B}_Y$, it is the same as $\tilde{B}_X$.

Let us consider computation of Hukuhara difference $Z_{12} = Z_1 -_h Z_2$ of Z-numbers $Z_1 = (\tilde{A}_1, \tilde{B}_1)$ and $Z_2 = (\tilde{A}_2, \tilde{B}_2)$. Hukuhara difference $Z_{12} = Z_1 -_h Z_2$ exists if and only if Hukuhara difference $\tilde{A}_{12} = \tilde{A}_1 -_h \tilde{A}_2$ (see Definition 2.35) exists. Suppose that $\tilde{A}_{12} = \tilde{A}_1 -_h \tilde{A}_2$ exists. Then, $A_{12}^\alpha, \alpha \in (0,1]$ will be computed as

$$A_{12}^\alpha = \bigcup_{i=1}^{r_\alpha - l_\alpha + 1}\left(A_{1,i}^\alpha -_h A_2^\alpha\right) = \bigcup_{i=1}^{r_\alpha - l_\alpha + 1}\left(\{x_{1\ i1}^\alpha, \ldots, x_{1\ im}^\alpha\} -_h \{x_{2\ 1_\alpha}^\alpha, \ldots, x_{2\ m_\alpha}^\alpha\}\right)$$

$$= \bigcup_{i=1}^{r_\alpha - l_\alpha + 1}\left(x_{1\ i1}^\alpha - x_{2\ 1_\alpha}^\alpha\right) = \ldots = \bigcup_{i=1}^{r_\alpha - l_\alpha + 1}\left(x_{1\ im}^\alpha - x_{2\ m_\alpha}^\alpha\right),$$

and $\text{supp}(\tilde{A}_{12}) = A_{12}^{\underline{\alpha}}$, where $\underline{\alpha} = \min \mu_{\tilde{A}_{12}}(x)$.

$\tilde{A}_{12}$ is then obtained as $\tilde{A}_{12} = \bigcup_{\alpha} \alpha A_{12}^{\alpha}$. Next it is needed to compute $\tilde{B}_{12}$. This requires to determine $\mu_{p_{12}}()$. The latter in turn requires to determine all the distributions p_{12}. Determination of p_{12} is implemented as follows. For any distribution p_1 (corresponds to Z_1) we should compute $P_1(A_{1,i}^{\underline{\alpha}}) = \sum_{j=1}^{m} p_1(x_{1\ ij}^{\underline{\alpha}})$, where $\underline{\alpha} = \min \mu_{\tilde{A}_1}(x)$. One can show that $P_1(A_{1,i}^{\underline{\alpha}}) = p_{12}(x_i)$, $i = 1,...,k$. Therefore, p_{12} is determined. Next, $\mu_{p_{12}}()$ is found as

$$\mu_{p_{12}}(p_{12}) = \max \mu_{p_1}(p_1) \tag{2.88}$$

subject to

$$\sum_{j=1}^{m} p_1(x_{1\ ij}^{\alpha}) = p_{12}(x_i),\ i = 1,...,k. \tag{2.89}$$

Finally, given $\mu_{p_{12}}()$ one can construct $\tilde{B}_{12}$ by solving (2.84)-(2.85). Thus, $Z_{12} = (\tilde{A}_{12}, \tilde{B}_{12})$ is obtained.

Now proceed to computation of a square and a square root of a Z-number. Let us consider computation of $Z_Y = Z_X^2$. Let $Z_X^+ = (\tilde{A}_X, R_X)$ where R_X is represented as

$$p_X = p_X(x_1) \setminus x_1 + p_X(x_2) \setminus x_2 + ... + p_X(x_n) \setminus x_n.$$

Then the discrete Z^+-number Z_Y^+ is determined as follows:

$$Z_Y^+ = (\tilde{A}_Y, R_Y)$$

where $\tilde{A}_Y = \tilde{A}_X^2$ with $\tilde{A}_X^2$ determined on the base of Definition 2.36 and R_Y is represented by a discrete probability distribution

$$p_Y = p_Y(y_1) \setminus y_1 + p_Y(y_2) \setminus y_2 + \ldots + p_Y(y_n) \setminus y_n \tag{2.90}$$

such that

$$y_k = x_k^2 \text{ and } p_Y(y_r) = \sum_{y_r = x^2} p_X(x), r = 1, \ldots, m \tag{2.91}$$

Next we compute $\mu_{p_X}(p_{X,l}) = \mu_{\tilde{B}_X}\left(\sum_{k=1}^{n} \mu_{\tilde{A}_X}(x_k) p_{X,l}(x_k)\right)$ by solving linear programming problem analogous to (2.80)-(2.81).

Now recalling (2.90)-(2.91), we realize that the fuzzy set of probability distributions p_X with membership function $\mu_{p_X}(p_{X,l})$ naturally induces the fuzzy set of probability distributions $p_{Y,l}$ with the membership function defined as

$$\mu_{p_Y}(p_{Y,l}) = \mu_{p_X}(p_{X,l}),$$

taking into account (2.91).

Next we should compute probability measure of $\tilde{A}_Y$ given p_Y on the base of Definition 2.29. Given a fuzzy restriction on p_Y described by the membership function μ_{p_Y} we construct a fuzzy set $\tilde{B}_Y$ with the membership function $\mu_{\tilde{B}_Y}$ defined as follows:

$$\mu_{\tilde{B}_Y}(b_{Y,l}) = \sup(\mu_{p_Y}(p_{Y,l}))$$

subject to

$$b_{Y,l} = \sum_k p_{Y,l}(x_k) \mu_{\tilde{A}_Y}(x_k).$$

As a result, Z^2 is obtained as $Z^2 = (\tilde{A}_Y, \tilde{B}_Y)$. for $x_i \geq 0, i = 1, \ldots, n$, one has $p_{Y,l}(y_k) = p_{X,l}(x_k)$, $\mu_{p_Y}(p_{Y,l}) = \mu_{p_X}(p_{X,l})$ and $\mu_{\tilde{A}_Y}(y_k) = \mu_{\tilde{A}_X}(x_k)$ with $y_k = x_k^2$. Thus one has

$$b_{Y,l} = b_{X,l} \text{ and } \mu_{\tilde{B}_Y}(b_{Y,l}) = \mu_{\tilde{B}_X}(b_{X,l}),$$

which means $\tilde{B}_Y = \tilde{B}_X$. Therefore, it is not needed to carry out computation of $\tilde{B}_Y$, it is the same as $\tilde{B}_X$.

Let us mention that computation of $Z_Y = Z_X^n$, where n is any natural number, is carried out analogously.

In [454] Zadeh asks a question: "What is a square root of a Z-number?". Let us consider computation of $Z_Y = \sqrt{Z_X}$. Let Z_X^+ and Z_X be the same as considered above for the case of a square of a Z-number. Then the discrete Z^+-number Z_Y^+ is determined as follows:

$$Z_Y^+ = (\tilde{A}_Y, R_Y)$$

where $\tilde{A}_Y = \sqrt{\tilde{A}_X}$ with $\sqrt{\tilde{A}_X}$ determined on the base of Definition 2.37 and R_Y is represented by a discrete probability distribution

$$p_{R_Y} = p_{R_Y}(y_1) \setminus y_1 + p_{R_Y}(y_2) \setminus y_2 + ... + p_{R_Y}(y_n) \setminus y_n, \tag{2.92}$$

such that

$$y_k = \sqrt{x_k} \text{ and } p_{R_Y}(y_k) = p_{R_X}(x_k). \tag{2.93}$$

Next we construct $\mu_{p_X}(p_{X,l}) = \mu_{\tilde{B}_X}\left(\sum_{k=1}^{n} \mu_{\tilde{A}_X}(x_k) p_{X,l}(x_k)\right)$ and recall that

$$\mu_{p_Y}(p_{Y,l}) = \mu_{p_X}(p_{X,l}),$$

taking into account (2.92)-(2.93).

Next we compute probability measure of $\tilde{A}_Y$ and given the membership function μ_{p_Y} we construct a fuzzy set $\tilde{B}_Y$ analogously to that we did above in computation of a square of a Z-number. As a result, $\sqrt{Z}$ is obtained as $\sqrt{Z} = (\tilde{A}_Y, \tilde{B}_Y)$. Let us mention that it is not needed to carry out computation of $\tilde{B}_Y$. One can easily verify that for the case of the square root of a discrete Z-number, $\tilde{B}_Y = \tilde{B}_X$ holds.

One another necessary operation in arithmetic of Z-numbers and a challenging practical issue is comparison of discrete Z-numbers. Zadeh addresses the problem of ranking Z-numbers as a very important problem and mentions a simple example: "*Is (approximately 100, likely) greater than (approximately 90, very likely)?*" [454]. Without doubt, this is a meaningful question, it is worth to mention that our everyday decisions are often characterized by imprecise and vague information both on future consequences and the related reliability.

In contrast to real numbers, Z-numbers are ordered pairs, for ranking of which there can be no unique approach. We suggest to consider comparison of Z-numbers on the base of fuzzy optimality (FO) principle [33,152]. Let Z-numbers $Z_1=(\tilde{A}_1,\tilde{B}_1)$ and $Z_2=(\tilde{A}_2,\tilde{B}_2)$ be given. First, it is needed to calculate the functions n_b, n_e, n_w which evaluate how much one of the Z-numbers is better, equivalent and worse than the other one with respect to the first and the second components:

$$
\begin{aligned}
n_b(Z_i,Z_j) &= P_b(\tilde{\delta}_{\tilde{A}}^{i,j})+P_b(\tilde{\delta}_{\tilde{B}}^{i,j})\\
n_e(Z_i,Z_j) &= P_e(\tilde{\delta}_{\tilde{A}}^{i,j})+P_e(\tilde{\delta}_{\tilde{B}}^{i,j})\\
n_w(Z_i,Z_j) &= P_w(\tilde{\delta}_{\tilde{A}}^{i,j})+P_w(\tilde{\delta}_{\tilde{B}}^{i,j})
\end{aligned}
\tag{2.94}
$$

where $\tilde{\delta}_{\tilde{A}}^{i,j}=\tilde{A}_i-\tilde{A}_j$, $\tilde{\delta}_{\tilde{B}}^{i,j}=\tilde{B}_i-\tilde{B}_j$, $P_l(\tilde{\delta}_{\tilde{A}}^{i,j})=\dfrac{Poss\left(\tilde{\delta}_{\tilde{A}}^{i,j}\,|\,\tilde{n}_l\right)}{\sum_{t\in\{b,e,w\}} Poss\left(\tilde{\delta}_{\tilde{A}}^{i,j}\,|\,\tilde{n}_t\right)}$,

$P_l(\tilde{\delta}_{\tilde{B}}^{i,j})=\dfrac{Poss\left(\tilde{\delta}_{\tilde{B}}^{i,j}\,|\,\tilde{n}_l\right)}{\sum_{t\in\{b,e,w\}} Poss\left(\tilde{\delta}_{\tilde{B}}^{i,j}\,|\,\tilde{n}_t\right)}$, $i,j=1,2,\ i\neq j$.

As $\sum_{t\in\{b,e,w\}} P_l(\tilde{\delta}_k^{i,j})=1$ always holds, one always has $n_b(Z_i,Z_j)+n_e(Z_i,Z_j)+n_w(Z_i,Z_j)=N$, where N is the number of components of a Z-number, i.e. $N=2$. The membership functions of $\tilde{n}_b,\tilde{n}_e,\tilde{n}_w$ are shown in Fig. 2.6.

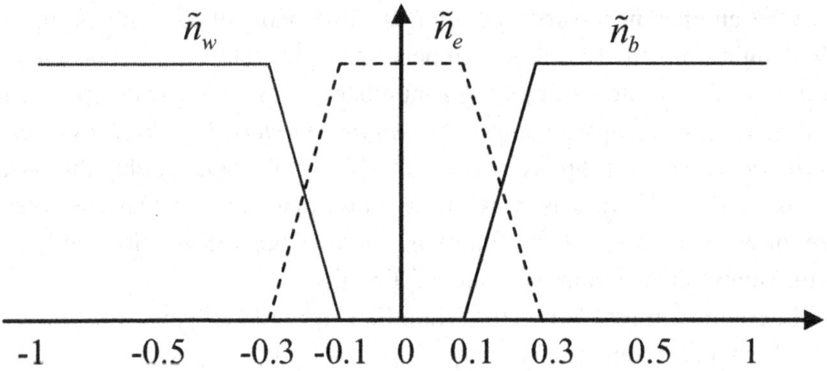

Fig. 2.6. The membership functions of $\tilde{n}_b, \tilde{n}_e, \tilde{n}_w$

Next it is needed to determine the greatest k such that Z_i Pareto dominates Z_j to the degree $(1-k)$. For this purpose, a function d is introduced:

$$d(Z_i, Z_j) = \begin{cases} 0, & \text{if } n_b(Z_i, Z_j) \le \dfrac{2 - n_e(Z_i, Z_j)}{2} \\ \dfrac{2 \cdot n_b(Z_i, Z_j) + n_e(Z_i, Z_j) - 2}{n_b(Z_i, Z_j)}, & \text{otherwise} \end{cases}. \tag{2.95}$$

Given d, the desired greatest k is found as $k = 1 - d(Z_i, Z_j)$, and then $(1-k) = d(Z_i, Z_j)$. $d(Z_i, Z_j) = 1$ implies Pareto dominance of Z_i over Z_j, whereas $d(Z_i, Z_j) = 0$ implies no Pareto dominance of Z_i over Z_j. The degree of optimality $do(Z_i)$ is determined as follows:

$$do(Z_i) = 1 - d(Z_j, Z_i). \tag{2.96}$$

Thus, in other words, $do(Z_i)$ is the degree to which one Z-number is higher than the other one. Then

$$Z_i > Z_j \text{ iff } do(Z_i) > do(Z_j),$$

$$Z_i < Z_j \text{ iff } do(Z_i) < do(Z_j)$$

and

$$do(Z_i) = do(Z_j) \text{ otherwise.}$$

Recall that comparison of fuzzy numbers is also a matter of a degree due to related vagueness. For Z-numbers, which are more complex constructs characterized by possibilistic-probabilistic uncertainty, degree-based comparison is even more desirable.

The suggested FO-based approach may be considered as basis of a human-oriented ranking of Z-numbers. In this viewpoint, we suggest to take into account degree of pessimism $\beta \in [0,1]$ as a mental factor which influences a choice of a preferred Z-number. The degree of pessimism is submitted by a human observer who wishes to compare the considered Z-numbers but does not completely rely on the results obtained by the above mentioned fuzzy optimality approach. In this viewpoint, given $do(Z_j) \le do(Z_i)$ we define for two Z-numbers Z_1 and Z_2:

$$r(Z_i, Z_j) = \beta do(Z_j) + (1-\beta) do(Z_i).$$

Then

$$Z_i > Z_j \text{ iff } r(Z_i, Z_j) > \frac{1}{2}(do(Z_i) + do(Z_j)),$$

$$Z_i < Z_j \text{ iff } r(Z_i, Z_j) < \frac{1}{2}(do(Z_i) + do(Z_j))$$

and $Z_i = Z_j$ otherwise.

The degree of pessimism β is submitted by a human being and adjust ranking of Z-numbers to reflect human attitude to the computed *do*. This attitude may result from the various importance of $\tilde{A}$ and $\tilde{B}$ components of Z-numbers for a human being and other issues.

Let us consider an example of an application of the suggested arithmetic of Z-numbers.

Example. Consider addition of two discrete Z-numbers $Z_1 = (\tilde{A}_1, \tilde{B}_1)$ and $Z_2 = (\tilde{A}_2, \tilde{B}_2)$ given:

$$\tilde{A}_1 = 0/1 + 0.3/2 + 0.5/3 + 0.6/4 + 0.7/5 + 0.8/6 + 0.9/7 + 1/8 + 0.8/9 + 0.6/10 + 0/11,$$

$$\tilde{B}_1 = 0/0 + 0.5/0.1 + 0.8/0.2 + 1/0.3 + 0.8/0.4 + 0.7/0.5 + 0.6/0.6 + 0.4/0.7 + 0.2/0.8 + 0.1/0.6 + 0/1;$$

$$\tilde{A}_2 = 0/1 + 0.5/2 + 0.8/3 + 1/4 + 0.8/5 + 0.7/6 + 0.6/7 + 0.4/8 + 0.2/9 + 0.1/10 + 0/11,$$

$$\tilde{B}_2 = 0/0 + 0.3/0.1 + 0.5/0.2 + 0.6/0.3 + 0.7/0.4 + 0.8/0.5 + 0.9/0.6 + 1/0.7 + 0.8/0.8 + 0.9/0.6 + 0/1.$$

According to the suggested approach, first we should proceed to the discrete Z^+-numbers. Let us consider $Z_1^+ = (\tilde{A}_1, R_1)$ and $Z_2^+ = (\tilde{A}_2, R_2)$ where R_1 and R_2 are represented by the following discrete probability distributions:

$$p_1 = 0.27\backslash 1 + 0\backslash 2 + 0\backslash 3 + 0.003\backslash 4 + 0.04\backslash 5 + 0.075\backslash 6 + 0.11\backslash 7 + 0.15\backslash 8 + 0.075\backslash 9 + 0.002\backslash 10 + 0.27\backslash 11,$$

$$p_2 = 0.09\backslash 1 + 0\backslash 2 + 0\backslash 3 + 0.32\backslash 4 + 0.18\backslash 5 + 0.1\backslash 6 + 0.036\backslash 7 + 0\backslash 8 + 0\backslash 9 + 0\backslash 10 + 0.09\backslash 11.$$

Next we should determine

$$Z_{12}^+ = (\tilde{A}_1 + \tilde{A}_2, R_1 + R_2).$$

In accordance with the suggested approach, first we compute $\tilde{A}_{12} = \tilde{A}_1 + \tilde{A}_2$ on the base of Definition 2.30. The resulting $\tilde{A}_{12}$ is as follows:

$$\tilde{A}_{12} = 0/1 + 0/2 + 0.19/3 + 0.36/4 + 0.5/5 + 0.58/6 + 0.65/7 + 0.73/8 + 0.8/9 + 0.87/10 + 0.93/11 + 1/12 + 0.9/13 + 0.8/14 + 0.73/15 + 0.7/16 + 0.6/17 + 0.45/18 + 0.3/19 + 0.17/20 + 0.086/21.$$

Next we compute $R_1 + R_2$ as a convolution $p_{12} = p_1 \circ p_2$ of the considered p_1 and p_2. $p_{12}(x)$ obtained in accordance with Definition 2.28 is given below:

$$\begin{aligned} p_{12} = & 0.025\backslash 1 + 0\backslash 2 + 0\backslash 3 + 0.87\backslash 4 + 0.52\backslash 5 + 0.036\backslash 6 + 0.028\backslash 7 + 0\backslash 8 \\ & + 0\backslash 9 + 0\backslash 10 + 0.14\backslash 11 + 0.07\backslash 12 + 0.082\backslash 13 + 0.1\backslash 14 + 0.055\backslash 15 \\ & + 0.036\backslash 16 + 0.02\backslash 17 + 0.014\backslash 18 + 0.007\backslash 19 + 0\backslash 20 + 0.05\backslash 21. \end{aligned}$$

Thus, $Z_{12}^{+} = (\tilde{A}_1 + \tilde{A}_2, p_{12}(x))$ is obtained.

Next we realize, that 'true' probability distributions p_1 and p_2 are not exactly known, but only fuzzy restrictions for p_1 and p_2 are available. We compute the membership degrees $\mu_{p_j}(p_j)$, $j = 1,2$ of the fuzzy restrictions given the solutions of the goal linear programming problems (2.80)-(2.81). For p_1 and p_2 considered above, these degrees are $\mu_{p_1}(p_1) = 0.8$ and $\mu_{p_2}(p_2) = 1$. Analogously, we computed the membership degrees of for all the considered p_1 and p_2.

Further, we should determine the induced fuzzy restriction over convolutions p_{12} based on (2.82)-(2.83). For example, the membership degree of this fuzzy restriction for the convolution p_{12} obtained above is $\mu_{p_{12}}(p_{12}) = 0.8$. Analogously, we computed the degrees for all the considered $p_{12}(x)$.

Now, based on Definition 2.29, we need to compute values of probability measure $P(\tilde{A}_{12})$ with respect to the obtained convolutions p_{12}. For example, $P(\tilde{A}_{12})$ with respect to p_{12} considered above is $P(\tilde{A}_{12}) = b_{12} = 0.63$.

At the final stage, we construct $\tilde{B}_{12}$ based on (2.84)-(2.85). For example, $\mu_{\tilde{B}_{12}}(0.63) = 0.8$. The constructed $\tilde{B}_{12}$ is given below:

$$\begin{aligned} \tilde{B}_{12} = & 0/0.56 + 0.5/0.60 + 0.8/0.63 + 1/0.66 + 0.8/0.69 + 0.7/0.72 \\ & + 0.6/0.75 + 0.4/0.78 + 0.2/0.81 + 0.1/0.84 + 0/0.86 + 0/1. \end{aligned}$$

Thus, $Z_{12} = (\tilde{A}_{12}, \tilde{B}_{12})$ as the result of addition is obtained where $\tilde{A}_{12}, \tilde{B}_{12}$ are shown in Fig. 2.7.

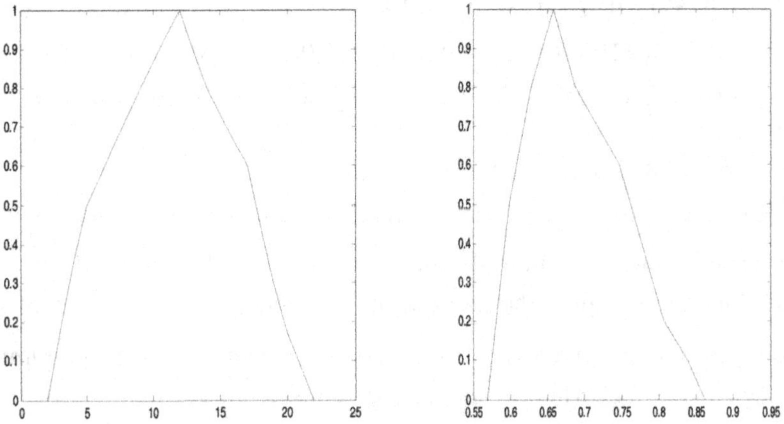

(a) (b)

Fig. 2.7. The result of addition of discrete Z-numbers: (a) $\tilde{A}_{12}$, (b) $\tilde{B}_{12}$

Computation with Z-numbers may be viewed as a generalization of computation with numbers, intervals, fuzzy numbers and random numbers. More concretely, the levels of generality are: computation with numbers (ground level); computation with intervals (level 1); computation with fuzzy numbers (level 2); and computation with Z-numbers (level 3). The higher the level of generality, the greater is the capability to construct realistic models of real-world systems, especially in the realms of economics and decision analysis.

It should be noted that many numbers, especially in fields such as economics and decision analysis are in reality Z-numbers, but they are not treated as such because it is much simpler to compute with numbers than with Z-numbers. Basically, the concept of a Z-number is a step toward formalization of the remarkable human capability to make rational decisions in an environment of imprecision and uncertainty.

2.1.8 *Fuzzy relations, linguistic variables*

In modeling systems the internal structure of a system must be described first. An internal structure is characterized by connections (associations) among the elements of system. As a rule these connections or associations are represented by means of relation. We will consider here fuzzy relations which gives us the representation about degree or strength of this connection.

There are several definitions of fuzzy relation [232, 438,459]. Each of them depends on various factors and expresses different aspects of modeling systems.

Definition 2.41. Type-1 fuzzy relation. Let $X_1, X_2, ..., X_n$ be nonempty crisp sets. Then, a $\tilde{R}(X_1, X_2, ..., X_n)$ is called a Type-1 fuzzy relation of sets $X_1, X_2, ..., X_n$, if $\tilde{R}(X_1, X_2, ..., X_n)$ is the fuzzy subset given on Cartesian product $X_1 \times X_2 \times \cdots \times X_n$.

If $n=2$, then fuzzy relation is called binary fuzzy relation, and is denoted as $\tilde{R}(X,Y)$. For three, four, or n sets the fuzzy relation is called ternary, quaternary, or n-ary, respectively.

In particular, if $X_1 = X_2 = \cdots = X_n = X$ we say that fuzzy relation R is given on set X among elements $x_1, x_2, ..., x_n \in X$.

Notice, that fuzzy relation can be defined in another way. Namely, by two ordered fuzzy sets.

Assume, two fuzzy sets $\mu_{\tilde{A}}(x)$ and $\mu_{\tilde{B}}(y)$ are given on crisp sets X and Y, respectively. Then, it is said, that fuzzy relation $R_{\tilde{A}\tilde{B}}(X,Y)$ is given on sets X and Y, if it is defined in the following way

$$\mu_{R_{\tilde{A}\tilde{B}}}(x,y) = \min_{x,y}[\mu_{\tilde{A}}(x), \mu_{\tilde{B}}(y)]$$

for all pairs (x,y), where $x \in X$ and $y \in Y$. As above, fuzzy relation $R_{\tilde{A}\tilde{B}}$ is defined on Cartesian product.

Let fuzzy binary relation on set X be given. Consider the following three properties of relation $\tilde{R}$:

1. Fuzzy relation $\tilde{R}$ is reflexive, if

$$\mu_{\tilde{R}}(x,x)=1$$

for all $x \in X$. If there exist $x \in X$ such that this condition is violated, then relation $\tilde{R}$ is irreflexive, and if $\tilde{R}(x,x)=0$ for all $x \in X$, the relation $\tilde{R}$ is antireflective;

2. A fuzzy relation $\tilde{R}$ is symmetric if it satisfies the following condition:

$$\mu_{\tilde{R}}(x,y)=\mu_{\tilde{R}}(y,x)$$

for all $x,y \in X$. If from $\tilde{R}(x,y)>0$ and $\tilde{R}(y,x)>0$ follows $x=y$ for all $x,y \in X$ relation $\tilde{R}$ is called antisymmetric;

3. A fuzzy relation $\tilde{R}$ is transitive (or, more specifically, max-min transitive) if

$$\mu_{\tilde{R}}(x,z) \geq \max_{y \in Y} \min(\mu_{\tilde{R}}(x,y),\ \mu_{\tilde{R}}(y,z))$$

is satisfied for all pairs $(x,z) \in X$.

Definition 2.42. Fuzzy proximity. A fuzzy relation is called a fuzzy proximity or fuzzy tolerance relation if it is reflexive and symmetric. A fuzzy relation is called a fuzzy similarity relation if it is reflexive, symmetric, and transitive.

Definition 2.43. Fuzzy composition. Let $\tilde{A}$ and $\tilde{B}$ be two fuzzy sets on $X \times Y$ and $Y \times Z$, respectively. A fuzzy relation $\tilde{R}$ on $X \times Z$ is defined as

$$\tilde{R}=\{((x,z),\mu_{\tilde{R}}(x,z) \,|\, (x,z) \in X \times Z\} \tag{2.97}$$

here

$$\mu_{\tilde{R}}: X \times Y \rightarrow [0,1]$$

$$(x,z) \mapsto \mu_{\tilde{R}}(x,z)=\mu_{\tilde{A}\circ\tilde{B}}(x,z)=\underset{y \in Y}{S}(\mathrm{T}(\mu_{\tilde{A}}(x,y),\mu_{\tilde{B}}(y,z))). \tag{2.98}$$

For $x \in X$ and $z \in Z$, "T" and "S" are triangular norms and triangular conorms, respectively.

Definition 2.44. Equivalence (similarity) relation. If fuzzy relation $\tilde{R}$ is reflexive, symmetric and transitive then relation $\tilde{R}$ is an equivalence relation or similarity relation.

A fuzzy relation $\tilde{R}$ is a fuzzy compatibility relation if it is reflexive and symmetric. This relation is cutworthy. Compatibility classes are defined by means of α-cut. In fact, using α-cut a class of compatibility relation is represented by means of crisp subset.

Therefore a compatibility relation can also be represented by reflexive undirected graph.

Now consider fuzzy partial ordering.

Let X be nonempty set. It is well known, that to order a set it is necessary to give an order relation on this set. But sometimes our knowledge and estimates of the elements of a set are not accurate and complete. Thus, to order such set the fuzzy order on set must be defined.

Definition 2.45. Fuzzy partial ordering relation. Let $\tilde{R}$ be binary fuzzy relation on X. Then fuzzy relation $\tilde{R}$ is called fuzzy partial ordering, if it satisfies the following conditions:

1. Fuzzy relation $\tilde{R}$ is reflexive;
2. Fuzzy relation $\tilde{R}$ is antisymmetric;
3. Fuzzy relation $\tilde{R}$ is fuzzy transitive.

If fuzzy partial order is given on set X then we will say that set X is fuzzy partially ordered.

Definition 2.46. Type-2 fuzzy relation. Let $X_1, X_2, \ldots, X_n$ be n universes. A Type-2 fuzzy relation in $X_1 \times X_2 \times \ldots \times X_n$ is Type-2 fuzzy subset of the Cartesian product space.

Let X and Y based on the Cartesian product $X \times Y$ be given. The binary Type-2 fuzzy relation $\tilde{\tilde{R}}$ between X and Y can be defined as follows:

$$\tilde{\tilde{R}}(X,Y) = \int_{X*Y} \mu_{\tilde{\tilde{R}}}(x,y)/(x,y), \tag{2.99}$$

where $x \in X$, $y \in Y$.

The membership function of $\tilde{\tilde{R}}(x,y)$ is given as follows:

$$\mu_{\tilde{\tilde{R}}(x,y)} = \int_{v \in J_{x,y}^{v}} r_{x,y}(v)/v,$$

where $r_{x,y}(v)$ is the secondary membership and $J_{x,y}^{v} \subset [0,1]$.

Let $\tilde{\tilde{R}}(X,Y)$ and $\tilde{\tilde{S}}(X,Y)$ are two Type-2 fuzzy relation on the same product space $X \times Y$. Their union and intersection can be defined as follows:

$$\mu_{\tilde{\tilde{R}} \cup \tilde{\tilde{S}}}(x,y) = \mu_{\tilde{\tilde{R}}}(x,y) \sqcup \mu_{\tilde{\tilde{S}}}(x,y) \tag{2.100}$$

$$\mu_{\tilde{\tilde{R}} \cap \tilde{\tilde{S}}}(x,y) = \mu_{\tilde{\tilde{R}}}(x,y) \sqcap \mu_{\tilde{\tilde{S}}}(x,y). \tag{2.101}$$

Composition of Type-2 fuzzy relations. Sup-star composition of two Type-2 fuzzy relations $\tilde{\tilde{R}}$ and $\tilde{\tilde{S}}$ is determined as

$$\mu_{\tilde{\tilde{R}} o \tilde{\tilde{S}}}(u,w) = \bigsqcup_{v \in V}[\mu_{\tilde{\tilde{R}}}(u,v) \sqcap \mu_{\tilde{\tilde{S}}}(v,w)].$$

The practice and experimental evidence have shown that decision theories developed for a perfect decision-relevant information and 'well-defined' preferences are not capable of adequate modeling of real-world decision making. The reason is that real decision problems are characterized by imperfect decision-relevant information and vaguely defined preferences. This leads to the fact that when solving real-world decision problems we need to move away from traditional decision approaches based on exact modeling which is good rather for decision analysis of thought experiments.

More concretely, the necessity to sacrifice the precision and determinacy is by the fact that real-world problems are characterized by perception-based information and choices, for which natural language is more covinient and close than precise formal approaches. Modeling decision making from this perspective is impossible without dealing with fuzzy categories near to human notions and imaginations. In this connection, it is valuable to use the notion of linguistic variable first introduced by L.Zadeh [440]. Linguistic variables allow an adequate reflection of approximate in-word descriptions of objects and phenomena in the case if there is no any precise deterministic description. It should be noted as well that many fuzzy categories described linguistically even appear to be more informative than precise descriptions.

Definition 2.47. Linguistic variable. A linguistic variable is characterized by the set (u,T,X,G,M), where u is the name of variable; T denotes the term-set of u that refer to as base variable whose values range over a universe X; G is a syntactic rule (usually in form of a grammar) genera-ting linguistic terms; M is a semantic rule that assigns to each linguistic term its meaning, which is a fuzzy set on X.

A certain $t \in T$ generated by the syntactic rule G is called a term. A term consisting of one or more words, the words being always used together, is named an atomary term. A term consisting of several atomary terms is named a composite term. The concatenation of some components of a composite term (i.e. the result of linking the chains of components of the composite term) is called a subterm. Here $t_1, t_2, \ldots$ are terms in the following expression

$$T = t_1 + t_2 + \cdots.$$

The meaning of $M(t)$ of the term t is defined as a restriction $R(t;x)$ on the basis variable x conditioned by the fuzzy variable X:

$$M(t) \equiv R(t;x),$$

it is assumed here that $R(t;x)$ and, consequently, $M(t)$ can be considered as a fuzzy subset of the set X named as t.

The assignment equation in case of linguistic variable takes the form in which t-terms in T are names generated by the grammar G, where the meaning assigned to the term t is expressed by the equality

$$M(t) = R(term\, in T).$$

In other words the meaning of the term t is found by the application of the semantic rule M to the value of term t assigned according to the right part of equation. Moreover, it follows that $M(t)$ is identical to the restriction associated with the term t.

It should be noted that the number of elements in T can be unlimited and then for both generating elements of the set T and for calculating their meaning, the application of the algorithm, not simply the procedure for watching term-set, is necessary.

We will say that a linguistic variable u is structured if its term-set T and the function M, which maps each element from the term-set into its meaning, can be given by means of algorithm. Then both syntactic and semantic rules connected with the structured linguistic variable can be considered algorithmic procedures for generating elements of the set T and calculating the meaning of each term in T, respectively.

However in practice we often encounter term-sets consisting of a small number of terms. This makes it easier to list the elements of term-set T and establishes a direct mapping from each element to its meaning. For axample, an intuitive description of possible economic conditions may be represented by linguistic terms like "strong econonmic growth", "weak economic growth" etc. Then the term set of linguistic variable "state of economy" can be written as follows:

T(state of economy) = "strong growth" + "moderate growth" + "static situation" + "recession".

The variety of economic conditions may also be described by ranges of the important economic indicators. However, numerical values of indicators may not be sufficiently clear even for experts and may arise questions and doubts. In contrast, linguistic description is well perceived by human intuition as qualitative and fuzzy.

2.2 Fuzzy Logic

2.2.1 *Classical fuzzy logic*

We will consider the logics with multi-valued and continuous values (fuzzy logic). Let's define the semantic truth function of this logic. Let P be statement and $T(P)$ its truth value, where $T(P) \in [0,1]$.

Negation values of the statement P are defined as:

$$T(\neg P) = 1 - T(P).$$

Hence

$$T(\neg\neg P) = T(P).$$

The implication connective is always defined as follows:

$$T(P \to Q) = T(\neg P \vee Q),$$

and the equivalence as

$$T(P \leftrightarrow Q) = T\left[(P \to Q) \wedge (Q \to P)\right].$$

It should be noted that exclusive disjunction ex, disjunction of negations (Shiffer's connective) |, conjunction of negations $\downarrow$ and $\sim\!\to$ (has no common name) are defined as negation of equivalence $\leftrightarrow$, conjunction $\wedge$, disjunction $\vee$, and implication $\to$, respectively.

The tautology denoted • and contradiction denoted ∘ will be, respectively:

$$T\left(\overset{\bullet}{P}\right) = T(P \vee \neg P); T\left(\overset{\circ}{P}\right) = T(P \wedge \neg P).$$

More generally

$$T\left(\overset{\bullet}{P}Q\right) = T((P \vee \neg P) \vee (Q \vee Q))$$

$$T\left(\overset{\circ}{P}Q\right) = T((P \wedge \neg P) \wedge (Q \wedge Q)).$$

Let us define the basic connectives of fuzzy logic in the following two fuzzy set theories.

Logic based on $(P(X), \cap, \cup, -)$. In this case disjunction and conjunct-tion are defined as:

$$T(P \vee Q) = \max(T(P), T(Q)); T(P \wedge Q) = \min(T(P), T(Q)).$$

It is clear, that $\vee$ and $\wedge$ are commutative, associative, idempotent and distributive and do not satisfy the law of excluded-middle, i.e. $T(P \vee \neg P) \neq 1$ and $T(P \vee \neg P) \neq 0$, but satisfy absorption law

$$T(P \vee (P \wedge Q)) = T(P); T(P \wedge (P \vee Q)) = T(P),$$

and also De Morgan's laws:

$$T(\neg(P \wedge Q)) = T(\neg P \vee \neg Q)$$

$$T(\neg(P \vee Q)) = T(\neg P \vee \neg Q).$$

Equivalence is defined as

$$T[(\neg P \vee Q) \wedge (P \vee \neg Q)] = T(\neg P \wedge Q) \vee (\neg P \vee \neg Q).$$

Law of excluded disjunction:

$$T[(\neg P \wedge Q) \vee (P \wedge \neg Q)] = [T(P \vee Q) \wedge (\neg P \vee \neg Q)].$$

The expressions for 16 connectives are presented in Table 2.2. It is assumed here that $T(P) = p$ and $T(Q) = q$.

Table 2.2. Expressions for connectives

PQ	$\dot{P}Q$	$P \vee Q$	$Q \to P$	P
pq PQ	$\max(p, 1-p, q, 1-q)$ $Q \to P$	$\max(p, q)$ Q	$\max(p, 1-q)$ $Q \leftrightarrow P$	p $P \wedge Q$
pq PQ	$\max(1-p, q)$ $P \mid Q$	q $P\,ex\,Q$	$\min(\max(1-p, q),$ $\max(p, 1-q))$ $\neg Q$	$\min(p, q)$ $Q - \to$
pq PQ	$\max(1-p, 1-q)$ $\neg P$	$\max(\min(1-p, q),$ $pq(p, 1-q))$ $P - \to Q$	$1-q$ $P \downarrow Q$	$\min(p, 1-q)$ $\overset{\circ}{P}Q$
pq	$\min(1-p, 1-q)$	$\min(1-p, q)$	$\min(1-p, 1-q)$	$\min(p, 1-q, q, 1-q)$

The quantifiers in the statements will be:

$$T(\exists x P(x)) = \sup(T(P(x))); T(\forall x P(x)) = \inf(T(P(x))),$$

where x denotes an element of the universe of discourse.

Multi-valued logic based on $\left(\tilde{P}(X), \cap, \cup, -\right)$ usually is called K-standard sequence logic. In this logic the connectives satisfy the following properties:

Implication $T\left[P \to (Q \to R)\right] = T\left[(P \wedge Q) \to R\right]$; tautology and contradiction

$$T(P \to P) = T\left(\overset{\bullet}{P}\right)$$

$$T\left(\overset{\circ}{P} \to P\right) = T(P)$$

$$T\left(P \to \overset{\circ}{P}\right) = T\left(\overset{\bullet}{P}\right)$$

$$T(P \leftrightarrow P) = T\left(\overset{\bullet}{P}\right)$$

$$T\left(\overset{\circ}{P} \to P\right) = T\left(\overset{\bullet}{P}\right)$$

$$T\left(P \to \overset{\circ}{P}\right) = T(\neg P)$$

$$T(P \leftrightarrow \neg P) = T\left(\overset{\circ}{P}\right).$$

The Shiffer's and Pierce's connectives

$$T(\neg P) = T(P \mid P)$$

$$T(P \to Q) = T(P \mid (Q / Q))$$

$$T\left(\overset{\circ}{P}\right) = T(P \mid (P \mid P)).$$

It is shown in [134, 240] that the multi-valued logic is fuzzification of the traditional propositional calculus (in sense of cxtension principle). In this logic each proposition P is assigned a normalized fuzzy set in [0,1], i.e. the pair $\{\mu_P(0), \mu_P(1)\}$ is interpreted as the degree of false or truth, respectively. Because the logical connectives of standard propositional calculus are functionals of truthness, that is they are represented as functions, they can be fuzzified.

Logic based on $\left(\tilde{P}(X), \underset{\bullet}{\cap}, \overset{\bullet}{\cup}, -\right)$. In this case disjunction and conjunction are defined as

$$T(P \overset{\bullet}{\vee} Q) = \min(1, T(P) + T(Q))$$

$$T(P \underset{\bullet}{\wedge} Q) = \max(0, T(P) + T(Q) - 1)$$

It is clear that $\overset{\bullet}{\vee}$ and $\underset{\bullet}{\wedge}$ are commutative, associative, not idempotent and not distributive and they satisfy De Morgan's laws

$$T(\neg(P \underset{\bullet}{\vee} Q)) = T(\neg P \vee \neg Q)$$

$$T(\neg(P \overset{\bullet}{\wedge} Q)) = T(\neg P \wedge \neg Q)$$

and the law of excluded-middle

$$T(P \vee \neg P) = 1, T(P \wedge \neg P) = 0$$

The 16 connectives are given in Table 2.3. Here $\vee$, $\rightarrow$, $\leftrightarrow$, $\wedge$, $|$, ex, $\sim\rightarrow$, $\downarrow$ are denoted by $\dot{\vee}$, $\Rightarrow$, $\Leftrightarrow$, $\underset{\bullet}{\wedge}$, $||$, ex, $\approx\Rightarrow$, $\downarrow\downarrow$, respectively.

Table 2.3. Expressions for connectives

PQ	$\dot{P}Q$	$Q \Rightarrow P$	$Q \Rightarrow P$	P
pq PQ	1 $P \Rightarrow Q$	$\min(1, p+q)$ Q	$\min(1, p+1-q)$ $P \Leftrightarrow Q$	p $P \underset{\bullet}{\wedge} Q$
pq PQ	$\min(1, 1-p+q)$ $P \parallel Q$	Q $P ex Q$	$1-\|p-q\|$ $\neg Q$	$\max(0, p+q-1)$ $Q \approx\Rightarrow P$
pq PQ	$\min(1, 1-p+1q)$ $\neg P\|$	$\|p-q\|$ $P \approx\Rightarrow Q$	$1-q$ $P \downarrow\downarrow Q$	$\max(0, p-q)$ $\mathring{P}Q$
pq	$1-p$	$\max(0, q-p)$	$\max(0, 1-p-q)$	0

Tautology and contradiction satisfy the following properties:

$$T(P \Rightarrow P) = T(\dot{P}),$$

$$T(\dot{P} \Rightarrow P) = T(P),$$

$$T(P \Rightarrow \dot{P}) = T(\dot{P}),$$

$$T(P \Leftrightarrow P) = T(\dot{P}),$$

$$T(\mathring{P} \Rightarrow P) = T(\dot{P}),$$

$$T(P \Leftrightarrow \mathring{P}) = T(\neg P).$$

In Zadeh's notation the implication $\Rightarrow$ corresponds to the usual inclusion for fuzzy sets, ex and $\approx\Rightarrow$ correspond to symmetric ∇ and bounded $|-|$ differences, respectively. This logic is known as Lukasiewicz logic (L-logic).

It should be noted that these two theories of fuzzy sets and logics constructed on the basis of these theories are not only known at the present time. In connection with this it is necessary to give semantic analysis of the major known multi-valued logics. For this purpose we will use power sets which are necessary for formalization of some operations on fuzzy sets.

Semantic Analysis of Different Fuzzy Logics. Let $\tilde{A}$ and $\tilde{B}$ be fuzzy sets of the subsets of non-fuzzy universe U ; in fuzzy set theory it is known that $\tilde{A}$ is a subset of $\tilde{B}$ iff

$$\mu_{\tilde{A}} \leq \mu_{\tilde{B}}, \text{ i.e. } \forall x \in U, \qquad \mu_{\tilde{A}}(x) \leq \mu_{\tilde{B}}(x).$$

Definition 2.48. Power fuzzy set[53]. For given fuzzy implication $\rightarrow$ and fuzzy set $\tilde{B}$ from the universe U, the power fuzzy set $\tilde{P}\tilde{B}$ from $\tilde{B}$ is given by membership function $\mu_{\tilde{P}\tilde{B}}$:

$$\mu_{\tilde{P}\tilde{B}}\tilde{A} = \underset{X \in U}{\wedge}(\mu_{\tilde{A}}(x) \rightarrow \mu_{\tilde{B}}(x)).$$

Then the degree to which $\tilde{A}$ is subset of $\tilde{B}$, is

$$\pi(\tilde{A} \subseteq \tilde{B}) = \mu_{\tilde{P}\tilde{B}}\tilde{A}.$$

Definition 2.49. Fuzzy implication operator [53]. Given a fuzzy implication operator $\rightarrow$ on the closed unit interval [0, 1], the operators $\leftarrow$ and $\leftrightarrow$ are defined by the conditions that, for all $a, b \in [0,1]$,

(1) $a \leftarrow b = b \rightarrow a$
(2) $a \leftrightarrow b = (a \rightarrow b) \wedge (a \leftarrow b) = (a \rightarrow b) \wedge (a \leftarrow b)$

Definition 2.50. Degree of "equivalency"[53]. Under the conditions of the definition of $P\tilde{B}$ the degree to which fuzzy sets $\tilde{A}$ and $\tilde{B}$ are equivalent is:

$$\pi\left(\tilde{A} \equiv \tilde{B}\right) = \pi\left(\tilde{A} \subseteq \tilde{B}\right) \wedge \pi\left(\tilde{B} \subseteq \tilde{A}\right);$$

or

$$\pi\left(\tilde{A} \equiv \tilde{B}\right) = \underset{x \in U}{\wedge} (\mu_{\tilde{A}} x \to \mu_{\tilde{B}} x) .$$

For practical purposes [53] in most cases it is advisable to work with multi-valued logics in which logical variable takes values from the real interval $I = [0,1]$ divided into 10 subintervals, i.e. by using set $V_{11} = [0, 0.1, 0.2, ..., 1]$.

We denote the truth values of premises $\tilde{A}$ and $\tilde{B}$ through $T(\tilde{A}) = a$ and $T(\tilde{B}) = b$. The implication operation in analyzed logics [5,344] has the following form:

1) min-logic

$$a \underset{\min}{\to} b = \begin{cases} a, & if \;\; a \le b \\ b, & otherwise. \end{cases}$$

2) $S^{\#}$ - logic

$$a \underset{S^{\#}}{\to} b = \begin{cases} 1, & if \;\; a \ne 1 \;\; or \;\; b = 1, \\ 0 & , otherwise. \end{cases}$$

3) S - logic ("Standard sequence")

$$a \underset{S}{\to} b = \begin{cases} 1, & if \;\; a \le b, \\ 0, & otherwise. \end{cases}$$

4) G - logic ("Gödelian sequence")

$$a \underset{G}{\to} b = \begin{cases} 1, & if \;\; a \le b, \\ b, & otherwise. \end{cases}$$

5) $G43$ - logic

$$a \underset{G43}{\to} b = \begin{cases} 1, & if \;\; a = 0, \\ \min(1, b/a), & otherwise. \end{cases}$$

6) L - logic(Lukasiewicz's logic)

$$a \underset{L}{\rightarrow} b = \min(1, 1-a+b).$$

7) *KD* - logic

$$a \underset{KD}{\rightarrow} b = ((1-a) \vee b = \max(1-a, b).$$

In turn ALI1-ALI4 - logics, suggested by us, which will be used in further chapters are characterized by the following implication operations [10,20]:

8) ALI1 - logic

$$a \underset{ALI1}{\rightarrow} b = \begin{cases} 1-a, & if \ \ a < b, \\ 1, & if \ \ a = b, \\ b, & if \ \ a > b \end{cases}$$

9) ALI2 - logic

$$a \underset{ALI2}{\rightarrow} b = \begin{cases} 1, & if \ \ a \le b, \\ (1-a) \wedge b, & if \ \ a > b \end{cases}$$

10) ALI3 - logic

$$a \underset{ALI3}{\rightarrow} b = \begin{cases} 1, & if \ \ a \le b, \\ b / [a + (1-b)], & otherwise. \end{cases}$$

11) ALI4 - logic

$$a \xrightarrow[ALI4]{} b = \begin{cases} \dfrac{1-\mathrm{a}+b}{2}, & \mathrm{a} > \mathrm{b}, \\ 1, & \mathrm{a} \le \mathrm{b}. \end{cases}$$

A necessary observation to be made in the context of this discussion is that with the only few exceptions for *S-logic* (3) and *G-logic* (4), and ALI1-ALI4 (8)-(11), all other known fuzzy logics (1)-(2), (5)-(7) do not satisfy either the classical "modus-ponens" principle, or other criteria which appeal to the human perception of mechanisms of a decision making process being formulated in [184]. The proposed fuzzy logics ALI1-ALI4 come with an implication operators, which satisfy the classical principle of "modus-ponens" and meets some additional criteria being in line with human intuition.

The comparative analysis of the first seven logics has been given in [53]. The analysis of these seven logics has shown that only S- and G-logics satisfy the classical principle of Modus Ponens and allow development of improved rule of fuzzy conditional inference. At the same time the value of truthness of the implication operation in G-logic is equal either to 0 or 1; and only the value of truthness of logical conclusion is used in the definition of the implication operation in S-logic. Thus the degree of "fuzziness" of implication is decreased, which is a considerable disadvantage and restricts the use of these logics in approximate reasoning.

Definition 2.51. Top of a fuzzy set. The top of fuzzy set $\tilde{B}$ is

$$H\tilde{B} = \vee_{U} \mu_{\tilde{B}}(x).$$

Definition 2.52. Bottom of a fuzzy set. The bottom of fuzzy set $\tilde{B}$ is

$$p\tilde{B} = \wedge_{U} \mu_{\tilde{B}}(x).$$

Definition 2.53. Nonfuzziness. Nonfuzziness $a \in U$ is $ka = a \vee (1-a)$. Then nonfuzziness of fuzzy set $\tilde{B}$ is defined as:

$$k\tilde{B} = \wedge_{U} k\mu_{\tilde{B}}(x).$$

Let us give a brief semantic analysis of the proposed fuzzy logics ALI1-ALI3 by using the terminology accepted in the theory of power fuzzy sets. For this purpose we formulate the following.

Proposal. Possibility degree of the inclusion of set $\pi(\tilde{A} \subseteq \tilde{B})$ in fuzzy logic ALI1-ALI3 is determined as:

$$\pi_1\left(\tilde{A} \subseteq \tilde{B}\right) = \begin{cases} 1-\mu_{\tilde{A}}(x), & if \quad \mu_{\tilde{A}}(x) < \mu_{\tilde{B}}(x), \\ 1, & if \quad \mu_{\tilde{A}}(x) = \mu_{\tilde{B}}(x), \\ \mu_{\tilde{B}}(x), & if \quad \mu_{\tilde{A}}(x) > \mu_{\tilde{B}}(x); \end{cases}$$

$$\pi_2\left(\tilde{A} \subseteq \tilde{B}\right) = \begin{cases} 1, & if \ \mu_{\tilde{A}}(x) \le \mu_{\tilde{B}}(x), \\ \left(1-\mu_{\tilde{A}}(x)\right) \wedge \mu_{\tilde{B}}(x), & if \ \mu_{\tilde{A}}(x) > \mu_{\tilde{B}}(x); \end{cases}$$

$$\pi_3\left(\tilde{A} \subseteq \tilde{B}\right) = \begin{cases} 1, & if \quad \mu_{\tilde{A}}(x) \le \mu_{\tilde{B}}(x), \\ \dfrac{\mu_{\tilde{B}}(x)}{\mu_{\tilde{A}}(x) + \left(1-\mu_{\tilde{B}}(x)\right)}, & if \quad \mu_{\tilde{A}}(x) > \mu_{\tilde{B}}(x). \end{cases}$$

We note, that if $\mu_{\tilde{A}}(x) = 0$ or $\tilde{A} \neq \varnothing$, then the crisp inclusion is possible for fuzzy logic ALI1. Below we consider the equivalence of fuzzy sets.

Proposal. Possibility degree of the equivalence of the sets $\pi(\tilde{A} \equiv \tilde{B})$ is determined as:

$$\pi_1\left(\tilde{A} \equiv \tilde{B}\right) = \begin{cases} 1-\left[\left(1-\mu_{\tilde{A}}(x)\right) \vee \mu_{\tilde{B}}(x)\right], & if \quad \mu_{\tilde{A}}(x) < \mu_{\tilde{B}}(x), \\ 1, & if \quad \tilde{A} = \tilde{B}, \\ 1-\left[\left(1-\mu_{\tilde{B}}(x)\right) \vee \mu_{\tilde{A}}(x)\right], & if \quad \mu_{\tilde{A}}(x) > \mu_{\tilde{B}}(x), \end{cases}$$

$$\pi_2\left(\tilde{A} \equiv \tilde{B}\right) = \begin{cases} 1, & if \quad \tilde{A} = \tilde{B}, \\ \underset{T}{\wedge}\left\{\left[\left(1-\mu_{\tilde{A}}(x)\right) \wedge \mu_{\tilde{B}}(x)\right], \left[\left(1-\mu_{\tilde{B}}(x)\right) \wedge \mu_{\tilde{A}}(x)\right]\right\} & if \quad \tilde{A} \neq \tilde{B}, \\ 0, \quad if\ \exists x \,|||\, \mu_{\tilde{A}}(x) = 0, \mu_{\tilde{B}}(x) \neq 0 & (or\ vice\ versa), \\ and \ \ also\ \exists x \,|||\, \mu_{\tilde{A}}(x) = 1, \ \mu_{\tilde{B}}(x) \neq 1 & (or\ vice\ versa), \end{cases}$$

$$\pi_3\left(\tilde{A}\subseteq\tilde{B}\right)=\begin{cases}1, & \textit{if} \quad \mu_{\tilde{A}}(x)\le\mu_{\tilde{B}}(x),\\ \dfrac{\mu_{\tilde{B}}(x)}{\mu_{\tilde{A}}(x)+\left(1-\mu_{\tilde{B}}(x)\right)}, & \textit{if} \quad \mu_{\tilde{A}}(x)>\mu_{\tilde{B}}(x).\end{cases}$$

Here the set $T=\{x\in U \,|\, \mu_{\tilde{A}}x\neq\mu_{\tilde{B}}x\}$ and $\tilde{A}=\tilde{B}$ means that $\forall x$ $\mu_{\tilde{A}}(x)=\mu_{\tilde{B}}(x)$ or in other words, $T=\varnothing$.

The symbol ||| means "such as". From the expression $\pi_i\left(\tilde{A}\equiv\tilde{B}\right)$, $i=\overline{1,3}$, it follows that for ALI1 fuzzy logic the equivalency $\pi_1\left(\tilde{A}\equiv\tilde{B}\right)=1$ takes place only when $\tilde{A}=\tilde{B}$. It is obvious that the equivalence possibility is equal to 0 only in those cases when one of the statements is crisp, i.e. either true or false, while the other is fuzzy.

Proposal. Degree to which fuzzy set $\tilde{B}$ is empty $\pi(\tilde{B}\equiv\varnothing)$ is determined as

$$\pi_1\left(\tilde{B}\equiv\varnothing\right)=\begin{cases}1, & \textit{if} \quad \tilde{B}=\varnothing,\\ 0, & \textit{otherwise};\end{cases}$$

$$\pi_2\left(\tilde{B}\equiv\varnothing\right)=\begin{cases}1, & \textit{if} \quad H\tilde{B}<1 \ \textit{or} \ \tilde{B}=\varnothing,\\ 0, & \textit{otherwise};\end{cases}$$

$$\pi_3\left(\tilde{B}\equiv\varnothing\right)=\begin{cases}1, & \textit{if} \ \tilde{B}=\varnothing,\\ 0, & \textit{otherwise}.\end{cases}$$

Here $\tilde{B}=\varnothing$ means that for $\forall x\,\mu_{\tilde{B}}(x)=0$, or equivalently $H\tilde{B}=0$.

We introduce the concept of disjointness of fuzzy sets. There are two kinds of the disjointness. For a set $\tilde{A}$ the first kind is defined by degree to which set $\tilde{A}$ is a subset of the complement of $\tilde{B}^c$. The second kind is the degree to which the intersection of sets is empty. Therefore, we formulate the following.

Proposal. Degree of disjointness of sets $\tilde{A}$ and $\tilde{B}$ is degree to which $\tilde{A}$ and $\tilde{B}$ are disjoint

$$\pi\left(\tilde{A}\ disj_1\ \tilde{B}\right)=\pi\left(\tilde{A}\subseteq\tilde{B}^C\right)\wedge\pi\left(\tilde{B}\subseteq\tilde{A}^C\right),$$

$$\pi\left(\tilde{A}\ disj_2\ \tilde{B}\right)=\pi\left(\left(\tilde{A}\cap\tilde{B}\right)=\varnothing\right).$$

Proposal. Disjointness grade of sets $\tilde{A}$ and $\tilde{B}$ is determined as

$$\pi_1\left(\tilde{A}\ disj_1\ \tilde{B}\right)=\begin{cases}1, & if\ \ \exists x\,|||\,\mu_{\tilde{A}}(x)=1-\mu_{\tilde{B}}(x),\\ \left(1-\mu_A(x)\right)\wedge\left(1-\mu_{\tilde{B}}(x)\right), & otherwise,\\ 0, & never;\end{cases}$$

$$\pi_2\left(\tilde{A}\ disj_1\ \tilde{B}\right)=\begin{cases}1, & if\ \mu_{\tilde{A}}(x)\le 1-\mu_{\tilde{B}}(x),\\ 0, & if\ \exists x\,|||\,\mu_{\tilde{A}}(x)=1,\ \ but\ \ \mu_{\tilde{B}}(x)\ne 0,\\ & or\ \mu_{\tilde{B}}(x)=1,\ but\ \mu_{\tilde{A}}(x)\ne 0,\\ \bigwedge_T\left[\left(1-\mu_{\tilde{A}}(x)\right),\left(1-\mu_{\tilde{B}}(x)\right)\right], & otherwise;\end{cases}$$

$$\pi_3\left(\tilde{A}\ disj_1\ \tilde{B}\right)=\begin{cases}1, & if\ \ \mu_{\tilde{A}}(x)=\mu_{\tilde{B}}(x)\ \ or\ \mu_{\tilde{B}}(x)=0,\\ \bigwedge_T\left[\dfrac{1-\mu_{\tilde{B}}(x)}{\mu_{\tilde{A}}(x)+\left(1-\mu_{\tilde{B}}(x)\right)},\dfrac{1-\mu_{\tilde{A}}(x)}{\mu_{\tilde{B}}(x)+\left(1-\mu_{\tilde{A}}(x)\right)}\right], & otherwise,\\ 0, & never,\end{cases}$$

where $$T=\{x\,|||\,\mu_{\tilde{A}}(x)>1-\mu_{\tilde{B}}(x)\}.$$

We note that, the disjointness degree of the set is equal to 0 only for fuzzy logic ALI2, when under the condition that one of the considered fuzzy sets is normal, the other is subnormal.

Proposal. Degree to which set is a subset of its complement for the considered fuzzy logics $\pi_i(\tilde{A} \subseteq \tilde{B}^C)$ takes the following form

$$\pi_1(\tilde{A} \subseteq \tilde{A}^C) = \begin{cases} 1, & \text{if } H\tilde{A} = 0, \\ 0, & \text{if } H\tilde{A} = 1, \\ 1 - H\tilde{A}, & \text{otherwise}; \end{cases}$$

$$\pi_2(\tilde{A} \subseteq \tilde{A}^C) = \begin{cases} 1, & \text{if } H\tilde{A} \le 0, \\ 0, & \text{if } H\tilde{A} = 1, \\ 1 - H\tilde{A}, & \text{otherwise}; \end{cases}$$

$$\pi_3(\tilde{A} \subseteq \tilde{A}^C) = \begin{cases} 1, & \text{if } H\tilde{A} \le 0.5, \\ 0, & \text{if } H\tilde{A} = 1, \\ (1 - H\tilde{A})/(2H\tilde{A}), & \text{otherwise}; \end{cases}$$

It is obvious that for the fuzzy logic ALI1 the degree to which a set is the subset of its complement is equal to the degree to which this set is empty. It should also be mentioned that the semantic analysis given in [10,20,24] as well as the analysis given above show a significant analogy between features of fuzzy logics ALI1 and KD. However, the fuzzy logic ALI1, unlike the KD logic, has a number of advantages. For example, ALI1 logic satisfies the condition $\mu_{\tilde{A}}x \wedge (\mu_{\tilde{A}}x \to \mu_{\tilde{B}}x) \le \mu_{\tilde{B}}x$ necessary for development of fuzzy conditional inference rules. ALI2 and ALI3 logics satisfy this inequality as well. This allows them to be used for the formalization of improved rules of fuzzy conditional inference and for the modeling of relations between main elements of a decision problem under uncertainty and interaction among behavioral factors.

2.2.2 *Extended fuzzy logic [453]*

Fuzzy logic adds to bivalent logic an important capability—a capability to reason precisely with imperfect information. In fuzzy logic, results of reasoning are expected to be provably valid, or p-valid for short. Extended fuzzy logic adds an equally important capability—a capability to reason imprecisely with imperfect information. This capability comes into play when precise reasoning is infeasible, excessively costly or unneeded. In extended fuzzy logic, p-validity of results is desirable but not required. What is admissible is a mode of reasoning which is fuzzily valid, or f-valid for short. Actually, much of everyday human reasoning is f-valid reasoning. What is important to note is that f-valid reasoning based on a realistic model may be more useful than p-valid reasoning based on an unrealistic model. In constructing better models of reality, a problem that has to be faced is that as the complexity of a system, S, increases, it becomes increasingly difficult to construct a model, $M(S)$, which is both cointensive, that is, close-fitting, and precise. This applies, in particular, to systems in which human judgment, perceptions and emotions play a prominent role. Economic systems, legal systems and political systems are cases in point. As the complexity of a system increases further, a point is reached at which construction of a model which is both cointensive and precise is not merely difficult—it is impossible. It is at this point that extended fuzzy logic comes into play. Actually, extended fuzzy logic is not the only formalism that comes into play at this point. The issue of what to do when an exact solution cannot be found or is excessively costly is associated with a vast literature. Prominent in this literature are various approximation theories [50], theories centered on bounded rationality [373], qualitative reasoning [413], commonsense reasoning [280,305] and theories of argumentation [382]. Extended fuzzy logic differs from these and related theories both in spirit and in substance. To develop an understanding of extended fuzzy logic, FLe, it is expedient to start with the following definition of fuzzy logic, FL. Fuzzy logic is a precise conceptual system of reasoning, deduction and computation in which the objects of discourse and analysis are, or are allowed to be, associated with imperfect information. In fuzzy logic, the results of reasoning, deduction and computation are expected to be provably valid (p-valid) within the conceptual structure of fuzzy logic. In fuzzy logic precision is achieved through association of fuzzy sets with membership functions and, more generally, association of granules with generalized constraints [297]. What this implies is that fuzzy logic is what may be called precisiated logic.

At this point, a key idea comes into play. The idea is that of constructing a fuzzy logic, FLu, which, in contrast to FL, is unprecisiated. What this means is that in FLu membership functions and generalized constraints are not specified, and are a matter of perception rather than measurement. To stress the contrast between FL and FLu, FL may be written as FLp, with p standing for precisiated. A question which arises is: What is the point of constructing FLu—a logic in which provable validity is off the table? But what is not off the table is what may be called fuzzy validity, or f-validity for short. As will be shown below, a model of FLu is f-geometry. Actually, everyday human reasoning is preponderantly f-valid reasoning. Humans have a remarkable capability to perform a wide variety of physical and mental tasks without any measurements and any computations. In this context, f-valid reasoning is perception-based. The concept of unprecisiated fuzzy logic provides a basis for the concept of extended fuzzy logic, FLe. More specifically, FLe is the result of adding FLu to FL (FLp). Basically, extended fuzzy logic, FLe, results from lowering of standards of cointension and precision in fuzzy logic, FL. In effect, extended fuzzy logic adds to fuzzy logic a capability to deal imprecisely with imperfect information when precision is infeasible, carries a high cost or is unneeded. This capability is a necessity when repeated attempts at constructing a theory which is both realistic and precise fail to achieve success. Cases in point are the theories of rationality, causality and decision-making under second order uncertainty, that is, uncertainty about uncertainty. There is an important point to be made. f-Validity is a fuzzy concept and hence is a matter of degree. When a chain of reasoning leads to a conclusion, a natural question is: What is the possibly fuzzy degree of validity, call it the validity index, of the conclusion? In most applications involving f-valid reasoning a high validity index is a desideratum. How can it be achieved? Achievement of a high validity index is one of the principal objectives of extended fuzzy logic. The importance of extended fuzzy logic derives from the fact that it adds to fuzzy logic an essential capability—the capability to deal with unprecisiated imperfect information.

In the existing fuzzy geometry formalisms [88, 193, 278, 279, 339, 347, 353], the underlying logic is precisiated fuzzy logic. In the world of f-geometry, suggested by Zadeh [453] the underlying logic is unprecisiated fuzzy logic, FLu. This f-Geometry differs both in spirit and in substance from Poston's fuzzy geometry [339], coarse geometry [347], fuzzy geometry of Rosenfeld [353], fuzzy geometry of Buckley and Eslami [88], fuzzy geometry of Mayburov [278], and fuzzy geometry of Tzafestas [193].

The counterpart of a crisp concept in Euclidean geometry is a fuzzy concept in this fuzzy geometry. Fuzzy concept may be obtained by fuzzy transformation (f-transform) of a crisp concept.

For example, the f-transform of a point is an f-point, the f-transform of a line is an f-line, the f-transform of a triangle is an f-triangle, the f-transform of a circle is an f-circle and the f-transform of parallel is f-parallel (Fig. 2.8). In summary, f-geometry may be viewed as the result of application of f-transformation to Euclidean geometry.

A key idea in f-geometry is the following: if C is p-valid then its f-transform, f-C, is f-valid with a high validity index.

An important f-principle in f-geometry, referred to as the validation principle, is the following. Let p be a p-valid conclusion drawn from a chain of premises $*p_1,...,*p_n$. Then, using the star notation, $*p$ is an f-valid conclusion drawn from $*p_1,...,*p_n$, and $*p$

has a high validity index. It is this principle that is employed to derive f-valid conclusions from a collection of f-premises.

A basic problem which arises in computation of f-transforms is the following. Let g be a function, a functional or an operator. Using the star

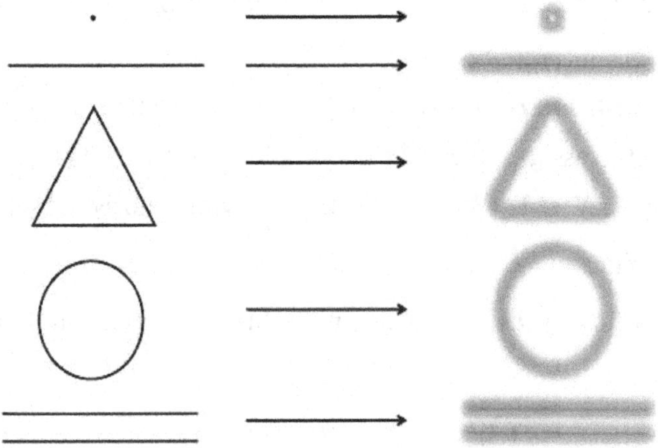

Fig 2.8. Examples of f-transformation

notation, let an f-transform, $*C$, be an argument of g. The problem is that of computing $g(*C)$. Generally, computing $g(*C)$ is not a trivial problem.

An f-valid approximation to $g(*C)$ may be derived through application of an f-principle which is referred to as precisiation/unprecisiation principle or P/I principle, for short [387]. More specifically, the principle may be expressed as

$$g(*C)^* = {}^*g(C)$$

where *= should be read as approximately equal. In words, $g(*C)$ is approximately equal to the f-transform of $g(C)$.

2.3 Fuzzy Functions

This section is concerned with the necessary concepts related to the calculus of fuzzy set-valued mappings, for short fuzzy functions. Let X be an arbitrary set. A family τ of fuzzy sets in X is called a fuzzy topology for X and the pair (X,τ) a fuzzy topological space if: (i)

$\mu_X \in \tau$ and $\mu_\phi \in \tau$; (ii) $\underset{i\in I}{\cup} \tilde{A}_i \in \tau$ whenever each $\tilde{A}_i \in \tau (i \in I)$; and (iii) $\tilde{A} \cap \tilde{B} \in \tau$ whenever $\tilde{A}, \tilde{B} \in \tau$ [64].

Definition 2.54. Fuzzy function [64]. A fuzzy function $\tilde{f}$ from a set X into a set Y assigns to each x in X a fuzzy subset $\tilde{f}(x)$ of Y. We denote it by $\tilde{f}: X \to Y$. We can identify $\tilde{f}$ with a fuzzy subset $G_{\tilde{f}}$ of $X \times Y$ and $\tilde{f}(x)(y) = G_{\tilde{f}}(x, y)$.

If $\tilde{A}$ is a fuzzy subset of X, then the fuzzy set $\tilde{f}(\tilde{A})$ in Y is defined by

$$\tilde{f}(\tilde{A})(y) = \sup_{x \in X}[G_{\tilde{f}}(x, y) \wedge A(x)].$$

The graph $\tilde{G}_{\tilde{f}}$ of $\tilde{f}$ is the fuzzy subset of X×Y associated with $\tilde{f}$,

$$\tilde{G}_{\tilde{f}} = \{(x, y) \in X \times Y : [\tilde{f}(x)](y) \neq 0 \}.$$

Let X be a fuzzy topological space. Neighborhood of a fuzzy set $\tilde{A} \subset X$ is any fuzzy set $\tilde{B}$ for which there is an open fuzzy set $\tilde{V}$ satisfying $\tilde{A} \subset \tilde{V} \subset \tilde{B}$. Any open fuzzy set $\tilde{V}$ that satisfies $\tilde{A} \subset \tilde{V}$ is called an open neighborhood of $\tilde{A}$.

A fuzzy function $\tilde{f}: X \to Y$ between two fuzzy topological spaces X and Y is: upper semicontinuous at the point x, if for every open neighborhood U of $\tilde{f}(x), \tilde{f}^u(U)$ is a neighborhood of x in X; lower semicontinuous at x, if for every open fuzzy set $\tilde{V}$ which intersects $\tilde{f}(x)$, $f^l(U)$ is a neighborhood of x; and continuous if it is both upper and lower semicontinuous.

Let $\mathcal{E}^n$ be a space of all fuzzy subsets of $\mathcal{R}^n$ [129,253]. These subsets satisfy the conditions of normality, convexity, and are upper semicontinuous with compact support.

Definition 2.55. Fuzzy closeness [64]. A function $\tilde{f}: X \to Y$ between two fuzzy topological spaces is fuzzy closed or has fuzzy closed graph if its graph is a closed fuzzy subset of $X \times Y$.

Definition 2.56. Composition [64]. Let $\tilde{f}: X \to Y$ and $\tilde{g}: Y \to Z$ be two fuzzy functions. The composition $\tilde{g} \circ \tilde{f}: X \to Z$ $\tilde{f}: X \to Z$ is defined by $(g \circ f)(x) = \; = \cup\{g(y) : [f(x)](y) \neq 0\}$.

Theorem 2.2. Convex hull of a fuzzy set [64]. *Let X, Y and Z be three fuzzy topological spaces. Let $\tilde{f}: X \to Y$ and $\tilde{g}: Y \to Z$ be two fuzzy functions. Then*

$$(i)\ (\tilde{g}_0\tilde{f})^u(\tilde{A}) = \tilde{f}^u(\tilde{g}^u(\tilde{A}))$$

and

$$(ii)\ (\tilde{g}_0\tilde{f})^l(\tilde{A}) = \tilde{f}^l(\tilde{g}^l(\tilde{A}))$$

where $\tilde{A}$ is an open fuzzy subset of Z.

A fuzzy set $\tilde{A}$ in $\mathcal{E}$ is called convex if for each $t \in [0,1], [t\tilde{A} + (1-t)\tilde{A}](x) \leq A(x)$. The convex hull of a fuzzy set $\tilde{B}$ is smallest convex fuzzy set containing $\tilde{B}$ and is denoted by $\tilde{c}_0(\tilde{B})$.

Definition 2.57. Fuzzy topological vector space [64]. A fuzzy linear topology on a vector space $\mathcal{E}$ over K is a fuzzy topology τ on $\mathcal{E}$ such that the two mappings:

$$f : \mathcal{E} \times \mathcal{E} \to \mathcal{E},\ f(x,y) = x + y,$$

$$h : K \times \mathcal{E} \to \mathcal{E},\ h(\lambda, x) = \lambda x,$$

are continuous when K has the usual fuzzy topology and $K \times E$, $E \times E$ the corresponding product fuzzy topologies. A linear space with a fuzzy linear topology is called a fuzzy topological vector space. A fuzzy topological vector space E is called locally convex if it has a base at origin of convex fuzzy sets.

Definition 2.58. Fuzzy multivalued functions [64]. If $\tilde{f}, \tilde{g}: X \to Y$ are two fuzzy multivalued functions, where Y is a vector space, then we define:

(1) The sum fuzzy multivalued function $\tilde{f}+\tilde{g}$ by

$$(\tilde{f}+\tilde{g})(x)=\tilde{f}(x)+\tilde{g}(x)=\left\{y+z: y\in\tilde{f}(x)\, and\, z\in\tilde{g}(x)\right\}.$$

(2) The convex hull of a fuzzy multivalued function $\tilde{c}_0(\tilde{f})$ of $\tilde{f}$ by

$$(\tilde{c}_0(\tilde{f}))(x)=\tilde{c}_0(\tilde{f}(x)).$$

(3) If Y is a fuzzy topological vector space, the closed convex hull of a fuzzy multivalued function $cl(\tilde{c}_0(\tilde{f}))$ of $\tilde{f}$ by

$$(cl(\tilde{c}_0(\tilde{f})))(x)=cl(\tilde{c}_0(\tilde{f}(x))).$$

Below a definition of measurability of fuzzy mapping $\tilde{F}:T\to\mathcal{E}^n$ is given.

Definition 2.59. Measurability of a fuzzy mapping [129,253]. We say that a mapping $\tilde{F}:T\to\mathcal{E}^n$ is strongly measurable if for all $\alpha\in[0,1]$ the set-valued mapping $F_\alpha:T\to P_K(\mathcal{R}^n)$ defined by

$$F_\alpha(t)=[F(t)]^\alpha$$

is (Lebesgue) measurable , when $P_K(\mathcal{R}^n)$ is endowed with the topology generated by the Hausdorff metric d_H .

If $\tilde{F}:T\to\mathcal{E}^n$ is continuous with respect to the metric d_H then it is strongly measurable [129,253].

A mapping $\tilde{F}:T\to\mathcal{E}^n$ is called integrably bounded if there exists an integrable function h such that $\|x\|\le h(t)$ for all $x\in\tilde{F}_0(t)$.

Definition 2.60. Integrability of fuzzy mapping [129,253]. Let $\tilde{F}:T\to\mathcal{E}^n$. The integral of $\tilde{F}$ over *T*, denoted $\int_T\tilde{F}(t)dt$ or $\int_a^b\tilde{F}(t)dt$, is defined levelwise by the equation

$$[\int_T\tilde{F}(t)dt]\;=\int_T F_\alpha(t)dt$$

$$= \{\int_T f(t)dt \mid f: T \to \mathcal{R}^n \text{ is a measurable selection for } F_\alpha\}$$

for all $0 < \alpha \leq 1$. A strongly measurable and integrably bounded mapping $\tilde{F}: T \to \mathcal{E}^n$ is said to be integrable over T if $\int_T \tilde{F}(t)dt \in \mathcal{E}^n$.

2.4 Approximate Reasoning

In our daily life we often make inferences where *antecedents* and *consequents* are represented by fuzzy sets. Such inferences cannot be realized adequately by the methods, which are based either on two-valued logic or many-valued logic. In order to facilitate such an inference, Zadeh [435,439,440,442,448,451] suggested an inference rule called a "compositional rule of inference". Using this inference rule, Zadeh, Mamdani [273], Mizumoto et al [160,184,301], R. Aliev and A. Tserkovny [18,25,30] suggested several methods for fuzzy reasoning in which the antecedent contain a conditional proposition involving fuzzy concepts:

Ant 1: If x is $\tilde{P}$ then y is $\tilde{Q}$

Ant2: x is $\tilde{P}'$ (2.102)

Cons: y is $\tilde{Q}'$.

Those methods are based on implication operators present in various fuzzy logics. This matter has been under a thorough discussion for the last couple decades. Some comparative analysis of such methods was presented in [54,55,56,160,163,184,217,224,225,226,275,276,301,367, 405,427,429]. A number of authors proposed to use a certain suite of fuzzy implications to form fuzzy conditional inference rules [25, 30, 160,184,244,263,273,301]. The implication operators present in the theory of fuzzy sets were investigated in [25, 30, 47, 51, 63, 66, 80, 81, 90, 97, 103, 118, 130, 176, 177, 205, 206, 218, 233, 247, 251, 255, 257, 262, 269,275, 283, 292, 303, 307, 310, 319, 327, 336, 370, 395, 396, 422, 423, 429, 466, 467, 468]. On the other hand, statistical features of fuzzy implication operators were studied in [322,412]. In turn, the properties of stability and continuity of fuzzy conditional inference rules were investigated in [154,219,236,263]. We will begin with a *formation* of a fuzzy logic regarded as an *algebraic system closed under all its operations*. In the sequel an investigation of statistical characteristics of the proposed fuzzy logic will be presented. Special attention will be paid to building a set of fuzzy conditional inference rules on the basis of the fuzzy logic proposed in this study. Next, continuity and stability features of the formalized rules will be investigated. Lately in fuzzy sets research the great attention is paid to the development of Fuzzy Conditional Inference Rules (CIR) [2, 10, 151, 236, 257, 283, 300, 310, 357]. This is connected with the feature of the natural language to contain a certain number of fuzzy concepts (F-concepts), therefore we have to make logical inference in which the preconditions and conclusions contain such F-concepts. The practice shows that there is a huge variety of ways in which the formalization of rules for such kind of inferences can be made. However, such inferences cannot be satisfactorily formalized using the classical Boolean Logic, i.e. here we need to use multi-valued logical systems. The development of the conditional logic rules embraces mainly three types of fuzzy propositions:

$$P_1 = IF\ x\ is\ \tilde{A}\ THEN\ y\ is\ \tilde{B}$$

$$P_2 = IF\ x\ is\ \tilde{A}\ THEN\ y\ is\ \tilde{B}$$

$$OTHERWISE\ \tilde{C}$$

$$P_3 = IF\ x_1\ is\ \tilde{A}_1\ AND\ x_2\ is\ \tilde{A}_2 \ldots AND \ldots AND\ x_n\ is\ \tilde{A}_n$$

$$THEN\ y\ is\ \tilde{B}.$$

The conceptual principle in the formalization of fuzzy rules is the Modus Ponens inference (separation) rule that states:

$IF(\alpha \to \beta)$ is true and α is true $THEN \beta$ is true.

The methodological base for this formalization is the compositional rule suggested by L. Zadeh [435,437]. Using this rule, he formulated some inference rules in which both the logical preconditions and consequences are conditional propositions including F-concepts. Later E. Mamdani [273] suggested inference rule, which like Zadeh's rule was developed for the logical proposition of type P_1. In other words the following type F-conditional inference is considered:

$$\begin{array}{l} \text{Proposition 1: } IF\ x\ is\ \tilde{A}\ THEN\ y\ is\ \tilde{B} \\ \text{Proposition 2: } x\ is\ \tilde{A}' \\ \hline \text{Conclusion: y is } \tilde{B}', \end{array} \tag{2.103}$$

where $\tilde{A}$ and $\tilde{A}'$ are F-concepts represented as F-sets in the universe U; $\tilde{B}$ is F-conceptions or F-set in the universe V. It follows that B' is the consequence represented as a F-set in V. To obtain a logical conclusion based on the CIR, the Propositions 1 and 2 must be transformed accordingly to the form of binary F-relation $\tilde{R}(A_1(x)), A_2(y))$ and unary F-relation $\tilde{R}(A_1(x))$. Here $A_1(x)$ and $A_2(y)$ are defined by the attributes x and y which take values from the universes U and V, respectively. Then

$$\tilde{R}\ (A_1(x)) = \tilde{A}'. \tag{2.104}$$

According to Zadeh-Mamdani's inference rule $\tilde{R}(A_1(x)), A_2(y))$ is defined as follows.

The maximin conditional inference rule

$$\tilde{R}_m(A_1(x),\ A_2(y)) = (\tilde{A} \times \tilde{B}) \cup (\neg\tilde{A} \times V) \tag{2.105}$$

The arithmetic conditional inference rule

$$\tilde{R}_a(A_1(x), A_2(y)) = (\neg\tilde{A} \times V) \oplus (U \times \tilde{B}) \tag{2.106}$$

The mini-functional conditional inference rule

$$\tilde{R}_c(A_1(x),\ A_2(y)) = \tilde{A} \times \tilde{B} \tag{2.107}$$

where $\times$, $\cup$ and $\neg$ are the Cartesian product, union, and complement operations, respectively; $\oplus$ is the limited summation.

Thus, in accordance with [273,435,437] the logical consequence $\tilde{R}(A_2(y))$, ($\tilde{B}'$in (2.103)) can be derived as follows:

$$\tilde{R}(A_2(y)) = \tilde{A}' \circ [(\tilde{A} \times \tilde{B})] \cup [\neg\tilde{A} \times U)]$$

$$\tilde{R}(A_2(y)) = \tilde{A}' \circ [(\neg\tilde{A} \times V)] \oplus [\neg U \times \tilde{B})]$$

or

$$\tilde{R}(A_2(y)) = \tilde{A}' \circ (\tilde{A} \times \tilde{B})$$

where $\circ$ – is the F-set maximin composition operator.

On the base of these rules the conditional inference rules for type P_2 were suggested in [48]:

$$\begin{aligned}&\tilde{R}_4(\tilde{A}_1(x), \tilde{A}_2(y))\\ &= [(\tilde{A} \times V) \oplus (U \times \tilde{B})] \cap [(\tilde{A} \times V) \oplus (U \times \tilde{C})]\end{aligned} \tag{2.108}$$

$$\begin{aligned}&\tilde{R}_5(A_1(x), A_2(y))\\ &= [(\neg\tilde{A} \times V) \cup (U \times \tilde{B})] \cap [(\tilde{A} \times V) \cup (U \times \tilde{C})]\end{aligned} \tag{2.109}$$

$$\tilde{R}_6(A_1(x),\ A_2(y)) = [(\tilde{A} \times \tilde{B}) \cup (\neg\tilde{A} \times \tilde{C})]. \tag{2.110}$$

Note that in [48] also the fuzzy conditional inference rules for type P_3 were suggested:

$$\tilde{R}_7(A_1(x),\ A_2(y)) = \left[\bigcap_{i=1,n}(\neg\tilde{A}_i \times V)\right] \oplus [(U \times \tilde{B})] \tag{2.111}$$

$$\tilde{R}_8(A_1(x),\ A_2(y)) = \left[\bigcap_{i=1,n}(\neg\tilde{A}_i \times V)\right] \cup [(U \times \tilde{B})] \tag{2.112}$$

$$\begin{aligned}\tilde{R}_9(A_1(x),\ A_2(y)) &= (\neg\tilde{A} \times V) \oplus (U \times \tilde{B}) \\ &= \int_{U\times V} 1 \wedge (1 - \mu_{\tilde{A}}(u) + \mu_{\tilde{B}}(v))/(u,v)\end{aligned} \tag{2.113}$$

In order to analyze the effectiveness of rules (2.103)-(2.113) we use some criteria for F-conditional logical inference suggested in [160]. The idea of these criteria is to compare the degree of compatibility of some fuzzy conditional inference rules with the human intuition when making approximate reasoning. These criteria are the following:

Criterion I

Precondition 1: IF x is $\tilde{A}$ THEN y is $\tilde{B}$

Precondition 2: x is $\tilde{A}$

Conclusion: y is $\tilde{B}$

Criterion II-1

Precondition 1: IF x is $\tilde{A}$ THEN y is $\tilde{B}$

Precondition 2: x is very $\tilde{A}$

Conclusion: y is very $\tilde{B}$

Criterion II-2

Precondition 1: IF x is $\tilde{A}$ THEN y is $\tilde{B}$

Precondition 2: x is very $\tilde{A}$

Conclusion: y is B

Criterion III

Precondition 1: IF x is $\tilde{A}$ THEN y is $\tilde{B}$

Precondition 2: x is more or less $\tilde{A}$

Conclusion: y is more or less $\tilde{B}$

Criterion IV-1

Precondition 1: IF x is $\tilde{A}$ THEN y is $\tilde{B}$

Precondition 2: x is not $\tilde{A}$

Conclusion: y is unknown

Criterion IV-2

Precondition 1: IF x is $\tilde{A}$ THEN y is $\tilde{B}$

Precondition 2: x is not $\tilde{A}$

Conclusion: y is not $\tilde{B}$

In [160] it was shown that in Zadeh-Mamdani's rules the relations $\tilde{R}_m$, $\tilde{R}_c$ and $\tilde{R}_c$ do not always satisfy the above criteria. For the case of mini-operational rule $\tilde{R}_c$ it has been found that criteria I and II-2 are satisfied while criteria II-1 and III are not.

In [160] an important generalization was made that allows some improvement to the mentioned F-conditional logical inference rules. It was shown there that for the conditional proposition arithmetical rule defined by Zadeh

$$P_1 = IF\ x\ is\ \tilde{A}\ THEN\ y\ is\ \tilde{B}$$

the following takes place

$$\begin{aligned}\tilde{R}_9(A_1(x),\ A_2(y)) &= (\neg\tilde{A}\times V)\oplus(U\times\tilde{B})\\ &= \int_{U\times V} 1\wedge(1-\mu_{\tilde{A}}(u)+\mu_{\tilde{B}}(v))/(u,v)\end{aligned}$$

The membership function for this F-relation is

$$1\wedge(1-\mu_{\tilde{A}}(u)+\mu_{\tilde{B}}(v))$$

that obviously meets the implication operation or the Ply-operator for the multi-valued logic L (by Lukasiewicz), i.e.

$$T(P \underset{L}{\rightarrow} Q), T(P) \tag{2.114}$$

where $T(P \underset{L}{\rightarrow} Q), T(P)$ and $T(Q)$ - are the truth values for the logical propositions $P \underset{L}{\rightarrow} Q, P$ and Q respectively.

In other words, these expressions can be considered as adaptations of implication in the L-logical system to a conditional proposition.

Having considered this fact, the following expression was derived:

$$\begin{aligned}
&\tilde{R}_a(A_1(x),\ A_2(y)) = (\neg\tilde{A}\times V)\oplus(U\times\tilde{B}) = \\
&= \int_{U\times V} 1\wedge(1-\mu_{\tilde{A}}(u)+\mu_{\tilde{B}}(v))/(u,v) = \\
&= \int_{U\in V} (\mu_{\tilde{A}}(u)\underset{L}{\rightarrow}\mu_{\tilde{B}}(v))/(u,v) = (\tilde{A}\times V)\rightarrow(U\times\tilde{B})
\end{aligned} \tag{2.115}$$

In [160] an opinion was expressed that the implication operation or the Ply-operator in the expression (2.115) may belong to any multi-valued logical system. The following are guidelines for deciding which logical system to select for developing F-conditional logical inference rules [160]. Let F-sets $\tilde{A}$ from U and $\tilde{B}$ from V are given in the form:

$$\tilde{A} = \int_U \mu_{\tilde{A}}(u)/u\,,\ \tilde{B} = \int_V \mu_{\tilde{B}}(v)/v$$

Then, as mentioned above, the conditional logical proposition P_1 can be transformed to the F-relation $\tilde{R}(A_1(x), A_2(y))$ by adaptation of the Ply-operator in multi-valued logical system, i.e.

$$\tilde{R}(A_1(x), A_2(y)) = \tilde{A}\times V \rightarrow U\times\tilde{B} = \int_{U\times V} (\mu_{\tilde{A}}(u)\rightarrow\mu_{\tilde{B}}(v))/(u,v) \tag{2.116}$$

where the values $\mu_{\tilde{A}}(u)\rightarrow\mu_{\tilde{B}}(v)$ are depending on the selected logical system.

Assuming $\tilde{R}(A_1(x)) = \tilde{A}$ we can conclude a logical consequence $\tilde{R}(A_2(y))$, then using the CIR for $\tilde{R}(A_1(x))$ and $\tilde{R}(A_1(x), A_2(y))$, then

$$\begin{aligned}
&\tilde{R}(A_2(y)) = \tilde{A}\circ\tilde{R}(A_1(x), A_2(y)) = \\
&= \int_U \mu_{\tilde{A}}(u)/u \circ \int_{U\times V} \mu_{\tilde{A}}(u)\rightarrow\mu_{\tilde{B}}(v))/(u,v) = \\
&= \int_V \vee_{u\in V}[\mu_{\tilde{A}}(u)\wedge(\mu_{\tilde{A}}(u)\rightarrow\mu_{\tilde{B}}(v))]
\end{aligned} \tag{2.117}$$

For the criterion I to be satisfied, one of the following equalities must hold true

$$\tilde{R}(A_2(y)) = \tilde{B},$$

$$\vee_{u\in V}[\mu_{\tilde{A}}(u) \wedge (\mu_{\tilde{A}}(u) \rightarrow \mu_{\tilde{B}}(v))] = \mu_{\tilde{B}}(v),$$

or

$$[\mu_{\tilde{A}}(u) \wedge (\mu_{\tilde{A}}(u) \rightarrow \mu_{\tilde{B}}(v))] \leq \mu_{\tilde{B}}(v). \tag{2.118}$$

the latter takes place for any u∈U and v∈V or in terms of truth values:

$$T(P \wedge (P \rightarrow Q)) \leq T(Q). \tag{2.119}$$

The following two conditions are necessary for formalization of F-conditional logical inference rules: the conditional logical inference rules (CIR) must meet the criteria I-IV; the conditional logical inference rules (CIR) satisfy the inequality (2.119). Now we consider formalization of the fuzzy conditional inference for a different type of conditional propositions. As was shown above, the logical inference for conditional propositions of type P_1 is of the following form:

Proposition 1: *IF x is* $\tilde{A}$ *THEN y is* $\tilde{B}$

Proposition 2: *x is* $\tilde{A}'$

(2.120)

Conclusion: *y is* $\tilde{B}'$

where $\tilde{A}$, $\tilde{B}$, and $\tilde{A}'$ are F-concepts represented as F-sets in *U, V*, and *V*, respectively, which should satisfy the criteria I, II-1, III, and IV-1.

For this inference if the Proposition 2 is transformed to an unary F-relation in the form $\tilde{R}(A_1(x)) = \tilde{A}'$ and the Proposition 1 is transformed to an F-relation $\tilde{R}(A_1(x), \tilde{R}(A_2(y))$ defined below, then the conclusion $\tilde{R}(A_2(y))$ is derived by using the corresponding F-conditional logical inference rule, i.e.

$$\tilde{R}(A_2(y) = \tilde{R}(A_1(x)) \circ \tilde{R}(A_1(x)) \tag{2.121}$$

where $\tilde{R}(A_2(y))$ is equivalent to $\tilde{B}'$ in (2.120).

Fuzzy Conditional Inference Rule 1

Theorem 2.3. *If the F-sets $\tilde{A}$ from U and $\tilde{B}$ from V are given in the traditional form:*

$$\tilde{A} = \int_U \mu_{\tilde{A}}(u)/u, \tilde{B} = \int_V \mu_{\tilde{B}}(v)/v \tag{2.122}$$

and the relation for the multi-valued logical system ALI1

$$\begin{aligned}\tilde{R}_1(A_1(x), A_2(y)) &= \tilde{A} \times V \xrightarrow[ALI1]{} U \times \tilde{B} = \\ &= \int_{U\times V} \mu_{\tilde{A}}(u)/(u,v) \xrightarrow[ALI1]{} \int_{U\times V} \mu_{\tilde{B}}(v)/(u,v) = \\ &= \int_{U\times V} (\mu_{\tilde{A}}(u) \xrightarrow[ALI1]{} \mu_{\tilde{B}}(v))/(u,v)\end{aligned} \tag{2.123}$$

where

$$\mu_{\tilde{A}}(u) \xrightarrow[ALI1]{} \mu_{\tilde{B}}(v) = \begin{Bmatrix} 1-\mu_{\tilde{A}}(u), \mu_{\tilde{A}}(u) < \mu_{\tilde{B}}(v) \\ 1, \quad \mu_{\tilde{A}}(u) = \mu_{\tilde{B}}(v) \\ \mu_{\tilde{B}}(v), \quad \mu_{\tilde{A}}(u) > \mu_{\tilde{B}}(v) \end{Bmatrix}$$

then the criteria I-IV are satisfied.

We will consider ALI4 in details.

Consider a continuous function $F(p,q) = p - q$ which defines a distance between p and q where p, q assume values in the unit interval. Notice that $F(p,q) \in [-1,1]$, where $F(p,q)^{\min} = -1$ and $F(p,q)^{\max} = 1$. The normalized version of $F(p,q)$ is defined as

$$F(p,q)^{norm} = \frac{F(p,q) - F(p,q)^{\min}}{F(p,q)^{\max} - F(p,q)^{\min}} = \frac{F(p,q)+1}{2} = \frac{p-q+1}{2}. \tag{2.124}$$

It is clear that $F(p,q)^{norm} \in [0,1]$. This function quantifies a concept of "closeness" between two values (potentially the ones for the truth values of *antecedent* and *consequent*), defined within unit interval, which therefore could play significant role in the formulation of the implication operator in a fuzzy logic.

Definition 2.61. Implication. An implication is a continuous function I from $[0,1]\times[0,1]$ into $[0,1]$ such that for $\forall p,\ p',\ q,\ q'\ r\in[0,1]$ the following properties are satisfied:

(I1) If $p\le p'$, then $I(p,q)\ge I(p',q)$ (Antitone in first argument),

(I2) If $q\le q'$, then $I(p,q)\le I(p,q')$ (Monotone in second argument),

(I3) $I(0,q)=1$, (Falsity),

(I4) $I(1,q)\le q$ (Neutrality),

(I5) $I(p,I(q,r))=I(q,I(p,r))$ (Exchange),

(I6) $I(p,q)=I(n(q),n(p))$ (Contra positive symmetry), where $n()$ - is a negation, which could be defined as $n(q)=T(\neg Q)=1-T(Q)$.

Let us define the implication operation

$$I(p,q)=\begin{cases}1-F(p,q)^{norm}, & p>q\\ 1, & p\le q\end{cases} \tag{2.125}$$

where $F(p,q)^{norm}$ is expressed by (2.124). Before showing that operation $I(p,q)$ satisfies axioms *(I1)-(I6),* let us show some basic operations encountered in proposed fuzzy logic.

Let us designate the truth values of the *antecedent* P and *consequent* Q as $T(P)=p$ and $T(P)=q$, respectively. The relevant set of proposed fuzzy logic operators is shown in Table 2.4.

To obtain the truth values of these expressions, we use well known logical properties such as

$p\to q=\neg p\vee q, p\wedge q=\neg(\neg p\vee\neg q)$ and alike.

In other words, we propose a new many-valued system, characterized by the set of *union* ($\cup$) and *intersection* ($\cap$) operations with relevant *complement*, defined as $T(\neg Q)=1-T(Q)$. In addition, the operators $\downarrow$ and $\uparrow$ are expressed as negations of the $\cup$ and $\cup$, respectively. It is well known that the *implication* operation in fuzzy logic supports the foundations of decision-making exploited in numerous schemes of approximate reasoning. Therefore let us prove that the proposed *implication* operation in (2.125) satisfies axioms *(I1)-(I6)*.

Table 2.4. Fuzzy logic operators

Name	**Designation**	**Value**
Tautology	$\overset{\bullet}{P}$	1
Controversy	$\overset{\circ}{P}$	0
Negation	$\neg P$	$1-P$
Disjunction	$P \vee Q$	$\begin{cases} \frac{p+q}{2}, p+q \neq 1, \\ 1, p+q=1 \end{cases}$
Conjunction	$P \wedge Q$	$\begin{cases} \frac{p+q}{2}, p+q \neq 1, \\ 0, p+q=1 \end{cases}$
Implication	$P \to Q$	$\begin{cases} \frac{1-p+q}{2}, p \neq q, \\ 1, p=q \end{cases}$
Equivalence	$P \leftrightarrow Q$	$\begin{cases} \min((p-q),(q-p)), p \neq q, \\ 1, p=q \end{cases}$
Pierce Arrow	$P \downarrow Q$	$\begin{cases} 1-\frac{p+q}{2}, p+q \neq 1, \\ 0, p+q=1 \end{cases}$
Shaffer Stroke	$P \uparrow Q$	$\begin{cases} 1-\frac{p+q}{2}, p+q \neq 1, \\ 1, p+q=1 \end{cases}$

For this matter, let us emphasize that we are working with a many-valued system, whose values for our purposes are the elements of the real interval $R=[0,1]$. For our discussion the set of truth values $V_{11}=\{0,0.1,0.2,...,0.9,1\}$ is sufficient. In further investigations, we use this particular set V_{11}.

Theorem 2.4. *Let a continuous function* $I(p,q)$ *be defined by (2.117) i.e.*

$$I(p,q)=\begin{Bmatrix}1-F(p,q)^{norm}, p>q \\ 1, \qquad p\leq q\end{Bmatrix}, p>q=\begin{cases}\frac{1-p+q}{2}, p>q \\ 1, p\leq q\end{cases} \quad (2.126)$$

where $F(p,q)^{norm}$ *is defined by (2.102). Then axioms (I1)-(I6) are satisfied and, therefore (2.126) is an implication operation.*

It should be mentioned that the proposed fuzzy logic could be characterized by yet some other three features:

$p\wedge 0\equiv 0, p\leq 1,$ whereas $p\wedge 1\equiv p, p\geq 0$ and $\neg\neg p=p$.

As a conclusion, we should admit that all above features confirm that *resulting system* can be applied to V_{11} for every finite and infinite n up to that $(V_{11},\neg,\wedge,\vee,\rightarrow)$ is then *closed* under all its operations.

Let us investigate Statistical Properties of the Fuzzy Logic. In this section, we discuss some properties of the proposed fuzzy implication operator (2.126), assuming that the two propositions (*antecedent/ consequent*) in a given compound proposition are independent of each other and the truth values of the propositions are uniformly distributed [257] in the unit interval. In other words, we assume that the propositions P and Q are independent from each other and the truth values $v(P)$ and $v(Q)$ are uniformly distributed across the interval $[0,1]$. Let $p=v(P)$ and $q=v(Q)$. Then the value of the implication $I=v(p\rightarrow q)$ could be represented as the function $I=I(p,q)$

Because p and q are assumed to be uniformly and independently distributed across $[0,1]$, the expected value of the implication is

$$E(I)=\iint_R I(p,q)dpdq. \quad (2.127)$$

Its variance is equal to

$$Var(I)=E[(I-E(I))^2]=\iint_R (I(p,q)-E(I))^2 dpdq=E[I^2]-E[I^2] \quad (2.128)$$

where $R=\{(p,q):0\leq p\leq 1, 0\leq q\leq 1\}$ From (2.127) and given (2.125) as well as the fact that

$$I(p,q)=\begin{cases} I_1(p,q), p>q, \\ I_2(p,q), p\leq q, \end{cases}$$

we have the following

$$E(I_1)=\iint_{\Re} I_1(p,q)dpdq=\int_0^1\int_0^1 \frac{1-p+q}{2}dpdq=\frac{1}{2}\int_0^1(\int_0^1(1-p+q)dp)dp=$$
$$=\frac{1}{2}\left[\int_0^1\left((p-\frac{p^2}{2}+p)\Bigg|_{p=0}^{p=1}\right)dq\right]=\frac{1}{2}\left[\frac{1}{2}+\frac{q^2}{2}\Bigg|_{q=0}^{q=1}\right]=\frac{1}{2} \qquad (2.129)$$

Whereas $E(I_2)=1$. Therefore $E(I)=(E(I_1)+E(I_2))/2=0.75$.

From (2.128) we have

$$I_1^2(p,q)=\frac{1}{4}(1-p+q)^2=\frac{1}{4}(1-2p+2q+p^2-2pq+q^2)$$

$$E(I_1^2)=\iint_{\Re} I_1^2(p,q)dpdq=\frac{1}{4}\int_0^1(\int_0^1(1-2p+2q+p^2-2pq+q^2)dp)dq=$$
$$\frac{1}{4}\int_0^1[p-2\frac{p^2}{2}+\frac{p^3}{3}-2\frac{p^2}{2}q+2q+q^2]\Bigg|_{p=0}^{p=1}dq=\frac{1}{4}\int_0^1(\frac{1}{3}+q+q^2)dq=$$
$$=\frac{1}{4}\left[\frac{q}{3}+\frac{q^2}{2}+\frac{q^3}{3}\right]\Bigg|_{q=0}^{q=1}=\frac{7}{24}$$

Here $E(I_2^2)=1$. Therefore $E(I^2)=(E(I_1^2)+E(I_2^2))/2=\frac{31}{48}$. From (2.128) and (2.129) we have $Var(I)=\frac{1}{12}=0.0833$.

Both values of $E(I)$ and $Var(I)$ demonstrate that the proposed fuzzy implication operator could be considered as one of the fuzziest from the list of the existing implications [206]. In addition, it satisfies the set of important Criteria I-IV, which is not the case for the most implication operators mentioned above.

As it was mentioned in [160] "in the semantics of natural language there exist a vast array of concepts and humans very often make inferences antecedents and consequences of which contain fuzzy concepts". A formalization of methods for such inferences is one of the most important issues in fuzzy sets theory. For this purpose, let U and V (from now on) be two *universes of discourses* and P and Q are corresponding fuzzy sets:

$$\tilde{P}=\int_U \mu_{\tilde{P}}(u)/u\,,\ \tilde{Q}=\int_V \mu_{\tilde{Q}}(v)/v. \tag{2.130}$$

Given (2.130), a *binary relationship* for the fuzzy conditional proposition of the type: "*If x is $\tilde{P}$ then y is $\tilde{Q}$*" for proposed fuzzy logic is defined as

$$\begin{aligned}\tilde{R}(A_1(x),A_2(y))=\tilde{P}\times V\to U\times\tilde{B}=\int_{U\times V}\mu_{\tilde{P}}(u)/(u,v)\to\int_{U\times V}\mu_{\tilde{Q}}(v)/(u,v)=\\ =\int_{U\times V}(\mu_{\tilde{P}}(u)\to\mu_{\tilde{Q}}(v))/(u,v)\end{aligned} \tag{2.131}$$

Given (2.125), expression (2.131) reads as

$$\mu_{\tilde{P}}(u)\to\mu_{\tilde{Q}}(v)=\begin{cases}\dfrac{1-\mu_{\tilde{P}}(u)+\mu_{\tilde{Q}}(v)}{2},\mu_{\tilde{P}}(u)>\mu_{\tilde{Q}}(v)\\ 1,\mu_{\tilde{P}}(u)\le\mu_{\tilde{Q}}(v)\end{cases}. \tag{2.132}$$

It is well known that given a *unary relationship* $\tilde{R}(A_1(x))$ one can obtain the consequence $\tilde{R}(A_2(y))$ by applying a compositional rule of inference (CRI) to $\tilde{R}(A_1(x))$ and $\tilde{R}(A_1(x),A_2(y))$ of type (2.131):

$$\begin{aligned}\tilde{R}(A_2(y))=\tilde{P}\circ\tilde{R}(A_1(x),A_2(y))=\int_U\mu_{\tilde{P}}(u)/u\circ\int_{U\times V}\mu_{\tilde{P}}(u)\to\mu_{\tilde{Q}}(v)/(u,v)=\\ \int_V\bigcup_{u\in V}[\mu_{\tilde{P}}(u)\wedge(\mu_{\tilde{P}}(u)\to\mu_{\tilde{Q}}(v))]/v\end{aligned} \tag{2.132}$$

In order to have Criterion I satisfied, that is $\tilde{R}(A_2(y)) = \tilde{Q}$ from (2.132), the equality

$$\int_V \bigcup_{u \in V} [\mu_{\tilde{P}}(u) \wedge (\mu_{\tilde{P}}(u) \to \mu_{\tilde{Q}}(v))] = \mu_{\tilde{Q}}(v) \tag{2.134}$$

has to be satisfied for any arbitrary v in V. To satisfy (2.134), it becomes necessary that the inequality

$$\mu_{\tilde{P}}(u) \wedge (\mu_{\tilde{P}}(u) \to \mu_{\tilde{Q}}(v)) \le \mu_{\tilde{Q}}(v) \tag{2.135}$$

holds for arbitrary $u \in U$ and $v \in V$. Let us define a new method of fuzzy conditional inference of the following type:

Ant 1: If x is $\tilde{P}$ then y is $\tilde{Q}$

Ant 2: x is $\tilde{P}'$ (2.136)

Cons: y is $\tilde{Q}'$

where $\tilde{P}, \tilde{P}' \subseteq U$ and $\tilde{Q}, \tilde{Q}' \subseteq V$. Fuzzy conditional inference in the form given by (2.136) should satisfy Criteria I-IV. It is clear that the inference (2.136) is defined by the expression (2.133), when $\tilde{R}(A_2(y)) = \tilde{Q}'$.

Theorem 2.5. *If fuzzy sets $\tilde{P} \subseteq U$ and $\tilde{Q} \subseteq V$ are defined by (2.131) and (2.132), respectively and*

$\tilde{R}(A_1(x), A_2(y))$ is expressed as

$$\tilde{R}(A_1(x), A_2(y)) = \tilde{P} \times V \xrightarrow[ALI4]{} U \times \tilde{Q}$$

$$= \int_{U \times V} \mu_{\tilde{P}}(u)/(u,v) \xrightarrow[ALI4]{} \int_{U \times V} \mu_{\tilde{Q}}(v)/(u,v)$$

$$= \int_{U \times V} (\mu_{\tilde{P}}(u) \xrightarrow[ALI4]{} \mu_{\tilde{Q}}(v))/(u,v)$$

where

$$\mu_{\tilde{P}}(u)\xrightarrow[ALI4]{}\mu_{\tilde{Q}}(v)=\begin{cases}\dfrac{1-\mu_{\tilde{P}}(u)+\mu_{\tilde{Q}}(v)}{2}, \mu_{\tilde{P}}(u)>\mu_{\tilde{Q}}(v)\\ 1, \mu_{\tilde{P}}(u)\le\mu_{\tilde{Q}}(v)\end{cases} \quad (2.137)$$

then Criteria I, II, III and IV-1 [160] are satisfied [19].

Theorem 2.6. *If fuzzy sets $\tilde{P}\subseteq U$ and $\tilde{Q}\subseteq V$ are defined by (2.131) and (2.132), respectively, and*

$\tilde{R}(A_1(x), A_2(y))$ *is defined as*

$$\begin{aligned}\tilde{R}_1(A_1(x), A_2(y)) &= (\tilde{P}\times V\xrightarrow[ALI4]{}U\times\tilde{Q})\cap(\neg\tilde{P}\times V\xrightarrow[ALI4]{}U\times\neg\tilde{Q})\\ &= \int_{U\times V}(\mu_{\tilde{P}}(u)\xrightarrow[ALI4]{}\mu_{\tilde{Q}}(v))\wedge((1-\mu_{\tilde{P}}(u))\xrightarrow[ALI4]{}(1-\mu_{\tilde{Q}}(v)))/(u,v)\end{aligned} \quad (2.138)$$

where

$$(\mu_{\tilde{P}}(u)\xrightarrow[ALI4]{}\mu_{\tilde{Q}}(v))\wedge((1-\mu_{\tilde{P}}(u))\xrightarrow[ALI4]{}(1-\mu_{\tilde{Q}}(v)))=$$

$$=\begin{cases}\dfrac{1-\mu_{\tilde{P}}(u)+\mu_{\tilde{Q}}(v)}{2}, \mu_{\tilde{P}}(u)>\mu_{\tilde{Q}}(v),\\ 1, \mu_{\tilde{P}}(u)=\mu_{\tilde{Q}}(v),\\ \dfrac{1-\mu_{\tilde{P}}(u)+\mu_{\tilde{Q}}(v)}{2}, \mu_{\tilde{P}}(u)<\mu_{\tilde{Q}}(v),\end{cases}$$

then Criteria I, II, III and IV-2 [160] are satisfied.

Theorems 2.4 and 2.5 show that fuzzy conditional inference rules, defined in (2.138) could adhere with human intuition to the higher extent as the one defined by (2.137). The major difference between mentioned methods of inference might be explained by the difference between *Criteria IV-1* and *IV-2*. In particular, a satisfaction of the *Criterion IV-1* means that in case of logical negation of an original antecedent we achieve an ambiguous result of an inference, whereas for the case of the *Criterion IV-2* there is a certainty in a logical inference. Let us to investigate stability and continuity of fuzzy conditional inference in this section. We revisit the fuzzy conditional inference rule (2.136). It will be shown that when the membership function of the observation $\tilde{P}$ is continuous, then the conclusion $\tilde{Q}$ depends continuously on the observation; and when the membership function of the relation $\tilde{R}$ is continuous then the observation $\tilde{Q}$ has a continuous membership function. We start with some definitions. A fuzzy set $\tilde{A}$ with membership function $\mu_{\tilde{A}}:\mathcal{R}\to[0,1]=I$ is called a fuzzy number if $\tilde{A}$ is normal, continuous, and convex. The fuzzy numbers represent the continuous possibility distributions of fuzzy terms of the following type

$$\tilde{A}=\int_{\mathcal{R}}\mu_A(x)/x$$

Let $\tilde{A}$ be a fuzzy number, then for any $\theta\geq 0$ we define $\omega_A(\theta)$ the modulus of continuity of $\tilde{A}$ by

$$\omega_{\tilde{A}}(\theta)=\max_{|x_1-x_2|\leq\theta}\left|\mu_{\tilde{A}}(x_1)-\mu_{\tilde{A}}(x_2)\right|. \quad (2.139)$$

An α-level set of a fuzzy interval $\tilde{A}$ is a non-fuzzy set denoted by $[A]^\alpha$ and is defined by $[A]^\alpha=\{t\in R|\mu_A(t)\geq\alpha\}$ for $\alpha=(0,1]$ and $[A]^{\alpha=0}=cl\left(\bigcup_{\alpha\in(0,1]}[A]^\alpha\right)$ for $\alpha=0$. Here we use a metric of the following type

$$D(\tilde{A},\tilde{B})=\sup_{\alpha\in[0,1]}d([A]^\alpha,[B]^\alpha) \quad (2.140)$$

where d denotes the classical Hausdorff metric expressed in the family of compact subsets of R^2, i.e.

$$d([A]^\alpha,[B]^\alpha)=\max\{|a_1(\alpha)-b_1(\alpha)|,|a_2(\alpha)-b_2(\alpha)|\},$$

whereas $[A]^\alpha=[a_1(\alpha),a_2(\alpha)],[B]^\alpha=[b_1(\alpha),b_2(\alpha)]$. When the fuzzy sets $\tilde{A}$ and $\tilde{B}$ have finite support $\{x_1,...,x_n\}$ then their Hamming distance is defined as

$$H(\tilde{A},\tilde{B}) = \sum_{i=1}^{n} \left| \mu_{\tilde{A}}(x_i) - \mu_{\tilde{B}}(x_i) \right| .$$

In the sequel we will use the following lemma.

Lemma 2.1 [81]. *Let $\delta \geq 0$ be a real number and let $\tilde{A}$, $\tilde{B}$ be fuzzy intervals. If*

$$D(\tilde{A},\tilde{B}) \leq \delta, \ \textit{Then}$$

$$\sup_{t \in \mathcal{R}} \left| \mu_{\tilde{A}}(t) - \mu_{B'}(t) \right| \leq \max\{\omega_{\tilde{A}}(\delta), \omega_{\tilde{B}}(\delta)\} .$$

Consider the fuzzy conditional inference rule with different observations $\tilde{P}$ and $\tilde{P}'$:

Ant 1: If x is $\tilde{P}$ then y is $\tilde{Q}$

Ant 2: x is $\tilde{P}$

Cons: y is $\tilde{Q}$.

Ant 1: If x is $\tilde{P}$ then y is $\tilde{Q}$

Ant 2: x is $\tilde{P}'$

Cons: y is $\tilde{Q}'$.

According to the fuzzy conditional inference rule, the membership functions of the conclusions are computed as

$$\mu_{\tilde{Q}}(v) = \bigcup_{u \in R} [\mu_{\tilde{P}}(u) \wedge (\mu_{\tilde{P}}(u) \rightarrow \mu_{\tilde{Q}}(v))],$$

$$\mu_{\tilde{Q}'}(v) = \bigcup_{u \in R} [\mu_{\tilde{P}'}(u) \wedge (\mu_{\tilde{P}}(u) \rightarrow \mu_{\tilde{Q}}(v))],$$

or

$$\mu_{\tilde{Q}}(v) = \sup[\mu_{\tilde{P}}(u) \wedge (\mu_{\tilde{P}}(u) \to \mu_{\tilde{Q}}(v))],$$
$$\mu_{\tilde{Q}'}(v) = \sup[\mu_{\tilde{P}'}(u) \wedge (\mu_{\tilde{P}}(u) \to \mu_{\tilde{Q}}(v))], \tag{2.141}$$

The following theorem shows the fact that when the observations are closed to each other in the metric $D(.)$ of (2.140) type, then there can be only a small deviation in the membership functions of the conclusions.

Theorem 2.7. *(Stability theorem) Let $\delta \geq 0$ and let $\tilde{P}$, $\tilde{P}'$ be fuzzy intervals and an implication operation in the fuzzy conditional inference rule (2.141) is of type (2.132). If $D(\tilde{P},\tilde{P}') \leq \delta$, then*

$$\sup_{v \in R} \left| \mu_{\tilde{P}}(v) - \mu_{\tilde{P}'}(v) \right| \leq \max\{\omega_{\tilde{P}}(\delta), \omega_{\tilde{P}'}(\delta)\}$$

Theorem 2.8. *(Continuity theorem) Let binary relationship $\tilde{R}(u,v) = \mu_{\tilde{P}}(u) \xrightarrow[ALI4]{} \mu_{\tilde{Q}}(v)$ be continuous. Then $\tilde{Q}$ is continuous and $\omega_{\tilde{Q}}(\delta) \leq \omega_{\tilde{R}}(\delta)$ for each $\delta \geq 0$.*

While we use extended fuzzy logic to reason with partially true statements we need to extend logics 1)-11) for partial truth. We consider here only extension at the Lukasewicz logic for partial truth. In order to deal with partial truth Pavelka [331] extended this logic by adding truth constants for all reals in $[0,1]$. Hajek [187] simplified it by adding these truth constants $\overline{r}$ only for each rational $r \in [0,1]$ (so $\overline{r}$ is an atomic formula with truth value r). They also added 'book - keeping axioms'

$$\overline{r \Rightarrow s} \equiv \overline{r} \to \overline{s} \text{ for rational r, s} \in [0,1] .$$

This logic is called Rational Pavelka logic (RPL). RPL was introduced in order to reason with partially true statements. In this section we note that this can already be done in Lukasiewicz logic, and that the conservative extension theorems allow us to lift the completeness theorem, that provability degree equals truth degree from RPL to Lukasiewicz logic. This may be regarded as an additional conservative extension theorem, confirming that, even for partial truth, Rational

Pavelka logic deals with exactly the same logic as Lukasiewicz logic - but in a very much more convenient way. RPL extends the language of infinite valued Łukasiewicz logic by adding to the truth constants 0 and 1 all rational numbers r of the unit interval $[0,1]$ *A graded formula* is a pair (φ, r) consisting of a formula φ of Lukasiewicz logic and a rational element $r \in [0,1]$, indicating that the truth value of φ is at least r, $\varphi \geq r$ [415]. For example, $\left(p(x), \frac{1}{2}\right)$ expresses the fact that the truth value of $p(x)$, $x \in Dom$, is at least $\frac{1}{2}$. The inference rules of RPL are the *generalization rule*

$$\frac{\varphi}{(\forall x)(\varphi)}, \tag{2.142}$$

and a modified version of the *modus ponens rule*,

$$\frac{(\varphi, r), (\varphi \rightarrow \psi, s)}{(\psi, r \otimes s)}. \tag{2.143}$$

Here $\otimes$ denotes the Lukasiewicz t-norm. Rule (2.143) says that if formula φ holds at least with truth value *r*, and the implication $\varphi \rightarrow \psi$ holds at least with truth value *s*, then formula ψ holds at least with truth value $r \otimes s$. The modified modus ponens rule is derived from the so-called *book-keeping axioms* for the rational truth constants *r*. The book-keeping axioms add to the axioms of Lukasiewicz logic and provide rules for evaluating compound formulas involving rational truth constants [188]. The use of fuzzy reasoning trades accuracy against speed, simplicity and interpretability for lay users. In the context of ubiquitous computing, these characteristics are clearly advantageous.

Chapter 3

Preferences Framework

3.1 Why Vague Preferences?

One of the main aspects defining solution of a decision problem is a preferences framework. In its turn one of the approaches to formally describe preferences is the use of utility function. Utility function is a quantitative representation of a DM's preferences and any scientifically ground utility model has its underlying preference assumptions.

The first approach to modeling human preferences was suggested by von Neumann and Morgenstern [397] in their expected utility (EU) model. This approach is based on axioms of weak order, independence and continuity of preferences over actions set $\mathcal{A}$. Further experiments and discussions conducted by economists and psychologists showed that the independence assumption in EU is non-realistic [36,91,144]. A lot of preference frameworks were suggested then which relax that of EU by modeling key aspects of a DM behavior. For example, in [362] independence is assumed for only comonotonic actions in $\mathcal{A}$.

Reconsideration of the preferences framework underlying EU resulted in development of various advanced preferences frameworks as generalizations of the former. These generalizations can be divided into two types: rank-dependence generalization and sign-dependence generalization [100]. Advanced preference frameworks include various reconsiderations and weakening of the independence axiom [147,167, 171,362], human attitudes to risk and uncertainty (rank-dependent generalization), gains and losses [222,387] (sign-dependent generalization) etc.

Various notions of uncertainty aversion (ambiguity aversion) in various formulations were included into many preference models starting from Schmeidler's Choquet expected utility (CEU) [362] preferences framework and Gilboa and Schmeidler's maxmin expected utility preferences framework [171], to more advanced uncertainty aversion formulations of Ghirardato, Maccheroni, Marinacci, Epstein, Klibanoff [93,106, 149,166,167,168,170,237,238].

In [168] they provide axiomatization for α-MMEU – a convex combination of minimal and maximal expected utilities, where minimal expected utility is multiplied by a degree of ambiguity aversion (ambiguity attitude). This approach allows differentiating ambiguity and ambiguity attitude. However, the approach in [168] allows to evaluate overall utility only comparing ambiguity attitudes of DMs with the same risk attitudes. The analogous features of comparative ambiguity aversion are also presented in [166]. Ambiguity aversion as an extra risk aversion is considered in [106, 148].

In [239] they suggested a smooth ambiguity model as a more general way to formalize decision making under ambiguity than MMEU. In this model probability-relevant information is described by assessment of DM's subjective probabilistic beliefs to various relevant probability distributions. In contrast to other approaches to decision making under ambiguity, the model provides a strong separation between ambiguity and ambiguity attitude. To describe whether a DM is an ambiguity averse, loving or neutral it is suggested to use well known technique of modeling risk attitudes. More concretely, to reflect a considered DM's reaction to ambiguity it is suggested to use a concave nonlinear function with a special parameter α as the degree of ambiguity aversion – the larger α correspond to a more ambiguity averse DM. In its turn ambiguity loving is modeled by a convex nonlinearity. As opposed to the models in [166,168,171], the model in [239] allows for comparison of ambiguity attitudes of DMs whose risk attitudes are different.

The other important property included into some modern preference frameworks is a trade-off-consistency which reflects strength of preferences with respect to coordinates of probabilistic outcomes.

The preference framework of the Cumulative Prospect Theory (CPT), suggested by Kahneman and Tversky [387], as opposed to the other existing frameworks includes both rank-dependence and sign-dependence features [100].

But are the modern preferences frameworks sufficiently adequate to model human attitudes to alternatives? Unfortunately, the modern preferences frameworks miss very important feature of human preferences: human preferences are vague [337]. Humans compare even simple alternatives linguistically using certain evaluation techniques such as "much better", "much worse", "a little better", "almost equivalent" etc. So, a preference is a matter of an imprecise degree and this issue should be taken into account in formulation of preferences framework. Let us consider an example.

Example. Suppose that Robert wants to decide among two possible jobs $\tilde{f}, \tilde{g}$ based on the following criteria: salary, excitement and travel time. The information Robert has is that the job $\tilde{f}$ offers notably higher salary, slightly less travel time and is significantly less interesting as compared to the job $\tilde{g}$. What job to choose?

Without doubt, evaluations like these are subjective and context-dependent but are often faced. If to suppose that for Robert salary is "notably" more important than the time issues and "slightly" more important than excitement then it may be difficult to him to compare these alternatives. The relevant information is too vague for Robert to clearly give preference to any of the alternatives. Robert may feel that superiority of the $\tilde{f}$ on the first criterion is approximately compensated by the superiority of the $\tilde{g}$ in whole on the second and the third criteria. But, at the same time Robert may not consider these jobs equally good. As a result, in contrast to have unambiguous preferences, Robert has some "distribution" of his preferences among alternatives. In other words, he may think that to some degree the job $\tilde{f}$ is as good as the job $\tilde{g}$ and, at the same time, that to some degree job $\tilde{g}$ is as good as the job $\tilde{f}$.

In this example we see that vagueness of subjective comparison of the alternatives on the base of some criteria naturally passes to the preferences among alternatives. For example, the term "notably higher" is not sharply defined but some vague term because various point estimates to various extents correspond to this term – for a given point estimate its correspondence to a "notably higher" term may not be true or false but partially true. This makes use of interval description of such estimates inadequate as no point may partially belong to an interval – it belongs or not. It is impossible to sharply differentiate "notably higher" and not "notably higher" points. As a result, vague estimates (in our case vague preferences) cannot be handled and described by classical logic and precise techniques. Fuzzy logic [11,243] is namely the tool to handle vague estimates and there is a solid number of works devoted to fuzzy and linguistic preference relations [328,407]. This is due to the fact that vagueness is more adequately measured by fuzziness. As a result, fuzzy degree-based preference axiomatization is more adequate representation from behavioral aspects point of view as it is closer to human thinking. In view of this, linguistic preference relations as a natural generalization of classical preference relations are an appropriate framework to underlie human-like utility model.

3.2 Fuzzy Preferences

Fuzzy preferences or fuzzy preference relations (FPRs)[79,135,196,200] are used to reflect the fact that in real-world problems, due to complexity of alternatives, lack of knowledge and information and some other reasons, a DM cannot give a full preference to one alternative from a pair. Preferences remain "distributed" reflecting that one alternative is to some extent better than another. In contrast to classical preference relations, FPR shows whether an alternative $\tilde{f}$ is more preferred to $\tilde{g}$ than alternative $\tilde{f}'$ is preferred to $\tilde{g}'$.

Given a set of alternatives $\mathcal{A}$, any fuzzy preference relation on $\mathcal{A}$ is a mapping $R:\mathcal{A}\times\mathcal{A}\to T$ where T is a totally ordered set. Very often a fuzzy preference relation is considered as $R:\mathcal{A}\times\mathcal{A}\to[0,1]$ which assigns to any pair of alternatives $\tilde{f},\tilde{g}\in\mathcal{A}$ a degree of preference $R(\tilde{f},\tilde{g})\in[0,1]$ to which $\tilde{f}$ is preferred to $\tilde{g}$. The higher $R(\tilde{f},\tilde{g})$ is, the more $\tilde{f}$ is preferred to $\tilde{g}$. In other words, FPR is characterized by a membership function $\mu_{\tilde{R}}(\tilde{f},\tilde{g})=R(\tilde{f},\tilde{g})$ which returns a degree of membership of a pair $(\tilde{f},\tilde{g})$ to $\tilde{R}$. FPR is a valued extension of classical preference relations. For example, a weak order is a special case of FPR when $R: \mathcal{A} \times \mathcal{A} \to \{0,1\}$ with $R(\tilde{f},\tilde{g})=1$ if and only if $\tilde{f} \succeq \tilde{g}$ and $R(\tilde{f},\tilde{g})=0$ otherwise.

Consider a general case of a classical preference relation (CPR) implying that $\tilde{f}$ is either strictly preferred, or equivalent or incomparable to $\tilde{g}$. This means that CPR is decomposed into a strict preference relation $\tilde{P}$, indifference preference relation $\tilde{I}$ and incomparability preference relation $\tilde{J}$, that is, $\forall \tilde{f},\tilde{g} \in \mathcal{A}$ either $(\tilde{f},\tilde{g}) \in \tilde{P}$, or $(\tilde{f},\tilde{g}) \in \tilde{I}$ or $(\tilde{f},\tilde{g}) \in \tilde{J}$. An important extension of this case to FPR can be defined as follows:

$$P(\tilde{f},\tilde{g}) + P(\tilde{g},\tilde{f}) + I(\tilde{f},\tilde{g}) + J(\tilde{f},\tilde{g}) = 1$$

where $P,I,J: \mathcal{A} \times \mathcal{A} \to [0,1]$ are fuzzy strict, fuzzy indifference and fuzzy incomparability preference relations respectively.

Another important type of FPR is that described by a function $R: \mathcal{A} \times \mathcal{A} \to [0,1]$ where $R(\tilde{f},\tilde{g})=1$ means full strict preference of $\tilde{f}$ over $\tilde{g}$, which is the same as $R(\tilde{g},\tilde{f})=0$ (full negative preference) and indifference between $\tilde{f}$ over $\tilde{g}$ is modeled as $R(\tilde{f},\tilde{g}) = R(\tilde{g},\tilde{f}) = 1/2$. In general, R is an additive reciprocal, i.e. $R(\tilde{f},\tilde{g}) + R(\tilde{g},\tilde{f}) = 1$. This is a degree-valued generalization of completeness property of classical relation, and $R(\tilde{f},\tilde{g}) > 1/2$ is a degree of a strict preference. However, such an R excludes incomparability.

Consider another important type of FPR within which indifference is written as $R(\tilde{f},\tilde{g}) = R(\tilde{g},\tilde{f}) = 1$, incomparability is written as $R(\tilde{f},\tilde{g}) = R(\tilde{g},\tilde{f}) = 0$ and completeness is written as $\max(R(\tilde{f},\tilde{g}), R(\tilde{g},\tilde{f})) = 1$.

For applications of FPR to model consistent choices, various consistency properties of the former are considered. One of the most important is transitivity of FPR. The idea of transitivity of FPR is a natural generalization of the transitivity of CPR and means that preference degree of one alternative over another is smaller than or equals to preference degrees between any two alternatives which are in indirect chain between the first two. Formally, transitivity of FPR is defined in terms of t-norm:

Definition 3.1. Transitivity of fuzzy preference relation [157]. A fuzzy preference relation R is T-transitive, where T is a T-norm, if

$$R(\tilde{f},\tilde{f}') \geq T(R(\tilde{f},\tilde{g}),R(\tilde{g},\tilde{f}')),\ \forall\tilde{f},\tilde{g},\tilde{f}' \in \mathcal{A}.$$

Below it is given some of the well-known transitivity properties of the FPR defined over a finite set of alternatives [108].

1. Triangle condition [201]:

$$\forall\tilde{f},\tilde{g},\tilde{f}' \in \mathcal{A}, R(\tilde{f},\tilde{g}) + R(\tilde{g},\tilde{f}') \geq R(\tilde{f},\tilde{f}').$$

This condition has the simple geometrical representation as a triangle whose vertices are alternatives $\tilde{f},\tilde{g},\tilde{f}'$ and the lengths of the sides are $R(\tilde{f},\tilde{g})$, $R(\tilde{g},\tilde{f}')$, $R(\tilde{f},\tilde{f}')$.

2. Weak transitivity [201]:

$$\forall\tilde{f},\tilde{g},\tilde{f}' \in \mathcal{A}: \min(R(\tilde{f},\tilde{g}),R(\tilde{g},\tilde{f}')) \geq 0.5 \Rightarrow R(\tilde{f},\tilde{f}') \geq 0.5.$$

The interpretation is as follows: If $\tilde{f}$ is preferred to $\tilde{g}$ and $\tilde{g}$ is preferred to $\tilde{f}'$, then $\tilde{f}$ should be preferred to $\tilde{f}'$. This is the usual transitivity condition that should be satisfied to exclude inconsistent choices. Any consistent fuzzy preference relation should satisfy this condition.

3. Max–min transitivity [116,134,155,470]:

$$R(\tilde{f},\tilde{f}') \geq \min(R(\tilde{f},\tilde{g}),R(\tilde{g},\tilde{f}')).$$

The interpretation is as follows. The preference degree of one alternative $\tilde{f}$ over another alternative $\tilde{f}'$ is higher than or equal to preference degrees between each of these two alternatives $\tilde{f}$ and $\tilde{f}'$ and any other alternative $\tilde{g} \in \mathcal{A}$. This is the traditional requirement to characterize consistency of FPRs [116]. However, this is a very strong requirement which may not be satisfied even for a FPR which is sufficiently consistent in practical sense. For example, let us consider a set of alternatives $\mathcal{A}=\{\tilde{f},\tilde{g},\tilde{h}\}$, such that $\tilde{h}\succ\tilde{g}\succ\tilde{f}$. Let the fuzzy comparison of the alternatives be given by the following reciprocal FPR:

$$\tilde{P}=\begin{pmatrix}0.5 & 0.1 & 0\\ 0.9 & 0.5 & 0.4\\ 1 & 0.6 & 0.5\end{pmatrix}.$$

It is easy to verify that this FPR satisfies weak transitivity and the triangle condition but does not satisfy max–min transitivity as $R(\tilde{f},\tilde{h})<\min(R(\tilde{f},\tilde{g}),R(\tilde{g},\tilde{h}))$.

4. Max–max transitivity [134,470]:

$$R(\tilde{f},\tilde{f}')\geq\max(R(\tilde{f},\tilde{g}),R(\tilde{g},\tilde{f}')).$$

This means that the degree of preference between two alternatives should be not smaller than the degrees of preference between these alternatives and any other alternative. This condition is stronger concept than max–min transitivity.

5. Restricted max–min transitivity [201,221]:

$$\min(R(\tilde{f},\tilde{g}),R(\tilde{g},\tilde{f}'))\geq 0.5\Rightarrow R(\tilde{f},\tilde{f}')\geq\min(R(\tilde{f},\tilde{g}),R(\tilde{g},\tilde{f}')).$$

This implies: if alternative $\tilde{f}$ is preferred to $\tilde{g}$ with a degree $R(\tilde{f},\tilde{g})$ and $\tilde{g}$ is preferred to $\tilde{f}'$ with a degree $R(\tilde{g},\tilde{f}')$, then $\tilde{f}$ should be preferred to $\tilde{f}'$ with at least a degree of preference $R(\tilde{f},\tilde{f}')$ equal to the maximum of the above values. The inequality in this condition should become equality only if there is indifference between at least two of the three alternatives. This transitivity condition is stronger than weak transitivity but it is milder than max–min transitivity.

6. Restricted max-max transitivity [201,221]:

$$\min(R(\tilde{f},\tilde{g}),R(\tilde{g},\tilde{f}'))\geq 0.5\Rightarrow R(\tilde{f},\tilde{f}')\geq\max(R(\tilde{f},g),R(g,\tilde{f}')).$$

As in the previous case, the equality holds only when there is indifference between at least two of the three alternatives and in this case max–max transitivity and restricted max–min transitivity coincide. This concept is stronger than restricted max–min transitivity and milder than max–max transitivity.

7. Multiplicative transitivity [200,221]

$$\frac{R(\tilde{f},\tilde{g})}{R(\tilde{g},\tilde{f})}\cdot\frac{R(\tilde{g},\tilde{f}')}{R(\tilde{f}',\tilde{g})}=\frac{R(\tilde{f},\tilde{f}')}{R(\tilde{f}',\tilde{f})}.$$

$\frac{R(\tilde{f},\tilde{g})}{R(\tilde{g},\tilde{f})}$ is interpreted as a ratio of the degrees of preference which means that $\tilde{f}$ is $\frac{R(\tilde{f},\tilde{g})}{R(\tilde{g},\tilde{f})}$ times as good as $\tilde{g}$. Multiplicative transitivity includes restricted max–max transitivity [201,221], and is rewritten as

$$R(\tilde{f},\tilde{g})R(\tilde{g},\tilde{f}')R(\tilde{f}',\tilde{f})=R(\tilde{f},\tilde{f}')R(\tilde{f}',\tilde{g})R(\tilde{g},\tilde{f}).$$

8. Additive transitivity [201,221]:
$(R(\tilde{f},\tilde{g})-0.5)+(R(\tilde{g},\tilde{f}')-0.5)=(R(\tilde{f},\tilde{f}')-0.5))$,
or, equivalently, $R(\tilde{f},\tilde{g})+R(\tilde{g},\tilde{f}')+R(\tilde{f}',\tilde{f})=1.5$.

The interpretation of this condition is as follows: assume you want to compare three alternatives $\tilde{f},\tilde{g},\tilde{f}'$. If you have no information on these alternatives, one assumption to start with is the indifference one: $\tilde{f}\sim\tilde{g}\sim\tilde{f}'$. Within FPR, this means $R(\tilde{f},\tilde{g})+R(\tilde{g},\tilde{f}')+R(\tilde{f},\tilde{f}')=0.5$. Assume now you have some information saying that $\tilde{f}\prec\tilde{g}$, which means $R(\tilde{f},\tilde{g})<0.5$. Then $R(\tilde{g},\tilde{f}')$ or $R(\tilde{f}',\tilde{f})$ have to change to exclude a contradiction $\tilde{f}\prec\tilde{g}\sim\tilde{f}'\sim\tilde{f}$. If to assume that $R(\tilde{g},\tilde{f}')=0$ then $\tilde{g}$ and $\tilde{f}'$ will be indifferent and given $\tilde{g}\succ\tilde{f}$ you have to conclude that $\tilde{f}'\succ\tilde{f}$. But as $\tilde{g}\sim\tilde{f}$ you have $R(\tilde{g},\tilde{f})=R(\tilde{f}',\tilde{f})=0$ which means $R(\tilde{f},\tilde{g})+R(\tilde{g},\tilde{f}')+R(\tilde{f}',\tilde{f})=R(\tilde{f},\tilde{g})+R(\tilde{g},\tilde{f}')+R(\tilde{g},\tilde{f})=$ $1+0.5=1.5$. W.l.o.g., suppose $R(\tilde{g},\tilde{f}')<0.5$. Then you have $\tilde{f}'\succ\tilde{g}$

and $\tilde{g} \succ \tilde{f}$, so $\tilde{f}' \succ \tilde{f}$. On the other hand, the value $R(\tilde{f}',\tilde{f})$ has to be equal to or greater than $R(\tilde{g},\tilde{f})$ (it is equal only if $R(\tilde{g},\tilde{f}')=0.5$ as it is shown above). If to interpret $R(\tilde{g},\tilde{f})=0.5$ as the extent of preference of $\tilde{g}$ over $\tilde{f}$ then it is reasonable to determine the extent of preference of $\tilde{f}'$ over $\tilde{f}$ as equal to the sum of the extents of preferences of $\tilde{f}'$ over $\tilde{g}$ and $\tilde{g}$ over $\tilde{f}$, i.e. $R(\tilde{f}',\tilde{f})-0.5=(R(\tilde{f}',\tilde{g})-0.5)+(R(\tilde{g},\tilde{f})-0.5)$.

One can easily find that the reciprocal fuzzy preference relation R, given above, verifies restricted max–min transitivity, restricted max–max transitivity and additive transitivity. It is also easy to prove that additive transitivity is stronger concept than restricted max–max transitivity [120].

Let us consider relations between the above mentioned concepts of transitivity. The weak transitivity is the minimum requirement on consistency of any FPR excluding that based on the triangle condition. The max–min transitivity and max–max transitivity are so strong that they may not be verified even for an FPR that can be very consistent in a practical sense. From this point of view, the restricted max–min and restricted max–max transitivity concepts may be good alternatives to them. Furthermore, restricted max–max transitivity is more intuitive in practical sense and is stronger than restricted max–min transitivity. The multiplicative transitivity is valid only if $R(\tilde{f},\tilde{g})>0$. As it is shown in [201], the multiplicative preference relations can be made equivalent to the additive transitivity property. Additive transitivity property also implies the triangle condition. An extensive description of the above mentioned properties and relations between them is given in [201].

3.3 Linguistic Preferences

FPR are a useful tool to handle vague preferences. Linguistic preferences, or linguistic preference relations (LPRs), sometimes called fuzzy linguistic preferences, are generalization of FPR used to account for a situations when a DM or an expert cannot assign precise degree of preference of one alternative to another, but express this degree in a form of linguistic terms like "much better", "a little worse" etc. Indeed, under imperfect environment where relevant information is NL-based, there is no sufficient information to submit exact degrees, but is natural to express degrees in NL corresponding to the kind of initial information.

To formalize linguistic preference relation it is first necessary to define a set of linguistic terms as a set of verbal expressions of preference degrees which would be appropriate for a considered problem. As a rule, they consider a finite and totally ordered linguistic term set $T=\{t_i\},\ i\in\{0,...,m\}$ with an odd cardinal ranging between 5 and 13. Each term is semantically represented by a fuzzy number, typically triangular or trapezoidal, placed over some predefined scale, e.g. [0,1]. For example: "no preference" – (0,0,0), "slightly better" – (0,0.3,0.5), "more or less better" – (0.3,0.5,0.7), "sufficiently better" – (0.5,0.7,1), "full preference" – (0.7,1,1). The cardinality of the term set is usually an odd.

Consider a finite set of alternatives $\mathcal{A}=\{\tilde{f}_i,\ i=1,2,...,n\ (n\geq 2)\}$. Then a linguistic preference relation is formally defined as follows:

Definition 3.2. Linguistic preference relation [197]. Let $\mathcal{A}$ be a finite set of alternatives, then a linguistic preference relation $\tilde{R}$ is a fuzzy set in $\mathcal{A}^2$ characterized by a membership function

$$\mu_{\tilde{R}}:\mathcal{A}^2\rightarrow T$$

$$\mu(\tilde{f}_i,\tilde{f}_j)=\tilde{r}_{ij},\ \forall\tilde{f}_i,\tilde{f}_j\in\mathcal{A}$$

indicating the linguistic preference degree of alternative $\tilde{f}_i$ over $\tilde{f}_j$, i.e. $\tilde{r}_{ij}\in T$.

So, linguistic preference relation is represented by a membership function whose values are not precise degrees in [0,1] but fuzzy numbers in [0,1]. This means that linguistic preference relation is a kind of FPR if to recall that the latter is in general defined by membership function whose range is an ordered structure.

Transitivity, completeness and other basic properties of preference relations are defined for linguistic preference relation by extending the corresponding properties of FPR on the base of extension principle. To illustrate this, consider max–min transitivity of FPR defined as $\tilde{r}_{ij} \geq \max_k \min(\tilde{r}_{ik}, \tilde{r}_{kj})$. Extension of this FPR to linguistic preference relation, when degrees of preferences are expressed as fuzzy numbers $\tilde{r}_{ij}$, $\tilde{r}_{ik}, \tilde{r}_{kj}$ may be achieved when min and max operations and $\geq$ are defined as follows:

$$\min(\tilde{A}, \tilde{B}) = \bigcup_{u,v \in U} \min(\mu_{\tilde{A}}(u), \mu_{\tilde{B}}(v)) / \min(u, v)$$

$$\max(\tilde{A}, \tilde{B}) = \bigcup_{u,v \in U} \min(\mu_{\tilde{A}}(u), \mu_{\tilde{B}}(v)) / \max(u, v)$$

$$\tilde{A} \geq \tilde{B} \text{ iff } \min(\tilde{A}, \tilde{B}) = \tilde{B}$$

where $\tilde{A}, \tilde{B} \in \{\tilde{r}_{ij}, \tilde{r}_{ik}, \tilde{r}_{kj}\}$.

For example, consider a linguistic preference relation given in Table 3.1.

Table 3.1. Linguistic preference relation

LPR	$\tilde{f}_1$	$\tilde{f}_2$	$\tilde{f}_3$
$\tilde{f}_1$	0	more or less better	sufficiently better
$\tilde{f}_2$	0	0	more or less better
$\tilde{f}_3$	0	0	0

Let the terms "more or less better" and "sufficiently better" be described by TFNs (0.5,0.7,0.8) and (0.8,0.9,1) respectively, and 0 be a singleton. Then one can verify that this linguistic preference relation satisfies max-min transitivity. For instance, $\tilde{r}_{\tilde{f}_3\tilde{f}_1} = (0.8, 0.9, 1) \geq \min(\tilde{r}_{\tilde{f}_3\tilde{f}_2}, \tilde{r}_{\tilde{f}_2\tilde{f}_1}) =$ $\min((0.5, 0.7, 0.8), (0.5, 0.7, 0.8)) = (0.5, 0.7, 0.8)$. Such an approach to model linguistic preference relation is a natural generalization of FPR and was suggested by L.A. Zadeh. In the successive literature this approach is referred to as the *traditional fuzzy linguistic approach* (*TFLA*). TFLA preserves fuzzy information about degrees of preference by direct computations over fuzzy numbers and, as a result, is of a higher computational complexity. There are also various other approaches to modeling linguistic preference relation, some of which allow reducing computational complexity of the TFLA or suggest some reasonable trade-off between preserving information and computational complexity. One of them is referred to as *ordinal fuzzy linguistic modeling* (OFLM). This approach is based on an idea of adopting symbolic computations [198] over indices of terms in a term set instead of direct computations over the terms themselves as fuzzy numbers. This makes the approach sufficiently simpler in terms of computational complexity than TFLA. In OFLM, they consider a finite linguistic term set with an odd cardinality and the terms described by fuzzy numbers over the unit interval [0,1]. Also, a mid term is used to express an approximate equivalence of alternatives by a fuzzy number with a mode equal to 0.5 and labeled like "almost equivalent". The other terms are distributed around the mid term expressing successively increasing preference degrees to the right and their symmetrical counterparts to the left. For example: "sufficiently worse", "more or less worse", "slightly worse", "almost equivalent", "slightly better", "more or less better", "sufficiently better". In OFLM, given a term set $T=\{\tilde{s}_0,\tilde{s}_1,...,\tilde{s}_m\}$ an LPR can be characterized by some of the following properties [197]:

1. Reflexive: $\tilde{r}_{ii}=\tilde{s}_m, \forall i$.
2. Irreflexive: $\tilde{r}_{ii}=\tilde{s}_0, \forall i$.
3. Symmetric: $\tilde{r}_{ij}=\tilde{r}_{ji}, \forall i,j$.
4. Antisymmetric: $\min(\tilde{r}_{ij},\tilde{r}_{ji})=\tilde{s}_0, \forall i,j, i\neq j$.
5. Complete: $\max(\tilde{r}_{ij},\tilde{r}_{ji})=\tilde{s}_m, \forall i,j, i\neq j$.
6. Transitive: $\tilde{r}_{ik}\geq \max(\tilde{r}_{ij},\tilde{r}_{jk}), \forall i,j,k$.
7. Negatively transitive: $\tilde{r}_{ik}\leq \max(\tilde{r}_{ij},\tilde{r}_{jk}), \forall i,j,k$.

Handling linguistic preference relation in OFLM is based on the total order of the linguistic terms in the term set and commonly is represented by means of a *negation operator*, a *comparison operator* and *aggregation operators*. Often, a negation operator is defined as

$$Neg(\tilde{s}_i) = \tilde{s}_j \text{, where } j = m - i;$$

and maximization and minimization operators (comparison operators) as:

$$Max(\tilde{s}_i, \tilde{s}_j) = \tilde{s}_j \text{ if } j \geq i;$$

$$Min(\tilde{s}_i, \tilde{s}_j) = \tilde{s}_i \text{ if } i \leq j.$$

In its turn, aggregation operators are defined on the base of the negation and comparison operators. However, we don't explain these operations and the OFLM in details. For detail description of the OFLM, one can refer to [199]. The main disadvantage of OFLM is that it leads to sufficient loss of information and decreases advantage of the idea of linguistic reasoning under imperfect information.

3.4 Methods of Uncertain Preferences Modeling

There exist also approaches to model uncertainty of preferences, other than FPR. These approaches account for comparison of ill-known alternatives under crisp (non-fuzzy) preference basis. In one of these approaches, which is used for modeling valued tournament relations, $R(f,g)$ measures the *likelihood of a crisp weak preference* $f \succeq g$ [119,133]. Formally, $R(f,g)$ is defined as follows:

$$R(f,g) = P(f \succ g) + \frac{1}{2} P(f \sim g),$$

where $f \sim g \Leftrightarrow f \succeq g$ and $g \succeq f$, which implies $R(f,g) + R(g,f) = 1$. Thus, uncertainty of preference is described by a probability distribution P over possible conventional preference relations, i.e. $R_i \subset \mathcal{A} \times \mathcal{A}$ with $f \succeq_i g \Leftrightarrow (f,g) \in R_i$ and $P(R_i) = P_i$, $i = 1,\dots,N$. Then

$$R(f,g) = \sum_{i: f \succ_i g} P_i + \sum_{i: f \sim_i g} \frac{1}{2} P_i.$$

For more details one can refer to [121]. This approach to modeling uncertain preferences was the first interpretation of fuzzy preference relations in the existing literature and was considered in the framework of the voting theory. It is needed to mention that such relations may be considered fuzzy because a degree of preference is used whereas the approach itself is probabilistic. However, this degree is a measured uncertainty about preferences which are themselves crisp but are not known with certainty. So, in its kernel, this approach does not support an idea underlying FPR – preference itself is a matter of a degree.

Another application of this approach may be implemented when there exists a utility function which quantifies preferences between alternatives f, g, f' on some numerical scale and the latter is supported by additional information in a form of a probability distribution. Then, $R(f,g) = P(u(f) > u(g))$, where $u : S \to \mathcal{R}$ is a utility function.

Other measures of uncertainty can also be used to describe uncertainty of preference. One of them is the possibility measure, by using thereof the uncertain preference is defined as

$$R(f,g) = P(f \succeq g),$$

where $P(f \succeq g)$ is the degree of possibility of preference. The use of the possibility theory defines $\max(R(f,g), R(g,f)) = 1$. At the same time, in terms of the possibility theory, $1 - R(f,g) = N(f \succeq g)$ is the degree of certainty of a strict preference.

A large direction in the realm of modeling uncertain preferences is devoted to modeling *incomplete preferences*[143,324]. In line with the transitivity, completeness of preferences is often considered as another reasonable assumption. However, transitivity is used as a consistency requirement whereas completeness is used as a requirement which exclude indecisiveness. The reasonability and intuitiveness of these basics are not the same: for completeness they may loss their strength as compared to transitivity because in real choice problems a lack of information, complexity of alternatives, psychological biases etc may hamper someone's choice up to indecisiveness. From the other side, indecisiveness may take place in group decision making when members' preferences disagree. The issue that completeness may be questionable was first addressed by Aumann [44]:

> "Of all the axioms of utility theory, the completeness axiom is perhaps the most questionable. Like others of the axioms, it is inaccurate as a description of real life; but unlike them, we find it hard to accept even from the normative

> viewpoint. ... For example, certain decisions that [an] individual is asked to make might involve highly hypothetical situations, which he will never face in real life; he might feel that he cannot reach an "honest" decision in such cases. Other decision problems might be extremely complex, too complex for intuitive "insight," and our individual might prefer to make no decision at all in these problems. Is it "rational" to force decisions in such cases?"

If to assume that preferences are not complete, one has to reject the use of numerical utility functions and has to deal with more complex representations. As it is argued in [324], the use of a numerical utility naturally leads to loss of information and then should not be dogmatic if one intends to model bounded rationality and imperfect nature of choice. In [324] they suggest to handle incomplete preferences by means of a vector-valued utility function as its range is naturally incompletely ordered. The other main argument for such an approach is that the use of a vector-valued utility is simpler than dealing with preferences themselves and in this case well-developed multi-objective optimization techniques may be applied. The idea of incomplete preferences underlying the approach in [324] is realized by the following assumption: given the set of alternatives $\mathcal{A}$ there exist at least one pair of alternatives $f, g \in \mathcal{A}$ for which neither $f \succeq g$ nor $g \succeq f$ is assumed.

There exist also other approaches dealing with incomplete preferences by means of imprecise beliefs and/or imprecise utilities. The following classification of these approaches is given in [312]:

1) Probabilities alone are considered imprecise. For this setting preferences are represented by a convex set of probability distributions and a unique, utility function $u()$. Such models are widely used in robust Bayesian statistics [211,346,401];

2) Utilities alone are considered imprecise. In this setting preferences are represented by a set of utility functions $\{u(c)\}$ and a unique probability distribution $p(s)$. Such representations were axiomatized and applied to economic models by Aumann [44] and Dubra, Maccheroni and Ok [137];

3) Both probabilities and utilities are considered imprecise. This is represented by sets of probability distributions $\{p(s)\}$ and utility functions $\{u()\}$. These sets are considered separately from each other allo-

wing for all arbitrary combinations of their elements. This is the traditional separation of imprecise information about beliefs and outcomes. Independence of two sets is practically justified and simplifies the decision analysis. However, this approach does not have axiomatic foundations. From the other side, the set of pairs may be non-convex and unconnected [210,211].

In order to compare adequacy of FPR and incomplete preferences models, we can emphasize the following classification of preference frameworks in terms of increasing uncertainty: complete orders, FPR, incomplete preferences. The first and the third one are idealized frameworks: the first implies that preference is absolutely clear, the third deals with the case when some alternatives are absolutely not comparable. Incomplete preference deals with lack of any information which can elucidate preferences. This is a very rare case in the sense that in most of situations some such information does exist, though it requires to be obtained. In its turn FPR implies that preference itself is not "single-valued" and should reflect competition of alternatives even if the related information is precise.

Chapter 4

Imperfect Decision-Relevant Information

4.1 What Is Imperfect Information?

In real decision making problems a DM is almost never provided with perfect, that is, ideal decision-relevant information to determine states of nature, outcomes, probabilities, utilities etc and has to construct decision background structure based on his/her perception and envision. In contrast, relevant information almost always comes imperfect. Imperfect information is information which in one or more respects is imprecise, uncertain, incomplete, unreliable, vague or partially true [452]. We will discuss these properties of imperfect information and their relations.

Two main concepts of imperfect information are imprecision and uncertainty. Imprecision is one of the widest concepts including variety of cases. For purposes of differentiation between imprecision and uncertainty, Prof. L.A. Zadeh suggested the following example:

> "For purposes of differentiation it is convenient to use an example which involves ethnicity. Assume that Robert's father is German and his mother's parents were German and French. Thus, Robert is 3/4 German and 1/4 French. Suppose that someone asks me: What is Robert's ethnicity. If my answer is: Robert is German, my answer is imprecise or, equivalently, partially true. More specifically, the truth value of my answer is 3/4. No uncertainty is involved. Next, assume that Robert is either German or French, and that I am uncertain about his ethnicity. Based on whatever information I have, my perception of the likelihood that Robert is German is 3/4. In this case, 3/4 is my subjective probability that Robert is German. No partiality of truth is involved."

In the first case imprecision is only represented by partial truth and no uncertainty is involved. As Prof. L.A. Zadeh defines, such imprecision is referred to as strict imprecision or s-imprecision for short.

In the second case, imprecision is only represented by uncertainty and no partial truth is involved.

Information is partially true if it is neither absolutely true nor absolutely false but in an intermediate closeness to reality. For example, suppose you needed to write down ten pages of a text and have already written 8 pages. Certainly 'the work is done' is not absolutely true and is not absolutely false, and, if to assume that all pages are written equivalently difficult, 'the work is done' is true with degree 0.8. From the other side, 'the work is not done' is not true and is not false from viewpoint of intuition because it is not informative and requires to be substituted by a more concrete evaluation.

Let us consider another example on imprecision and uncertainty which is suggested by P. Smets [375]:

> "To illustrate the difference between imprecision and uncertainty, consider the following two situations:
>
> 1. John has at least two children and I am sure about it.
>
> 2. John has three children but I am not sure about it."
>
> In case 1, the number of children is imprecise but certain. In case 2, the number of children is precise but uncertain. Both aspects can coexist but are distinct. Often the more imprecise you are, the most certain you are, and the more precise, the less certain. There seems to be some Information Maximality Principle that requires that the 'product' of precision and certainty cannot be beyond a certain critical level. Any increase in one is balanced by a decrease in the other."

Imprecision is a property of the content under consideration: either more than one or no realization is compatible with the available information [375].

One realization of imprecise information is **ambiguous** information. Ambiguous information is information which may have at least two different meanings. For example, a statement 'you are aggressive' is ambiguous because aggressive may mean 'belligerent' or 'energetic'. For example, homonyms are typical carriers of ambiguity.

Ambiguous information may be approximate, e.g. 'the temperature of water in the glass is between 40°C and 50°C' is approximate if the temperature is 47°C. Ambiguous information like 'the temperature is close to 60°C' is **vague**. Such vague information is **fuzzy**, because in this case the temperature is not sharply bounded. Both 59°C and 63°C corresponds to this, but the first corresponds stronger. Correspondence of a temperature value to 'the 'temperature is close to 60°C' smoothly decreases as this value moves away from 60°C. In general, vague information is information which is not well-defined, it is carried by a 'loose concept'. The worst case of vague information is unclear information. Ambiguous information may also be **incomplete**: "the vacation will be in a summer month" because a summer month may be either June, or July or August.

Uncertain information is commonly defined as information which is not certain. P. Smets defines uncertainty as a property that results from a lack of information about the world for deciding if the statement is true or false [375]. The question on whether uncertainty is objective or subjective property is still rhetoric.

Objective uncertainty may be probabilistic or non-probabilistic. Probabilistic uncertainty is uncertainty related to randomness – probability of an event is related to its tendency to occur. Main kinds of non-probabilistic uncertainty are possibilistic uncertainty and complete ignorance. Possibilistic uncertainty reflects an event's 'ability' to occur. To be probable, an event has to be possible. At the same time, very possible events may be a little probable. The dual concept of possibility is necessity. Necessity of an event is impossibility of the contrary event to occur. Complete ignorance is related to situations when no information on a variable of interest (e.g. probability) is available. For case of probability complete ignorance may be described by a set of all probability distributions.

Objective uncertainty relates to evidence on a likelihood of phenomena. Subjective uncertainty relates to DM's opinion on a likelihood of phenomena. More specifically, subjective uncertainty is a DM's belief on occurrence of an event. Classification of subjective uncertainty is very wide and its primitive forms are, analogously to that of objective uncertainty, subjective probability, subjective possibility and subjective necessity. The structures of these forms of subjective uncertainty are the same as those of objective probability, possibility and necessity. However, the sources of them differ: subjective uncertainty is a DM's opinion, whereas objective uncertainty is pure evidence. For example, mathematical structure of subjective probability is a probability measure but the values of this measure are assigned on the base of a DM's opinion under lack of evidence. Analogously, subjective possibility and necessity are a DM's opinions on possibility and necessity of an event.

Unreliable information is information to which an individual does not trust or trusts weakly due to the source of this information. As a result, an individual does not rely on this information. For example, you may not trust to the meteorological forecast if it is done by using old technology and equipment.

Imperfect information is impossible to be completely caught in terms of understanding what this concept means (e.g. uncertainty concept), and thus, cannot be perfectly classified. Any classification may have contradictions, flows and changes of concepts.

In real-world, imperfect information is commonly present in all components of the decision making problem. States of nature reflects possible future conditions which are commonly ill-known whereas the existing theories are based on perfect construction – on partition of the future objective conditions into mutually exclusive and exhaustive states. Possible realizations of future are not completely known. The future may result in a situation which was not thought and unforeseen contingencies commonly take place [164]. From the other side, those states of nature which are supposed as possible, are themselves vaguely defined and it is not always realistic to strictly differentiate among them. The outcomes and probabilities are also not well known, especially taking into account that they are related to ill-known states of nature. However, the existing theories do not pay significant attention to these issues. The most of the theories, including the famous and advanced theories, take into account only imperfect information related to probabilities. Moreover, this is handled by coarse description of ambiguity – either by exact constraints on probabilities (a set of priors) or by using subtle techniques like probabilistic constraints or specific non-linear functions. These are, however, approaches rather for frameworks of the designed experiments but not for real-world decision problems when information is not sufficiently good to apply such techniques. In Table 4.1 below we tried to classify decision situations on the base of different types of decision relevant information that one can be faced with and the utility models that can be applied.

Table 4.1. Classification of decision-relevant information

		Probabilities			
Outcomes	Utilities	Precise	Complete Ignorance	Ambiguous	Imperfect
Precise	Precise	Situation 1	Situation 2	Situation 3	Situation 4
	Fuzzy	Situation 5	Situation 6	Situation 7	Situation 8
Complete Ignorance	Precise	Situation 9	Situation 10	Situation 11	Situation 12
	Fuzzy	Situation 13	Situation 14	Situation 15	Situation 16
Ambiguous	Precise	Situation 17	Situation 18	Situation 19	Situation 20
	Fuzzy	Situation 21	Situation 22	Situation 23	Situation 24
Imperfect	Precise	Situation 25	Situation 26	Situation 27	Situation 28
	Fuzzy	Situation 29	Situation 30	Situation 31	Situation 32

In this table, we identify three important coordinates (dimensions). The first one concerns information available for probabilities, the second captures information about outcomes, while the third looks at the nature of utilities and their description. The first two dimensions include precise information (risk), complete ignorance (absence of information), ambiguous information, and imperfect information. Two main types of utilities are considered, namely precise and fuzzy. Decision-relevant information setups are represented at the crossing of these coordinates; those are cells containing Situations from 1 to 32. They capture combinations of various types of probabilities, outcomes, and utilities.

The most developed scenarios are those positioned in entries from 1 to 4 (precise utility models). A limited attention is paid to situations 5-8 with fuzzy utilities [37,82,169,277]. For situations 9-12 with complete ignorance with respect to outcomes and with precise utilities a few works on interactive obtaining of information were suggested. For situations 13-16, to our knowledge, no works were suggested. Few studies are devoted to the situations with ambiguous outcomes (situations 17-20) [203,206,208] and precise utilities and no works to ambiguous outcomes with fuzzy utilities are available (situations 21-24). For situations 25-32 very few studies were reported including the existing fuzzy utility models [37,82,169,277]. The case with imperfect probabilities, imperfect outcomes, and fuzzy utilities (situation 32) generalizes all the other situations. An adequate utility model for this situation is suggested in [34] and is expressed in Chapter 6 of the present book.

4.2 Imprecise Probabilities

The probability theory has a large spectrum of successful applications. However, the use of a single probability measure for quantification of uncertainty has severe limitations main of which are the following [34]: 1) precise probability is unable to describe complete ignorance (total lack of information); 2) one can determine probabilities of some subsets of a set of possible outcomes but cannot always determine probabilities for all the subsets; 3) one can determine probabilities of all the subsets of a set of possible outcomes but it will require laborious computations.

Indeed, classical probability imposes too strong assumptions that significantly limit its use even in simple real-world or laboratory problems. Famous Ellsberg experiments and Schmeidler's coin example are good illustrative cases when available information appears insufficient to determine actual probabilities. Good discussion of real-world tasks which are incapable to be handled within probabilistic framework is given in [170]. In real problems, quality of decision-relevant information does not require the use of a single probability measure. As a result, probabilities cannot be precisely determined and are imprecise. For such cases, they use constraints on a probability of an event H in form of lower and upper probabilities denoted $\underline{P}(H)$ and $\overline{P}(H)$ respectively. That is, a probability $P(H)$ of an event H is not known precisely but supposed to be somewhere between $\underline{P}(H)$ and $\overline{P}(H)$: $P(H) \in [\underline{P}(H), \overline{P}(H)]$ where $0 \leq \underline{P}(H) \leq \overline{P}(H) \leq 1$; in more general formulation, constraints in form of lower and upper expectations for a random variable are used. In special case when $\underline{P}(H) = \overline{P}(H)$ a framework of lower and upper probabilities degenerates to a single probability $P(H)$. Complete lack of knowledge about likelihood of H is modeled by $\underline{P}(H) = 0$ and $\overline{P}(H) = 1$. This means that when likelihood of an event is absolutely unknown, they suppose that probability of this event may take any value from [0,1] (from impossibility to occur up to certain occurrence).

Constraints on probabilities imply existence of a set of probability distributions, that is, multiple priors, which are an alternative approach to handle incomplete information on probabilities. Under the certain consistency requirements the use of multiple priors is equivalent to the use of lower and upper probabilities. Approaches in which imprecise probabilities are handled in form of intervals $[\underline{p}, \overline{p}]$ are unified under the name *interval probabilities*.

An alternative way to handle incomplete information on probabilities is the use of non-additive probabilities, typical cases of which are lower probabilities and upper probabilities and their convex combinations. However, multiple priors are more general and intuitive approach to handle incomplete probability information than non-additive probabilities.

The most fundamental axiomatization of imprecise probabilities was suggested by Peter Walley who suggested the term *imprecise probabilities* [399]. The behavioral interpretation of Walley's axiomatization is based on buying and selling prices for gambles. Walley's axiomatization is more general than Kolmogorov's axiomatization of the standard probability theory. The central concept in Walley's theory is the lower prevision concept which generalizes standard (additive) probability, lower and upper probabilities and non-additive measures. However, in terms of generality, the concept of lower prevision is inferior to multiple priors. Another disadvantage of lower prevision theory is its high complexity that limits its practical use.

Alternative axiomatizations of imprecise probabilities were suggested by Kuznetsov [249] and Weichselberger [410] for the framework of interval probabilities. Weichselberger generalizes Kolmogorov's axioms to the case of interval probabilities but, as compared to Walley, does not suggest a behavioral interpretation. However, his theory is more tractable in practical sense.

What is the main common disadvantage of the existing imprecise probability theories? This disadvantage is missing the intrinsic feature of probability-related information which was pointed out by L. Savage even before emergence of the existing imprecise probability theories. Savage wrote [360]:

"...there seem to be some probability relations about which we feel relatively 'sure' as compared with others.... The notion of 'sure' and 'unsure' introduced here is vague, and my complaint is precisely that neither the theory of personal probability as it is developed in this book, nor any other device known to me renders the notion less vague".

Indeed, in real-world situations we don't have sufficient information to be definitely sure or unsure in whether that or another value of probability is true. Very often, our sureness stays at some level and does not become complete being hampered by a lack of knowledge and information. That is, sureness is a matter of a strength, or in other words, of a degree. Therefore, 'sure' is a loose concept, a vague concept. In our opinion, the issue is that in most real-world decision-making problems, relevant information perceived by DMs involves possibilistic uncertainty. Fuzzy probabilities are the tools for resolving this issue to a large extent because they represent a degree of truth of a considered numeric probability.

Fuzzy probabilities are superior from the point of view of human reasoning and available information in real-world problems than interval probabilities which are rather the first departs from precise probabilities frameworks. Indeed, interval probabilities only show that probabilities are imprecise and no more. In real-world, the bounds of an interval for probability are subjectively 'estimated' but not calculated or actually known as they are in Ellsberg experiment. Subjective assignments of probability bounds will likely inconsistent with human choices in real-world problems as well as subjective probabilities do in Ellsberg experiment. Reflecting imperfect nature of real-world information, probabilities are naturally soft-constrained.

As opposed to second-order probabilities which are also used to differentiate probability values in terms of their relevance to available information, fuzzy probabilities are more relaxed constructs. Second-order probabilities are too exigent to available information and are more suitable for designed experiments.

Fuzzy probability is formally a fuzzy number defined over [0,1] scale to represent an imprecise linguistic evaluation of a probability value. Representing likelihoods of mutually exclusive and exhaustive events, fuzzy probabilities are tied together by their basic elements summing up to one. Fuzzy probabilities define a fuzzy set $\tilde{P}^{\rho}$ of probability distributions ρ which is an adequate representation of imprecise probabilistic information related to objective conditions especially when the latter are vague. As compared to the use of second-order probabilities, the use of possibility distribution over probability distributions [8,23,34] is appropriate and easier for describing DM's (or experts') confidence. This approach does not require from a DM to assign beliefs over priors directly. Possibility distribution can be constructed computationally from fuzzy probabilities assigned to states of nature [82,458]. This means that a DM or experts only need to assign linguistic evaluations of probabilities to states of nature as they usually do. For each linguistic evaluation a fuzzy probability can then be defined by construction of a membership function. After this possibility distribution can be obtained computationally [82,458] without involving a DM.

We can conclude that fuzzy probabilities [87,264,338,379,426] are a successful interpretation of imprecise probabilities which come from human expertise and perceptions being linguistically described. For example, in comparison to multiple priors consideration, for majority of cases, a DM has some linguistic additional information coming from his experience or even naturally present which reflects unequal levels of belief or possibility for different probability distributions. This means, that it is more adequate to consider sets of probability distributions as fuzzy sets which allow taking into account different degrees of belief or possibility for different probability distributions. Really, for many cases, some probability distributions are more relevant, some probability distributions are less relevant to the considered situation and also it is difficult to sharply differentiate probabilities that are relevant from those that are irrelevant. This type of consideration involves second-order uncertainty, namely, probability-possibility modeling of decision-relevant information.

4.3 Granular States of Nature

The existing utility theories are based on Savage's formulation of states of nature as "*a space of* ***mutually exclusive*** *and* ***exhaustive*** *states*" [360]. This is a perfect consideration of environment structure. However, in real-world problems it is naïve to suppose that we can so perfectly partition future into mutually exclusive objective conditions and predict all possible objective conditions. Future is hidden from our eyes and only some indistinct, approximate trends can be seen. From the other side, unforeseen contingencies are commonly met which makes impossible to determine exhaustive states and also rules out sharp differentiation to exclusive objective conditions. This requires tolerance in describing each objective condition to allow for mistakes, misperceptions, flaws, that are due to imperfect nature of information about future. From the other side, tolerance may also allow for dynamic aspects due to which a state of nature may deviate from its initial condition.

In order to see difficulties with determination of states of nature let us consider a problem of differentiating future economic conditions into states of economy. Commonly, states of economy can be considered as "strong growth", "moderate growth", "stable economy", "recession". These are not 'single-valued' and cannot be considered as 'mutually exclusive' (as it is defined in Savage's formulation of state space): for example, moderate growth and stable economy don't have sharp boundaries and as a result, may not be "exclusive" – they may overlap. The same concerns 'moderate growth' and 'strong growth' states. For instance, when analyzing the values of the certain indicators that determine a state of economy it is not always possible to definitely label the latter as a 'moderate growth' or 'strong growth'. Observing some actual situation an expert may conclude that it is "somewhere between" 'strong growth' and 'moderate growth', but "closer" to the latter. This means that to a larger extent the actual situation concerns the "moderate growth" and to a smaller extent to the "strong growth". It is not adequate to sharply differentiate the values related to "moderate growth" from those related to the "strong growth". In other words, various conditions labeled as "strong growth" with various extents concerns it, but not equally. How to take into account the inherent vagueness of states of nature and the fact that they are intrinsically not exclusive but overlapping? Savage's definition is an idealized view on formalization of objective conditions for such cases. Without doubt, in real-life decision making it is often impossible to construct such an ideal formalization, due to uncertainty of relevant information. In general, a DM cannot exhaustively determine each objective condition that may be faced and cannot precisely differentiate them. Each state of nature is, essentially, some area under consideration which collects in some sense similar objective conditions one can face, that is some set of "elementary" states or quantities [164]. Unfortunately, in the existing decision making theories a small attention is paid to the essence and structure of states of nature, consideration of them is very abstract (formal) and is unclear from human perception point of view.

Formally speaking, a state of nature should be considered as a granule - not some single point or some object with abstract content. This will result to some kind of information granulation of objective conditions. Construction of states of nature on the base of similarity, proximity etc of objective conditions may be adequately modeled by using fuzzy sets and fuzzy information granulation concepts [241,444]. This will help to model vague and overlapping states of nature. For example, in the considered problem, economic conditions may be partitioned into overlapping fuzzy sets defined over some relative scale representing levels of economic welfare. Such formalization will be more realistic for vagueness, ambiguity, partial truth, impreciseness and other imperfectness of future-related information.

4.4 Imprecise Outcomes

In real-life decision making DM almost always cannot precisely determine future possible outcomes and have to use imprecise quantities like, for example, *high profit*, *medium cost* etc. Such quantities can be adequately represented by ranges of numerical values with possibility distribution among them. From the other side, very often outcomes and utilities are considered in monetary sense, whereas a significantly smaller attention is paid to other types of outcomes and utilities. Indeed, utilities are usually subjectively assigned and, as a result, are heuristic evaluations. In extensive experiments conducted by Kahneman and Tversky, which uncovered very important aspects of human behavior, only monetary outcomes are used. Without doubt, monetary consideration is very important, but it is worth to investigate also other types of outcomes which are naturally present in real-life decision activity. In this situation it is not suitable to use precise quantities because subjective evaluations are conditioned also by non-monetary issues such as health, time, reputation, quality etc. The latter are usually described by linguistic evaluations.

In order to illustrate impreciseness of outcomes in real-world problems, let us consider a case of an evaluation of a return from investing into bonds of an enterprise which will produce new products the next year. Outcomes (returns) of investment will depend on future possible economic conditions. Let us suppose these conditions of economy be partitioned into states of nature labeled as "strong growth", "moderate growth", "stable economy", and "recession" which we considered above. It is impossible to precisely know values of outcomes of the investment under these states of nature. For example, the outcome of the investment obtained under "strong growth" may be evaluated "high" (off course with underlying range of numerical values). The vagueness of outcomes evaluations are resulted from uncertainty about future: impreciseness of a demand for the products produced by the enterprise in the next year, future unforeseen contingencies, vagueness of future economic conditions, political processes etc. Indeed, the return is tightly connected to the demand the next year which cannot be precisely known in advance. The investor does not really know what will take place the next year, but still approximately evaluate possible gains and losses by means of linguistic terms. In other words, the investor is not completely sure in some precise value of the outcome – the future is too uncertain for precise estimation to be reasonably used. The investor sureness is 'distributed' among various possible values of the perceived outcome. One way to model is the use of a probabilistic outcome, i.e. to use probability distribution (if a discrete set of numerical outcomes is considered) or probability density function (for continuous set) over possible basic outcomes [170] to encode the related objective probabilities or subjective probabilities. However, this approach has serious disadvantages. Using objective probabilities requires good representative data which don't exist as a demand for a new product is considered. Even for the case of a common product, a good statistics does not exist because demands for various years take place in various environmental conditions. The use of subjective probabilities is also not suitable as they commonly fail to describe human behavior and perception under ambiguity of information.

The use of probabilistic outcomes does not also match human perceptions which are expressed in form of linguistic evaluations of outcomes. Humans don't think within the probabilistic framework as this is too strong for computational abilities of a human brain; thus, it is needed to use a more flexible formalization. Fuzzy set theory provides more adequate representation of linguistic evaluations. By using this theory, a linguistic evaluation of an outcome may be formalized by a membership function (a fuzzy set) representing a soft constraint on possible basic outcomes. In contrast to probabilistic constraint, a membership function is not based on strong assumptions and does not require good data. A membership function is directly assigned by a DM to reflect his/her experience, perception, envision etc. which cannot be described by classical mathematics but may act well under imperfect information. Fuzzy sets theory helps to describe future results as imprecise and overlapping, especially under imprecise essence of states of nature. Also, a membership function may reflect various basic outcomes' possibilities, which are much easier to determine than probabilities.

From the other side, the use of fuzzy sets allows to adequately describe non-monetary outcomes like health, reputation, quality which are often difficult to be defined in terms of precise quantities.

Chapter 5

Uncertainty Measures in Decision Making

5.1 Objective and Subjective Probabilities

Uncertainty is intrinsic to decision making environment. No matter whether we deal with numerical or non-numerical events, we are not completely sure in their occurrence. Numerical events are commonly regarded as values of a random variable. Non-numerical events can be encoded by, for example, natural numbers and then treated as values of a random variable. To formally take into account uncertainty in decision analysis, we need to use some mathematical constructs which will measure quantitatively an extent to what that or another event is likely to occur. Such constructs are called uncertainty measures. The most famous measure is the probability measure. Probability measure assigns its values to events to reflect degrees to which events are likely to occur. These values are called probabilities. Probability is a real number from [0,1], and the more likely an event to occur the higher is its probability. Probability equal to 0 implies that it is impossible for an event to occur or we are completely sure that it cannot occur, and probability equal to 1 means that an event will necessary occur or we are completely sure in its occurrence. The axiomatization of the standard probability measure was suggested by Kolmogorov [248]. Prior to proceeding to axiomatization of Kolmogorov, let us introduce the necessary concepts. The first concept is the space of elementary events. Elementary event, also called an atomic event, is the minimal event that may occur, that is, an event that cannot be divided into smaller events. Denote $\mathcal{S}$ the space of elementary events and denote $S \in \mathcal{S}$ an elementary event. A subset

$H \subseteq \mathcal{S}$ of the space of elementary events $S \in \mathcal{S}$ is called an event. An event H occurs if any $\mathcal{S} \in H$ occurs. The next concept is a σ-algebra of subsets denoted $\mathcal{F}$:

Definition 5.1. σ **-algebra** [248]. A set $\mathcal{F}$, elements of which are subsets of $\mathcal{S}$ (not necessarily all) is called σ-algebra if the following hold:

(1) $\mathcal{S} \in \mathcal{F}$

(2) if $H \in \mathcal{F}$ then $H^c \in \mathcal{F}$

(3) if $H_1, H_2, \ldots \in \mathcal{F}$ then $H_1 \cup H_2 \cup \ldots \in \mathcal{F}$

Now let us proceed to the Kolmogorov's axiomatization of a probability measurc.

Definition 5.2. Probability measure [248]. Let $\mathcal{S}$ be a space of elementary events and $\mathcal{F}$ is a σ-algebra of its subsets. The probability measure is a function $P: \mathcal{F} \to [0,1]$ satisfying:

(1) $P(H) \geq 0$ for any $H \in \mathcal{F}$.

(2) For any sequence $H_1, H_2, \ldots \in \mathcal{F}$ with $H_i \cap H_j \neq \varnothing$:

$$P(\bigcup_{i=1}^{\infty} H_i) = \sum_{i=1}^{\infty} P(H_i)$$

(3) $P(\mathcal{S}) = 1$

The first condition is referred to as non-negativity. The second condition is referred to as additivity condition. The third condition implies that the event $\mathcal{S}$ will necessary occur. Conditions (1)-(3) are called probability axioms. From (1)-(3) it follows $P(\varnothing) = 0$ which means that it is impossible that no elementary event $S \in \mathcal{S}$ will occur. Let us mention that probability of a union $H \cup G$ of two arbitrary events is $P(H \cup G) = P(H) + P(G) - P(H \cap G)$. For the case $H \cap G = \varnothing$ one has $P(H \cup G) = P(H) + P(G)$.

Definition 5.2 provides mathematical structure of a probability measure. Consider now natural interpretations of a probability measure. There exist two main types of probabilities: objective probabilities and subjective probabilities. Objective probabilities, also called empirical probabilities, are quantities which are calculated on the base of real evidence: experimentations, observations, logical conclusions. They also can be obtained by using statistical formulas. Objective probabilities are of two types: experimental probabilities and logical probabilities. Experimental probability of an event is a frequency of its occurrence. For example, a probability that a color of a car taken at random in a city is white is equal to the number of white cars divided by the whole number of the cars in the city. Logical probability is based on a reasonable conclusion on a likelihood of an event. For instance, if a box contains 70 white and 30 black balls, a probability that a ball drawn at random is white is 70/100=0.7.

The use of objective probabilities requires very restrictive assumptions. For experimental probabilities the main assumptions are as follows:

(1) Experimentation (or observations) must take place under the same conditions and it must be assumed that the future events will also take place under these conditions. Alternatively, there need to be present clear dynamics of conditions in future;

(2) Observations of the past behavior must include representative data (e.g., observations must be sufficiently large).

As to logical probabilities, their use must be based on quite reasonnable conclusions. For example, if to consider the box with balls mentioned above, an assumption must be made that the balls are well mixed inside the box (not a layer of white balls is placed under the layer of black balls) to calculate probability of a white ball drawn as 70/100=0.7.

From the other side, as Kahneman, Tversky and others showed [222] that even if objective probabilities are known, beliefs of a DM don't coincide with them. As being perceived by humans, objective probabilities are affected by some kind of distortion – they are transformed into so-called decision weights and mostly small probabilities are overweighted, whereas high probabilities are underweighted. Also, the overweighting and underweighting of probabilities are different for positive and negative outcomes [387].

Subjective probability is a degree of belief of an individual in a likelihood of an event. Formally, subjective probabilities are values of a probability measure. From interpretation point of view, subjective probability reflects an individual's experience, perceptions and is not based on countable and, sometimes, detailed facts like objective probability. Subjective probabilities are more appropriate and 'smart' approach for measuring likelihood of events in real-life problems because in such problems the imperfect relevant information conflicts with the very strong assumptions underlying the use of objective probabilities. Real-life relevant information is better handled by experience and knowledge that motivates the use of a subjective basis.

Subjective probability has a series of disadvantages. One of the main disadvantages is that different people would assign different subjective probabilities. It is difficult to reason uniquely accurate subjective probabilities among those assigned by different people. Indeed, given a lack of information, people have to guess subjective probabilities as they suppose. As it is mentioned in [295], using subjective probabilities is a "symptom of the problem, not a solution". Subjective probability is based not only on experience but also on feelings, emotions, psychological and other factors which can distort its accuracy. The other main disadvantage is that subjective probability, due to its preciseness and additivity, fails to describe human behavior under ambiguity.

5.2 Non-Additive Measures

The use of the additive probability measure is unsuitable to model human behavior conditioned by uncertainty of the real world, psychological, mental and other factors. In presence of uncertainty, when true probabilities are not exactly known, people often tend to consider each alternative in terms of the worst case within the uncertainty and don't rely on good cases. In other words, most of people prefer those decisions for which more information is available. This behavior is referred to as ambiguity aversion – people don't like ambiguity and wish certainty. Even when true probabilities are known, most people exhibit non-linear attitude to probabilities – change of likelihood of an event from impossibility to some chance or from a very good chance to certainty are treated much more strongly than the same change somewhere in the range of medium probabilities. Therefore, attitude to values of probabilities is qualitative.

Due to its additivity property, the classical (standard) probability measure cannot reflect the above mentioned evidence. Axiomatizations of such evidence required to highly weaken assumptions on a DM's belief which was considered as the probability measure. The resulted axiomatizations are based either on non-uniqueness of probability measure or on non-additivity of a measure of uncertainty reflecting humans' beliefs. The first axiomatization of choices based on a non-additive measure was suggested by Schmeidler [362]. This is a significant generalization of additive measures-based decisions because the uncovered non-additive measure inherited only normalization and monotonicity properties from the standard probability measure.

Nowadays non-additive measures compose a rather wide class of measures of uncertainty. Below we list non-additive measures used in decision making under ambiguity. For these measures a unifying term *non-additive probability* is used.

We will express the non-additive probabilities in the framework of decision making under ambiguity. Let $\mathcal{S}$ be a non-empty set of states of nature and $\mathcal{F}$ be a family of subsets of $\mathcal{S}$. We will consider w.l.o.g. $\mathcal{F}=2^{\mathcal{S}}$.

The definition of a non-additive probability is as follows [362].

Definition 5.3. Non-additive probability[362]. A set function $\eta:\mathcal{F}\to[0,1]$ is referred to as a non-additive probability if it satisfies the following:

(1) $\eta(\varnothing)=0$;

(2) $\forall H,G\in\mathcal{F}$, $H\subset G$ implies $\eta(H)\le\eta(G)$;

(3) $\eta(\mathcal{S})=1$.

The non-additive probability is also referred to as *Choquet capacity*. Condition (2) is called monotonicity with respect to set inclusion and conditions (1) and (3) are called normalization conditions. Thus, a non-additive probability does not have to satisfy $\eta(H\cup G)=\eta(H)+\eta(G)$. A non-additive probability is called *super-additive* if $\eta(H\cup G)\ge\eta(H)+\eta(G)$ and is called *sub-additive* if $\eta(H\cup G)\le\eta(H)+\eta(G)$, provided $H\cap G=\varnothing$.

There exist various kinds of non-additive probability many of which are constructed on the base of a set C of probability measures P over

$\mathcal{S}$. The one of the well known non-additive probabilities is the *lower envelope* $\eta_* : \mathcal{F} \to [0,1]$ which is defined as follows:

$$\eta_*(H) = \min_{P \in \mathcal{C}} P(H). \tag{5.1}$$

The dual concept of the lower envelope is the *upper envelope* $\eta^* : \mathcal{F} \to [0,1]$ which is defined by replacing $\min$ operator in (5.1) by $\max$ operator. Lower and upper envelopes are respectively minimal and maximal probabilities of an event $H \subset \mathcal{S}$. Therefore, $\eta_*(H) \le P(H) \le \eta^*(H), \quad \forall H \subset \mathcal{S}, P \in \mathcal{C}$. A lower envelope is a super-additive measure, whereas an upper envelope is a sub-additive measure. A non-additive probability can also be defined as a convex combination of $\eta_*(H)$ and $\eta^*(H)$: $\eta(H) = \alpha\eta_*(H) + (1-\alpha)\eta^*(H)$, $\alpha \in [0,1]$. The parameter α is referred to as a degree of ambiguity aversion. Indeed, α is an extent to which belief $\eta(H)$ is based on the smallest possible probability of an event H; $1-\alpha$ is referred to as a degree of ambiguity seeking.

The generalizations of lower and upper envelopes are *lower* and *upper probabilities* which are super-additive and sub-additive probabilities respectively. Lower and upper probabilities, denoted $\underline{\eta}$ and $\overline{\eta}$ respectively, satisfy $\underline{\eta}(H) = 1 - \overline{\eta}(H^c) \ \forall H \in \mathcal{S}$, where $H^c = \mathcal{S} \setminus H$.

The special case of lower envelopes and, therefore, of lower probabilities are *2-monotone Choquet capacities*, also referred to as *convex capacities*. A non-additive probability is called 2-monotone Choquet capacity if it satisfies $\eta(H \cup G) \ge \eta(H) + \eta(G) - \eta(H \cap G), \forall H, G \subset \mathcal{S}$.

A generalization of *2-monotone* capacity is an *n-monotone* capacity. A capacity is an *n-monotone*, if for any sequence $H_1, ..., H_n$ of subsets of $\mathcal{S}$ the following holds:

$$\eta(H_i \cup ... \cup H_n) \ge \sum_{\substack{I \subset \{1,...,n\} \\ I \ne \varnothing}} (-1)^{|I|-1} \eta\left(\bigcap_{i \in I} H_i\right).$$

A capacity which is *n-monotone* for all n is called *infinite monotone capacity* or a *belief function*.

The belief function theory, also known as Dempster-Shafer theory, or mathematical theory of evidence, or theory of random sets, was suggested by Dempster in [128], and developed by Shafer in [369]. Belief functions are aimed to be used for describing subjective degrees of belief to an event, phenomena, or object of interest. We will not explain this theory but just mention that it was not directly related to decision making. As it was shown in [189,190], axiomatization of this theory is a generalization of the Kolmogorov's axioms of the standard probability theory. Due to this fact, a value of a belief function denoted $Bel()$ for an event H can be considered as a lower probability, that is, as a lower bound on a probability of an event H. An upper probability in the belief function theory is termed as a *plausibility function* and is denoted Pl. So, in the belief functions theory probability $P(H)$ of an event H is evaluated as $Bel(H) \le P(H) \le Pl(H)$.

The motivation of using non-additive probabilities in decision making problems is the fact that information on probabilities is imperfect, which can be incomplete, imprecise, distorted by psychological factors etc. A non-additive measure can be determined from imprecise objective or subjective probabilities of states of nature. Impreciseness of objective probabilities can be conditioned by the lack of information ruling out determination of actual exact probabilities (as in Ellsberg experiments). Impreciseness of subjective probabilities can be conditioned by natural impreciseness of human beliefs. Let us consider the case when imprecise information is represented in form of interval probabilities. Given a set $\mathcal{S} = \{S_1, S_2, ..., S_n\}$, interval probabilities are defined as follows [183].

Definition 5.4. Interval probability[183]. The intervals $P(S_i) = [\underline{p}_i, \overline{p}_i]$ $i = 1,...,n$ are called the interval probabilities of $\mathcal{S}$ if for any $p_i \in [\underline{p}_i, \overline{p}_i]$ there exist $p_1 \in [\underline{p}_1, \overline{p}_1], \ldots, p_{i-1} \in [\underline{p}_{i-1}, \overline{p}_{i-1}]$, $p_{i+1} \in [\underline{p}_{i+1}, \overline{p}_{i+1}]$, ..., $p_n \in [\underline{p}_n, \overline{p}_n]$ such that

$$\sum_{i=1}^{n} p_i = 1 .$$

In this definition p_i denotes a basic probability, i.e. a numeric probability from an interval $P(S_i) = [\underline{p}_i, \overline{p}_i]$. From Definition 5.4 it follows, in particular, that interval probabilities cannot be directly assigned as numerical probabilities. The issue is that in the case of interval probabilities, the requirement to numerical probabilities to sum up to one must be satisfied throughout all the probability ranges. Sometimes, interval probabilities $P(S_i) = P_i$ can be directly assigned consistently to $n-1$ states of nature $S_1, S_2, ..., S_{j-1}, \ S_{j+1}, ..., S_n$, and on the base of these probabilities, an interval probability $P(S_j) = P_j$ for the rest one state of nature S_j will be calculated. For example, consider a set of states of nature with three states $S = \{S_1, S_2, S_3\}$. Let interval probabilities for S_2 and S_3 be assigned as follows:

$$P_2 = [0.2, 0.3], \ P_3 = [0.5, 0.6].$$

Then, according to the conditions in Definition 5.4, P_1 will be determined as follows:

$$P_1 = [1 - 0.3 - 0.6, 1 - 0.2 - 0.5] = [0.1, 0.3].$$

Given interval probabilities of states of nature $P_i = [\underline{p}_i, \overline{p}_i]$ a value $\eta_*(H)$ of a lower probability for an event H can be determined as follows:

$$\eta_*(H) = \min \sum_{S_i \in H} p_i$$

$$s.t.$$

$$\sum_{i=1}^{n} p_i = 1 \tag{5.2}$$

$$p_i \leq \overline{p}_i$$

$$p_i \geq \underline{p}_i$$

A value $\eta^*(H)$ of an upper probability for an event H can be determined by replacing *min* operator by *max* operator in the above mentioned problem. Consider an example. Given interval probabilities $P_1 = [0.1, 0.3]$, $P_2 = [0.2, 0.3]$, $P_3 = [0.5, 0.6]$, the values of the lower and upper probabilities η_* and η^* for $H = \{S_1, S_3\}$, obtained as solutions of the problem (5.2), are $\eta_*(H) = 0.7$ and $\eta^*(H) = 0.8$.

The above mentioned measures of uncertainty can be listed in terms of the increasing generality between the probability measure and the Choquet capacity as follows:

probability measure $\Rightarrow$ belief function $\Rightarrow$ convex capacity $\Rightarrow$ lower envelope $\Rightarrow$ lower probability $\Rightarrow$ Choquet capacity

Based on this, we can conclude that probability measure models human beliefs as purely additive likelihoods, whereas Choquet capacity models the largest spectrum of non-additivity of human beliefs which may be conditioned by ambiguity attitudes, psychological, mental and other influential factors.

An important extension of capacities was suggested by Grabisch and Labreuche for multicriteria decisions [250]. They provide a motivating example showing an intuitive choice that cannot be described by means of a Choquet capacity. The example concerns evaluating overall skills of students in a high school on the base of their grades in mathematics (M), physics (P), and literature (L). The director as a DM considers that mathematics and physics are more important than literature. At the same time, the director would disagree with sufficient flaw in literature no matter what skills are exhibited in M and P. Yet another natural issue underlying the director's reasoning is that M and P are of a redundancy as mathematics is a language of physics. Therefore, the reasoning of the director is described by the following rules of choice [250]:

Rule 1: For a student good in M, L is more important than P

Rule 2: For a student bad in M, P is more important than L

Consider the following students SA, SB, SC, SD with the marks in M, L, P varying in-between 0 and 20 (Table 5.1):

Table 5.1 Students' grades

S	M	P	L
SA	15	18	6
SB	15	16	8
SC	6	13	2
SD	6	11	4

Rules 1 and 2 can be used for easy comparison of the students:

According to Rule 1, $\mathrm{SB} \succ \mathrm{SA}$

According to Rule 2, $\mathrm{SC} \succ \mathrm{SD}$

These common preferences cannot be described neither by Choquet integral not by CPT. As it is shown in [250], the use of Choquet integral requires the capacity η to satisfy contradictory conditions:

$$\mathrm{SC} \succ \mathrm{SD} \text{ implies } \eta(\{\mathrm{M,P}\})+\eta(\{\mathrm{P}\})>1$$

$$\mathrm{SB} \succ \mathrm{SA} \text{ implies } \eta(\{\mathrm{M,P}\})+\eta(\{\mathrm{P}\})<1$$

To use CPT it is needed to transform the scale [0,20] using a neutral level 10 to the scale [-10,10]. Then, the use of the CPT with the capacities η_1 (for positive part) and η_2 (for negative part) also results in contradiction:

$$\mathrm{SB} \succ \mathrm{SA} \text{ implies } \eta_1(\{\mathrm{P}\})>\eta_2(\{\mathrm{L}\})$$

$$\mathrm{SC} \succ \mathrm{SD} \text{ implies } \eta_1(\{\mathrm{P}\})<\eta_2(\{\mathrm{L}\})$$

The reason that both Choquet integral and CPT fail to represent the considered preferences is that these models are unable to measure comparative importance of two criteria on the base of whether another criterion has positive or negative value. In the considered example, the comparison of importance of P and L depends on the value of M.

In [250], it is suggested a decision model based on a new kind of measure called bi-capacity. Bi-capacity is used to model interaction between 'good' and 'bad' performances with respect to criteria. As compared to capacity, bi-capacity is a two-place set function. The values the bi-capacity takes are from [-1,1]. More formally, the bi-capacity is defined as a set function

$$\eta : W \to [-1,1], \textit{where} \quad W=\{(H,G): H,G \subset I, H \cap G=\varnothing\}$$

satisfying

$$H \subset H' \Rightarrow \eta(H,G) \le \eta(H',G),\ G \subset G' \Rightarrow \eta(H,G') \le \eta(H,G)$$

and

$$\eta(I,\varnothing)=1,\ \eta(\varnothing,I)=-1,\ \eta(\varnothing,\varnothing)=0,$$

I is the set of indexes of criteria. The attributes in H are satisfied attributes whereas the attributes in G are dissatisfied ones. The integral with respect to bi-capacity as a representation of an overall utility of an alternative $f: I \to \mathcal{R}$ is defined as follows:

$$U(f) = \sum_{l=1}^{n} (u(f_{(l)}) - u(f_{(l+1)}))\eta(\{(1),...,(l)\} \cap I^{+}, \{(1),...,(l)\} \cap I^{-}), \quad (5.3)$$

provided $u(f_{(l)}) \geq u(f_{(l+1)})$ and $u(f_{(n+1)}) = 0$ by convention; $I^{+} = \{i \in I : u(f_i) \geq 0\}, I^{-} = I \setminus I^{+}$ where $u(f_{(l)})$ is a utility of a value of *(l)*-th criterion for f, $\eta(\cdot,\cdot)$ is a bi-capacity.

In the example above, the choice $\text{SB} \succ \text{SA}$ and $\text{SC} \succ \text{SD}$ on the base rules 1 and 2 is represented by the following inequalities in terms of η:

$$\eta(\{\text{M,P}\},\varnothing) - \eta(\{\text{M,P}\},\{\text{L}\}) > \eta(\{\text{P}\},\varnothing),$$
$$-\eta(\varnothing,\{\text{L}\}) < \eta(\{\text{P}\},\{\text{M,L}\}) - \eta(\varnothing,\{\text{M,L}\})$$

These conditions do not contradict the properties of bi-capacity $\eta(\cdot,\cdot)$. So, bi-capacity based aggregation (5.3) is able to compare P and L depending on performance in M, which cannot be done nor by Choquet integral neither by CPT.

In special case, when η is equal to the difference of two capacities η_1 and η_2 as $\eta(H,G) = \eta_1(H) - \eta_2(G)$, (5.3) reduces to the CPT model. In general case, as compared to CPT, (5.3) is not an additive representation of separately aggregated satisfied and dissatisfied criteria that provides more smart way for decision making.

The disadvantage of a bi-capacity relates to difficulties of its determination, in particular, to computational complexity. In details the issues are discussed in [250].

The bi-capacity-based aggregation which was axiomatized for multicriteria decision making [250] can also be applied for decisions under uncertainty due to formal parallelism between these two problems [302]. Indeed, states of nature are criteria on base of which alternatives are evaluated.

The non-additive measures provide a considerable success in modeling of decision making. However, the non-additive measures only reflect the fact that human choices are non-additive and monotone, which may be due to attitudes to uncertainty, distortion of probabilities etc, but nothing more. However, in real-world it is impossible to accurately determine precisely the 'shape' of a non-additive measure due to imperfect relevant information. Indeed, real-world probabilities of subsets and subsets themselves, outcomes, interaction of criteria, etc are imprecisely and vaguely defined. From the other side, attitudes to uncertainty, extent of probabilities distortion and other behavioral issues violating additivity are also imperfectly known. These aspects rule out exact determination of a uniquely accurate non-additive measure.

5.3 Fuzzy Measures and Fuzzy-Valued Fuzzy Measures

In the previous section we considered non-additive measures which are used in the existing decision theories to model non-additivity of DM's behavior. Main shortcoming of using non-additive measures is the difficulty of the underlying interpretation. One approach to overcome this difficulty is to use a lower envelope of a set of priors as a non-additive probability and then to use it in CEU model. However, in real-world problems determination of the set of priors itself meets difficulty of imposing precise constraint determining what prior should be included and what should not be included into this set. In other words, due to lack of information, it is impossible to sharply constraint a range for a probability of a state of nature, that is, to assign accurate interval probability. From the other side, if the set of priors is defined, why to construct lower envelope and use it in the CEU? It is computationally simpler to use the equivalent model – MMEU. In this Section, we start with a class of non-additive measures called *fuzzy measures*. Fuzzy measures have their own interpretations that do not require using a set of priors to define them and makes construction of these measures computationally simple. Finally, we will consider an effective extension of non-additive measures called *fuzzy-valued* fuzzy measures which have a good suitability for measuring vague real-world information.

The first fuzzy measure we consider is a *possibility measure.* Possibility means an ability of an event to occur. It was recently mentioned that probability of an event can hardly be determined due to a series of reasons, whereas possibility of occurrence of an event is easier to be evaluated. Possibility measure has also its interpretation in terms of multiple priors.

Possibility measure is a non-additive set function $\Pi:\mathcal{F}(\mathcal{S})\to[0,1]$ defined over a σ-algebra $\mathcal{F}(\mathcal{S})$ of subsets of $\mathcal{S}$ and satisfying the following conditions [441]:

(1) $\Pi(\varnothing)=0$;

(2) $\Pi(\mathcal{S})=1$;

(3) For any collection of subsets $H_i\in\mathcal{F}(\mathcal{S})$ and any set of indexes I the following holds:

$$\Pi\Big(\bigcup_{i\in I}H_i\Big)=\sup_{i\in I}\Pi(H_i)$$

Possibility measure Π can be represented by *possibility distribution function,* or possibility distribution, for short. Possibility distribution is a function $\pi:\mathcal{S}\to[0,1]$ and by means of π possibility measure Π is determined as follows:

$$\Pi(H)=\sup_{S\in H}\pi(S)$$

Condition (2) predetermines normalization condition $\sup_{S\in\mathcal{S}}\pi(S)=1$. Given $\mathcal{S}$ as a set of states of nature, possibility measure provides information on possibility of occurrence of an event $H\subset\mathcal{S}$. A possibility distribution π_1 is more informative than π_2 if $\pi_1(S)\le\pi_2(S),\ \forall S\in\mathcal{S}$.

The dual concept of the possibility is the concept of necessity. Necessity measure is a set function $N:P(\mathcal{S})\to[0,1]$ that is defined as $N(H)=1-\Pi(H^c),H^c=\mathcal{S}\setminus H$. This means, for example, that if an event H is necessary (will necessary happen), then the opposite event H^c is impossible.

From the definitions of possibility and necessity measures one can find that the following hold:

(1) $N(H)\le\Pi(H)$;

(2) if $\Pi(H)<1$ then $N(H)=0$;

(3) if $N(H) > 0$ then $\Pi(H) = 1$;

(4) $\max(\Pi(H), \Pi(H^c)) = 1$;

(5) $\min(N(H), N(H^c)) = 0$.

The possibility differs from probability in various aspects. First, possibility of two sets H and G provided $H \cap G = \varnothing$ is equal to the maximum possibility among those of H and G, that is: $\Pi(H \cup G) = \max(\Pi(H), \Pi(G))$. In its turn probability $H \cap G$ is equal to the sum of those of H and G: $P(H \cup G) = P(H) + P(G)$.

Another difference between possibility measure and probability measure is that the first is compositional that make it more convenient from computational point of view. For example, given $P(H)$ and $P(G)$, we cannot determine precisely $P(H \cup G)$, but can only determine its lower bound which is equal to $\max(P(H), P(G))$ and an upper bound which is equal to $\min(P(H) + P(G), 1)$. At the same time possibility of $H \cup G$ is exactly determined based on $\Pi(H)$ and $\Pi(G)$: $\Pi(H \cup G) = \max(\Pi(H), \Pi(G))$. However, the possibility of an intersection is not exactly defined: it is only known that $\Pi(G \cap H) \leq \min(\Pi(G), \Pi(H))$. As to necessity measure, it is exactly defined only for an intersection of sets: $N(H \cap G) = \min(N(H), N(G))$.

Yet another difference is that as compared to probability, possibility is able to model complete ignorance, that is, absence of any information. Absence of any information about H is modeled in the possibility theory as $\Pi(H) = \Pi(H^c) = 1$ and $N(H) = N(H^c) = 0$. From this it follows $\max(\Pi(H), \Pi(H^c)) = 1$ and $\min(N(H), N(H^c)) = 0$.

The essence of the possibility is that it models rather qualitative information about events than quantitative one. Possibility measure only provides ranking of events in terms of their comparative possibilities. For example, $\pi(S_1) \leq \pi(S_2)$ implies that S_1 is more possible than S_2. $\pi(S) = 0$ implies that occurrence of S is impossible whereas $\pi(S) = 1$ implies that S is one of the most possible realizations. The fact that possibility measure may be used only for analysis at qualitative, comparative level [393], was proven by Pytyev in [340], and referred to as the principle of relativity in the possibility theory. This principle implies that possibility measure cannot be used to measure actual possibility of an event but can only be used to determine whether the possibility of one event is higher, equal to, or lower than the possibility of another event. Due to this feature, possibility theory is less self-descriptive than probability theory but requires much less information for analysis of events than the latter.

One of the interpretations of possibility measure is an upper bound of a set of probability measures [136,340,400]. Let us consider the following set of probability measures coherent with possibility measure Π :

$$\mathcal{P}(\Pi)=\{P:P(H)\leq\Pi(H),\forall H\subseteq\mathcal{S}\}$$

Then the upper bound of probability for an event H is

$$\overline{P}(H)=\sup_{P\in\mathcal{P}(\Pi)}P(H)$$

and is equal to possibility $\Pi(H)$. The possibility distribution is then defined as

$$\pi(S)=\overline{P}(\{S\}),\forall S\in\mathcal{S}$$

Due to normalization condition $\sup_{S\in\mathcal{S}}\pi(S)=1$, the set $\mathcal{P}(\Pi)$ is always not empty. In [136,400] they show when one can determine a set of probability measures given possibility measure.

Analogous interpretation of possibility is its representation on the base of lower and upper bounds of a set of distribution functions. Let information about unknown distribution function F for a random variable X be described by means of a lower $\underline{F}$ and an upper $\overline{F}$ distribution functions: $\underline{F}(X)\leq F(X)\leq\overline{F}(X),\forall X\in\mathcal{X}$. The possibility distribution π then may be defined as

$$\pi(X)=\min(\overline{F}(X),1-\underline{F}(X)).$$

Baudrit and Dubois showed that a set of probabilities generated by possibility distribution π is more informative than a set of probabilities generated by equivalent distribution functions.

In order to better explain what possibility and necessity measures are, consider an example with a tossed coin. If to suppose that heads and tails are equiprobable, then the probabilities of heads and tails will be equal to 0.5. As to possibilities, we can accept that both heads and tails are very possible. Then, we can assign the same high value of possibility to both events, say 0.8. At the same time, as the result of tossing the coin is not intentionally designed, we can state that the necessity of both events is very small. It also follows from $\mathrm{N}(\{heads\}) = 1 - \Pi(\{tails\})$, $\mathrm{N}(\{tails\}) = 1 - \Pi(\{heads\})$. As this example suggests, we can state that possibility measure may model ambiguity seeking (hope for a good realization of uncertainty), where as necessity measure may model ambiguity aversion.

One of the most practically efficient and convenient fuzzy measures are *Sugeno* fuzzy measures. Sugeno fuzzy measure $g: \mathcal{F}(\mathcal{S}) \to [0,1]$ is a fuzzy measure that satisfies:

(1) $g(\varnothing) = 0$;
(2) $g(\mathcal{S}) = 1$;
(3) $H \subset G \Rightarrow g(H) \le g(G)$;
(4) $H_i \uparrow H$ or $H_i \downarrow H \Rightarrow \lim_{i \to +\infty} g(H_i) = g(H)$.

From these conditions it follows $g(H \cup G) \ge \max(g(H), g(G))$ and $g(H \cap G) \le \min\,(g(H), g(G))$. In special cases, when $g(H \cup G) = \max(g(H), g(G))$, Sugeno measure is the possibility measure and when $g(H \cap G) = \min(g(H), g(G))$, Sugeno measure g is the necessity measure.

The class of Sugeno measures that became very widespread due to its practical usefulness are g_λ measures. g_λ measure is defined by the following condition referred to as the λ-rule:

$$g_\lambda(H \cup G) = g_\lambda(H) + g_\lambda(G) + \lambda g_\lambda(H) g_\lambda(G),\ \lambda \in [-1, +\infty)$$

For the case of $H = \mathcal{S}$, this condition is called normalization rule. λ is called normalization parameter of g_λ measure. For $\lambda > 0$, g_λ measure satisfies $g_\lambda(H \cup G) > g_\lambda(H) + g_\lambda(G)$ that generates a class of superadditive measures. For $\lambda > 0$ one gets a class of subadditive measures:

$g_{\lambda}(H \cup G) < g_{\lambda}(H) + g_{\lambda}(G)$. The class of additive measures is obtained for $\lambda = 0$.

One type of fuzzy measures is defined as a linear combination of possibility measure and probability measure. This type is referred to as g_v measure. g_v measure is a fuzzy measure that satisfies the following:

(1) $g_v(\varnothing) = 0;$

(2) $g_v(S) = 1;$

(3) $\forall i \in N, H_i \in \mathcal{F}(S), \forall i \neq j;$

(4) $H_i \cap H_j = \varnothing \Rightarrow g_v\left(\underset{i\in N}{\cup} H_i\right) = (1-v) \underset{i\in N}{\vee} g_v(H_i) + v\sum_{i\in N} g_v(H_i),\ v \geq 0;$

(5) $\forall H, G \in \mathcal{F}(S): H \subseteq G \Rightarrow g_v(H) \leq g_v(G).$

g_v is an extension of a measure suggested by Tsukamoto which is a special case obtained when $v \in [0,1]$ [386]. For $v \in [0,1]$ one has a convex combination of possibility and probability measures. For purposes of decision making this can be used to model behavior which is inspired by a mix of probabilistic judgement and an extreme non-additive reasoning, for instance, ambiguity aversion. Such modeling may be good as reflecting that a person is not only an uncertainty averse but also thinks about some 'average', i.e. approximate precise probabilities of events. This may be justified by understanding that, from one side, in real-world situations we don't know exactly the boundaries for a probability of an event. From the other, we don't always exhibit pure ambiguity aversion by try to guess some reasonable probabilities in situations of ambiguity.

g_v is the possibility measure when $v = 0$, and g_v is the probability measure when $v = 1$. For $v \in (0,1)$, g_v describes uncertainty that differs from both probability and possibility [46,386].

Fuzzy measures are advantageous type of non-additive measures as they mainly have clear interpretation and some of them are "self-contained". The latter means that some fuzzy measures, like possibility measure, don't require a set of priors for their construction. Moreover, a fuzzy measure can be more informative than a set of priors or a set of priors can be obtained from it. Despite of these advantages, fuzzy measures are also not sufficiently adequate for solving real-world decision problems. The issue is that fuzzy measures suffer from the disadvantage of all the widespread additive and non-additive measures: fuzzy measures are numerical representation of uncertainty. In contrast, real-world uncertainty cannot be precisely described – it is not to be caught by a numerical function. This aspect is, in our opinion, one of the most essential properties of real-world uncertainty.

The precise non-additive measures match well the backgrounds of decision problems of the existing theories which are characterized by perfect relevant information: mutually exclusive and exhaustive states of nature, sharply constrained probabilities. However, as we discussed in the previous chapter, real-world decision background is much more 'ill-defined'. Essence of information about states of nature makes them rather blurred and overlapping but not perfectly separated. For example, evaluations like 'moderate growth' and 'strong growth' of economy cannot be precisely bounded and may overlap to that or another extent. This requires to use fuzzy sets as more adequate descriptions of real objective conditions. Probabilities of states of nature are also fuzzy as they cannot be sharply constrained. This is conditioned by lack of specific information, by the fact that human sureness in occurrence of events stays in form of linguistic estimations like "very likely", "probability is medium", "probability is small" etc which are fuzzy. From the other side, this is conditioned by fuzziness of states of nature themselves. When the "strong growth" and "moderate growth" and their likelihoods are vague and, therefore, relations between them are vague, – how to obtain a precise measure? Natural impreciseness, fuzziness related to states of nature must be kept as the useful data medium in passing from probabilities to a measure – the use of precise measure cannot be sufficiently reasonable and leads to loss of information. From the other side, shape of non-additivity of a DM's behavior cannot be precisely determined, whereas some linguistic, approximate, but still ground relevant information can be obtained. Fuzziness of the measure in this case serves as a good interpretation.

Thus, a measure which models human behavior under real-world imperfect information should be considered not only as non-additive, but also as fuzzy imprecise quantity that will reflect human evaluation technique based on, in general, linguistic assessments. In this sense a more adequate construction that better matches imperfect real-world information is *a fuzzy number-valued fuzzy measure.* Prior to formally express what is a fuzzy number-valued measure, let us introduce some formal concepts. First concept is a set of fuzzy states of nature $\mathcal{S}=\{\tilde{S}_1,...,\tilde{S}_n\}$, where $\tilde{S}_i, i=1,...,n$ is a fuzzy set defined over a universal set U in terms of membership function $\mu_{\tilde{S}_i}:U\to[0,1]$. The second concept relates to comparison of fuzzy numbers. For two fuzzy numbers $\tilde{A}_1,\tilde{A}_2\in\mathcal{E}^1$, we say that $\tilde{A}_1\le\tilde{A}_2$, if for every $\alpha\in(0,1]$ [11,465]:

$$A_{11}^{\alpha}\le A_{21}^{\alpha}\text{ and }A_{12}^{\alpha}\le A_{22}^{\alpha}.$$

We consider that $\tilde{A}_1<\tilde{A}_2$, if $\tilde{A}_1\le\tilde{A}_2$, and there exists an $\alpha_0\in(0,1]$ such that $A_{11}^{\alpha_0}<A_{21}^{\alpha_0}$, or $A_{12}^{\alpha_0}<A_{22}^{\alpha_0}$. We consider that $\tilde{A}_1=\tilde{A}_2$ if $\tilde{A}_1\le\tilde{A}_2$, and $\tilde{A}_2\le\tilde{A}_1$ [465].

Denote $\mathcal{E}^1_{[0,1]}$ a set of all fuzzy numbers defined over the unit interval [0,1] and denote $\mathcal{F}$ a σ-algebra of subsets of $\mathcal{S}$. A fuzzy number-valued fuzzy measure ((*z*) fuzzy measure) on $\mathcal{F}$ is a fuzzy number-valued fuzzy set function $\tilde{\eta}:\mathcal{F}\to\mathcal{E}^1_{[0,1]}$ with the properties [465]:

(1) $\tilde{\eta}(\varnothing)=0$;

(2) if $H\subset G$ then $\tilde{\eta}(H)\le\tilde{\eta}(G)$;

(3) if $H_1\subset H_2\subset...,H_n\subset...\in\mathcal{F}$, then $\tilde{\eta}(\bigcup_{n=1}^{\infty}H_n)=\lim_{n\to\infty}\tilde{\eta}(H_n)$;

(4) if $H_1\supset H_2\supset...,H_n\in\mathcal{F}$,

and there exists n_0 such that $\tilde{\eta}(H_{n_0})\ne\tilde{\infty}$, then $\tilde{\eta}(\bigcap_{n=1}^{\infty}H_n)=\lim_{n\to\infty}\tilde{\eta}(H_n)$.

Here limits are taken in terms of supremum metric d [129,253], $\tilde{\infty}$ denotes fuzzy infinity[465] concept of which is formally defined in Chapter 6 (Definition 6.3).

So, a fuzzy number-valued fuzzy measure $\tilde{\eta}:\mathcal{F}\to\mathcal{E}^1_{[0,1]}$ assigns to every subset of $\mathcal{S}$ a fuzzy number defined over [0,1]. Condition (2) is called monotonicity condition. $\tilde{\eta}$ is free of the additivity requirement.

Let us consider $\tilde{\eta}$ as a fuzzy number-valued lower probability constructed from linguistic probability distribution $\tilde{P}^l$:

$$\tilde{P}^{l} = \tilde{P}_1 / \tilde{S}_1 + \tilde{P}_2 / \tilde{S}_2 + \cdots + \tilde{P}_n / \tilde{S}_n.$$

Linguistic probability distribution $\tilde{P}^{l}$ implies that a state $\tilde{S}_i \in \mathcal{S}$ is assigned a linguistic probability $\tilde{P}_i$ that can be described by a fuzzy number defined over [0,1]. Let us shortly mention that the requirement for numeric probabilities to sum up to one is extended for a linguistic probability distribution to a wider requirement which includes degrees of consistency, completeness and redundancy which will be described in details in Chapter 6. Given $\tilde{P}^{l}$, we can obtain from it a fuzzy set $\tilde{P}^{\rho}$ of possible probability distributions $\rho(s)$, $s \in \mathrm{S}$, S is a universe of discourse. We can construct a fuzzy-valued fuzzy measure from $\tilde{P}^{\rho}$ as its lower probability function [317] by taking into account a degree of correspondence of $\rho(s)$ to $\tilde{P}^{l}$. A degree of membership of an arbitrary probability distribution $\rho(s)$ to $\tilde{P}^{\rho}$ (a degree of correspondence of $\rho(s)$ to $\tilde{P}^{l}$) can be obtained by the formula

$$\pi_{\tilde{P}}(\rho(s)) = \min_{i=1,n}(\pi_{\tilde{P}_i}(p_i)),$$

where $p_i = \int_{\mathrm{S}} \rho(s)\mu_{\tilde{S}_i}(s)ds$ is numeric probability of a fuzzy state $\tilde{S}_i$ defined by $\rho(s)$. $\pi_{\tilde{P}_i}(p_i) = \mu_{\tilde{P}_i}\left(\int_{\mathrm{S}} \rho(s)\mu_{\tilde{S}_i}(s)ds\right)$ is a membership degree of p_i to $\tilde{P}_i$. To derive a fuzzy-number-valued fuzzy measure $\tilde{\eta}_{\tilde{P}^{l}}$ we suggest using the following formulas [34]:

$$\eta(H) = \bigcup_{\alpha \in (0,1]} \alpha\left[\eta_1^{\alpha}(H), \eta_2^{\alpha}(H)\right] \tag{5.4}$$

where

$$\eta_1^{\alpha}(H) = \inf\left\{\int_{\mathrm{S}} \rho(s)\max_{\tilde{S}\in H}\mu_{\tilde{S}}(s)ds \,\middle|\, \rho(s) \in P^{\rho^{\alpha}}\right\}, \tag{5.5}$$

$$\eta_2^{\alpha}(H) = \inf\left\{\int\limits_{S} \rho(s)\max_{\tilde{S}\in H}\mu_{\tilde{S}}(s)ds \,\middle|\, \rho(s)\in core(\tilde{P}^{\rho})\right\},$$

$$P^{\rho^{\alpha}} = \left\{\rho(s)\,\middle|\, \min_{i=1,n}(\pi_{\tilde{P}_i}(p_i)) \geq \alpha\right\},\ core(\tilde{P}^{\rho}) = P^{\rho^{\alpha=1}},\ H\subset \mathcal{S}$$

The support of $\tilde{\eta}$ is defined as $\operatorname{supp}\tilde{\eta} = cl\left(\bigcup_{\alpha\in(0,1]}\eta^{\alpha}\right)$. So, $\tilde{\eta}_{\tilde{P}^l}$ is constructed by using $\mu_{\tilde{S}}(s)$ which implies that in construction of the non-additive measure $\tilde{\eta}_{\tilde{P}^l}$ we take into account impreciseness of the information on states of nature themselves. Detailed examples on construction of a fuzzy number-valued measure are considered in the upcoming chapters.

5.4 Comparative Analysis of the Existing Measures of Uncertainty

In this section we will discuss features of various existing precise additive and non-additive measures and fuzzy-valued fuzzy measures. The discussion will be conducted in terms of a series of criteria suggested in [400]: interpretation, calculus, consistency, imprecision, assessment, computation. The emphasis will be given to situations in which all the relevant information is described in NL.

Interpretation, Calculus and Consistency. Linguistic probabilities-based fuzzy-valued lower and upper probabilities and their convex combinations have clear behavioral interpretation: they represent ambiguity aversion, ambiguity seeking and their various mixes when decision relevant information is described in NL. Updating these measures is to be conducted as updating the underlying fuzzy probabilities according to fuzzy Bayes' rule and new construction of these measures from the updated fuzzy probabilities.

Formal validity of the considered fuzzy-valued measures is defined from verification of degrees of consistency, completeness and redundancy of the underlying fuzzy probabilities as initial judgments.

Among the traditional measures, Bayesian probability and coherent lower previsions suggested by Walley [400] (these measures are crisp, non-fuzzy) are only measures which satisfy the considered criteria. Bayesian probability has primitive behavioral interpretation, on base of which the well-defined rules of combining and updating are constructed. Coherent lower previsions have a clear and more realistic behavioral interpretation. The rules for updating, combining and verification of consistency for lower previsions are based on the natural extension principle [399,400] which is a general method. However, it is very complex both from analytical and computational points of view.

Possibility theory and the Dempster-Shafer theory, as it is mentioned in [399,400], suffer from lack of the methods to verify consistency of initial judgments and conclusions.

Imprecision. Fuzzy-valued lower and upper previsions and their convex combinations are able to transfer additional information in form of possibilistic uncertainty from states of nature and associated probabilities to the end up measuring of events. As a result, these measures are able to represent vague predicates in NL and partial and complete ignorance as degenerated cases of linguistic ambiguity.

Dempster-Shafer theory is a powerful tool for modeling imprecision and allows to model complete ignorance. However, this theory suffers from series of significant disadvantages [393]. Determination of basic probabilities in this theory may lead to contradictory results. From the other side, under lack of information on some elements of universe of discourse, values of belief and plausibility functions for these elements become equal to zero which means that occurrence of them will not take place. However, this is not justified if the number of observations is small.

Possibility theory is able to model complete ignorance and requires much less information for modeling than probability theory does. Possibility measure, as opposed to probability measure, is compositional, which makes it computationally more convenient. However, possibility measure has a serious disadvantage relative to the probability measure. This theory allows only for qualitative comparative analysis of events – it allows determining whether one event is more or less possible than another, but does not allow determining actual possibilities of events.

Dempster-Shafer theory, lower prevision theory and possibility theory can be considered as special cases of multiple priors representations [393]. In this sense, belief and plausibility functions can be considered as an upper and lower bounds of probability respectively. Possibility theory also can be used for representation of bounds of multiple priors and is used in worst cases of statistical information.

Possibility theory, Dempster-Shafer theory and coherent lower previsions as opposed to Bayesian probabilities are able to model ignorance, impreciseness and NL-based vague evaluations. However, as these theories are based on precise modeling of uncertainty, use of them lead to significant roughening of NL-based information. For example, linguistic description of information on states of nature and their probabilities creates a too high vagueness for these precise measures to be believable or reliable in real-life problems.

Assessment. Fuzzy-valued lower probability is obtained from the linguistic probability assessments which are practical and human-like estimations for real-world problems. Coherent lower prevision can also be obtained from the same sources, but, as a precise quantity, it will be not reliable as very much deviated from vague and imprecise information on states of nature and probabilities.

The other main advantage of fuzzy-valued lower probabilities and fuzzy probabilities constructed for NL-based information is that they, as opposed to all the other measures, don't require independence or non-interaction assumptions on the measured events, which are not accurate when we deal with overlapping and similar objective conditions.

Computation. The construction of unknown fuzzy probability, the use of fuzzy Bayes' formula and construction of a fuzzy-valued lower prevision are quite complicated variational or nonlinear programming problems. However, the complexity here is the price we should pay if we want to adequately formalize and compute from linguistic descriptions. As opposed to the natural extension-based complex computations of coherent lower previsions which involves linear programming, the computation of fuzzy-valued previsions is more intuitive, although arising the well known problems of nonlinear optimization.

Computations of coherent lower previsions (non-fuzzy) can be reduced to simpler computations of possibility measures and belief functions as their special cases, but it will lead to the loss of information.

Adequacy of the use of a fuzzy-valued lower (upper) probability consists in its ability to represent linguistic information as the only adequate relevant information on dependence between states of nature in real-life problems. The existing non-additive measures, being numerical-valued, cannot adequately represent such information. To some extent this can be done by lower previsions, but in this case one deals with averaging of linguistic information to precise values which leads to loss of information.

Chapter 6

Fuzzy Logic-Based Decision Theory with Imperfect Information

6.1 Decision Model

6.1.1 *Fuzzy decision environment*

In real-world decision making problems usually we are not provided with precise and credible information. In contrast, available information is vague, imprecise, partial true and, as a result, is described in natural language (NL). NL-based information creates fuzzy environment in which decisions are commonly made. The existing decision theories are not developed for applications in fuzzy environment and consequently require more deterministic information. There exist a series of fuzzy approaches to decision making like fuzzy AHP [145,265], fuzzy TOPSIS [265,408], fuzzy Expected Utility [82,169,277]. However, they are mainly fuzzy generalizations of the mathematical structures of the existing theories used with intent to account for vagueness, impreciseness and partial truth. Direct fuzzification of the existing theories often leads to inconsistency and loss of properties of the latter (for example, loss of consistency and transitivity of preference matrices in AHP method when replacing their numerical elements by fuzzy numbers). Let us consider the existing works devoted to the fuzzy utility models and decisions under fuzzy uncertainty [4,37,76,82,126,169,180,182,277]. In [82] they presented axioms for linguistic preference relation (LPR) in terms of linguistic probability distributions over fuzzy outcomes and defined fuzzy expected utility on this basis. But, unfortunately, an existence of a fuzzy utility function has not been proved. [76] is an extensive work devoted to the representation of fuzzy preference relation (FPR). In this paper, an existence of a utility function representing a fuzzy preorder is proved. However, in this work a utility function itself is considered as a non-fuzzy real-valued function. In [277] it is formulated conditions for existence and continuity of a numerical and fuzzy-valued expected utility under some standard conditions of a FPR (viz. reflexivity, transitivity, continuity, etc.). The author proves theorems on existence of a fuzzy expected utility for the cases of probabilistic and possibilistic information on states of nature. The possibilistic case, as it is correctly identified by the author, appears to be more adequate to deal with real-world problems. However, in this model, probabilities and outcomes are considered as numerical entities. This notably limits the use of the suggested model for real-life decision problems where almost all the information is described in NL. A new approach for decision making under possibilistic information on states of nature when probabilistic information is absent is considered in [180]. In [169] they suggest representation of a fuzzy preference relation by fuzzy number-valued expected utility on the basis of fuzzy random variables. However, an existence of a fuzzy utility function has not been shown. In [37] they consider a fuzzy utility as a fuzzy-valued Choquet integral with respect to a real-valued fuzzy measure obtained based on a set of possible probability distributions and with a fuzzy integrand. Unfortunately, the existence of the suggested fuzzy utility is not proved.

We can conclude that the existing fuzzy approaches to decision making have significant disadvantages. Fuzzy approaches in which an existence of a utility function is proved, uses fuzzy sets to describe only a part of the components of decision problems. Those approaches that are based on fuzzy description of the most part of a decision problem are lack of mathematical proof of an existence of a utility function. From the other side, many of the existing fuzzy approaches follow too simple models like EU model.

It is needed to develop original and mathematically grounded fuzzy decision theories which are based on initial fuzzy information on all the components of a decision problem. Such fuzzy theories should take into account initial information stemming from fuzzy environment in end-up comparison of alternatives.

In the present chapter we present a fuzzy-logic-based decision theory with imperfect information. This theory is developed for the framework of mix of fuzzy information and probabilistic information and is based on a fuzzy utility function represented as a fuzzy-valued Choquet integral. Being developed for imperfect information framework, the suggested theory differs from the CEU theory as follows:

1) Spaces of fuzzy sets [8,129,253] instead of a classical framework are used for modeling states of nature and outcomes 2) Fuzzy probabilities are considered instead of numerical probability distributions 3) Linguistic preference relation [8,82,243] is used instead of binary logic-based preference relations 4) Fuzzy number-valued utility functions [8,34,129,253] are used instead of real-valued utility functions 5) Fuzzy number-valued fuzzy measure [8,465] is used instead of a real-valued non-additive probability.

These aspects form fundamentally a new statement of the problem – the problem of decision making with imperfect information. This problem is characterized by second-order uncertainty, namely by fuzzy probabilities. In this framework, we prove representation theorems for a fuzzy-valued utility function. Fuzzy-valued utility function will be described as a fuzzy-valued Choquet integral [8,21,34,433] with a fuzzy number-valued integrand and a fuzzy number-valued fuzzy measure. Fuzzy number-valued integrand will be used to model imprecise linguistic utility evaluations. It is contemplated that fuzzy number-valued fuzzy measure that can be generated by fuzzy probabilities will better reflect the features of impreciseness and non-additivity related to human behavior. The fuzzy utility model we consider is more suitable for human evaluations and vision of decision problem and related information.

6.1.2 *Statement of the problem*

Prior to formally state a problem of decision making with imperfect information as the problem of decision making under mix of fuzzy and probabilistic uncertainties, we will provide the necessary mathematical background. This is the background of spaces of fuzzy numbers and fuzzy functions and the related operations described below.

The first concept we consider is the space of all fuzzy subsets of $\mathcal{R}^n$ denoted $\mathcal{E}^n$ [129,253] which satisfy the conditions of normality, convexity, and are upper semicontinuous with compact support. It is obvious that $\mathcal{E}^1$ is the set of fuzzy numbers defined over $\mathcal{R}$. Then let us denote by $\mathcal{E}^1_{[0,1]}$ the corresponding space of fuzzy numbers defined over the unit interval $[0,1]$. Once the space of fuzzy sets is chosen, a metrics on it must be chosen to define other concepts such as limits, closures and continuity. We suggest to use a fuzzy-valued metrics (the use of which is more adequate to measure distances between fuzzy objects) definition of which is given below.

Definition 6.1. Fuzzy Hausdorff distance [16,34]. Let $\tilde{A},\tilde{B} \in \mathcal{E}^n$. The fuzzy Hausdorff distance $\tilde{d}_{fH}$ between $\tilde{A}$ and $\tilde{B}$ is defined as

$$\tilde{d}_{fH}(\tilde{A},\tilde{B}) = \bigcup_{\alpha\in[0,1]} \alpha \left[d_H(A^1,B^1), \sup_{\alpha\le\bar{\alpha}\le 1} d_H(A^{\bar{\alpha}},B^{\bar{\alpha}}) \right],$$

where d_H is the Hausdorff distance [129,253] and A^1, B^1 denote the cores ($\alpha = 1$ level sets) of fuzzy sets $\tilde{A},\tilde{B}$ respectively.

Let us consider a small example. Let $\tilde{A}$ and $\tilde{B}$ be triangular fuzzy sets $\tilde{A} = (2,3,4)$ and $\tilde{B} = (6,8,12)$. Then the fuzzy Hausdorff distance d_{fH} between $\tilde{A}$ and $\tilde{B}$ is defined as a triangular fuzzy set $\tilde{d}_{fH}(\tilde{A},\tilde{B}) = (5,5,8)$.

The next necessary concept that will be used in the sequel is the concept of difference of two elements of $\mathcal{E}^n$ referred to as Hukuhara difference:

Definition 6.2. Hukuhara difference [16,129,253]. Let $\tilde{X},\tilde{Y} \in \mathcal{E}^n$. If there exists $\tilde{Z} \in \mathcal{E}^n$ such that $\tilde{X} = \tilde{Y} + \tilde{Z}$, then $\tilde{Z}$ is called a Hukuhara difference of $\tilde{X}$ and $\tilde{Y}$ and is denoted as $\tilde{X} -_h \tilde{Y}$.

Note that with the standard fuzzy difference for $\tilde{Z}$ produced of $\tilde{X}$ and $\tilde{Y}$, $\tilde{X} \neq \tilde{Y} + \tilde{Z}$. We use Hukuhara difference when we need $\tilde{X} = \tilde{Y} + \tilde{Z}$.

Example. Consider $\tilde{X}$ and $\tilde{Y}$ as the following TFNs: $\tilde{X} = (3,7,11)$ and $\tilde{Y} = (1,2,3)$. Hukuhara difference of $\tilde{X}$ and $\tilde{Y}$ exists and is equal to $\tilde{X} -_h \tilde{Y} = (3,7,11) -_h (1,2,3) = (3-1, 7-2, 11-3) = (2,5,8)$. Indeed,

$$\tilde{Y} + \left(\tilde{X} -_h \tilde{Y}\right) = (1,2,3) + (2,5,8) = (3,7,11) = \tilde{X} .$$

Now we need to proceed to a concept of a fuzzy number-valued fuzzy measure. Let Ω be a nonempty finite set and $\mathcal{F}$ be σ-algebra of subsets of Ω. The values of a fuzzy number-valued fuzzy measure are fuzzy numbers for which the concepts defined below will be used.

Definition 6.3. Fuzzy infinity [465]. Let $\tilde{A}$ be a fuzzy number. For every positive real number M, there exists a $\alpha_0 \in (0,1]$ such that $M < A_2^{\alpha_0}$ or $A_1^{\alpha_0} < -M$. Then $\tilde{A}$ is called fuzzy infinity, denoted by $\tilde{\infty}$.

Definition 6.4. Comparison of fuzzy numbers [465]. For $\tilde{A}_1, \tilde{A}_2 \in \mathcal{E}^1$, we say that $\tilde{A}_1 \le \tilde{A}_2$, if for every $\alpha \in (0,1]$,

$$A_{11}^{\alpha} \le A_{21}^{\alpha} \text{ and } A_{12}^{\alpha} \le A_{22}^{\alpha} .$$

We consider that $\tilde{A}_1 < \tilde{A}_2$, if $\tilde{A}_1 \le \tilde{A}_2$, and there exists an $\alpha_0 \in (0,1]$ such that

$$A_{11}^{\alpha_0} < A_{21}^{\alpha_0}, \text{or } A_{12}^{\alpha_0} < A_{22}^{\alpha_0} .$$

We consider that $\tilde{A}_1 = \tilde{A}_2$ if $\tilde{A}_1 \le \tilde{A}_2$, and $\tilde{A}_2 \le \tilde{A}_1$.

Denote $\mathcal{E}_+^1 = \left\{\tilde{A} \in \mathcal{E} \middle| \tilde{A} \ge 0\right\}$. Thus, $\mathcal{E}_+^1$ is a space of fuzzy numbers defined over $\mathcal{R}_+$. A definition of a fuzzy number-valued fuzzy measure as a monotone fuzzy number-valued set function suggested by Zhang [465], and also referred to as a (z)-fuzzy measure, is as follows.

Definition 6.5. Fuzzy number-valued fuzzy measure [465]. A ((z) fuzzy measure) on $\mathcal{F}$ is a fuzzy number-valued fuzzy set function $\tilde{\eta} : \mathcal{F} \to \mathcal{E}_+^1$ with the properties:

(1) $\tilde{\eta}(\varnothing) = 0$;

(2) if $H \subset G$ then $\tilde{\eta}(H) \le \tilde{\eta}(G)$;

(3) if $H_1 \subset H_2 \subset ..., H_n \subset ... \in \mathcal{F}$, then $\tilde{\eta}(\bigcup_{n=1}^{\infty} H_n) = \lim_{n\to\infty} \tilde{\eta}(H_n)$;

(4) if $H_1 \supset H_2 \supset ..., H_n \in \mathcal{F}$, and there exists n_0 such that $\tilde{\eta}(H_{n_0}) \ne \tilde{\infty}$, then $\tilde{\eta}(\bigcap_{n=1}^{\infty} H_n) = \lim_{n\to\infty} \tilde{\eta}(H_n)$.

Here limits are taken in terms of the $\tilde{d}_{fH}$ distance.

Consider an example. Let $\Omega=\{\omega_1,\omega_2,\omega_3\}$. The values of the fuzzy number-valued set function $\tilde{\eta}$ for the subsets of Ω can be as the triangular fuzzy numbers given in Table 6.1:

Table 6.1. The values of the fuzzy number-valued set function $\tilde{\eta}$

$H\subset\Omega$	$\{\omega_1\}$	$\{\omega_2\}$	$\{\omega_3\}$	$\{\omega_1,\omega_2\}$	$\{\omega_1,\omega_3\}$	$\{\omega_2,\omega_3\}$
$\tilde{\eta}(H)$	(0.3,0.4,0.4)	(0,0.1,0.1)	(0.3,0.5,0.5)	(0.3,0.5,0.5)	(0.6,0.9,0.9)	(0.3,0.6,0.6)

Fuzzy number-valued set function $\tilde{\eta}$ is a fuzzy number-valued fuzzy measure. For instance, one can verify that condition 2 of Definition 6.5 for $\tilde{\eta}$ is satisfied.

A pair $(\Omega,\tilde{\mathcal{F}}(\Omega))$ is called a fuzzy measurable space and a triple $(\Omega,\tilde{\mathcal{F}}(\Omega),\tilde{\eta})$ is called a (z) fuzzy measure space. Let us provide a definition of a fuzzy-valued Choquet integral as a Choquet integral of a fuzzy-valued function [433] with respect to a fuzzy number valued fuzzy measure:

Definition 6.6. Fuzzy-valued Choquet integral. Let $\tilde{\varphi}:\Omega\to\mathcal{E}^1$ be a measurable fuzzy-valued function on Ω and $\tilde{\eta}$ be a fuzzy-number-valued fuzzy measure on $\mathcal{F}$. The Choquet integral of $\tilde{\varphi}$ with respect to $\tilde{\eta}$ is defined as

$$\int_{\Omega}\tilde{\varphi}d\tilde{\eta}=\sum_{i=1}^{n}\left(\tilde{\varphi}(\omega_{(i)}))-_h\tilde{\varphi}(\omega_{(i+1)})\right)\cdot\tilde{\eta}(H_{(i)})$$

where index (i) implies that elements $\omega_i\in\Omega,i=1,...,n$ are permuted such that $\tilde{\varphi}(\omega_{(i)}))\geq\tilde{\varphi}(\omega_{(i+1)})$, $\tilde{\varphi}(\omega_{(n+1)})=0$ by convention and $H_{(i)}\subseteq\Omega$.

In the suggested theory $\tilde{\eta}$ will be constructed on the base of the linguistic information on distribution of probabilities over Ω. This requires using the following concepts:

Definition 6.7. Linguistic probabilities of a random variable [82]. The set of linguistic probabilities $\tilde{P}^l=\{\tilde{P}_1,...,\tilde{P}_i,...,\tilde{P}_n\}$ and corresponding values $\{X_1,...,X_i,...,X_n\}$ of a random variable X are called a distribution of linguistic probabilities of this random variable.

Definition 6.8. Fuzzy set-valued random variable [82]. Let a discrete variable $\tilde{X}$ take a value from the set $\{\tilde{X}_1,...,\tilde{X}_n\}$ of possible linguistic values, each of which is a fuzzy variable $\langle x_i, U_x, \tilde{X}_i \rangle$ described by a fuzzy set $\tilde{X}_i = \int_{U_x} \mu_{\tilde{X}_i}(x)/x$. Let the probability that $\tilde{X}$ takes a linguistic value $\tilde{X}_i$ be characterized by a linguistic probability $\tilde{P}_i \in \tilde{P}^l$, $\tilde{P}^l =$ $\{\tilde{P} | \tilde{P} \in \mathcal{E}^1_{[0,1]}\}$. The variable $\tilde{X}$ is then called a fuzzy set-valued random variable.

Definition 6.9. Linguistic lottery [82]. Linguistic lottery is a fuzzy set-valued random variable with known linguistic probability distribution. Linguistic lottery is represented by a vector:

$$\tilde{L} = \left(\tilde{P}_1, \tilde{X}_1; ...; \tilde{P}_i, \tilde{X}_i; ...; \tilde{P}_n, \tilde{X}_n\right).$$

Let us consider an example. Let us have the linguistic lottery $\tilde{L} = \left(\tilde{P}_1, \tilde{X}_1; \tilde{P}_2, \tilde{X}_2; \tilde{P}_3, \tilde{X}_3\right)$, where $\tilde{P}_i$ and $\tilde{X}_i$ are described by triangular and trapezoidal fuzzy numbers defined over [0,1]: $\tilde{X}_1 = (0.1, 0.3, 0.5)$ ('small'), $\tilde{X}_2 = (0.3, 0.5, 0.7)$ ('medium'), $\tilde{X}_3 = (0.5, 0.7, 0.9)$ ('large'), $\tilde{P}_1 = (0.5, 0.7, 0.9)$ ('high'), $\tilde{P}_2 = (0.0, 0.2, 0.4)$ ('low'), $\tilde{P}_3 = (0.0, 0.0, 0.1, 0.4)$ ('very low'). Then the considered linguistic lottery is:

$$\tilde{L} = \begin{pmatrix} (0.5, 0.7, 0.9), (0.1, 0.3, 0.5); \\ (0.0, 0.2, 0.4), (0.3, 0.5, 0.7); \\ (0.0, 0.0, 0.1, 0.4), (0.5, 0.7, 0.9) \end{pmatrix}.$$

On the base of the above mentioned concepts we can proceed to the formal statement of problem of decision making with imperfect information.

Let $\mathcal{S} = \{\tilde{S}_1, ..., \tilde{S}_m\} \subset \mathcal{E}^n$ be a set of fuzzy states of nature, $\mathcal{X} = \{\tilde{X}_1, ..., \tilde{X}_l\}$ $\subset \mathcal{E}^n$ be a set of fuzzy outcomes, $\mathcal{Y}$ be a set of distributions of linguistic probabilities over $\mathcal{X}$, i.e. $\mathcal{Y}$ is a set of fuzzy number-valued functions

[31,34,62,129,253]: $\mathcal{Y}=\left\{\tilde{y}\,\middle|\,\tilde{y}:\tilde{\mathcal{X}}\to\mathcal{E}^1_{[0,1]}\right\}$. For notational simplicity we identify $\mathcal{X}$ with the subset $\left\{\tilde{y}\in\mathcal{Y}\,\middle|\,\tilde{y}(\tilde{X})=1 \text{ for some } \tilde{X}\in\mathcal{X}\right\}$ of $\mathcal{Y}$. Denote by $\mathcal{F}_S$ a σ-algebra of subsets of $\mathcal{S}$. Denote by $\mathcal{A}_0$ the set of all $\mathcal{F}_S$-measurable [304,433] fuzzy finite valued step functions [404] from $\mathcal{S}$ to $\mathcal{Y}$ and denote by $\mathcal{A}_c$ the constant fuzzy functions in $\mathcal{A}_0$. We call a function $\tilde{f}:\mathcal{S}\to\mathcal{Y}$ a fuzzy finite valued step function if there is a finite partition of $\mathcal{S}$ to $H_i\subset\mathcal{S}, i=1,2,...,m$, $H_j\cap H_k=\varnothing$, for $j\neq k$, such that $\tilde{f}(\tilde{S})=\tilde{y}_i$ for all $\tilde{S}\in H_i$. In this case $\tilde{g}:\mathcal{S}\to\mathcal{Y}$ is called a constant fuzzy function if for some $\tilde{y}\in\mathcal{Y}$ one has $\tilde{g}(\tilde{S})=\tilde{y}$ for all $\tilde{S}\in\mathcal{S}$. Thus the constant fuzzy function is a special case of a fuzzy finite valued step function.

Let $\mathcal{A}$ be a convex subset [311] of $\mathcal{Y}^S$ which includes $\mathcal{A}_c$. $\mathcal{Y}$ can be considered as a subset of some linear space, and $\mathcal{Y}^S$ can then be considered as a subspace of the linear space of all fuzzy functions from $\mathcal{S}$ to the first linear space. Let us now define convex combinations in $\mathcal{Y}$ pointwise [311]: for $\tilde{y}$ and $\tilde{z}$ in $\mathcal{Y}$, and $\lambda\in(0,1)$, $\lambda\tilde{y}+(1-\lambda)\tilde{z}=\tilde{r}$, where $\tilde{r}(\tilde{X})=\lambda\tilde{y}(\tilde{X})+(1-\lambda)\tilde{z}(\tilde{X})$, $\tilde{y}(\tilde{X}),\tilde{z}(\tilde{X})\in\mathcal{E}^1_{[0,1]}$. The latter expression is defined based on the Zadeh's extension principle. Let $\mu_{\tilde{r}(\tilde{X})},\mu_{\tilde{y}(\tilde{X})},\mu_{\tilde{z}(\tilde{X})}:[0,1]\to[0,1]$ denote the membership functions of fuzzy numbers $\tilde{r}(\tilde{X}),\tilde{y}(\tilde{X}),\tilde{z}(\tilde{X})$, respectively. Then for $\mu_{\tilde{r}(\tilde{X})}:[0,1]\to[0,1]$ we have:

$$\mu_{\tilde{r}(\tilde{X})}(r(\tilde{X}))=\sup\min_{\substack{r(\tilde{X})=\lambda y(\tilde{X})+(1-\lambda)z(\tilde{X})\\ y(\tilde{X})+z(\tilde{X})\leq 1}}(\mu_{\tilde{y}(\tilde{X})}(y(\tilde{X})),\mu_{\tilde{z}(\tilde{X})}(z(\tilde{X}))),$$
$$r(\tilde{X}),y(\tilde{X}),z(\tilde{X})\in[0,1].$$

Convex combinations in $\mathcal{A}$ are also defined pointwise, i.e. for $\tilde{f}$ and $\tilde{g}$ in $\mathcal{A}$: $\lambda\tilde{f}+(1-\lambda)\tilde{g}=\tilde{h}$, where $\lambda\tilde{f}(\tilde{S})+(1-\lambda)\tilde{g}(\tilde{S})=\tilde{h}(\tilde{S})$ on $\mathcal{S}$.

To model LPR, let's introduce a linguistic variable "degree of preference" with term-set $\mathcal{T}=(T_1,...,T_K)$. Terms can be labeled, for example, as "equivalence", "little preference", "high preference", and can each be described by a fuzzy number defined over some scale, for example, [0,1]. The fact that preference of $\tilde{f}$ against $\tilde{g}$ is described by some $T_i \in T$ is expressed as $\tilde{f}\, T_i\, \tilde{g}$. We denote LPR as $\succsim_l$ and below we sometimes, for simplicity, write $\tilde{f} \succsim_l^i \tilde{g}$ or $\tilde{f} \succ_l^i \tilde{g}$ instead of $\tilde{f}\, T_i\, \tilde{g}$.

In the suggested framework, we extend a classical neo-Bayesian nomenclature as follows: elements of $\mathcal{X}$ are fuzzy outcomes; elements of $\mathcal{Y}$ are linguistic lotteries; elements of $\mathcal{A}$ are fuzzy acts; elements of $\mathcal{S}$ are fuzzy states of nature; and elements of $\tilde{\mathcal{F}}_S$ are fuzzy events.

Definition 6.10. Comonotonic fuzzy acts [34,37]. Two fuzzy acts $\tilde{f}$ and $\tilde{g}$ in $\mathcal{Y}^S$ are said to be comonotonic if there are no $\tilde{S}_i$ and $\tilde{S}_j$ in $\mathcal{S}$ for which $\tilde{f}(\tilde{S}_i) \succ_l \tilde{f}(\tilde{S}_j)$ and $\tilde{g}(\tilde{S}_j) \succ_l \tilde{g}(\tilde{S}_i)$ hold.

Two real-valued functions $a:\mathcal{S}\to\mathcal{R}$ and $b:\mathcal{S}\to\mathcal{R}$ are comonotonic iff $(a(\tilde{S}_i)-a(\tilde{S}_j))(b(\tilde{S}_i)-b(\tilde{S}_j))\geq 0$ for all $\tilde{S}_i$ and $\tilde{S}_j$ in $\mathcal{S}$.

For a fuzzy number-valued function $\tilde{a}:\mathcal{S}\to\mathcal{E}^1$ denote by a^α, $\alpha\in(0,1]$ its α-cut and note that $a^\alpha=\left[a_1^\alpha,a_2^\alpha\right]$, where $a_1^\alpha,a_2^\alpha:\mathcal{S}\to\mathcal{R}$.

Two fuzzy functions $\tilde{a},\tilde{b}:\mathcal{S}\to\mathcal{E}^1$ are said to be comonotonic iff the real-valued functions $a_1^\alpha,b_1^\alpha:\mathcal{S}\to\mathcal{R}$ and also $a_2^\alpha,b_2^\alpha:\mathcal{S}\to\mathcal{R}$, $\alpha\in(0,1]$ are comonotonic.

A constant act $\tilde{f}=\tilde{y}^S$ for some $\tilde{y}$ in $\mathcal{Y}$, and any act $\tilde{g}$ are comonotonic. An act $\tilde{f}$ whose statewise lotteries $\{\tilde{f}(\tilde{S})\}$ are mutually indifferent, i.e. $\tilde{f}(\tilde{S})\sim_l \tilde{y}$ for all $\tilde{S}$ in $\mathcal{S}$, and any act $\tilde{g}$ are comonotonic.

It is common knowledge that under degrees of uncertainty humans evaluate alternatives or choices linguistically using certain evaluation techniques such as "much worse", "a little better", "much better", "almost equivalent" etc. In contrast to the classical preference relation, imposed on choices made by humans, LPR consistently expresses "degree of preference" allowing the analysis of preferences under uncertainty.

Below we give a series of axioms of the LPR $\succsim_l$ over $\mathcal{A}$ [8,23,31,34].

(i) *Weak-order:*

(a) *Completeness. Any two alternatives are comparable with respect to LPR: for all* $\tilde{f}$ *and* $\tilde{g}$ *in* $\mathcal{A}$: $\tilde{f} \succsim_l \tilde{g}$ *or* $\tilde{g} \succsim_l \tilde{f}$. *This means that for all* $\tilde{f}$ *and* $\tilde{g}$ *there exists such* $T_i \in \mathcal{T}$ *that* $\tilde{f} \succsim_l^i \tilde{g}$ *or* $\tilde{g} \succsim_l^i \tilde{f}$.

(b) *Transitivity. For all* $\tilde{f}, \tilde{g}$ *and* $\tilde{h}$ *in* $\mathcal{A}$: *If* $\tilde{f} \succsim_l \tilde{g}$ *and* $\tilde{g} \succsim_l \tilde{h}$ *then* $\tilde{f} \succsim_l \tilde{h}$. *This means that if there exist such* $T_i \in \mathcal{T}$ *and* $T_j \in \mathcal{T}$ *that* $\tilde{f} \succsim_l^i \tilde{g}$ *and* $\tilde{g} \succsim_l^j \tilde{h}$, *then there exists such* $T_k \in \mathcal{T}$ *that* $\tilde{f} \succsim_l^k \tilde{h}$. Transitivity of LPR is defined on the base of the extension principle and fuzzy preference relation [243]. This axiom states that any two alternatives are comparable and assumes one of the fundamental properties of preferences (transitivity) for the case of fuzzy information;

(ii) *Comonotonic Independence*: *For all pairwise comonotonic acts* $\tilde{f}, \tilde{g}$ *and* $\tilde{h}$ *in* $\mathcal{A}$ *if* $\tilde{f} \succsim_l \tilde{g}$, *then* $\sigma\tilde{f} + (1-\sigma)\tilde{h} \succsim_l \sigma\tilde{g} + (1-\sigma)\tilde{h}$ *for all* $\sigma \in (0,1)$. *This means that if there exist such* $T_i \in \mathcal{T}$ *that* $\tilde{f} \succsim_l^i \tilde{g}$ *then there exists such* $T_k \in \mathcal{T}$ *that* $\sigma\tilde{f} + (1-\sigma)\tilde{h} \succsim_l^k \sigma\tilde{g} + (1-\sigma)\tilde{h}$, *with* $\tilde{f}, \tilde{g}$ *and* $\tilde{h}$ *pairwise comonotonic.*

The axiom extends the independency property for comonotonic actions for the case of fuzzy information;

(iii) *Continuity*: *For all* $\tilde{f}, \tilde{g}$ *and* $\tilde{h}$ *in* $\mathcal{A}$: *if* $\tilde{f} \succ_l \tilde{g}$ *and* $\tilde{g} \succ_l \tilde{h}$ *then there are* σ *and* β *in* $(0,1)$ *such that* $\sigma\tilde{f} + (1-\sigma)\tilde{h} \succ_l \tilde{g} \succ_l \beta\tilde{f} + (1-\beta)\tilde{h}$. *This means that if there exist such* $T_i \in \mathcal{T}$ *and* $T_j \in \mathcal{T}$ *that* $\tilde{f} \succsim_l^i \tilde{g}$ *and* $\tilde{g} \succsim_l^j \tilde{h}$ *then there exist such* $T_k \in \mathcal{T}$ *and* $T_m \in \mathcal{T}$ *that define preference of* $\sigma\tilde{f} + (1-\sigma)\tilde{h} \succsim_l^k \tilde{g} \succsim_l^m \beta\tilde{g} + (1-\beta)\tilde{h}$;

(iv) *Monotonicity*: *For all* $\tilde{f}$ *and* $\tilde{g}$ *in* $\mathcal{A}$: *If* $\tilde{f}(\tilde{S}) \succsim_l \tilde{g}(\tilde{S})$ *on* $\mathcal{S}$ *then* $\tilde{f} \succsim_l \tilde{g}$. *This means that if for any* $\tilde{S} \in \mathcal{S}$ *there exists such* $T \in \mathcal{T}$ *that* $\tilde{f}(\tilde{S}) \succsim_l \tilde{g}(\tilde{S})$, *then there exists* $T_i \in \mathcal{T}$ *such that* $\tilde{f} \succsim_l^i \tilde{g}$;

(v) *Nondegeneracy*: *Not for all* $\tilde{f}, \tilde{g} \in \mathcal{A}$, $\tilde{f} \succsim_l \tilde{g}$.

LPR $\succsim_l$ on $\mathcal{A}$ induces LPR denoted also by $\succsim_l$ on $\mathcal{Y}$: $\tilde{y} \succsim_l \tilde{z}$ iff $\tilde{y}^S \succsim_l \tilde{z}^S$, where $\tilde{y}^S$ and $\tilde{z}^S$ denotes the constant functions $\tilde{y}$ and $\tilde{z}$ on $\mathcal{S}$.

The presented axioms are formulated to reflect human preferences under a mixture of fuzzy and probabilistic information. Such formulation requires the use of a fuzzy-valued utility function. Formally, it is required to use a fuzzy-valued utility function $\tilde{U}$ such that

$$\forall \tilde{f}, \tilde{g} \in \mathcal{A}, \tilde{f} \succsim_l \tilde{g} \Leftrightarrow \tilde{U}(\tilde{f}) \geq \tilde{U}(\tilde{g}).$$

The problem of decision making with imperfect information is formalized as a 4-tuple $D_{DMII} = (\mathcal{S}, \mathcal{Y}, \mathcal{A}, \succsim_l)$ and consists in determination of an optimal $\tilde{f}^* \in \mathcal{A}$, that is, $\tilde{f}^* \in \mathcal{A}$ for which $\tilde{U}(\tilde{f}^*) = \max_{\tilde{f} \in \mathcal{A}} \tilde{U}(\tilde{f})$.

Fuzzy utility function $\tilde{U}$ we adopt will be described as a fuzzy number-valued Choquet integral with respect to a fuzzy number-valued fuzzy measure. In its turn fuzzy number-valued fuzzy measure can be obtained from NL-described knowledge about probability distribution over $\mathcal{S}$. NL-described knowledge about probability distribution over $\mathcal{S}$ is expressed as $\tilde{P}^l = \tilde{P}_1 / \tilde{S}_1 + \tilde{P}_2 / \tilde{S}_2 + \tilde{P}_3 / \tilde{S}_3$= *small/small* + *high/medium* + *small/large*, with the understanding that a term such as *high/medium* means that the probability, that $\tilde{S}_2 \in \mathcal{S}$ is medium, is high. So, $\tilde{P}^l$ is a *linguistic (fuzzy) probability distribution.*

6.1.3 *Fuzzy utility function*

In the discussions above, we have mentioned the necessity of the use of a fuzzy utility function as a suitable quantifying representation of vague preferences. Below we present a definition of a fuzzy number-valued utility function representing LPR (i)-(v) over an arbitrary set $\mathcal{Z}$ of alternatives.

Definition 6.11. Fuzzy utility function [8,23,27,31,34]. Fuzzy number-valued function $\tilde{U}(\cdot): \mathcal{Z} \to \mathcal{E}^1$ is a fuzzy utility function if it represents linguistic preferences $\succsim_l$ such that for any pair of alternatives

$\tilde{Z}_1, \tilde{Z}_2 \in \mathcal{Z}$, $\tilde{Z}_1 \succsim_l^i \tilde{Z}_2$ holds if and only if $\tilde{U}(\tilde{Z}_1) \geq \tilde{U}(\tilde{Z}_2)$, where T_i is determined on the base of $\tilde{d}_{fH}\left(\tilde{U}(\tilde{Z}_1), \tilde{U}(\tilde{Z}_2)\right)$.

Here we consider a set $\mathcal{Z}$ of alternatives as if they are a set $\mathcal{A}$ of actions $\tilde{f}: \mathcal{S} \to \mathcal{Y}$.

Below we present representation theorems showing the existence of a fuzzy number-valued Choquet-integral-based fuzzy utility function [23,31,34] that represents LPR defined over the set $\mathcal{A}$ of alternatives.

Theorem 6.1 [31,34]. *Assume that LPR $\succsim_l$ on $\mathcal{A} = \mathcal{A}_0$ satisfies (i) weak order, (ii) continuity, (iii) comonotonic independence, (iv) monotonicity, and (v) nondegeneracy. Then there exists a unique fuzzy number-valued fuzzy measure $\tilde{\eta}$ on $\tilde{\mathcal{F}}_S$ and an affine fuzzy number-valued function $\tilde{u}$ on $\mathcal{Y}$ such that for all $\tilde{f}$ and $\tilde{g}$ in $\mathcal{A}$:*

$$\tilde{f} \succsim_l \tilde{g} \quad iff \quad \int_{\mathcal{S}} \tilde{u}(\tilde{f}(\tilde{S}))d\tilde{\eta} \geq \int_{\mathcal{S}} \tilde{u}(\tilde{g}(\tilde{S}))d\tilde{\eta}$$

where $\tilde{u}$ is unique up to positive linear transformations.

Theorem 6.2 [31,34]. *For a nonconstant affine fuzzy number-valued function $\tilde{u}$ on $\mathcal{Y}$ and a fuzzy number-valued fuzzy measure $\tilde{\eta}$ on $\tilde{\mathcal{F}}_S$ a fuzzy number-valued Choquet integral $\tilde{U}(\tilde{f}) = \int_{\mathcal{S}} \tilde{u}(\tilde{f}(\tilde{S}))d\tilde{\eta}$ induces such LPR on $\mathcal{A}_0$ that satisfies conditions (i)-(v). Additionally, $\tilde{u}$ is unique up to positive linear transformations.*

The direct theorem (Theorem 6.1) provides conditions for existence of the suggested fuzzy utility function representing LPR defined over a set of fuzzy actions under conditions of fuzzy probabilities. LPR formulated by using a series of axioms reflects the essence of human-like preferences under conditions of imperfect information. The converse theorem (Theorem 6.2) provides conditions under which a fuzzy utility function described as a fuzzy number-valued Choquet integral with a fuzzy number-valued integrand and a fuzzy number-valued fuzzy measure induces the formulated LPR.

In order to prove these theorems we need to use a series of mathematical results [31,34] we present below. These results are obtained for a fuzzy-valued Choquet integral [433] of a fuzzy number-valued function with respect to a fuzzy number-valued fuzzy measure. The general expression of the considered fuzzy-valued Choquet integral is

$$\tilde{I}(\tilde{a}) = \int_{\mathcal{S}} \tilde{a} d\tilde{\eta} = \int_{0}^{\infty} \tilde{\eta}(\{\tilde{S} \in \mathcal{S} | \tilde{a}(\tilde{S}) \geq \tilde{\delta}\}) d\tilde{\delta}, \tag{6.1}$$

where $\tilde{a}: \mathcal{S} \to \mathcal{E}^1$. In α-cuts we will have

$$\left[\tilde{I}(\tilde{a})\right]^{\alpha} = \left[I_1^{\alpha}(a_1^{\alpha}), I_2^{\alpha}(a_2^{\alpha})\right], \text{ where}$$

$$I_1^{\alpha}(a_1^{\alpha}) = \int_{\mathcal{S}} a_1^{\alpha} d\eta_1^{\alpha} = \int_{0}^{\infty} \eta_1^{\alpha}(\{\tilde{S} \in \mathcal{S} | a_1^{\alpha}(\tilde{S}) \geq \delta_1^{\alpha}\}) d\delta_1^{\alpha},$$

$$I_2^{\alpha}(a_2^{\alpha}) = \int_{\mathcal{S}} a_2^{\alpha} d\eta_2^{\alpha} = \int_{0}^{\infty} \eta_2^{\alpha}(\{\tilde{S} \in \mathfrak{S} | a_2^{\alpha}(\tilde{S}) \geq \delta_2^{\alpha}\}) d\delta_2^{\alpha}.$$

Here $I_1^{\alpha}, I_2^{\alpha}: \mathcal{C} \to \mathcal{R}$ are monotonic and homogenous functions, where $\mathcal{C}$ is the space of bounded, $\tilde{\mathcal{F}}_{\mathcal{S}}$-measurable, and real-valued functions on $\mathcal{S}$. $\left[\tilde{I}(\tilde{a})\right]^{\alpha} = \left[I_1^{\alpha}(a_1^{\alpha}), I_2^{\alpha}(a_2^{\alpha})\right]$ is an α-cut of a fuzzy number because $I_1^{\alpha}(a_1^{\alpha}) \leq I_1^{\bar{\alpha}}(a_1^{\bar{\alpha}})$, $I_2^{\alpha}(a_2^{\alpha}) \geq I_2^{\bar{\alpha}}(a_2^{\bar{\alpha}})$ for $\alpha \leq \bar{\alpha}$ and $I_1^{\alpha}(a_1^{\alpha}) \leq I_2^{\alpha}(a_2^{\alpha})$ due to monotonicity property of $I_1^{\alpha}, I_2^{\alpha}: \mathcal{C} \to \mathcal{R}$ and the fact that $\eta_1^{\alpha}(a_1^{\alpha}) \leq \eta_2^{\alpha}(a_2^{\alpha})$.

Denote $\mathcal{S}^*$ the indicator function of $\mathcal{S}$. Consider the following result related to a fuzzy number-valued fuzzy measure $\tilde{\eta}$.

Theorem 6.3. *Let $\tilde{I}: \mathcal{B} \to \mathcal{E}^1$, where $\mathcal{B}$ is the space of bounded, $\tilde{\mathcal{F}}_{\mathcal{S}}$-measurable, fuzzy number-valued functions on $\mathcal{S}$, satisfying $\tilde{I}(\mathcal{S}^*) = 1$, be given. Assume also that the functional $\tilde{I}$ satisfies:*

(i) Comonotonic additivity: for comonotonic $\tilde{a}, \tilde{b} \in \mathcal{B}$, $\tilde{I}(\tilde{a} + \tilde{b}) = \tilde{I}(\tilde{a}) + \tilde{I}(\tilde{b})$ holds;

(ii) Monotonicity: if $\tilde{a}(\tilde{S}) \geq \tilde{b}(\tilde{S})$ for all $\tilde{S} \in \mathcal{S}$ then $\tilde{I}(\tilde{a}) \geq \tilde{I}(\tilde{b})$.

Under these conditions, defining $\tilde{\eta}(H)=\tilde{I}(H^*)$ for all $H\in\tilde{\mathcal{F}}_S$, where H^* denotes the indicator function of H, we have

$$\tilde{I}(\tilde{a})=\int_0^{\infty}\tilde{\eta}(\tilde{a}\geq\tilde{\delta})d\tilde{\delta}+\int_{-\infty}^{0}\left(\tilde{\eta}(\tilde{a}\geq\tilde{\delta})-1\right)d\tilde{\delta},\ \forall\tilde{a}\in\mathcal{B},\tag{6.2}$$

such that

$$I_1^{\alpha}(a_1^{\alpha})=\int_0^{\infty}\eta_1^{\alpha}(a_1^{\alpha}\geq\delta_1^{\alpha})d\delta_1^{\alpha}+\int_{-\infty}^{0}\left(\eta_1^{\alpha}(a_1^{\alpha}\geq\delta_1^{\alpha})-1\right)d\delta_1^{\alpha}$$

$$I_2^{\alpha}(a_2^{\alpha})=\int_0^{\infty}\eta_2^{\alpha}(a_2^{\alpha}\geq\delta_2^{\alpha})d\delta_2^{\alpha}+\int_{-\infty}^{0}\left(\eta_2^{\alpha}(a_2^{\alpha}\geq\delta_2^{\alpha})-1\right)d\delta_2^{\alpha}.$$

Note that comonotonically additive and monotonic $\tilde{I}$ on $\mathcal{B}$ satisfies $\tilde{I}(\lambda\tilde{a})=\lambda\tilde{I}(\tilde{a})$ for $\lambda>0$. Indeed, α-cut of $\tilde{I}(\lambda\tilde{a})$ is defined as $\left[\tilde{I}(\lambda\tilde{a})\right]^{\alpha}=\left[I_1^{\alpha}([\lambda\tilde{a}]_1^{\alpha}),I_2^{\alpha}([\lambda\tilde{a}]_2^{\alpha})\right]$, where $[\lambda\tilde{a}]_1^{\alpha}=\lambda a_1^{\alpha}$, $[\lambda\tilde{a}]_2^{\alpha}=\lambda a_2^{\alpha}$ because $\lambda>0$. So, $I_1^{\alpha}(\lambda a_1^{\alpha})=\lambda I_1^{\alpha}(a_1^{\alpha}),I_2^{\alpha}(\lambda a_2^{\alpha})=\lambda I_2^{\alpha}(a_2^{\alpha})$.

Thus, we will have:

$$\begin{aligned}\left[\tilde{I}(\lambda\tilde{a})\right]^{\alpha}&=\left[I_1^{\alpha}(\lambda a_1^{\alpha}),I_2^{\alpha}(\lambda a_2^{\alpha})\right]=\left[\lambda I_1^{\alpha}(a_1^{\alpha}),\lambda I_2^{\alpha}(a_2^{\alpha})\right]\\&=\lambda\left[I_1^{\alpha}(a_1^{\alpha}),I_2^{\alpha}(a_2^{\alpha})\right]=\lambda\left[\tilde{I}(\tilde{a})\right]^{\alpha}\end{aligned}$$

So, $\tilde{I}(\lambda\tilde{a})=\lambda\tilde{I}(\tilde{a}),\lambda>0$.

In order to prove Theorem 6.3 we need to use the following remark.

Remark 6.1. *The integrand in (6.2) can be compactly expressed as follows:*

$$\tilde{a}^*(\tilde{\delta})=\begin{cases}\tilde{\eta}(\tilde{a}\geq\tilde{\delta}),\tilde{\delta}\geq 0\\ \tilde{\eta}(\tilde{a}\geq\tilde{\delta})-\tilde{\eta}(S),\tilde{\delta}<0\end{cases},$$

in sense that

$$a^{*\alpha}_1(\tilde{\delta}) = a^{*\alpha}_1(\delta_1^\alpha) = \begin{cases} \eta_1^\alpha(a_1^\alpha \geq \delta_1^\alpha), \delta_1^\alpha \geq 0 \\ \eta_1^\alpha(a_1^\alpha \geq \delta_1^\alpha) - \eta_1^\alpha(\mathcal{S}), \delta_1^\alpha < 0 \end{cases}$$

$$a^{*\alpha}_2(\tilde{\delta}) = a^{*\alpha}_2(\delta_2^\alpha) = \begin{cases} \eta_2^\alpha(a_2^\alpha \geq \delta_2^\alpha), \delta_2^\alpha \geq 0 \\ \eta_2^\alpha(a_2^\alpha \geq \delta_2^\alpha) - \eta_2^\alpha(\mathcal{S}), \delta_2^\alpha < 0 \end{cases}$$

If a_1^α, a_2^α are nonnegative, then $a^{*\alpha}_1, a^{*\alpha}_2 = 0$ for $\delta_1^\alpha, \delta_2^\alpha < 0$. If θ_1^α, θ_2^α are negative lower bounds of a_1^α, a_2^α respectively then $a^{*\alpha}_1(\delta_1^\alpha) = 0$ and $a^{*\alpha}_2(\delta_2^\alpha) = 0$ for $\delta_1^\alpha \leq \theta_1^\alpha$ and $\delta_2^\alpha \leq \theta_2^\alpha$ respectively. If $\vartheta_1^\alpha, \vartheta_2^\alpha$ are upper bound of a_1^α, a_2^α respectively, then α-cuts of (6.2) are equivalent to

$$I_1^\alpha(a_1^\alpha) = \int_{\theta_1^\alpha}^{\vartheta_1^\alpha} a^{*\alpha}_1(\delta_1^\alpha) d\delta_1^\alpha,$$

$$I_2^\alpha(a_2^\alpha) = \int_{\theta_2^\alpha}^{\vartheta_2^\alpha} a^{*\alpha}_2(\delta_2^\alpha) d\delta_2^\alpha.$$

So, (6.2) is equivalent to $\tilde{I}(\tilde{a}) = \int_{\tilde{\theta}}^{\tilde{\vartheta}} \tilde{a}^*(\tilde{\delta}) d\tilde{\delta}$ (the fact that $\vartheta_1^\alpha, \vartheta_2^\alpha$ and θ_1^α, θ_2^α can be considered as endpoints of α-cut of a fuzzy number is obvious). As $I_1^\alpha, I_2^\alpha : \mathcal{C} \to \mathcal{R}$ are comonotonically additive and monotonic, then, based on the results in [362], we can claim that α-cuts of (6.2) are implied by α-cuts of (6.1), and hence, (6.2) is implied by (6.1).

Proof of Theorem 6.3. Remark 6.1 allows for proof of (6.1) for nonnegative fuzzy number-valued functions only. Assuming that (6.1) holds for any fuzzy finite step function, we will prove it for an arbitrary nonnegative $\tilde{\mathcal{F}}_S$-measurable fuzzy number-valued function [433] $\tilde{a}$ bounded by some $\tilde{\lambda} \in \mathcal{E}^1$ (that is, $0 \leq \tilde{a}(\tilde{S}) \leq \tilde{\lambda}$, hold for all $\tilde{S} \in \mathcal{S}$). For $n = 1, 2, \ldots$ and $1 \leq k \leq 2^n$ we define

$$\mathfrak{H}_n^{k,1,\alpha} = \left\{ \tilde{S} \in \mathfrak{S} \middle| \lambda_1^\alpha (k-1)/2^n < \left[\tilde{a}(\tilde{S})\right]_1^\alpha \leq \lambda_1^\alpha k/2^n \right\} \text{ and}$$

$$\mathfrak{H}_n^{k,2,\alpha} = \left\{ \tilde{S} \in \mathfrak{S} \middle| \lambda_2^\alpha (k-1)/2^n < \left[\tilde{a}(\tilde{S})\right]_2^\alpha \le \lambda_2^\alpha k/2^n \right\}.$$

Define also

$$\left[\tilde{a}_n(\tilde{S})\right]_1^\alpha = \lambda_1^\alpha (k-1)/2^n,\ \left[\tilde{a}_n(\tilde{S})\right]_2^\alpha = \lambda_2^\alpha (k-1)/2^n,\ \left[\tilde{b}_n(\tilde{S})\right]_1^\alpha = \lambda_1^\alpha k/2^n,$$
$$\left[\tilde{b}_n(\tilde{S})\right]_2^\alpha = \lambda_2^\alpha k/2^n.$$

Thus, for all $\tilde{S}$ and n:

$$\left[\tilde{a}_n(\tilde{S})\right]_1^\alpha \le \left[\tilde{a}_{n+1}(\tilde{S})\right]_1^\alpha \le \left[\tilde{a}(\tilde{S})\right]_1^\alpha \le \left[\tilde{b}_{n+1}(\tilde{S})\right]_1^\alpha \le \left[\tilde{b}_n(\tilde{S})\right]_1^\alpha \text{ and}$$

$$\left[\tilde{a}_n(\tilde{S})\right]_2^\alpha \le \left[\tilde{a}_{n+1}(\tilde{S})\right]_2^\alpha \le \left[\tilde{a}(\tilde{S})\right]_2^\alpha \le \left[\tilde{b}_{n+1}(\tilde{S})\right]_2^\alpha \le \left[\tilde{b}_n(\tilde{S})\right]_2^\alpha$$

hold. So, for all $\tilde{S}$ and n $\tilde{a}_n(\tilde{S}) \le \tilde{a}_{n+1}(\tilde{S}) \le \tilde{a}(\tilde{S}) \le \tilde{b}_{n+1}(\tilde{S}) \le \tilde{b}_n(\tilde{S})$ hold. Monotonicity for $I_1^\alpha, I_2^\alpha : \mathcal{C} \to \mathcal{R}$ implies that $I_1^\alpha(a_{n1}^\alpha) \le I_1^\alpha(a_1^\alpha)$ $\le I_1^\alpha(b_{n1}^\alpha)$, $I_2^\alpha(a_{n2}^\alpha) \le I_2^\alpha(a_2^\alpha) \le I_2^\alpha(b_{n2}^\alpha)$, in turn comonotonic additivity of $I_1^\alpha, I_2^\alpha :\ \mathcal{C} \to \mathcal{R}$ implies

$$0 \le I_1^\alpha(b_{n1}^\alpha) - I_1^\alpha(a_{n1}^\alpha) = \lambda_1^\alpha / 2^n \to 0 \text{ and}$$

$$0 \le I_2^\alpha(b_{n2}^\alpha) - I_2^\alpha(a_{n2}^\alpha) = \lambda_2^\alpha / 2^n \to 0,\ \ n \to \infty.$$

Based on the assumption about fuzzy finite step functions, it follows that

$$I_1^\alpha(a_{n1}^\alpha) = \int_0^{\lambda_1^\alpha} \eta_1^\alpha(a_{n1}^\alpha \ge \delta_1^\alpha) d\delta_1^\alpha\ ,\ I_2^\alpha(a_{n2}^\alpha) = \int_0^{\lambda_2^\alpha} \eta_2^\alpha(a_{n2}^\alpha \ge \delta_2^\alpha) d\delta_2^\alpha \text{ and}$$

$$I_1^\alpha(b_{n1}^\alpha) = \int_0^{\lambda_1^\alpha} \eta_1^\alpha(b_{n1}^\alpha \ge \delta_1^\alpha) d\delta_1^\alpha\ ,\ I_2^\alpha(b_{n2}^\alpha) = \int_0^{\lambda_2^\alpha} \eta_2^\alpha(b_{n2}^\alpha \ge \delta_2^\alpha) d\delta_2^\alpha\ .$$

The monotonicity of $\eta_1^\alpha, \eta_2^\alpha$ and the definitions of $a_{n1}^\alpha, b_{n1}^\alpha, a_{n2}^\alpha, b_{n2}^\alpha$,

$n = 1,2,...,$ imply $\eta_1^\alpha(a_{n1}^{\ \alpha} \geq \delta_1^\alpha) \leq \eta_1^\alpha(a_1^\alpha \geq \delta_1^\alpha) \leq \eta_1^\alpha(b_{n1}^{\ \alpha} \geq \delta_1^\alpha)$, $\eta_2^\alpha(a_{n2}^{\ \alpha} \geq \delta_2^\alpha)$ $\leq \eta_2^\alpha(a_2^\alpha \geq \delta_2^\alpha) \leq \eta_2^\alpha(b_{n2}^{\ \alpha} \geq \delta_2^\alpha)$. From these inequalities it follows that

$$\int_0^{\lambda_1^\alpha} \eta_1^\alpha(a_{n1}^{\ \alpha} \geq \delta_1^\alpha)d\delta_1^\alpha \leq \int_0^{\lambda_1^\alpha} \eta_1^\alpha(a_1^\alpha \geq \delta_1^\alpha)d\delta_1^\alpha \leq \int_0^{\lambda_1^\alpha} \eta_1^\alpha(b_{n1}^{\ \alpha} \geq \delta_1^\alpha)d\delta_1^\alpha \text{ and}$$

$$\int_0^{\lambda_2^\alpha} \eta_2^\alpha(a_{n2}^{\ \alpha} \geq \delta_2^\alpha)d\delta_2^\alpha \leq \int_0^{\lambda_2^\alpha} \eta_2^\alpha(a_2^\alpha \geq \delta_2^\alpha)d\delta_2^\alpha \leq \int_0^{\lambda_2^\alpha} \eta_2^\alpha(b_{n2}^{\ \alpha} \geq \delta_2^\alpha)d\delta_2^\alpha$$

hold.

So, $I_1^\alpha(a_1^\alpha) = \int_0^{\lambda_1^\alpha} \eta_1^\alpha(a_1^\alpha \geq \delta_1^\alpha)d\delta_1^\alpha$, $I_2^\alpha(a_2^\alpha) = \int_0^{\lambda_2^\alpha} \eta_2^\alpha(a_2^\alpha \geq \delta_2^\alpha)d\delta_2^\alpha$, that is,

$$\tilde{I}(\tilde{a}) = \int_0^{\tilde{\lambda}} \tilde{\eta}(\tilde{a} \geq \tilde{\delta})d\tilde{\delta}.$$

Let us now prove that (6.1) holds for fuzzy finite step functions. Any nonnegative fuzzy step function $\tilde{a} \in \mathcal{B}$ has a unique α-cut representation $a_1^\alpha = \sum_{i=1}^k \delta_{i1}^{\ \alpha} H_i^*$, $a_2^\alpha = \sum_{i=1}^k \delta_{i2}^{\ \alpha} H_i^*$ for some k, where $\delta_{11}^{\ \alpha} > \delta_{21}^{\ \alpha} > \cdots$ $> \delta_{k1}^{\ \alpha}, \delta_{12}^{\alpha} > \delta_{22}^{\alpha} > \cdots > \delta_{k2}^{\ \alpha}$ and the sets H_i, $i = 1,...,k$ are pairwise disjoint. Defining $\delta_{k+11}^{\ \ \alpha} = 0$, $\delta_{k+12}^{\ \ \alpha} = 0$ we have:

$$\int_0^{\delta_{11}^\alpha} \eta_1^\alpha(a_1^\alpha \geq \delta_1^\alpha)d\delta_1^\alpha = \sum_{i=1}^k \left(\delta_{i1}^\alpha - \delta_{i+11}^{\ \ \alpha}\right)\eta_1^\alpha\left(\bigcup_{j=1}^i H_j\right),$$

$$\int_0^{\delta_{12}^\alpha} \eta_2^\alpha(a_2^\alpha \geq \delta_2^\alpha)d\delta_2^\alpha = \sum_{i=1}^k \left(\delta_{i2}^\alpha - \delta_{i+12}^{\ \ \alpha}\right)\eta_2^\alpha\left(\bigcup_{j=1}^i H_j\right).$$

So,

$$\int_0^{\tilde{\delta}_1} \tilde{\eta}(\tilde{a} \geq \tilde{\delta})d\tilde{\delta} = \sum_{i=1}^k \left(\tilde{\delta}_i -_h \tilde{\delta}_{i+1}\right)\tilde{\eta}\left(\bigcup_{j=1}^i \mathfrak{H}_j\right). \tag{6.3}$$

Note that throughout the study we use the Hukuhara difference. The induction hypothesis implies that for $k < n$

$$\tilde{I}(\tilde{a}) = \sum_{i=1}^{k}\left(\tilde{\delta}_i -_h \tilde{\delta}_{i+1}\right)\tilde{\eta}\left(\bigcup_{j=1}^{i} H_j\right). \tag{6.4}$$

We need to prove it for $k = n$. Note that for $k = 1$ $I_1^\alpha(\delta_1^\alpha \mathfrak{H}^*) = \delta_1^\alpha \eta_1^\alpha(\mathfrak{H})$, and $I_2^\alpha(\delta_2^\alpha H^*) = \delta_2^\alpha \eta_2^\alpha(H)$ hold, i.e, $\tilde{I}(\tilde{\delta}H^*) = \tilde{\delta}\tilde{\eta}(H)$ holds.

Given endpoints of α-cut of $\tilde{a}$ as $a_1^\alpha = \sum_{i=1}^{k}\delta_{i1}^\alpha H_i^*$, $a_2^\alpha = \sum_{i=1}^{k}\delta_{i2}^\alpha H_i^*$, $\tilde{a} = \tilde{b} + \tilde{c}$, where $b_1^\alpha = \sum_{i=1}^{k-1}(\delta_{i1}^\alpha - \delta_{i+11}{}^\alpha)H_i^*$, $b_2^\alpha = \sum_{i=1}^{k-1}(\delta_{i2}^\alpha - \delta_{i+12}{}^\alpha)H_i^*$, $c_1^\alpha = \delta_{k1}{}^\alpha\left(\sum_{i=1}^{k}H_j^*\right)$, $c_2^\alpha = \delta_{k2}{}^\alpha\left(\sum_{i=1}^{k}H_j^*\right)$. From the induction hypothesis ($k-1 < n$),

$$\tilde{I}(\tilde{b}) = \sum_{i=1}^{k-1}\left(\left(\tilde{\delta}_i -_h \tilde{\delta}_k\right) -_h \left(\tilde{\delta}_{i+1} -_h \tilde{\delta}_k\right)\right)\tilde{\eta}\left(\bigcup_{j=1}^{i} H_j\right) = \sum_{i=1}^{k-1}\left(\tilde{\delta}_i -_h \tilde{\delta}_{i+1}\right)\tilde{\eta}\left(\bigcup_{j=1}^{i} H_j\right) \text{ and}$$

$$\tilde{I}(\tilde{c}) = \tilde{\delta}_k\tilde{\eta}\left(\bigcup_{j=1}^{i} H_j\right).$$

Thus, $\tilde{I}(\tilde{b}) + \tilde{I}(\tilde{c}) = \sum_{i=1}^{k}\left(\tilde{\delta}_i -_h \tilde{\delta}_{i+1}\right)\tilde{\eta}\left(\bigcup_{j=1}^{i} H_j\right)$. From the other side, as $\tilde{b}$ and $\tilde{c}$ are comonotonic, $\tilde{I}(\tilde{a}) = \tilde{I}(\tilde{b}) + \tilde{I}(\tilde{c})$ and (6.4) for $k = n$ has been proved. The proof is completed. □

Remark 6.2. *From the opposite direction of Theorem 6.3 it follows that if a fuzzy functional* $\tilde{I}$ *is defined by (6.2) with respect to some fuzzy number-valued fuzzy measure, then it satisfies comonotonic additivity and monotonicity. One can easily obtain the proof by reversing the proof of Theorem 6.3 as follows. For a functional* $\tilde{I}$ *defined by (6.2) with respect to some fuzzy number-valued fuzzy measure* $\tilde{\eta}$, *it is needed to prove that it is comonotonically additive and monotonic. Monotonicity of* $\tilde{I}$ *follows from the fact that* $\tilde{a} \geq \tilde{b}$ *on* S *implies* $\tilde{a}^* \geq \tilde{b}^*$ *on* $\mathcal{E}^1$.

So, at first it is needed to show comonotonic additivity for fuzzy finite step functions in $\mathcal{B}$. To this end the following two claims are given.

Claim 6.1. *Two fuzzy finite step functions* $\tilde{b}, \tilde{c} \in \mathcal{B}$ *are comonotonic iff there exists an integer* k, *a partition of* $\mathcal{S}$ *into* k *pairwise disjoint elements* $(H_i)_{i=1}^{k}$ *of* $\tilde{\mathcal{F}}_{\mathcal{S}}$, *and two* k *-lists of fuzzy numbers* $\tilde{\beta}_1 \geq \tilde{\beta}_2 \geq \ldots \geq \tilde{\beta}_k$ *and* $\tilde{\gamma}_1 \geq \tilde{\gamma}_2 \geq \ldots \geq \tilde{\gamma}_k$ *such that* $\tilde{b} = \sum_{i=1}^{k} \tilde{\beta}_i H_i^*$ *and* $\tilde{c} = \sum_{i=1}^{k} \tilde{\gamma}_i H_i^*$. *The proof is obvious.*

Claim 6.2. *Let* $(H_i)_{i=1}^{k}$ *be* $\tilde{\mathcal{F}}_{\mathcal{S}}$*-measurable finite partition of* $\mathcal{S}$ *(if* $i \neq j$, *then* $H_i \cap H_j = \varnothing$*) and let* $\tilde{a} = \sum_{i=1}^{k} \tilde{\delta}_i H_i^*$ *with* $\tilde{\alpha}_1 \geq \tilde{\alpha}_2 \geq \ldots \geq \tilde{\alpha}_k$. *Then for any fuzzy number-valued fuzzy measure* $\tilde{\eta}: \tilde{\mathcal{F}}_{\mathcal{S}} \to \mathcal{E}^1$ *we have:*

$$\int_{-\infty}^{\infty} \tilde{a}^*(\tilde{\delta}) d\tilde{\delta} = \sum_{i=1}^{k} (\tilde{\delta}_i -_h \tilde{\delta}_{i+1}) \tilde{\eta}\left(\bigcup_{j=1}^{i} H_j \right) \tag{6.5}$$

with $\tilde{\delta}_{k=1} = 0$.

For $\tilde{I}(\tilde{a})$ defined by the left side of (6.5) for fuzzy finite step functions, the formula (6.5) and Claim 6.6 imply additivity for comonotonic fuzzy finite step functions. Extension of this result to any comonotonic functions in $\mathcal{B}$ is obtained by computing appropriate limits in metrics $\tilde{d}_{fH}$.

It can be easily shown that Theorem 6.3 and its converse hold if $\mathcal{B}$ is substituted by $\mathcal{B}_0$, the set of all fuzzy finite step functions in $\mathcal{B}$. Also, for comonotonically additive and monotonic $\tilde{I}: \mathcal{B}_0 \to \mathcal{E}^1$ there exists a unique extension to all of $\mathcal{B}$, which satisfies comonotonic additivity and monotonicity. To prove this it is needed to pass to α -cuts of $\tilde{I}$ and then easily apply the facts that $\mathcal{B}$ is the (sup) norm closure of $\mathcal{B}_0$ in $(\mathcal{E}^1)^{\mathcal{S}}$ in metrics $\tilde{d}_{fH}$ and that monotonicity implies norm continuity.

Now let $\mathcal{B}(\mathcal{K})$ denote the set of functions in $\mathcal{B}$ with values in $\mathcal{K}$, and suppose that $\mathcal{K} \supset \left\{ \tilde{v} \in \mathcal{E}^1 \middle| -\tilde{\gamma} \leq \tilde{v} \leq \tilde{\gamma} \right\}$, where $\tilde{\gamma} \geq 0, -\tilde{\gamma} = -1\tilde{\gamma}$.

Corollary 6.1. *Let* $\tilde{I}:\mathcal{B}(\mathcal{K})\to\mathcal{E}^1$ *be given such that*

1) *for all* $\tilde{\lambda}\in\mathcal{K}$ $\tilde{I}(\tilde{\lambda}\mathcal{S}^*)=\tilde{\lambda}$
2) *if* $\tilde{a},\tilde{b}$ *and* $\tilde{c}$ *are pairwise comonotonic, and* $\tilde{I}(\tilde{a})>\tilde{I}(\tilde{b})$, *then* $\tilde{I}(\sigma\tilde{a}+(1-\sigma)\tilde{c})>\tilde{I}(\sigma\tilde{b}+(1-\sigma)\tilde{c})$, $\sigma\in(0,1)$,
3) *if* $\tilde{a}\ge\tilde{b}$ *on* $\mathcal{S}$, *then* $\tilde{I}(\tilde{a})\ge\tilde{I}(\tilde{b})$.

Then, defining $\tilde{\eta}(H)=\tilde{I}(H^*)$ on $\tilde{\mathcal{F}}_S$ we will have for all $\tilde{a}\in\mathcal{B}(\mathcal{K})$:

$$\tilde{I}(\tilde{a})=\int_0^\infty\tilde{\eta}(\tilde{a}\ge\tilde{\delta})d\tilde{\delta}+\int_{-\infty}^0\left(\tilde{\eta}(\tilde{a}\ge\tilde{\delta})-1\right)d\tilde{\delta}.$$

The proof consists in extending $\tilde{I}$ on $\mathcal{B}(\mathcal{K})$ to $\tilde{I}$ on $\mathcal{B}$ and showing that conditions of Theorem 6.3 are satisfied. As $\tilde{I}$ is homogeneous on $\mathcal{B}(\mathcal{K})$ it can be uniquely extended to a homogeneous function on $\mathcal{B}$. Next, by homogeneity, the extended functional $\tilde{I}$ satisfies monotonicity on $\mathcal{B}$. Comonotonic additivity of $\tilde{I}$ on $\mathcal{B}$ follows from the following Lemma and homogeneity property.

Lemma. *Given the conditions of the Corollary, let* $\tilde{a}$ *and* $\tilde{b}$ *in* $\mathcal{B}(\mathcal{K})$ *be comonotonic such that* $\tilde{d}_{fH}(\tilde{a}(\tilde{S}),0)\ge-1+\varepsilon$, $\tilde{d}_{fH}(\tilde{b}(\tilde{S}),0)\le1-\varepsilon$ *for some* $\varepsilon>0$ *and let* $0<\lambda<1$. *Then* $\tilde{I}(\lambda\tilde{a}+(1-\lambda)\tilde{b})=\lambda\tilde{I}(\tilde{a})+(1-\lambda)\tilde{I}(\tilde{b})$.

Proof. Denote $\tilde{I}(\tilde{a})=\tilde{\sigma}$ and $\tilde{I}(\tilde{b})=\tilde{\beta}$. By the condition of the Lemma, and by (i) and (iii) of the Corollary it is true that $\tilde{\sigma}\mathcal{S}^*,\tilde{\beta}\mathcal{S}^*\in\mathcal{B}(\mathcal{K})$, $\tilde{I}(\tilde{\sigma}\mathcal{S}^*)=\tilde{\sigma}$ and $\tilde{I}(\tilde{\beta}\mathcal{S}^*)=\tilde{\beta}$.

We need to prove that $\tilde{I}(\lambda\tilde{a}+(1-\lambda)\tilde{b})=\lambda\tilde{I}(\tilde{a})+(1-\lambda)\tilde{I}(\tilde{b})$. Suppose that $\tilde{I}(\lambda\tilde{a}+(1-\lambda)\tilde{b})>\lambda\tilde{I}(\tilde{a})+(1-\lambda)\tilde{I}(\tilde{b})$ (the case of the other inequality is treated in a similar manner).

Let $0<\xi<\varepsilon$. Then by (i) $\tilde{I}(\tilde{\sigma})<\tilde{I}((\tilde{\sigma}+\xi)\mathcal{S}^*)$, $\tilde{I}(\tilde{b})<\tilde{I}((\tilde{\beta}+\xi)\mathcal{S}^*)$. Now

$$\lambda\tilde{\sigma}+(1-\lambda)\tilde{\beta}+\xi=\tilde{I}(\lambda(\tilde{\sigma}+\xi)\mathcal{S}^*+(1-\lambda)(\tilde{\beta}+\xi)\mathcal{S}^*)>$$
$$>\tilde{I}(\lambda\tilde{a}+(1-\lambda)(\tilde{\beta}+\xi)\mathcal{S}^*)>\tilde{I}(\lambda\tilde{a}+(1-\lambda)\tilde{b}).$$

The equality follows from (i) and each of the two inequalities follows from (ii). The inequality above holds for any ξ ($0<\xi<\varepsilon$), so we get the required contradiction. The proof is completed. □

Remark 6.3. *The Corollary holds if $\mathcal{B}(\mathcal{K})$ is replaced by $\mathcal{B}_0(\mathcal{K})$ the set of bounded, $\tilde{\mathcal{F}}_S$-measurable, fuzzy finite step functions on $\mathcal{S}$ with values in $\mathcal{K}$. The same is true for the Lemma.*

Given the above mentioned auxiliary results on a fuzzy number-valued Choquet integral [433] of a fuzzy number-valued function with respect to a fuzzy number-valued fuzzy measure $\tilde{\eta}$ we can prove the theorems 6.1 and 6.2. Let us proceed to the proof of theorem 6.1.

Proof of Theorem 6.1.

Step 1. At this step we show the existence of an affine fuzzy-number-valued function defined over $\mathcal{Y}$.

Affinity of $\tilde{u}$ implies $\tilde{u}(\tilde{y})=\sum_{\tilde{X}\in\mathcal{X}}\tilde{y}(\tilde{X})\tilde{u}(\tilde{X})$ defined as follows:

$$\mu_{\tilde{u}(\tilde{y})}(u(\tilde{y}))=\sup_{\substack{u(\tilde{y})=\sum_{\tilde{X}\in\mathcal{X}}y(\tilde{X})u(\tilde{X})\\ \sum_{\tilde{X}\in\mathcal{X}}y(\tilde{X})=1}}\min(\mu_{\tilde{u}(\tilde{X})}(u(\tilde{X})),\mu_{\tilde{y}(\tilde{X})}(y(\tilde{X}))).$$

Positive linear transformation $\tilde{u}'$ of $\tilde{u}$ implies $\tilde{u}'=\tilde{A}\tilde{u}(\tilde{y})+\tilde{B}$, $\tilde{A}\in\mathcal{E}^1_+,\tilde{B}\in\mathcal{E}^1$, where addition and multiplication is defined on the base of Zadeh's extension principle.

Using the implications from von Neumann-Morgenstern theorem, we suppose that there exists a fuzzy-number-valued function $\tilde{u}$ representing LPR $\succsim_l$ induced on $\mathcal{Y}$. Now, from the nondegeneracy axiom it follows that there exist such $\tilde{f}^*$ and $\tilde{f}_*$ in $\mathcal{A}_0$ that $\tilde{f}^*\succ_l\tilde{f}_*$. From the monotonicity axiom it follows existence of a state $\tilde{S}$ in $\mathcal{S}$ such that $\tilde{f}^*(\tilde{S})\equiv\tilde{y}^*\succ_l\tilde{f}_*(\tilde{S})\equiv\tilde{y}_*$. Since $\tilde{u}$ is given up to a positive linear transformation, suppose that $\tilde{u}(\tilde{y}_*)=-\tilde{v}$ and $\tilde{u}(\tilde{y}^*)=\tilde{v}$, $\tilde{v}\in\mathcal{E}^1_+$. We denote $\mathcal{K}=\tilde{u}(\mathcal{Y})$ which is a convex subset [311] of $\mathcal{E}^1$ with $-\tilde{v},\tilde{v}\in\mathcal{K}$.

Step 2. At this step we show the existence of an affine fuzzy-number-valued function defined over $\mathcal{A}_0$.

Denote by $\mathcal{M}_{\tilde{f}}=\{\sigma\tilde{f}+(1-\sigma)\tilde{y}^S\mid\tilde{y}\in\mathcal{Y}\ and\ \sigma\in[0,1]\}$ for an arbitrary $\tilde{f} \in \mathcal{A}_0$. It is clear that $\mathcal{M}_{\tilde{f}}$ is convex and any two acts in $\mathcal{M}_{\tilde{f}}$ are comonotonic. So we can claim that there exists an affine fuzzy number-valued function over $\mathcal{M}_{\tilde{f}}$ representing the corresponding LPR $\succsim_l$. By using positive linear transformation we can define for this function denoted $\tilde{J}_{\tilde{f}}$: $\tilde{J}_{\tilde{f}}(\tilde{y}_*^S) = -\tilde{v}$ and $\tilde{J}_{\tilde{f}}(\tilde{y}^{*S}) = \tilde{v}$. For any $\tilde{h} \in \mathcal{M}_{\tilde{f}} \cap \mathcal{M}_{\tilde{g}}$, $\tilde{J}_{\tilde{f}}(\tilde{h}) = \tilde{J}_{\tilde{g}}(\tilde{h})$ holds. This allows to define fuzzy number- valued function $\tilde{J}(\tilde{f}) = \tilde{J}_{\tilde{f}}(\tilde{f})$ on $\mathcal{A}_0$, which represents the LPR $\succsim_l$ on $\mathcal{A}_0$ and satisfies for all $\tilde{y}$ in $\mathcal{Y}: \tilde{J}(\tilde{y}^S) = \tilde{u}(\tilde{y})$.

Step 3. At this step we show the existence of a fuzzy-number-valued functional [404] defined on the base of $\tilde{u}$ and $\tilde{J}_{\tilde{f}}$.

Denote by $\mathcal{B}_0(\mathcal{K})$ the $\tilde{\mathcal{F}}_S$-measurable, $\mathcal{K}$-valued fuzzy finite step functions on $\mathcal{S}$. By means of $\tilde{u}$ let us define an onto function $\tilde{\Phi}: \mathcal{A}_0 \to \mathcal{B}_0(\mathcal{K})$ as $\tilde{\Phi}(\tilde{f})(\tilde{S}) = \tilde{u}(\tilde{f}(\tilde{S}))$, $\tilde{S} \in \mathcal{S}, \tilde{f} \in \mathcal{A}_0$. If $\tilde{\Phi}(\tilde{f}) = \tilde{\Phi}(\tilde{g})$ then $\tilde{f} \sim_l \tilde{g}$ (it follows from monotonicity). So, $\tilde{\Phi}(\tilde{f}) = \tilde{\Phi}(\tilde{g})$ implies $\tilde{J}(\tilde{f}) = \tilde{J}(\tilde{g})$.

Define a fuzzy number-valued function $\tilde{I}$ on $\mathcal{B}_0(\mathcal{K})$ as follows: $\tilde{I}(\tilde{a}) = \tilde{J}(\tilde{f})$ for $\tilde{a} \in \mathcal{B}_0(\mathcal{K})$, where $\tilde{f} \in \mathcal{A}_0$ is such that $\tilde{\Phi}(\tilde{f}) = \tilde{a}$. $\tilde{I}$ is well defined as $\tilde{J}$ is constant fuzzy number-valued function (that is, $\exists \tilde{v} \in \mathcal{E}^1$, $\tilde{J}(\tilde{f}) = \tilde{v}$, $\forall \tilde{f} \in \mathcal{A}$) on $\tilde{\Phi}^{-1}(\tilde{a})$.

Fuzzy number-valued function $\tilde{I}$ satisfies the following conditions:

(i) for all $\tilde{\sigma}$ in $\mathcal{K}: \tilde{I}(\tilde{\sigma}\mathcal{S}^*) = \tilde{\sigma}$. Indeed, let $\tilde{y} \in \mathcal{Y}$ be such that $\tilde{u}(\tilde{y}) = \tilde{\sigma}$, hence $\tilde{J}(\tilde{y}^S) = \tilde{\sigma}$ and $\tilde{\Phi}(\tilde{y}^S) = \tilde{\sigma}\mathcal{S}^*$ implying $\tilde{I}(\tilde{\sigma}\mathcal{S}^*) = \tilde{\sigma}$;

(ii) for all pairwise comonotonic functions $\tilde{a}$, $\tilde{b}$ and $\tilde{c}$ in $\mathcal{B}_0(\mathcal{K})$ and $\sigma \in [0,1]$: if $\tilde{I}(\tilde{a}) > \tilde{I}(\tilde{b})$, then $\tilde{I}(\sigma\tilde{a} + (1-\sigma)\tilde{c}) > \tilde{I}(\sigma\tilde{b} + (1-\sigma)\tilde{c})$. This is true because $\tilde{\Phi}$ preserves comonotonicity;

(iii) if $\tilde{a}(\tilde{S}) \geq \tilde{b}(\tilde{S})$ on $\mathcal{S}$ for $\tilde{a}$ and $\tilde{b}$ in $\mathcal{B}_0(\mathcal{K})$ then $\tilde{I}(\tilde{a}) \geq \tilde{I}(\tilde{b})$. This is true because $\tilde{\Phi}$ preserves monotonicity.

Step 4. This step completes the proof of the Theorem 6.1.

From the Corollary and Remark 6.3 for a fuzzy number-valued

function on $\mathcal{B}_0(\mathcal{K})$, which satisfies conditions (i), (ii), and (iii) above, it follows that the fuzzy number-valued fuzzy measure $\tilde{\eta}$ on $\tilde{\mathcal{F}}_S$ defined by $\tilde{\eta}(H) = \tilde{I}(H^*)$ satisfies

$$\tilde{I}(\tilde{a}) \geq \tilde{I}(\tilde{b}) \text{ iff } \int_S \tilde{a}d\tilde{\eta} \geq \int_S \tilde{b}d\tilde{\eta}, \; \forall \tilde{a}, \tilde{b} \in \mathcal{B}_0(\mathcal{K}) \tag{6.6}$$

Hence, for all $\tilde{f}$ and $\tilde{g}$ in $\mathcal{A}_0$:

$$\tilde{f} \succsim_l \tilde{g} \text{ iff} \int_S \tilde{\Phi}(\tilde{f})d\tilde{\eta} \geq \int_S \tilde{\Phi}(\tilde{g})d\tilde{\eta}.$$

The proof is completed. □

Proof of Theorem 6.2.

Step 1. At this step we show that LPR, which is induced by $\tilde{u}$ and $\tilde{\eta}$ on $\mathcal{A}_0$, satisfies axioms (i)-(v).

To prove this theorem we use Remarks 6.1-6.3, Theorem 6.3 and other results given above, which show that $\tilde{I}$ on $\mathcal{B}_0(\mathcal{K})$ defined by (6.6) satisfies conditions (i)-(iii). Secondly, we can see that $\tilde{J}$ is defined as a combination of $\tilde{\Phi}$ and $\tilde{I}$. Thus, the LPR on $\mathcal{A}_0$ induced by $\tilde{J}$ satisfies all the required conditions because $\tilde{\Phi}$ preserves monotonicity and comonotonicity and $\int_S \tilde{a}d\tilde{\eta}$ is a (sup) norm continuous function on $\tilde{a}$ in metrics $\tilde{d}_{fH}$ (this is based on the analogous property of endpoints for α-cuts of $\int_S \tilde{a}d\tilde{\eta}$ that are classical functionals of the type considered in [361]).

Step 2. At this step we show the uniqueness of the fuzzy utility representation.

In order to prove the uniqueness property of the utility representation suppose that there exists an affine fuzzy number-valued function $\tilde{u}'$ on $\mathcal{Y}$ and a fuzzy number-valued fuzzy measure $\tilde{\eta}'$ on $\tilde{\mathcal{F}}_S$ such that for all $\tilde{f}$ and $\tilde{g}$ in $\mathcal{A}_0$:

$$\tilde{f} \succsim_l \tilde{g} \text{ iff } \int_{\mathcal{S}} \tilde{u}'(\tilde{f}(\tilde{S}))d\tilde{\eta}' \geq \int_{\mathcal{S}} \tilde{u}'(\tilde{g}(\tilde{S}))d\tilde{\eta}'. \tag{6.7}$$

Monotonicity of $\tilde{\eta}'$ can be derived. Considering (6.7) for all $\tilde{f},\tilde{g} \in \mathcal{A}_c$ we obtain, based on implications of von Neumann and Morgenstern theorem and Zadeh's extension principle, that $\tilde{u}'$ is a positive linear transformation of $\tilde{u}$. But (6.7) is preserved for positive linear transformation of a fuzzy utility. Hence, to prove that $\tilde{\eta}' = \tilde{\eta}$ we may assume w.l.o.g. that $\tilde{u}' = \tilde{u}$. For an arbitrary H in $\tilde{\mathcal{F}}_S$ let $\tilde{f}$ in $\mathcal{A}_0$ be such that $\tilde{\Phi}(\tilde{f}) = \tilde{\lambda} H^*, \tilde{\lambda} \in \mathfrak{E}^1$. Then $\int_{\mathcal{S}} \tilde{\Phi}(\tilde{f})d\tilde{\eta} = \tilde{\lambda}\tilde{\eta}(H)$ and $\int_{\mathcal{S}} \tilde{\Phi}(\tilde{f})d\tilde{\eta}' = \tilde{\lambda}\tilde{\eta}'(H)$. Let $\tilde{y}$ in $\mathcal{Y}$ be such that $\tilde{u}(\tilde{y}) = \tilde{\lambda}\tilde{\eta}(H)$. Then $\tilde{f} \sim_l \tilde{y}^{\mathcal{S}}$, which implies $\tilde{u}(\tilde{y}) = \tilde{u}'(\tilde{y}) = \int_{\mathcal{S}} \tilde{u}'(\tilde{y})d\tilde{\eta}' = \tilde{\lambda}\tilde{\eta}'(H)$. So, $\tilde{\lambda}\tilde{\eta}(H) = \tilde{\lambda}\tilde{\eta}'(H)$, and therefore, $\tilde{\eta}(H) = \tilde{\eta}'(H)$. The proof is completed. □

In brief, a value of a fuzzy utility function $\tilde{U}$ for action $\tilde{f}$ is determined as a fuzzy number-valued Choquet integral [21,23,27,31,34]:

$$\tilde{U}(\tilde{f}) = \int_{\mathcal{S}} \tilde{u}(\tilde{f}(\tilde{S}))d\tilde{\eta}_{\tilde{P}^l} = \sum_{i=1}^{n} \left(\tilde{u}(\tilde{f}(\tilde{S}_{(i)})) -_h \tilde{u}(\tilde{f}(\tilde{S}_{(i+1)}))\right) \cdot \tilde{\eta}_{\tilde{P}^l}(H_{(i)}). \tag{6.8}$$

Here $\tilde{\eta}_{\tilde{P}^l}()$ is a fuzzy number-valued fuzzy measure obtained from linguistic probability distribution over $\mathcal{S}$ [21,23,27,31,34] and $\tilde{u}(\tilde{f}(\tilde{S}))$ is a fuzzy number-valued utility function used to describe NL-based evaluations of utilities, (i) means that utilities are ranked such that $\tilde{u}(\tilde{f}(\tilde{S}_{(1)})) \geq \ldots \geq \tilde{u}(\tilde{f}(\tilde{S}_{(n)}))$, $H_{(i)} = \left\{\tilde{S}_{(1)},\ldots,\tilde{S}_{(i)}\right\}$, $\tilde{u}(\tilde{f}_j(\tilde{S}_{(n+1)})) = 0$, and for each (i) there exists $\tilde{u}(\tilde{f}(\tilde{S}_{(i)})) -_h \tilde{u}(\tilde{f}(\tilde{S}_{(i+1)}))$. Mutliplication $\cdot$ is realized in the sense of the Zadeh's extension principle. An optimal $\tilde{f}^* \in \mathcal{A}$, that is $\tilde{f}^* \in \mathcal{A}$ for which $\tilde{U}(\tilde{f}^*) = \max_{\tilde{f} \in \mathcal{A}} \left\{\int_{\mathcal{S}} \tilde{u}(\tilde{f}(\tilde{S}))d\tilde{\eta}_{\tilde{P}^l}\right\}$, can be determined by using a suitable fuzzy ranking method.

Note that for a special case the suggested decision making model and utility representation reduces to the model and representation suggested by Schmeidler in [362].

6.1.4 *Fuzzy-valued measure construction from linguistic probabilities*

The crucial problem in the determination of an overall fuzzy utility of an alternative is a construction of a fuzzy number-valued fuzzy measure $\tilde{\eta}$. We will consider $\tilde{\eta}$ as a fuzzy number-valued lower probability constructed from linguistic probability distribution $\tilde{P}^l$. Linguistic probability distribution $\tilde{P}^l$ implies that a state $\tilde{S}_i \in \mathcal{S}$ is assigned a linguistic probability $\tilde{P}_i$ that can be described by a fuzzy number defined over [0,1]. However, fuzzy probabilities $\tilde{P}_i$ cannot initially be assigned for all $\tilde{S}_i \in \mathcal{S}$ [31,34]. Initial data are represented by fuzzy probabilities for $n-1$ fuzzy states of nature whereas for one of the given fuzzy states the probability is unknown. Subsequently, it becomes necessary to determine unknown fuzzy probability $\tilde{P}(\tilde{S}_j)=\tilde{P}_j$ [27,31,34]. In the framework of Computing with Words [25,290,445,446], the problem of obtaining the unknown fuzzy probability for state $\tilde{S}_j$ given fuzzy probabilities of all other states is a problem of propagation of generalized constraints [443, 449,451]. Formally this problem is formulated as [449]:

Given

$$\tilde{P}\left(\tilde{S}_i\right)=\tilde{P}_i;\ \tilde{S}_i \in \mathcal{E}^n,\ \tilde{P}_i \in \mathcal{E}^1_{[0,1]},\ i=\{1,\dots,j-1,j+1,\dots,n\} \tag{6.9}$$

find unknown

$$\tilde{P}\left(\tilde{S}_j\right)=\tilde{P}_j,\ \tilde{P}_j \in \mathcal{E}^1_{[0,1]}. \tag{6.10}$$

It reduces to a variational problem of constructing the membership function $\mu_{\tilde{P}_j}(\cdot)$ of an unknown fuzzy probability $\tilde{P}_j$:

$$\mu_{\tilde{P}_j}(p_j)=\sup_\rho \min_{i=\{1,\dots,j-1,j+1,\dots,n\}}(\mu_{\tilde{P}_i}(\int_S \mu_{\tilde{S}_i}(s)\rho(s)ds)) \tag{6.11}$$

subject to

$$\int_S \mu_{\tilde{S}_j}(s)\rho(s)ds = p_j,\ \int_S \rho(s)ds = 1. \quad (6.12)$$

here $\mu_{\tilde{S}_j}(s)$ is the membership function of a fuzzy state $\tilde{S}_j$.

When $\tilde{P}_j$ has been determined, linguistic probability distribution $\tilde{P}^l$ for all states $\tilde{S}_i$ is determined:

$$\tilde{P}^l = \tilde{P}_1/\tilde{S}_1 + \tilde{P}_2/\tilde{S}_2 + \cdots + \tilde{P}_n/\tilde{S}_n.$$

If we have linguistic probability distribution over fuzzy values of some fuzzy set-valued random variable $\tilde{S}$, the important problem that arises is the verification of its consistency, completeness, and redundancy [4,82].

Let the set of linguistic probabilities $\tilde{P}^l = \{\tilde{P}_1,...,\tilde{P}_n\}$ correspond to the set of linguistic values $\{\tilde{S}_1,...,\tilde{S}_n\}$ of the fuzzy set-valued random variable $\tilde{S}$. For special case, a fuzzy probability distribution $\tilde{P}^l$ is inconsistent when the condition

$$p_i = \int_S \mu_{\tilde{S}_i}(s)\rho(s)ds \quad (6.13)$$

or

$$\mu_{\tilde{P}_i}\left(\int_S \mu_{\tilde{S}}(s)\rho(s)ds\right) = 1 \quad (6.14)$$

is not satisfied for any density ρ from the set of evaluations of densities.

The degree of inconsistency (denoted **contr**) of a linguistic probability distribution $\tilde{P}^l$ could be determined as

$$\text{contr}\,\tilde{P}^l = \min_{\rho}\left[1 - \int_S \rho(s)ds\right] \quad (6.15)$$

where ρ satisfies conditions (6.13) and (6.14). Obviously, contr $\tilde{P}^l = 0$ if the required density ρ exists.

Let a fuzzy probability distribution $\tilde{P}^l$ be consistent, that is contr $\tilde{P}^l = 0$. If this distribution is given as a set of crisp probabilities p_i, then its incompleteness (denoted **in**) and redundancy (denoted **red**) can be expressed as

$$\text{in}\,\tilde{P}^l = \max\left\{0, 1 - \sum_i p_i\right\} \tag{6.16}$$

$$\text{red}\,\tilde{P}^l = \max\left\{0, \sum_i p_i - 1\right\}. \tag{6.17}$$

If $\tilde{P}^l$ is given using linguistic probabilities $\tilde{P}_i$ then its incompleteness and redundancy can be expressed as

$$\text{in}\,\tilde{P}_S = \max\left\{0, 1 - \sup_{\gamma \in \Gamma} \gamma\right\} \tag{6.18}$$

$$\text{red}\,\tilde{P}_S = \max\left\{0, \inf_{\gamma \in \Gamma} \gamma - 1\right\} \tag{6.19}$$

where $\Gamma = \{\gamma | \mu_\Lambda(\gamma) = 1\}$. Here Λ is a sum of linguistic probabilities $\tilde{P}_i \in \tilde{P}^l$.

Given consistent, complete and not redundant linguistic probability distribution $\tilde{P}^l$ we can obtain from it a fuzzy set $\tilde{P}^\rho$ of possible probability distributions $\rho(s)$. We can construct a fuzzy measure from $\tilde{P}^\rho$ as its lower probability function (lower prevision) [317] by taking into account a degree of correspondence of $\rho(s)$ to $\tilde{P}^l$. Lower prevision is a unifying measure as opposed to the other existing additive and non-additive measures [400,403]. We denote the fuzzy-number-valued fuzzy measure by $\tilde{\eta}_{\tilde{P}^l}$ [21,23,27,34] because it is derived from the given linguistic probability distribution $\tilde{P}^l$. A degree of membership of an arbitrary probability distribution $\rho(s)$ to $\tilde{P}^{\rho}$ (a degree of correspondence of $\rho(s)$ to $\tilde{P}^{l}$) can be obtained by the formula

$$\pi_{\tilde{P}}(\rho(s)) = \min_{i=1,n}(\pi_{\tilde{P}_i}(p_i)),$$

where $p_i = \int_S \rho(s)\mu_{\tilde{S}_i}(s)ds$ is numeric probability of fuzzy state $\tilde{S}_i$ defined by $\rho(s)$, $s \in S$, S is a universe of discourse. Furthermore, $\pi_{\tilde{P}_i}(p_i) = \mu_{\tilde{P}_i}\left(\int_S \rho(s)\mu_{\tilde{S}_i}(s)ds\right)$ is the membership degree of p_i to $\tilde{P}_i$.

To derive a fuzzy-number-valued fuzzy measure $\tilde{\eta}_{\tilde{P}^l}$ we suggest the following formulas [8,27,31,34]:

$$\eta_{\tilde{P}^l}(H) = \bigcup_{\alpha \in (0,1]} \alpha\left[\eta_{\tilde{P}^l{}_1}^{\alpha}(H), \eta_{\tilde{P}^l{}_2}^{\alpha}(H)\right], \tag{6.20}$$

where

$$\begin{aligned}\eta_{\tilde{P}^l{}_1}^{\alpha}(H) &= \inf\left\{\int_S \rho(s)\max_{\tilde{S}\in H}\mu_{\tilde{S}}(s)ds \,\middle|\, \rho(s) \in P^{\rho^{\alpha}}\right\}\\ \eta_{\tilde{P}^l{}_2}^{\alpha}(H) &= \inf\left\{\int_S \rho(s)\max_{\tilde{S}\in H}\mu_{\tilde{S}}(s)ds \,\middle|\, \rho(s) \in core(\tilde{P}^{\rho})\right\}\end{aligned}, \tag{6.21}$$

where $P^{\rho^{\alpha}} = \left\{\rho(s) \,\middle|\, \min_{i=1,n}(\pi_{\tilde{P}_i}(p_i)) \ge \alpha\right\}$, $core(\tilde{P}^{\rho}) = P^{\rho^{\alpha=1}}$, $H \subset S$. The support of $\tilde{\eta}_{\tilde{P}^l}$ is defined as supp $\tilde{\eta}_{\tilde{P}^l} = cl\left(\bigcup_{\alpha\in(0,1]} \eta_{\tilde{P}^l}^{\alpha}\right)$.

For special case, when states of nature are just some elements, fuzzy number-valued fuzzy measure $\tilde{\eta}_{\tilde{P}^l}$ is defined as

$$\tilde{\eta}_{\tilde{P}^l}(H) = \bigcup_{\alpha \in (0,1]} \alpha\left[\eta_{\tilde{P}^l{}_1}^{\alpha}(H), \eta_{\tilde{P}^l{}_2}^{\alpha}(H)\right],\ H \subset S = \{S_1, \ldots, S_n\} \tag{6.22}$$

where

$$\begin{aligned}&\eta_{\tilde{P}^{l}{}_1}^{\alpha}(H)=\inf\left\{\sum_{S_i\in H}p(S_i)\middle|(p(S_1),...,p(S_n))\in P^{\rho^{\alpha}}\right\},\\&\eta_{\tilde{P}^{l}{}_2}^{\alpha}(H)=\inf\left\{\sum_{S_i\in H}p(S_i)\middle|(p(S_1),...,p(S_n))\in core(P^{\rho})\right\}\end{aligned}. \tag{6.23}$$

Here $P^{\rho\alpha}=\left\{(p(S_1),...,p(S_n))\in P_1^{\alpha}\times...\times P_n^{\alpha}\middle|\sum_{i=1}^{n}p(S_i)=1\right\}$, and $P_1^{\alpha},...,P_n^{\alpha}$ are α-cuts of fuzzy probabilities $\tilde{P}_1,...,\tilde{P}_n$ respectively, $p(S_1),...,p(S_n)$ are basic probabilities for $\tilde{P}_1,...,\tilde{P}_n$ respectively, $\times$ denotes the Cartesian product.

6.1.5 *Type-2 fuzzy decision modeling*

Let $S=\left\{\tilde{\tilde{S}}_1,...,\tilde{\tilde{S}}_n\right\}$ be a set of states of nature and $\mathcal{X}=\left\{\tilde{\tilde{X}}_1,...,\tilde{\tilde{X}}_l\right\}$ be a set of Type-2 fuzzy outcomes. The set of Type-2 fuzzy actions is defined as $\mathcal{A}=\{\tilde{\tilde{f}}\mid\tilde{\tilde{f}}:S\rightarrow\mathcal{X}\}$ We will use utility function $\tilde{\tilde{U}}$ to describe preferences over $\mathcal{A}$. The problem is to find an optimal action as an action $\tilde{\tilde{f}}^*\in\mathcal{A}$ for which $\tilde{\tilde{U}}(\tilde{\tilde{f}}^*)=\max_{\tilde{\tilde{f}}\in\mathcal{A}}\tilde{\tilde{U}}(\tilde{\tilde{f}})$. Utility function $\tilde{\tilde{U}}$ is described by Type-2 fuzzy Choquet integral. In this study we use fuzzy Choquet integral, where the integrand takes an interval Type-2 fuzzy number and the fuzzy measure is real number-valued [194]. It is obvious that Choquet integral with an IT2 FN-valued integrand $\tilde{\tilde{f}}$ produces an IT2 FN. An IT2 FN may be described as as an IT2 FS where the UMF and LMF are Type-1 FNs. The embedded Type-1 FN-valued functions $\tilde{f}_e^j$ is described as the functions $\tilde{f}_e^j(\tilde{\tilde{S}}_i)\in FOU(\tilde{\tilde{f}}(\tilde{\tilde{S}}_i)),\ \forall i,j.$

Thus, we define the FOU of $\int_S\tilde{\tilde{f}}d\eta$ as the union of all $\int_S\tilde{f}_e^j d\eta$:

$$FOU\left(\int_S\tilde{\tilde{f}}d\eta\right)\equiv\bigcup_j\int_S\tilde{f}_e^j d\eta, \tag{6.24}$$

$\int_S \tilde{\tilde{f}} d\eta$ may be defined as

$$\int_S \tilde{\tilde{f}} d\eta = 1 \Big/ FOU\left(\int_S \tilde{\tilde{f}} d\eta\right), \tag{6.25}$$

where $\int_S \tilde{\tilde{f}} d\eta$ is an IT2 FN.

If $\tilde{\tilde{U}} = \int_S \tilde{\tilde{f}} d\eta$ then

$$UMF_{\tilde{\tilde{U}}} = \int_S UMF_{\tilde{\tilde{f}}} d\eta \tag{6.26}$$

$$LMF_{\tilde{\tilde{U}}} = \int_S LMF_{\tilde{\tilde{f}}} d\eta \tag{6.27}$$

where $UMF_{\tilde{\tilde{U}}}$ is the function where $\overline{\tilde{f}}(\tilde{\tilde{S}}_i) = UMF_{\tilde{\tilde{f}}}(\tilde{\tilde{S}}_i), \forall i$ and $LMF_{\tilde{\tilde{U}}}$ is the function where $\underline{\tilde{f}}(\tilde{\tilde{S}}_i) = LMF_{\tilde{\tilde{f}}}(\tilde{\tilde{S}}_i), \forall i$.

We can build $\int_S UMF_{\tilde{\tilde{f}}} d\eta$ and $\int_S LMF_{\tilde{\tilde{f}}} d\eta$ from the α-cuts, ${}^{\alpha}UMF_{\tilde{\tilde{f}}}$ and ${}^{\alpha}LMF_{\tilde{\tilde{f}}}$. So, we can write

$$UMF_{\int_S \tilde{\tilde{f}} d\eta} = \overline{\int_S \tilde{\tilde{f}} d\eta} = \int_S UMF_{\tilde{\tilde{f}}} d\eta \tag{6.28}$$

$$LMF_{\int_S \tilde{\tilde{f}} d\eta} = \underline{\int_S \tilde{\tilde{f}} d\eta} = \int_S LMF_{\tilde{\tilde{f}}} d\eta \tag{6.29}$$

One can build the UMF and LMF of $FOU\left(\int_S \tilde{\tilde{f}} d\eta\right)$ by performing the Choquet integral on the respective functions on the UMFs and LMFs of $\tilde{\tilde{f}}$.

In practice, the type-2 fuzzy Choquet integral can be calculated by performing the Choquet integral on the UMFs and LMFs of the IT2 FN-valued evidence.

6.1.6 *A General methodology for decision making with imperfect information*

The problem of decision making with imperfect information consists in determination of an optimal action $\tilde{f}^* \in \mathcal{A}$, that is $\tilde{f}^* \in \mathcal{A}$ for which $\tilde{U}(\tilde{f}^*) = \max_{\tilde{f} \in \mathcal{A}} \left\{ \int_{\mathcal{S}} \tilde{u}(\tilde{f}(\tilde{S})) d\tilde{\eta}_{\tilde{P}^l} \right\}$. In this section we present the methodology for solving this problem. The methodology consists of the several stages described below.

At the first stage it becomes necessary to assign linguistic utility values $\tilde{u}(\tilde{f}_j(\tilde{S}_i))$ to every action $\tilde{f}_j \in \mathcal{A}$ taken at a state $\tilde{S}_i \in \mathcal{S}$.

The second stage consists in construction of a fuzzy number-valued fuzzy measure over $\mathcal{F}_S$ based on partial knowledge available in form of linguistic probabilities. First, given known probabilities $P(\tilde{S}_i) = \tilde{P}_i$; $\tilde{S}_i \in \mathcal{E}^n$, $\tilde{P}_i \in \mathcal{E}^1_{[0,1]}$, $i = \{1,\dots,j-1,j+1,\dots,n\}$ one has to find an unknown probability $P(\tilde{S}_j) = \tilde{P}_j, \tilde{P}_j \in \mathcal{E}^1_{[0,1]}$ by solving the problem described by (6.9)-(6.10) (or (6.11)-(6.12)). As a result, one would obtain a linguistic probability distribution $\tilde{P}^l$ expressed over all the states of nature. If some additional information about the probability over $\mathcal{S}$ is received (e.g. from indicator events), it is required to update $\tilde{P}^l$ on the base of this information by using fuzzy Bayes' formula [87]. Then based on the latest $\tilde{P}^l$ it is necessary to construct fuzzy number-valued fuzzy measure $\tilde{\eta}_{\tilde{P}^l}$ by solving the problem expressed by (6.20)-(6.21).

At the next stage the problem of calculation of a fuzzy-valued Choquet integral [433] for every action $\tilde{f}_j$ is solved. At this stage, first it is required for an action $\tilde{f}_j$ to rearrange indices of states $\tilde{S}_i$ on the base of Definition 6.4 and find such new indices (i) that $\tilde{u}(\tilde{f}_j(\tilde{S}_{(1)})) \geq \cdots \geq \tilde{u}(\tilde{f}_j(\tilde{S}_{(n)}))$. Next it is needed to calculate fuzzy values $\tilde{U}(\tilde{f}_j)$ of a fuzzy-valued Choquet integral for every action $\tilde{f}_j$ by using (6.8).

Finally, by using a suitable fuzzy ranking method, an optimal $\tilde{f}^* \in \mathcal{A}$, that is $\tilde{f}^* \in \mathcal{A}$ for which $\tilde{U}(\tilde{f}^*) = \max_{\tilde{f} \in \mathcal{A}} \left\{ \int_{\mathcal{S}} \tilde{u}(\tilde{f}(\tilde{S}))d\tilde{\eta}_{\tilde{P}^l} \right\}$ is determined.

6.2 Multicriteria Decision Analysis with Imperfect Information

As it was shown in [302], there exists a formal parallelism between decision making under uncertainty and multicriteria decision making [41,104,308,314,356,377,380].

Let us consider a problem of decision making with imperfect information $D_{DMII} = (\mathcal{S}, \mathcal{Y}, \mathcal{A}, \succsim_l)$ and multicriteria decision making $D_{MCDM} = (\mathcal{X}, \succsim_l)$, with $\mathcal{X} = \mathcal{X}_1 \times ... \times \mathcal{X}_n$. As we consider $\mathcal{S}$ as a finite set, we can identify acts $\tilde{f} \in \mathcal{A}$ with the elements of $\mathcal{X}$ by considering them as $(\tilde{\varphi}_1, ..., \tilde{\varphi}_n)$, where $\tilde{\varphi}_i \in \mathcal{X}_i$ denotes $\tilde{f}(\tilde{S}_i)$. Then the preference relation $\succsim_l$ over the acts becomes a preference relation over $\mathcal{X}$. For decision making with imperfect information, the preference is formally expressed as

$$\forall \tilde{f}, \tilde{g} \in \mathcal{A}, \tilde{f} \succsim_l \tilde{g} \Leftrightarrow (\tilde{\varphi}_1, ..., \tilde{\varphi}_n) \succsim_l (\tilde{\psi}_1, ..., \tilde{\psi}_n)$$

and for multicriteria decision making, the fact that an alternative $\tilde{X}$ is preferred to $\tilde{X}'$ is expressed as

$$\tilde{X} \succsim_l \tilde{X}' \Leftrightarrow (\tilde{X}_1, ..., \tilde{X}_n) \succsim_l (\tilde{X}'_1, ..., \tilde{X}'_n), \tilde{X}_i, \tilde{X}'_i \in \mathcal{X}_i, \forall i \in I.$$

The problem of decision analysis with imperfect information can be written as multiattribute decision making problem using the following identifications [302]:

1) States of the nature and criteria: $\mathcal{S} \leftrightarrow \mathcal{I}$; 2) acts and alternatives as values of criteria $\mathcal{A} \leftrightarrow \mathcal{X}$, and $\tilde{f} \succsim_l \tilde{g} \Leftrightarrow (\tilde{\varphi}_1, ..., \tilde{\varphi}_n) \succsim_l (\tilde{\psi}_1, ..., \tilde{\psi}_n)$.

Let us now recall the statement of the multiattribute decision making problem. Let us assume that unidimensional utility functions $\tilde{u}_i : \mathcal{X}_i \to \mathcal{E}^1$, for $i = 1, ..., n$ are defined. In order to represent the preference relation $\succsim_l$

we need to find an appropriate aggregate operator $\mathrm{H}:\mathcal{E}^{\mathrm{n}} \to \mathcal{E}^{1}$ such that $\tilde{X} \succsim_l \tilde{X}'$ holds iff

$$\tilde{U}(\tilde{X}) = \mathrm{H}(\tilde{u}_1(\tilde{X}_1),...,\tilde{u}_n(\tilde{X}_n)) \geq \tilde{U}(\tilde{X}') = \mathrm{H}(\tilde{u}_1(\tilde{X}_1'),...,\tilde{u}_n(\tilde{X}_n')).$$

In the framework of the methodology proposed here, we use the operator $\mathrm{H}(\cdot)$ as a fuzzy-valued Choquet integral and hence

$$\begin{aligned}\tilde{U}(\tilde{X}) &= \sum_{i=1}^{n}\left[\tilde{u}_{(i)}(\tilde{X}_{(i)}) - \tilde{u}_{(i+1)}(\tilde{X}_{(i+1)})\right]\tilde{\eta}_{\tilde{P}^l}(\mathcal{H}_{(i)}) \geq \tilde{U}(\tilde{X}') \\ &= \sum_{i=1}^{n}\left[\tilde{u}_{(i)}(\tilde{X}'_{(i)}) - \tilde{u}_{(i+1)}(\tilde{X}'_{(i+1)})\right]\tilde{\eta}_{\tilde{P}^l}(\mathcal{H}_{(i)}), \mathcal{H}_{(i)} \subset 2^{\mathcal{I}}.\end{aligned} \tag{6.30}$$

Here $\tilde{\eta}_{\tilde{P}^l}$ on $2^{\mathcal{I}}$ is obtained from linguistic probability $\tilde{P}^l$ by solving the problem (6.11)-(6.12).

Chapter 7

Hierarchical Models for Decision Making with Imperfect Information

7.1 Multi-Agent Fuzzy Hierarchical Model for Decision Making

Economy as a complex system is composed of a number of agents interacting in a distributed mode. Advances in distributed artificial intelligence, intelligent agent theory and soft computing technology make it possible for these agents as components of a complex system to interact, cooperate, contend and coordinate in order to form global behavior of economic system. Recently, there has been great interest in development of Intelligent Agents and Multi-agent systems in economics, in particular in decision analysis and control of economic systems [26,153, 191,220,235,261,265,272,385,414,464].

It should be noted that economic agents often deal with incomplete, contradictory, missing and inaccurate data and knowledge [15,132, 216,223]. Furthermore, the agents have to make decisions in uncertain situations, i.e. multi-agent economical systems in the real world function within an environment of uncertainty and imprecision.

In this section we consider approach to decision analysis in multi-agent economic system suggested in [15,28].

In this approach to multi-agent distributed intelligent systems the main idea is granulation of functions and powers from a central authority to local authorities. In these terms, economy is composed of several agents, which can perform their own functions independently, and, therefore, have information, authority and power necessary to perform only their own functions. These intelligent agents can communicate together to work, cooperate and be coordinated in order to reach a common goal of economy in a system [15].

Below we present the formalism of this approach.

For simplicity, we will mainly consider systems with so-called "fan" structure in which the economic system consists of N agents at the lower level and one element at the higher level (which we call a center). A hierarchy has two levels: the focus or overall goal of the decision making problem at the top, and competing alternatives at the bottom.

The state of i-th agent ($i = 1,...,N$) is characterized by vector $\tilde{X}_i$. The vector $\tilde{X}_i$ should meet the local constraints

$$\tilde{X}_i \in \mathcal{X}_i \subset \mathcal{E}^{n_i} \tag{7.1}$$

where $\mathcal{X}_i$ – is a set in n_i dimensional space $\mathcal{E}^{n_i}$. A specificity of these hierarchical systems is information aggregation at the higher level. This means that the only agent of the higher level, the center, is concerned not on individual values of variables $\tilde{X}_i$, but some indexes evaluating elements' activities produced from those values. Let's denote the vector of such indexes as:

$$\tilde{F}_i(\tilde{X}_i) = (\tilde{f}_{i1}(\tilde{X}_i),...,\tilde{f}_{im_i}(\tilde{X}_i)), i = 1,...,N. \tag{7.2}$$

The local concerns of i-th agent are represented by vector criteria $\tilde{\Phi}_i(\tilde{X}_i) = (\tilde{\varphi}_{i_1}(\tilde{X}_i),...,\tilde{\varphi}_{i_{K_i}}(\tilde{X}_i))$. Let's assume that the agents concern in increased values of the fuzzy criteria: $\tilde{\varphi}_{i_k}(\tilde{X}_i), k = 1,...,K_i$. Sometimes the indexes may directly mimic the criteria, but in general, the indexes can be related to these criteria in a specific manner. It is worth noting that the number of indexes m_i and criteria K_i is much less than the dimension of vector $\tilde{X}_i$.

Note that the center only receives the information about the indexes $\tilde{F}_i$, not about the vector $\tilde{X}_i$. Because the dimension of $\tilde{F}_i$ is usually significantly less than the dimension of vector $\tilde{X}_i$, it considerably reduce amount of data circulating between the levels.

The state of the center is characterized by vector $\tilde{F}_0$, the components of which are the indexes of the agents of the lower level:

$$\tilde{F}_0 = (\tilde{F}_1, ..., \tilde{F}_N), \tag{7.3}$$

where

$$\tilde{F}_i = \tilde{F}_i(\tilde{X}_i). \tag{7.4}$$

The vector $\tilde{F}_0$ should satisfy the global constraints:

$$\tilde{F}_0 \in \mathcal{X}_0 \subset \mathcal{E}^{m_0}, \text{ where } m_0 = \sum_{i=1}^{N} m_i . \tag{7.5}$$

Let's assume that the set $\mathcal{X}_0$ is defined on the constraint set:

$$\mathcal{X}_0 = \left\{ \tilde{F}_0 / \tilde{H}(\tilde{F}_0) \geq \tilde{B} \right\}, \tag{7.6}$$

where $\tilde{H}(\tilde{F}_0)$ is some fuzzy vector-function, $\tilde{B} = (\tilde{B}_1, ..., \tilde{B}_M)$ is a vector. The objective of the center is to maximize the vector criteria:

$$\tilde{\varphi}_0(\tilde{F}_0) = (\tilde{\varphi}_{01}(\tilde{F}_0), ..., \tilde{\varphi}_{0K_0}(\tilde{F}_0)) \rightarrow \max.$$

We have to use the following notions for solving the optimization problem.

Definition 7.1. Fuzzy complete optimal solution [15,265]. $\tilde{X}^*$ is said to be a *fuzzy complete optimal solution*, if and only if there exists an $\tilde{X}^* \in \mathcal{X}$ such that $\tilde{f}_i(\tilde{X}^*) \geq \tilde{f}_i(\tilde{X})$, $i = 1, ..., K$, for all $\tilde{X} \in \mathcal{X}$.

In general, such a complete optimal solution that simultaneously maximizes (or minimizes) all objective functions does not always exist when the objective functions conflict with each other. Thus, a concept of a *fuzzy Pareto optimal solution* is taken into consideration.

Definition 7.2. Fuzzy Pareto optimal solution [15,265]. $\tilde{X}^*$ is said to be a *fuzzy Pareto optimal solution*, if and only if there does not exist another $\tilde{X} \in \mathcal{X}$ such that $\tilde{f}_i(\tilde{X}) \geq \tilde{f}_i(\tilde{X}^*)$ for all i and $\tilde{f}_j(\tilde{X}) \neq \tilde{f}_j(\tilde{X}^*)$ for at least one j.

Definition 7.3. A weak fuzzy optimal solution [15,265]. $\tilde{X}^*$ is said to be a *weak fuzzy Pareto optimal solution*, if and only if there does not exist another $\tilde{X} \in \mathcal{X}$ such that $\tilde{f}_i(\tilde{X}) > \tilde{f}_i(\tilde{X}^*)$, $i = 1,...,K$.

Let $\mathcal{X}^{CO}$, $\mathcal{X}^P$ or $\mathcal{X}^{WP}$ denote fuzzy complete optimal, fuzzy Pareto optimal, or weak fuzzy Pareto optimal solution sets respectively. Then from above definitions, we can easily get the following relations:

$$\mathcal{X}^{CO} \subseteq \mathcal{X}^P \subseteq \mathcal{X}^{WP} \tag{7.7}$$

A fuzzy satisfactory solution is a reduced subset of the feasible set that exceeds all of the aspiration levels of each attribute. A set of satisfactory solutions is composed of acceptable alternatives. Satisfactory solutions do not need to be non-dominated. And a preferred solution is a non-dominated solution selected as the final choice through decision makers' involvement in the information processing.

Commonly, the decision making process implies the existence of a person making the final decision (Decision Maker-agent) at the higher level.

As our primary goal is to coordinate the center and the agents of the lower level to align their objectives, we consider the objective function of the center as known:

$$\tilde{\tilde{H}}(\tilde{\Phi}_0(\tilde{F}_0)) = \tilde{H}_0(\tilde{F}_0) \to \max \tag{7.8}$$

or

$$\tilde{\tilde{H}}(\tilde{\Phi}_0(\tilde{F}_0)) = \int_0^T \tilde{H}_0(\tilde{F}_0)dt \to \max.$$

The coordination (overall optimization) problem can be formulated as follows:

$$\tilde{H}_0(\tilde{F}_1,...,\tilde{F}_N) \to \max; \tag{7.9}$$

$$\tilde{H}(\tilde{F}_1,...,\tilde{F}_N) \geq \tilde{B}; \tag{7.10}$$

$$\tilde{F}_i \in \mathcal{I}_i^{\tilde{F}} = \left\{ \tilde{F}_i / \tilde{F}_i = \tilde{F}_i(\tilde{X}_i), \tilde{X}_i \in P_i^{\tilde{X}} \left(\text{or } \tilde{X}_i \in R_i^{\tilde{X}} \right) \right\}, \tag{7.11}$$

where $P_i^{\tilde{X}} (R_i^{\tilde{X}})$ is the set of effective (semi-effective) solutions of the problem

$$\tilde{\Phi}_i(\tilde{X}_i) = (\tilde{\varphi}_{i1}(\tilde{X}_i), \ldots, \tilde{\varphi}_{iK_i}(\tilde{X}_i)) \to \max; \tag{7.12}$$

$$\tilde{X}_i \in \mathcal{X}_i . \tag{7.13}$$

Because the sets $P_i^{\tilde{X}} (R_i^{\tilde{X}})$ and accordingly the set $\mathcal{I}_i^{\tilde{F}}$ can have rather complex structures, the condition (7.11) can be replaced by

$$\tilde{F}_i \in Q_i^{\tilde{F}} \tag{7.14}$$

where $Q_i^{\tilde{F}}$ is the set satisfying the condition:

$$\mathcal{I}_i^{\tilde{F}} \subset Q_i^{\tilde{F}} \subset \mathcal{J}_i^{\tilde{F}} = \left\{ \tilde{F}_i / \tilde{F}_i = \tilde{F}_i(\tilde{X}_i), \tilde{X}_i \in \mathcal{X}_i \right\}. \tag{7.15}$$

We suggest two methods to solution to (7.9)-(7.11).

a) Non-iterative method

Non-iterative optimization method includes three main phases. At the first stage, the local problems of vector optimization are dealt with. The solutions of these problems are sets $P_i^{\tilde{X}}$ and sets $\mathcal{I}_i^{\tilde{F}} (Q_i^{\tilde{F}})$ or any approximations of these sets. The second stage implies the implementation of the center's task (7.9)-(7.11) as a result of which we get the optimal values of the agents' criteria $\tilde{F}^* = (\tilde{F}_1^* \ldots, \tilde{F}_N^*)$. Vector $\tilde{F}_i^*$ is then passed to i-th agent which implements the third stage by solving the problem:

$$\tilde{F}_i(\tilde{X}_i) = \tilde{F}_i^*; \tilde{X}_i \in \mathcal{X}_i . \tag{7.16}$$

A solution of (7.16) represents local variables $\tilde{X}_i^*$. In case of several existing solutions, one is selected based on preferences of the element.

b) Iterative method

Let $\Omega_i \subset \mathcal{E}^{K_i}$ be a subset in the space of criteria. Let's call the elements $\tilde{\omega}_i \in \Omega_i$ from this subset as coordinating signals.

Definition 7.4. Coordinating function [15]. The function $\tilde{\bar{F}}_i(\tilde{\omega}_i) = (\tilde{\bar{f}}_{i1}(\tilde{\omega}_i),...,\tilde{\bar{f}}_{im_i}(\tilde{\omega}_i))$ is named a coordinating function if the following conditions are satisfied:

a) for $\forall \tilde{\omega}_i \in \Omega_i$ there exists such element $\tilde{\bar{X}}_i(\tilde{\omega}_i) \in R_i^{\tilde{X}}$, for which $\tilde{\bar{F}}_i(\tilde{\omega}_i) = \tilde{F}_i(\tilde{\bar{X}}_i(\tilde{\omega}_i))$;

b) inversely, for any element $\tilde{X}_i^0$ – of subset $P_i^{\tilde{X}}$, there exists such coordinating signal $\tilde{\omega}_i^0 \in \Omega_i$, for which $\tilde{\bar{F}}_i(\tilde{\omega}_i^0) = \tilde{F}_i(\tilde{X}_i^0)$.

From the definition above, it follows that the problem (7.9)-(7.11) is equivalent to the problem given below:

$$\left.\begin{aligned} &\tilde{H}_0(\bar{F}_1(\tilde{\omega}_1),...,\bar{F}_N(\tilde{\omega}_N)) \to \max;\\ &\tilde{H}(\tilde{\bar{F}}_i(\tilde{\omega}_i),...,\tilde{\bar{F}}_N(\tilde{\omega}_N)) \geq \tilde{B};\\ &\tilde{\omega}_i \in \Omega_i, i=1,...,N. \end{aligned}\right\} \tag{7.17}$$

Thus, the variables of problem (7.17) are coordinating signals $\tilde{\omega}_i$, defined on the set of acceptable coordinating signals Ω_i. The rationale for such transformation is simpler structure of set Ω_i compared to the set of effective elements (points).

Choosing among different coordinating functions $\tilde{\bar{F}}_i(\tilde{\omega}_i)$ and different solution approaches of problem (7.17) it is possible to construct a large number of iterative decomposition coordinating methods [15,28]. It can be shown that for crisp case the known decomposition algorithms such as Dantzig-Wolf algorithm or the algorithm based on the interaction predicttion principle[296] are special cases of the more general suggested algorithm [15].

Let's consider the procedure of optimization in two-level multi-agent decision making systems [15]. The agents send their solutions to the center for further global decision making. Each solution represents a vector of criteria of the agent, acceptable within the local constraints. On the basis of the received alternatives the center creates a solution optimal to the system as a whole. This solution is forwarded to the agents who then implement it. In this case the task of the center is in the determination of the optimal values for weight coefficients of the agents' solutions and can be written as follows:

$$\tilde{H}_0 = \sum_{i=1}^{N}\sum_{j=1}^{R_i} \lambda_{ij}\tilde{Z}_{0ij} \to \max; \tag{7.18}$$

$$\tilde{H}_m = \sum_{i=1}^{N}\sum_{j=1}^{R_i} \lambda_{ij}\tilde{Z}_{mij} \geq \tilde{B}_m,\ m = 1,\ldots,M; \tag{7.19}$$

$$\sum_{j=1}^{R_i} \lambda_{ij} = 1,\ i = [1,\ldots,N], \tag{7.20}$$

here λ_{ij} is the weight coefficient sought for j-th alternative of an i-th agent; $\tilde{Z}_{mij} =< \tilde{A}_{mij}, \tilde{F}_{ij} >$, $m = 0,\ldots,M$; $\tilde{A}_{mij}$ are constant coefficients in the model of the center; $\tilde{F}_{ij}$ is the vector criteria of the solution of i-th agent in j-th alternative.

Definition 7.5. Fuzzy optimality [15]. Vector λ^* giving the maximum of the membership function for the set $\tilde{D}$, "desirability of λ from the viewpoint of satisfaction of all indices" is fuzzy optimal solution to (7.18)-(7.20).

Thus, the decision making process in the center is reduced to solving the fuzzy linear programming problem (7.18)-(7.20). Agents' alternatives are created by Pareto optimality (PO) procedures. The complexity of the solution of (7.18)-(7.20) rapidly increases as the number of agents' alternatives increases. In the interactive procedure given below we use the fuzzy optimality principle in the decision making process on the base of (7.18)-(7.20).

In some cases decision makers prefer an interactive approach to find an optimal solution for a decision problem as such an approach enables decision makers to directly engage in the problem solving process. In this section, we propose an interactive method, which not only allows decision makers to give their fuzzy goals, but also allows them to continuously revise and adjust their fuzzy goals. In this way, decision makers can explore various optimal solutions under their goals, and then choose the most satisfactory one.

First of all Decision Maker analyzes agents' individual solutions received by the center. At this preliminary stage the opinion of Decision Maker on the agents' activity, which can be evaluated qualitatively, is taken into consideration.

Based on the extension principle, for a fixed $\lambda=\{\lambda_{ij}, i=1,\dots,N,\ j=1,\dots,R_i\}$ it is possible to obtain the "value of m-th criteria for this λ":

$$\tilde{H}_{m\lambda} = \lambda_{11}\tilde{Z}_{m11} + \cdots + \lambda_{NR_N}\tilde{Z}_{mNR_N}$$

Then the fuzzy values $\tilde{B}_m$ are constructed having sense of "the value of m-th criteria desirable for Decision Maker", $m=1,\dots,M$. Note that in accordance with the principle of Bellmann-Zadeh [65], the $\tilde{H}_0$, which is the objective of the problem (7.18)-(7.20) and $\tilde{H}_m, m=1,\dots,M$ (constraints), are represented by fuzzy sets. The sets $\tilde{b}_m$ are constructed by processing preferences of Decision Maker such as "it is necessary that m-th criteria be not less than c_m^1 and it is desired that it is not less than c_m^2, while the allowable range is $c_m \pm \Delta c_m$". The membership function of the fuzzy set $\tilde{B}_m$ corresponding to the last clause can be set as follows:

$$\mu(B_m) = \left\{ \begin{array}{l} 0,\ if\ \ B_m \le c_m - \Delta c_m \ \ or\ \ B_m \ge c_m + \Delta c_m; \\ \dfrac{B_m - c_m + \Delta c_m}{\Delta c_m},\ if\ \ c_m - \Delta c_m \le B_m \le c_m; \\ \dfrac{c_m + \Delta c_m - B_m}{\Delta c_m}, \quad if\ \ c_m \le B_m \le c_m + \Delta c_m. \end{array} \right\}$$

Then for each a fixed λ it can be related the fuzzy set $\tilde{\Phi}_{m\lambda} \triangleq$ $\triangleq \tilde{H}_{m\lambda} \cap \tilde{B}_m$. The membership function of this set $\mu_{\tilde{\Phi}_{m\lambda}}()$ for argument $\Phi_{m\lambda}$ is equal to the smaller of the two values: the first value defines the possibility of the fact that m-th criteria would take the value of $\tilde{\Phi}_{m\lambda}$ considering the fuzziness of the parameters that determine it and the second value defines the degree of desire ability of this value for the Decision Maker.

Let's consider the fuzzy sets $\tilde{D}_m$ such as "desirability of λ from the viewpoint of $m-$th criteria", $m=[0,...,M]$, defined on the domain set λ given by (7.20).

The membership function of a fuzzy set $\tilde{D}_m$ denoted as $\tilde{\nu}_m(\lambda)$ is determined as the height of the fuzzy set $\tilde{\Phi}_{m\lambda}$

$$\nu_m(\lambda) \triangleq \max \mu_{\tilde{\Phi}_{m\lambda}}(\Phi_{m\lambda}) = \mu_{\tilde{\Phi}_{m\lambda}}(\Phi^*_{m\lambda}).$$

Let $\tilde{H}_{m\lambda}$ and $\tilde{B}_m$ be LR fuzzy numbers [11] $\tilde{H}_{m\lambda} = \left(H_{m\lambda}, \underline{H}_{m\lambda}, \overline{H}_{m\lambda}\right)$ and $\tilde{B}_m = \left(B_m, \underline{B}_m, \overline{B}_m\right)$. Then from formula (7.20), for determining the height of intersection of two fuzzy numbers, we have:

$$\mu\left(\Phi^*_{m\lambda}\right) = \begin{cases} R\left[\dfrac{B_m - H_{m\lambda}}{\overline{H}_{m\lambda} - \underline{\tilde{B}}_m}\right], \text{ if } B_m - H_{m\lambda} \geq 0; \\ L\left[\dfrac{H_{m\lambda} - B_m}{\underline{H}_{m\lambda} - \overline{B}_m}\right], \text{ if } B_m - H_{m\lambda} \leq 0. \end{cases}$$

Thus, we obtained the formulas for the membership functions of $\tilde{D}_m$ "desirability of λ from the viewpoint of m-th criterion", $m=0,...,M$. Then it is necessary to construct the membership function of the fuzzy set $\tilde{D}$ "desirability of λ from the viewpoint of satisfaction of all indices". Let's assume that the membership function of this fuzzy set which we will denote $\nu(\lambda)$ is defined via membership functions $\nu_m(\lambda)$, $m=0,...,M$ and vector $\pi=(\pi_0,...,\pi_M)$, where $\pi_m, m \in 0,\dots,M$ is the degree of importance of m-th index or the function $\nu_m(\lambda)$ related to this index:

$$\nu(\lambda,\pi) = \overline{\nu}(\mu_0(\lambda),...,\mu_M(\lambda),\pi_0,...,\pi_M).$$

Functions $\overline{\nu}$ can take different forms, such as, for example,

$$\bar{v}^1 = \sum_k \pi_k \mu_k(\lambda);\ \bar{v}^2 = \min_k \{\pi_k \mu_k(\lambda)\};$$

$$\bar{v}^3 = \prod_k \mu_k(\lambda)^{\pi_k};\ \bar{v}^4 = \min_k \{\mu_k(\lambda)^{\pi_k}\}.$$

The weight coefficients π_k is determined by way of processing of Decision Maker responses to stated questions. The success of such human-centered procedure depends mainly on understandability of the questions to the Decision Maker. In our view, the procedure in which Decision Maker is presented two alternatives q_1 and q_2 for comparison by using a predefined set of linguistic terms is appropriate. We can use the following set: "Can not say which of the alternatives is better (worse)", "Alternative q_1 is somewhat better (worse) than alternative q_2", "Alternative q_1 is noticeably better (worse) that alternative q_2", "Alternative q_1 is considerably better (worse) that alternative q_2".

The linguistic expressions presented to Decision Maker can be considered as linguistic labels for corresponding fuzzy sets, defined on the universe of discourse

$$R = \{r \,/\, r = v(\lambda_1, \pi) - v(\lambda_2, \pi) \,/\, \lambda_1, \lambda_2 \text{ are allowable}\}.$$

Because $0 \le v(\lambda, \pi) \le 1$, then $R \subset [-1,1]$. Hence, the membership function for the expression "Alternatives q_1 and q_2 are equivalent" can be given by formula:

$$\rho_4(r) = \begin{cases} 1 - 25r^2,\ if\ |r| \le 0,2; \\ 0,\ if\ |r| \ge 0,2. \end{cases}$$

And the membership function for the expression "Alternative q_1 is somewhat better than alternative q_2" can be given by formula:

$$\rho_5(r) = \begin{cases} 1 - 25(r - 0.3)^2,\ if\ 0.1 \le r \le 0,5; \\ 0,\ if\ |r| \ge 0,5. \end{cases}$$

Membership functions $\rho_s(r)$ of linguistic terms labeled by *s=1,2,...,7* (*4* – "alternatives q_1 and q_2 are equivalent"; *5* – "alternative q_1 is somewhat better than alternative q_2") for comparison of alternatives are shown in Fig. 7.1.

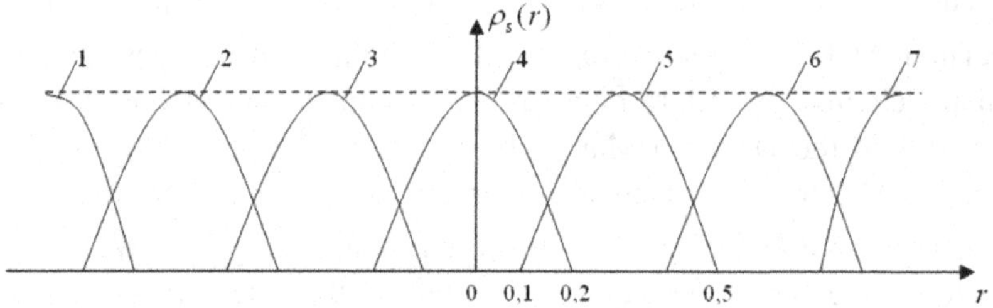

Fig. 7.1. Linguistic terms for comparison of alternatives

Let a Decision Maker compare Q pairs of alternatives. The alternative q is characterized by the vector of decision variables λ corresponding to this vector by values of membership functions $\nu_m(\lambda)$ of fuzzy sets $\tilde{D}_m$ "desirability of λ from the viewpoint of m-th criterion" as well as fuzzy sets $\tilde{H}_{m\lambda}$ "value of m-th criterion for current λ".

If comparing alternatives q_1 and q_2, Decision Maker chooses linguistic label s with the membership function $\rho_s(r)$, then a fuzzy set $\rho_q(\pi)$ is defined in space of weight coefficients π, which can be called as "consistent with the q-th response of Decision Maker". The corresponding membership function is defined as:

$$\bar{\rho}_q(\pi) = \rho_s(r),\ r = \nu(\lambda_{q_1}, \pi) - \nu(\lambda_{q_2}, \pi).$$

Then, consecutively we determine:

1) Intersection of fuzzy sets $\bar{p}_q(\pi)$:

$$\bar{p}(\pi) = \bigcap_{q \in [1:Q]} \bar{p}_q(\pi)$$

2) Vector π^* giving the maximum of the function $\bar{p}(\pi)$

$$\pi^* = Arg \max_{\pi} \overline{p}(\pi^*).$$

3) Membership function $\nu(\lambda, \pi^*)$ for fuzzy set $\tilde{D}$ "desirability of λ from the viewpoint of satisfaction of all objectives"

4) Vector λ^* giving the maximum of this membership function

$$\lambda^* = Arg \max_{\lambda} \nu(\lambda, \pi^*).$$

By revising fuzzy goals, this method will provide decision makers with a series of optimal solutions. Hence, decision makers can select the most suitable one on the basis of their preference, judgment, and experience.

7.2 Decision Making with Second-Order Imprecise Probability

The realm we consider in this section is hierarchical imprecise probability models. Such models allow taking into account an imprecision and imperfection of our knowledge, expressed by interval values of probabilities of states of nature and interval degrees of trust to such values. A decision-making process analysis and a choice of the most preferable alternative subject to variation of intervals at the lower and upper levels of models and the types of distribution on the sets of random values of probabilities of states of nature is of most interest.

As it is mentioned above, most of the existing utility models assume the utility function and probability distribution to be accurately known. But in reality, human preferences, events, probabilities are not exactly known – they are imprecise, and therefore, should be considered as granules. In real world decision-making problems we also often encounter uncertainty about uncertainty, or uncertainty square (uncertainty^2), for short [450]. Instances of uncertainty^2 are fuzzy sets of type 2, imprecise probabilities [105,124,162,173,185,186,334,384, 426] etc. There exist a huge number of methods able to handle first-order uncertainty, but there is no general theory of decision analysis under uncertainty square. Most parts of the existing decision theory assume a decision maker (DM) has complete knowledge about the distribution on states of nature and does not offer methodology to deal with partial or fuzzy information. The standard probability theory is more than an adequate tool to deal with physical, inanimate systems where human judgment, perceptions, and emotions do not play a role, but is not designed to deal with perceptions which play a prominent role for humanistic systems and which are intrinsically imprecise [444,451].

Natural and useful interpretations of imprecise probabilities as second-order information granules are interval probabilities, fuzzy (linguistic) probabilities [142,333,426] etc. Handling imprecise probabilities include such problems as describing imprecise priors and sampling distributions; proceeding from approximate priors and sampling distributions to approximate posteriors and posterior related quantities; making decisions with imprecise probabilities etc. Today, computation with imprecise probabilities [43,140,142,214,426] is an active field of research. However, much of the literature is concerned with elicitation rather than computation and imprecise probabilities are considered in isolation [450].

Adequate and intuitively meaningful models for describing information structures of decision making problem are the second-order imprecise hierarchical models. First a hierarchical model where probabilities were normally imprecise was proposed in [174]. It is argued in [124,156] that more general hierarchical models are Bayesian models. Unfortunately, probabilities in these models are supposed to be exact that significantly limits the use of this type of models. Further the hierarchical models were modified and developed in [122,313,401]. In [122] a hierarchical uncertainty model that presents vague probability assessment and inference on its base is considered. This model is based on Walley's theory of imprecise probabilities. In [124,393] the various decision making criteria with imprecise probabilities are discussed. In [42,45] the unified behavioral theory of lower prevision and some open problems in the theory are discussed. In [45,59] the problem of combination of experts' beliefs represented by imprecise probabilities is considered. The possibilistic imprecise second-order probability model is considered in [70,101,401]. Modeling linguistic uncertainty in terms of upper probabilities which are given in behavioral interpretation is considered in [403]. A quasi-Bayesian model of subjective uncertainty where beliefs are represented by lower and upper probabilities is investigated in [71].

Shortcomings of the mentioned models are that they require using exact probability distribution at the second level of a hierarchical model. It limits a practical use of these models. Further development of a hierarchical model is related to creation of hierarchical models that have interval probabilities at the second level. More comprehensive review and some new results are shown in [393]. More universal and popular model for interval probabilities processing is Walley's theory of imprecise probabilities and a principle of natural extension [399]. Main drawback of this approach is impossibility to use it when experts' beliefs are contradictory. Other drawback is related to a huge amount of optimization problems.

In this section hierarchical interval imprecise probability models are considered. Such models allow taking into account an imprecision and imperfection of our knowledge, expressed by interval values of probabilities of states of nature and degrees of trust to such values. Taking into account review of state-of-the-art of decision making problems with hierarchical probability models, we consider the decision making problem with the second-order uncertainty where beliefs at the first and the second levels of hierarchical probability models are represented by interval probabilities. Imprecise hierarchical models of Walley may be considered as a special case of the considered model.

The assessed intervals of probabilities are often concern of expert's or DM's experience. His/her confidence is also imprecise and can be described as an interval. A decision making problem with the second-order information granules, where the probabilities at the first and at the second levels are given as intervals is considered in this section.

Denote by $\underline{a}_i, \overline{a}_i$ the lower and upper bounds respectively of interval probability of a state of nature at the first level, i.e. a state $S_i \in \mathcal{S}$ is assigned a probability P_i that can be described by a interval $[\underline{a}_i, \overline{a}_i]$. Denote by $\underline{b}_i, \overline{b}_i$ the lower and upper bounds respectively of interval probability describing expert's confidence at the second level, i.e. an expert's confidence can be described by interval $[\underline{b}_i, \overline{b}_i]$. Then we can express the imprecise hierarchical probability model as

$$\text{Prob}\{P_i = [\underline{a}_i; \overline{a}_i]\} = [\underline{b}_i; \overline{b}_i], i = \overline{1,n}. \tag{7.21}$$

Probability distributions of the second level of the hierarchical model are defined on a set of probability distributions of the first level. The suggested decision making methodology based on a given information structure (7.21) uses utility function for description of preferences. To represent the utility function we use Choquet integral with non-additive measure:

$$U(f) = \int_S u(f_i(S))d\eta \tag{7.22}$$

where η is a non-additive measure represented by lower prevision [399] which is constructed from (7.21), $f_k : \mathcal{S} \to \mathcal{R}$, $i = 1,...,K$, is an alternative.

Then the decision making problem consists in determination of an optimal action $f^* \in \mathcal{A}$ such that

$$U(f^*) = \max_{f_k \in \mathcal{A}} \{\int_S u(f_k(S))d\eta\}. \tag{7.23}$$

The suggested decision making method includes the following stages. At first stage it is needed to assign utility values for actions $f_k \in \mathcal{A}$ taken at a state $S_i \in \mathcal{S}$. The second stage consists in construction of lower prevision to calculate value of utility function for $f_k \in \mathcal{A}$. In this study lower prevision is determined as

$$\eta(B) = \inf_{\rho \in M} \int_B \rho(S)dS, \; B \subset \mathcal{S} \tag{7.24}$$

where ρ is a probability density function over $\mathcal{S}$ and M is a set of probability density functions describing probability-relevant information. M is defined taking into account the following constraints:

$$\underline{b} \le \int_{\underline{a}}^{\overline{a}} \phi(\rho)d\rho \le \overline{b}, \tag{7.25}$$

$$\int_0^1 \phi(\rho)d\rho = 1, \tag{7.26}$$

and $\phi(\rho)$ is pdf over M. Relevant information on imprecise probability is represented by interval probabilities for n-1 states of nature. It is required to obtain unknown imprecise probability $P(S_j) = P_j$ given $P(S_i) = P_i$, $i \in \{1,\dots,j-1,j+1,\dots,n\}$. The lower and the upper bounds of $P_j = [\underline{a}_j; \overline{a}_j]$ are determined as follows:

$$\underline{a}_j = \underline{a}(S_j) = \min(1 - \sum_{i=1,i\neq j}^{n} p(S_i)) \tag{7.27}$$

$$\overline{a}_j = \overline{a}(S_j) = \max(1 - \sum_{i=1,i\neq j}^{n} p(S_i)). \tag{7.28}$$

Here $p(S_i) \in [\underline{a}_i, \overline{a}_i]$ is a basic value of the probability at the first level of the hierarchical model.

Next the problem of calculation of a value of utility function described as a Choquet integral for each $f_k \in \mathcal{A}$ in accordance with (7.22) is performed. Finally, an optimal action $f^* \in \mathcal{A}$ is obtained in accordance with (7.23).

For calculations in accordance with the presented methodology the following tools have been developed:

1) The solver for unknown probability calculation.
2) The module for lower prevision calculation in accordance with (7.24)-(7.26) on the base of a non-linear programming approach.
3) The module for Choquet integral calculation.
4) The module for ranking values of utility function to determine preferences among alternatives.

Chapter 8

Decision Making Model without Utility

1. 8.1 State of the Art

In the realm of formal methods of decision making, the general approach is the use of the utility theories which are based on an evaluation of a vector-valued alternative by means of an appropriate scalar-valued quantity. In real-life, human being does not proceed from vectors of attributes' values to scalar values for comparison in reasoning or decision making. Also, preferences as human judgments are often described in natural language (NL) and cannot be described by exact numerical values. For such cases, when application of utility function meets significant difficulties, scoring of alternatives may be conducted by direct ranking of alternatives. Then, as a rule, instead of a utility function it is used binary relations that provide finding an optimal or near to optimal alternative(s). There exists a spectrum of works in this area.

For performing outranking of alternatives, some methods had been developed for the traditional multiattribute decision making (MADM) problem [265,462]. One of the first among these methods was ELECTRE method [207,354,355]. The general scheme of this method can be described as follows. A DM assigns a weight for each criterion and concordance and discordance indices are constructed. After this, a decision rule is constructed including construction of a binary relation on the base of information received from a DM. Once a binary relation is constructed, a DM is provided with a set of non-dominated alternatives and chooses one alternative from among them as a final decision.

One of the most famous approaches is the Analytical Hierarchy

Process (AHP) [209]. In the AHP approach, criteria weights and criteria values are obtained by an intensive involving a DM. A DM chooses a value from a predefined scale to compare criteria between each other in terms of their importance. The same procedure is performed for pairwise comparison of alternatives with respect to each criterion. Performing these procedures creates several matrices, for which eigenvalues are computed to measure consistency of human's subjective comparison. If consistency is not satisfactory, the corresponding comparison performed again until the required consistency is reached. If it is so, an eigenvector is calculated to arrive at the desired estimations (weights or criteria values).

Similar methods like TOPSIS [209,325,434], VIKOR [325,326] are based on the idea that optimal vector-valued alternative(s) should have the shortest distance from the positive ideal solution and farthest distance from the negative ideal solution. An optimal alternative in the VIKOR is based on the measure of "closeness" to the positive ideal solution. TOPSIS and VIKOR methods use different aggregation functions and different normalization methods. There exists a series of works based on applying interval and fuzzy techniques to extend AHP [145,265], TOPSIS [256,260,265,408] and VIKOR [259,330] to fuzzy environment.

In [394] a fuzzy balancing and ranking method for MADM is suggested. They appraise the performance of alternatives against criteria via linguistic variables precisiated as triangular fuzzy numbers (TFNs).

The above mentioned approaches including the classical MADM methods and their fuzzy extensions suffer from serious disadvantages. Classical MADM methods require to provide perfect decision relevant information (e.g. to assign precise weights to criteria). This difficult problem sometimes is resolved by intensive involving of a DM. The fuzzy extensions of the existing methods are more tolerant. However, the fuzzy set theory does not play in these methods a main role, the main role is again belongs to the framework of the classical methods although equipped with ability to process linguistic information. Another important issue is that all these approaches are not developed to solve problems of decision making under uncertainty.

The above mentioned circumstances mandate necessity to develop new decision approaches which, from one side, may be based on a direct pairwise comparison of vector-valued alternatives. From the other side, there is a need to model the way humans actually think and reason with information described in NL in making decisions, for which it is adequate to use original capabilities of the fuzzy set theory[133].

In order to address the above mentioned problems, it is adequate to use computing with words (CW) approaches [198,290,443,445,452,454] to provide an intuitive, human friendly way to decision making. In [152] they suggest a fuzzy Pareto optimality (FPO) concept for MADM problems. This concept is an implementation of the ideas of CW-based redefinitions of the existing scientific concepts [449]. In this approach, by directly comparing alternatives, they arrive at total degrees to which one alternative is better than, is equivalent to, and is worse than another one. These degrees are determined as graded sums of differences between criteria values for considered alternatives. Such comparison is closer to the way humans compare alternatives by confronting their criteria values.

In the present chapter we suggest FPO concept-based approach to decision making under uncertainty in which relevant information on states of nature, probabilities and outcomes is imperfect as described in NL. As compared to the existing approaches, the suggested approach has a fundamental capability to conduct a direct comparison of NL-described alternatives by using linguistic preference degrees. Linguistic degrees are obtained by soft constraining of a Pareto optimal set of alternatives on the base of their degrees of optimality. The decision analysis in this approach is free from complex operations like construction of utility function or intensive involving of a DM. Computations with linguistic information is mainly based on simple operations.

8.2 Decision Making Model Without Utility

Let $\mathcal{S}=\{\tilde{S}_1,\tilde{S}_2,...,\tilde{S}_M\}\subset\mathcal{E}^n$ be a set of fuzzy states of nature and $\mathcal{X}\subset\mathcal{E}^n$ be a set of fuzzy outcomes. Fuzziness of states of nature is used for a fuzzy granulation of objective conditions when pure partitioning of the latter is impossible due to vagueness of the relevant information described in NL. A set of alternatives is considered as a set $\mathcal{A}$ of fuzzy functions $\tilde{f}$ from $\mathcal{S}$ to $\mathcal{X}$ [23,33,458]. Linguistic information on likelihood $\tilde{P}^l$ of the states of nature is formalized by fuzzy probabilities $\tilde{P}_j$ of the states $\tilde{S}_j$:

$$\tilde{P}^l = \tilde{P}_1 / \tilde{S}_1 + \tilde{P}_2 / \tilde{S}_2 + \ldots + \tilde{P}_M / \tilde{S}_M,$$

where $\tilde{P}_j \in \mathcal{E}^1_{[0,1]}$.

Due to vagueness of real-world objective conditions and uncertainty of future, relevant information on states of nature and the related probabilities is often described in NL. These are the cases when objective probabilities are not known due to absence of good statistical data and precise subjective probabilities are not reliable. Assuming three states of nature, NL-described information about corresponding probability distribution *Prob*() can be expressed as follows:

Prob(State1)/State1+Prob(State2)/State2+Prob(State3)/State3

= small/small + high/medium + very small/large,

with the understanding that a term *high/medium* means that the probability that the state of nature is *medium* is *high*. The considered linguistic description can be precisiated by using fuzzy sets with typical membership functions, say triangular-shaped one. Then the precisiation will be formally written as:

$$\tilde{P}^l = \tilde{P}_1 / \tilde{S}_1 + \tilde{P}_2 / \tilde{S}_2 + \tilde{P}_3 / \tilde{S}_3.$$

Here, for instance, $\tilde{S}_2$ and $\tilde{P}_2$ are TFNs used as precisiation for the terms *medium* and *high* respectively. Thus $\tilde{P}^l$ is a distribution of the fuzzy probabilities over the fuzzy states of nature. Let us mention that construction of this distribution does not consist in just assessing appropriate fuzzy numbers but requires solving a complex optimization problem[449] which is described in Chapter 6.

Vague preferences over a set of imprecise alternatives is modeled by a linguistic preference relation over $\mathcal{A}$. For this purpose it is adequate to introduce a linguistic variable "degree of preference" [33,82] with a term-set $\mathcal{T} = (T_1,...,T_K)$. Terms can be labeled as, for example, "equivalence", "little preference", "high preference", and each can be described by a fuzzy number defined over some scale like [0,1] or [0,10] etc. The fact that $\tilde{f}_i$ is linguistically preferred to $\tilde{f}_k$ is written as $\tilde{f}_i \succsim_l \tilde{f}_k$. The latter means that there exist some $T_i \in \mathcal{T}$ as a linguistic degree $Deg(\tilde{f}_i \succsim_l \tilde{f}_k)$ to which $\tilde{f}_i$ is preferred to $\tilde{f}_k$: $Deg(\tilde{f}_i \succsim_l \tilde{f}_k) \approx T_i$.

A decision making problem with imperfect information is formalized as a 4-tuple $\left(\mathcal{S}, \tilde{P}^l, \mathcal{A}, \succsim_l\right)$ and consists in determination of $\succsim_l$. The latter are described on the base of degrees of optimality of alternatives. A degree of optimality of an alternative $\tilde{f}_i$ denoted $do(\tilde{f}_i)$ is an overall degree to which $\tilde{f}_i$ dominates all the other alternatives. The linguistic preference $\tilde{f}_i \succsim_l \tilde{f}_k$ of $\tilde{f}_i$ with respect to $\tilde{f}_k$ is described by a degree $Deg(\tilde{f}_i \succsim_l \tilde{f}_k) = do(\tilde{f}_i) - do(\tilde{f}_k)$ iff $do(\tilde{f}_i) > do(\tilde{f}_k)$ and $Deg(\tilde{f}_i \succsim_l \tilde{f}_k) = 0$ otherwise [33].

The FPO formalism suggested in [152] is developed for a perfect information structure, i.e. when all the decision relevant information is represented by precise numerical evaluations. From the other side, this approach is developed for multiattribute decision making. We extend the FPO formalism for the considered framework of decision making with imperfect information[33]. The method of solution is described below.

The solution of the considered problem consists in determination of a linguistic degree of preference of $\tilde{f}_i$ to $\tilde{f}_k$ for all $\tilde{f}_i, \tilde{f}_k \in \mathcal{A}$ by direct comparison of $\tilde{f}_i$ and $\tilde{f}_k$ as vector-valued alternatives.

At the first stage it is needed for fuzzy probabilities $\tilde{P}_j$ to be known for each fuzzy state of nature $\tilde{S}_j$. However, it can be given only partial information represented by fuzzy probabilities for all fuzzy states except one. The unknown fuzzy probability cannot be assigned but must be computed based on the known fuzzy probabilities. Computation of an unknown fuzzy probability is an optimization problem as it requires construction of a membership function (see Chapter 6, (6.9)-(6.12)). When an unknown fuzzy probability is found, linguistic probability distribution $\tilde{P}^l$ for all states $\tilde{S}_j$ is determined:

$$\tilde{P}^l = \tilde{P}_1 / \tilde{S}_1 + \tilde{P}_2 / \tilde{S}_2 + \cdots + \tilde{P}_M / \tilde{S}_M$$

The important problem that arises for the obtained $\tilde{P}^l$, is to verify its consistency, completeness and redundancy (Chapter 6, (6.13)-(6.19)).

At the second stage, given consistent, complete and not-redundant distribution of the fuzzy probabilities over all the states of nature it is needed to determine the total degrees of statewise superiority, equivalence and inferiority of $\tilde{f}_i$ with respect to $\tilde{f}_k$ taking into account fuzzy probability $\tilde{P}_j$. The total degree nbF of statewise superiority, the total degree neF of statewise equivalence, and the total degree nwF of statewise inferiority of $\tilde{f}_i$ with respect to $\tilde{f}_k$ are determined on the base of differences between fuzzy outcomes of $\tilde{f}_i$ and $\tilde{f}_k$ at each fuzzy state of nature as follows:

$$nbF(\tilde{f}_i, \tilde{f}_k) = \sum_{j=1}^{M} \mu_b^j (gmv((\tilde{f}_i(\tilde{S}_j) - \tilde{f}_k(\tilde{S}_j)) \cdot \tilde{P}_j)), \tag{8.1}$$

$$neF(\tilde{f}_i, \tilde{f}_k) = \sum_{j=1}^{M} \mu_e^j (gmv((\tilde{f}_i(\tilde{S}_j) - \tilde{f}_k(\tilde{S}_j)) \cdot \tilde{P}_j)), \tag{8.2}$$

$$nwF(\tilde{f}_i, \tilde{f}_k) = \sum_{j=1}^{M} \mu_w^j (gmv((\tilde{f}_i(\tilde{S}_j) - \tilde{f}_k(\tilde{S}_j)) \cdot \tilde{P}_j)), \tag{8.3}$$

where $\mu_b^j, \mu_e^j, \mu_w^j$ are membership functions for linguistic evaluations "better", "equivalent" and "worse" respectively, determined as in [152], gmv is the generalized mean value of a fuzzy number[394]. For any j-th state $\mu_b^j, \mu_e^j, \mu_w^j$ are constructed such that Ruspini condition holds, which, in turn, results in the following condition [33]:

$$nbF(\tilde{f}_i, \tilde{f}_k) + neF(\tilde{f}_i, \tilde{f}_k) + nwF(\tilde{f}_i, \tilde{f}_k) = \sum_{j=1}^{M} (\mu_b^j + \mu_e^j + \mu_w^j) = M\,. \tag{8.4}$$

On the base of $nbF(\tilde{f}_i, \tilde{f}_k)$, $neF(\tilde{f}_i, \tilde{f}_k)$, and $nwF(\tilde{f}_i, \tilde{f}_k)$, $(1-kF)$ dominance is determined as dominance in the terms of its degree. This concepts suggests that $\tilde{f}_i$ $(1-kF)$-dominates $\tilde{f}_k$ iff

$$neF(\tilde{f}_i,\tilde{f}_k) < M\,,\ nbF(\tilde{f}_i,\tilde{f}_k) \geq \frac{M - neF(\tilde{f}_i,\tilde{f}_k)}{kF+1}\,, \tag{8.5}$$

with $kF \in [0,1]$. In order to determine the greatest kF such that $\tilde{f}_i$ $(1-kF)$- dominates $\tilde{f}_k$, a function d is introduced:

$$d(\tilde{f}_i,\tilde{f}_k) = \begin{cases} 0, & if\ \ nbF(\tilde{f}_i,\tilde{f}_k) \leq \dfrac{M - neF(\tilde{f}_i,\tilde{f}_k)}{2} \\ \dfrac{2\cdot nbF(\tilde{f}_i,\tilde{f}_k) + neF(\tilde{f}_i,\tilde{f}_k) - M}{nbF(\tilde{f}_i,\tilde{f}_k)}, & otherwise. \end{cases} \tag{8.6}$$

Given d, the desired greatest kF is found as $1-d(\tilde{f}_i,\tilde{f}_k)$. $d(\tilde{f}_i,\tilde{f}_k)=1$ implies Pareto dominance of $\tilde{f}_i$ over $\tilde{f}_k$ whereas $d(\tilde{f}_i,\tilde{f}_k)=0$ implies no Pareto dominance of $\tilde{f}_i$ over $\tilde{f}_k$.

In contrast to determine whether $\tilde{f}^*$ is Pareto optimal, in FPO they determine whether $\tilde{f}^*$ is Pareto optimal with the considered degree kF. $\tilde{f}^*$ is kF optimal if and only if there is no $\tilde{f}_i \in \mathcal{A}$ such that $\tilde{f}_i$ $(1-kF)$- dominates $\tilde{f}^*$. The main idea of FPO concept suggests to consider $\tilde{f}^*$ in terms of its degree of optimality $do(\tilde{f}^*)$ determined as

$$do(\tilde{f}^*) = 1 - \max_{\tilde{f}_i \in \mathcal{A}} d(\tilde{f}_i,\tilde{f}^*)\,. \tag{8.7}$$

do can be considered as the membership function of a fuzzy set describing the notion of kF-optimality.

We call kF-Optimal Set $\mathcal{D}_{kF}$ and kF-Optimal Front $\mathcal{A}_{kF}$ the set of kF-optimal solutions in the design domain and the objective domain respectively.

Let $\mu_{\tilde{D}}(\tilde{f}_i,\tilde{f}_k)$ be a membership function defined as follows:

$$\mu_{\tilde{D}}(\tilde{f}_i,\tilde{f}_k) = \varphi_{\mu_{\tilde{D}}}(nbF(\tilde{f}_i,\tilde{f}_k), neF(\tilde{f}_i,\tilde{f}_k), nwF(\tilde{f}_i,\tilde{f}_k))\,. \tag{8.8}$$

Then $\mu_{\tilde{D}}(\tilde{f}_i,\tilde{f}_k)$ is a fuzzy dominance relation if for any $\alpha \in [0,1]$,

$\mu_{\tilde{D}}(\tilde{f}_i, \tilde{f}_k) > \alpha$ implies that $\tilde{f}_i$ $(1-kF)$-dominates $\tilde{f}_k$. Particularly, $\varphi_{\mu_{\tilde{D}}}$ is defined as follows:

$$\varphi_{\mu_{\tilde{D}}} = \frac{2 \cdot nbF(\tilde{f}_i, \tilde{f}_k) + neF(\tilde{f}_i, \tilde{f}_k)}{2M}. \tag{8.9}$$

A membership function $\mu_{\tilde{D}}(\tilde{f}_i, \tilde{f}_k)$ represents the fuzzy optimality relation if for any $0 \le kF \le 1$ $\tilde{f}^*$ belongs to the kF-cut of $\mu_{\tilde{D}}$ if and only if there is no $\tilde{f}_i \in \mathcal{A}$ such that

$$\mu_{\tilde{D}}(\tilde{f}_i, \tilde{f}^*) > kF. \tag{8.10}$$

At the third stage, on the base of values of $nbF(\tilde{f}_i, \tilde{f}_k)$, $neF(\tilde{f}_i, \tilde{f}_k)$, and $nwF(\tilde{f}_i, \tilde{f}_k)$, the value of degree of optimality $do(\tilde{f}_i)$ as a degree of membership to a fuzzy Pareto optimal set, is determined by using formulas (8.5)-(8.9) for each $\tilde{f}_i \in \mathcal{A}$. The obtained $do()$ allows for justified determination of linguistic preference relation $\succsim_l$ over $\mathcal{A}$.

At the fourth stage, the degree $Deg(\tilde{f}_i \succsim_l \tilde{f}_k)$ of preference of $\tilde{f}_i$ to $\tilde{f}_k$ for any $\tilde{f}_i, \tilde{f}_k \in \mathcal{A}$ should be determined based on $do()$. For simplicity, one can calculate $Deg(\tilde{f}_i \succsim_l \tilde{f}_k)$ as follows:

$$Deg(\tilde{f}_i \succsim_l \tilde{f}_k) = do(\tilde{f}_i) - do(\tilde{f}_k).$$

8.3 Related Works

The main existing theories of decision making under uncertainty are based on the use of utility function. These theories include Subjective Expected Utility [360], Choquet Expected Utility [362], multiple priors-based models like Maximin Expected Utility [171], smooth ambiguity model [239] and others, Cumulative Prospect Theory [387] etc and fuzzy utility models [9,76,169,277]. The disadvantages of the utility-based theories consist in the use of very restrictive assumptions on preferences and in a loss of information intrinsic to any transformation of a vector-valued alternative into a scalar value. Very restrictive assumptions make the resulting utility model simple but not adequate; less restrictive and, as a result, more adequate ones make a utility model more complicated. There also exist situations for which utility function cannot be applied (for example, lexicographic ordering).

In order to compare the approach suggested in this study with the existing theories of decision making under uncertainty it is needed to take into account several important aspects. The first aspect implies that the existing methods require detailed and complete information on alternatives provided by a DM and intensive involving of the latter into choosing an optimal or suboptimal alternative(s). The suggested approach does not require intensive involving of a DM or an expert into decision analysis; he/she only needs to provide intuitively meaningful linguistic information on states of nature, outcomes and probabilities. Particularly, the use of linguistic information is convenient to account for vagueness of future when describing outcomes of alternatives. Second, such methods as TOPSIS [209,325,434], ELECTRE, VIKOR [325,326] and similar approaches require posing the weights of effective decision criteria that may not be always realizable. In the suggested approach, a DM needs to provide not precise but linguistic evaluation of probabilities. Moreover, partial information is required: a DM linguistically evaluates all the probabilities except the least known one. The latter is then computed without involving of a DM. Third, classical Pareto optimality principle which underlies the existing methods makes it necessary to deal with a large space of non-dominated alternatives that complicates a choice. The suggested approach is based on the fuzzy Pareto optimality principle which is developed to differentiate among 'more optimal' and 'less optimal' non-dominated alternatives. Fourth, all the methods like AHP [145,265], TOPSIS [256,265,408] etc are developed only for MADM problems and not for problems of decision making under risk or uncertainty. Although a parallelism between these problems exists, these methods cannot be directly applied for decision making under uncertainty. The suggested approach is developed directly for decision making under uncertainty and allows for application of the FPO. The method suggested in [394] does not take into account importance of criteria which is analogous to likelihoods of states of nature for decision under uncertainty. In our approach likelihoods of states of nature is taken into account by using linguistic probabilities. Fifth aspect uncovers that the existing methods are characterized by an absence of a significant impact of the fuzzy sets theory for decision making. The existing decision approaches are mainly fuzzy extensions of the well-known MADM approaches like AHP [228], TOPSIS [215,260,469], PROMETHEE, ELECTRE [207,354,355] and others. These are approaches where fuzzy sets are applied to the original numerical techniques to account for impreciseness and vagueness[133]. Some of these extensions suffer from disadvantages of direct, artificial replacement of numerical quantities by fuzzy numbers. This leads to loss of the properties of the original numerical approaches (for example loss of consistency and transitivity of preference matrices in AHP when replacing their numerical elements by fuzzy numbers)[133]. Also, when directly fuzzifying existing approaches one meets hard computational problems or even problems which don't have solutions (some fuzzy equations), or arrives at counterintuitive formal constructs. At the same time, it is necessary to mention that there exist mathematically correct and tractable extensions of the existing approaches to the fuzzy environment. For example, these are constraint-based method [84] or an approach in [342] as fuzzy versions of AHP. However, these methods don't resolve disadvantages of the original crisp approaches but only model imprecision within these approaches. The suggested approach does not utilize fuzzification of some existing method. It is developed for dealing with linguistic information which is formalized by fuzzy sets. The fuzzy optimality principle is applied for such formalization to rank alternatives by providing their degrees of optimality.

Chapter 9

Behavioral Decision Making with Combined States under Imperfect Information

9.1 State of the Art

Decision making is a behavioral process. During the development of decision theories scientists try to take into account features of human choices in formal models to make the latter closer to human decision activity. Risk issues were the first basic behavioral issues which became necessary to consider in construction of decision methods. Three main categories of risk-related behaviors: risk aversion, risk seeking and risk neutrality were introduced. Gain-loss attitudes [222] and ambiguity attitudes [171] were revealed as other important behavioral features. Prospect theory, developed for decision under risk [222], was the first decision theory incorporating both risk and gain-loss attitudes into a single utility model. Cumulative Prospect theory (CPT) [387], as its development, can be applied both for decision under risk and uncertainty and is one of the most successful decision theories. CPT is based on the use of Choquet integrals and, as a result, is able to represent not only risk and gain-loss attitudes but also ambiguity attitudes. Choquet Expected Utility (CEU) is a well-known typical model which can be used both for ambiguity and risk situations.

The first model developed for ambiguity aversion was Maximin expected utility (MMEU) [171]. Its generalization, α-MMEU, is able to represent both ambiguity aversion and ambiguity seeking [168]. Smooth ambiguity model [239] is a more advanced decision model for describing ambiguity attitudes.

A large stream of investigations led to development of parametric and non-parametric decision models taking into account such important psychological, moral and social aspects of decisions as reciprocity [114,115,150], altruism [39,114], trust [68,115] and others.

A large area of research in modeling decision makers (agents) in line with nature (environment) is mental-level models [85,92,112,252], idea of which was suggested in [316]. In these models a DM is modeled by a set of states. Each state describes his/her possible decision-relevant condition and is referred to as "mental state", "state of mind" etc. In these models, they consider relations between mental state and state of environment (nature) [113,191,418]. In [85,252] a mental state and a state of nature compose a state of the whole system called a "global state". Within the scope of mental-level models there are two main research areas of a mental state modeling: internal modeling [85,428] and implementation-independent (external) modeling [85]. The first is based on modeling a mental state by a set of characteristics (variables) and the second is based on modeling a mental state on the base of beliefs, preferences and decision criterion [85,343,371].

Now we observe a significant progress in development of a series of successful decision theories based on behavioral issues. Real-life human choices are based on simultaneous influence of main aspects of decision situations like risk, ambiguity and others. The question arises of how to adequately model joint influence of these factors on human choices and whether we should confine ourselves to assuming that these determinants influence choices independently. Due to highly constrained computational ability of human brain, independent influence of these factors can hardly be met. Humans conduct an intelligent, substantive comparison of real-life alternatives in whole, i.e. as some mixes of factors without pure partitioning of them. This implies interaction of the mentioned aspects in their influence on human choices. However, one of the disadvantages of the existing theories of decisions under uncertainty is an absence of a due attention to interaction of the factors. A vector of variables describing the factors is used in a decision model without fundamental consideration of how these factors really interact, they are considered separately. Also, information on intensity of the factors and their interaction is rather uncertain and vague and can mainly be described qualitatively and not quantitatively. The mentioned issues are the main reasons of why humans are not completely rational but partially, or bounded rational DMs[373] and why the existing decision models based on pure mathematical formalism become inconsistent with human choices.

9.2. Combined States Concept and Behavioral Decision Making

9.2.1 *Motivation*

The necessity to take into account that humans are not fully rational DMs was first conceptually addressed by Herbert Simon [373]. He proposed the concept of bounded rationality which reflects notable limitations of humans' knowledge and computational abilities. Despite their significant importance, the ideas of bounded rationality did not found its mathematical fundamentals to form a new consistent formal basis adequate to real decisions. The theory which can help to form an adequate mathematical formalism for bounded rationality-based decision analysis is the fuzzy set theory suggested by L.A. Zadeh [435]. The reason for this is that fuzzy set theory and its developments deal with formalization of linguistically (qualitatively) described imprecise or vague information and partial truth. Indeed, limitation of human knowledge, taken as one of the main aspects in bounded rationality, in real world results in the fact that humans use linguistic evaluations because the latter, as opposed to precise numbers, are tolerant for impreciseness and vagueness of real decision-relevant information. In fuzzy sets theory this is formalized by using fuzzy sets and fuzzy numbers. The other aspect – limitation of computational ability of humans – leads to the fact that humans think and reason in terms of propositions in natural language (NL), but not in terms of pure mathematical expressions. Such activity results in arriving at approximate solutions and satisfactory results but not at precise optimal solutions. This coincides with what is stated in bounded rationality ideas. In fuzzy logic, this is termed as approximate reasoning [41,440,451]. Fuzzy sets theory was initially suggested for an analysis of humanistic systems where perceptions play a pivotal role. Perceptions are imprecise, they have fuzzy boundaries [318], and, as a result, are often described linguistically. Fuzzy sets theory and its successive technologies [443] as tools for correct formal processing of perception-based information may help us to arrive at perceptions-friendly and mathematically consistent decisions. So, there is an evident connection between ideas of bounded rationality theory and fuzzy set theory [318].

So, in addition to missing interaction of behavioral factors in the existing theories they don't extensively take into account that information on a DM's behavior is imperfect. To be more concrete, in CPT they imperatively consider that a DM is risk averse when dealing with gains and risk seeking when dealing with losses. However it is too simplified view and in reality we don't have such complete information concerning risk attitudes of a considered DM in a considered situation. In α -MMEU they consider a balance of ambiguity aversion and ambiguity seeking that drives a DM's choices, but this is modeled by a precise value α , whereas real information about the ambiguity attitudes is imprecise. This all means that it is needed to model possibilistic uncertainty reflecting incomplete and imprecise relevant information on decision variables and not only probabilistic uncertainty.

Necessity of considering interaction of behavioral factors under imperfect information is the main insight for development of new decision approaches. Following this, we suggest considering a space of vectors of variables describing behavioral factors (for example, risk and ambiguity attitudes) as composed of main subspaces each describing one principal DM's behavior. Each subspace we suggest to consider as a DM's state in which he/she may be when making choices [7,32]. Such formalization is in the direction of internal modeling of DMs (or agents) within the scope of the mental-level models. However, we suggest to consider these subspaces as not exclusive, but as some overlapping sets to reflect the facts that principal behaviors may have indeed some similarity and proximity, which should not be disregarded because the state of a DM is uncertain itself and cannot be sharply bounded. For this case we suggest to use fuzzy granulation of the considered space, i.e. granulation into fuzzy sets each describing one state of a DM. This helps to closer model a DM's condition as the relevant information is mainly described in linguistic (qualitative) form and could not be reliably described by precise dependencies.

In our approach, uncertainty related to what state of a DM is likely to occur is described by a linguistic (fuzzy) probability. Fuzzy probability describes impreciseness of beliefs coming from uncertainty and complexity of interaction of the factors, from absence of ideal information.

Concerning states of nature, in many real problems there is also no sufficient information to consider them as "mutually exclusive": for example, if one considers states of economy, the evaluations like "moderate growth" and "strong growth" don't have sharp boundaries and, as a result, may not be "exclusive" – they may overlap. Observing some actual situation an expert may conclude that to a larger extent it concerns the moderate growth and to a smaller extent to the strong growth. An appropriate way to model this is the use of fuzzy sets. In real-life it is often impossible to construct exclusive and exhaustive states of nature, due to uncertainty of relevant information [164]. In general, a DM cannot exhaustively determine each objective condition that may be faced and precisely differentiate them. Each state of nature is, essentially, some area which collects similar objective conditions, that is some set of "elementary" states or quantities. Unfortunately, in the existing decision theories a small attention paid to the essence and structure of states of nature.

We suggest to consider the space of states of nature and space of DM's states as constituting a single space of combined states [7,13,32], i.e. to considering Cartesian product of these two important spaces as basis for comparison of alternatives. Likelihood of occurrence of each combined space as a pair consisting of one state of nature and one DM's state is to be described by fuzzy probability of their joint occurrence. This fuzzy joint probability (FJP) is to be found on the base of fuzzy marginal probabilities of a state of nature and a state of a DM and, if possible, on the base of some information about dependence of these states. Utilities of outcomes are also to be distributed over the combined states reflecting naturally various evaluation of the outcomes by a DM in his/her various states.

Consideration of DM's behavior by space of states and its Cartesian product with space of states of nature [7,13,32] will allow for transparent analysis of decisions. In contrast, in the existing utility models human attitudes to risk, ambiguity and others are included using complex mathematical expressions – nonlinear transformations, second-order probabilities etc. Indeed, most of the existing decision theories are based on parametric modeling of behavioral features. As a result, they cannot adequately describe human decision activity; they are mathematically complex and not transparent. The existing non-parametric approaches are more fundamental, but, they also are based on perfect and precise description of human decision activity. This is non-realistic because human thinking and motivation are perception-based [452] and cannot be captured by precise techniques. Real-life information related to a DM behavior and objective conditions is intrinsically imperfect. We mostly make decisions under vagueness, impreciseness, partial truth etc. of decision-relevant information and ourselves think in categories of "smooth" concepts even under perfect information.

So, our approach is based on three justifications: necessity of considering dependence between various behavioral determinants, necessity to take into account uncertainty of what behavior will be present in making choices (e.g. what risk attitude), a need for construction transparent model of behavioral decision analysis.

In the present study we develop investigations started in [6,7,12,13]. We suggest a new approach to behavioral decision making under imperfect information, namely under mix of probabilistic and possibilistic uncertainties. We show that the expected utility(EU) [397], CEU [362] and CPT [387] are special cases of the combined states-based approach. For a representation in the suggested model we adopt the generalized fuzzy Choquet-like aggregation with respect to a fuzzy-valued bi-capacity.

9.2.2 *Statement of the problem [32]*

Let $\mathcal{S}=\{\tilde{S}_1,\tilde{S}_2,...,\tilde{S}_M\}\subset\mathcal{E}^n$ be a space of fuzzy states of nature and $\mathcal{X}$ be a space of fuzzy outcomes as a bounded subset of $\mathcal{E}^n$. Denote by $\mathcal{H}=\left\{\tilde{h}_1,\tilde{h}_2,...,\tilde{h}_N\right\}\subset\mathcal{E}^n$ a set of fuzzy states of a DM [7,12,32]. Then we call $\Omega = \mathcal{S} \times \mathcal{H}$ a space "nature-DM", elements of which are combined states $\tilde{w} = (\tilde{S}, \tilde{h})$ where $\tilde{S} \in \mathcal{S}, \tilde{h} \in \mathcal{H}$.

Denote $\mathcal{F}_\Omega$ a σ-algebra of subsets of Ω. Let us consider a set of fuzzy actions as the set $\mathcal{A} = \left\{ \tilde{f} \in \mathcal{A} \middle| \tilde{f} : \Omega \to \mathcal{X} \right\}$ of all $\mathcal{F}_\Omega$-measurable fuzzy functions from Ω to $\mathcal{X}$ [7,12].

A problem of behavioral decision making with combined states under imperfect information (BDMCSII) can be formally described as a 4-tuple $D_{BDMCSII} = (\Omega, \mathcal{X}, \mathcal{A}, \succsim_l)$ where $\succsim_l$ are linguistic preferences of a DM.

In general, it is not known which state of nature will take place and what state of a DM will present at the moment of decision making. Only some partial knowledge on probability distributions on $\mathcal{S}$ and $\mathcal{H}$ is available. An information relevant to a DM can be formalized as a linguistic probability distribution over his/her states: $\tilde{P}_1 / \tilde{h}_1 + \tilde{P}_2 / \tilde{h}_2 + \cdots + \tilde{P}_N / \tilde{h}_N$, where $\tilde{P}_i$ is a linguistic belief degree or a linguistic probability. So, $\tilde{P}_i / \tilde{h}_i$ can be formulated as, for example, "a probability that a DM's state is $\tilde{h}_i$ is $\tilde{P}_i$".

For closer description of human behavior and imperfect information on Ω we use a fuzzy number-valued bi-capacity $\tilde{\eta} = \tilde{\eta}(G, H), G, H \subset \Omega$. A fuzzy-valued bi-capacity is defined as follows.

Definition 9.1. Fuzzy number-valued bi-capacity. A fuzzy number-valued bi-capacity on $\mathcal{F}_\Omega^2 = \mathcal{F}_\Omega \times \mathcal{F}_\Omega$ is a fuzzy number-valued set function $\tilde{\eta} : \mathcal{F}_\Omega^2 \to \mathcal{E}^1_{[-1,1]}$ with the following properties:

(1) $\tilde{\eta}(\varnothing, \varnothing) = 0$;

(2) if $\mathcal{V} \subset \mathcal{V}'$ then $\tilde{\eta}(\mathcal{V}, \mathcal{W}) \le \tilde{\eta}(\mathcal{V}', \mathcal{W})$;

(3) if $\mathcal{W} \subset \mathcal{W}'$ then $\tilde{\eta}(\mathcal{V}, \mathcal{W}) \ge \tilde{\eta}(\mathcal{V}, \mathcal{W}')$;

(4) $\tilde{\eta}(\Omega, \varnothing) = 1$ and $\tilde{\eta}(\varnothing, \Omega) = -1$.

In special case, values of a fuzzy-valued bi-capacity $\tilde{\eta}(\mathcal{V}, \mathcal{W})$ can be determined as the difference of values of two fuzzy-valued measures

$\tilde{\eta}_1(\mathcal{V})-\tilde{\eta}_2(\mathcal{W})$, where "$-$" is defined on the base of Zadeh's extension principle[129].

Value or utility of an outcome $\tilde{X}=\tilde{f}(\tilde{S},\tilde{h})$ in various DM's states will also be various, and then can be formalized as a function $\tilde{u}(\tilde{X})=$ $=\tilde{u}(\tilde{f}(\tilde{S},\tilde{h}))$. We can claim that the value function of Kahneman and Tversky $v=v(f())$ [222] appears then as a special case. So, an overall utility $\tilde{U}(\tilde{f})$ of an action $\tilde{f}$ is to be determined as a fuzzy number-valued bi-capacity-based aggregation of $\tilde{u}(\tilde{f}(\tilde{S},\tilde{h}))$ over space Ω. Then the BDMCSII problem consists in determination of an optimal action as an action $\tilde{f}^{*}\in\mathcal{A}$ with $\tilde{U}(\tilde{f}^{*})=\max_{f\in\mathcal{A}}\int_{\Omega}\tilde{u}(\tilde{f}(\tilde{w}))d\tilde{\eta}$.

9.2.3 *Model*

Axiomatization. As the basis for our model we use the framework of bi-capacity formulated by Labreuche and Grabisch[250]. The bi-capacity is a natural generalization of capacities and is able to describe interaction between attractive and repulsive values (outcomes, criteria values), particularly, gains and losses. We extend this framework to the case of imperfect information by using linguistic preference relation [32]. The linguistic preference means that the preference among actions $\tilde{f}$ and $\tilde{g}$ is modeled by a degree $Deg(\tilde{f}\succsim_l\tilde{g})$ to which $\tilde{f}$ is at least as good as $\tilde{g}$ and a degree $Deg(\tilde{g}\succsim_l\tilde{f})$ to which $\tilde{g}$ is at least as good as $\tilde{f}$. The degrees $Deg()$ are from [0,1]. The closer $Deg(\tilde{f}\succsim_l\tilde{g})$ to 1 the more $\tilde{f}$ is preferred to $\tilde{g}$. These degrees are used to represent vagueness of preferences, that is, situations when decision relevant information is too vague to definitely determine preference of one alternative against another. For special case, when $Deg(\tilde{g}\succsim_l\tilde{f})=0$ and $Deg(\tilde{f}\succsim_l\tilde{g})\neq 0$ we have the classical preference, i.e. we say that $\tilde{f}$ is preferred to $\tilde{g}$.

We use bi-capacity-adopted integration at the space "nature-DM" for determination of an overall utility of an alternative. The base for our model is composed by intra-combined state information and inter-combined states information. Intra-combined state information is used to form utilities representing preference over outcomes $\tilde{f}(\tilde{w}_i)=\tilde{X}_i$, where $\tilde{w}_i=(\tilde{S}_{i_1},\tilde{h}_{i_2})$ of an act $\tilde{f}\in\mathcal{A}$ with understanding that these are preferences at state of nature $\tilde{S}_{i_1}$ conditioned by a state $\tilde{h}_{i_2}$ of a DM.

Inter-combined states information will be used to form fuzzy-valued bi-capacity representing dependence between combined states as human behaviors under incomplete information.

Proceeding from these assumptions, for an overall utility $\tilde{U}$ of action $\tilde{f}$ we use an aggregation operator based on the use of a bi-capacity. Bi-capacity is a more powerful tool to be used in a space "nature-DM". More concretely, we use a fuzzy-valued generalized Choquet-like aggregation with respect to fuzzy-valued bi-capacity over Ω [32]:

$$\tilde{U}(\tilde{f})=\sum_{l=1}^{L}\left(\left|\tilde{u}(\tilde{f}(\tilde{w}_{(l)}))\right|-_h\left|\tilde{u}(\tilde{f}(\tilde{w}_{(l+1)}))\right|\right)\tilde{\eta}(\{\tilde{w}_{(1)},\dots,\tilde{w}_{(l)}\}\cap N^+,\{\tilde{w}_{(1)},\dots,\tilde{w}_{(l)}\}\cap N^-),\quad (9.1)$$

where $(\cdot)$ implies that the indices are permuted in order to have $\left|\tilde{u}(\tilde{f}(\tilde{w}_{(l)}))\right|\geq\left|\tilde{u}(\tilde{f}(\tilde{w}_{(l+1)}))\right|$; $\tilde{u}(\tilde{f}(\tilde{w}_{(L+1)}))=0$ by convention. The set is N^+ is defined as $N^+=\{\tilde{w}\in\Omega\,|\,\tilde{u}(\tilde{f}(\tilde{w}))\geq 0\}$, $N^-=\Omega\setminus N^+$, $\tilde{\eta}(\cdot,\cdot)$ is a fuzzy number-valued bi-capacity.

In (9.1) under level α we have an interval $U^\alpha(\tilde{f})=[U_1^\alpha(\tilde{f}),U_2^\alpha(\tilde{f})]$ of possible precise overall utilities, where $U_1^\alpha(\tilde{f}),\,U_2^\alpha(\tilde{f})$ are described as follows:

$$\begin{aligned}U_1^\alpha(\tilde{f})&=\left(\left|u_1^\alpha(\tilde{f}(\tilde{w}_{(1)}))\right|-\left|u_1^\alpha(\tilde{f}(\tilde{w}_{(2)}))\right|\right)\eta_1^\alpha(\{\tilde{w}_{(1)}\}\cap N^+,\{\tilde{w}_{(1)}\}\cap N^-)\\&+\left(\left|u_1^\alpha(\tilde{f}(\tilde{w}_{(2)}))\right|-\left|u_1^\alpha(\tilde{f}(\tilde{w}_{(3)}))\right|\right)\eta_1^\alpha(\{\tilde{w}_{(1)},\tilde{w}_{(2)}\}\cap N^+,\{\tilde{w}_{(1)},\tilde{w}_{(2)}\}\cap N^-)\\&+\cdots+\left|u_1^\alpha(\tilde{f}(\tilde{w}_{(L)}))\right|\eta_1^\alpha(\{\tilde{w}_{(1)},\tilde{w}_{(2)},\dots,\tilde{w}_{(L)}\}\cap N^+,\{\tilde{w}_{(1)},\tilde{w}_{(2)},\dots,\tilde{w}_{(L)}\}\cap N^-),\end{aligned}$$

$$\begin{aligned}U_2^\alpha(\tilde{f})&=\left(\left|u_2^\alpha(\tilde{f}(\tilde{w}_{(1)}))\right|-\left|u_2^\alpha(\tilde{f}(\tilde{w}_{(2)}))\right|\right)\eta_2^\alpha(\{\tilde{w}_{(1)}\}\cap N^+,\{\tilde{w}_{(1)}\}\cap N^-)\\&+\left(\left|u_2^\alpha(\tilde{f}(\tilde{w}_{(2)}))\right|-\left|u_2^\alpha(\tilde{f}(\tilde{w}_{(3)}))\right|\right)\eta_2^\alpha(\{\tilde{w}_{(1)},\tilde{w}_{(2)}\}\cap N^+,\{\tilde{w}_{(1)},\tilde{w}_{(2)}\}\cap N^-)\\&+\cdots+\left|u_2^\alpha(\tilde{f}(\tilde{w}_{(L)}))\right|\eta_2^\alpha(\{\tilde{w}_{(1)},\tilde{w}_{(2)},\dots,\tilde{w}_{(L)}\}\cap N^+,\{\tilde{w}_{(1)},\tilde{w}_{(2)},\dots,\tilde{w}_{(L)}\}\cap N^-),\end{aligned}$$

where $\left|u_1^\alpha(\tilde{f}(\tilde{w}_{(1)}))\right|\geq\cdots\geq\left|u_1^\alpha(\tilde{f}(\tilde{w}_{(L)}))\right|$, $\left|u_2^\alpha(\tilde{f}(\tilde{w}_{(1)}))\right|\geq\cdots\geq\left|u_2^\alpha(\tilde{f}(\tilde{w}_{(L)}))\right|$ and

$u_1^\alpha(\tilde{f}(\tilde{w}_{(L)})) = u_2^\alpha(\tilde{f}(\tilde{w}_{(L)})) = 0$ by convention. Thus, $U_i^\alpha(\tilde{f}), i = 1,2$ is a Choquet-like precise bi-capacity based functional, with u_i^α and η_i^α $i = 1,2$ being a precise utility function and a precise bi-capacity respectively. This representation captures impreciseness of both a utility and a bi-capacity arising from impreciseness of outcomes and probabilities in real-world decision problems.

An optimal action $\tilde{f}^* \in \mathcal{A}$, that is $\tilde{f}^* \in \mathcal{A}$ for which $\tilde{U}(\tilde{f}^*) = \max_{\tilde{f}\in}\left\{\int_\Omega \tilde{u}(\tilde{f}(\tilde{S},\tilde{h})d\tilde{\eta}\right\}$ is found by a determination of $Deg(\tilde{f} \succsim_l \tilde{g})$, $\tilde{f},\tilde{g} \in \mathcal{A}$: optimal action $\tilde{f}^* \in \mathcal{A}$ is an action for which $Deg(\tilde{f}^* \succsim_l \tilde{f}) \geq Deg(\tilde{f} \succsim_l \tilde{f}^*)$ is satisfied for all $\tilde{f} \in \mathcal{A}, \tilde{f} \neq \tilde{f}^*$. The determination of $Deg(\tilde{f} \succsim_l \tilde{g})$ is based on comparison of $U(\tilde{f})$ and $U(\tilde{g})$ as the basic values of $\tilde{U}(\tilde{f})$ and $\tilde{U}(\tilde{g})$ respectively as follows. Membership functions of $\tilde{U}(\tilde{f})$ and $\tilde{U}(\tilde{g})$ describe possibilities of their various basic values $U(\tilde{f})$ and $U(\tilde{g})$ respectively, that is, possibilities for various precise values of overall utilities of $\tilde{f}$ and $\tilde{g}$. In accordance with these membership functions, there is possibility $\alpha \in (0,1]$ that precise overall utilities of $\tilde{f}$ and $\tilde{g}$ are equal to $U_1^\alpha(\tilde{f}), U_2^\alpha(\tilde{f})$ and $U_1^\alpha(\tilde{g}), U_2^\alpha(\tilde{g})$ respectively. Therefore, we can state that there is possibility $\alpha \in (0,1]$ that the difference between precise overall utilities of $\tilde{f}$ and $\tilde{g}$ is $U_i^\alpha(\tilde{f}) - U_j^\alpha(\tilde{g}), i, j = 1,2$. As $\tilde{f}$ is preferred to $\tilde{g}$ when overall utility of $\tilde{f}$ is larger than that of $\tilde{g}$, we will consider only positive $U_i^\alpha(\tilde{f}) - U_i^\alpha(\tilde{g})$. Consider now the following functions:

$$\sigma(\alpha) = \sum_{i=1}^{2}\sum_{j=1}^{2} \max(U_i^\alpha(\tilde{f}) - U_j^\alpha(\tilde{g}), 0);$$

$$\delta_{ij}(\alpha) = \begin{cases} \dfrac{\max(U_i^\alpha(\tilde{f}) - U_j^\alpha(\tilde{g}), 0)}{\left|U_i^\alpha(\tilde{f}) - U_j^\alpha(\tilde{g})\right|}, & if\ U_i^\alpha(\tilde{f}) - U_j^\alpha(\tilde{g}) \neq 0 \\ 0, & else \end{cases} \quad i, j = 1,2;$$

$$\delta(\alpha) = \sum_{i}^{2}\sum_{j}^{2} \delta_{ij}(\alpha).$$

$\sigma(\alpha)$ shows the sum of all positive differences between $U_1^\alpha(\tilde{f}), U_2^\alpha(\tilde{f})$ and $U_1^\alpha(\tilde{g}), U_2^\alpha(\tilde{g})$ and $\delta(\alpha)$ shows the number of these differences. Consider now the quantity $\frac{\int_0^1 \alpha\sigma(\alpha)d\alpha}{\int_0^1 \alpha\delta(\alpha)d\alpha}$ as a weighted average of differences $U_i^\alpha(\tilde{f})-U_j^\alpha(\tilde{g}),\ i,j=1,2$ where weights are their possibilities $\alpha\in(0,1]$. The degree $Deg(\tilde{f}\succsim_l \tilde{g})$ is determined then as follows:

$$Deg(\tilde{f}\succsim_l \tilde{g})=\frac{\int_0^1 \alpha\sigma(\alpha)d\alpha}{(u_{\max}-u_{\min})\int_0^1 \alpha\delta(\alpha)d\alpha} \tag{9.2}$$

In other words, $Deg(\tilde{f}\succsim_l \tilde{g})$ is determined as a percentage of a weighted average of differences $U_i^\alpha(\tilde{f})-U_j^\alpha(\tilde{g}),\ i,j=1,2$ with respect to $u_{\max}-u_{\min}$ being maximally possible difference ($u_{\min}$ and $u_{\max}$ are respecttively the lower and upper bounds of the universe of discourse for utility $\tilde{u}$, and, therefore, $u_{\max}\le\tilde{U}(\tilde{f})\le u_{\min}$ as $\tilde{U}(\tilde{f})$ is an aggregation of $\tilde{u}$). By other words, the closer the difference $U_i^\alpha(\tilde{f})-U_j^\alpha(\tilde{g})$ of the equally possible values of precise overall utilities of $\tilde{f}$ and $\tilde{g}$ to $u_{\max}-u_{\min}$ the higher is the extent to which $\tilde{f}$ is better than $\tilde{g}$.

Let us show that the famous existing utility models are special cases of the proposed combined states-based fuzzy utility model[32]. To do this, we simplify our model to its non-fuzzy variant and consider its relation with the existing utility models. Bi-capacity-based aggregation of $u(f(S,h))$ on a space Ω would be a natural generalization of an aggregation of $u(f(S))$ on a space $\mathcal{S}$. We will show this by comparing of EU and CEU applied on space $\mathcal{S}=\{S_1,S_2,...S_m\}$ with the same models applied on a combined states space Ω. For obvious illustration let us first look at a general representation of combined states space $\Omega=\mathcal{S}\times\mathcal{H}$ given in Table 9.1.

Table 9.1. Combined states space

	S_1	...	S_i	...	S_M
h_1	(S_1,h_1)	...	(S_i,h_1)	...	(S_M,h_1)
...	...	...	...	...	...
h_j	(S_1,h_j)	...	(S_i,h_j)	...	(S_M,h_j)
...	...	...	...	...	...
h_N	(S_1,h_N)	...	(S_i,h_N)	...	(S_M,h_N)

EU criterion used for combined states space (Table 9.1) will have the following form[32]:

$$U(f)=\sum_{l=1}^{MN}u(f(w_l))p(w_l)=\sum_{i=1}^{M}\sum_{j=1}^{N}u(f(S_i,h_j))p(S_i,h_j)\,. \tag{9.3}$$

In traditional EU (i.e. EU applied on a space S only) they consider that a DM exhibits the same behavior in any state of nature. In our terminology this means that only one state of a DM can exist. Then, to model a classical EU within (9.3) we should exclude all h_j except one, say h_k. This immediately means that $P(S_i,h_j)=0,\forall j\neq k$ (as we consider that all $h_j, j\neq k$ don't exist) and we have

$$U(f)=\sum_{i=1}^{M}u(f(S_i,h_k))p(S_i,h_k)\,.$$

Now, as a DM is always at a state h_k whatever state S_i takes place, we have $p(S_i,h_k)=p(S_i)$. Furthermore, in common EU only risk attitudes as behavioral aspects are taken into account. A DM is considered as either risk averse or risk seeking or risk neutral. So, h_k can represent one of these behaviors. For example, if h_k represents risk aversion then $u()$ will be concave, if h_k represents risk seeking then $u()$ will be convex etc. So, h_k determines form of $u()$. If we use notation $u^*(f(\cdot))$ for $u(f(\cdot,h_k))$ when h_k represents, for example, risk aversion, we have (9.3) as $U(f)=\sum_{i=1}^{N}u^*(f(S_i))p(S_i)$ which is nothing but the traditional EU. So, the traditional EU is a special case of the EU criterion used for Ω.

Combined-states based approach as opposed to classical EU allows to take into account that a DM can exhibit various risk attitudes at various states of nature. This usually takes place in real life and is taken into account in PT and CPT (these models are based on experimental observations demonstrating that people exhibit risk aversion for gains and risk seeking for losses).

Let us now show that CEU used for space S is a special case of the analogous aggregation over Ω. CEU used for Ω will have the following form:

$$U(f)=\sum_{l=1}^{MN}(u(f(w_{(l)}))-u(f(w_{(l+1)})))\eta(\{w_{(1)},...,w_{(l)}\}) \tag{9.4}$$

$w_{(l)}=(S_j,h_k)$, $u(f(w_{(l)}))\geq u(f(w_{(l+1)}))$. Assuming now that only some h_k exists, we have that $\forall w\in\Omega, w=(S_i,h_k)$, that is $\Omega=S\times\{h_k\}$. Then we will have $u(f(w_{(l)}))-u(f(w_{(l+1)}))=0$ whenever $w_{(l)}=(S_i,h_k), w_{(l+1)}=(S_i,h_k)$. Only differences $u(f(w_{(l)}))-u(f(w_{(l+1)}))$ for which $w_{(l)}=(S_i,h_k), w_{(l+1)}=(S_j,h_k)$, $i\neq j$ may not be equal to zero. As a result, making simple transformations, we will have:

$$U(f)=\sum_{i=1}^{n}(u(f(S_{(i)},h_k))-u(f((S_{(i+1)},h_k))))\eta(\{(S_{(1)},h_k),...,(S_{(i)},h_k)\}).$$

Now, using notations $u^*(f(\cdot))$ for $u(f(\cdot,h_k))$ and $\eta^*(\{S_{(1)},...,S_{(j)}\})=\eta(\{(S_{(1)},h_k),...,(S_{(j)},h_k)\})$ we can write[32]

$$U(f)=\sum_{i=1}^{N}(u^*(f(S_{(i)}))-u^*(f(S_{(i+1)})))\eta^*(\{S_{(1)},...,S_{(i)}\}).$$

This is nothing but a traditional CEU. Traditional CEU is often used to represent uncertainty attitude as an important behavioral aspect. In the suggested setting, if h_k represents uncertainty aversion (uncertainty seeking) then $\eta(\{(S_{(1)},h_k),...,(S_{(j)},h_k)\})$ can be chosen as lower prevision (upper prevision).

It can also be shown that the utility model used in the CPT is also a special case of the combined states approach. This follows from the fact that representation used in CPT is a sum of two Choquet integrals.

9.2.4 *Solution of the problem*

The solution of the problem consists in determination of an optimal action $\tilde{f}^* \in \mathcal{A}$ with $\tilde{U}(\tilde{f}^*) = \max_{\tilde{f} \in \mathcal{A}} \left\{ \int_\Omega \tilde{u}(\tilde{f}(\tilde{S},\tilde{h}))d\tilde{\eta} \right\}$. The problem is solved as follows. At the first stage it becomes necessary to assign linguistic utility values $\tilde{u}(\tilde{f}(\tilde{S}_i,\tilde{h}_j))$ to every action $\tilde{f} \in \mathcal{A}$ taken at a state of nature $\tilde{S}_i \in \mathcal{S}$ when a DM's state is $\tilde{h}_j$. The second stage consists in construction of a FJP distribution $\tilde{P}^l$ on Ω proceeding from partial information on marginal distributions over $\mathcal{S}$ and $\mathcal{H}$ which is represented by given fuzzy probabilities for all states except one. This requires constructing unknown fuzzy probability for each space [31,34]. Given marginal distribution of fuzzy probabilities for all the states, it is needed to verify consistency, completeness and redundancy of this distribution [82]. Finally, on the base of fuzzy marginal distributions (for $\mathcal{S}$ and $\mathcal{H}$) and information on dependence between states of nature $\tilde{S} \in \mathcal{S}$ and a DM's states $\tilde{h} \in \mathcal{H}$ it is needed to construct FJP distribution $\tilde{P}^l$ on Ω.

At the third stage it is necessary to construct a fuzzy-valued bi-capacity $\tilde{\eta}(\cdot,\cdot)$ based on FJP $\tilde{P}^l$ on Ω. For simplicity one can determine a fuzzy-valued bi-capacity as the difference of two fuzzy-valued capacities.

Next an overall utility $\tilde{U}(\tilde{f})$ for every action $\tilde{f} \in \mathcal{A}$ is computed by using formula (9.1). In (9.1) differences between absolute values of fuzzy utilities $\left|\tilde{u}(\tilde{f}(\tilde{S},\tilde{h}))\right|$ assigned at the first stage are multiplied on the base of the Zadeh's extension principle by the values of the fuzzy valued bi-capacity $\tilde{\eta}(\cdot,\cdot)$ constructed at the third stage.

Finally, an optimal action $\tilde{f}^* \in \mathcal{A}$ as the action with the maximal fuzzy valued utility $\tilde{U}(\tilde{f}^*) = \max_{\tilde{f} \in \mathcal{A}} \left\{ \int_\Omega \tilde{u}(\tilde{f}(\tilde{S},\tilde{h}))d\tilde{\eta} \right\}$ is determined by comparing fuzzy overall utilities $\tilde{U}(\tilde{f})$ for all $\tilde{f} \in \mathcal{A}$ (see formula (9.2)).

9.2.5 *Construction of a fuzzy joint probability distribution over a space of combined states*

As we mentioned in the previous section, in order to solve the considered problem of behavioral decision making we need to construct a fuzzy-valued bi-capacity over a space of combined states Ω. This fuzzy-valued bi-capacity is used to model relations between combined states under imperfect relevant information. One natural informational basis to construct a fuzzy-valued bi-capacity is a FJP over combined states. The FJP distribution describes dependence of states of a DM on states of nature, that is, dependence of a human behavior on objective conditions that is a quite natural phenomenon. In order to proceed to construction of FJP we need to consider some preliminary concepts that are given below.

There exist mainly two approaches to construction of a joint probability distribution: approaches for modeling dependence among events (e.g. the chance that it will be cloudy and it will rain) and approaches modeling dependence among random variables (e.g. the chance that an air temperature is in-between 20°C and 30°C and air humidity is in-between 90%-95%). In modeling dependence of states of a DM on states of nature we will follow dependence of events framework. This framework is more suitable as states of a DM and states of nature are not numerical but are rather qualitative.

To measure a joint probability of two events H and G we need two kinds of information: marginal probabilities for H and G and information on a type of dependence between H and G referred to as a *sign of dependence*. There exist three types of dependence[417,419]: positive dependence, independence and negative dependence. Positive dependence implies that H and G have tendency to occur together, e.g. one favors occurrence of another. For example, cloudiness and rain are positively dependent. Negative dependence implies they don't commonly occur together, e.g. one precludes occurrence of another. For example, sunny day and raining are negatively dependent. Independence implies that occurrence of one does not affect an occurrence of another. The extreme case of a positive dependence is referred to as a perfect dependence. The extreme case of a negative dependence is referred to as opposite dependence. It is well known that given numerical probabilities

$P(H)$ and $P(G)$ of independent events H and G, the joint probability $P(H,G)$ is determined as

$$P(H,G) = P(H)P(G). \tag{9.5}$$

The perfect dependence is determined as [417,419]

$$P(H,G) = \min(P(H), P(G)). \tag{9.6}$$

For explanation of this fact one may refer to [417,419]. It is clear that $P(H)P(G) \le \min(P(H), P(G))$. Positive dependence among H and G is modeled as [417,419]

$$P(H,G) \in [P_1(H,G), P_2(H,G)] = \left[P(H)P(G), \min(P(H), P(G))\right]. \tag{9.7}$$

Indeed, positively dependent events occur together more often that independent ones.

Opposite dependence among H and G is determined as

$$P(H,G) = \max(P(H) + P(G) - 1, 0). \tag{9.8}$$

It is known that $\max(P(H) + P(G) - 1, 0) \le P(H)P(G)$. Negative dependence among H and G is modeled as.

$$\begin{aligned} &P(H,G) \in [P_1(H,G), P_2(H,G)] \\ &= [\max(P(H) + P(G) - 1, 0), P(H)P(G)]. \end{aligned} \tag{9.9}$$

Indeed, negatively dependent events occur together less often that independent ones.

Unknown dependence is modeled as

$$\begin{aligned} &P(H,G) \in [P_1(H,G), P_2(H,G)] \\ &= [\max(P(H) + P(G) - 1, 0), \min(P(H), P(G))]. \end{aligned} \tag{9.10}$$

For the case of interval-valued probabilities of H and G, i.e. when $P(H) \in [P_1(H), P_2(H)]$ and $P(G) \in [P_1(G), P_2(G)]$ the formulas (9.5)-(9.10) are generalized as follows:

$$P(H,G) \in [P_1(H,G), P_2(H,G)] = [P_1(H)P_1(G), P_2(H)P_2(G)]. \tag{9.11}$$

$$\begin{aligned} &P(H,G) \in [P_1(H,G), P_2(H,G)] \\ &= [\min(P_1(H), P_1(G)), \min(P_2(H), P_2(G))]. \end{aligned} \tag{9.12}$$

$$P(H,G) \in [P_1(H,G), P_2(H,G)] = \left[P_1(H)P_1(G), \min(P_2(H), P_2(G))\right]. \tag{9.13}$$

$$\begin{aligned} &P(H,G) \in [P_1(H,G), P_2(H,G)] \\ &= [\max(P_1(H) + P_1(G) - 1, 0), \max(P_2(H) + P_2(G) - 1, 0)]. \end{aligned} \tag{9.14}$$

$$\begin{aligned} &P(H,G) \in [P_1(H,G), P_2(H,G)] \\ &= [\max(P_1(H) + P_1(G) - 1, 0), P_2(H)P_2(G)]. \end{aligned} \tag{9.15}$$

$$\begin{aligned} &P(H,G) \in [P_1(H,G), P_2(H,G)] \\ &= [\max(P_1(H) + P_1(G) - 1, 0), \min(P_2(H), P_2(G))]. \end{aligned} \tag{9.16}$$

The above mentioned formulas may be extended for the case of fuzzy probabilities $\tilde{P}(H)$ and $\tilde{P}(G)$ as follows. The fuzzy joint probability $\tilde{P}(H,G)$ may be defined as

$$\tilde{P}(H,G) = \bigcup_{\alpha \in [0,1]} \alpha [P_1^\alpha(H,G), P_2^\alpha(H,G)]$$

where endpoints of an interval $[P_1^\alpha(H,G), P_2^\alpha(H,G)]$ are determined from endpoints $P_1^\alpha(H)$, $P_1^\alpha(G)$, $P_2^\alpha(H)$ and $P_2^\alpha(G)$ on the base of one of formulas (9.11)-(9.16) depending on a sign of dependence. For example, positive dependence is modeled as

$$\tilde{P}(H,G) = \bigcup_{\alpha \in [0,1]} \alpha \left[P_1^\alpha(H)P_1^\alpha(G), \min(P_2^\alpha(H), P_2^\alpha(G))\right]$$

and negative dependence as

$$\tilde{P}(H,G) = \bigcup_{\alpha\in[0,1]} \alpha\left[\max(P_1^{\alpha}(H)+P_1^{\alpha}(G)-1,0), P_2^{\alpha}(H)P_2^{\alpha}(G)\right].$$

9.3 Agent's Behavior Models

We suggest to model an economic agent, a DM, by a set of states. An important issue that arises here is a determination of a state of a DM h. As far as this concept is used to model human behavior which is conditioned by psychological, mental and other behavioral factors, in general, it should not have an abstract or atomic content but should have substantial basis. One approach is a consideration of h as a 'personal quality' of a DM which is formalized as a value of a multivariable function. Each input variable of this function is to be used for measuring one of behavioral factors like risk attitude, ambiguity attitude, altruism, trust, fairness, social responsibility. Thus, a personal quality will have different 'levels' h_i each determined by a vector of measured behavioral factors that describes a behavioral condition of a DM.

Another approach is to consider a state of a DM h_i as a vector of variables describing behavioral factors without converting it into a single generalized value.

The first approach is simpler, i.e. more convenient as a state of a DM will enter decision model as a single value. However a question arises on how to convert a vector into a single value. Anyway, this will lead to a loss of information. The second approach is more adequate, however it is more complex. Consider a small example. Let a DM consider three possible alternatives for investment: to buy stocks, to buy bonds of enterprise or to deposit money in a bank. The results of the alternatives are subject to a state of nature as one of the three possible economic conditions: growth, stagnation, inflation. As the factors underlying behavioral condition of a DM, that is, a state of a DM, we will consider attitudes to risk and ambiguity which are main issues and are especially important for investment problems. The first approach to model a state of a DM is a convolution of the values of the considered factors into a personal quality as a single resulting value. For example, a personal quality of a risk averse and an ambiguity averse investor may be characterized by the typical term "conservative investor", the other combinations will be described by other personal qualities like "aggressive investor" etc. Given such a 'single-valued' reference, it is needed to determine both a joint probability and a utility of any alternative for this state of a DM and any state of nature (economy) – growth, stagnation, inflation. As the state of a DM and a state of nature are both 'single-valued' it will be rather easy to do this. However, this easiness is conditioned by simplistic approach which deprives us of useful information. Influence of each factor will be substantially driven out by convolution to a single value. The second approach models a state of a DM 'as is' – as a pair of risk and ambiguity attitudes without a convolution. Such modeling is more intuitive and transparent. The determination of joint probability and a utility of any alternative as measures of relations between state of nature and state of a DM will then be more adequate because greater useful information is considered. Indeed, even in the first approach, a researcher may have to 'return back' to the behavioral factors in order to more substantially model the relations between the corresponding single-valued personal quality and states of nature. However, the second approach is more complex in terms of mathematical realization – the number of the variables in a model is larger – and this is a price for more adequate modeling.

In the next sections we consider two kinds of the first approach to modeling a DM.

9.3.1 *Model based on fuzzy "if-then" rules*

Let us consider an approach to agent behavior modeling under second order uncertainty [11,25]. It is very difficult to precisely define a term like agent [267,268,306,320,420]. There are tens definitions of agent. A definition similar to those in [195,320,420] was suggested by us in 1986 [17] and we will use this definition in this work which embraces the following features: autonomy; interaction with an environment and other agents; perception capability; learning; reasoning capability. In [17] an agent with the mentioned characteristics was called a smart agent.

The architecture of a smart agent in accordance with this definition is given in Fig. 9.1.

The mathematical description of knowledge in the knowledge base (KB) of agent is based on fuzzy interpretation of antecedents and consequents in production rules.

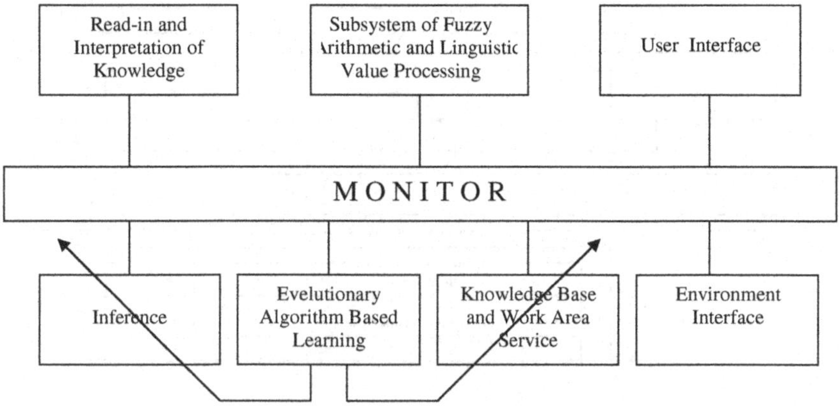

Fig. 9.1. Structure of an intelligent agent

For the knowledge representation the antecedent of each rule contains a conjunction of logical connectives like (Fig. 9.2): <name of object> $\left\{\begin{matrix} = \\ \neq \end{matrix}\right\}$ <linguistic value> named elementary antecedent .

The consequent of the rule is a list of imperatives, among which may be some operator-functions (i.e. input and output of objects' values, operations with segments of a knowledge base, etc). Each rule may be complemented with a confidence degree $Cf \in [0,100]$. Each linguistic value has a corresponding membership function. The subsystem of fuzzy arithmetic and linguistic values processing (see Fig. 9.1) provides automatic interpretation of linguistic values like "high", "low", "OK", "near...", "from ... to..." and so on; i.e. for each linguistic value this subsystem automatically computes parameters of membership functions using universes of corresponding variable. The user of the system may define new linguistic values, modify built-in ones and explicitly prescribe a membership function in any place where linguistic values are useful.

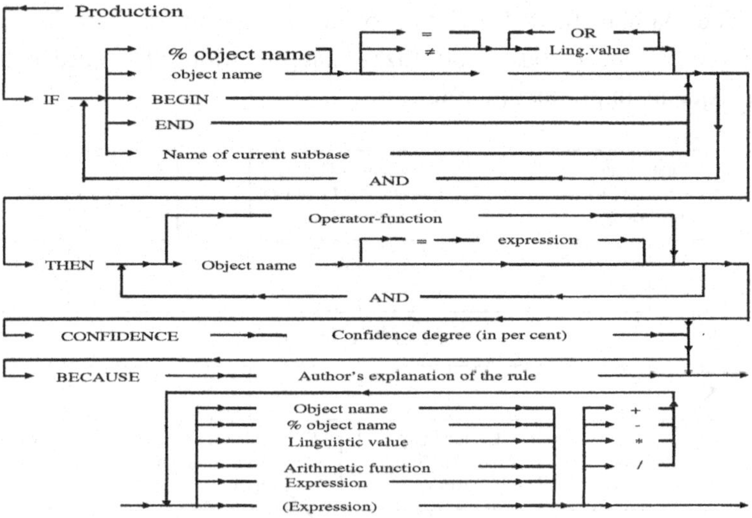

Fig. 9.2. Production rules

Learning of agents is based on evolutionary algorithms[11] which includes adjusting of agent's KB. The agents are described by a KB that consists of a certain number of fuzzy rules related through "ALSO":

$$R^k : IF\ X_1\ is\ \tilde{A}_{k1}\ and\ X_2\ is\ \tilde{A}_{k2}\ and\ ...\ and\ X_m\ is\ \tilde{A}_{km}\ THEN$$
$$u_{k1}\ is\ \tilde{B}_{k1}\ and\ u_{k2}\ is\ \tilde{B}_{k2}\ and\ ...\ and\ u_{kl}\ is\ \tilde{B}_{kl},\quad k=\overline{1,K}$$

where $X_i, i=\overline{1,m}$ and $u_j, j=\overline{1,l}$ are total input and local output variables $\tilde{A}_{ki}, \tilde{B}_{kj}$ are fuzzy sets, and K is the number of rules. Note, that inputs $X_1, X_2, ..., X_m$ may be crisp or fuzzy variables.

Efficiency of inference engine considerably depends on the knowledge base internal organization. That is why an agent's model implements paradigm of "network of production rules" similar to semantic network. Here the nodes are rules and vertexes are objects. Inference mechanism acts as follows. First, some objects take some values (initial data). Then, all production rules, containing each of these objects in antecedent, are chosen from the knowledge base. For these rules the truth degree is computed (in other words, the system estimates the truth degree of the fact that current values of objects correspond to values fixed in antecedents). If the truth degree exceeds some threshold then imperatives from consequent are executed. At that time the same objects as well as a new one take new values and the process continues till work area contains "active" objects ("active" object means untested one).

The assigned value of the object is also complemented by a number, named confidence degree, which is equal to the truth degree of the rule.

A truth degree of a rule's antecedent is calculated according to the following algorithm [38].

Let us consider an antecedent of a rule in the form:

$$\text{IF ... AND } \tilde{w}_i \begin{Bmatrix} = \\ \neq \end{Bmatrix} \tilde{A}_{ij} \text{ AND ... AND } \tilde{w}_k \begin{Bmatrix} = \\ \neq \end{Bmatrix} \tilde{A}_{jk} \text{ AND ...}$$

Confidence degree of the rule is $Cf \in [0,100]$.

Objects $\tilde{w}_i$, $\tilde{w}_k$ have current values of the form $(\tilde{v}, cf)$ in the work area ($\tilde{v}$ is linguistic value with its membership function, $cf \in [0,100]$ is confidence degree of the value $\tilde{v}$). Truth value of k-th elementary antecedent is:

$r_k = Poss\left(\tilde{v}_k \middle| \tilde{A}_{jk}\right) cf_k$, if the sign is "=" and $r_k = \left(1 - Poss\left(\tilde{v}_k \middle| \tilde{A}_{jk}\right)\right) cf_k$, if the sign is "≠". *Poss* is defined as

$$Poss\left(\tilde{v} \middle| \tilde{A}\right) = \max_u \min(\mu_{\tilde{v}}(u), \mu_{\tilde{A}}(u)) \in [0,1].$$

The truth degree of the rule:

$$R_j = (\min_k r_k) \frac{Cf_j}{100}.$$

After the inference is over, the user may obtain for each object the list of its values with confidence degree which are accumulated in the work area. The desirable value of the object may be obtained using one of the following procedures:

I. Last - $\tilde{v}_i^N$

II. The value with maximum confidence degree- $\tilde{v}_i^m / cf_i^m = \max_n cf_i^n$

III. The value $\tilde{v}_i = \wedge_n(\tilde{v}_i^n cf_i^n)$, or $\tilde{v}_i = \vee_n(\tilde{v}_i^n cf_i^n)$

IV. The average value $\bar{\tilde{v}}_i = \dfrac{\sum_n \tilde{v}_i^n cf_i^n}{\sum_n cf_i^n}$

This model has a built-in function AVRG which calculates the average value. This function simplifies the organization of compositional inference with possibility measures. As a possibility measure here a confidence degree is used. So, the compositional relation is given as a set of production rules like:

$$\text{IF } X_1 = \tilde{A}_1^j \text{ AND } X_2 = \tilde{A}_2^j \text{ AND ... THEN } y_1 = \tilde{B}_1^j \text{ AND } y_2 = \tilde{B}_2^j \text{ AND ...}$$

where j is a number of a rule (similar to the row of the compositional relation matrix). After all these rules have been executed (with different truth degrees) the next rule (rules) ought to be executed:

$$\text{IF THEN } Y_1 = AVRG(y_1) \text{ AND } Y_2 = AVRG(y_2) \text{ AND ...}$$

Fuzzy hypotheses generating and accounting systems. Using this model one may construct hypotheses generating and accounting systems. Such system contains the rules:

IF <condition$_j$> THEN $X = \tilde{A}_j$ CONFIDENCE cf_j.

Here "$X = \tilde{A}_j$" is a hypothesis that the object X takes the value $\tilde{A}_j$. Using some preliminary information, this system generates elements $X = (\tilde{A}_j, R_j)$, where R_j is a truth degree of j-th rule. In order to account for the hypothesis (i.e. to estimate the truth degree that X takes the value $\tilde{A}_j$) the recurrent Bayes-Shortliffe (BS) formula, generalized for the case of fuzzy hypotheses, is used [372]:

$$P_0 = 0$$

$$P_j = P_{j-1} + cf_j Poss(\tilde{A}_0 / \tilde{A})\left(1 - \frac{P_{j-1}}{100}\right).$$

This formula is realized as a built-in function BS :

$$\text{IF END THEN } P = BS(X, \tilde{A}_0).$$

The above described model is realized by using the ESPLAN expert system shell [11].

Let us consider an example.

Let us describe the model taking into account the private characteristic features of a DM by using the following rules:

Rule 1:

IF altruism level of a DM is *about 45* and emotion level of a DM is *about 40*

THEN personal quality of a DM ($\tilde{D}_i$) is *about 35* and CF is *90%*

Rule 2:

IF altruism level of a DM is *about 45* and emotion level of a DM is *about 60*

THEN personal quality of a DM ($\tilde{D}_i$) is *about 45* and CF is *55%*

⋮

Rule 15:

IF altruism level of a DM is *about 65* and emotion level of a DM is *about 20*

THEN personal quality of a DM ($\tilde{D}_i$) is *about 75* and CF is *60%*.

It is required to determine the DM personal quality (output).

The linguistic terms used in the considered if-then rules are described by trapezoidal fuzzy numbers. For example, *about 45* is described as follows

$$about\,45=\begin{cases}\dfrac{X-30}{12}, 30\le X<42\\ 1, 42\le X\le 48\\ \dfrac{50-X}{2}, 48<X\le 50\\ 0, otherwise\end{cases}$$

By applying the suggested methodology, in case of *altruism level* being *about* 65 and *emotion level* being about 60, the *personal quality* is computed as *about* 45.

9.3.2 *Model based on the Dempster-Shafer theory*

Human behavioral modeling requires an ability to represent and manipulate imprecise cognitive concepts. It also needs to include the uncertainty and unpredictability of human action [428]. Human behavioral modeling requires an ability to formally represent sophisticated cognitive concepts that are often at best described in imprecise linguistic terms. Fuzzy sets provide a powerful tool for enabling the semantical modeling of these imprecise concepts within computer based systems [117,447]. With the aid of a fuzzy set we can formally represent sophisticated imprecise linguistic concepts in a manner that allows for the types of computational manipulation needed for reasoning in behavioral models based on human cognition and conceptualization.

In addition to the imprecision of human conceptualization reflected in language many situations that arise in human behavioral modeling entail aspects of probabilistic uncertainty [428]. Now we consider an agent behavioral modeling using fuzzy and Dempster-Shafer theories suggested in [428].

The Dempster-Shafer approach fits nicely into the fuzzy logic since both techniques use sets as their primary data structure and are important components of the emerging field of granular computing [58,258]. In [428] the behavioral model is represented by partitioning the input space. We can represent relationship between input and output variables by a collection of n "IF-THEN" rules of the form:

$$\text{If } X_1 \text{ is } \tilde{A}_{i1} \text{ and } X_2 \text{ is } \tilde{A}_{i2}, \ldots \text{ and } X_r \text{ is } \tilde{A}_{ir} \text{ then } Y \text{ is } D_i. \tag{9.17}$$

Here each $\tilde{A}_{ij}$ typically indicates a linguistic term corresponding to a value of its associated variable, furthermore each $\tilde{A}_{ij}$ is formally repre-ented as a fuzzy subset defined over the domain of the associated variab-le X_j. Similarly $\tilde{D}_i$ is a value associated with the consequent variable that is formally defined as a fuzzy subset of the domain of Y. To find the output of an agent described by (9.17) for given values of the input variables the Mamdani-Zadeh reasoning paradigm is used [8,432].

It is needed now to add further modeling capacity to model (9.17) by allowing for probabilistic uncertainty in the consequent. For this we consider the consequent to be a fuzzy Dempster-Shafer granule. Thus we shall now consider the output of each rule to be of the form Y is m_i where m_i is a belief structure with focal elements $\tilde{D}_{ij}$ which are fuzzy subsets of the universe of Y, and associated weights $m_i(\tilde{D}_{ij})$. Thus a typical rule is now of the form

$$\text{If } X_1 \text{ is } \tilde{A}_{i1} \text{ and } X_2 \text{ is } \tilde{A}_{i2}, \ldots \text{ and } X_r \text{ is } \tilde{A}_{ir} \text{ then } Y \text{ is } m_i(). \tag{9.18}$$

Using a belief structure to model the consequent of a rule is essentially saying that $m_i(\tilde{D}_{ij})$ is the probability that the output of the *i-th* rule lies in the set $\tilde{D}_{ij}$. So rather than being certain as to the output set of a rule we have some randomness in the rule. We note that with $m_i(\tilde{D}_{ij}) =$ 1 for some $\tilde{D}_{ij}$ we get the (9.17).

Let us describe the reasoning process in this situation with belief structure consequents. Assume the inputs to the system are the values for the antecedent variables, $X_j = x_j$. For each rule we obtain the firing level, $\tau_i = \text{Min}[A_{ij}(x_j)]$.

The output of each rule is a belief structure $m'_i = \tau_i \wedge m$. The focal elements of m'_i are $\tilde{F}_{ij}$, a fuzzy subset of Y where $F_{ij}(y) = Min[\tau_i, D_{ij}(y)]$, here $\tilde{D}_{ij}$ is a focal element of m_i. The weights associated with these new focal elements are simply $m'_i(\tilde{F}_{ij}) = m'_i(\tilde{D}_{ij})$. The overall output of the system m is obtained by taking a union of the individual rule outputs, $m = \bigcup_{i=1}^{n} m'_i$.

For every collection $< \tilde{F}_{1j_1}, \ldots \tilde{F}_{nj_1} >$ where $\tilde{F}_{ij_1}$ is a focal element of m_i we obtain a focal element of m, $\tilde{E} = \bigcup_i \tilde{F}_{ij_1}$, and the associated weight is

$$m(\tilde{E}) = \prod_{i=1}^{n} m'_i(\tilde{F}_{ij_1}).$$

As a result of this third step it is obtained a fuzzy Dempster-Shafer belief structure "*V* is *m*" as output of the agent. We denote the focal elements of m as the fuzzy subsets $\tilde{E}_j$, j = 1 to q, with weights $m(\tilde{E}_j)$.

Let us describe the model taking into account the characteristic features of an economic agent (DM). Here the basic problem is to evaluate personal quality of a DM by using his psychological determinants. For determining psychological determinants as basic factors (inputs of a model) influencing to DM's performance, total index of DM (output of a model), we used the fuzzy Delphi method[25]. We have obtained that main psychological determinants (inputs) are following factors: trust, altruism, reciprocity, emotion, risk, social responsibility, tolerance to ambiguity.

For a total index (resulting dimension) of a DM as an overall evaluation to be determined on the base of the determinants we obtained personal quality, or power of decision, or DM's performance. So, DM's behavioral model can be described as (for simplicity we use 2 inputs):

Rule 1: IF trust level of a DM is *about 76* and altruism level of a DM *about 45* THEN personal quality of a DM (V) is m_1.

Rule 2: IF trust level of a DM is *about 35* and altruism level of a DM *about 77* THEN personal quality of a DM (V) is m_2.

Let us determine the output (personal quality of a DM) if trust level of a DM is *about 70* and altruism level of a DM is *about 70*:

$$m_1 \text{ has focal elements } \tilde{D}_{11} = \tilde{46} \text{ with } m(\tilde{D}_{11}) = 0.7 \text{ and}$$
$$\tilde{D}_{12} = \tilde{48} \text{ with } m(\tilde{D}_{11}) = 0.3,$$

$$m_2 \text{ has focal elements } \tilde{D}_{21} = \tilde{76} \text{ with } m(\tilde{D}_{21}) = 0.2 \text{ and}$$
$$\tilde{D}_{22} = \tilde{81} \text{ with } m(\tilde{D}_{22}) = 0.8.$$

The values of linguistic variables are trapezoidal fuzzy numbers:

$$\tilde{46} = \begin{cases} \dfrac{x-40}{6}, 40 \le x < 46 \\ 1, x = 46 \\ \dfrac{65-x}{19}, 46 < x \le 65 \\ 0, otherwise \end{cases} \qquad \tilde{48} = \begin{cases} \dfrac{x-40}{8}, 40 \le x < 48 \\ 1, x = 48 \\ \dfrac{65-x}{17}, 48 \le x \le 65 \\ 0, otherwise \end{cases}$$

$$\tilde{76} = \begin{cases} \dfrac{x-61}{15}, 61 \le x < 76 \\ 1, x = 76 \\ \dfrac{95-x}{19}, 76 < x \le 95 \\ 0, otherwise \end{cases} \qquad \tilde{81} = \begin{cases} \dfrac{x-61}{20}, 61 \le x < 81 \\ 1, x = 81 \\ \dfrac{95-x}{14}, 81 < x \le 95 \\ 0, otherwise \end{cases}$$

Let us calculate the belief values for each rule. By using approach suggested in [428] we found that the empty set takes the value 0.09. But in accordance with Dempster-Shafer theory *m*-value of the empty set should be zero. In order to achieve this, *m* values of the focal elements should be normalized and m value of the empty set made equal to zero. The normalization process is as follows:

1) Determine $T = \sum_{A_i \cap B_i = \varnothing} m_1(\tilde{A}_i) \cdot m_2(\tilde{B}_i)$

2) For all $\tilde{A}_i \cap \tilde{B}_i = \varnothing$ weights

$$m(\tilde{E}_k) = \frac{1}{1-T} m_1(\tilde{A}_i) \cdot m_2(\tilde{B}_j)$$

3) For all $\tilde{E}_k = \varnothing$ sets $m(\tilde{E}_k) = 0$

In accordance with the procedures described above:

$$m(\{\tilde{46}\}) = 0.230769,$$

$$m(\{\tilde{46}, y\}) = 0.384615,$$

$$Bel(\{\tilde{46}, y\}) = 0.615385.$$

For the second rule: $Bel(\{\tilde{76}, y\}) = 0.753425$. Firing level of the i-th rule is equal to the minimum among all degrees of membership of a system input to antecedent fuzzy sets of this rule: $\tau_i = \min_{j=1}^{n}[\max_{X_j}(A'(x_j) \wedge A_{ij}(x_j))]$. The firing levels of each rule are $\tau_1 = 0.26$ and $\tau_2 = 0.28$. The defuzzified values of focal elements obtained by using the center of gravity method are the following: $Defuz(\tilde{E}_1) = \overline{y}_1 = 61.56$; $Defuz(\tilde{E}_2) = \overline{y}_2 = 64.15$; $Defuz(\tilde{E}_4) = \overline{y}_4 = 65.11$. The defuzzified value of m is $\overline{y} = 63.92$.

By using the framework described above we arrive at the following Dempster-Shafer structure:

IF trust level of a DM is *about 70* and altruism level of a DM *about 70* THEN personal quality of a DM (V) is equal to 63.92.

Chapter 10

Decision Making under Unprecisiated Imperfect Information

Decision making is conditioned by relevant information. This information very seldom has reliable numerical representation. Usually, decision relevant information is perception-based. A question arises of how to proceed from perception-based information to a corresponding mathematical formalism. When perception-based information is expressed in NL, the fuzzy set theory can be used as a corresponding mathematical formalism and then the theories presented in Chapters 6,7,8,9 can be applied for decision analysis. However, sometimes perception-based information is not sufficiently clear to be modeled by means of membership functions. In contrast, it remains at a level of some cloud images which are difficult to be caught by words. This imperfect information caught in perceptions cannot be precisiated by numbers or fuzzy sets and is referred to as *unprecisiated* information[453]. To better understand a spectrum of decision relevant information ranging from numbers to unprecisiated information, let us consider a problem of decision making under imperfect information suggested by Prof. Lotfi Zadeh that is known as Zadeh's two boxes problem. The problem is as follows.

Assume that we have two open boxes, A and B, each containing twenty black and white balls. A ball is picked at random. If I pick a white ball from A, I win a1 dollars; if I pick a black ball, I lose a2 dollars. Similarly, if I pick a white ball from B, I win b1 dollars; and if I pick a black ball, I lose b2 dollars. Then, we can formulate the five problems dependent on the accuracy of the available information:

Case 1. I can count the number of white balls and black balls in each box. Which box should I choose?

Case 2. I am shown the boxes for a few seconds, not enough to count the balls. I form a perception of the number of white and black balls in each box. These perceptions lead to perception-based imprecise probabilities which allow to be described as fuzzy probabilities. The question is the same: which box should I choose?

Case 3. I am given enough time to be able to count the number of white and black balls, but it is the gains and losses that are perception-based and can be described as fuzzy numbers. The question remains the same.

Case 4. Probabilities, gains and losses are perception-based and can be described as fuzzy probabilities and fuzzy numbers. The question remains the same.

Case 5. The numbers of balls of each color in each box cannot be counted. All I have are visual perceptions which cannot be precisiated by fuzzy probabilities.

Let us discuss these cases. Case 1 can be successfully solved by the existing theories because it is stated in numerical information. Cases 2-4 are characterized by linguistic decision-relevant information, and therefore, can be solved by the decision theory suggested in Chapter 6. No theory can be used to solve Case 5 as it is stated, including the theory suggested in Chapter 6, because this case is initially stated in informational framework of visual perceptions for which no formal decision theory is developed. However, humans are able to make decisions based on visual perceptions. Modeling of this outstanding capability, even to some limited extent, becomes a difficult yet a highly promising research area. In this regard, development of new decision models should be aimed at ability of these models to provide results which can be effectively analyzed and intuitively interpreted. In turn, for human perceptions in many practical situations visual representations becomes the most adequate formal description. At the same time, visual images describing human perceptions would be relatively simple. The reason is that perceptions are, as a rule, not very detailed due to highly constrained computational ability of a human brain. However, let us mention that visual representation may naturally have a wide spectrum of forms depending on a problem at hand. Therefore, the choice of a suitable representation is an important and context-dependent task. As it is mentioned in [73], visualization can be defined as a human activity on development of mental images and the tools for improvement of this ability. Images related to a problem at hand are naturally composed of entities with various degrees of correspondence. In this regard, the visual representation has the following advantages from the viewpoint of expressive power[127]:

- a wide variety of forms and the possibility to use additional visual and geometric attributes to transform available pieces of information into representative images (graphic forms). Taking into account feasible additions and modifications, such attributes can be directly associated with visual variables[73,271].
- intuitive, self-descriptive expression of both quantitative and qualitative information;
- possibility of convenient description of multidimensionality of uncertainty by using 2D images;
- suitable means for generation of new ideas in information exchange and transparent representation of a DM's vision of relationships between predefined variables in a considered decision problem [73].

Development of new decision models able to deal with perception-based information in the form of visual representation arises as a motivation of the research suggested in this chapter. In this chapter we use new fuzzy geometry and the extended fuzzy logic of Prof. Zadeh [453] to cope with uncertain situations coming with unprecisiated information (see Section 2.2.2). In this approach, the objects of computing and reasoning are geometrical primitives, which model human perceptions when the latter cannot be defined in terms of membership functions. The fuzzified axioms of Euclidean geometry are used. A method of decision making with outcomes and probabilities described by geometrical primitives is developed. In this method, geometrical primitives like fuzzy points and fuzzy lines represent the main elements of a decision problem as information granules each representing truth degrees distributed along a set of basic values. The decision model considers a knowledge base with fuzzy geometrical "if-then" rules.

10.1 State of the Art

All works on decision analysis assume availability of either some numeric or measurement-based information. In other words, the available imperfect information is always considered to admit required precision. The fundamental question remains: what if the information is not only imperfect and perception-based, but also unprecisiated?

As stated in [453] while fuzzy logic delivers an important capability to reason precisely in presence of imperfect information, the extended (or unprecisiated) fuzzy logic delivers a unique ability to reason imprecisely with imperfect information. The capability to reason imprecisely is used by human being when precise reasoning is infeasible, excessively costly or not required at all. A typical real-world case example is a case when the only available information is perception-based and no trustworthy precision or fuzzy numeric models (e.g. articulated through membership functions) are possible to obtain. As a model of unprecisiated fuzzy logic we consider fuzzy geometry [453].

The concept of fuzzy geometry is not new. Many authors suggest various versions of fuzzy geometry. Some of well-known ones are the Poston's fuzzy geometry [339], coarse geometry [347], fuzzy geometry of Rosenfeld [349,350,351,352,353], fuzzy geometry of Buckley and Eslami [88], fuzzy geometry of Mayburov [278,279], fuzzy geometry of Tzafestas [193], and fuzzy incidence geometry of Wilke [415]. Along this line of thought, many works are devoted to model spatial objects with fuzzy boundaries [110,138,363].

The study reported in [363] proposes a general framework to represent ill-defined information regarding boundaries of geographical regions by using the concept of relatedness measures for fuzzy sets. Regions are represented as fuzzy sets in a two-dimensional Euclidean space, and the notions of nearness and relative orientation are expressed as fuzzy relations. To support fuzzy spatial reasoning, the authors derive transitivity rules and provide efficient techniques to deal with the complex interactions between nearness and cardinal directions.

The work presented in [110] introduces a geometric model for uncertain lines that is capable of describing all the sources of uncertainty in spatial objects of linear type. Uncertain lines are defined as lines that incorporate uncertainty description both in the boundary and interior and can model all the uncertainty by which spatial data are commonly affected and allow computations in presence of uncertainty without oversimplification of the reality.

Qualitative techniques for spatial reasoning are adopted in [138]. The author formulates a computational model for defining spatial constraints for geographic regions, provided a set of imperfect quantitative and qualitative constraints.

What is common in all currently known fuzzy geometries is that the underlying logic is the fuzzy logic. Fuzzy logic implies existence of a valid numerical information (qualitative or quantitative) regarding the geometric objects under consideration. In situations, when source information is very unreliable to benefit from application of computationally-intensive mathematical operations of the fuzzy logic, some new method is needed. The new fuzzy geometry, the concept of which is proposed by Zadeh and referred to as F-Geometry, could be regarded as a highly suitable vehicle to model unprecisiated or extended fuzzy logic [453].

Of the geometries mentioned above, the fuzzy incidence geometry of Wilke [415] can be used to form a starting point for developing a new F-Geometry. Thus fuzzy incidence geometry extends the Euclidean geometry by providing concepts of extended points and lines as subsets of coordinate space, providing fuzzy version of incidence axioms, and reasoning mechanism by taking into account the positional tolerance and truth degree of relations among primitives. To allow for partially true conclusions from partially true conditions, the graduated reasoning with Rational Pavelka Logic (RPL) is used [331,415].

The purpose of this chapter is to develop a concept and a technique that can be used to more adequately reflect the human ability to formally describe perceptions for which he/she could hardly suggest acceptable linguistic approximations due to their highly uncertain nature or for which such precision, if provided, would lead to a loss or degradation of available information. Such unprecisiatable perceptions many times form an underlying basis for everyday human reasoning as well as decision making in economics and business.

It is suggested that Fuzzy Geometry or F-geometry (or geometry for extended primitives) can be used to more adequately reflect the human ability to describe decision-relevant information by means of geometrical primitives. Classical geometry is not useful in this case. As it was mentioned in [321], the classical geometry fails to acknowledge that visual space is not an abstract one but its properties are defined by perceptions.

The main idea is to describe uncertain data (which are perceptions of human observer, researcher, or a decision maker) in geometric language using extended primitives: points, lines, bars, stripes, curves etc. to prevent possible loss of information due to the precisiation of such data to classical fuzzy sets based models (e.g. when using membership functions etc.).

10.2 Fuzzy F-marks

10.2.1 *Hierarchy of visual representation of uncertainty*

For a wide spectrum of problems, relevant information about variables of interest is supported by perceptions in form of blurred images. Therefore, for such problems an idea of a new fuzzy geometry suggested by Zadeh[453] is a natural approach for formalization of relevant information so that it can be used in further processing with minimal distortion and loss.

Let us set out the main principles underlying a new fuzzy geometry and its application to modeling of perception based information.

For the simplest case, values on the considered domain of discourse, e.g. interval [0,1], can be represented as intersecting intervals, with each interval associated with a particular linguistic label. Such partition seems convenient for software implementation, but a reasonable question arises on whether all points of an interval equally correspond to a considered perceived value. Typical imperfection intrinsic to these questions requires paying special attention to structure of information granules describing ranges of variables of interest.

Unprecisiated visual images can be visualized using geometrical primitives such as the *extended points* and *lines*[110,416]. The use of geometrical primitives serving as representation of information granules that combine description of both *imprecise values of variables* and the related *expert's truth degrees* provides the opportunity to apply ideas of fuzzy geometry in decision analysis applications. Fuzzy geometry primitives provide a basis of meaningful semantic interpretation of values in the context of suggested combinations of visual variables. A space where a fuzzy geometry primitive exists can be considered as 2D space one dimension of which represents an ordered set of possible values of a variable of interest, and the other dimension is of an expert truth degree. Then a typical fuzzy geometrical primitive can be considered as a convex compact set in the considered 2D space. The length of this set is measured along the first dimension and represents an imprecision of perception-based information on a value of a variable considered. The width of the set is measured along the second dimension and represents a truth degree related to the imprecise value. A special attention has to be paid to variable widths of a fuzzy geometrical primitive for the points at the first dimension axe. Indeed, when assigning some range of possible values on the base of perception, we often agree that the points close to the center of a range are more likely than those closer to its ends. Therefore, the truth degree $\varphi^{(i)} = \varphi^{(i)}(x)$ is variable, and $\underline{\varphi}^{(i)} \le \varphi^{(i)} \le \overline{\varphi}^{(i)}$, $x \in [a,b]$.

The variable width $\varphi^{(i)} = \varphi^{(i)}(x)$ reflects *positional uncertainty*[110] of a value as an unprecisiated granule in the universe of discourse $[\mathrm{a},\mathrm{b}]$. If for a considered value a fuzzy point is chosen as the best formal description then geometrical primitive in form of a circle may be used. If a more general formalization like a fuzzy line is chosen, the form of ellipse is a noteworthy option as well.

Let us emphasize that values $\varphi^{(i)}$ are precise. Precise values are indicators of successful modeling when they are accurate. However, this can hardly be met in practice due to the presence of information imprecision and subjective biases. For taking into account this imperfect features, shading can be used as an appropriate graphical fuzzy 'tool' to express *approximation* of truth as a soft constraint $\hat{\varphi}(x)$ over a precise estimates $\varphi(x)$. The shading used means darkening of varying density by means of spray can or some 'fuzzy' pencil. Indeed, shading or color values is powerful and well-developed mean to visualize uncertain boundaries of objects.

Thus, truth degrees form a hierarchy[457]. Truth degrees of a first order are precise numbers from a unit interval. Truth degrees of a second order are shading-based restriction on first order truth degrees. Truth degrees of an n-th order are restrictions on truth degrees of an (n-1)th order. Based on the above mentioned, we use an hierarchy of truth degrees: numeric truth degree $\varphi(x) \to$ second-order truth degree $\hat{\varphi}(x)$.

As an illustration of an hierarchy of truth degrees, let us consider a fuzzy geometrical primitive in Fig. 10.1 with two truth dimensions. At any point x the first truth dimension is the width $\varphi = \varphi(x)$ of the ellipse. The second dimension is expressed by color shading which is a soft constraint on precise estimates. A more likely numerical truth is expressed by a darker color.

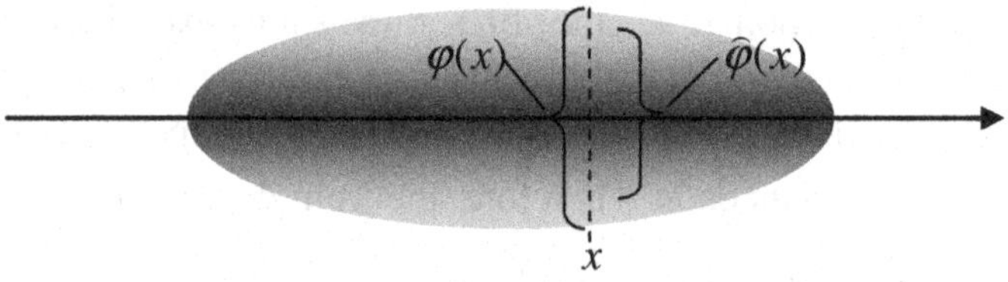

Fig. 10.1. Fuzzy geometry primitive with two truth dimensions

In the study suggested in the present chapter we consider perception-based information described by fuzzy geometrical primitives with numeric truth degrees.

10.2.2 *Definitions*

In this section we provide definitions of fuzzy geometrical primitives with numeric truth degrees and operators for their treatment. The basic primitives are F-points and F-lines for which a general concept of F-mark is used. The considered primitives are defined as two-dimensional sets, which are subsets of $\mathcal{R}^2$.

Definition 10.1. F-mark [179,415]. An ***F-mark*** is a bounded subset of $\mathcal{R}^2$, representing a graphical hand-mark drawn by human being to indicate visually a value of a perception-based information granule.

So, formally an F-mark A can be represented as a bounded subset of $\mathcal{R}^2 : A \subset \mathcal{R}^2$. But an F-mark is more than just a physical area as it is meant to hold a perception of a measurable value. Usually, an area A, representing an F-mark is assumed to be a convex set [415].

Let us define some basic primitives that we will use in context of decision making.

Any F-mark, which represents a convex subset A of $\mathcal{R}^2$, can be approximately defined by its center $c = (x_c, y_c)$ (which is a Euclidean point) and two diameters ($\phi_{\min}, \phi_{\max}$) [415]:

$$A = P(c, \phi_{\min}, \phi_{\max}). \tag{10.1}$$

The center c can be computed as a center of gravity of an F-mark's convex hull: $c=C(ch(A))$ while the two diameters are [415]:

$$\phi_{\min} = \min_t \left| ch(A) \cap \{c + t \cdot R_\alpha (0,1)^T\} \right|$$

$$\phi_{\max} = \max_t \left| ch(A) \cap \{c + t \cdot R_\alpha (0,1)^T\} \right|,$$

$t \in \mathcal{R}$ and $\mathcal{R}_\alpha$ is the rotation matrix describing rotation by angle α.

The illustration of the concept of an F-mark is presented in Fig. 10.2.

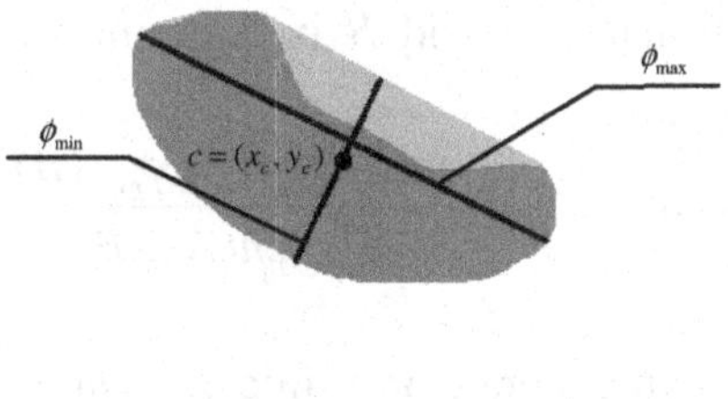

Fig. 10.2. An F-mark and its convex hull with two diameters

Definition 10.2. F-point. The degree to which an F-mark $A=P(c,\phi_{\min},\phi_{\max})$ is an ***F-point*** is determined as follows [415]:

$$p(A) = \phi_{\min} / \phi_{\max} \ . \tag{10.2}$$

Definition 10.3. F-line. The degree to which an F-mark A is an ***F-line*** is determined as[415]:

$$l(A) = 1 - p(A) \ .$$

Definition 10.4. Truth degree of an incidence of two F-marks. The truth degree of predicate for the incidence of F-marks A and B is determined as [415]:

$$inc(A,B) = \max\left(\frac{|ch(A) \cap ch(B)|}{|ch(A)|}, \frac{|ch(A) \cap ch(B)|}{|ch(B)|} \right), \tag{10.3}$$

here $ch(A)$ is a convex hull of an F-mark A, $|ch(A)|$ is the area covered by $ch(A)$.

Definition 10.5. Truth degree of an equality of two F-marks. The truth degree of a predicate defining the equality of F-marks A and B, is determined as follows [415]:

$$eq(A,B) = \min\left(\frac{|ch(A) \cap ch(B)|}{|ch(A)|}, \frac{|ch(A) \cap ch(B)|}{|ch(B)|} \right). \tag{10.4}$$

Definition 10.6. Measure of distinctness of two f-marks. The measure of distinctness of F-marks A and B is determined as [415]:

$$dp(A,B) = \max\left(0, 1 - \frac{\max\left(\phi_{\max}(A), \phi_{\max}(B)\right)}{\phi_{\max}(ch(A \cup B))} \right). \tag{10.5}$$

F-points A, B can generate an F-line $L = ch(A \cup B)$ as follows (Fig. 10.3):

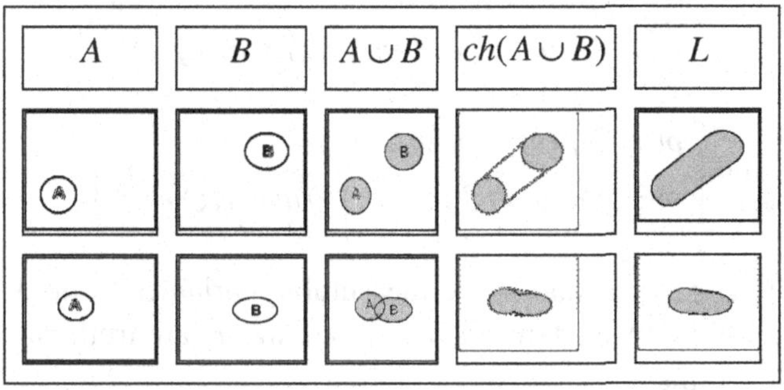

Fig. 10.3. Generation of an F-line from two F-points

10.3 Axioms of the Fuzzy Incidence Geometry

The following axioms formalize the behavior of points and lines in incident geometry [415]:

(A1) For every two distinct points *p* and *q*, at least one line *l* exists that is incident with *p* and *q*.
(A2) Such a line is unique.
(A3) Every line is incident with at least two points.
(A4) At least three points exist that are not incident with the same line.

For fuzzy version of incident geometry each of the above axioms may not evaluate to absolute truth for all possible inputs.

A fuzzy version of the incident geometry, which is suitable to work with F-marks can be axiomatized as follows [415]:

$$\text{(A1')} \quad \left(dp(x,y) \to \sup_{z} \left[l(z) \otimes inc(x,z) \otimes inc(y,z) \right], r_1 \right)$$

$$\text{(A2')} \quad \begin{array}{l} \left(dp(x,y) \left[\to l(z) \to \left[inc(x,z) \to \left[inc(y,z) \to l(z') \right.\right.\right.\right. \\ \qquad \left.\left.\left.\left. \to \left[inc(x,z') \to \left[inc(y,z') \to eq(z,z') \right] \right] \right] \right], r_2 \right) \end{array} \tag{10.6}$$

(A3') $$\left(l(z) \to \sup_{x,y} \left\{ \begin{matrix} p(x) \otimes p(y) \otimes \\ \otimes \neg eq(x,y) \otimes inc(x,z) \otimes inc(y,z) \end{matrix} \right\}, r_3 \right)$$

(A4') $$\left(\sup_{u,v,w,z} \left[\begin{matrix} p(u) \otimes p(v) \otimes p(w) \otimes l(z) \\ \to \neg\left(inc(u,z) \otimes inc(v,z) \otimes inc(w,z)\right) \end{matrix} \right], r_4 \right),$$

where x, y, z, z', u, v, and w are measurable variables to hold F-marks, $\otimes$ denotes Lukasiewicz T-norm, r_1, r_2, r_3, and r_4 are truth values of the associated axioms.

10.4 Statement of a Decision Making Problem

F-geometry can be effectively used in decision-making. The decision-making "if-then" rules for an uncertain environment can be composed on the basis of F-geometry concepts used to more adequately reflect the perceived information granules and relationships. F-geometry based decision-making allows for better modeling of the knowledge of human observer, researcher, or a DM, thereby making the inference system's output more realistic (through minimizing losses of meaning and distortion of source information).

Let us start with a formal problem statement. In an unprecisiated perception-based information setting we consider a decision making problem as a 4-tuple $(\mathcal{S},\mathcal{P},\mathcal{X},\mathcal{A},\succsim)$ where a set of states of nature $\mathcal{S}$, a corresponding imprecise probability distribution $\mathcal{P}$, a set of outcomes $\mathcal{X}$ are generally considered as spaces of F-lines[461]. The set of actions $\mathcal{A}$ is considered then as a set of mappings from $\mathcal{S}$ to $\mathcal{X}$. Preferences $\succsim$ in its turn is to be implicit in some knowledge base described as "if-then" rules which include $\mathcal{S},\mathcal{P},\mathcal{X},\mathcal{A}$-based description of various decision making situations faced before and a DM's or experts' opinion-based evaluations of corresponding intrinsic values $V(f)$ of alternatives $f \in \mathcal{A}$.

The problem of decision making consists in determination of the best alternative as an alternative $f^* \in \mathcal{A}$ for which $V(f^*) = \max_{f \in \mathcal{A}} V(f)$ [461].

10.5 F-mark Based If-Then Rules

Assume that fuzzy geometrical "if-then" rules based knowledge base for decision making have the following form[14]:

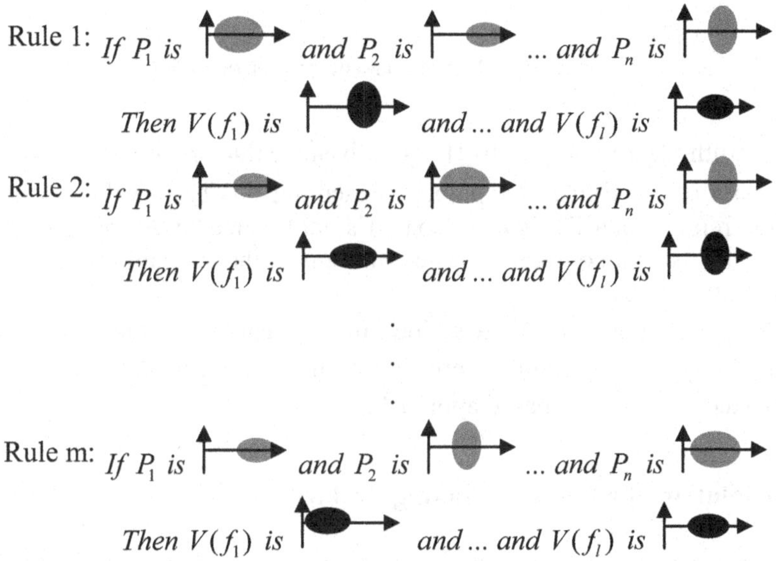
Rule 1: If P_1 is … and P_2 is … ... and P_n is …
Then $V(f_1)$ is … and ... and $V(f_l)$ is …
Rule 2: If P_1 is … and P_2 is … ... and P_n is …
Then $V(f_1)$ is … and ... and $V(f_l)$ is …
Rule m: If P_1 is … and P_2 is … ... and P_n is …
Then $V(f_1)$ is … and ... and $V(f_l)$ is …

A current perception-based input information on values of variables of interest is introduced by a user in form of F-lines. An entered F-line is situated in a 2D space one dimension of which supports a basic (numerical) value of probability and the other dimension supports a truth degree associated with this basic value. Every F-line is approximated by its convex hull which represents a set of basic values of a variable of interest with the associated truth degrees. In accordance with the hierarchy of visual representation of uncertainty (Section 10.2.1, Fig. 10.1), numeric truth degree-based fuzzy geometrical primitive which decribes, for instance, perception-based probability estimate can be represented as follows (see Fig. 10.4).

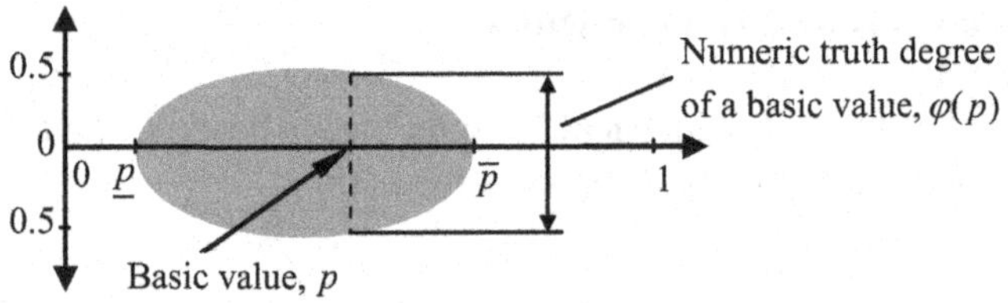

Fig. 10.4. An F-line as a description of a value

A truth degree $\varphi(p)\in[0,1]$ of a basic value p is defined as a thickness of the F-line at a point representing this basic value. A truth degree represents a DM's or an expert's confidence-based evaluation of the truthness of a considered basic value given the available perception-based information.

The following steps describe the essence of the suggested methodology and reasoning procedure of decision-making using the suggested F-Geometry based approach.

10.6 Solution of a Decision Making Problem

Let us describe the proposed methodology of decision analysis on the base of fuzzy geometrical "if-then" rules[14]:

1. Construct fuzzy geometrical if-then rules and assign a confidence degree $Cf^{j}, j=1,...,m$ for each rule which represents confidence degree of the adequacy of a rule.
2. Set threshold r'^{kb} for a truth value $\underline{r}^{kb}$ (say, $r'^{kb}=0.5$) as the minimal required degree of satisfaction of the axioms for the primitives in the "if-then" rules knowledge base.
3. For each fuzzy geometrical primitive of the fuzzy geometrical "if-then" rules determine satisfaction of the axioms (A1′)-(A4′) by calculating $r_i^j(P_k),\ i=1,...,4,\quad k=1,...,n,\quad j=1,...,m$ and $\underline{r}_k^j=\min\limits_{i=1,...,4} r_{k\,i}^j$ as the minimal degree of satisfaction of the axioms.
4. Verify whether the threshold condition is satisfied for all primitives in each "if-then" rule. If it is so, then the "if-then" rules

knowledge base can be used for decision analysis. If for a considered primitive $\underline{r}_k^j$ is smaller than a predefined threshold r'^{kb} then re-enter corresponding visual information until threshold is satisfied.

5. For each rule $j=1,...,m$ calculate a minimal partial truth $\underline{r}^j$ of satisfaction of the axioms for primitives describing all the n inputs (probabilities) and l outputs (values of alternatives) $\underline{r}^j = \min\limits_{k=1,...,n+l} \underline{r}_k^j$ and a partial truth for the aggregated relation matrix $r = \min\limits_{j=1,...,m} \underline{r}^j$.
6. Calculate a confidence degree of the aggregated relation matrix: $Cf = \min\limits_{j=1,...,m} Cf^j$.
7. Calculate a partial truth of the aggregated outputs of the rules: $s = r \otimes Cf$.
8. Aggregate inputs of every rule on the base of Lukasiewicz T-norm as in the suggested approach RPL is used.
9. For every rule compute the relation matrix between the aggregated inputs and each output (value of alternative) on the base of Lukasiewicz implication as in the suggested approach RPL is used.
10. Aggregate the relation matrices by using Lukasiewicz t-conorm (as RPL is used) into one aggregated relation matrix for a value of each alternative.
11. Obtain fuzzy geometrical information describing perception-based evaluation of probabilities of a DM and construct convex hulls.
12. Set threshold r'^{DM} for a truth value $\underline{r}^{DM}$ (say, $r'^{DM} = 0.1$) as the minimal required degree of satisfaction of the axioms for the convex hulls constructed at the previous step.
13. For each convex hull verify satisfaction of the axioms (A1′)-(A4′) by calculating $r_{ki}, i=1,...,4, k=1,...,n$ and $\underline{r}_k = \min\limits_{i=1,...,4} r_{ki}$.
14. Verify whether $\underline{r}_k$ it exceeds a predefined threshold r'^{DM}. If a threshold condition is satisfied then the reasoning within the fuzzy geometrical "if-then" rules is performed on base of RPL. If a

threshold condition is not satisfied then a DM reenter corresponding visual information until threshold is satisfied.

15. Aggregate fuzzy geometrical inputs provided by a DM into one input by using Lukasiewicz T-norm.
16. Compute a composition of new input information with the aggregated relation by using Lukasiewicz T-norm and Lukasiewicz t-conorm and obtain resulting fuzzy geometrical values of alternatives.
17. Calculate a partial truth of the fuzzy geometrical outputs computed at the previous step: $s_{new} = \min(r, \underline{r}_k) \otimes Cf$.
18. Arrive at values of alternatives $V(f)$ multiplied by the associated partial truth s_{new} calculated at the previous step: $V_s(f) = s_{new}V(f)$.
19. Compare the weighted overall values on the base of their distances to the upper bound of the universe of discourse. The best alternative is that with the minimal distance to the upper bound as an ideal point.

Chapter 11

The General Theory of Decisions

11.1 State of the Art

The evolution of decision theories passed a long way starting from the famous work of von Neumann and Morgenstern [397] and the present state of the art is represented by a wide spectrum of theories. As a result of evolution of decision analysis, the three main directions are formed: normative theories, descriptive theories and prescriptive theories. Normative theories are developed to model fully rational decisions inspired by monetary issues and do not allow for any psychological, mental or other factors, and require precise and completely reliable decision-relevant information. On one hand, these theories are rather one-sided, utopian and are not adequate to real decision problems. On the other hand, however, these theories contain principles of strong analysis and computations in order to take aim at strongly adjusted decision. The normative theories answer the question "what a DM should do". Descriptive theories are more realistic as they account for a lot of important humanistic factors, including psychology, perception, attitudes of a DM toward people, tolerance to imprecision and uncertainty, understanding of imperfect nature of decision environment. The descriptive theories answer the question "what a DM really does". It should be noted that the majority of decision theories cannot be considered as purely normative or descriptive. For example, the Prospect theory can be considered as synthesis of normative expected paradigm and formalization of psychological biases. The same can be referred to the other theories. This situation formed a concept of a prescriptive theory which composes strong theoretical basis of normative approach in line with the important influential factors observed in real-world decisions. The related research is formed under the title *neuroeconomics* where they study brain activity which concerns decision making and economic behavior. In general, the scope of neuroeconomics is study of decision activity at neuronal, genetic, anatomic, social and other levels of humans and animals.

The important direction of analysis of economic decisions which may be considered as a part of prescriptive models research is referred to as *discrete choice models* [67,234,274,281,282,374]. These models are based on the evidence that in real-world decision problems one usually has a discrete and finite set of mutually exclusive alternatives. Moreover, a choice among alternatives is conditioned by both attributes of alternatives and attributes of a DM (behavioral determinants). In discrete choice models, a researcher tries to approximately determine a DM's actual utility on the base of two types of attributes. The possible deviation of an approximately determined utility of an alternative from its actual utility is considered as random quantity. For treating of all the deviations a precise joint probability distribution is used taking into account all the alternatives.

It should be mentioned that the main tendency of evolution of decision analysis is that development of decision theories is carried out along particular directions. Despite that a series of the existing theories simultaneously include important issues as risk, gain-loss and ambiguity attitudes, altruism, trust and other behavioral determinants the latter are mainly considered independently of each other. There is no theory in existence which would be developed to describe a human behavioral model as a single whole, as an ensemble of both imperfect decision relevant information issues from one side and behavioral determinants from the other. In this regard, let us pay attention at the principal restrictions of the existing decision approaches: 1) the use of numerical, precise techniques whereas real-world information is imprecise and constraints are soft; 2) requirement of the use of mutually exclusive and exhaustive states of nature whereas our knowledge about future and its possible forms is quite dim; 3) the strong accent on the use of precise probability measures even in advanced models, whereas a long time ago J. Keynes mentioned that real probabilities are imprecise; 4) the use of mainly binary logic-based preference relations, whereas real preferences may be vague as humans may find difficulty to make choices due to incomplete information; 5) the fact that a human being reasons with linguistic description of information is not taken into account; 6) parametrical modeling of behavioral determinants without taking into account their interaction as a driving force of decision making; 7) a small attention is paid to account for reliability of decision-relevant information despite that it is, as a rule, partially reliable.

The above-mentioned disadvantages imply that the existing decision theories are developed for solving particular decision problems. There are a lot of real-world decision problems in existence which cannot be solved by the existing decision theories. It is needed to develop a general theory of decisions that would be free of the mentioned restrictions. This theory would be of a higher expressive power than the existing theories. This requires creating a unified decision model for decision making under uncertainty, for multicriteria decision making and for group decision making under risk, uncertainty, imprecise and incomplete information.

In the present chapter, we suggest the basics of the new general theory of decisions which is based on complex consideration of imperfect decision-relevant information issues and behavioral aspects. We illustrate that the existing theories including Expected Utility (EU) of von Neumann and Morgenstern, Choquet Expected Utility (CEU), Cumulative Prospect Theory (CPT) and other theories are special cases of the suggested general theory of decisions. We provide axioms and principles, the corresponding mathematical methodologies of decision analysis and auxiliary formal techniques. Let us mention an important issue related to generality. The main criticism addressed to general theories is concentrated at their analytical and computational complexities and, as a result, particular theories are considered as more effective. However, an increased computational power of information processing systems nowadays allows for effective computations with imperfect information, particularly, imprecise, partially true and partially reliable information, which are much more complex than computations over numbers and probabilities. At this point, the main criticism of general theories begins to loss its topicality.

11.2 Principles of the Suggested General Theory of Decisions

We can mention that the main directions of decision analysis are not yet pieced together. However, the existing approaches, along their development and improvement, tend to merge into one mainstream. In common, any general theory of decisions should have the following properties [159,376]: 1) Generality; 2) Congruence with reality; 3) Tractability.

Let us discuss what these properties imply. *Generality* of a theory implies that every existing decision making theory would be its particular case. This requires using a unified decision model at its nutshell which could unite the existing models into a single whole. As a result, the existing decision theories would be particular cases of a new general theory of decisions, because they are developed for modeling particular evidences. A unified decision model will help us understand more about how various interacting factors of decision making including behavioral determinants compose an ensemble inspiring real-world decisions.

In order to achieve *congruence with reality* it is needed to understand what is the basis of real-world decision making. Due to imprecision, vagueness, partial truth and partial reliability of real-world decision-relevant information and complexity of considered phenomena, this information is supported by perceptions. Often, perception-based information has linguistic, i.e. natural language-based representation. Initially, any problem is described verbally, and then they try to construct a formal model reflecting observed regularities. However, formalisms of the majority of the existing theories account for imperfect nature of only probability-relevant information. Indeed, the imperfect information related to states of nature, outcomes, behavioral determinants and other elements of a decision problem, is missed. The problem is that when we proceed from imperfect information to a precise numerical model we deal with inevitable coarsening, loss and distortion of information. Concerning behavioral determinants like risk, ambiguity and losses attitudes, fairness, reciprocity and others, the most important issue in development of a new general theory is modeling of their interaction. Indeed, a mental state of a DM is a complex system of these factors. The main disadvantage of the existing theories is that this issue is not fundamentally addressed.

It should be mentioned that the properties of generality and congruence with reality are closely related. Without taking into account interaction of behavioral determinants and imperfect nature of decision relevant information, a general theory of decisions cannot be created. It is reasonable to recall that taking into account real-world ambiguity of probabilities resulted in construction of the theories more general than the expected utility theories. Subsequent introduction of ambiguity attitudes and human expertise lead to the further generalization.

The main difficulty related to the use of general theories is related to computational complexities. However, modern computational resources allow achieving *tractability*[411] of a general theory by overcoming the problems of decision analysis under second-order uncertainty and linguistic information.

Taking into account the properties of a general theory, let us proceed to formulation of main principles of the general theory we intend to develop[9]. The evolution of modeling decision-relevant information has led to formation of the following hierarchy with increase of adequacy: numerical information (ground level), interval-valued information (first level), fuzzy information (second-level), information with second-order uncertainty (third level), Z-information and visual information (fourth level)[453,454]. In the existing theories, information is mainly considered at the ground, first, second, and, sometimes, at the third levels. Unfortunately a small attention is paid to such important aspect as reliability of information. It is often assumed, especially in the most famous theories, that the relevant information is trustful. However, real-world information is, as a rule, partially reliable. Therefore, the obtained results of decision analysis will naturally be partially reliable.

Concerning the behavioral aspects, as we suggest in Chapter 9, behavioral determinants, i.e. subjective conditions, should be considered at the same fundamental level of decision analysis as states of nature, i.e. objective conditions. Moreover, objectives and subjective conditions should be linked together as a human behavior naturally depends on objective conditions. However, in the existing approaches the basis of decision analysis is the space of states of nature only, whereas behavioral determinants are just introduced parametrically. Taking into account these important issues we intend to develop the new general theory of decisions which will have the following principles:

1) General theory of decisions should be based on fuzzy logic, not on binary logic. There is a need to shift the foundations of decision analysis and economic behavior from bivalent logic to fuzzy logic. This shift opens the door to construction of much better models of reality — reality in which uncertainty and imprecision lie at the center rather than on the periphery, as it is mentioned by Prof. L.A. Zadeh.

2) New modeling language in a basis of the general theory. In real-world decisions, motivations, intuition, human knowledge and human behaviour, such as perception, emotions and norms, play dominant roles. Consequently, real-world decision problems are too complex to be translated into classical mathematical and bivalent logic languages, and then being solved and interpreted in the language of the real world. The traditional modeling methodology (science deals with models of reality) is perhaps not relevant or at least not powerful enough to satisfy the requirements of human reasoning and decision making activities. A new much more effective modelling language is needed to capture the decisions reality. In general, Fuzzy logic-based modelling languages have higher power of cointension than their bivalent logic based counterparts and present the potential for playing an essential role in modelling economic, social and political systems.

3) Solving paradoxes. A series of paradoxes exists which show an insufficient expressive power of that or another theory to model human choices inspired by separate behavioral determinants of a DM. In order to overcome a drawback of decision theory uncovered by some paradox, a new theory is developed as an extension of the former in a separate direction. As a result, a more general, but still a particular theory is created. The general theory should definitely solve the existing paradoxes subject to the corresponding conditions.

4) Systematic foundation of unified multidisciplinary model and easiness of its application for various fields. Decision making is activity which is based on psychological, mental, cultural, intellectual, social, material and other incentives. Decision making is also one of the broadest human activities. Therefore, any general theory of decisions

should definitely rely on a multidisciplinary basis. Any different view on a general theory will result in a very particular, unrealistic theory. Thus, an adequate theoretical formalism should be developed to represent multidisciplinary basis of a general theory of decisions. This should be systematic formalism which models decision making as an interaction of influential issues including behavioral determinants, factors of environment and properties of decision-relevant information. From the other side, due to complexity of multidisciplinary basis, this formalism should be 'transparent' for mathematical analysis and intuition. A systematic, multidisciplinary and transparent formalism would help to easily apply a general theory in realms of various disciplines.

5) Taking into account vague preferences. Real-world preferences are vague because they involve a combination of fuzzy and probabilistic uncertainties. This means that comparing two alternatives, a DM often cannot give preference to one alternative solely, but the preference is in some sense 'distributed' among alternatives. The concept of a vague preference relation is intended to serve as a better model of preference in realistic settings. Treatment of vague preferences will go far beyond all that has been previously done in the realm of decision analysis. This will be a good representation of limited knowledge of a human being, especially when a DM considers future results of decisions.

6) Joint consideration of environment conditions and human behavior at a new fundamental level. We suggest describing a human behavior by a space of states of a DM. The states of a DM represent his/her principal mental conditions inspired by various intensities of underlying behavioral determinants. The latter have an inextricable link with factors of an external environment. In view of this, we suggest to consider the space of states of a DM and the space of states of nature composing a whole space of combined states as a basis of decision analysis. A combined state should reflect whether the considered human subjective condition can take place at the considered objective condition and to what degree of likelihood.

7) Taking into account non-additivity of real-world preferences. Modeling of non-additivity of DM's preferences should be based on the use of a bi-capacity [250]. The bi-capacity is a natural generalization of capacities where we are able to describe interaction between attractive

and repulsive values (outcomes, criteria values), particularly, gains and losses. It is well-known that utility function in the Cumulative Prospect Theory is a particular case of bi-capacity-based utility function. In the Cumulative Prospect Theory, gains and losses are aggregated separately. The use of a bi-capacity would allow for a more reasonable comparison of 'gains' and 'losses' than the common capacity does.

8) The use of Z-information. Real-world information is often partially reliable. The reasons are partial reliability of the source of information, misperceptions, psychological biases, incompetence etc. Z-information[454] represents an NL-described value of a variable of interest in line with the related NL-described reliability. What is important is that Z-information is not only the most general representation of real-world imperfect information but also has the highest descriptive power from human perception point of view. The use of Z-information is very important to describe both decision environment and behavioral determinants. The reason is that information on states of nature, future outcomes and behavioral determinants is naturally not completely known, and, therefore, taking into account reliability of estimated values is necessary.

Behavioral decision analysis in the general theory of decisions will be based on a concept of a combined state (see Chapter 9). The space of combined states is both more fundamental and a more transparent basis of behavioral decision analysis. A state of a DM should in general be considered as a vector whose components are behavioral factors which are important for the problem at hand. For example, a state of an investor may be characterized by risk attitude, ambiguity attitude, reciprocity and social responsibility. The same applies to a state of nature (e.g. economy), for which such indexes as inflation rate, GDP, unemployment level may be considered. Consideration of a combined state, therefore, becomes a promising task.

The principle of a combined state is very close to the idea underlying discrete choice models. However, let us contrast these two approaches. At first we should mention, that discrete choice is considered for the cases of qualitative decision-relevant information. In real-world, qualitative information about alternatives is described by people using NL, as it is indeed imprecise, partially true and, sometimes, is vague. As a result, in contrast to assumptions of the existing discrete choice models, it is not possible to perfectly differentiate among values of attributes of alternatives. It is known, that there exist three important issues that complicates construction of a discrete choice model. First, a DM often has incomplete and partially true information on alternatives. Second, a researcher often has incomplete and partially true information on alternatives. Third, a researcher often has imperfect information about behavioral determinants of a DM. In the existing discrete choice model these problems are treated by applying probabilistic models. However, as it was shown by simple laboratory experiments, a probability measure often fails to model decision phenomena[36,144]. The use of only a probabilistic approach is not sufficient to treat imprecision, ambiguity, partial truth. The approach suggested in the present chapter is more adequate for dealing with qualitative information about a decision environment and a DM because it is based on sinergy of probability theory and fuzzy set theory. This allows to deal with imprecise probabilities as importnat constituent of real choices.

The proposed principles of the new general theory of decisions open a door to improvement and progress of such important directions as group decision making and multicriteria decisions. For group decision making, the use of a formalism of states of a DM may help to discover at a more fundamental level an expertise and professionalism of members of a group. This, in turn would lead to more adequate and clear ranking of them and, therefore, a better determination of an optimal group decision. For multicriterial decisions, the use of states of a DM would help to overcome incorrect, improper choices of a human being which can be conditioned by the fact that emotions, biases etc may hinder constructive consideration of criteria and their importance.

The suggested general theory of decisions may help to better understand the phenomena of motivation, bounded rationality and imperfect information as leading factors of economic agents behavior.

Let us now proceed to formalization of the suggested general theory of decisions. The suggested theory is based on a framework of discrete information processing. In the next section we give a prerequisite material including definitions of such concepts as a Z-number valued probability measure, a Z-number valued random variable, a Z-number valued function and others which will be used in the sequel.

11.3 Preliminaries

Denote $\mathcal{Z}$ the space of discrete Z-numbers:

$$\mathcal{Z}=\left\{Z=(\tilde{A},\tilde{B})\middle|\tilde{A}\in\mathcal{D}^1,\tilde{B}\in\mathcal{D}^1_{[0,1]}\right\}.$$

Then denote $\mathcal{Z}^n$ the space elements of which are n-vectors of Z-numbers $\mathbf{Z}=(Z_1,Z_2,...,Z_n)=((\tilde{A}_1,\tilde{B}_1),(\tilde{A}_2,\tilde{B}_2),....,(\tilde{A}_n,\tilde{B}_n))$. Also, we denote $\mathcal{Z}^{\{\tilde{B}\}}=\left\{(\tilde{A},\tilde{B})\in\mathcal{Z}\middle|\tilde{B}=const\right\}$ as a set of Z-numbers with fixed $\tilde{B}$. Denote $\mathcal{Z}_{[c,d]}=\left\{(\tilde{A},\tilde{B})\middle|\tilde{A}\in\mathcal{D}^1_{[c,d]},\tilde{B}\in\mathcal{D}^1_{[0,1]}\right\}$, $[c,d]\subset\mathcal{R}$, and $\mathcal{Z}_+=\left\{(\tilde{A},\tilde{B})\in\mathcal{Z}^1\middle|\tilde{A}\in\mathcal{D}^1_{[0,\infty)}\right\}$, $\mathcal{Z}_-=\mathcal{Z}\backslash\mathcal{Z}_+$. Below we will indicate a Z-number by the hat above the character, such as $\hat{Z}$.

Definition 11.1. A Z-number valued infinity. Let $(\tilde{A},\tilde{B})$ be a Z-number. For every positive real number M, there exists $\alpha_0\in(0,1]$ such that $M<A_2^{\alpha_0}$ or $A_1^{\alpha_0}<-M$. Then $(\tilde{A},\tilde{B})$ is called Z-number valued infinity, denoted by $\hat{\infty}$.

Definition 11.2. Supremum metrics for Z-numbers. The supremum metrics in $\mathcal{Z}^n$ is defined as

$$D\left(\hat{Z}_1,\hat{Z}_2\right)=d\left(\tilde{A}_1,\tilde{A}_2\right)+d\left(\tilde{B}_1,\tilde{B}_2\right) \tag{11.1}$$

where $d(\cdot,\cdot)$ is the supremum metrics for fuzzy sets [129,253]. $(\mathcal{Z}^n,D)$ is a complete metric space. $D\left(\hat{Z}_1,\hat{Z}_2\right)$ has the following properties:

$$D\left(\hat{Z}_1+\hat{Z},\ \hat{Z}_2+\hat{Z}\right)=D\left(\hat{Z}_1,\ \hat{Z}_2\right),$$
$$D\left(\hat{Z}_2,\hat{Z}_1\right)=D\left(\hat{Z}_1,\ \hat{Z}_2\right),$$
$$D\left(\lambda\hat{Z}_1,\lambda\hat{Z}_2\right)=|\lambda|D\left(\hat{Z}_1,\hat{Z}_2\right),\ \lambda\in\mathcal{R},$$
$$D\left(\hat{Z}_1,\hat{Z}_2\right)\le D\left(\hat{Z}_1,\hat{Z}\right)+D\left(\hat{Z},\hat{Z}_2\right).$$

Denote $\mathcal{F}$ a σ-algebra of Ω. Let us define for two Z-numbers

$\hat{Z}_1=(\tilde{A}_1,\tilde{B}_1)$ and $\hat{Z}_2=(\tilde{A}_2,\tilde{B}_2)$ that $\hat{Z}_1=\hat{Z}_2$ iff $\tilde{A}_1=\tilde{A}_2$ and $\tilde{B}_1=\tilde{B}_2$, where equality of fuzzy numbers is defined in terms of Definition 6.4 (see Chapter 6).

Definition 11.3. A Z-number valued probability measure. The probability measure is a function $\hat{P}:\mathcal{F}\to\mathcal{Z}_{[0,1]}$ satisfying:

(1) $\hat{P}(\mathcal{V})\ge(0,1)$ for any $\mathcal{V}\in\mathcal{F}$;

(2) For any sequence $\mathcal{V}_1,\mathcal{V}_2,...\in\mathcal{F}$ with $\mathcal{V}_i\cap\mathcal{V}_j\neq\varnothing$: $\hat{P}(\bigcup_{i=1}^{\infty}\mathcal{V}_i)=\sum_{i=1}^{\infty}\hat{P}(\mathcal{V}_i)$;

(3) $\hat{P}(\Omega)=(1,1)$.

Definition 11.4. A Z-number valued random variable. Given a probability space $(\Omega,\mathcal{F},P)$, a mapping $\mathcal{X}:\Omega\to\mathcal{Z}$ is said to be a Z-valued random variable if it is D-Borel measurable, that is, it is a measurable mapping w.r.t. the Borel σ-field generated on $\mathcal{Z}$ by the topology associated with D.

Definition 11.5. A Z-number valued function. In general, a Z-number valued function is a mapping $\hat{f}:\Omega\to\mathcal{Z}$, where Ω is a universe of discourse.

Given a Z-number valued function $\hat{f}:\Omega\to\mathcal{Z}$, a fuzzy number valued function $\tilde{\varphi}:\Omega\to\mathcal{D}^1$ is called its $\tilde{A}$-valued function whenever for any $\omega\in\Omega$ one has $\tilde{\varphi}(\omega)=\tilde{A}\in\mathcal{D}^1$ iff $\hat{f}(\omega)=(\tilde{A},\tilde{B})\in\mathcal{Z}$. A fuzzy number valued function $\tilde{\gamma}:\Omega\to\mathcal{D}^1_{[0,1]}$ is called $\tilde{B}$-valued function for $\hat{f}:\Omega\to\mathcal{Z}$ whenever for any $\omega\in\Omega$ one has $\tilde{\gamma}(\omega)=\tilde{B}\in\mathcal{D}^1_{[0,1]}$ iff $\hat{f}(\omega)=(\tilde{A},\tilde{B})\in\mathcal{Z}$.

We suggest following definition of measurability of a Z-number valued function on the base of a concept of measurability of a fuzzy mapping (see Section 2.3) [129,253,433]:

Definition 11.6. Measurability of a Z-number valued function. A Z-valued mapping $\hat{f}:\Omega\to\mathcal{Z}$ is called a measurable Z-valued function if its $\tilde{A}$-valued function and $\tilde{B}$-valued function are measurable fuzzy mappings.

Definition 11.7. ***A Z-number valued capacity.*** A Z-number valued capacity on $\mathcal{F}$ is a Z-number valued set function $\hat{\eta}:\mathcal{F}\to\mathcal{Z}_{[0,1]}$ with the properties:

(1) $\hat{\eta}(\varnothing)=(0,1)$;

(2) if $\mathcal{V}\subset\mathcal{W}$ then $\hat{\eta}(\mathcal{V})\leq\hat{\eta}(\mathcal{W})$;

(3) if $\mathcal{V}_1\subset\mathcal{V}_2\subset...,\mathcal{V}_n\subset...\in\mathcal{F}$, then $\hat{\eta}(\bigcup_{n=1}^{\infty}\mathcal{V}_n)=\lim_{n\to\infty}\hat{\eta}(\mathcal{V}_n)$;

(4) if $\mathcal{V}_1\supset\mathcal{V}_2\supset...,\mathcal{V}_n\in\mathcal{F}$, and there exists n_0 such that if $\hat{\eta}(\mathcal{V}_{n_0})\neq\hat{\infty}$, then $\hat{\eta}(\bigcap_{n=1}^{\infty}\mathcal{V}_n)=\lim_{n\to\infty}\hat{\eta}(\mathcal{V}_n)$.

Definition 11.8. ***A Z-number valued bi-capacity.*** A Z-number valued bi-capacity on $\mathcal{F}^2=\mathcal{F}\times\mathcal{F}$ is a Z-number valued set function $\hat{\eta}:\mathcal{F}^2\to\mathcal{Z}_{[-1,1]}$ with the properties:

(1) $\tilde{\eta}(\varnothing,\varnothing)=(0,1)$;

(2) if $\mathcal{V}\subset\mathcal{V}'$ then $\hat{\eta}(\mathcal{V},\mathcal{W})\leq\hat{\eta}(\mathcal{V}',\mathcal{W})$;

(3) if $\mathcal{W}\subset\mathcal{W}'$ then $\hat{\eta}(\mathcal{V},\mathcal{W})\geq\hat{\eta}(\mathcal{V},\mathcal{W}')$;

(4) $\hat{\eta}(\Omega,\varnothing)=(1,1)$ and $\hat{\eta}(\varnothing,\Omega)=(-1,1)$.

11.4 A Uunified Decision Model

11.4.1 *Formal framework*

In the majority of the existing theories, a formal decision framework includes the following elements: a set of states of nature $\mathcal{S}$ that describes external environment conditions, a set of outcomes $\mathcal{X}$, a set of alternatives $\mathcal{A}$ as a set of actions $\mathcal{A}=\{f|f:\mathcal{S}\to\mathcal{X}\}$ generating outcomes $\mathcal{X}$ subject to external environment conditions $\mathcal{S}$, and preferences of a DM $\succsim$ representing choice over a set $\mathcal{A}$. In the suggested formal framework, we introduce a set of states of a DM $\mathcal{H}$ in order to model subjective conditions of a choice in line with the objective conditions in an evident manner.

The suggested framework is a framework of processing of discrete information. Taking into account the fact that real problems are characterized by linguistic information which is, as a rule, described by a discrete set of meaningful linguistic terms, in our study we consider discrete Z-numbers.

Let $\mathcal{S}=\{\boldsymbol{S}|\boldsymbol{S}\in\mathcal{S}\}$ be a discrete space of vector-valued states of nature and $\mathcal{H}=\{\hat{\boldsymbol{h}}|\hat{\boldsymbol{h}}\in\mathcal{H}\}$ a discrete space of vector-valued states of a DM, such that

$$\boldsymbol{S}=(S_1,...,S_m),\ \hat{\boldsymbol{h}}=(\hat{h}_1,...,\hat{h}_n),$$

where components $S_i, i=1,...,m$ are important factors of decision environment (for economic problems the factors like *GDP*, *interest rates* etc) and components $\hat{h}_j=(\tilde{A}_{h_j},\tilde{B}_{h_j})\ j=1,...,n,$ are behavioral determinants (for example, *risk attitude*, *ambiguity attitude*, *reciprocity*, *trust* etc). Denote $\mathrm{S}^{(i)}=\{S_1^{(i)},...,S_{m_i}^{(i)}\}$ a discrete set of values of S_i and denote $\mathrm{H}^{(j)}=\{\hat{h}_1^{(j)},...,\hat{h}_{n_j}^{(j)}\}$ a discrete set of values of $\hat{h}_j$.

Let us denote $\mathcal{X}=\{\hat{X}_1,...,\hat{X}_l\}$, $\hat{X}_k\in\mathcal{Z}, k=1,...,l$, a space of Z-valued vector outcomes. We call $\Omega=\mathcal{S}\times\mathcal{H}$ a space "nature-DM", elements of which are combined states $\hat{\boldsymbol{\omega}}=(\boldsymbol{S},\hat{\boldsymbol{h}})$ where $\boldsymbol{S}\in\mathcal{S},\hat{\boldsymbol{h}}\in\mathcal{H}$. Consider $\mathcal{A}=\{\hat{f}|\hat{f}:\Omega\to\mathcal{X}\}$ the set of Z-valued actions as the set of Z-valued functions from Ω to $\mathcal{X}$. Let us denote $\hat{X}_i=\{\hat{f}(\hat{\boldsymbol{\omega}}_i)|\hat{f}\in\mathcal{A},\hat{\boldsymbol{\omega}}_i\in\Omega\}$. It is obvious that $\mathcal{X}=\bigcup_{i=1}^{nm}\hat{X}_i$.

In the suggested framework, linguistic preference relation (LPR) is used to account for vagueness of real-world preferences. The LPR used in our general model is composed by intra-combined state information and inter-combined states information. Intra-combined state information is used to form utilities representing preferences over outcomes $\hat{f}(\hat{\boldsymbol{\omega}}_i)=\hat{X}_i$, where $\hat{\boldsymbol{\omega}}_i=(\boldsymbol{S}_{i_1},\hat{\boldsymbol{h}}_{i_2})$, of an act $\hat{f}\in\mathcal{A}$ with understanding that these are preferences at state of nature $\boldsymbol{S}_{i_1}$ conditioned by a state $\hat{\boldsymbol{h}}_{i_2}$ of a DM.

Inter-combined states information is used to represent preferences inspired by dependence between combined states as human behaviors under imperfect information.

To model LPR, let's introduce a linguistic variable "*degree of preference*" with term-set $\mathcal{T}=(T_1,...,T_n)$. The fact that preference of $\hat{f}$ against $\hat{g}$ is described by some $T_i \in \mathcal{T}$ is expressed as $\hat{f}\, T_i\, \hat{g}$. We denote LPR as $\succsim_l$ and below we sometimes, for simplicity, write $\hat{f} \succsim_l^i \hat{g}$ or $\hat{f} \succ_l^i \hat{g}$ instead of $\hat{f}\, T_i\, \hat{g}$. Denote $0_i \in \mathcal{X}_i$ neutral, $-1_i \in \mathcal{X}_i$ the worst and $1_i \in \mathcal{X}_i$ the best outcomes from $\mathcal{X}_i$.

Intra-combined state information. Z-valued utilities of outcomes $\hat{u}_i^{\varsigma}:\mathcal{X}_i \to \mathcal{Z}_{\varsigma}, \varsigma \in \{+,-\}$, satisfy

(i) *Monotonicity* $\forall \hat{X}_i, \hat{Y}_i$, $(\hat{X}_i, 0_i) \succsim_l (\hat{Y}_i, 0_i) \Leftrightarrow \hat{u}_i(\hat{X}_i) \ge \hat{u}_i(\hat{Y}_i)$.

(ii) *Interval scale condition*

$\forall \hat{X}_i, \hat{Y}_i, \hat{Z}_i, \hat{W}_i$ such that $\hat{u}_i(\hat{X}_i) > \hat{u}_i(\hat{Y}_i)$ and $\hat{u}_i(\hat{W}_i) > \hat{u}_i(\hat{Z}_i)$ one has

$$\frac{\hat{u}_i(\hat{X}_i)-\hat{u}_i(\hat{Y}_i)}{\hat{u}_i(\hat{Z}_i)-\hat{u}_i(\hat{W}_i)} = \hat{k}(\hat{X}_i, \hat{Y}_i, \hat{Z}_i, \hat{W}_i) \in \mathcal{D}^1_{[0,\infty)} \times \{1\}$$

iff the difference of satisfaction degree that the DM feels between $(\hat{X}_i, 0_i)$ and $(\hat{Y}_i, 0_i)$ is $\hat{k}(\hat{X}_i, \hat{Y}_i, \hat{Z}_i, \hat{W}_i)$ as large as the difference of satisfaction between $(\hat{W}_i, 0_i)$ and $(\hat{Z}_i, 0_i)$.

(iii) *Normalization*

$\hat{u}_i^{+}(0_i)=(0,1), \hat{u}_i^{+}(1_i)=(1,1), \hat{u}_i^{-}(0_i)=(0,1)$ and $\hat{u}_i^{-}(-1_i)=(-1,0)$.

(iv) *Multiplicative transitivity*

$\forall \hat{X}_i, \hat{Y}_i, \hat{Z}_i, \hat{W}_i, \hat{R}_i, \hat{V}_i$ such that $\hat{u}_i(\hat{X}_i) > \hat{u}_i(\hat{Y}_i)$, $\hat{u}_i(\hat{W}_i) > \hat{u}_i(\hat{Z}_i)$ and $\hat{u}_i(\hat{R}_i) > \hat{u}_i(\hat{V}_i)$ we have

$$\hat{k}(\hat{X}_i, \hat{Y}_i, \hat{Z}_i, \hat{W}_i) \times \hat{k}(\hat{Z}_i, \hat{W}_i, \hat{R}_i, \hat{V}_{ii}) = \hat{k}(\hat{X}_i, \hat{Y}_i, \hat{R}_i, \hat{V}_i).$$

(v) *$\hat{u}_i^{\varsigma}$ is stable under positive linear transformation*

The ratio $\dfrac{\hat{u}_i(\hat{X}_i)-\hat{u}_i(\hat{Y}_i)}{\hat{u}_i(\hat{Z}_i)-\hat{u}_i(\hat{W}_i)}$ does not change if $\hat{u}_i$ is changed to $\alpha\hat{u}_i+\beta$, $\alpha>0, \beta\ge 0$.

Inter-combined states information. Z-valued bi-capacity $\hat{\eta}$ satisfies:

(i) *Monotonicity*

$$\hat{\eta}(\mathcal{V},\mathcal{V}') \geq \hat{\eta}(\mathcal{W},\mathcal{W}') \Leftrightarrow (1_{\mathcal{V}},-1_{\mathcal{V}'},0_{\neg(\mathcal{V}\cup\mathcal{V}')}) \succsim_l (1_{\mathcal{W}},-1_{\mathcal{W}'},0_{\neg(\mathcal{W}\cup\mathcal{W}')})$$

(ii) *Interval scale condition*

$$\frac{\hat{\eta}(\mathcal{V},\mathcal{V}')-\hat{\eta}(\mathcal{W},\mathcal{W}')}{\hat{\eta}(\bar{\mathcal{V}},\bar{\mathcal{V}}')-\hat{\eta}(\bar{\mathcal{W}},\bar{\mathcal{W}}')}=\hat{k}(\mathcal{V},\mathcal{V}',\mathcal{W},\mathcal{W}',\bar{\mathcal{V}},\bar{\mathcal{V}}',\bar{\mathcal{W}},\bar{\mathcal{W}}')$$

iff the difference of satisfaction degrees that the DM feels between $(1_{\mathcal{V}},-1_{\mathcal{V}'},0_{\neg(\mathcal{V}\cup\mathcal{V}')})$ and $(1_{\mathcal{W}},-1_{\mathcal{W}'},0_{\neg(\mathcal{W}\cup\mathcal{W}')})$ is as large as the difference of satisfaction between $(1_{\bar{\mathcal{V}}},-1_{\bar{\mathcal{V}}'},0_{\neg(\bar{\mathcal{V}}\cup\bar{\mathcal{V}}')})$ and $(1_{\bar{\mathcal{W}}},-1_{\bar{\mathcal{W}}'},0_{\neg(\bar{\mathcal{W}}\cup\bar{\mathcal{W}}')})$.

(iii) *Normalization*

$\hat{\eta}(\varnothing,\varnothing)=(0,1), \hat{\eta}(N,\varnothing)=(1,1)$ and $\forall(\mathcal{V},\mathcal{V}')\in \mathfrak{A}^{*}(N)$, $\hat{\eta}(\mathcal{V},\mathcal{V}')\in \mathcal{Z}^{1}_{[-1,1]}$.

(iv) *Multiplicative transitivity*

$\forall \mathcal{V},\mathcal{V}',\mathcal{W},\mathcal{W}',\bar{\mathcal{V}},\bar{\mathcal{V}}',\bar{\mathcal{W}},\bar{\mathcal{W}}',\mathcal{K},\mathcal{K}',\mathcal{L},\mathcal{L}' \subset N$ such that $\hat{\eta}(\mathcal{V},\mathcal{V}') > \hat{\eta}(\mathcal{W},\mathcal{W}')$, $\hat{\eta}(\bar{\mathcal{V}},\bar{\mathcal{V}}') > \hat{\eta}(\bar{\mathcal{W}},\bar{\mathcal{W}}')$ and $\hat{\eta}(\mathcal{K},\mathcal{K}') > \hat{\eta}(\mathcal{L},\mathcal{L}')$ one has

$$\hat{k}(\mathcal{V},\mathcal{V}',\mathcal{W},\mathcal{W}',\bar{\mathcal{V}},\bar{\mathcal{V}}',\bar{\mathcal{W}},\bar{\mathcal{W}}')\times\hat{k}(\bar{\mathcal{V}},\bar{\mathcal{V}}',\bar{\mathcal{W}},\bar{\mathcal{W}}',\mathcal{K},\mathcal{K}',\mathcal{L},\mathcal{L}')=$$
$$=\hat{k}(\mathcal{V},\mathcal{V}',\mathcal{W},\mathcal{W}',\mathcal{K},\mathcal{K}',\mathcal{L},\mathcal{L}')$$

(v) *Homogeneity*

The ratio $\dfrac{\hat{u}_i(\hat{X}_i)-\hat{u}_i(\hat{Y}_i)}{\hat{u}_i(\hat{Z}_i)-\hat{u}_i(\hat{W}_i)}$ does not change if $\hat{\eta}$ changes to $\gamma\hat{\eta}$, $\gamma\in R$

If the preferences $\succsim_l$ of a DM over $\mathcal{A}$ satisfies the above mentioned assumptions then they can be described by a Z-valued overall utility $\hat{U}(\hat{f})$ of $\hat{f}\in\mathcal{A}$ expressed as a Z-valued Choquet-like aggregation of $\hat{u}(\hat{f}(\boldsymbol{S},\hat{\boldsymbol{h}}))$ w.r.t. Z-number-valued bi-capacity:

$$\hat{U}(\hat{f})=\sum_{l=1}^{L}(\hat{u}(\hat{f}(\hat{\omega}_{(l)}))-_h\hat{u}(\hat{f}(\hat{\omega}_{(l+1)})))\hat{\eta}(\mathcal{V},\mathcal{W})=$$
$$=\sum_{l=1}^{n}((\tilde{A}_{u(f(\hat{\omega}_{(l)}))},\tilde{B}_{u(f(\hat{\omega}_{(l)}))})-_h(\tilde{A}_{u(f(\hat{\omega}_{(l+1)}))},\tilde{B}_{u(f(\hat{\omega}_{(l+1)}))}))(\tilde{A}_{\eta(\mathcal{V},\mathcal{W})},\tilde{B}_{\eta(\mathcal{V},\mathcal{W})}), \tag{11.2}$$

where indices (l) implies $\hat{u}(\hat{f}(\hat{\omega}_{(l)}))\geq\hat{u}(\hat{f}(\hat{\omega}_{(l+1)}))$; $\hat{u}(\hat{f}(\hat{\omega}_{(L+1)}))=(0,1)$ by convention; $\mathcal{V}=\{\hat{\omega}_{(1)},...,\hat{\omega}_{(l)}\}\cap N^+$, $\mathcal{W}=\{\hat{\omega}_{(1)},...,\hat{\omega}_{(l)}\}\cap N^-$, $N^+=\{\hat{\omega}\in\Omega:\hat{u}(\hat{f}(\hat{\omega}))\geq(0,1)\}$, $N^-=\Omega\setminus N^+$. $\hat{\eta}:\Omega\times\Omega\to\mathcal{Z}_{[-1,1]}$ is a Z-number-valued bi-capacity.

An optimal $\hat{f}^*\in\mathcal{A}$, that is, such $\hat{f}^*\in\mathcal{A}$ that $\hat{U}(\hat{f}^*)=\max_{\hat{f}\in\mathcal{A}}\left\{\int_{\Omega}\hat{u}(\hat{f}(S,\hat{h}))d\hat{\eta}\right\}$, is determined by using the method of ranking of Z-numbers (Section 2.1.7).

11.4.2 *Comparison of the suggested general theory of decisions with the existing theories*

Let us show that the existing decision theories like EU, CEU and CPT are special cases of the suggested general theory of decisions. First, let us suppose that all the decision relevant information is completely reliable, that is, for any Z-number $Z=(\tilde{A},\tilde{B})$, the part $\tilde{B}$ is taken as a singleton $\tilde{B}=1$. In this case the framework of decision making under Z-valued information (partially reliable information) will reduce to decision making under fuzzy information and the utility model will reduce to fuzzy-valued aggregation with respect to fuzzy-valued bi-capacity:

$$\hat{U}(\hat{f})=\sum_{l=1}^{L}(\hat{u}(\hat{f}(\hat{\omega}_{(l)}))-_h\hat{u}(\hat{f}(\hat{\omega}_{(l+1)})))\hat{\eta}(\mathcal{V},\mathcal{W})=$$
$$=\sum_{l=1}^{L}((\tilde{A}_{u(f(\omega_{(l)}))},\tilde{B}_{u(f(\omega_{(l)}))})-_h(\tilde{A}_{u(f(\omega_{(l+1)}))},\tilde{B}_{u(f(\omega_{(l+1)}))}))(\tilde{A}_{\eta(\mathcal{V},\mathcal{W})},\tilde{B}_{\eta(\mathcal{V},\mathcal{W})})=$$
$$=\sum_{l=1}^{L}((\tilde{A}_{u(f(\omega_{(l)}))},1)-_h(\tilde{A}_{u(f(\omega_{(l+1)}))},1))(\tilde{A}_{\eta(\mathcal{V},\mathcal{W})},1)=$$

$$=\sum_{l=1}^{L}(\tilde{A}_{u(f(\boldsymbol{\omega}_{(l)}))} -_h \tilde{A}_{u(f(\boldsymbol{\omega}_{(l+1)}))})\tilde{A}_{\eta(\mathcal{V},\mathcal{W})} =$$

$$=\sum_{l=1}^{L}(\tilde{u}(\tilde{f}(\tilde{\boldsymbol{\omega}}_{(l)})) -_h \tilde{u}(\tilde{f}(\tilde{\boldsymbol{\omega}}_{(l+1)})))\tilde{\eta}(\mathcal{V},\mathcal{W}) =$$

Thus, a fuzzy-valued utility functional is obtained:

$$\tilde{U}(\tilde{f}) = \sum_{l=1}^{L}(\tilde{u}(\tilde{f}(\tilde{\boldsymbol{\omega}}_{(l)})) -_h \tilde{u}(\tilde{f}(\tilde{\boldsymbol{\omega}}_{(l+1)})))\tilde{\eta}(\mathcal{V},\mathcal{W})\cdot$$

This is a decision model suggested in Chapter 9. Thus, simplifying the obtained fuzzy decision model to its non-fuzzy variant and applying the results obtained in Section 9.2.3 one can find that the existing decision theories are special cases of the suggested general theory of decisions.

11.5 Methodology for the General Theory of Decisions

An application of the suggested general theory requires solving of several related problems. As the basis of decision analysis in the suggested theory is the space of combined states, the adequate determination of the structure of a state of nature and a state of a DM is important. This begins with determination of influential factors $S_1,...,S_m$ of objective conditions which are influential for the considered alternatives. On the base of analysis of the considered alternatives and factors $S_1,...,S_m$, a vector of behavioral determinants $\hat{\boldsymbol{h}}=(\hat{h}_1,...,\hat{h}_n)$ which are important for a considered choice, should be determined. In turn, for each component $S_i, i=1,...,m$ and $\hat{h}_j, j=1,...,n$ it is needed to determine discrete sets $S^{(i)}$ and $H^{(j)}$ of their possible values. For example, if $\hat{h}_j$ is *risk attitude* then the set $H^{(j)}$ may be

$$H^{(j)}=\{\hat{h}_1^{(j)}=(risk\,averse, high), \hat{h}_2^{(j)} =$$
$$=(risk\,neutral, high),\ \hat{h}_3^{(j)}=(risk\,seeking, high)\}.$$

If S_i is *GDP* then the set $S^{(i)}$ may be

$$S^{(i)} = \{S_1^{(i)} = low, S_2^{(i)} = medium, S_3^{(i)} = high\}.$$

A space of combined states as a space of multidimensional vectors $(\boldsymbol{S},\hat{\boldsymbol{h}}) = (S_{i_1}^{(1)},...,S_{i_m}^{(m)},\hat{h}_{j_1}^{(1)},...,\hat{h}_{j_n}^{(n)}) = (S_{k_1}^{(1)},...,S_{k_m}^{(m)},\hat{h}_{k_{m+1}}^{(m+1)},...,\hat{h}_{k_{m+n}}^{(m+n)})$ can then be used for comparison of alternatives. For this purpose, for each alternative it is necessary to determine Z-valued utilities $\hat{u}(\hat{f}(\boldsymbol{S},\hat{\boldsymbol{h}}))$ of its Z-valued outcomes at all the combined states. These utilities measure attractiveness or repulsiveness of each outcome from a DM's condition point of view. This can be done by using experience based-evaluation or by applying well-known techniques. The other necessary information for comparison of alternatives is measuring degrees of dependence of a DM's condition on objective conditions. These degrees will be represented by means of Z-valued joint probabilities. For determination of Z-valued joint probabilities, it is needed to estimate Z-valued marginal probabilities of $(S_1,...,S_m),(\hat{h}_1,...,\hat{h}_n)$. In turn, this requires to use information on Z-valued probability distributions over $S^{(i)}$ and $H^{(j)}$:

$$\hat{P}(S_i) = \hat{P}_1^{(i)}/S_1^{(i)} + ... + \hat{P}_{m_i}^{(i)}/S_{m_i}^{(i)},\ i = 1,...,m,$$
$$\hat{P}(\hat{h}_j) = \hat{P}_1^{(j)}/\hat{h}_1^{(j)} + ... + \hat{P}_{n_j}^{(j)}/\hat{h}_{n_j}^{(j)},\ j = 1,...,n,$$

where $\hat{P}_1^{(i)} = (\tilde{A}_{P_1^{(i)}},\tilde{B}_{P_1^{(i)}}),...,$ $\hat{P}_{m_i}^{(i)} = (\tilde{A}_{P_{m_i}^{(i)}},\tilde{B}_{P_{m_i}^{(i)}})$, $\hat{P}_1^{(j)} = (\tilde{A}_{P_1^{(j)}},\tilde{B}_{P_1^{(j)}}),...,$ $\hat{P}_{n_j}^{(j)} = (\tilde{A}_{P_{n_j}^{(j)}},\tilde{B}_{P_{n_j}^{(j)}})$. Note that the condition $\tilde{B}_{P_1^{(i)}} = ... = \tilde{B}_{P_{m_i}^{(i)}} = \tilde{B}_{P^{(i)}}$, $\tilde{B}_{P_1^{(j)}} = ... = \tilde{B}_{P_{nj}^{(j)}} = \tilde{B}_{P^{(j)}}$ should be satisfied for the purpose of consistency of Z-valued probability distributions. Given $\hat{P}(S_i)$ and $\hat{P}(\hat{h}_j)$, the Z-valued marginal probability distributions $\hat{P}(\boldsymbol{S})$ and $\hat{P}(\hat{\boldsymbol{h}})$ will be represented as follows:

$$\hat{P}(\boldsymbol{S}) = \hat{P}(S_1)/S_1 + ... + \hat{P}(S_m)/S_m,$$
$$\hat{P}(\hat{\boldsymbol{h}}) = \hat{P}(\hat{h}_1)/\hat{h}_1 + ... + \hat{P}(\hat{h}_n)/\hat{h}_n.$$

Given marginal $\hat{P}(\boldsymbol{S})$ and $\hat{P}(\hat{\boldsymbol{h}})$, and information about signs of dependences between components of $\boldsymbol{S}$ and $\hat{\boldsymbol{h}}$, it is needed to

determine the Z-valued joint probabilities over combined states $\hat{P}(\boldsymbol{S},\hat{\boldsymbol{h}}) = \hat{P}(S_{i_1}^{(1)},...,S_{i_m}^{(m)},\hat{h}_{j_1}^{(1)},...,\hat{h}_{j_n}^{(n)}) = \hat{P}(S_{k_1}^{(1)},...,S_{k_m}^{(m)},\hat{h}_{k_{m+1}}^{(m+1)},...,\hat{h}_{k_{m+n}}^{(m+n)})$:
$\hat{P}(S_{k_1}^{(1)},...,S_{k_m}^{(m)},\hat{h}_{k_{m+1}}^{(m+1)},...,\hat{h}_{k_{m+n}}^{(m+n)}) = \phi(\hat{P}(S_{k_1}^{(1)}),...,\hat{P}(S_{k_m}^{(m)}),\hat{P}(\hat{h}_{k_{m+1}}^{(m+1)}),...,\hat{P}(\hat{h}_{k_{m+n}}^{(m+n)}))$.
The main problem in determination of $\hat{P}(\boldsymbol{S},\hat{\boldsymbol{h}})$ is to obtain an information about interdependencies of $S_{k_1}^{(1)},...,S_{k_m}^{(m)},\hat{h}_{k_{m+1}}^{(m+1)},...,\hat{h}_{k_{m+n}}^{(m+n)}$. Taking into account the complexity of relations between $S_{k_1}^{(1)},...,S_{k_m}^{(m)},\hat{h}_{k_{m+1}}^{(m+1)},...,\hat{h}_{k_{m+n}}^{(m+n)}$, an adequate approach to obtain such information is the use of some intelligent procedure based on expert evaluations[60,72,75,161,254,323,348,460].

On the base of the Z-valued joint probabilities $\hat{P}(\hat{\boldsymbol{\omega}}) = \hat{P}(\boldsymbol{S},\hat{\boldsymbol{h}}) = (\tilde{A}_{P(\boldsymbol{\omega})},\tilde{B}_P)$, a Z-valued bi-capacity $\hat{\eta}$ is then constructed to model relation between combined states under imprecise and partially reliable information, especially taking into account interaction between attractive and repulsive outcomes. A Z-valued bi-capacity $\hat{\eta}$ is to be constructed as the difference between two Z-valued capacities:

$$\hat{\eta}(\mathcal{V},\mathcal{W}) = \hat{\upsilon}_1(\mathcal{V}) - \hat{\upsilon}_2(\mathcal{W}).$$

Z-valued fuzzy capacities $\hat{\upsilon}_1(\mathcal{V}),\hat{\upsilon}_2(\mathcal{W})$ can be constructed as lower or upper probabilities or their convex combinations. As lower and upper probabilities, one can use lower and upper envelops of the set of priors which is defined by Z-valued restrictions $\hat{P}(\hat{\boldsymbol{\omega}}) = \hat{P}(\boldsymbol{S},\hat{\boldsymbol{h}}) = (\tilde{A}_{P(\boldsymbol{\omega})},\tilde{B}_P)$. The lower envelope $\hat{\upsilon}(\mathcal{V})$ can be found as

$$\hat{\upsilon}(\mathcal{V}) = (\tilde{A}_\upsilon(\mathcal{V}),\tilde{B}_\upsilon),\ \tilde{B}_\upsilon = \tilde{B}_P$$
$$\tilde{A}_\upsilon(\mathcal{V}) = \bigcup_{\alpha\in(0,1]} \alpha\left[A_{\upsilon1}^{\alpha}(\mathcal{V}), A_{\upsilon2}^{\alpha}(\mathcal{V})\right],\ \mathcal{V}\subset\Omega=\{\hat{\omega}_1,...,\hat{\omega}_L\} \quad (11.3)$$

where

$$A_{\upsilon1}^{\alpha}(\mathcal{V}) = \inf\left\{\sum_{\hat{\omega}_i\in V} p(\hat{\omega}_i) \middle| (p(\hat{\omega}_1),...,p(\hat{\omega}_L))\in A_{\mathrm{P}}^{\alpha}\right\},$$
$$A_{\mathrm{P}}^{\alpha} = \left\{(p(\hat{\omega}_1),...,p(\hat{\omega}_L))\in A_{P(\boldsymbol{\omega}_1)}^{\alpha}\times...\times A_{P(\boldsymbol{\omega}_L)}^{\alpha} \middle| \sum_{l=1}^{L} p(\hat{\omega}_l) = 1\right\}. \quad (11.4)$$

Here $A_{P(\omega_1)}{}^{\alpha},...,A_{P(\omega_L)}{}^{\alpha}$ are α-cuts of fuzzy probabilities $\tilde{A}_{P(\omega_1)},...,\tilde{A}_{P(\omega_L)}$ respectively, $p(\hat{\omega}_1),...,p(\hat{\omega}_L)$ are basic probabilities for $\tilde{A}_{P(\omega_1)},...,\tilde{A}_{P(\omega_L)}$ respectively, $\times$ denotes the Cartesian product. The upper prevision can be obtained by substituting inf by sup in (11.4).

For each alternative $\hat{f}$, given its utilities for all the combined states and the Z-valued bi-capacity modeling dependence between combined states, the overall utility $\hat{U}(\hat{f})$ can be determined according to (11.2). The best alternative is further found by determining the highest value of the Z-valued utility $\hat{U}:\mathcal{A}\to\mathcal{Z}$. The determination of the highest value of $\hat{U}$ can be done by applying fuzzy Pareto optimality principle-based comparison of Z-numbers suggested in Chapter 2.

11.6 Related Works

Let us consider the existing works which to that or another extent utilize application of Z-numbers-based and analogous ideas to decision analysis. Works [35,332] as well as the study in Section 7.2 is devoted to decision making based on hierarchical model with second order interval probabilities. The authors apply the suggested approach to benchmark decision problem and real-world decision problem (investment problem). In the considered approach, DM's subjective evaluation of a likelihood of a state of nature is represented by a pair of intervals. The first interval is used to describe imprecise probability of a state of nature. However, as an estimation of probability is always subject to DM's confidence (which is also cannot be exactly measured), the latter is introduced into the model in form of the second interval. This second interval is formalized as an imprecise probability measure of the first interval and may be considered as a reliability of the latter. In other words, this structure can be considered as a special reduced case of a Z-number, components of which are intervals and not fuzzy numbers. In the considered paper a decision rule is a CEU with a non-additive measure constructed on the base of the second-order interval probability. The research suggested in the paper suffers from a series of disadvantages which limits its use for solving of real decision problems. The first disadvantage is that the approach is able to deal with imperfect information related to probabilities only. Moreover, for this purpose sharp constraints (intervals) are used which don't correspond to real-world information described in NL. Particularly, it is difficult to exactly constrain DM's confidence. The second disadvantage is absence of consideration of a series of important behavioral determinants, which become apparent in real problems, especially in investment problems.

In [227] they considered an approach to multi-criteria decision making in which criteria weights and criteria evaluations of alternatives are described by informational constructs which are analogous to Z-numbers. The considered informational construct is represented by a pair of fuzzy numbers, where the second component is intended to represent reliability of the first component. However, it is not openly mentioned whether the second component is a probability measure of the first, as it is assumed in the Z-number idea suggested by Zadeh [454]. In the considered approach a pair of fuzzy numbers is reduced to one fuzzy number. Moreover, the overall performance evaluations of alternatives are computed as crisp numbers. This implies significant loss of information contained in the original informational constructs and, therefore, the comparison of alternatives may not be adequate or trustful.

Papers [430,431] are devoted to new representations, approaches and applications of Z-numbers in various important fields, including decision making. It is suggested to consider a Z-valuation $(X, \tilde{A}, \tilde{B})$ in terms of a possibility distribution over probability distributions which underlie the corresponding Z-number $Z = (\tilde{A}, \tilde{B})$. The author also suggests an alternative formulation of Z-information in terms of a Dempster-Shafer belief structure [128,369] which involves Type-2 fuzzy sets. However, in the suggested approach only typical distributions are considered. In order to use any typical distribution, the corresponding assumptions must be initially verified which are adequate to the considered phenomena. In general, this is not always possible when the relevant information is imperfect and the properties of the phenomena are not well-known. For example, in many real-life applications the part $\tilde{B}$ of a Z-number, the reliability, is subjectively assigned by a human being. Indeed, we may not know the pattern that subjective probabilities underlying $\tilde{B}$ follow. From the other side, if a suitable typical distribution is known, one will deal with high computational complexity conditioned by non-linear variational problems. In the paper, it is considered to choose among alternatives each having one Z-number-valued payoff. As a result, the suggested decision rule is comparing Z-numbers. The comparison of Z-numbers is conducted by reducing them to fuzzy numbers. Each fuzzy number is obtained from a Z-valuation $(X, \tilde{A}, \tilde{B})$ as a fuzzy expected value of X calculated by using a fuzzy set of probability distributions induced by $\tilde{A}$ and $\tilde{B}$. The resulting fuzzy numbers are then compared on the base of their defuzzified values. However, this comparison is based on reducing a Z-number to a crisp value which is naturally characterized by sufficient loss of information. The other important disadvantage of the suggested decision making with Z-numbers is that single-valued alternatives (with one payoff) are considered, whereas real-world alternatives are vector-valued.

The work [456] is devoted to the issues of computation over continuous Z-numbers and several important practical problems in the area of control, decision making and other areas. The suggested investigation is based on the use of normal density functions for modeling random variables. However, it should be mentioned that the author of [456] aim at suggestion of ideas and recommendations on application of computations with Z-numbers rather on development of decision making approaches.

Paper [181] is devoted to decisions under uncertainty when information is described by Z-numbers. The authors formulate the problem of decision making when probabilities of states of nature and outcomes of alternatives are described by Z-numbers. The suggested decision analysis is based on two main stages. At the first stage, based on approach suggested in [227], Z-numbers are reduced to fuzzy numbers. At the second stage, values of fuzzy utility function for alternatives are computed and an alternative with the highest fuzzy utility value is chosen as the best one. As fuzzy utility models a fuzzy expected utility and a fuzzy Choquet expected utility [31,34] are considered. The main disadvantage of the suggested research is related to the loss of information resulting from converting Z-numbers to fuzzy numbers.

In [378] they suggest several approaches of approximate evaluation of a Z-number in order to reduce computational complexity. For example, one of the suggested approaches is based on approximation of set of convolutions by means of fuzzy "if-then" rules.

We can conclude that there is a small number of works related to Z-information-based general approaches to decision making. In Section 12.2.5 we provide an example of application of the suggested general theory of decisions to solving of a real-world decision problem.

Chapter 12

Simulations and Applications

In real-world problems, as a rule, perceptions are original sources of decision relevant information on environment and a DM's behavior. Perception-based information is intrinsically imperfect and, as a result, is usually described in NL or in form of visual images. In this chapter we provide solutions of decision making problems with perception-based imperfect information by applying decision theories suggested in the previous chapters. The considered decision making problems include benchmark problems and real-world decision problems in the areas of business, economics, production and medicine. The NL-based and visual imperfect information in these problems makes the use of the existing decision theories inapplicable to solve them.

12.1 Decision Simulations for Benchmark Problems

12.1.1 *Zadeh's two boxes problem[34]*

Prof. Lotfi Zadeh suggested a benchmark problem of decision making under imperfect information [34] which is described in Chapter 10. Let us solve this problem by applying the suggested decision theory with imperfect information [31,34].

We will not consider Case 1 of this problem as it falls within the classical framework of a decision making problem, and, therefore, can be solved by using the existing decision theories. Let us consider solving Case 4 and also Cases 2, 3. These cases fall within the category of decision problems for which fuzzy logic-based decision theory suggested in Chapter 6 is developed. Let us denote boxes as A and B and colors of balls as w (white) and b (black).

The set of possible events will be represented as $\{Aw, Bw, Ab, Bb\}$, where Aw means "a white ball picked from box A", Bb means "a black ball picked from box B" etc. Then the set of the states of nature is: $S = \{S_1, S_2, S_3, S_4\}$,where $S_1 = (Aw, Bw)$, $S_2 = (Aw, Bb)$, $S_3 = (Ab, Bw)$, $S_4 = (Ab, Bb)$.

Denote probabilities of the events as $\tilde{P}(Aw), \tilde{P}(Bw), \tilde{P}(Ab), \tilde{P}(Bb)$. Then the probabilities of the states are defined as:

$$\tilde{P}_1 = \tilde{P}(Aw, Bw) = \tilde{P}(Aw)\tilde{P}(Bw);$$
$$\tilde{P}_2 = \tilde{P}(Aw, Bb) = \tilde{P}(Aw)\tilde{P}(Bb);$$
$$\tilde{P}_3 = \tilde{P}(Ab, Bw) = \tilde{P}(Ab)\tilde{P}(Bw);$$
$$\tilde{P}_4 = \tilde{P}(Ab, Bb) = \tilde{P}(Ab)\tilde{P}(Bb).$$

Denote the outcomes of the events as $\tilde{X}(Aw), \tilde{X}(Bw), \tilde{X}(Ab), \tilde{X}(Bb)$, where $\tilde{X}(Aw)$ denotes the outcome faced when a white ball is picked from box A etc.

The alternatives are: $\tilde{f}_1$ (means choosing box A), $\tilde{f}_2$ (means choosing box B).

As alternatives map states to outcomes, we write:

$$\tilde{f}_1(S_1) = \tilde{X}(Aw);$$
$$\tilde{f}_1(S_2) = \tilde{X}(Aw);$$
$$\tilde{f}_1(S_3) = \tilde{X}(Ab);$$
$$\tilde{f}_1(S_4) = \tilde{X}(Ab);$$

$$\tilde{f}_2(S_1) = \tilde{X}(Bw);$$
$$\tilde{f}_2(S_2) = \tilde{X}(Bb);$$
$$\tilde{f}_2(S_3) = \tilde{X}(Bw);$$
$$\tilde{f}_2(S_4) = \tilde{X}(Bb).$$

Assume that imperfect decision-relevant information is treated by using fuzzy outcomes and fuzzy probabilities given in form of the following triangular and trapezoidal fuzzy numbers, respectively:

$$\begin{aligned}
&\tilde{X}(Aw) = \$(15,20,25),\\
&\tilde{X}(Ab) = \$(-10,-5,0),\\
&\tilde{X}(Bw) = \$(80,100,120),\\
&\tilde{X}(Bb) = \$(-25,-20,-15).
\end{aligned}$$

$$\tilde{P}(Aw) - (0.25,0.35,0.5,0.6)\,,\ \tilde{P}(Bw) = (0.1,0.2,0.25,0.35)\,.$$

Then the unknown probabilities are:

$$\tilde{P}(Ab) = (0.4,0.5,0.65,0.75)\,,\ \tilde{P}(Bb) = (0.65,0.75,0.8,0.9)\,.$$

The probabilities of the states of nature are computed as follows:

$$\begin{aligned}
\tilde{P}(Aw,Bw) &= (0.25,0.35,0.5,0.6)\cdot(0.1,0.2,0.25,0.35)\\
&= (0.025,0.07,0.125,0.21);\\
\tilde{P}(Aw,Bb) &= (0.25,0.35,0.5,0.6)\cdot(0.65,0.75,0.8,0.9)\\
&= (0.1625,0.2625,0.4,0.54);\\
\tilde{P}(Ab,Bw) &= (0.4,0.5,0.65,0.75)\cdot(0.1,0.2,0.25,0.35)\\
&= (0.04,0.1,0.1625,0.2625);\\
\tilde{P}(Ab,Bb) &= (0.4,0.5,0.65,0.75)\cdot(0.65,0.75,0.8,0.9)\\
&= (0.26,0.375,0.52,0.675).
\end{aligned}$$

An overall utility for an alternative $\tilde{f}_j,\ j=1,2$ will be determined as a fuzzy-valued Choquet integral (see Chapter 6):

$$\begin{aligned}
&\tilde{U}(\tilde{f}_j) = (\tilde{u}(\tilde{f}_j(S_{(1)})) -_h \tilde{u}(\tilde{f}_j(S_{(2)})))\tilde{\eta}_{\tilde{P}^l}\left(\{S_{(1)}\}\right)\\
&+(\tilde{u}(\tilde{f}_j(S_{(2)})) -_h \tilde{u}(\tilde{f}_j(S_{(3)})))\tilde{\eta}_{\tilde{P}^l}\left(\{S_{(1)},S_{(2)}\}\right)\\
&+(\tilde{u}(\tilde{f}_j(S_{(3)})) -_h \tilde{u}(\tilde{f}_j(S_{(4)})))\tilde{\eta}_{\tilde{P}^l}\left(\{S_{(1)},S_{(2)},S_{(3)}\}\right)\\
&+(\tilde{u}(\tilde{f}_j(S_{(4)})))\tilde{\eta}_{\tilde{P}^l}\left(\{S_{(1)},S_{(2)},S_{(3)},S_{(4)}\}\right).
\end{aligned}$$

Here (i) means that the states are ordered such that $\tilde{u}(\tilde{f}_j(S_{(1)})) \geq \tilde{u}(\tilde{f}_j(S_{(2)})) \geq \tilde{u}(\tilde{f}_j(S_{(3)})) \geq \tilde{u}(\tilde{f}_j(S_{(4)}))$, $\tilde{u}(\tilde{f}_j(S_{(i)}))$ denotes utility of an outcome we face taking action $\tilde{f}_j$ at a state $S_{(i)}$, $\tilde{\eta}_{\tilde{P}^l}(\cdot)$ is a fuzzy number-valued fuzzy measure. For simplicity, we define $\tilde{u}(\tilde{f}_j(S_i))$ to be numerically equal to the corresponding outcomes $\tilde{f}_j(S_i)$. Then the overall utilities of the alternatives are determined as follows:

$$\tilde{U}(\tilde{f}_1) = (25,25,25)\tilde{\eta}_{\tilde{P}^l}\left(\{S_1,S_2\}\right) + (-10,-5,0);$$

$$\tilde{U}(\tilde{f}_2) = (105,120,135)\tilde{\eta}_{\tilde{P}^l}\left(\{S_1,S_3\}\right) + (-25,-20,-15).$$

The α-cuts of $\tilde{\eta}_{\tilde{P}^l}\left(\{S_1,S_2\}\right)$, $\tilde{\eta}_{\tilde{P}^l}\left(\{S_1,S_3\}\right)$ are found as numerical solutions to problem (6.22)-(6.23) (Chapter 6):

$$\eta^{\alpha}_{\tilde{P}^l}(\{S_1,S_2\}) =$$
$$= \inf\left\{ P(S_1) + P(S_2) \middle| (P(S_1),...,P(S_4)) \in P_1^{\alpha} \times,...,\times P_4^{\alpha}, \sum_{i=1}^{4} P(S_i) = 1 \right\},$$

$$\eta^{\alpha}_{\tilde{P}^l}(\{S_1,S_3\}) =$$
$$= \inf\left\{ p(S_1) + p(S_3) \middle| (P(S_1),...,P(S_4)) \in P_1^{\alpha} \times,...,\times P_4^{\alpha}, \sum_{i=1}^{4} P(S_i) = 1 \right\}.$$

The values of $\tilde{\eta}_{\tilde{P}^l}\left(\{S_1,S_2\}\right)$, $\tilde{\eta}_{\tilde{P}^l}\left(\{S_1,S_3\}\right)$ we found are triangular fuzzy numbers $\tilde{\eta}_{\tilde{P}^l}\left(\{S_1,S_2\}\right) = (0.25,0.35,0.35)$, $\tilde{\eta}_{\tilde{P}^l}\left(\{S_1,S_3\}\right) = (0.1,0.2,0.2)$.

Now we can compute fuzzy overall utilities $\tilde{U}(\tilde{f}_1), \tilde{U}(\tilde{f}_2)$. The computed $\tilde{U}(\tilde{f}_1), \tilde{U}(\tilde{f}_2)$ approximated by triangular fuzzy numbers are shown in Fig. 12.1.

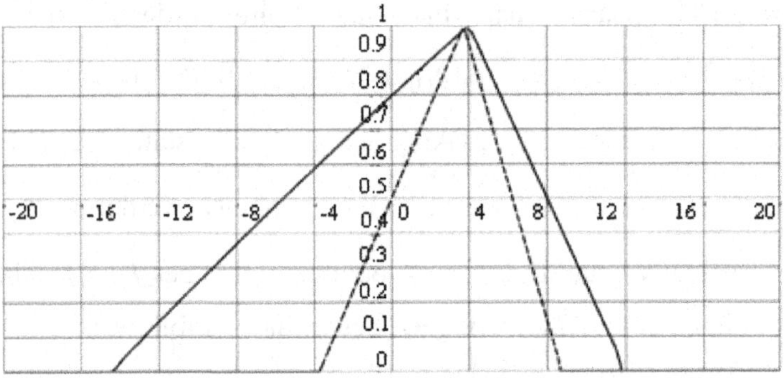

Fig. 12.1. Computed fuzzy overall utilities $\tilde{U}(\tilde{f}_1)$ (dashed), $\tilde{U}(\tilde{f}_2)$ (solid)

Applying Jaccard comparison method [368] we find that:

$$\tilde{U}(\tilde{f}_1) \geq \tilde{U}(\tilde{f}_2) \text{ with degree } 0.83$$

$$\tilde{U}(\tilde{f}_2) \geq \tilde{U}(\tilde{f}_1) \text{ with degree } 0.59$$

We determine the linguistic degree of the preference as it is shown in the Fig. 12.2 below. According to the Fig. 12.2, $\tilde{f}_1$ (choosing box A) has small preference over $\tilde{f}_2$ (choosing box B).

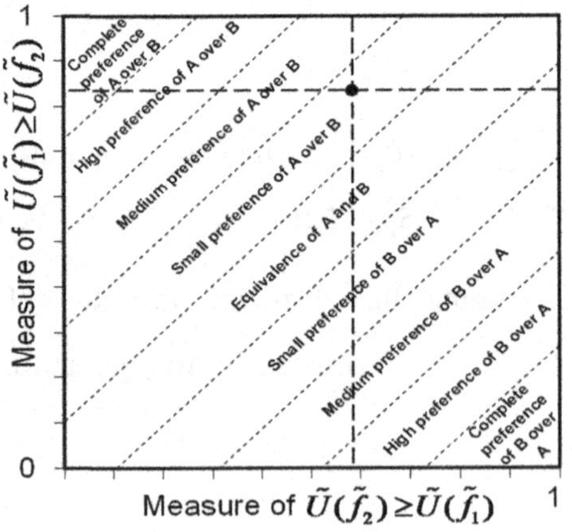

Fig. 12.2. Linguistic preferences

The decision relevant information we considered in this problem is characterized by imperfect (fuzzy) probabilities, imperfect (fuzzy) outcomes and fuzzy utilities. Such type of decision-relevant information is presented in Cell 32 of Table 4.1 (see Chapter 4). Below we shortly present the results of solving the Zadeh's problem for its special cases – Cases 2 and 3 when only probabilities or outcomes are imprecise.

1. The case of imprecise probabilities described as trapezoidal fuzzy numbers $\tilde{P}(Aw)=T(0.25,0.35,0.5,0.6)$, $\tilde{P}(Bw)=T(0.1,0.2,0.25,0.35)$ and precise outcomes $\tilde{X}(Aw)=\$20$, $\tilde{X}(Ab)=\$5$, $\tilde{X}(Bw)=\$100$, $\tilde{X}(Bb)=\$20$. This is the situation presented in Cell 4 in Table 4.1 (see Chapter 4) – information on probabilities is imperfect and information on outcomes and utilities is precise (as we determine utilities to be numerically equal to outcomes). In this case the suggested fuzzy utility model degenerates to a fuzzy-valued utility described as Choquet integral with *numeric* integrand and *fuzzy number-valued* fuzzy measure. The obtained fuzzy overall utilities for this case are $\tilde{U}(f_1)=(1.25,3.75,3.75)$ and $\tilde{U}(f_2)=(-8,4,4)$. According to the Jaccard index [368], $\tilde{U}(f_1)\geq\tilde{U}(f_2)$ with degree 0.708 and $\tilde{U}(f_2)\geq\tilde{U}(f_1)$ with degree 0.266, which implies the medium preference of f_1 over f_2. In this case we have more strong preference of f_1 over f_2 than that obtained for the case of fuzzy probabilities and fuzzy outcomes (small preference of f_1 over f_2). The reason for this is that in the present case information is more precise (outcomes are exactly known) and also ambiguity aversion resulted from fuzzy probabilities is more clearly observed (whereas in the previous case it is weaken behind impreciseness of outcomes).

2. The case of imprecise outcomes described as fuzzy numbers $\tilde{X}(Aw)=\$(15,20,25)$, $\tilde{X}(Ab)=\$(-10,-5,0)$, $\tilde{X}(Bw)=\$(80,100,120)$, $\tilde{X}(Bb)=\$(-25,-20,-15)$ and precise probabilities $P(Aw)=0.4$, $P(Bw)=0.2$. This is the situation presented in Cell 29 in Table 4.1 – information on probabilities is precise and information on outcomes and utilities is imperfect (as we determine utilities to be numerically equal to outcomes). In this case the suggested fuzzy utility model degenerates to a fuzzy-valued expected utility with *fuzzy number-valued* integrand and

crisp probability measure. The obtained fuzzy overall utilities are $\tilde{U}(\tilde{f}_1)=(0,5,10)$ and $\tilde{U}(\tilde{f}_2)=(-4,4,12)$. According to the Jaccard index, $\tilde{U}(\tilde{f}_1)\geq\tilde{U}(\tilde{f}_2)$ with degree 0.915 and $\tilde{U}(\tilde{f}_2)\geq\tilde{U}(\tilde{f}_1)$ with degree 0.651, which implies small preference of $\tilde{f}_1$ over $\tilde{f}_2$. So, despite that in this case the situation is less uncertain than for the case with fuzzy probabilities and fuzzy outcomes, we have in essence the same preference of $\tilde{f}_1$ over $\tilde{f}_2$. The reason for this is that for this case ambiguity aversion is absent (due to exact probabilities) and impreciseness of outcomes does not allow for a higher preference.

Consider now solving Case 5. This case takes place when after having a look at boxes (Fig. 12.3), a DM has visual perceptions which are not sufficiently detailed to be described by membership functions.

A DM can only graphically evaluate the probabilities as F-marks. Such essence of the relevant information requires the use of fuzzy geometry-based decision theory suggested in Chapter 10 for solution of Case 5.

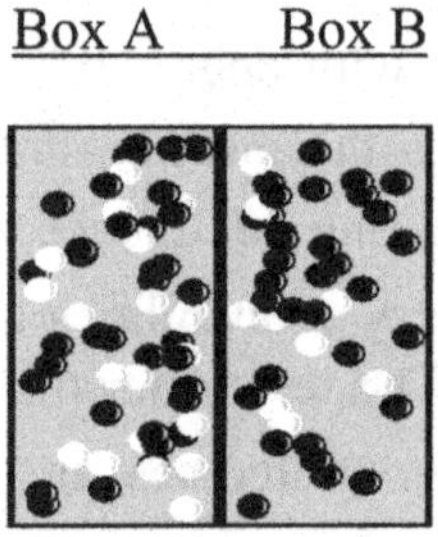

Fig. 12.3. Two boxes with large number of black and white balls

12.1.2 ***Bingo game [32]***

In this example we conduct experimental investigations on application of the combined states-based approach as a more general approach than CPT to behavioral decision making in a benchmark decision problem – the famous Bingo game [8,32,202]. The considered behavioral aspects are risk issues.

Let a transparent Bingo Blower box contain red, blue and green balls, numbers of which cannot be visually defined exactly but can only be defined by means of imprecise linguistic evaluations as follows: "the number of blue balls is medium, the number of red balls is about thirty percent and the number of green balls is the least". Let us consider two alternative games to choose from:

$100 is given if a red ball is extracted, $10 is given if a blue ball is extracted and $10 is taken if a green ball is extracted;

$10 is given if a red ball is extracted, $10 is taken if a blue ball is extracted and $100 is given if a green ball is extracted.

CPT theory can not be applied to solve this problem as it is stated because in this problem the information relevant to probabilities is linguistic. Another important issue related to application of CPT is that in this theory they imperatively consider a DM as risk averse in domain of gains and risk seeking in domain of losses. However, these assumptions on human behavior underlying CPT should not be considered as dogma. A DM, who is risky in his character, would likely exhibit risk seeking also in domain of gains. There may also be other behaviors which are not considered in CPT.

The above mentioned issues of the considered problem make the use of CPT unsuitable and require applying the combined states-based approach suggested in Chapter 9. The reason is that this approach is more powerful and flexible in modeling behavior aspects and is able to deal with imperfect information described in NL. We will consider application of combined states-based approach.

The set of states of nature is $S = \{S_1, S_2, S_3\}$, where S_1, S_2, S_3 – extraction of a red, extraction of a blue and extraction of a green balls respectively.

To formally construct this decision problem we need to precisiate linguistic information related to probabilities of the states of nature. To do this, we use triangular fuzzy numbers (TFNs) to describe probabilities of blue and green balls and on base of them calculate fuzzy probability of a red ball extraction. As a result, we have constructed the following TFNs-described probabilities:

$$\tilde{P}(S_1) = (0.15, 0.2, 0.25), \tilde{P}(S_2) = (0.45, 0.5, 0.55), \tilde{P}(S_3) = (0.25, 0.3, 0.35).$$

The alternatives we have are as follows

$$f_1 = \left(f_1(S_1) = 100; f_1(S_2) = 10; f_1(S_3) = -10\right),$$

$$f_2 = \left(f_2(S_1) = 10; f_2(S_2) = -10; f_2(S_3) = 100\right).$$

Let us reveal preferences over these alternatives by applying combined states-based approach [32]. According to the behavioral basics of CPT, a DM is risk averse for gains and risk seeking for losses. Thus, we model a DM in our approach by a set of two possible states $\mathcal{H} = \{h_1, h_2\}$, where h_1 and h_2 (for simplicity, considered binary – non-fuzzy) are a DM's states representing risk aversion and risk seeking respectively [32]. Then the ideas underlying CPT can be realized in combined states-based approach as follows. For the case of alternative f_1 there may be only the following combined states: $(S_1,h_1),(S_2,h_1)$, (S_3,h_2). Indeed, in S_1 and S_2 a gain takes place, and, therefore, in these conditions a DM will be risk averse, that is a DM's state will be h_1. In its turn, in S_3 a loss takes place and then a DM is a risk seeking, that is a DM's state will be h_2. Any other combined state, for example (S_1,h_2) is impossible – in CPT they don't consider a DM risk seeking in domain of gains. However, we will consider all combinations of states of nature and states of a DM for more powerful modeling. Then a combined states space will be as it is shown in Table 12.1 [32]:

Table 12.1. Combined states for the risk attitudes

	S_1	S_2	S_3
h_1	(S_1,h_1)	(S_2,h_1)	(S_3,h_1)
h_2	(S_1,h_2)	(S_2,h_2)	(S_3,h_2)

In our approach we determine an overall utility of an alternative as Choquet-like bi-capacity-based aggregation of its utilities $u(f(S_i,h_j))$ $(f \in \{f_1,f_2\}; i=1,2,3;\ j=1,2)$ with respect to a fuzzy-valued bi-capacity $\tilde{\eta}$ over combined states space. $u(f(S_i,h_j))$ will be chosen concave for h_1 and convex for h_2 by applying for simplicity the technique adopted to construct a value function in CPT:

$$u(f(S_i,h_1))=\begin{cases}(f(S_i))^{\alpha},\ f(S_i)\ge 0\\ -\lambda(-f(S_i))^{\beta},\ f(S_i)<0\end{cases}$$
$$u(f(S_i,h_2))=\begin{cases}(f(S_i))^{\beta},\ f(S_i)\ge 0\\ -\lambda(-f(S_i))^{\alpha},\ f(S_i)<0\end{cases} \qquad (12.1)$$

$\alpha=0.88,\ \beta=1.25$. This means that $u(f(\cdot,h_1))$ is concave and $u(f(\cdot,h_2))$ is convex both for gains and losses. $\tilde{\eta}$ will be obtained from FJPs $\tilde{P}(s,h)$ of combined states $(S,h),\ S\in\mathcal{S}, h\in\mathcal{H}$.

The next step, according to the methodology given in Chapter 9 is to define FJPs $\tilde{P}(S_i,h_j)$ over combined states given fuzzy marginal probabilities for states of nature and states of a DM: $\tilde{P}(S_i)$ and $\tilde{P}(h_j)$. Therefore, we need to assign fuzzy probabilities $\tilde{P}(h_j)$ over states of a DM. Exact information on intensity of risk attitudes of a person is naturally not known to assign precise actual probabilities to h_1 and h_2. Available information on intensities is usually described in NL. Let us consider a DM risk aversion (h_1) of which dominates risk seeking (h_2) and let the imprecise relevant information is described by fuzzy probabilities: $\tilde{P}(h_1)=(0.65,0.7,0.75),\ \tilde{P}(h_2)=(0.25,0.3,0.35)$. Given fuzzy marginal distributions $\tilde{P}(S)$, $\tilde{P}(h)$ we will calculate FJP $\tilde{P}(S,h)$ taking into account any of the combined states that may occur. The FJP distribution will be obtained on the base of concepts of positive dependence and negative dependence for events [417,419]. For alternative f_1 we suppose positive dependence between elements (considered as events) of the pairs $(S_1,h_1),(S_2,h_1),(S_3,h_2)$ (as these are combinations of states nature and DM's behaviors that take place according to CPT) and negative dependence between elements (considered as events) of $(S_1,h_2),(S_2,h_2),(S_3,h_1)$ (as these are combinations of states of nature and a DM's behavior that can not take place according to CPT). Then the FJPs are obtained from fuzzy marginal probabilities as the following trapezoidal fuzzy numbers [32]:

$$\tilde{P}(S_1,h_1)=(0.0825,0.12,0.2,0.25)\,;\tilde{P}(S_2,h_1)=(0.2475,0.3,0.5,0.55)\,;$$
$$\tilde{P}(S_3,h_1)=(0,0,0.18,0.26);\tilde{P}(S_1,h_2)=(0,0,0.08,0.1125)\,;$$
$$\tilde{P}(S_2,h_2)=(0,0,0.2,0.2475)\,;\;\tilde{P}(S_3,h_2)=(0.07,0.12,0.3,0.4)\,.$$

Analogously, for f_2 supposing positive dependence between ele-ments of (S_1,h_1), (S_2,h_2), (S_3,h_1) and negative dependence between ele-ments of (S_1,h_2), (S_2,h_1), (S_3,h_2) we obtained the following FJPs:

$$\tilde{P}(S_1,h_1)=(0.0825,0.12,0.2,0.25)\,;\tilde{P}(S_2,h_1)=(0.1,0.2,0.3,0.3575)\,;$$
$$\tilde{P}(S_3,h_1)=(0.11,0.18,0.3,0.4)\,;\tilde{P}(S_1,h_2)=(0,0,0.08,0.1125)\,;$$
$$\tilde{P}(S_2,h_2)=(0.1575,0.2,0.4,0.45);\;\tilde{P}(S_3,h_2)=(0,0,0.12,0.18)\,.$$

Now we need to obtain fuzzy overall utilities $\tilde{U}(f_1)$ and $\tilde{U}(f_2)$, which are to be calculated as follows:

$$\begin{aligned}
&\tilde{U}(f_1)=(|u(f_1(S_1,h_2))|-|u(f_1(S_1,h_1))|)\tilde{\eta}(\{(S_1,h_2)\},\varnothing)+\\
&(|u(f_1(S_1,h_1))|-|u(f_1(S_3,h_1))|)\tilde{\eta}(\{(S_1,h_2),(S_1,h_1)\},\varnothing)+\\
&(|u(f_1(S_3,h_1))|-|u(f_1(S_2,h_2))|)\tilde{\eta}(\{(S_1,h_2),(S_1,h_1)\},\{(S_3,h_1)\})+\\
&(|u(f_1(S_2,h_2))|-|u(f_1(S_3,h_2))|)\times\\
&\times\tilde{\eta}(\{(S_1,h_2),(S_1,h_1),(S_2,h_2)\},\{(S_3,h_1)\})+\\
&(|u(f_1(S_3,h_2))|-|u(f_1(S_2,h_1))|)\times\\
&\times\tilde{\eta}(\{(S_1,h_2),(S_1,h_1),(S_2,h_2)\},\{(S_3,h_1),(S_3,h_2)\})+\\
&+|u(f_1(S_2,h_1))|\tilde{\eta}(\{(S_1,h_2),(S_1,h_1),(S_2,h_2),(S_2,h_1)\},\{(S_3,h_1),(S_3,h_2)\})
\end{aligned}\tag{12.2}$$

$$\begin{aligned}
&\tilde{U}(f_2)=(|u(f_2(S_3,h_2))|-|u(f_2(S_3,h_1))|)\tilde{\eta}(\{(S_3,h_2)\},\varnothing)+\\
&(|u(f_2(S_3,h_1))|-|u(f_2(S_2,h_1))|)\tilde{\eta}(\{(S_3,h_2),(S_3,h_1)\},\varnothing)+\\
&(|u(f_2(S_2,h_1))|-|u(f_2(S_1,h_2))|)\tilde{\eta}(\{(S_3,h_2),(S_3,h_1)\},\{(S_2,h_1)\})+\\
&(|u(f_2(S_1,h_2))|-|u(f_2(S_2,h_2))|)\tilde{\eta}(\{(S_3,h_2),(S_3,h_1),(S_1,h_2)\},\\
&\{(S_2,h_1)\})+(|u(f_2(S_2,h_2))|-|u(f_2(S_1,h_1))|)\tilde{\eta}(\{(S_3,h_2),(S_3,h_1),\\
&(S_1,h_2),\},\{(S_2,h_1),(S_2,h_2)\})+|u(f_2(S_1,h_1))|\tilde{\eta}(\{(S_1,h_2),(S_1,h_1),\\
&(S_3,h_2),(S_3,h_1)\},\{(S_2,h_1),(S_2,h_2)\})
\end{aligned}\tag{12.3}$$

where utilities are determined by (12.1).

We define fuzzy-valued bi-capacity $\tilde{\eta}_{\tilde{P}^l}(\mathcal{V},\mathcal{W})$ in (12.2),(12.3) as a difference $\tilde{\eta}_{\tilde{P}^l}(\mathcal{V},\mathcal{W})=\tilde{\eta}_{\tilde{P}^l}(\mathcal{V})-\tilde{\eta}_{\tilde{P}^l}(\mathcal{W})$ of values of a fuzzy-valued lower probability $\tilde{\eta}_{\tilde{P}^l}$. The latter are defined as it is shown in [27,34]. The values of $\tilde{\eta}_{\tilde{P}^l}(\mathcal{V},\mathcal{W})$ for f_1 and f_2 are given in Tables 12.2 and 12.3:

Table 12.2. Fuzzy-valued bi-capacity obtained for f_1

$\mathcal{V},\mathcal{W}\subset\Omega$	$\tilde{\eta}_{\tilde{P}^l}(\mathcal{V},\mathcal{W})$	$\tilde{\eta}_{\tilde{P}^l}(\mathcal{V})$	$\tilde{\eta}_{\tilde{P}^l}(\mathcal{W})$
$\{(S_1,h_2)\},\varnothing$	(0,0,0)	(0,0,0)	(0,0,0)
$\{(S_1,h_2),(S_1,h_1)\},\varnothing$	(0,0.0825,0.12)	(0,0.0825,0.12)	(0,0,0)
$\{(S_1,h_2),(S_1,h_1)\},\{(S_3,h_1)\}$	(0,0.0825,0.12)	(0,0.0825,0.12)	(0,0,0)
$\{(S_1,h_2),(S_1,h_1),(S_2,h_2)\},\{(S_3,h_1)\}$	(0,0.0825,0.12)	(0,0.0825,0.12)	(0,0,0)
$\{(S_1,h_2),(S_1,h_1),(S_2,h_2)\},\{(S_3,h_1),(S_3,h_2)\}$	(0,0.0825,0.12)	(0,0.0825,0.12)	(0,0,0)
$\{(S_1,h_2),(S_1,h_1),(S_2,h_2),(S_2,h_1)\},\{(S_3,h_1),(S_3,h_2)\}$	(0.22,0.3,0.35)	(0.34,0.34,0.42)	(0.07,0.12,0.12)

Table 12.3. Fuzzy-valued bi-capacity obtained for f_2

$\mathcal{V},\mathcal{W}\subset\Omega$	$\tilde{\eta}_{\tilde{P}^l}(\mathcal{V},\mathcal{W})$	$\tilde{\eta}_{\tilde{P}^l}(\mathcal{V})$	$\tilde{\eta}_{\tilde{P}^l}(\mathcal{W})$
$\{(S_3,h_2)\},\varnothing$	(0,0,0)	(0,0,0)	(0,0,0)
$\{(S_3,h_2),(S_3,h_1)\},\varnothing$	(0.11,0.11,0.18)	(0.11,0.11,0.18)	(0,0,0)
$\{(S_3,h_2),(S_3,h_1)\},\{(S_2,h_1)\}$	(0.11,0.11,0.18)	(0.11,0.11,0.18)	(0,0,0)
$\{(S_3,h_2),(S_3,h_1),(S_1,h_2)\},\{(S_2,h_1)\}$	(0.11,0.11,0.18)	(0.11,0.11,0.18)	(0,0,0)
$\{(S_3,h_2),(S_3,h_1),(S_1,h_2)\},\{(S_2,h_1),(S_2,h_2)\}$	(-0.19,-0.12,0.0225)	(0.11,0.11,0.18)	(0.1575,0.3,0.3)
$\{(S_1,h_2),(S_1,h_1),(S_3,h_2),(S_3,h_1)\},\{(S_2,h_1),(S_2,h_2)\}$	(-0.1075,0,0.1425)	(0.1925,0.3,0.3)	(0.1575,0.3,0.3)

The overall fuzzy utilities obtained as TFNs by (12.2) and (12.3) are:

$$\tilde{U}(f_1)=(5.8,8.3,8.7),\ \tilde{U}(f_2)=(1.8,6.15,8.6).$$

Comparing these fuzzy utilities by using formula (9.2) (see Chapter 9) we obtained: $Deg(f_1 \succ_l f_2) = 0.059$, $Deg(f_2 \succ_l f_1) = 0.023$. So, as $Deg(f_1 \succ_l f_2) > Deg(f_2 \succ_l f_1)$ then, formally, the best solution is f_1.

Let us solve this problem by applying CPT. As the exact objective probabilities $P(S_1), P(S_2), P(S_3)$ are not known we need to precisiate DM's probability-related perceptions to some approximate values like $P(S_1) = 0.2, P(S_2) = 0.5, P(S_3) = 0.3$. Applying CPT for this case, we obtained the following overall utilities of our alternatives:

$$U(f_1) = 12.4, \quad U(f_2) = 11.35$$

So, $f_1 \succ f_2$. When solving the considered problem by CPT, we used such numerical values for probabilities which result in the same best alternative as that obtained by the combined states-based approach – f_1. However, in general, it is impossible to use precise numbers as equivalents to qualitative information. In the considered problem and many real-world problems qualitative, imperfect information supported by perceptions are used to cover uncertainty as the accurate precise values are not known. In turn, approximate precise numbers and even intervals used to replace perceptions-based information are often erroneous. This approximation is a mere guesswork disregarding a lot of useful information. This, as a result, naturally leads to improper decisions. According to CPT, f_1 is unambiguously better than f_2. In the suggested approach, in comparison to CPT, imprecision and vagueness of information is better kept and takes a part in a final comparison of alternatives – there remains some vagueness on what alternative is better.

12.2 Applications in Business and Economics

12.2.1 *Business development for a computer firm*

A manager of a computer firm needs to make a decision concerning his business over the next five years. There has been good sales growth over the past couple of years. The owner sees three options. The first is to enlarge the current store, the second is to move to a new site, and the third is simply wait and do nothing. The decision to expand or move would take little time, and, so, the store would not lose revenue. If nothing were done the first year and strong growth occurred, then the decision to expand would be reconsidered. Waiting longer than one year would allow competition to move in and would make expansion no longer feasible.

The description of assumptions and conditions the manager consider is NL-based and includes linguistically described values of revenues, costs and probabilities for the problem are as follows:

"Strong growth as a result of the increased population of computer buyers from the electronics new firm has "*a little higher than medium*" probability. Strong growth with a new site would give annual returns of "*strong revenue*" per year. Weak growth with a new site would give annual returns of "*weak revenue*". Strong growth with an expansion would give annual returns of an "*about strong revenue*" per year. Weak growth with an expansion would mean annual returns of a "*lower than weak*". At the existing store with no changes, there would be returns of "*medium revenue*" per year if there is strong growth and of a "*higher than weak revenue*" per year if growth is weak. Expansion at the current site would cost "*low*". The move to the new site would cost "*high*". If growth is strong and the existing site is enlarged during the second year, the cost would still be "*low*". Operating costs for all options are equal."

The considered problem is characterized by NL-described imperfect information on all its elements: alternatives, outcomes, states of nature and probabilities. Really, in a broad variety of economic problems relevant information cannot be represented by precise evaluations. Moreover, the considered problem is characterized by second-order uncertainty represented in form of fuzzy probabilities. Such essence of the problem makes it impossible to apply the existing decision theories for solving it. In order to apply any existing theory, one needs to precisiate the NL-described information to precise numbers that leads to distortion and loss of information. As a result, one will arrive at a decision problem which is not equivalent to the original one and the resulted solution will not be trustful. For solving this problem it is more adequate to apply decision theory suggested in Chapter 6 which is able to deal with NL-described information. Below we consider application of this theory to solving the considered problem.

Let us provide representation of linguistic evaluations of revenues and costs in form of triangular fuzzy numbers. Revenues: "strong revenue" = (175.5;195;214.5); "weak revenue" = (103.5; 115; 126.5); "about strong revenue" = (171; 190; 209); lower than weak" = (90;100;110); "medium revenue" = (153;170;187); "higher than weak revenue"= (94.5;105;115.5). Costs: "high"=(189;210;231); "low"=(78.3; 87; 95.7); "zero"=(0;0;5). In Table 12.4 linguistic description of revenues, costs and final values (outcomes) for each decision is given. The fuzzy outcomes calculated based on fuzzy revenues and costs as "**Value of an outcome = revenue – cost**" based on the, are as follows: "about large" = (646.5;765;841.5); "about medium" = (286.5;365;401.5); "large 1" = (759.3;863;949.3); "medium" = (354.3; 413;454.3); "large2" = (741.3;843;927;3); "large3" = (760;850;930); "higher than medium" = (472.5;525;577.5).

Table 12.4. Linguistic description of revenues, costs and final values

Alternative	**Revenue**	**Cost**	**Value of an outcome = revenue – cost**
Move to new location, strong growth	"strong revenue" × 5 yrs	"high" "high"	"about large" "about medium"
Move to new locations, weak growth	"weak revenue" × 5 yrs	"low"	"large1"
Expand store, strong growth	"about strong revenue" × 5 yrs	"low"	"medium"
Expand store, weak growth	"lower than weak" × 5 yrs	"low"	"large3"
Do nothing now, strong growth, expand next year	"medium revenue" × 1 yr + "about strong revenue" × 4 yrs	"zero"	"large2"
Do nothing now, strong growth, do not expand next year	"medium revenue" × 5 yr	"zero"	"higher than medium"
Do nothing now, weak growth	"higher than weak revenue"	"zero"	

The set of the fuzzy states of the nature is $\mathcal{S}=\{\tilde{S}_1,\tilde{S}_2\}$, where $\tilde{S}_1$ – "strong growth", $\tilde{S}_2$ – "weak growth". The membership functions of $\tilde{S}_1$ and $\tilde{S}_2$ are shown in the Fig. 12.4:

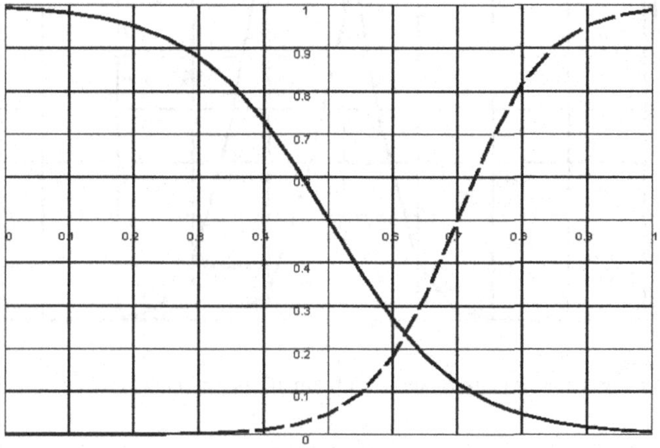

Fig.12.4. Fuzzy states of the nature: $\tilde{S}_1$ (dashed), $\tilde{S}_2$ (solid)

The linguistic probability distribution $\tilde{P}^l$ over the states of the nature that corresponds with the knowledge the manager has is:

$$\tilde{P}^l=\tilde{P}_1/\tilde{S}_1+\tilde{P}_2/\tilde{S}_2$$

$\tilde{P}_1$ = "a little higher than medium" , described by triangular fuzzy number $(0.45;0.55;0.65)$ and $\tilde{P}_2$ is unknown.

The set of the manager's possible actions is $\mathcal{A}=\{\tilde{f}_1,\tilde{f}_2,\tilde{f}_3\}$, where $\tilde{f}_1$ denotes "move" decision, $\tilde{f}_2$ denotes "expand" decision, $\tilde{f}_3$ denotes "do nothing" decision.

Fuzzy probabilities $\tilde{P}_1$(given) and $\tilde{P}_2$ (obtained on the base of solving the problem (6.11)-(6.12) (Chapter 6)) are given in the Fig.12.5:

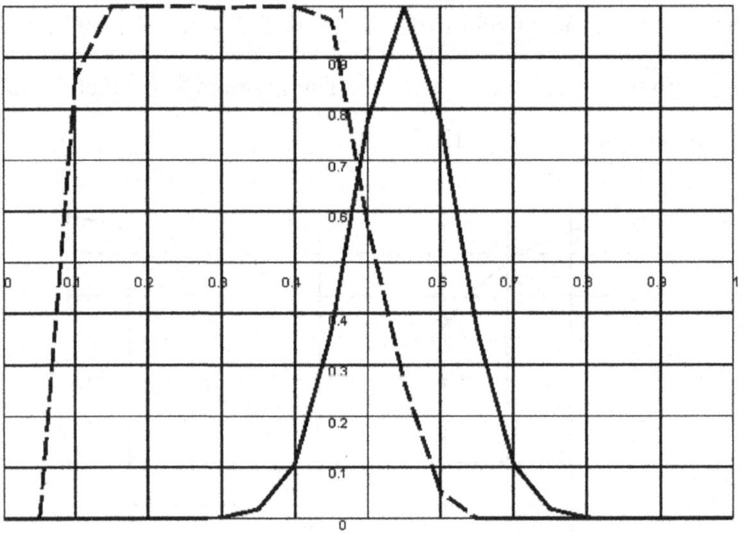

Fig.12.5.The given (solid curve) and the obtained (dashed curve) fuzzy probabilities

The defuzzified values of the fuzzy-valued measure $\tilde{\eta}_{\tilde{P}^l}$ obtained from $\tilde{P}^l$ on the base of formulas (6.20)-(6.21) (Chapter 6) by using the approach suggested in [309,458] are given in Table 12.5. The defuzzified values are used for simplicity of further calculations.

Table 12.5. Fuzzy measure $\tilde{\eta}_{\tilde{P}^l}$

$\mathcal{H}$	$\{\tilde{S}_1\}$	$\{\tilde{S}_2\}$	$\{\tilde{S}_1,\tilde{S}_2\}$
$\tilde{\eta}_{\tilde{P}^l}(\mathcal{H})$	0.47	0.38	1

Utility values are calculated as follows:

$$\tilde{U}(\tilde{f})=\tilde{\eta}_{\tilde{P}^l}(\{\tilde{S}_{(1)},\tilde{S}_{(2)}\})\tilde{u}(\tilde{f}(\tilde{S}_{(2)}))+\tilde{\eta}_{\tilde{P}^l}(\{\tilde{S}_{(1)}\})(\tilde{u}(\tilde{f}(\tilde{S}_{(1)}))-_h\tilde{u}(\tilde{f}(\tilde{S}_{(2)})))$$

The calculated fuzzy utility values of $\tilde{f}_i, i=\overline{1,3}$ are

$$\tilde{U}(\tilde{f}_1)=(419.52;\ 516.2;\ 612.8)\,;\tilde{U}(\tilde{f}_2)=(480.5;\ 583.1;\ 684{,}7)\,;$$

$$\tilde{U}(\tilde{f}_3)=(559.4;\ 647.85;\ 750.65)\,.$$

These fuzzy utility values are shown in Fig. 12.6.

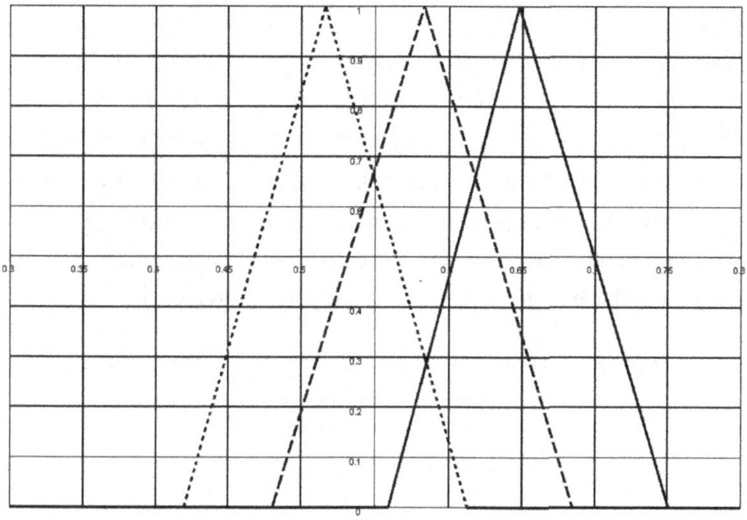

Fig. 12.6. Fuzzy utility values of the manager's possible actions: $\tilde{U}(\tilde{f}_1)$ (dotted), $\tilde{U}(\tilde{f}_2)$ (dashed), $\tilde{U}(\tilde{f}_3)$ (solid)

Using the Fuzzy Jaccard compatibility-based ranking method [368] we got the following results on ranking the alternatives:

$\tilde{U}(\tilde{f}_1)\geq\tilde{U}(\tilde{f}_2)$ is satisfied with the degree 0.377;

$\tilde{U}(\tilde{f}_2)\geq\tilde{U}(\tilde{f}_1)$ is satisfied with the degree 0.651;

$\tilde{U}(\tilde{f}_2)\geq\tilde{U}(\tilde{f}_3)$ is satisfied with the degree 0.3032;

$\tilde{U}(\tilde{f}_3)\geq\tilde{U}(\tilde{f}_2)$ is satisfied with the degree 0.6965.

As can be seen, the best alternative is $\tilde{f}_3$ - "Do nothing".

12.2.2 *Decision making in investment problem with second-order imprecise probabilities* [35,332]

Let us consider a problem of decision making on investment under imperfect information described by the second-order hierarchical uncertainty model [35,332] given in Section 7.2.

Suppose that we have three mutually exclusive and exhaustive states of nature representing three possible states of economy during a year: economic growth (S_1), static economic situation (S_2), and economic recession (S_3). The possible alternatives are the following: to buy bonds (f_1), to buy stocks of enterprise (f_2), to deposit money at a bank (f_3). The result of the each act depends on a state of economy that will actually take place. The utilities described by precise numbers for the each act taken at various states of economy are provided in Table 12.6.

Table 12.6. The utility values of actions under various states

	S_1	S_2	S_3
f_1	8	7	5
f_2	7	4	7
f_3	7	8	5

Let uncertainty about states of nature be described as follows. An expert assigns interval probabilities for S_1 (economic growth) and S_2 (static economic situation) be $P(S_1)=$ [0.3;0.4] and $P(S_2)=$ [0.2;0.4], respectively. As these interval assignments are subjective, an interval probability equal to [0.7; 0.9] is used to measure an imprecise evaluation degree of confidence of the expert's interval probabilities.

Therefore, this problem is characterized by modeling uncertainty with the use of two levels. The first level of uncertainty is represented by interval probabilities of states of nature assigned by an expert. The second level is represented by interval probabilities measuring degrees of confidences of an expert in assignment of interval probabilities to states of nature. In other respects, the decision problem considered here follows the classical framework: we will consider mutually exclusive and exhaustive states of nature and precise outcomes. Despite of this, the considered problem cannot be solved adequately by the existing decision theories because they are incapable to deal with second-order uncertainty model two levels of which are imprecise. For example, smooth ambiguity model and the other models of ambiguity which follow second order uncertainty framework, are developed for precise description of uncertainty at its second level. Therefore, we will apply a hierarchical second-order imprecise probability model suggested in Section 7.2 which is developed for describing imprecision at the both levels of second-order uncertainty.

The problem is to determine an optimal action for investment. Following the methodology introduced in Section 7.2, we have to find interval probability for S_3 (economic recession). For this, by making use of (7.27)-(7.28) we obtain the interval probability [0.2; 0.5]. The information structure for the given decision making problem may be described as:

$$\text{Prob}\{P(S_1) = [0.3; 0.4]\} = [0.7; 0.9],$$

$$\text{Prob}\{P(S_2) = [0.2; 0.4]\} = [0.7; 0.9],$$

$$\text{Prob}\{P(S_3) = [0.2; 0.5]\} = [0.7; 0.9].$$

Given these data and following the decision making method proposed in Section 7.2, we calculate the lower prevision measure. The results are shown in Table 12.7.

Table 12.7. Values of lower prevision η

Events	**Lower prevision** η
$\{S_1\}$	0.31
$\{S_2\}$	0.21
$\{S_3\}$	0.21
$\{S_1, S_2\}$	0.51
$\{S_2, S_3\}$	0.41
$\{S_1, S_3\}$	0.51

Following (7.22) we calculate the values of the utility function defined as the Choquet integral for the each act. The values of the utility function for the corresponding alternatives are as follows:

$$U(f_1) = 6.33, \quad U(f_2) = 6.13, \quad U(f_3) = 6.23$$

we have $f_1 \succ f_3 \succ f_2$.

A process of decision-making cannot be considered completed unless we complete a thorough sensitivity analysis showing optimal decision's (decisions') dependence on possible variations of the parameters of the problem [83].

We have investigated an influence of interval probabilities present at the first and the second levels of the hierarchical imprecise probability model to values of the utility function for each act. The results are reported in Tables 12.8 and 12.9 respectively.

Table 12.8. Values of the utility function for the acts under variation of interval probabilities present at the first level

CASES	f_1		f_3		f_2
$P(S_1)=[0.6;0.7]$ $P(S_2)=[0.1;0.2]$ $P(S_3)=[0.1;0.3]$	$U_1=7.03$	$\succ$	$U_3=6.53$	$\succ$	$U_2=6.13$
$P(S_1)=[0.2;0.3]$ $P(S_2)=[0.3;0.5]$ $P(S_3)=[0.2;0.5]$	$U_1=6.23$	$\prec$	$U_3=6.33$	$\succ$	$U_2=5.23$
$P(S_1)=[0.1;0.2]$ $P(S_2)=[0.8;0.9]$ $P(S_3)=[0.0;0.1]$	$U_1=6.93$	$\prec$	$U_3=7.63$	$\succ$	$U_2=4.33$
$P(S_1)=[0.1;0.3]$ $P(S_2)=[0.5;0.6]$ $P(S_3)=[0.1;0.4]$	$U_1=6.33$	$\prec$	$U_3=6.73$	$\succ$	$U_2=4.63$
$P(S_1)=[0.9;0.95]$ $P(S_2)=[0.0;0.02]$ $P(S_3)=[0.03;0.1]$	$U_1=7.73$	$\succ$	$U_3=6.83$	$\succ$	$U_2=6.73$

Table 12.9. Values of the utility function for the acts under variation of interval probabilities occurring at the second level

CASES	f_1		f_3		f_2
$\Pr=[0.1;0.3]$	$U(f_1)=6.3$	$\prec$	$U(f_3)=6.356$	$\succ$	$U(f_2)=5.5$
$\Pr=[0.2;0.5]$	$U(f_1)=6.3$	$\succ$	$U(f_3)=6.2$	$\succ$	$U(f_2)=5.5$
$\Pr=[0.4;0.6]$	$U(f_1)=6.3$	$\prec$	$U(f_3)=6.81$	$\succ$	$U(f_2)=5.5$
$\Pr=[0.6;0.8]$	$U(f_1)=6.31$	$\succ$	$U(f_3)=6.22$	$\succ$	$U(f_2)=5.51$
$\Pr=[0.9;0.95]$	$U(f_1)=6.36$	$\succ$	$U(f_3)=6.352$	$\succ$	$U(f_2)=5.57$

The plot of relationship between the values of the utility function and the probability interval for S_1 (economic growth) for the first case is shown in Fig.12.7.

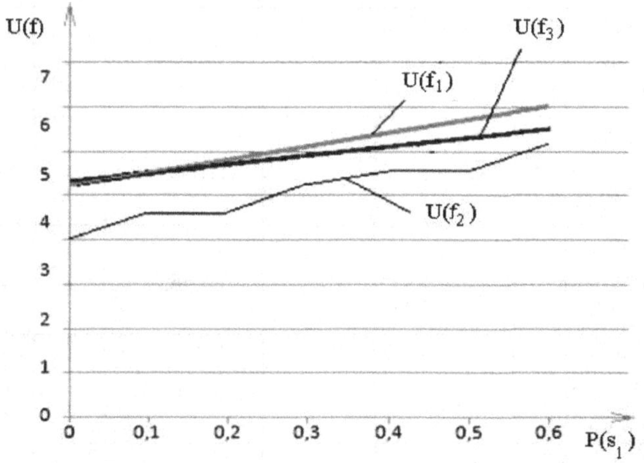

Fig.12.7. Plot of utility function values' dependence on probabilities in case of experiment 1

The values of the utility function subject to variation of interval probabilities given at the first level for the first case are provided in Table 12.10.

Table 12.10. Values of the utility function for different values of interval probabilities presented at the first level

	f_1		f_3		f_2
$P(S_1)=[0.5;0.8]$ $P(S_2)=[0.1;0.2]$ $P(S_3)=[0.0;0.4]$	U_1=6.73	$\succ$	U_3 =6.33	$\succ$	U_2=5.53
$P(S_1)=[0.4;0.7]$ $P(S_2)=[0.1;0.2]$ $P(S_3)=[0.1;0.5]$	U_1=6.43	$\succ$	U_3 =6.13	$\succ$	U_2=5.53
$P(S_1)=[0.3;0.7]$ $P(S_2)=[0.1;0.2]$ $P(S_3)=[0.1;0.6]$	U_1=6.13	$\succ$	U_3 =5.93	$\succ$	U_2=5.23
$P(S_1)=[0.2;0.8]$ $P(S_2)=[0.1;0.2]$ $P(S_3)=[0.0;0.7]$	U_1=5.83	$\succ$	U_3 =5.73	$\succ$	U_2=4.63
$P(S_1)=[0.1;0.7]$ $P(S_2)=[0.1;0.2]$ $P(S_3)=[0.1;0.8]$	U_1=5.53	=	U_3=5.53	$\succ$	U_2=4.63
$P(S_1)=[0.0;0.8]$ $P(S_2)=[0.1;0.3]$ $P(S_3)=[0.0;0.1]$	U_1=5.27	$\prec$	U_3 =5.33	$\succ$	U_2=4.078
$P(S_1)=[0.6;0.7]$ $P(S_2)=[0.0;0.2]$ $P(S_3)=[0.1;0.4]$	U_1=6.83	$\succ$	U_3 =6.27	$\succ$	U_2=6.13
$P(S_1)=[0.6;0.7]$ $P(S_2)=[0.2;0.3]$ $P(S_3)=[0.0;0.2]$	U_1=7.23	$\succ$	U_3 =6.83	$\succ$	U_2 =5.83
$P(S_1)=[0.6;0.7]$ $P(S_2)=[0.3;0.4]$ $P(S_3)=[0.0;0.1]$	U_1 =7.43	$\succ$	U_3 =7.13	$\succ$	U_2 =5.83

The analysis of such plots helps us to gain a detailed insight into the nature of the solutions being produced. For the first case and for any $P(S_1)>[0.1;0.3]$ we have $f_1 \succ f_3, f_3 \succ f_2$. If the value of the interval probability for s_1 satisfies the condition $P(S_1) <[0.1;0.3]$ then $f_1 \prec f_3$, $f_2 \prec f_3$ and for any $P(S_2)<[0.6;0.7]: f_1, f_3 \succ f_2$. Having such plots, for every case we can estimate the values of utility function for every value of probabilities $P(S_1)$ and $P(S_2)$.

It should be noted, that if the groups of events are stochastically dependent then we can overestimate only the total probabilities of events of interest by varying the values of probabilities. Furthermore such analysis can be of interest to deal with more complicated scenarios of decision-making.

The graphical representation of influence of changes of interval probabilities on the values of utility function for acts is given in Figs. 12.8 and 12.9, respectively.

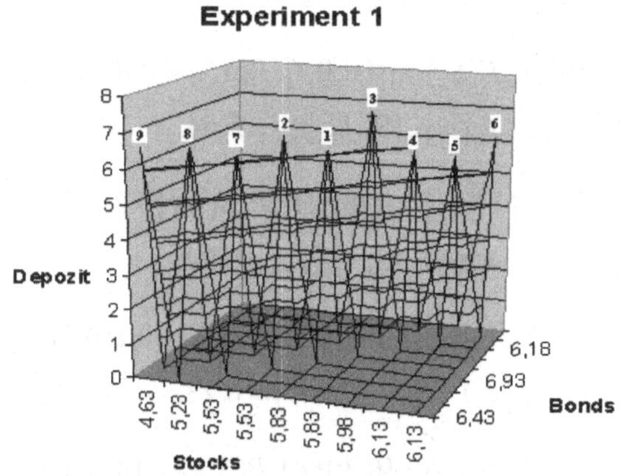

Fig.12.8. The plot of surface of deposit for experiment 1

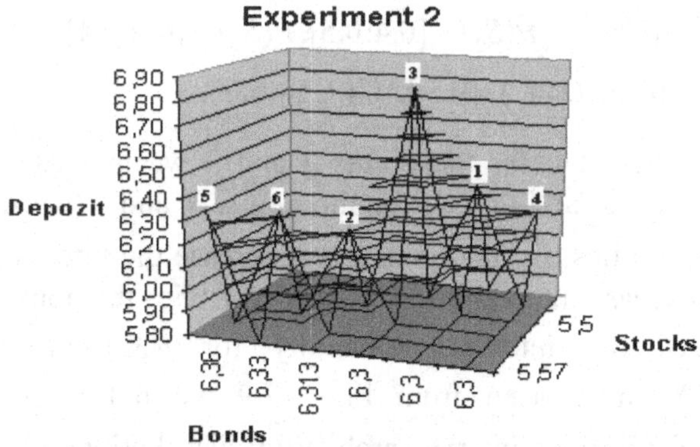

Fig.12.9. The plot of surface of deposit for experiment 2

1- $P(S_1)=[0.4;0.6], P(S_2)=[0.1;0.2], P(S_3)=[0.2;0.5]$
$U(f_1)=6.43,\ U(f_2)=5.83,\ U(f_3)=6.13;$

2- $P(S_1)=[0.5;0.7], P(S_2)=[0.2;0.3], P(S_3)=[0.0;0.3]$
$U(f_1)=6.93,\ U(f_2)=5.53,\ U(f_3)=6.63;$

3- $P(S_1)=[0.6;0.7], P(S_2)=[0.3;0.4], P(S_3)=[0.0;0.1]$
$U(f_1)=7.43,\ U(f_2)=5.83,\ U(f_3)=7.13;$

4- $P(S_1)=[0.35;0.55], P(S_2)=[0.05;0.15], P(S_3)=[0.3;0.6]$
$U(f_1)=6.18,\ U(f_2)=5.98,\ U(f_3)=5.88;$

5- $P(S_1)=[0.3;0.5], P(S_2)=[0.0;0.1], P(S_3)=[0.4;0.7]$
$U(f_1)=5.93,\ U(f_2)=6.13,\ U(f_3)=5.64.$

6- $P(S_1)=[0.5;0.7], P(S_2)=[0.0;0.1], P(S_3)=[0.2;0.5]$
$U(f_1)=6.53,\ U(f_2)=6.13,\ U(f_3)=6.04.$

7- $P(S_1)=[0.3;0.5], P(S_2)=[0.2;0.3], P(S_3)=[0.2;0.5]$
$U(f_1)=6.33,\ U(f_2)=5.53,\ U(f_3)=6.23.$

8- $P(S_1)=[0.3;0.5], P(S_2)=[0.3;0.4], P(S_3)=[0.1;0.4]$
$U(f_1)=6.53,\ U(f_2)=5.23,\ U(f_3)=6.53.$

9- $P(S_1)=[0.2;0.5], P(S_2)=[0.4;0.5], P(S_3)=[0.0;0.4]$
$U(f_1)=6.43,\ U(f_2)=4.63,\ U(f_3)=6.63.$

As it can be seen, for the points 2 and 3 we increase the interval probabilities $P(S_1)$ and $P(S_2)$, for the points 4 and 5 we decrease the interval probabilities, for the point 6 we increase the interval probability $P(S_1)$ and decrease interval probability $P(S_2)$. For the points 7, 8, and 9 we decreased the interval probability for $P(S_1)$ and increased it for $P(S_2)$. As it is seen from Fig. 12.9 we obtain the following preferences for various interval probability distributions encountered at the first level: for all points, except the point 5, 8 and 9, the first alternative is more preferable.

1- $\text{Prob} = [0.9; 0.95]$
$U(f_1) = 6.36,\ U(f_2) = 5.57,\ U(f_3) = 6.352;$

2 - $\text{Prob} = [0.7; 0.9]$
$U(f_1) = 6.33,\ U(f_2) = 5.53,\ U(f_3) = 6.32;$

3- $\text{Prob} = [0.6; 0.8]$
$U(f_1) = 6.31,\ U(f_2) = 5.51,\ U(f_3) = 6.22;$

4 - $\text{Prob} = [0.4; 0.6]$
$U(f_1) = 6.3,\ U(f_2) = 5.5,\ U(f_3) = 6.81;$

5- $\text{Prob} = [0.2; 0.5]$
$U(f_1) = 6.3,\ U(f_2) = 5.5,\ U(f_3) = 6.2;$

6- $\text{Prob} = [0.1; 0.3]$
$U(f_1) = 6.3,\ U(f_2) = 5.5,\ U(f_3) = 6.356;$

Figure 12.9 demonstrates that the changes of interval probabilities at the second level of hierarchical model lead to changes of utilities and sometimes to the changes of preferences. This graphical visualization offers us an ability to assess how an actual economic situation may change the investment decisions.

To analyze robustness of the decisions generated by the introduced method, we have conducted investigations on influence of interval probabilities at the first and second level of imprecise hierarchical probability model on the preferences being produced. We made small changes to interval probabilities at the first and the second level and observed stability of preferences to these changes.

Let us recall that the model is said to be robust if under slight change of the interval probabilities of states S_1, S_2, S_3 the values of the utility function for the acts also slightly change. In this study, we define robustness as the maximum deviation of the values of the utility function being a result of the deviation from the consistent interval probabilities. In the most existing models, the robustness has not been considered in the design process. Therefore, it becomes of a great importance to determine the robustness of the model to the variations of its parameters. The issue we are trying to address in this study is how the model is robust to the perturbations of the training data or operating points. In this sense, the robustness analysis [74,212] is more appealing for practical applications as we always face with uncertainty, noise, and disturbances in the design of a decision model.

To analyze robustness of the suggested approach, we made slight changes to interval probabilities of states S_1, S_2, S_3 and for these changes calculated the values of the utility function.

Let the interval assessments for states "Growth", "Static economic situation" be equal to:

1) [0.6; 0.7], [0.1; 0.2]; 2)[0.1; 0.3], [0.5; 0.6];

3) [0.9; 0.95],[0.0; 0.02].

Then the preferences are shown in Table 12.11 (see the results of experiment 1).

Table 12.11. Initial Preferences

CASES	f_1		f_3		f_2
$P(S_1)=[0.6;0.7]$ $P(S_2)=[0.1;0.2]$ $P(S_3)=[0.1;0.3]$	$U(f_1)$=7.03	$\succ$	$U(f_3)$=6.53	$\succ$	$U(f_2)$=6.13
$P(S_1)=[0.1;0.3]$ $P(S_2)=[0.5;0.6]$ $P(S_3)=[0.1;0.4]$	$U(f_1)$=6.33	$\prec$	$U(f_3)$=6.73	$\succ$	$U(f_2)$=4.63
$P(S_1)=[0.9;0.95]$ $P(S_2)=[0.0;0.02]$ $P(S_3)=[0.03;0.1]$	$U(f_1)$=7.73	$\succ$	$U(f_3)$=6.83	$\succ$	$U(f_2)$=6.73

We slightly change these interval assessments. Let the interval assessments for events "Growth", "Static economic situation" be equal to:

1)[0.59; 0.69], [0.09; 0.19]; 2)[0.09; 0.29], [0.49; 0.59];
3)[0.89; 0.94], [0;0.01].

The results are summarized in Table 12.12 and 12.13.

Table 12.12. Robustness analysis: the change of $P(S_1)$

CASES	f_1		f_3		f_2
$P(S_1)=[0.59;0.69]$ $P(S_2)=[0.09;0.19]$ $P(S_3)=[0.12;0.32]$	$U(f_1)$=6.98	$\succ$	$U(f_3)$=6.48	$\succ$	$U(f_2)$=5.86
$P(S_1)=[0.89;0.94]$ $P(S_2)=[0.0;0.01]$ $P(S_3)=[0.05;0.11]$	$U(f_1)$=7.7	$\succ$	$U(f_3)$=6.85	$\succ$	$U(f_2)$=6.826

Table 12.13. Robustness analysis: the change of $P(S_2)$

CASE	f_1		f_3		f_2
$P(S_1)=[0.09;0.29]$ $P(S_2)=[0.49;0.59]$ $P(S_3)=[0.12;0.42]$	$U(f_1)$=6.28	$\prec$	$U(f_3)$=6.68	$\succ$	$U(f_2)$=4.66

To better investigate robustness of the considered model we will consider change of a preference degree among alternatives under change of interval probabilities. For simplicity we describe the preference degree of alternative f_i to alternative f_j as the ratio of their corresponding utilities $U(f_i)$ and $U(f_j)$: $U(f_i)/U(f_j)$.

Let us consider the changes of preference degrees for each alternative (Table 12.14).

As we can see from Tables 12.11-12.14 the preferences remain stable.

Table 12.14. Preference degrees - robustness analysis

	CASES	f_1	f_3	f_2
1	$P(S_1)=[0.6;0.7]$ $P(S_2)=[0.1;0.2]$ $P(S_3)=[0.1;0.3]$	1.14	0.93	0.92
	$P(S_1)=[0.59;0.69]$ $P(S_2)=[0.09;0.19]$ $P(S_3)=[0.12;0.32]$	1.19	0.9	0.92
2	$P(S_1)=[0.1;0.3]$ $P(S_2)=[0.5;0.6]$ $P(S_3)=[0.1;0.4]$	1.36	0.68	1.06
	$P(S_1)=[0.09;0.29]$ $P(S_2)=[0.49;0.59]$ $P(S_3)=[0.12;0.42]$	1.34	0.68	1.06
3	$P(S_1)=[0.9;0.95]$ $P(S_2)=[0.0;0.02]$ $P(S_3)=[0.03;0.1]$	1.14	0.99	0.88
	$P(S_1)=[0.89;0.94]$ $P(S_2)=[0.0;0.01]$ $P(S_3)=[0.05;0.11]$	1.12	1.00	0.88

12.2.3 *Behavioral decision making in investment problem with fuzzy imperfect information [32]*

In Section 12.1.2 we conducted behavioral decision analysis in Bingo game by taking into account risk attitudes of a DM. In this section we will consider behavioral decision making conditioned by risk attitudes in an investment problem described below [8,32].

An economic agent considers the following alternatives to make a decision for short-term investment of up to 1 year: common bonds, stocks of enterprise, time deposit. Suppose that the agent evaluates each alternative under the following states of economy that may take place during a year: strong growth, moderate growth, stable economy, recession. Having examined the relationships between the yields on the alternative investments and the states of economy on the base of the past experience, the economic agent notes the following trends:

the first action will yield high income if there is strong growth in economy, medium income – if there is moderate growth in economy, less than medium income under stable economy and small income if recession occurs;
the second action will yield very high income if there is strong growth in economy, medium income if there is moderate growth in economy, small income under stable economy and a notable loss if recession occurs;
the third action will yield approximately the same medium income in all the considered states of economy.

It is also supposed that strong growth will take place with a medium probability, moderate growth will take place with a less than medium probability, stable economy – with a small probability and recession – with a very small probability.

What option to choose?

Let us solve this problem following the approach suggested in Chapter 9 (Section 9.2) by taking into account risk issues. In contrast to analysis in Section 12.1.2 we consider DM's states as fuzzy sets to describe impreciseness of concepts of "risk seeking", "risk averse" and "risk neutrality" as these are qualitative and are matter of a degree.

Let us name the three possible actions (alternatives) as $\tilde{f}_1$ (common bonds), $\tilde{f}_2$ (stocks of enterprise), $\tilde{f}_3$ (time deposit). We denote the states of the world (the economy) as follows: $\tilde{S}_1$ ("strong growth"), $\tilde{S}_2$ ("moderate growth"), $\tilde{S}_3$ ("stable"), $\tilde{S}_4$ ("recession") (Fig. 12.10).

The fuzzy probabilities of states of nature $-\tilde{P}_1$ ("medium", given), $\tilde{P}_2$ ("less than medium", given), $\tilde{P}_3$ ("small", given), $\tilde{P}_4$ ("very small", calculated on base of $\tilde{P}_1, \tilde{P}_2, \tilde{P}_3$) are shown in Fig. 12.11.

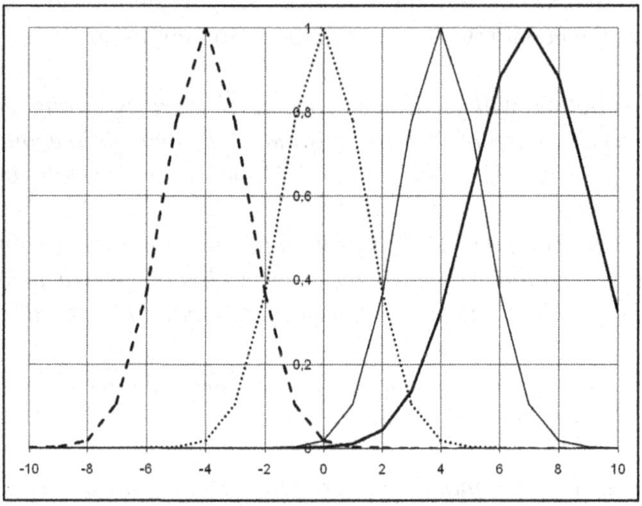

Fig. 12.10. Fuzzy states of economy: $\tilde{S}_1$ (thick line), $\tilde{S}_2$ (thin line), $\tilde{S}_3$ (dotted line), $\tilde{S}_4$ (dashed line)

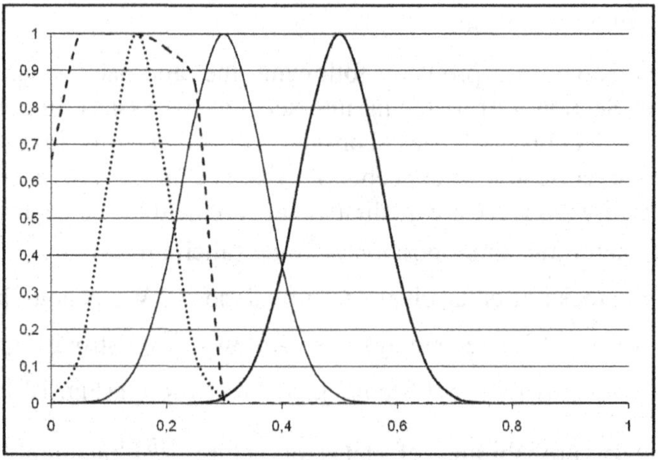

Fig. 12.11. Fuzzy probabilities $\tilde{P}_1$ (thick line), $\tilde{P}_2$ (thin line), $\tilde{P}_3$ (dotted), $\tilde{P}_4$ (dashed).

Let us denote the considered three fuzzy states of a DM as follows: $\tilde{h}_1$ – risk aversion, $\tilde{h}_2$ – risk neutrality, and $\tilde{h}_3$ – risk seeking. Fuzziness of these states reflects impreciseness of the information on the each of the risk attitudes levels. The fuzzy states $\tilde{h}_1$, $\tilde{h}_2$, $\tilde{h}_3$ are given in the Fig.12.12:

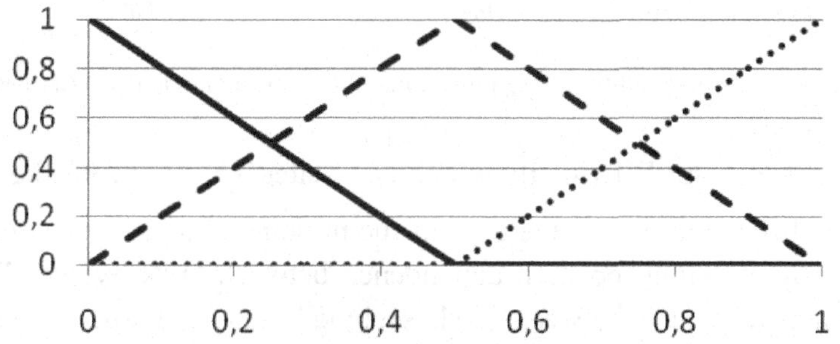

Fig. 12.12. Fuzzy states of a DM: $\tilde{h}_1$ (solid), $\tilde{h}_2$ (dashed), $\tilde{h}_3$ (dotted)

Further, in accordance with Section 9.2.4, we need to assign fuzzy utilities over combined states space Ω. We obtain fuzzy utilities $\tilde{u}(\tilde{f}(\tilde{S}_i, \tilde{h}_j))$ on the base of Zadeh's extension principle and the ideas used in Prospect theory.

The next step in solving the considered problem is to determine FJPs for the combined states from fuzzy marginal probabilities over the states of nature and the DM's states. As the majority of people are risk averse, we consider a DM with $\tilde{h}_1$ (risk aversion) as the most probable state. Let the fuzzy probabilities of fuzzy states $\tilde{h}_1$, $\tilde{h}_2$, $\tilde{h}_3$ be defined as follows: $\tilde{P}(\tilde{h}_1)$ ("high" – given), $\tilde{P}(\tilde{h}_2)$ ("small" – given), $\tilde{P}(\tilde{h}_3)$ ("very small" – computed) – see Fig.12.13:

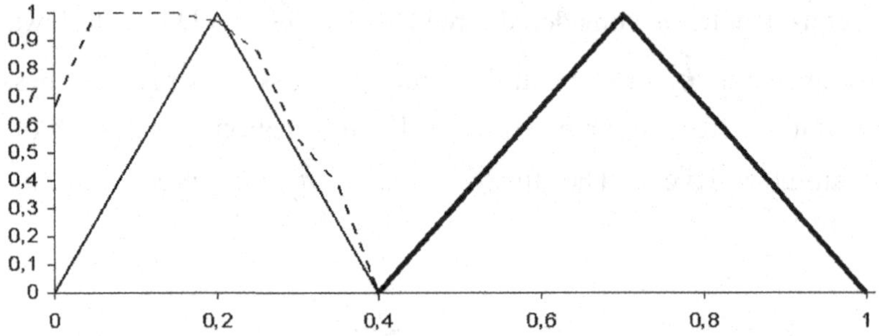

Fig. 12.13. Fuzzy probabilities: $\tilde{P}(\tilde{h}_1)$ (thick line), $\tilde{P}(\tilde{h}_2)$ (thin line), $\tilde{P}(\tilde{h}_3)$ (dashed line)

We determine FJPs of the combined states $(\tilde{S}_i, \tilde{h}_j)$ from the fuzzy marginal probabilities on the base of the notions of dependence between events by assuming positive dependence between "risk aversion" state and gains and also between "risk seeking" state and losses, negative dependence – between "risk aversion" state and losses and also between "risk seeking" state and gains, and independence between "risk neutrality" and both gains and losses. For example, the FJPs of combined states for the case of $\tilde{f}_1$ action (common bonds) are described by the following trapezoidal fuzzy numbers:

$$\tilde{P}(\tilde{S}_1,\tilde{h}_1)=(0.12,0.35,0.5,0.7), \tilde{P}(\tilde{S}_2,\tilde{h}_1)=(0.04,0.21,0.3,0.5),$$
$$\tilde{P}(\tilde{S}_3,\tilde{h}_1)=(0,0.105,0.15,0.3), \tilde{P}(\tilde{S}_4,\tilde{h}_1)=(0,0.035,0.15,0.3);$$

$$\tilde{P}(\tilde{S}_1,\tilde{h}_2)=(0,0.1,0.1,0.28), \tilde{P}(\tilde{S}_2,\tilde{h}_2)=(0,0.06,0.06,0.2),$$
$$\tilde{P}(\tilde{S}_3,\tilde{h}_2)=(0,0.03,0.03,0.12), \tilde{P}(\tilde{S}_4,\tilde{h}_2)=(0,0.01,0.03,0.12);$$

$$\tilde{P}(\tilde{S}_1,\tilde{h}_3)=(0,0,0.05,0.28), \tilde{P}(\tilde{S}_2,\tilde{h}_3)=(0,0,0.03,0.2),$$
$$\tilde{P}(\tilde{S}_3,\tilde{h}_3)=(0,0,0.015,0.12), \tilde{P}(\tilde{S}_4,\tilde{h}_3)=(0,0,0.015,0.12).$$

Given these FJPs, in accordance with Chapter 9, we need to determine fuzzy-valued bi-capacity $\tilde{\eta}_{\tilde{P}^l}(\cdot,\cdot)$ over subsets of the combined states space to be used in determination of the fuzzy overall utility for each alternative. The fuzzy overall utility $\tilde{U}(\tilde{f}_1)$ is expressed as follows [32]:

$$\tilde{U}(\tilde{f}_1)=(\left|\tilde{u}(\tilde{f}_1(\tilde{S}_1,\tilde{h}_1))\right|-_h\left|\tilde{u}(\tilde{f}_1(\tilde{S}_1,\tilde{h}_2))\right|)\tilde{\eta}_{\tilde{P}^l}(\{(\tilde{S}_1,\tilde{h}_1)\},\varnothing)+$$

$$(\left|\tilde{u}(\tilde{f}_1(\tilde{S}_1,\tilde{h}_2))\right|-_h\left|\tilde{u}(\tilde{f}_1(\tilde{S}_1,\tilde{h}_3))\right|)\tilde{\eta}_{\tilde{P}^l}(\{(\tilde{S}_1,\tilde{h}_1),(\tilde{S}_1,\tilde{h}_2)\},\varnothing)$$

$$(\left|\tilde{u}(\tilde{f}_1(\tilde{S}_1,\tilde{h}_3))\right|-_h\left|\tilde{u}(\tilde{f}_1(\tilde{S}_2,\tilde{h}_1))\right|)\tilde{\eta}_{\tilde{P}^l}(\{(\tilde{S}_1,\tilde{h}_1),(\tilde{S}_1,\tilde{h}_2),(\tilde{S}_1,\tilde{h}_3)\},\varnothing)+$$

$$+(\left|\tilde{u}(\tilde{f}_1(\tilde{S}_2,\tilde{h}_1))\right|-_h\left|\tilde{u}(\tilde{f}_1(\tilde{S}_2,\tilde{h}_2))\right|)\tilde{\eta}_{\tilde{P}^l}(\{(\tilde{S}_1,\tilde{h}_1),(\tilde{S}_1,\tilde{h}_2),(\tilde{S}_1,\tilde{h}_3),(\tilde{S}_2,\tilde{h}_1)\},\varnothing\})+$$

$$+(\left|\tilde{u}(\tilde{f}_1(\tilde{S}_2,\tilde{h}_2))\right|-_h\left|\tilde{u}(\tilde{f}_1(\tilde{S}_2,\tilde{h}_3))\right|)\times$$

$$\times\tilde{\eta}_{\tilde{P}^l}(\{(\tilde{S}_1,\tilde{h}_1),(\tilde{S}_1,\tilde{h}_2),(\tilde{S}_1,\tilde{h}_3),(\tilde{S}_2,\tilde{h}_1),(\tilde{S}_2,\tilde{h}_2)\},\varnothing)+$$

$$+(\left|\tilde{u}(\tilde{f}_1(\tilde{S}_2,\tilde{h}_3))\right|-_h\left|\tilde{u}(\tilde{f}_1(\tilde{S}_3,\tilde{h}_1))\right|)\times$$

$$\times\tilde{\eta}_{\tilde{P}^l}(\{(\tilde{S}_1,\tilde{h}_1),(\tilde{S}_1,\tilde{h}_2),(\tilde{S}_1,\tilde{h}_3),(\tilde{S}_2,\tilde{h}_1),(\tilde{S}_2,\tilde{h}_2),(\tilde{S}_2,\tilde{h}_3)\},\varnothing)+$$

$$(\left|\tilde{u}(\tilde{f}_1(\tilde{S}_3,\tilde{h}_1))\right|-_h\left|\tilde{u}(\tilde{f}_1(\tilde{S}_3,\tilde{h}_2))\right|)\tilde{\eta}_{\tilde{P}^l}(\{(\tilde{S}_1,\tilde{h}_1),(\tilde{S}_1,\tilde{h}_2),(\tilde{S}_1,\tilde{h}_3),(\tilde{S}_2,\tilde{h}_1),(\tilde{S}_2,\tilde{h}_2),(\tilde{S}_2,\tilde{h}_3),(\tilde{S}_3,\tilde{h}_1)\},\varnothing)$$

$$+(\left|\tilde{u}(\tilde{f}_1(\tilde{S}_3,\tilde{h}_2))\right|-_h\left|\tilde{u}(\tilde{f}_1(\tilde{S}_3,\tilde{h}_3))\right|)\tilde{\eta}_{\tilde{P}^l}(\{(\tilde{S}_1,\tilde{h}_1),(\tilde{S}_1,\tilde{h}_2),(\tilde{S}_1,\tilde{h}_3),(\tilde{S}_2,\tilde{h}_1),(\tilde{S}_2,\tilde{h}_2),(\tilde{S}_2,\tilde{h}_3),(\tilde{S}_3,\tilde{h}_1),(\tilde{S}_3,\tilde{h}_2)\},\varnothing)$$

$$(\left|\tilde{u}(\tilde{f}_1(\tilde{S}_3,\tilde{h}_1))\right|-_h\left|\tilde{u}(\tilde{f}_1(\tilde{S}_3,\tilde{h}_2))\right|)\tilde{\eta}_{\tilde{P}^l}(\{(\tilde{S}_1,\tilde{h}_1),(\tilde{S}_1,\tilde{h}_2),(\tilde{S}_1,\tilde{h}_3),(\tilde{S}_2,\tilde{h}_1),(\tilde{S}_2,\tilde{h}_2),(\tilde{S}_2,\tilde{h}_3),(\tilde{S}_3,\tilde{h}_1)\},\varnothing)$$

$$+(\left|\tilde{u}(\tilde{f}_1(\tilde{S}_3,\tilde{h}_2))\right|-_h\left|\tilde{u}(\tilde{f}_1(\tilde{S}_3,\tilde{h}_3))\right|)\tilde{\eta}_{\tilde{P}^l}(\{(\tilde{S}_1,\tilde{h}_1),(\tilde{S}_1,\tilde{h}_2),(\tilde{S}_1,\tilde{h}_3),(\tilde{S}_2,\tilde{h}_1),(\tilde{S}_2,\tilde{h}_2),(\tilde{S}_2,\tilde{h}_3),(\tilde{S}_3,\tilde{h}_1),(\tilde{S}_3,\tilde{h}_2)\},\varnothing)$$

$$+(\left|\tilde{u}(\tilde{f}_1(\tilde{S}_3,\tilde{h}_3))\right|-_h\left|\tilde{u}(\tilde{f}_1(\tilde{S}_4,\tilde{h}_1))\right|)\tilde{\eta}_{\tilde{P}^l}(\{(\tilde{S}_1,\tilde{h}_1),(\tilde{S}_1,\tilde{h}_2),(\tilde{S}_1,\tilde{h}_3),(\tilde{S}_2,\tilde{h}_1),(\tilde{S}_2,\tilde{h}_2),(\tilde{S}_2,\tilde{h}_3),(\tilde{S}_3,\tilde{h}_1),(\tilde{S}_3,\tilde{h}_2),(\tilde{S}_3,\tilde{h}_3)\},\varnothing)$$

$$+(\left|\tilde{u}(\tilde{f}_1(\tilde{S}_4,\tilde{h}_1))\right|-_h\left|\tilde{u}(\tilde{f}_1(\tilde{S}_4,\tilde{h}_2))\right|\tilde{\eta}_{\tilde{P}^l}(\{(\tilde{S}_1,\tilde{h}_1),(\tilde{S}_1,\tilde{h}_2),(\tilde{S}_1,\tilde{h}_3),(\tilde{S}_2,\tilde{h}_1),(\tilde{S}_2,\tilde{h}_2),(\tilde{S}_2,\tilde{h}_3),(\tilde{S}_3,\tilde{h}_1),(\tilde{S}_3,\tilde{h}_2),(\tilde{S}_3,\tilde{h}_3),(\tilde{S}_4,\tilde{h}_1)\},\varnothing)$$

$$=(\left|\tilde{u}(\tilde{f}_1(\tilde{S}_4,\tilde{h}_2))\right|-_h\left|\tilde{u}(\tilde{f}_1(\tilde{S}_4,\tilde{h}_3))\right|\tilde{\eta}_{\tilde{P}^l}(\{(\tilde{S}_1,\tilde{h}_1),(\tilde{S}_1,\tilde{h}_2),(\tilde{S}_1,\tilde{h}_3),(\tilde{S}_2,\tilde{h}_1),(\tilde{S}_2,\tilde{h}_2),(\tilde{S}_2,\tilde{h}_3),(\tilde{S}_3,\tilde{h}_1),(\tilde{S}_3,\tilde{h}_2),(\tilde{S}_3,\tilde{h}_3),(\tilde{S}_4,\tilde{h}_1),(\tilde{S}_4,\tilde{h}_2)\},\varnothing)$$

$$=\left|\tilde{u}(\tilde{f}_1(\tilde{S}_4,\tilde{h}_3))\right|\tilde{\eta}_{\tilde{P}^l}(\{(\tilde{S}_1,\tilde{h}_1),(\tilde{S}_1,\tilde{h}_2),(\tilde{S}_1,\tilde{h}_3),(\tilde{S}_2,\tilde{h}_1),(\tilde{S}_2,\tilde{h}_2),(\tilde{S}_2,\tilde{h}_3),(\tilde{S}_3,\tilde{h}_1),(\tilde{S}_3,\tilde{h}_2),(\tilde{S}_3,\tilde{h}_3),(\tilde{S}_4,\tilde{h}_1),(\tilde{S}_4,\tilde{h}_2),(\tilde{S}_4,\tilde{h}_3)\},\varnothing)$$

$$=(\left|\tilde{u}(\tilde{f}_1(\tilde{S}_1,\tilde{h}_3))\right|-_h\left|\tilde{u}(\tilde{f}_1(\tilde{S}_2,\tilde{h}_1))\right|)\tilde{\eta}_{\tilde{P}^l}(\{(\tilde{S}_1,\tilde{h}_1),(\tilde{S}_1,\tilde{h}_2),(\tilde{S}_1,\tilde{h}_3)\},\varnothing)$$

$$+(\left|\tilde{u}(\tilde{f}_1(\tilde{S}_2,\tilde{h}_3))\right|-_h\left|\tilde{u}(\tilde{f}_1(\tilde{S}_3,\tilde{h}_1))\right|)\tilde{\eta}_{\tilde{P}^l}(\{(\tilde{S}_1,\tilde{h}_1),(\tilde{S}_1,\tilde{h}_2),(\tilde{S}_1,\tilde{h}_3),(\tilde{S}_2,\tilde{h}_1),(\tilde{S}_2,\tilde{h}_2),(\tilde{S}_2,\tilde{h}_3)\},\varnothing)$$

$$+(\left|\tilde{u}(\tilde{f}_1(\tilde{S}_3,\tilde{h}_3))\right|-_h\left|\tilde{u}(\tilde{f}_1(\tilde{S}_4,\tilde{h}_1))\right|)\tilde{\eta}_{\tilde{P}^l}(\{(\tilde{S}_1,\tilde{h}_1),(\tilde{S}_1,\tilde{h}_2),(\tilde{S}_1,\tilde{h}_3),(\tilde{S}_2,\tilde{h}_1),(\tilde{S}_2,\tilde{h}_2),(\tilde{S}_2,\tilde{h}_3),(\tilde{S}_3,\tilde{h}_1),(\tilde{S}_3,\tilde{h}_2),(\tilde{S}_3,\tilde{h}_3)\},\varnothing)$$

$$+\left|\tilde{u}(\tilde{f}_1(\tilde{S}_4,\tilde{h}_3))\right|\tilde{\eta}_{\tilde{P}^l}(\{(\tilde{S}_1,\tilde{h}_1),(\tilde{S}_1,\tilde{h}_2),(\tilde{S}_1,\tilde{h}_3),(\tilde{S}_2,\tilde{h}_1),(\tilde{S}_2,\tilde{h}_2),(\tilde{S}_2,\tilde{h}_3),(\tilde{S}_3,\tilde{h}_1),(\tilde{S}_3,\tilde{h}_2),(\tilde{S}_3,\tilde{h}_3),(\tilde{S}_4,\tilde{h}_1),(\tilde{S}_4,\tilde{h}_2),(\tilde{S}_4,\tilde{h}_3)\},\varnothing)$$

We will determine the fuzzy-valued bi-capacity $\tilde{\eta}_{\tilde{P}^l}(\cdot,\cdot)$ as $\tilde{\eta}_{\tilde{P}^l}(\mathcal{V},\mathcal{W}) = \tilde{\eta}_{\tilde{P}^l}(\mathcal{V}) - \tilde{\eta}_{\tilde{P}^l}(\mathcal{W}),\ \mathcal{V},\mathcal{W} \in \Omega$, where $\tilde{\eta}_{\tilde{P}^l}$ is the fuzzy-valued lower probability constructed from the FJPs (as it was done in the previous example). The calculated fuzzy overall utilities $\tilde{U}(\tilde{f}_1),\ \tilde{U}(\tilde{f}_2),\ \tilde{U}(\tilde{f}_3)$ approximated by TFNs are given in the Fig.12.14:

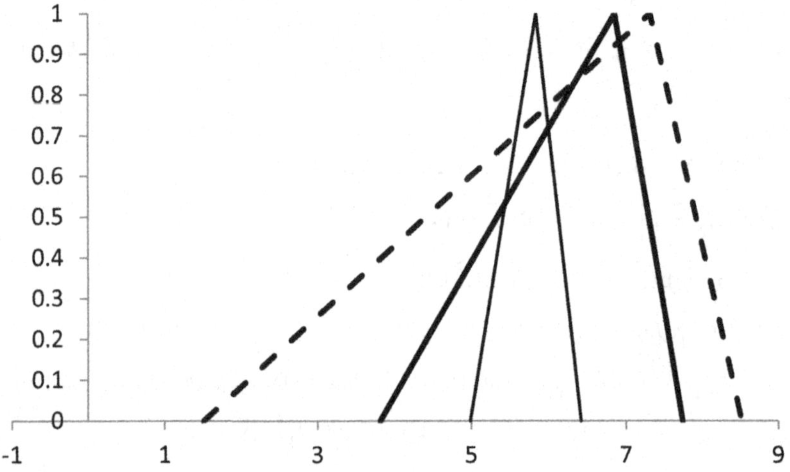

Fig. 12.14. Fuzzy overall utilities: $\tilde{U}(\tilde{f}_1)$ (thick line) $\tilde{U}(\tilde{f}_2)$ (thin line), $\tilde{U}(\tilde{f}_3)$ (dashed line).

Conducting pairwise comparison by using formula (9.2) (see Chapter 9), we got the following results [32]:

$$Deg(\tilde{f}_1 \succsim_l \tilde{f}_2) = 0.038;$$

$$Deg(\tilde{f}_2 \succsim_l \tilde{f}_1) = 0.0247;$$

$$Deg(\tilde{f}_1 \succsim_l \tilde{f}_3) = 0.026;$$

$$Deg(\tilde{f}_3 \succ_l \tilde{f}_1) = 0.01;$$

$$Deg(\tilde{f}_2 \succ_l \tilde{f}_3) = 0.035;$$

$$Deg(\tilde{f}_3 \succ_l \tilde{f}_2) = 0.027.$$

So, as $Deg(\tilde{f}_1 \succ_l \tilde{f}_i) > Deg(\tilde{f}_i \succ_l \tilde{f}_1),\ i = 2,3$, then the best solution is $\tilde{f}_1$.

12.2.4 *The supplier selection problem [33]*

Consider a problem of decision making with imperfect information as a problem of a supplier selection [33,394] by taking into account possible economic conditions.

The set of alternatives is represented by a set of five suppliers: $\mathcal{A}=\{\tilde{f}_1,\tilde{f}_2,\tilde{f}_3,\tilde{f}_4,\tilde{f}_5\}$. The set of states of nature is represented by five possible economic conditions: $\mathcal{S}=\{S_1,S_2,S_3,S_4,S_5\}$. Each economic condition S_j is characterized by requirements to profitability, relationship closeness, technological capability, conformance quality and conflict resolution aspects of a supplier. For simplicity, states of nature are considered in classical sense. Payoff table containing TFN-based evaluations of outcomes of the alternatives under the economic conditions is given below (Table 12.15):

Table 12.15. Payoff table with fuzzy outcomes

	S_1	S_2	S_3	S_4	S_5
$\tilde{f}_1$	(5.0,7.0,9.0)	(7.0,9.0,10.0)	(3.0,5.0,7.0)	(9.0,10.0,10.0)	(5.0,7.0,9.0)
$\tilde{f}_2$	(1.0,3.0,5.0)	(3.0,5.0,7.0)	(5.0,7.0,9.0)	(7.0,9.0,10.0)	(1.0,3.0,5.0)
$\tilde{f}_3$	(3.0,5.0,7.0)	(5.0,7.0,9.0)	(7.0,9.0,10.0)	(5.0,7.0,9.0)	(3.0,5.0,7.0)
$\tilde{f}_4$	(0.0,1.0,3.0)	(1.0,3.0,5.0)	(0.0,1.0,3.0)	(1.0,3.0,5.0)	(7.0,9.0,10.0)
$\tilde{f}_5$	(7.0,9.0,10.0)	(0.0,1.0,3.0)	(1.0,3.0,5.0)	(3.0,5.0,7.0)	(0.0,1.0,3.0)

Let linguistic information on probabilities of the economic conditions be described as follows:

$$\tilde{P}^l=(0.2,\ 0.3,\ 0.4)/S_1+(0.1,\ 0.2,\ 0.3)/S_2+(0.0,\ 0.1,\ 0.2)/S_3$$
$$+(0.3,\ 0.3,\ 0.5)/S_4+(0.0,\ 0.1,\ 0.4)/S_5.$$

This problem can be solved by the fuzzy logic-based decision theory suggested in Chapter 6. However, application of this theory in this case, as compared to the cases in Sections 12.1.1, 12.2.1, will lead to an increased complexity and time consuming computations of a fuzzy number valued fuzzy measure due to a large number of states of nature – 5 states of nature. In this respect, it is more convenient to apply fuzzy optimality-based approach to decision making under imperfect information without a utility function which is suggested in [33] and presented in Chapter 8. Application of this approach to the considered problem will provide valid results at a notably less complex and time consuming computations.

By applying fuzzy optimality concept-based approach, the considered problem can be solved as follows. At first, according to (8.11), (8.12), (8.13), we calculated nbF, neF, nwF [33]:

$$nbF = \begin{bmatrix} 0 & 0.28667 & 0.21 & 0.55667 & 0.42667 \\ 0.02 & 0 & 0.056667 & 0.35667 & 0.28 \\ 0.033333 & 0.14667 & 0 & 0.41333 & 0.31 \\ 0.02 & 0.086667 & 0.053333 & 0 & 0.15667 \\ 0.046667 & 0.16667 & 0.10667 & 0.31333 & 0 \end{bmatrix},$$

$$neF = \begin{bmatrix} 5 & 4.6933 & 4.7567 & 4.4233 & 4.5267 \\ 4.6933 & 5 & 4.7967 & 4.5567 & 4.5533 \\ 4.7567 & 4.7967 & 5 & 4.5333 & 4.5833 \\ 4.4233 & 4.5567 & 4.5333 & 5 & 4.53 \\ 4.5267 & 4.5533 & 4.5833 & 4.53 & 5 \end{bmatrix},$$

$$nwF = \begin{bmatrix} 0 & 0.02 & 0.033333 & 0.02 & 0.046667 \\ 0.28667 & 0 & 0.14667 & 0.086667 & 0.16667 \\ 0.21 & 0.056667 & 0 & 0.053333 & 0.10667 \\ 0.55667 & 0.35667 & 0.41333 & 0 & 0.31333 \\ 0.42667 & 0.28 & 0.31 & 0.15667 & 0 \end{bmatrix}.$$

Next we calculated $\mu_{\tilde{D}}$ and $d(\tilde{f}_i, \tilde{f}_k)$ (see formulas (8.8),(8.6)):

$$\mu_{\tilde{D}} = \begin{bmatrix} 0.5 & 0.47333 & 0.48233 & 0.44633 & 0.462 \\ 0.52667 & 0.5 & 0.509 & 0.473 & 0.48867 \\ 0.51767 & 0.491 & 0.5 & 0.464 & 0.47967 \\ 0.55367 & 0.527 & 0.536 & 0.5 & 0.51567 \\ 0.538 & 0.51133 & 0.52033 & 0.48433 & 0.5 \end{bmatrix},$$

$$d(\tilde{f}_i, \tilde{f}_k) = \begin{bmatrix} 0 & 0.93023 & 0.84127 & 0.96407 & 0.89062 \\ 0 & 0 & 0 & 0.75701 & 0.40476 \\ 0 & 0.61364 & 0 & 0.87097 & 0.65591 \\ 0 & 0 & 0 & 0 & 0 \\ 0 & 0 & 0 & 0.5 & 0 \end{bmatrix}.$$

Finally we calculated degree of optimality for each of the considered alternatives (see formula(8.7)):

$$do = \begin{bmatrix} 1 \\ 0.069767 \\ 0.15873 \\ 0.035928 \\ 0.10938 \end{bmatrix}.$$

So, the preferences obtained are: $\tilde{f}_1 \succsim \tilde{f}_3 \succsim \tilde{f}_5 \succsim \tilde{f}_2 \succsim \tilde{f}_4$. The degrees of preferences are the following[33]:

$$Deg(\tilde{f}_1 \succsim_l \tilde{f}_3) = 0.84,$$

$$Deg(\tilde{f}_3 \succsim_l \tilde{f}_5) = 0.05,$$

$$Deg(\tilde{f}_5 \succsim_l \tilde{f}_2) = 0.04,$$

$$Deg(\tilde{f}_2 \succsim_l \tilde{f}_4) = 0.034.$$

We have also solved this problem by applying the method suggested in [394].

The preference obtained by this method is: $\tilde{f}_1 \succsim \tilde{f}_3 \succsim \tilde{f}_2 \succsim \tilde{f}_5 \succsim \tilde{f}_4$. This is almost the same ordering as that obtained by the method suggested in this paper. However, the suggested method, as compared to the method in [394] has several advantages. The first is that our method not only determines ordering among alternatives, but also determines to what degree the considered alternative is optimal. This degree is an overall extent to which the considered alternative is better than all the other. The second when one has alternatives which are equivalent according to the method in [394], by using our approach it is possible to differentiate them into more and less optimal ones by determining the corresponding value of k_F. Given these two advantages, the method suggested in Chapter 8 is of almost the same computational complexity as the method in [394].

12.2.5 *Business behavioral decision under Z-information*

In Section 12.2.3 we considered decision making in investment problem under fuzzy information. In this section we consider application of a general theory of decisions suggested in Chapter 11 to solving of a more general problem which is characterized by Z-valued decision information and vector-valued states of nature and DM. The problem is described below.

An economic agent considers a problem of decision making on choosing one of the three alternatives for a short-term investment of up to 1 year: common bonds, stocks of enterprise, fixed-term deposit. These alternatives are evaluated under the three assumed economic conditions characterized by various values of GDP level and inflation rate: high GDP and low inflation rate, medium GDP and medium inflation rate, low GDP and high inflation rate. Having examined the relationships between the yields on the alternative investments and the economic conditions on the base of the past experience, the economic agent *is very sure* that the following trends will take place:

the first action will yield high income under the first economic condition, medium income under the second economic condition, less than medium income under the third economic condition;

the second action will yield very high income in the first economic condition, medium income in the second economic condition, small income in the third economic condition;

the third action will yield approximately the same medium income in all the considered states of economy.

At the same time, an economic agent is *sure* that the likelihoods of the assumed values of the considered economic indicators are as follows:

probability of high GDP is higher than medium, probability of medium GDP is about thirty percent, probability of low GDP is the smallest;

probability of low inflation rate is about seventy percent, probability of medium inflation rate is about twenty percent, probability of high inflation rate is the smallest.

Let us suppose that in the considered problem a DM will always think about uncertainty of future and various risks related to investment problems. In other words, the choice of an economic agent (DM) will depend on his risk and ambiguity attitudes. Consequently, we will consider a DM's state as vector of two behavioral determinants: risk attitude and ambiguity attitude. Further, we will consider that the following states of the DM (subjective conditions) may take place: risk and ambiguity aversion, risk aversion and ambiguity seeking, risk seeking and ambiguity aversion, risk and ambiguity seeking. The DM is sure that the likelihoods of the assumed intensities of the considered behavioral determinants are as follows::

probability of risk aversion is about sixty to seventy percent and probability of ambiguity aversion is about sixty percent.

What option for investment to choose?

Formal description of the problem. The considered problem is formally described as follows. The set of alternatives is

$$\mathcal{A}=\{\hat{f}_1,\hat{f}_2,\hat{f}_3\}$$

where $\hat{f}_1$ is common bonds, $\hat{f}_2$ is stocks of enterprise, $\hat{f}_3$ is time deposit.

The set of states of nature is

$$\mathcal{S}=\{\boldsymbol{S}_1,\boldsymbol{S}_2,\boldsymbol{S}_3\}$$

where $\boldsymbol{S}_1=(S_1^{(3)},S_2^{(1)})$ is *high* GDP and *low* inflation rate, $\boldsymbol{S}_2=(S_1^{(2)},S_2^{(2)})$ is *medium* GDP and *medium* inflation rate, $\boldsymbol{S}_3=(S_1^{(1)},S_2^{(3)})$ *low* GDP and *high* inflation rate.

Now let us formalize the states of a DM. For simplicity, we will consider classical (not Z-valued states). The set of states of the DM is

$$\mathcal{H}=\{\boldsymbol{h}_1,\boldsymbol{h}_2,\boldsymbol{h}_3,\boldsymbol{h}_4\},$$

where $\boldsymbol{h}_1=(h_1^{(1)},h_2^{(1)})$ is risk and ambiguity aversion, $\boldsymbol{h}_2=(h_1^{(1)},h_2^{(2)})$ is risk aversion and ambiguity seeking, $\boldsymbol{h}_3=(h_1^{(2)},h_2^{(1)})$ is risk seeking and ambiguity aversion, $\boldsymbol{h}_4=(h_1^{(2)},h_2^{(2)})$ is risk and ambiguity seeking.

Given imprecise and partially reliable information about possible outcomes of the considered alternatives let us assign the Z-valued utilities of these outcomes over the set of combined states as it is shown in Tables 12.16,12.17 and 12.18:

Table 12.16. Z-valued utilities for $\hat{f}_1$

	$\boldsymbol{S}_1=(S_1^{(3)},S_2^{(1)})$	$\boldsymbol{S}_2=(S_1^{(2)},S_2^{(2)})$	$\boldsymbol{S}_3=(S_1^{(1)},S_2^{(3)})$
$\boldsymbol{h}_1=(h_1^{(1)},h_2^{(1)})$	About8, very sure	About 4, very sure	About 3, very sure
$\boldsymbol{h}_2=(h_1^{(1)},h_2^{(2)})$	About 12, very sure	About 7, very sure	About 4, very sure
$\boldsymbol{h}_3=(h_1^{(2)},h_2^{(1)})$	About 9, very sure	About 5, very sure	About 3, very sure
$\boldsymbol{h}_4=(h_1^{(2)},h_2^{(2)})$	About 14, very sure	About 8, very sure	About 5, very sure

Table 12.17. Z-valued utilities for $\hat{f}_2$

	$\boldsymbol{S}_1=(S_1^{(3)},S_2^{(1)})$	$\boldsymbol{S}_2=(S_1^{(2)},S_2^{(2)})$	$\boldsymbol{S}_3=(S_1^{(1)},S_2^{(3)})$
$\boldsymbol{h}_1=(h_1^{(1)},h_2^{(1)})$	About 11.5, very sure	About 3.5, very sure	About -3.3, very sure
$\boldsymbol{h}_2=(h_1^{(1)},h_2^{(2)})$	About 16.5, very sure	About 6.5, very sure	About -1.5, very sure
$\boldsymbol{h}_3=(h_1^{(2)},h_2^{(1)})$	About 12.5, very sure	About 4.5, very sure	About -2.5, very sure
$\boldsymbol{h}_4=(h_1^{(2)},h_2^{(2)})$	About 23, very sure	About 7.5, very sure	About -1, very sure

Table 12.18. Z-valued utilities for $\hat{f}_3$

	$\boldsymbol{S}_1=(S_1^{(3)},S_2^{(1)})$	$\boldsymbol{S}_2=(S_1^{(2)},S_2^{(2)})$	$\boldsymbol{S}_3=(S_1^{(1)},S_2^{(3)})$
$\boldsymbol{h}_1=(h_1^{(1)},h_2^{(1)})$	About 3.5, verysure	About 4, verysure	About 6.5, verysure
$\boldsymbol{h}_2=(h_1^{(1)},h_2^{(2)})$	About 8.5, very sure	About 6.5, verysure	About 8.5, verysure
$\boldsymbol{h}_3=(h_1^{(2)},h_2^{(1)})$	About 4.25, verysure	About 4.25, verysure	About 7.5, verysure
$\boldsymbol{h}_4=(h_1^{(2)},h_2^{(2)})$	About 11, verysure	About 7.5, verysure	About 9.5, verysure

In order to determine the DM's preferences over the considered alternatives we need to adequately model relation between his behavioral determinants and the considered economic indicators. This relation will be described by Z-valued joint probabilities of the combined states. In turn, construction of Z-valued joint probabilities requires to determine sign of dependence between the states of a DM $\boldsymbol{h}$ and the states of nature $\boldsymbol{S}$. The determined sign of dependence is shown in Table 12.19.

Table 12.19. Dependence between $\boldsymbol{S}$ and $\boldsymbol{h}$

	$\boldsymbol{S}_1=(S_1^{(3)},S_2^{(1)})$	$\boldsymbol{S}_2=(S_1^{(2)},S_2^{(2)})$	$\boldsymbol{S}_3=(S_1^{(1)},S_2^{(3)})$
$\boldsymbol{h}_1=(h_1^{(1)},h_2^{(1)})$	negative	negative	positive
$\boldsymbol{h}_2=(h_1^{(1)},h_2^{(2)})$	neutral	neutral	positive
$\boldsymbol{h}_3=(h_1^{(2)},h_2^{(1)})$	neutral	neutral	negative
$\boldsymbol{h}_4=(h_1^{(2)},h_2^{(2)})$	positive	positive	negative

Assume that the Z-valued joint probabilities determined on the base of the revealed dependence are as it is shown in Table 12.20:

Table 12.20. Z-valued joint probabilities

	$S_1 = (S_1^{(3)}, S_2^{(1)})$	$S_2 = (S_1^{(2)}, S_2^{(2)})$	$S_3 = (S_1^{(1)}, S_2^{(3)})$
$h_1 = (h_1^{(1)}, h_2^{(1)})$	About 0.18, sure	About 0.22, sure	About 0.05, sure
$h_2 = (h_1^{(1)}, h_2^{(2)})$	About 0.09, sure	About 0.1, sure	About 0.05, sure
$h_3 = (h_1^{(2)}, h_2^{(1)})$	About 0.014, sure	About 0.01, sure	About 0.0025, sure
$h_4 = (h_1^{(2)}, h_2^{(2)})$	About 0.22, sure	About 0.22, sure	About 0.02, sure

Let us now compute the Z-valued overall utilities for the alternatives on the base of (11.2). For example, for $\hat{f}_1$ it has the following form:

$$\hat{U}(\hat{f}_1) = \left(\left|\hat{u}(\hat{f}_1(\omega_{14}))\right| -_h \left|\hat{u}(\hat{f}_1(\omega_{12}))\right|\right)\hat{\eta}(\{\omega_{14}\},\varnothing)$$

$$+\left(\left|\hat{u}(\hat{f}_1(\omega_{12}))\right| -_h \left|\hat{u}(\hat{f}_1(\omega_{13}))\right|\right)\hat{\eta}(\{\omega_{14},\omega_{12}\},\varnothing)$$

$$\left(\left|\hat{u}(\hat{f}_1(\omega_{13}))\right| -_h \left|\hat{u}(\hat{f}_1(\omega_{11}))\right|\right)\hat{\eta}(\{\omega_{14},\omega_{12},\omega_{13}\},\varnothing)$$

$$+\left(\left|\hat{u}(\hat{f}_1(\omega_{11}))\right| -_h \left|\hat{u}(\hat{f}_1(\omega_{24}))\right|\right)\hat{\eta}(\{\omega_{14},\omega_{12},\omega_{13},\omega_{11}\},\varnothing)$$

$$+\left(\left|\hat{u}(\hat{f}_1(\omega_{24}))\right| -_h \left|\hat{u}(\hat{f}_1(\omega_{22}))\right|\right)\hat{\eta}(\{\omega_{14},\omega_{12},\omega_{13},\omega_{11},\omega_{24}\},\varnothing)$$

$$+\left(\left|\hat{u}(\hat{f}_1(\omega_{22}))\right| -_h \left|\hat{u}(\hat{f}_1(\omega_{23}))\right|\right)\hat{\eta}(\{\omega_{14},\omega_{12},\omega_{13},\omega_{11},\omega_{24},\omega_{22}\},\varnothing)$$

$$+\left(\left|\hat{u}(\hat{f}_1(\omega_{23}))\right| -_h \left|\hat{u}(\hat{f}_1(\omega_{34}))\right|\right)\hat{\eta}(\{\omega_{14},\omega_{12},\omega_{13},\omega_{11},\omega_{24},\omega_{22},\omega_{23}\},\varnothing\})$$

$$+\left(\left|\hat{u}(\hat{f}_1(\omega_{34}))\right| -_h \left|\hat{u}(\hat{f}_1(\omega_{32}))\right|\right)\hat{\eta}(\{\omega_{14},\omega_{12},\omega_{13},\omega_{11},\omega_{24},\omega_{22},\omega_{23},\omega_{34}\},\varnothing\})$$

$$+\left(\left|\hat{u}(\hat{f}_1(\omega_{32}))\right| -_h \left|\hat{u}(\hat{f}_1(\omega_{21}))\right|\right)\hat{\eta}(\{\omega_{14},\omega_{12},\omega_{13},\omega_{11},\omega_{24},\omega_{22},\omega_{23},\omega_{34},\omega_{32}\},\varnothing\})$$

$$+\left(\left|\hat{u}(\hat{f}_1(\omega_{21}))\right| -_h \left|\hat{u}(\hat{f}_1(\omega_{33}))\right|\right)\hat{\eta}(\{\omega_{14},\omega_{12},\omega_{13},\omega_{11},\omega_{24},\omega_{22},\omega_{23},\omega_{34},\omega_{32},\omega_{21}\},\varnothing\})$$

$$+\left(\left|\hat{u}(\hat{f}_1(\omega_{33}))\right| -_h \left|\hat{u}(\hat{f}_1(\omega_{31}))\right|\right)\hat{\eta}(\{\omega_{14},\omega_{12},\omega_{13},\omega_{11},\omega_{24},\omega_{22},\omega_{23},\omega_{34},\omega_{32},\omega_{21},\omega_{33}\},\varnothing\})$$

$$+\left|\hat{u}(\hat{f}_1(\omega_{31}))\right|\hat{\eta}(\{\omega_{14},\omega_{12},\omega_{13},\omega_{11},\omega_{24},\omega_{22},\omega_{23},\omega_{34},\omega_{32},\omega_{21},\omega_{33},\omega_{31}\},\varnothing\})$$

where $\omega_{ij} = (S_i, h_j)$ is a combined state. The Z-valued bi-capacity $\hat{\eta}(\cdot,\cdot)$ was computed as the difference of Z-valued capacities by using

(11.3)-(11.4).

For the other alternatives $\hat{U}()$ is determined analogously. The obtained Z-valued utilities $\hat{U}()$ are shown in Figs. 12.15, 12.16 and 12.17):

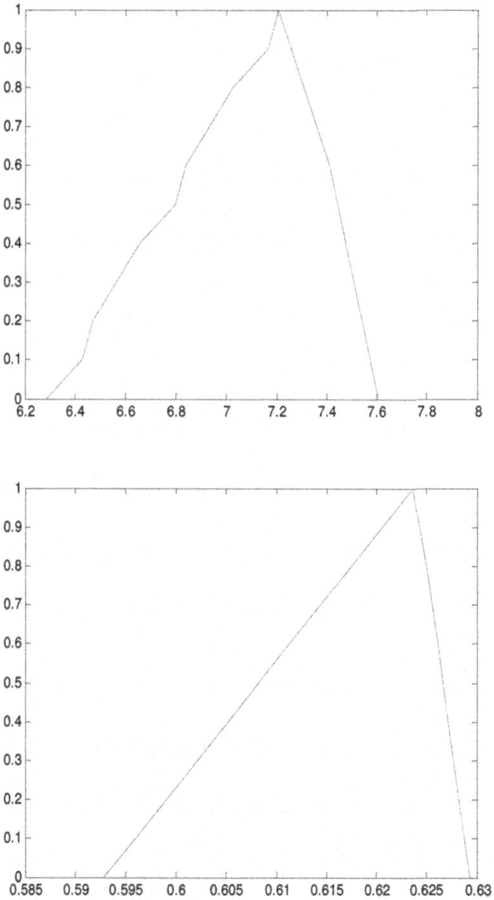

$\hat{U}(\hat{f}_1) = (about\,7.6, about\,0.62)$

Fig. 12.15. Z-valued overall utility for $\hat{f}_1$

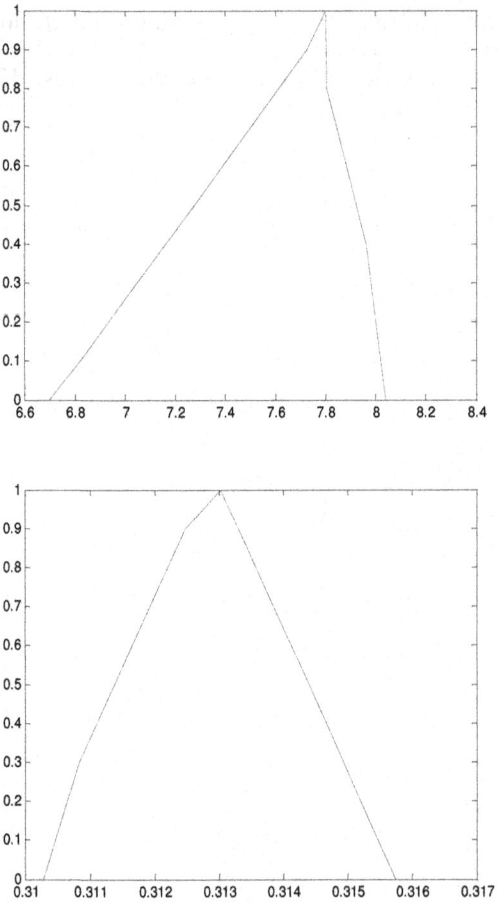

$$\hat{U}(\hat{f}_2) = (about\,7.8, about\,0.31)$$

Fig. 12.16. Z-valued overall utility for $\hat{f}_2$

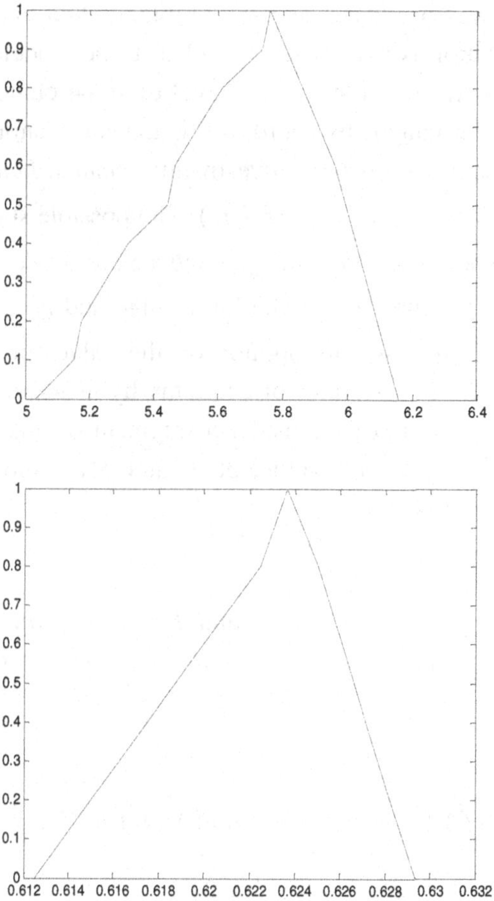

$$\hat{U}(\hat{f}_3) = (\textit{about}\,5.76, \textit{about}\,0.62)$$

Fig. 12.17. Z-valued overall utility for $\hat{f}_3$

By comparing the Z-valued overall utilities on the base of FO concept-based approach (see Section 2.1.7) we obtained the following results: $do(\hat{f}_1) = 1, do(\hat{f}_2) = 0.13, do(\hat{f}_3) = 0$. Assuming the degree of pessimism $\beta = 0.3$ we found that the best alternative is $\hat{f}_1$ (common bonds).

12.2.6. *Business decision with visual information*

In this section we consider a decision problem when imperfect decision relevant information is not sufficiently clear to be modeled by means of membership functions but stays at a level of some cloud images which are difficult to be caught by words [22]. Let an economic agent have three alternatives for short-term investment: *common bonds* (f_1), *stocks of enterprise* (f_2) and *time deposit* (f_3). The possible states of economy are*strong growth* (S_1), *moderate growth* (S_2), *stable economy* (S_3), *recession* (S_4). On the base of the knowledge and past experience, the economic agent expresses his opinion on the values of the alternatives under probabilities of the states of economy by using fuzzy geometrical IF-THEN rules base. Let us consider a fragment of this rules base with two rules (for simplicity only values of f_1 and f_2 are shown):

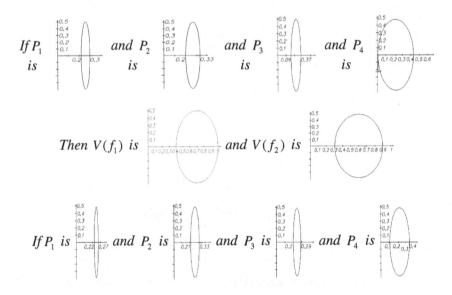

If P_1 *is* 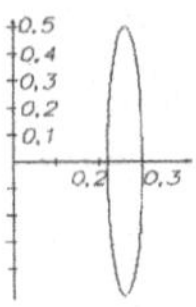

and P_2 *is* 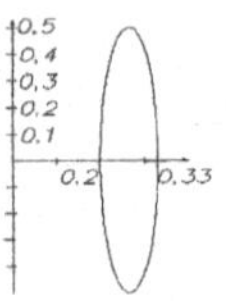

and P_3 *is* 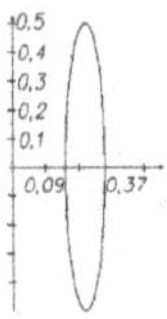

and P_4 *is* 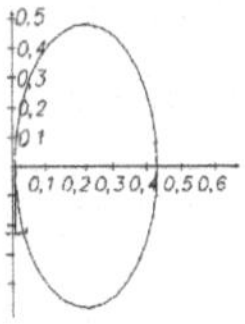

Then $V(f_1)$ *is* 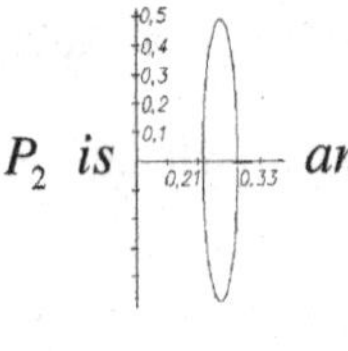
and $V(f_2)$ *is* 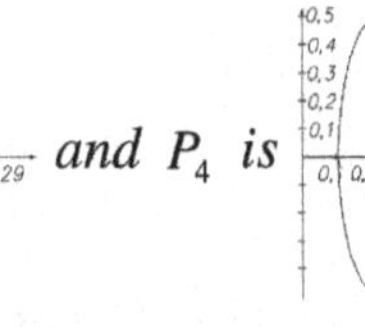

If P_1 *is*

and P_2 *is*

and P_3 *is*

and P_4 *is*

Then $V(f_1)$ *is* 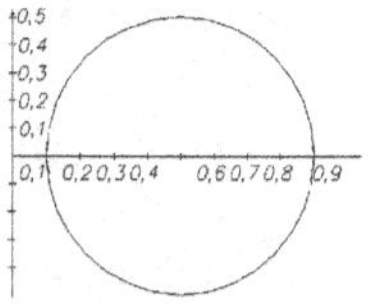

and $V(f_2)$ *is* 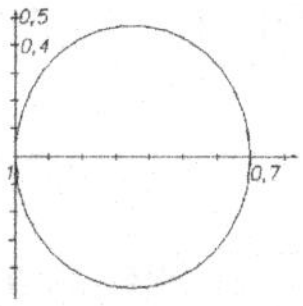

The four antecedents as fuzzy geometrical objects in each rule represent perception of the values of probabilities of four states of nature. The consequent of each rule represents the value of the alternative. The problem is to determine the best alternative by applying reasoning within the considered rules given current perception based information on probabilities. The problem is solved on the base of the methodology described in Section 10.6 as follows. Given the considered fuzzy geometrical "if-then" rules we set a threshold $r'^{kb} = 0.4$ (Step 2). Next we determine satisfaction of the axioms (A1′)-(A4′)for each fuzzy geometrical primitive and verify if the threshold condition is met (Steps 3 and 4). The computed $\underline{r}_k{}^j{}_i$ for rule $\underline{r}_k{}^j{}_i$ are the following:

Rule 1: $\underline{r}^1(P_1) = 0.49$; $\underline{r}^1(P_2) = 0.6$; $\underline{r}^1(P_3) = 0.58$; $\underline{r}^1(P_4) = 0.7$;

$$\underline{r}^1(V(f_1)) = 0.8,\ \underline{r}^1(V(f_2)) = 0.82$$

Rule 2: $\underline{r}^2(P_1) = 0.47$; $\underline{r}^2(P_2) = 0.56$; $\underline{r}^2(P_3) = 0.53$; $\underline{r}^2(P_4) = 0.55$;

$$\underline{r}^2(V(f_2)) = 0.73,\ \underline{r}^2(V(f_2)) = 0.79.$$

As one can see, $\underline{r}^j \geq r'^{kb}$, $j = 1,2$ holds in all the cases and, therefore, the 'if-then' rules can be used for solving the considered decision problem.

Now we compute a partial truth $\underline{r}^j$ for each rule and a partial truth r for the "if-then" rules base (Step 5):

$$r = \min\{\min_{k=1,\dots,n} \underline{r}_k^1, \min_{k=1,\dots,n} \underline{r}_k^2\} = \min\{0.49, 0.47\} = 0.47.$$

Next we calculate partial truth of the "if-then" rules base (Step 6):

$$Cf = \min(0.8, 0.9) = 0.8.$$

and a partial truth to the aggregated outputs of the rules (Step 7):

$$s = r \otimes Cf = \max\{0.47 + 0.8 - 1, 0\} = 0.27.$$

At the next stage (Step 8) inputs in each rule are aggregated into one input by using Lukasiewicz t-norm (Tables 12.21 and 12.22):

Table 12.21. Aggregation of the inputs of the first rule

Basic value	Truth degrees of the inputs				Aggregation results (truth degrees)
	$P(S_1)$	$P(S_2)$	$P(S_3)$	$P(S_4)$	
0.21	0.54	0	0.98	0	0
0.22	0.72	0	1	0	0
0.23	0.84	0.66	0.98	0	0
0.24	0.92	0.86	0.94	0.8	0.52
0.25	0.992	0.96	0.86	0.86	0.672
0.26	0.998	1	0.74	0.74	0.478
0.27	0.998	0.96	0.56	0.56	0.078
0.28	0.972	0.86	0	0	0
0.29	0.92	0.66	0	0	0
0.3	0.84	0	0	0	0

Table 12.22. Aggregation of the inputs of the second rule

Basic value	Truth degrees of the inputs				Aggregation results (truth degrees)
	$P(S_1)$	$P(S_2)$	$P(S_3)$	$P(S_4)$	
0.21	0	0	0.62	0.92	0
0.22	0	0.58	0.84	0.98	0
0.23	0.8	0.78	0.94	1	0.52
0.24	0.98	0.9	0.994	0.98	0.854
0.25	0.98	0.96	0.994	0.92	0.854
0.26	0.8	0.996	0.94	0.8	0.536
0.27	0	0.996	0.84	0.6	0
0.28	0	0.96	0.62	0	0
0.29	0	0.9	0	0	0
0.3	0	0.78	0	0	0

Next we construct the fuzzy geometrical relation matrices between the aggregated inputs and the two outputs $V(f_i), i=1,2$ of the rules (Step 9): $R_1^i, i=1,2$ (1st rule) and $R_2^i, i=1,2$ (2nd rule) by using Lukasiewicz implication (Tables 12.23, 12.24, 12.25 and 12.26).

Table 12.23. Fuzzy geometrical relation matrix R_1^1

	0	0	0	0	0.74	0.94	1	0.94	0.74	0
0	1	1	1	1	1	1	1	1	1	1
0	1	1	1	1	1	1	1	1	1	1
0	1	1	1	1	1	1	1	1	1	1
0.52	0.480	0.480	0.480	0.480	1	1	1	1	1	0.480
0.672	0.328	0.328	0.328	0.328	1	1	1	1	1	0.328
0.478	0.522	0.522	0.522	0.522	1	1	1	1	1	0.522
0.078	0.922	0.922	0.922	0.922	1	1	1	1	1	0.922
0	1	1	1	1	1	1	1	1	1	1
0	1	1	1	1	1	1	1	1	1	1
0	1	1	1	1	1	1	1	1	1	1

Table 12.24. Fuzzy geometrical relation matrix R_1^2

	0	0	0	0	0	0	0.980	1	0.980	0.920
0	1	1	1	1	1	1	1	1	1	1
0	1	1	1	1	1	1	1	1	1	1
0	1	1	1	1	1	1	1	1	1	1
0.52	0.480	0.480	0.480	0.480	0.480	0.480	1	1	1	1
0.672	0.328	0.328	0.328	0.328	0.328	0.328	1	1	1	1
0.478	0.522	0.522	0.522	0.522	0.522	0.522	1	1	1	1
0.078	0.922	0.922	0.922	0.922	0.922	0.922	1	1	1	1
0	1	1	1	1	1	1	1	1	1	1
0	1	1	1	1	1	1	1	1	1	1
0	1	1	1	1	1	1	1	1	1	1

Table 12.25. Fuzzy geometrical relation matrix R_2^1

	0	0.68	0.884	0.98	1	0.98	0.884	0.68	0	0
0	1	1	1	1	1	1	1	1	1	1
0	1	1	1	1	1	1	1	1	1	1
0.52	0.480	1	1	1	1	1	1	1	0.480	0.480
0.854	0.146	0.826	1	1	1	1	1	0.826	0.146	0.146
0.854	0.146	0.826	1	1	1	1	1	0.826	0.146	0.146
0.536	0.464	1	1	1	1	1	1	1	0.464	0.464
0	1	1	1	1	1	1	1	1	1	1
0	1	1	1	1	1	1	1	1	1	1
0	1	1	1	1	1	1	1	1	1	1
0	1	1	1	1	1	1	1	1	1	1

Table 12.26. Fuzzy geometrical relation matrix R_2^2

	0	0	0.5	0.57	0.62	0.7	0.8	0.98	0.98	0.8
0	1	1	1	1	1	1	1	1	1	1
0	1	1	1	1	1	1	1	1	1	1
0.52	0.480	0.48	0.98	1	1	1	1	1	1	1
0.854	0.146	0.146	0.646	0.716	0.766	0.846	0.946	1	1	0.946
0.854	0.146	0.146	0.646	0.716	0.766	0.846	0.946	1	1	0.946
0.536	0.464	0.464	0.964	1	1	1	1	1	1	1
0	1	1	1	1	1	1	1	1	1	1
0	1	1	1	1	1	1	1	1	1	1
0	1	1	1	1	1	1	1	1	1	1
0	1	1	1	1	1	1	1	1	1	1

At the next step (Step 10), we determine aggregated fuzzy relation matrices R^1, R^2 for two rules as the unions $R^1 = R_1^1 \cup R_2^1$ and $R^2 = R_1^2 \cup R_2^2$ by using Lukasiewicz t-conorm (Tables 12.27 and 12.28).

Table 12.27. Aggregated fuzzy relation matrix R^1

1	1	1	1	1	1	1	1	1	1
1	1	1	1	1	1	1	1	1	1
1	1	1	1	1	1	1	1	1	1
0.626	1	1	1	1	1	1	1	1	0.626
0.474	1	1	1	1	1	1	1	1	0.474
0.986	1	1	1	1	1	1	1	1	0.986
1	1	1	1	1	1	1	1	1	1
1	1	1	1	1	1	1	1	1	1
1	1	1	1	1	1	1	1	1	1
1	1	1	1	1	1	1	1	1	1
1	1	1	1	1	1	1	1	1	1
1	1	1	1	1	1	1	1	1	1

Table 12.28. Aggregated fuzzy relation matrix R^2

1	1	1	1	1	1	1	1	1	1
1	1	1	1	1	1	1	1	1	1
1	1	1	1	1	1	1	1	1	1
0.626	0.626	1	1	1	1	1	1	1	1
0.474	0.474	0.974	1	1	1	1	1	1	1
0.986	0.986	1	1	1	1	1	1	1	1
1	1	1	1	1	1	1	1	1	1
1	1	1	1	1	1	1	1	1	1
1	1	1	1	1	1	1	1	1	1
1	1	1	1	1	1	1	1	1	1
1	1	1	1	1	1	1	1	1	1
1	1	1	1	1	1	1	1	1	1

Matrices R^1 and R^2 will be used for computation of the first and second aggregated outputs respectively given a current input.

Now assume that a DM has provided fuzzy geometrical information of his/her perception-based probabilities for a new decision making situation (Step 11). Given this information we construct the corresponding convex hulls (Step 12). The constructed convex hulls are shown in Fig.12.18:

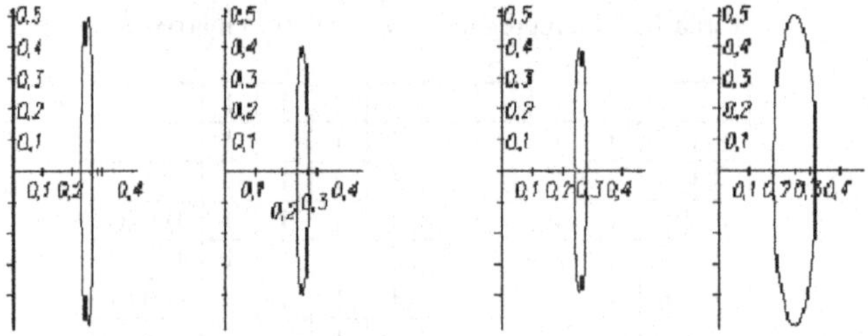

Fig. 12.18. Entered information approximated by convex hulls

Next we set threshold $r'^{DM} = 0.1$ for satisfaction of the axioms for the considered convex hulls and verified satisfaction of the axioms A1'-A4' (Steps 12, 13 and 14):

$$\underline{r}_1 = 0.52,\ \underline{r}_2 = 0.49,\ \underline{r}_3 = 0.53,\ \underline{r}_4 = 0.6.$$

So, a threshold condition $\underline{r}_k \geq r'^{DM},\ k = 1,...,4$ holds and the information entered by a DM can be used for solving the problem.

Now it is needed to aggregate fuzzy geometrical inputs provided by a DM into one input to use them in the further computations (Step 15). The aggregation of these inputs is shown in Table 12.29.

Table 12.29. Aggregation of the current inputs

Basic values	Truth degrees of the inputs				Aggregation results on the inputs
	$P(S_1)$	$P(S_2)$	$P(S_3)$	$P(S_4)$	
0.21	0.96	0.8	0	0.992	0
0.22	0.996	0.72	0.5	0.998	0.214
0.23	0.996	0.64	0.52	0.998	0.154
0.24	0.96	0.56	0.56	0.972	0.052
0.25	0.9	0.48	0.6	0.92	0
0.26	0.78	0.4	0.64	0.84	0
0.27	0.58	0.32	0.7	0.72	0
0.28	0	0.24	0.78	0.54	0
0.29	0	0.16	0.7	0	0
0.3	0	0.08	0.64	0	0

At the next step (Step 16) we compute maximin composition of the aggregated current inputs by using Lukasiewicz t-conorm and t-norm and arrive at resulting outputs for the rules (Tables 12.30 and 12.31).

Table 12.30. Calculation of the resulting output for f_1

0	1	1	1	1	1	1	1	1	1	1
0.214	1	1	1	1	1	1	1	1	1	1
0.154	1	1	1	1	1	1	1	1	1	1
0.052	0.626	1	1	1	1	1	1	1	1	0.626
0	0.474	1	1	1	1	1	1	1	1	0.474
0	0.986	1	1	1	1	1	1	1	1	0.986
0	1	1	1	1	1	1	1	1	1	1
0	1	1	1	1	1	1	1	1	1	1
0	1	1	1	1	1	1	1	1	1	1
0	1	1	1	1	1	1	1	1	1	1
	0.368	***0.42***	***0.42***	***0.42***	***0.42***	***0.42***	***0.42***	***0.42***	***0.42***	***0.368***

Table 12.31. Calculation of the resulting output for f_2

0	1	1	1	1	1	1	1	1	1	1
0.214	1	1	1	1	1	1	1	1	1	1
0.154	1	1	1	1	1	1	1	1	1	1
0.052	0,626	0,626	0,726	1	1	1	1	1	0,726	0,626
0	0,474	0,474	0,574	0,974	1	1	1	1	0,574	0,474
0	0,986	0,986	1	1	1	1	1	1	1	0,986
0	1	1	1	1	1	1	1	1	1	1
0	1	1	1	1	1	1	1	1	1	1
0	1	1	1	1	1	1	1	1	1	1
0	1	1	1	1	1	1	1	1	1	1
	0.368	***0.368***	***0.368***	***0.42***	***0.42***	***0.42***	***0.42***	***0.42***	***0.368***	***0.368***

Thus we get the resulting outputs as the overall values of the considered alternatives:

$$V(f_1)=\{(h_1(v_1),v_1);...;(h_1(v_n),v_n)\}$$
$$=\{(0.368,0.1);(0.42,0.2);(0.42,0.3);(0.42,0.4);(0.42,0.5); \quad (12.4)$$
$$(0.42,0.6);(0.42,0.7);(0.42,0.8);(0.42,0.9);(0.368,1)\},$$

$$V(f_2)=\{(h_2(v_1),v_1);...;(h_2(v_n),v_n)\}$$
$$=\{(0.368,0.1);(0.368,0.2);(0.368,0.3);(0.42,0.4);(0.42,0.5); \quad (12.5)$$
$$(0.42,0.6);(0.42,0.7);(0.42,0.8);(0.368,0.9);(0.368,1)\}.$$

Graphical representations of the computed overall values of the alternatives are shown below (Fig.12.19):

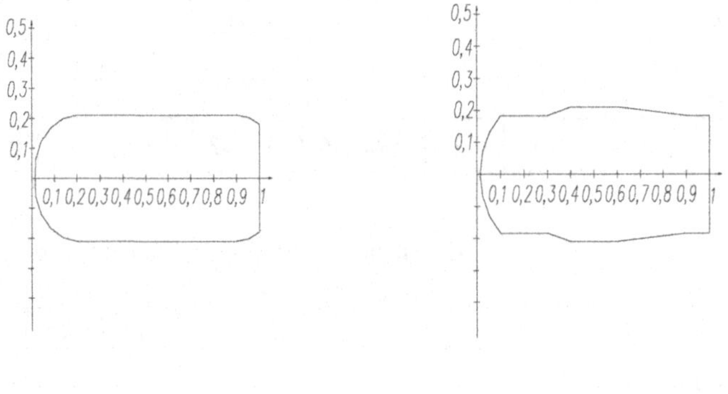

Fig. 12.19. The computed overall values of the alternatives: (a) $V(f_1)$, (b) $V(f_2)$

Next we calculate a partial truth of the fuzzy geometrical outputs (Step 17):

$$s_{new}=\min(r,\underline{r}_k)\otimes Cf=\max\{0.47+0.8-1,0\}=0.27.$$

Now it is needed to compare the obtained overall values of alternatives (12.4)-(12.5) in order to determine the best alternative. Here we need to take into account that each overall value $V(f_i)$ is graded by the degree of belief s_{new}. One approach to do it is to multiply $V(f_i)$ by s_{new} and arrive at a weighted overall value $V_s(f_i)$. Then we will determine the best alternative as an alternative whose overall value's distance to the upper bound of the universe of discourse V is the smallest. A distance-based comparison is an adequate approach for comparison of quantities described by geometrical figures. We will use an expected value of the Hausdorff, distance suggested in [101] for fuzzy sets. For our case of geometrical figures this distance is described by the formula (12.6) where a truth value $h_i(v)$ is used instead of a membership degree used in [101]:

$$d_w(V_s(f_i),\overline{v}) = \frac{\sum_{k=1}^{n} \alpha_k d([V_S(f_i)]^{\alpha_k},\overline{v})}{\sum_{k=1}^{n} \alpha_k}, \tag{12.6}$$

where $[V_s(f_i)]^{\alpha_k} = \{v \in \mathrm{V} | h_i(v) \geq \alpha_k, \alpha_k = \frac{k}{n}, k = 1,...,n|\}$, $\overline{v}$ is the upper bound of V, V is the universe of discourse, $d()$ is the Haussdorf distance[129].

Now we proceed to computation of $V_s(f_i)$ (Step 18):

$$\begin{aligned}V_s(f_1) &= s_{new} \cdot V(f_1)\\ &= \{(0.368,0.027);(0.42,0.054);(0.42,0.081);(0.42,0.108);(0.42,0.135);\\ &(0.42,0.162);(0.42,0.189);(0.42,0.216);(0.42,0.243);(0.368,0.27)\},\end{aligned}$$

$$\begin{aligned}V_s(f_2) &= s_{new} \cdot V(f_2)\\ &= \{(0.368,0.027);(0.368,0.054);(0.368,0.081);(0.42,0.108);(0.42,0.135);\\ &(0.42,0.162);(0.42,0.189);(0.42,0.216);(0.368,0.243);(0.368,0.27)\}.\end{aligned}$$

Let us now calculate the considered distances (12.6) (Step 19):

$$d_w(V_s(f_1),\overline{v}) = 0.76, \; d_w(V_s(f_2),\overline{v}) = 0.73.$$

Therefore, $d_w(V_s(f_2),\overline{v}) < d_w(V_s(f_1),\overline{v})$ and the best alternative is f_2.

12.3 Applications in Production

12.3.1 *Multi-criteria decision making on optimal planning of oil refinery under fuzzy information*

We consider a problem of multiattribute decision making on an oil-refinery manufacturing optimal planning under fuzzy information. An integrated plant flow diagram of the considered oil-refinery manufacturing is given in the Fig. 12.20:

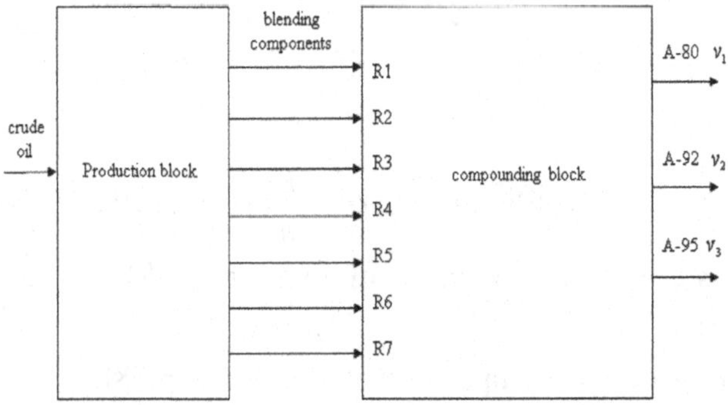

Fig. 12.20. The main blocks of oil refinery manufacturing

Oil refinery manufacturing consists of two blocks: the production block and the compounding block. At the production block, two-stage technological scheme of oil refinery is performed. At the first stage, the primary oil refining is performed by two units. At the second stage the secondary oil refinery is performed in catalytic cracking, carbonization and catalytic reforming units.

In the production block it is produced the following fractions necessary for gasoline production: fraction OP-85 (R1), stable platformate (R2), coke gasoline (R3), high-antiknock rating base fuel (R4), virgin gasoline (R5), fraction OP-85-180 (R6), hydrofined gasoline (R7). In the compounding block it is produced three motor gasolines – A-80, A-92, A-95. Their values are denoted by $x_1(v_1)$, $x_2(v_2)$, $x_3(v_3)$ respectively.

Statement of the problem. Nowadays in economics it is more and more realized that it is not adequate to construct utility function based only on economic (monetary etc) indicators. They sound necessity to take into account also other aspects, such as ecological, social and other matters. In view of this, in our planning problem we will consider utility as a function of three indices: profit, quality of products (quality, for short) and worker satisfaction.

Let $x = (x_1, x_2, x_3)$ denote the vector of decision variables to be quantities of produced A-80, A-92, A-95 respectively. The planning problem is characterized by three criteria:

1) Profit:

$$\tilde{X}_1(x) = \tilde{c}_{11}x_1 + \tilde{c}_{12}x_2 + \tilde{c}_{13}x_3,$$

where $\tilde{c}_{11}, \tilde{c}_{12}, \tilde{c}_{13}$ denote market prices for A-80, A-92, A-95 respectively.

2) Quality:

$$\tilde{X}_2(x) = \tilde{c}_{21}x_1 + \tilde{c}_{22}x_2 + \tilde{c}_{23}x_3,$$

where $\tilde{c}_{21}, \tilde{c}_{22}, \tilde{c}_{23}$ denote fuzzy quality ratings for produced A-80, A-92, A-95 respectively, assigned by experts from [0,10] scale. In our case these ratings are described by triangular fuzzy numbers $\tilde{c}_{21} = (7.2;8;8.8)$, $\tilde{c}_{22} = (4.5;5;5.5)$, $\tilde{c}_{23} = (2.7;3;3.3)$.

3) Worker satisfaction:

$$\tilde{X}_3(x) = \tilde{c}_{31}x_1 + \tilde{c}_{32}x_2 + \tilde{c}_{33}x_3,$$

where $\tilde{c}_{31}, \tilde{c}_{32}, \tilde{c}_{33}$ denote worker satisfaction fuzzy ratings from [0,10] related to production A-80, A-92, A-95 respectively. These ratings are assigned on the base of questionnaire design results and reflect such important matters as safety measures, insalubrities of manufacturing etc. In our case these ratings are described by the following triangular fuzzy numbers: $\tilde{c}_{31} = (3.6;4;4.4)$, $\tilde{c}_{32} = (7.2;8;8.8)$, $\tilde{c}_{33} = (5.4;6;6.6)$.

Using these notations the considered optimal planning problem is formulated as fuzzy multiobjective linear programming (FMOLP) problem [265]:

$$\max \tilde{X}(x) = \max \begin{pmatrix} \tilde{X}_1(x) \\ \tilde{X}_2(x) \\ \tilde{X}_3(x) \end{pmatrix} = \max \begin{pmatrix} \tilde{c}_{11}x_1 + \tilde{c}_{12}x_2 + \tilde{c}_{13}x_3 \\ \tilde{c}_{21}x_1 + \tilde{c}_{22}x_2 + \tilde{c}_{23}x_3 \\ \tilde{c}_{31}x_1 + \tilde{c}_{32}x_2 + \tilde{c}_{33}x_3 \end{pmatrix}$$

$$= \max \begin{pmatrix} 28\tilde{8}x_1 + 2\tilde{9}0x_2 + 3\tilde{0}0x_3 \\ \tilde{8}x_1 + \tilde{5}x_2 + \tilde{3}x_3 \\ \tilde{4}x_1 + \tilde{8}x_2 + \tilde{6}x_3 \end{pmatrix} \tag{12.7}$$

subject to:

resource constraints:

for fraction OP-85:

$$\tilde{a}_{11}x_1 + \tilde{a}_{12}x_2 + \tilde{a}_{13}x_3 = 0.2\tilde{2}89x_1 + 0.0\tilde{1}028x_2 \le \tilde{b}_1 = 27\tilde{6}12 \tag{12.8}$$

for stable platformate:

$$\tilde{a}_{21}x_1 + \tilde{a}_{22}x_2 + \tilde{a}_{23}x_3 = 0.0\tilde{6}91x_1 + 0.3\tilde{4}94x_2 + 0.7\tilde{8}57x_3 \le \tilde{b}_2 = 386\tilde{2}14 \tag{12.9}$$

for coke gasoline:

$$\tilde{a}_{31}x_1 + \tilde{a}_{32}x_2 + \tilde{a}_{33}x_3 = 0.08\tilde{4}6591x_1 \le \tilde{b}_3 = 69\tilde{2}5 \tag{12.10}$$

for high-antiknock rating base fuel:

$$\tilde{a}_{41}x_1 + \tilde{a}_{42}x_2 + \tilde{a}_{43}x_3 = 0.4\tilde{9}01x_1 + 0.\tilde{6}402x_2$$
$$+0.2\tilde{1}42x_3 \le \tilde{b}_4 = 61\tilde{4}955 \tag{12.11}$$

for virgin gasoline:

$$\tilde{a}_{51}x_1 + \tilde{a}_{52}x_2 + \tilde{a}_{53}x_3 = 0.\tilde{0}4718x_1 \le \tilde{b}_5 = 38\tilde{5}8 \tag{12.12}$$

for fraction OP-85-180:

$$\tilde{a}_{61}x_1 + \tilde{a}_{62}x_2 + \tilde{a}_{63}x_3 = 0.0\tilde{1}289x_1 \le \tilde{b}_6 = 10\tilde{5}4 \tag{12.13}$$

for hydrofined gasoline:

$$\tilde{a}_{71}x_1 + \tilde{a}_{72}x_2 + \tilde{a}_{73}x_3 = 0.\tilde{0}671x_1 \le \tilde{b}_7 = 54\tilde{8}8\sqrt{2} \tag{12.14}$$

constraints on plan of end products:

on motor gasoline A-80:

$$\tilde{a}_{81}x_1 + \tilde{a}_{82}x_2 + \tilde{a}_{83}x_3 = \tilde{1}x_1 \ge \tilde{b}_8 = 20\tilde{0}0 \tag{12.15}$$

on motor gasoline A-92:

$$\tilde{a}_{91}x_1 + \tilde{a}_{92}x_2 + \tilde{a}_{93}x_3 = \tilde{1}x_2 \ge \tilde{b}_9 = 20\tilde{0}0 \tag{12.16}$$

on motor gasoline A-95:

$$\tilde{a}_{101}x_1 + \tilde{a}_{102}x_2 + \tilde{a}_{103}x_3 = \tilde{1}x_3 \ge \tilde{b}_{10} = 20\tilde{0}0 \tag{12.17}$$

quality constraints:

$$\left.\begin{aligned} \tilde{a}_{111}x_1 + \tilde{a}_{112}x_2 + \tilde{a}_{113}x_3 &= 0.27\tilde{7}569x_1 \ge \tilde{b}_{11} \\ \tilde{a}_{121}x_1 + \tilde{a}_{122}x_2 + \tilde{a}_{123}x_3 &= 0.07\tilde{3}72x_2 \ge \tilde{b}_{12} \\ \tilde{a}_{131}x_1 + \tilde{a}_{132}x_2 + \tilde{a}_{133}x_3 &= 0.0\tilde{0}62x_3 \ge \tilde{b}_{13} \end{aligned}\right\} \tag{12.18}$$

balance constraints:

$$\tilde{a}_{141}x_1 + \tilde{a}_{142}x_2 + \tilde{a}_{143}x_3 = \tilde{1}x_1 + \tilde{1}x_2 + \tilde{1}x_3 \le \tilde{b}_{14} = 104\tilde{6}107. \tag{12.19}$$

To obtain the best solution of this problem we will use fuzzy group decision making (GDM) method. GDM considers the way people work together in reaching a decision [265]. Often a group decision process is influenced by uncertain factors such as decision makers' roles, preferences for alternatives etc. A group satisfactory solution is the solution which is the most acceptable by the group of individuals as a whole.

To solve the production-planning problem in a group we have first to create a decision group, with John as the group leader and Phillip and Nick as group members. The group members generate different solutions (alternatives) $\tilde{X}^1, \tilde{X}^2, \tilde{X}^3$ by solving the above described FMOLP (12.7)-

(12.19). Assume that John uses FMOLP method [265], Phillip uses fuzzy multiobjective linear goal programming (FMOLGP) method [265], Nick uses Interactive FMOLP method [265] respectively to generate individual solutions. All group members then presented their individual solutions to the group level for further group decision making. The group leader, John, considers the individual solutions as the group alternatives. The generated alternatives are given in the Table 12.32.

Table 12.32. Fuzzy alternatives

	Criterion 1 ($\tilde{X}_1$)	Criterion2 ($\tilde{X}_2$)	Criterion 3 ($\tilde{X}_3$)
John's alternative, ($\tilde{X}^1$)	$\tilde{X}_1^1$ =Very High	$\tilde{X}_2^1$ = Low	$\tilde{X}_3^1$ = Below medium
Phillip'salternative($\tilde{X}^2$)	$\tilde{X}_1^2$ =Medium	$\tilde{X}_2^2$ = Low	$\tilde{X}_3^2$ = Medium
Nick'salternative ($\tilde{X}^3$)	$\tilde{X}_1^3$ =High	$\tilde{X}_2^3$ = Lowest	$\tilde{X}_3^3$ = Medium

The corresponding membership functions of normalized values of the criteria are given in the Figs. 12.21, 12.22 and 12.23:

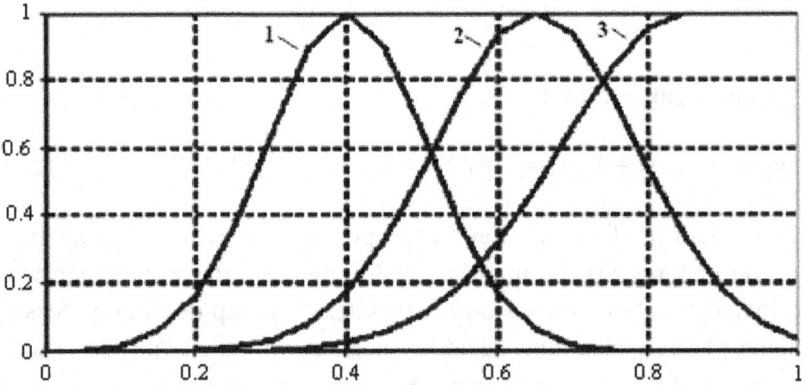

Fig. 12.21. Membership functions of the fuzzy values for the Criterion 1 (Profit): Medium (curve 1), High (curve 2), Very High (curve 3)

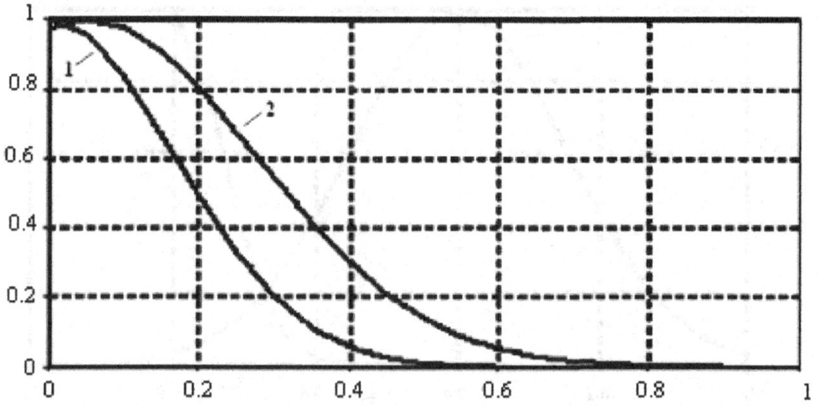

Fig. 12.22. Membership functions of the fuzzy values for the Criterion 2 (Quality): Very Low (curve 1),Low (curve 2)

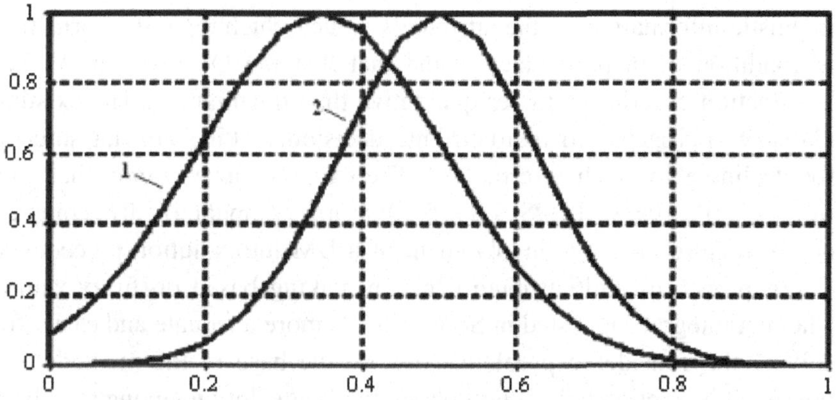

Fig. 12.23. Membership functions of the fuzzy values for the Criterion 3 (Worker satisfaction): Below medium (curve 1), Medium (curve 2)

In our case partial information is described by linguistic probability distribution defined over the set 2^I, where $I = \{1,2,3\}$. We assume that it is only known linguistic probabilities $\tilde{P}_1$ and $\tilde{P}_2$ for the criteria $\tilde{X}_1$ and $\tilde{X}_2$ which are given in the Fig.12.24:

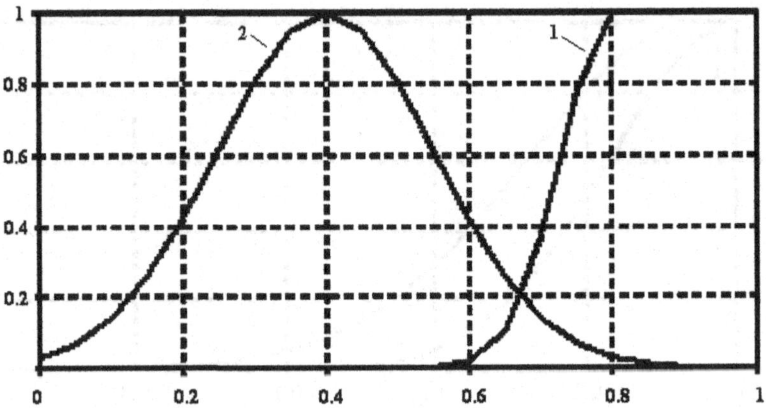

Fig. 12.24. Given linguistic probabilities $\tilde{P}_1$ (curve 1) and $\tilde{P}_2$ (curve 2)

The considered multiattribute decision problem is characterized by linguistic information on the attribute's values. Such type of information is conditioned, in particular, by the fact that the Quality and Worker Satisfaction criteria are rather qualitative than quantitative. The existing classical approaches to multiattribute decision making are not suitable for dealing with such information. The existing fuzzy approaches like fuzzy AHP, fuzzy TOPSIS [145,408] are computationally complex and/or require intensive involvement of a DM into solution procedures. The approach to multiattribute decision making based on fuzzy-valued Choquet integral suggested in Section 6.2 is more adequate and easier for solving the considered problem. Now on the base of the methodology presented in Section 6.2 we will obtain the best solution among the given alternatives using the proposed fuzzy Choquet integral based utility model. To calculate utility of an alternative we will use formula (6.9).

At first we defined $\tilde{P}_3$ by solving problem (6.4)-(6.5) (see Chapter 6). All the linguistic probabilities $\tilde{P}_1$, $\tilde{P}_2$, $\tilde{P}_3$ are shown in the Fig.12.25.

On the base of the methodology presented in Chapter 6 utility of an alternative $\tilde{X}^j$ is determined as

$$\tilde{U}(\tilde{X}^j) = \mathrm{H}(\tilde{u}_1(\tilde{X}_1^j), \tilde{u}_2(\tilde{X}_2^j), \tilde{u}_3(\tilde{X}_3^j)),$$

where $\mathrm{H}(\cdot)$ is defined as a fuzzy Choquet integral (Chapter 6).

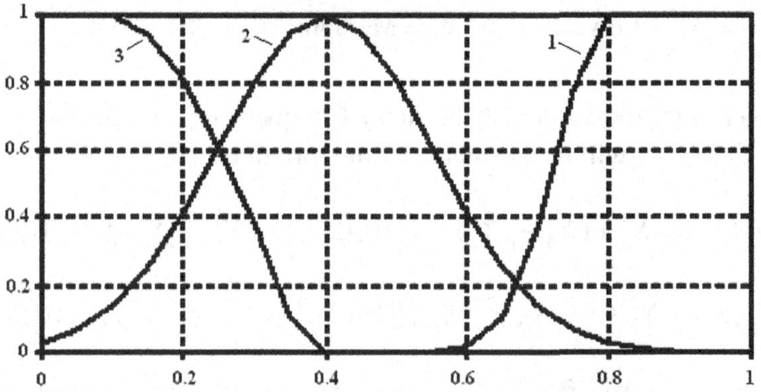

Fig. 12.25. Linguistic probabilities: given $\tilde{P}_1$ (curve 1), $\tilde{P}_2$ (curve 2) and the obtained $\tilde{P}_3$ (curve 3)

For simplicity, we define utilities $\tilde{u}_i(\tilde{X}_i^j)$ as $\tilde{u}_i(\tilde{X}_i^j) = \tilde{u}_i^j = \tilde{X}_i^j$. So, the fuzzy Choquet integral representing for $\tilde{X}^j$ will be calculated by the formula

$$\tilde{U}(\tilde{X}^j) = \tilde{u}^j_{(3)}\tilde{\eta}_{\tilde{P}^l}\left(\{(1),(2),(3)\}\right)^j + (\tilde{u}^j_{(2)} - \tilde{u}^j_{(3)})\tilde{\eta}_{\tilde{P}^l}\left(\{(1),(2)\}^j\right) + (\tilde{u}^j_{(1)} - \tilde{u}^j_{(2)})\left(\{(1)\}^j\right).$$

To calculate fuzzy Choquet integral we rank the terms participating in the individual alternative evaluations:

Alternative 1: $\tilde{X}_2^1 = \text{Low} < \tilde{X}_3^1 = \text{Below Medium} < \tilde{X}_1^1 = \text{Very High}$.
Alternative 2: $\tilde{X}_2^2 = \text{Low} < \tilde{X}_1^2 = \text{Medium} < \tilde{X}_3^2 = \text{Medium}$.
Alternative 3: $\tilde{X}_2^3 = \text{Lowest} < \tilde{X}_3^3 = \text{Medium} < \tilde{X}_1^3 = \text{High}$.

Therefore, the ranked utilities $\tilde{u}^j_{(i)}$ (that are components in the fuzzy Choquet integrals evaluating alternatives) are as follows.

Alternative 1:
$\tilde{u}^1_{(1)} = \tilde{X}_2^1 = \text{Low}$; $\tilde{u}^1_{(2)} = \tilde{X}_3^1 = \text{Below Medium}$; $\tilde{u}^1_{(3)} = \tilde{X}_1^1 = \text{Very High}$.
Alternative 2:
$\tilde{u}^2_{(1)} = \tilde{X}_2^2 = \text{Low}$; $\tilde{u}^2_{(2)} = \tilde{X}_1^2 = \text{Medium}$; $\tilde{u}^2_{(3)} = \tilde{X}_3^2 = \text{Medium}$.
Alternative 3:

$\tilde{u}^3_{(1)} = \tilde{X}^3_2 =$ Lowest; $\tilde{u}^3_{(2)} = \tilde{X}^3_3 =$ Medium; $\tilde{u}^3_{(3)} = \tilde{X}^3_1 =$ High.

Therefore, the values of the fuzzy Choquet integrals for the alternatives $\tilde{X}^j, j = \overline{1,3}$ will be calculated by the formulas:

$$\tilde{U}(\tilde{X}^1) = \tilde{X}^1_2 + (\tilde{X}^1_3 -_h \tilde{X}^1_2)\tilde{\eta}_{\tilde{P}^l}\left(\{(1),(2)\}^1\right) + (\tilde{X}^1_1 -_h \tilde{X}^1_3)\tilde{\eta}_{\tilde{P}^l}\left(\{(1)\}^1\right)$$

$$\tilde{U}(\tilde{X}^2) = \tilde{X}^2_2 + (\tilde{X}^2_1 -_h \tilde{X}^2_2)\tilde{\eta}_{\tilde{P}^l}\left(\{(1),(2)\}^2\right) + (\tilde{X}^2_3 -_h \tilde{X}^2_1)\tilde{\eta}_{\tilde{P}^l}\left(\{(1)\}^2\right)$$

$$\tilde{U}(\tilde{X}^3) = \tilde{X}^3_2 + (\tilde{X}^3_3 -_h \tilde{X}^3_2)\tilde{\eta}_{\tilde{P}^l}\left(\{(1),(2)\}^3\right) + (\tilde{X}^3_1 -_h \tilde{X}^3_3)\tilde{\eta}_{\tilde{P}^l}\left(\{(1)\}^3\right)$$

Now it is needed to obtain a fuzzy measure $\tilde{\eta}_{\tilde{P}^l}$ from the linguistic probability $\tilde{P}^l$ on 2^I as a solution of the problem (6.13)-(6.14) (where instead of a set S we will consider the set of indexes I). After this we calculated fuzzy utilities $\tilde{U}(\tilde{X}^j), j = \overline{1,3}$ the membership functions of which are shown in the Fig. 12.26:

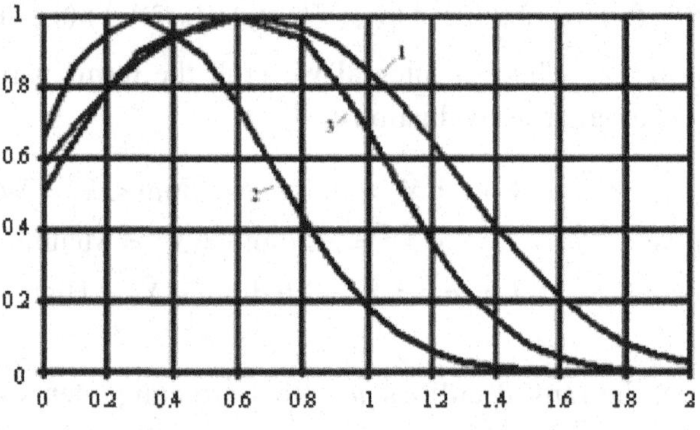

Fig. 12.26. Fuzzy utilities: $\tilde{U}(\tilde{X}^1)$ (curve 1), $\tilde{U}(\tilde{X}^2)$ (curve 2), $\tilde{U}(\tilde{X}^3)$ (curve 3)

By ranking the overall fuzzy utilities $\tilde{U}(\tilde{X}^j), j = \overline{1,3}$ using Center-of-Gravity method:

$\tilde{U}(\tilde{X}^1)$(defuzz)=0.7284>$\tilde{U}(\tilde{X}^3)$(defuzz)=0.6181>$\tilde{U}(\tilde{X}^2)$(defuzz)=0.4251 we determined the best alternative as John's alternative.

12.3.2 *Decision making with imperfect information on the base of a two-level hierarchical model*

Let us consider decision making for an oil refinery plant which includes three units: preliminary distillation unit; cat cracker unit; cocker unit (see Fig.12.27)

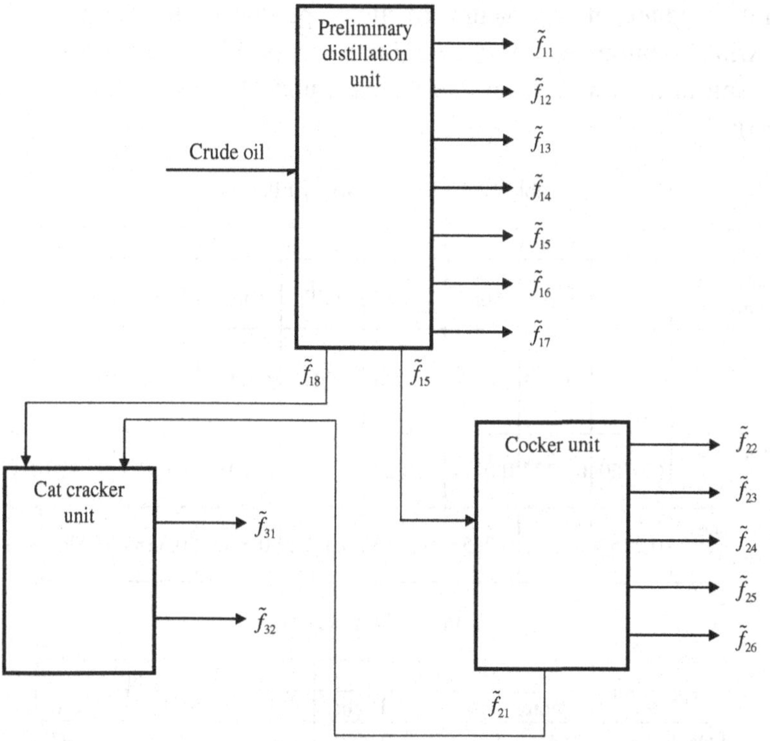

Fig. 12.27. Manufacturing scheme of oil refinery

Let us provide short description for the manufacturing that is schematically shownin Fig. 12.27. Preliminary distillation unit produces eight products: fraction OP-85, $\tilde{x}_{11}(\tilde{f}_{11})$, fraction OP-85-180, $\tilde{x}_{12}(\tilde{f}_{12})$, kerosene, $\tilde{x}_{13}(\tilde{f}_{13})$, diesel oil, $\tilde{x}_{14}(\tilde{f}_{14})$, tar $\tilde{x}_{15}(\tilde{f}_{15})$, liquid petroleum gas $\tilde{x}_{16}(\tilde{f}_{16})$, scrubber gas $\tilde{x}_{17}(\tilde{f}_{17})$, vacuum gasoil $\tilde{x}_{18}(\tilde{f}_{18})$. Tar enters cocker unit which produces gasoil, $\tilde{x}_{21}(\tilde{f}_{21})$, coke $\tilde{x}_{22}(\tilde{f}_{22})$, heavy gasoil $\tilde{x}_{23}(\tilde{f}_{23})$, coke light gasoil, $\tilde{x}_{24}(\tilde{f}_{24})$, waste, $\tilde{x}_{25}(\tilde{f}_{25})$, dry gas, $\tilde{x}_{26}(\tilde{f}_{26})$. Vacuum gasoil and gasoil enter cat cracker unit which produces petrol, $\tilde{x}_{31}(\tilde{f}_{31})$ and reflux, $\tilde{x}_{32}(\tilde{f}_{32})$.

The considered decision making problem is maximization of an overall amount of petroleum fractions produced at the plant. The following solutions to a Pareto-optimization problem were obtained for each unit at the micro-level, i.e. for each unit (Tables 12.33, 12.34 and 12.35):

Table 12.33. Preliminary distillation unit

Preliminary distillation unit	1st variant			2nd variant			3rd variant		
	Center	Left	Right	Center	Left	Right	Center	Left	Right
fraction OP-85 ($\tilde{x}_{11}$)	0.0378	0.0367	0.0390	0.0224	0.0217	0.0231	0.0335	0.0325	0.0345
OP-85-180 ($\tilde{x}_{12}$)	0.0750	0.0727	0.0772	0.1023	0.0992	0.1054	0.0916	0.0889	0.0944
Kerosene ($\tilde{x}_{13}$)	0.2852	0.2767	0.2938	0.3115	0.3022	0.3209	0.3385	0.3283	0.3486

Table 12.34. Cocker unit

Cocker unit	1st variant			2nd variant		
	Center	Left	Right	Center	Left	Right
Gas oil ($\tilde{x}_{21}$)	0.4164	0.4039	0.4228	0.4075	0.3953	0.4198
Coke ($\tilde{x}_{22}$)	0.2357	0.2287	0.2428	0.2450	0.2376	0.2523

Table 12.35. Cat cracker

Cat cracker unit	1st variant			2nd variant		
	Center	Left	Right	Center	Left	Right
Petrol ($\tilde{x}_{31}$)	0.1525	0.1479	0.1571	0.1438	0.1395	0.1481
Reflux ($\tilde{x}_{32}$)	0.3834	0.3719	0.3949	0.3917	0.3887	0.4117

For solving this decision making problem on coordination of the functioning of the three units we use the conventional approach to decision making in multi-agent systems [15] explained in Section 7.1.1. A DM expresses $\tilde{H}_0$ and $\tilde{H}_1$ according to (7.18)-(7.19):

$\tilde{H}_0$ is an overall amount of petroleum fractions that should be about $\tilde{b}_0 = (0.65, 0.58, 0.715)$,

$\tilde{H}_1$ is an overall amount of gas oil fractions that should be about $\tilde{b}_1 = (0.78, 0.702, 0.858)$.

At the next step $v_0(\bar{\lambda})$, $v_1(\bar{\lambda})$ and $v(\bar{\lambda}) = \pi_0 v_1 + \pi_1 v_2$ functions are constructed. The importance weights π_0 and π_1 are obtained according to the procedure of an involvement of a DM into a decision making process that was described in Section 7.1. In our case $\pi_0 = 0.6$ and $\pi_1 = 0.4$.

A vector λ is determined by solving the maximization problem: $\max_{\bar{\lambda}}(v(\bar{\lambda}))$. The results of solving this problem are given below:

$$\lambda_{11} = 0.09; \lambda_{12} = 0.45; \lambda_{13} = 0.46; \lambda_{21} = 0.81; \lambda_{22} = 0.19; \lambda_{31} = 0.75; \lambda_{32} = 0.25.$$

On the base of calculated λ_{ij} the scheduled tasks desired in terms of an overall goal are calculated for each unit:

$$\tilde{x}_{11} = (0.0345, 0.0335, 0.0356); \tilde{x}_{12} = (0.0850, 0.0824, 0.0875);$$
$$\tilde{x}_{13} = (0.3119, 0.3026, 0.3213);$$
$$\tilde{x}_{21} = (0.1509, 0.1463, 0.1554); \tilde{x}_{22} = (0.23, 0.2070, 0.253);$$
$$\tilde{x}_{31} = (0.4142, 0.4017, 0.4220); \tilde{x}_{32} = (0.2380, 0.2309, 0.2452).$$

The obtained values of $\tilde{x}_{ij}$ are sent to the micro-level to be implemented by solving goal programming problems that completes solving the considered problem. The vector of technological parameters ξ_i determined by solving goal programming problems is sent further for realization.

12.3.3 *Decision making on oil extraction under imperfect information [31]*

Assume that a manager of an oil-extracting company needs to make a decision on oil extraction at a potentially oil-bearing region. Knowledge about oil occurrence the manager has is described in NL and has the following form[31]:
"probability of 'occurrence of commercial oil deposits' is lower than medium"

The manager can make a decision based on this information, or at first having conducted seismic investigation of the region. Concerning the seismic investigation used, its accuracy is such that it with the probability "*very high*" confirms occurrence of commercial oil deposits and with the probability "*high*" confirms absence of commercial oil deposits. The manager has a set of alternative actions to choose from. The goal is to find the optimal action.

The considered problem comes within the same information framework as the problems considered in Sections 12.1.1, 12.1.2 – this problem is characterized by imperfect information described in NL. We will use the theory suggested in Chapter 6 for solving of this problem.

Let us develop a general formal description of the problem. The set of the fuzzy states of nature is

$$\mathcal{S}=\{\tilde{S}_1,\tilde{S}_2\}$$

where $\tilde{S}_1$ denotes "occurrence of commercial oil deposits" and $\tilde{S}_2$ denotes "absence of commercial oil deposits". The states $\tilde{S}_1$ and $\tilde{S}_2$ are represented by triangular fuzzy numbers $\tilde{S}_1=(1;1;0)$, $\tilde{S}_2=(0;1;1)$.

The linguistic probability distribution $\tilde{P}^l$ over the states of nature that corresponds the knowledge of the manager is

$$\tilde{P}^l=\tilde{P}_1/\tilde{S}_1+\tilde{P}_2/\tilde{S}_2$$

where $\tilde{P}_1$ is a triangular fuzzy number $\tilde{P}_1=(0.3;0.4;0.5)$ that represents linguistic term "lower than medium" and $\tilde{P}_2$ is unknown.

Taking into account the opportunities available to the manager, we consider the following set of the manager's possible actions: $\mathcal{A}=\{\tilde{f}_1,\tilde{f}_2,\tilde{f}_3,\tilde{f}_4,\tilde{f}_5,\tilde{f}_6\}$. The NL-based description of the manager actions $\tilde{f}_i$, $i=\overline{1,6}$ is given below in Table 12.36.

Table 12.36. Possible actions of the manager

Notation	NL-based description
$\tilde{f}_1$	Conduct seismic investigation and extract oil if seismic investigation shows occurrence of commercial oil deposits
$\tilde{f}_2$	Conduct seismic investigation and do not extract oil if seismic investigation shows occurrence of commercial oil deposits
$\tilde{f}_3$	Conduct seismic investigation and extract oil if seismic investigation shows absence of commercial oil deposits
$\tilde{f}_4$	Conduct seismic investigation and do not extract oil if seismic investigation shows absence of commercial oil deposits
$\tilde{f}_5$	Extract oil without seismic investigation
$\tilde{f}_6$	Abandon seismic investigation and oil extraction

In the problem, we have two types of events: geological events (states of the nature) - "occurrence of commercial oil deposits" ($\tilde{S}_1$) and "absence of commercial oil deposits" ($\tilde{S}_2$) and two seismic events (results of seismic investigation) - "seismic investigation shows occurrence of commercial oil deposits" (B_1) and "seismic investigation shows absence of commercial oil deposits" (B_2). Below we list possible combinations of geological and seismic events with fuzzy probabilities of their occurrence by taking into account NL-described information about accuracy of results of seismic investigation :

$B_1 / \tilde{S}_1$ - there are indeed commercial oil deposits and seismic investigation confirms their occurrence, $\tilde{P}(B_1 / \tilde{S}_1) = (0.7;0.8;0.9)$

$B_2 / \tilde{S}_1$ - there are indeed commercial oil deposits but seismic investigation shows their absence, $\tilde{P}(B_2 / \tilde{S}_1)$ is unknown;

$B_1 / \tilde{S}_2$ - there are almost no commercial oil deposits but seismic investigation shows their occurrence, $\tilde{P}(B_1 / \tilde{S}_2)$ is unknown;

$B_2 / \tilde{S}_2$ - there are almost no commercial oil deposits and seismic investigation shows their absence, $\tilde{P}(B_2 / \tilde{S}_2) = (0.6; 0.7; 0.8)$

According to (6.4) – (6.5) in Chapter 6 we have obtained unknown conditional probabilities $\tilde{P}(B_2 / \tilde{S}_1) = (0.1; 0.2; 0.3)$ and $\tilde{P}(B_1 / \tilde{S}_2) = (0.2; 0.3; 0.4)$.

Seismic investigation allows updating the prior knowledge about actual state of the nature with the purpose to obtain more credible information. Given a result of seismic investigation, the manager can revise prior probabilities of the states of the nature on the base of linguistic probabilities $\tilde{P}(B_j / \tilde{S}_k), k = \overline{1,2}, j = \overline{1,2}$ of possible combinations $\tilde{S}_k / B_j$ of geological and seismic events. These combinations are shown in Table 12.37.

Table 12.37. Possible combinations of seismic and geological events

Seismic events	Geological events	Notation
Seismic investigation shows occurrence of commercial oil	occurrence of commercial oil deposits	$\tilde{S}_1 / B_1$
Seismic investigation shows absence of commercial oil	occurrence of commercial oil deposits	$\tilde{S}_1 / B_2$
Seismic investigation shows occurrence of commercial oil	absence of commercial oil deposits	$\tilde{S}_2 / B_1$
Seismic investigation shows absence of commercial oil	absence of commercial oil deposits	$\tilde{S}_2 / B_2$

To revise probability of a state $\tilde{S}_k$ given seismic investigation result B_j we obtain a fuzzy posterior probability $\tilde{P}(\tilde{S}_k / B_j)$ of $\tilde{S}_k$ based on the fuzzy Bayes' formula (in α-cuts):

$$P^{\alpha}(\tilde{S}_k / B_j) = \left\{ \frac{P_{jk}P_k}{\sum_{k=1}^{K} P_{jk}P_k} \middle| P_k \in P_k^{\alpha}, P_{jk} \in P_{jk}^{\alpha}, \sum_{k=1}^{K} P_k = 1 \right\}$$

The calculated $\tilde{P}(\tilde{S}_1 / B_j)$, $j = \overline{1,2}$ are shown in Figs. 12.28 and 12.29

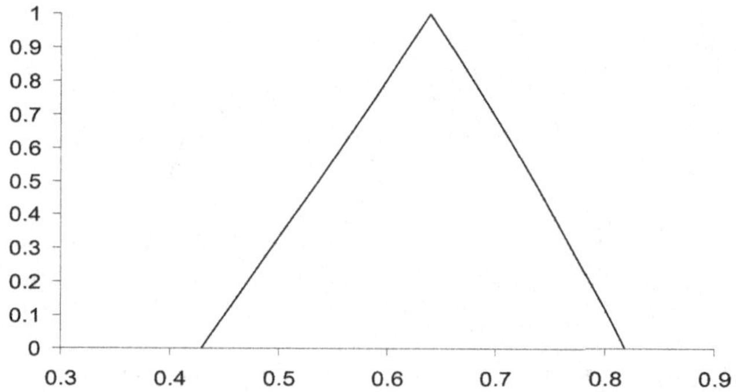

Fig. 12.28. Posterior probability $\tilde{P}(\tilde{S}_1 / B_1)$

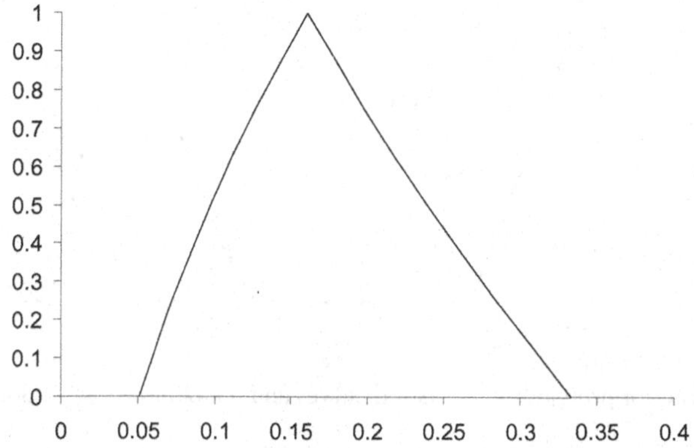

Fig. 12.29. Posterior probability $\tilde{P}(\tilde{S}_1 / B_2)$

Now we have new, revised (posterior) linguistic probabilities $\tilde{P}(\tilde{S}_1 / B_1)$ and $\tilde{P}(\tilde{S}_1 / B_2)$ for the state $\tilde{S}_1$ obtained on the basis of possible seismic investigation results B_1, B_2, respectively. We will denote them by $\tilde{P}_{1rev}^{B_1}$ and $\tilde{P}_{1rev}^{B_2}$, respectively. For these cases we have obtained unknown probabilities of absence of commercial oil deposits $\tilde{P}_{2rev}^{B_1}$ and $\tilde{P}_{2rev}^{B_2}$. The membership functions for $\tilde{P}_{1rev}^{B_1}$ and $\tilde{P}_{2rev}^{B_1}$ are shown in Fig. 12.30 and for $\tilde{P}_{1rev}^{B_2}$ and $\tilde{P}_{2rev}^{B_2}$ in Fig. 12.31.

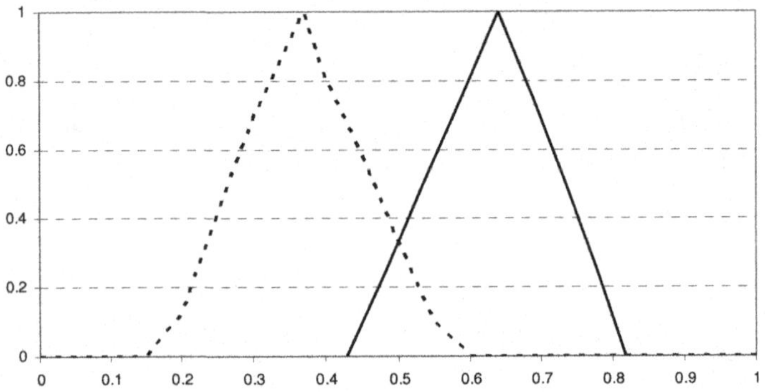

Fig. 12.30. Posterior probability $\tilde{P}_{1rev}^{B_1}$ (solid curve) and the obtained $\tilde{P}_{2rev}^{B_1}$ (dotted curve)

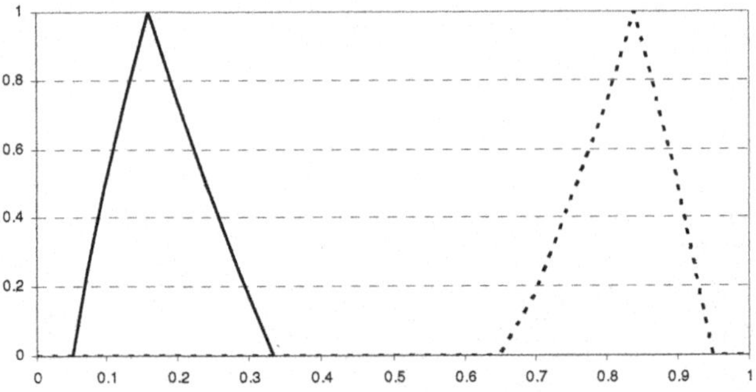

Fig. 12.31. Posterior probability $\tilde{P}_{1rev}^{B_2}$ (solid curve) and the obtained $\tilde{P}_{2rev}^{B_2}$ (dotted curve)

For actions $\tilde{f}_1, \tilde{f}_2, \tilde{f}_3, \tilde{f}_4$ depending on seismic investigations, the manager will use $\tilde{P}_{1rev}^{B_1}$ and $\tilde{P}_{2rev}^{B_1}$ or $\tilde{P}_{1rev}^{B_2}$ and $\tilde{P}_{2rev}^{B_2}$ instead of prior $\tilde{P}_1$.

For action $\tilde{f}_5$ the unknown $\tilde{P}_2$ is obtained from the $\tilde{P}_1$ as traingular fuzzy number (0.5;0.6;0.7) (by using neuro-fuzzy-evolutionary approach described in [309,458]).

Now we have all required probabilities of the states $\tilde{S}_1$ and $\tilde{S}_2$. Assume that the manager evaluates utilities for various actions taken at various states of the nature from some scale. Because of incomplete and uncertain information about possible values of profit from oil sale and possible costs for seismic investigation and drilling of a well, the manager linguistically evaluates utilities for various actions taken at various states of the nature. Assume that the manager's linguistic utility evaluations for various actions taken at various states of the nature are as shown in the Table 12.38:

Table 12.38. Lingustic utility evaluations

	$\tilde{f}_1$	$\tilde{f}_2$	$\tilde{f}_3$	$\tilde{f}_4$	$\tilde{f}_5$	$\tilde{f}_6$
$\tilde{S}_1$	Positive significant	Negative very high	High	Negative very high	Positive high	0
$\tilde{S}_2$	Negative low	Negative very low	Negative low	Negative very low	Negative insignificant	

Below we give the representation of linguistic utilities for actions $\tilde{f}_i$ made at the states $\tilde{S}_k$ by triangular fuzzy numbers $\tilde{u}(\tilde{f}_i(\tilde{S}_k)) = \tilde{u}_{ik}$ defined on the scale $[-1,1]$:

$$\tilde{u}_{11} = (0.65;0.75;0.85)\,;\tilde{u}_{12} = (-0.11;-0.1;-0.09)\,;$$
$$\tilde{u}_{21} = (-0.88;-0.85;-0.82)\,;\tilde{u}_{22} = (-0.07;-0.04;-0.01)\,;$$
$$\tilde{u}_{31} = (0.65;0.75;0.85)\,;\tilde{u}_{32} = (-0.11;-0.1;-0.09)\,;$$
$$\tilde{u}_{41} = (-0.88;-0.85;-0.82)\,;\tilde{u}_{42} = (-0.07;-0.04;-0.01)\,;$$
$$\tilde{u}_{51} = (0.7;0.8;0.9)\,;\ \tilde{u}_{52} = (-0.08;-0.07;-0.06)\,;\ \tilde{u}_6 = 0.$$

To find the optimal action based on the methodology suggested in Section 6.1.5 we first calculate for each action $\tilde{f}_i$ its utility as a fuzzy-valued Choquet integral

$$\tilde{U}(\tilde{f}_i) = \int_S \tilde{u}(\tilde{f}_i(\tilde{S}))d\tilde{\eta}_{\tilde{P}^l}\,,$$

where $\tilde{\eta}_{\tilde{P}^l}$ is a fuzzy-valued fuzzy measure obtained from the linguistic probability distribution as a solution to the problem (6.13) – (6.14) (Chapter 6) based on the neuro-fuzzy-evolutionary technique covered in [309,458]. Let us note that depending upon actions, a fuzzy-valued measure will be constructed by considering either prior or posterior probability distributions. For actions $\tilde{f}_1, \tilde{f}_2$, fuzzy-valued measure will be constructed on the basis of $\tilde{P}^{B_1}_{rev}$ and for actions $\tilde{f}_3, \tilde{f}_4$ fuzzy-valued measure will be constructed based on $\tilde{P}^{B_2}_{rev}$ (as the seismic investigation has been involved). For action $\tilde{f}_5$ a fuzzy measure will be constructed on the basis of prior distribution. For action $\tilde{f}_6$ its utility, i.e. Choquet integral, is obviously equal to zero.

Fuzzy measures $\tilde{\eta}_1$ and $\tilde{\eta}_2$ defined on the base of $\tilde{P}^{B_1}_{rev}$ and $\tilde{P}^{B_2}_{rev}$ respectively are shown in Table 12.39:

Table 12.39. Fuzzy number-valued measures obtained from the posterior probabilities

$\mathcal{H} \subset \mathcal{S}$	$\{\tilde{S}_1\}$	$\{\tilde{S}_2\}$	$\{\tilde{S}_1, \tilde{S}_2\}$
$\tilde{\eta}_1(\mathcal{H})$	(0.43, 0.64, 0.64)	(0.18, 0.36, 0.36)	1
$\tilde{\eta}_2(\mathcal{H})$	(0.05, 0.16, 0.16)	(0.67, 0.84, 0.84)	1

The fuzzy-valued measure $\tilde{\eta}$ obtained on the base of prior probability is shown in Table 12.40:

Table 12.40. Fuzzy measure (approximated to triangular fuzzy numbers) obtained from the prior probabilities.

$\mathcal{H} \subset \mathcal{S}$	$\{\tilde{S}_1\}$	$\{\tilde{S}_2\}$	$\{\tilde{S}_1, \tilde{S}_2\}$
$\tilde{\eta}(\mathcal{H})$	(0.3, 0.4, 0.4)	(0.5, 0.6, 0.6)	1

As utilities for $\tilde{u}_{ik}$ are fuzzy numbers, the corresponding values of Choquet integrals will also be fuzzy. We calculate a fuzzy utility for every action $\tilde{f}_i$ as a fuzzy value of a Choquet integral. Then using the fuzzy Jaccard compatibility-based ranking method, we find an action with the highest value of a fuzzy utility as an optimal one. The form of a Choquet integral for action $\tilde{f}_1$ reads as

$$\tilde{U}(\tilde{f}_1)=\sum_{i=1}^{2}\left(\tilde{u}(\tilde{f}_1(\tilde{S}_{(i)}))-_h\tilde{u}(\tilde{f}_1(\tilde{S}_{(i+1)}))\right)\tilde{\eta}_{\tilde{P}^l}\left(\mathcal{H}_{(i)}\right)=$$
$$=\left(\tilde{u}(\tilde{f}_1(\tilde{S}_{(1)}))-_h\tilde{u}(\tilde{f}_1(\tilde{S}_{(2)}))\right)\tilde{\eta}_1\left(\left\{\tilde{S}_{(1)}\right\}\right)+\tilde{u}(\tilde{f}_1(\tilde{S}_{(2)}))\tilde{\eta}_1\left(\left\{\tilde{S}_{(1)},\tilde{S}_{(2)}\right\}\right)$$

As $\tilde{u}(\tilde{f}_1(\tilde{S}_{(1)}))=\tilde{u}_{11}=(0.65;0.75;0.85)$, $\tilde{u}(\tilde{f}_1(\tilde{S}_2))=\tilde{u}_{12}=(-0.11;-0.1;-0.09)$ we find that $\tilde{u}_{11}\geq\tilde{u}_{12}$. Then $\tilde{u}(\tilde{f}_1(\tilde{S}_{(1)}))=\tilde{u}_{11}$, $\tilde{u}(\tilde{f}_1(\tilde{S}_{(2)}))=\tilde{u}_{12}$ and $\tilde{S}_{(1)}=\tilde{S}_1$, $\tilde{S}_{(2)}=\tilde{S}_2$. The Choquet integral for action f_1 is equal to

$$\tilde{U}(\tilde{f}_1)=\left(\tilde{u}(\tilde{f}_1(\tilde{S}_1))-_h\tilde{u}(\tilde{f}_1(\tilde{S}_2))\right)\tilde{\eta}_1\left(\left\{\tilde{S}_1\right\}\right)+$$
$$+\tilde{u}(\tilde{f}_1(\tilde{S}_2))\tilde{\eta}_1\left(\left\{\tilde{S}_1,\tilde{S}_2\right\}\right)=\left(\tilde{u}_{11}-_h\tilde{u}_{12}\right)\tilde{\eta}_1\left(\left\{\tilde{S}_1\right\}\right)+\tilde{u}_{12}\tilde{\eta}_1\left(\left\{\tilde{S}_1,\tilde{S}_2\right\}\right)=$$
$$=\left(\tilde{u}_{11}-_h\tilde{u}_{12}\right)\tilde{\eta}_1\left(\left\{\tilde{S}_1\right\}\right)+\tilde{u}_{12}=\left((0.65;0.75;0.85)-_h(-0.11;-0.1;-0.09)\right)\times$$
$$\times(0.43,\ 0.64,\ 0.64)+(-0.11;-0.1;-0.09).$$

The obtained result is approximated by a triangular fuzzy number comes as $\tilde{U}(\tilde{f}_1)=(0.2168,0.444,0.5116)$.

Based on this procedure, we have computed the fuzzy values of Choquet integrals also for the other actions $f_i, i=\overline{1,5}$ obtaining the following results:

$$\tilde{U}(\tilde{f}_2)=\sum_{i=1}^{2}\left(\tilde{u}(\tilde{f}_2(\tilde{S}_{(i)}))-_h\tilde{u}(\tilde{f}_2(\tilde{S}_{(i+1)}))\right)\tilde{\eta}_{\tilde{P}^l}\left(\mathcal{H}_{(i)}\right)=$$
$$=\left(\tilde{u}(\tilde{f}_2(\tilde{S}_{(1)}))-_h\tilde{u}(\tilde{f}_2(\tilde{S}_{(2)}))\right)\tilde{\eta}_1\left(\left\{\tilde{S}_{(1)}\right\}\right)+\tilde{u}(\tilde{f}_2(\tilde{S}_{(2)}))\tilde{\eta}_1\left(\left\{\tilde{S}_{(1)},\tilde{S}_{(2)}\right\}\right)=$$
$$=\left(\tilde{u}(\tilde{f}_2(\tilde{S}_2))-_h\tilde{u}(\tilde{f}_2(\tilde{S}_1))\right)\tilde{\eta}_1\left(\left\{\tilde{S}_2\right\}\right)+\tilde{u}(\tilde{f}_2(\tilde{S}_1))\tilde{\eta}_1\left(\left\{\tilde{S}_1,\tilde{S}_2\right\}\right)=$$
$$=\left(\tilde{u}_{22}-_h\tilde{u}_{21}\right)\tilde{\eta}_1\left(\left\{\tilde{S}_2\right\}\right)+\tilde{u}_{21}\tilde{\eta}_1\left(\left\{\tilde{S}_1,\tilde{S}_2\right\}\right)=$$
$$=\left((-0.07;-0.04;-0.01)-_h(-0.88;-0.85;-0.82)\right)\cdot(0.67,\ 0.84,\ 0.84)+$$
$$+(-0.88;-0.85;-0.82),$$

$$\tilde{U}(\tilde{f}_3)=\sum_{i=1}^{2}\left(\tilde{u}(\tilde{f}_3(\tilde{S}_{(i)}))-_h\tilde{u}(\tilde{f}_3(\tilde{S}_{(i+1)}))\right)\tilde{\eta}_{\tilde{P}^l}\left(\mathcal{H}_{(i)}\right)=$$
$$=\left(\tilde{u}(\tilde{f}_3(\tilde{S}_{(1)}))-_h\tilde{u}(\tilde{f}_3(\tilde{S}_{(2)}))\right)\tilde{\eta}_2\left(\{\tilde{S}_{(1)}\}\right)+\tilde{u}(\tilde{f}_3(\tilde{S}_{(2)}))\tilde{\eta}_2\left(\{\tilde{S}_{(1)},\tilde{S}_{(2)}\}\right)=$$
$$=\left(\tilde{u}(\tilde{f}_3(\tilde{S}_1))-_h\tilde{u}(\tilde{f}_3(\tilde{S}_2))\right)\tilde{\eta}_2\left(\{\tilde{S}_1\}\right)+\tilde{u}(\tilde{f}_3(\tilde{S}_2))\tilde{\eta}_2\left(\{\tilde{S}_1,\tilde{S}_2\}\right)=$$
$$=\left(\tilde{u}_{31}-_h\tilde{u}_{32}\right)\tilde{\eta}_2\left(\{\tilde{S}_1\}\right)+\tilde{u}_{32}\tilde{\eta}_2\left(\{\tilde{S}_1,\tilde{S}_2\}\right)=$$
$$=\left((0.65;0.75;0.85)-_h(-0.11;-0.1;-0.09)\right)\cdot(0.43,\ 0.64,\ 0.64)+$$
$$+(-0.11;-0.1;-0.09),$$

$$\tilde{U}(\tilde{f}_4)=\sum_{i=1}^{2}\left(\tilde{u}(\tilde{f}_4(\tilde{S}_{(i)}))-_h\tilde{u}(\tilde{f}_4(\tilde{S}_{(i+1)}))\right)\tilde{\eta}_{\tilde{P}^l}\left(\mathcal{H}_{(i)}\right)=$$
$$=\left(\tilde{u}(\tilde{f}_4(\tilde{S}_{(1)}))-_h\tilde{u}(\tilde{f}_4(\tilde{S}_{(2)}))\right)\tilde{\eta}_2\left(\{\tilde{S}_{(1)}\}\right)+\tilde{u}(\tilde{f}_4(\tilde{S}_{(2)}))\tilde{\eta}_2\left(\{\tilde{S}_{(1)},\tilde{S}_{(2)}\}\right)=$$
$$=\left(\tilde{u}(\tilde{f}_4(\tilde{S}_2))-_h\tilde{u}(\tilde{f}_4(\tilde{S}_1))\right)\tilde{\eta}_2\left(\{\tilde{S}_2\}\right)+\tilde{u}(\tilde{f}_4(\tilde{S}_1))\tilde{\eta}_2\left(\{\tilde{S}_1,\tilde{S}_2\}\right)=$$
$$=\left(\tilde{u}_{42}-_h\tilde{u}_{41}\right)\tilde{\eta}_2\left(\{\tilde{S}_2\}\right)+\tilde{u}_{21}\tilde{\eta}_2\left(\{\tilde{S}_1,\tilde{S}_2\}\right)=$$
$$=\left((-0.07;-0.04;-0.01)-_h(-0.88;-0.85;-0.82)\right)\cdot(0.67,\ 0.84,\ 0.84)+$$
$$+(-0.88;-0.85;-0.82),$$

$$\tilde{U}(\tilde{f}_5)=\sum_{i=1}^{2}\left(\tilde{u}(\tilde{f}_5(\tilde{S}_{(i)}))-_h\tilde{u}(\tilde{f}_5(\tilde{S}_{(i+1)}))\right)\tilde{\eta}_{\tilde{P}^l}\left(\mathcal{H}_{(i)}\right)=$$
$$=\left(\tilde{u}(\tilde{f}_5(\tilde{S}_{(1)}))-_h\tilde{u}(\tilde{f}_5(\tilde{S}_{(2)}))\right)\tilde{\eta}\left(\{\tilde{S}_{(1)}\}\right)+\tilde{u}(\tilde{f}_5(\tilde{S}_{(2)}))\tilde{\eta}\left(\{\tilde{S}_{(1)},\tilde{S}_{(2)}\}\right)=$$
$$=\left(\tilde{u}(\tilde{f}_5(\tilde{S}_1))-_h\tilde{u}(\tilde{f}_5(\tilde{S}_2))\right)\tilde{\eta}\left(\{\tilde{S}_1\}\right)+\tilde{u}(\tilde{f}_5(\tilde{S}_2))\tilde{\eta}\left(\{\tilde{S}_1,\tilde{S}_2\}\right)=$$
$$=\left(\tilde{u}_{51}-_h\tilde{u}_{52}\right)\tilde{\eta}\left(\{\tilde{S}_1\}\right)+\tilde{u}_{52}\tilde{\eta}\left(\{\tilde{S}_1,\tilde{S}_2\}\right)=$$
$$=\left((0.7;0.8;0.9)-_h(-0.08;-0.07;-0.06)\right)\cdot(0.3,\ 0.4,\ 0.4)+$$
$$+(-0.08;-0.07;-0.06).$$

The obtained results approximated by TFNs are as follows:

$\tilde{U}(\tilde{f}_2)=(-0.5317,-0.3316,-0.3016)$; $\tilde{U}(\tilde{f}_3)=(-0.072,0.036,0.0604)$;
$\tilde{U}(\tilde{f}_4)=(-0.8395,-0.7204,-0.6904)$; $\tilde{U}(\tilde{f}_5)=(0.154,0.278,0.324)$.

These fuzzy numbers are shown in Fig. 12.32.

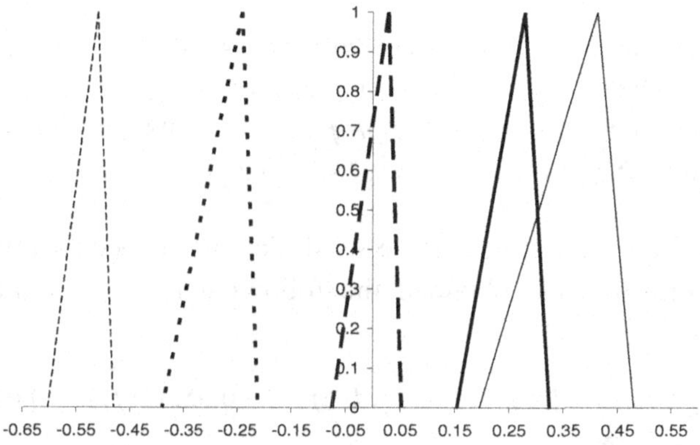

Fig. 12.32. Fuzzy values of Choquet integral for possible actions (for $\tilde{f}_1$ - thin solid line, for $\tilde{f}_2$ - thick dotted line, for $\tilde{f}_3$ - thick dashed line, for $\tilde{f}_4$ - thin dashed line, for $\tilde{f}_5$ - thick solid line)

As it can be seen the highest fuzzy utilities are those of alternatives $\tilde{f}_1$ and $\tilde{f}_5$. The application of the fuzzy Jaccard compatibility-based ranking method [26,368] to compare the fuzzy utility values for $\tilde{f}_1$ and $\tilde{f}_5$ gave rise to the following results:

$$\tilde{U}(\tilde{f}_1) \geq \tilde{U}(\tilde{f}_5) \text{ is satisfied with the degree } 0.8748;$$

$$\tilde{U}(\tilde{f}_5) \geq \tilde{U}(\tilde{f}_1) \text{ is satisfied with the degree } 0.1635.$$

The best action is $\tilde{f}_1$ "Conduct seismic investigation and extract oil if seismic investigation shows occurrence of commercial oil deposits" as one with the highest fuzzy utility value being equal to $\tilde{U}(\tilde{f}_1) = (0.1953, 0.412, 0.4796)$.

We also considered the possibility of applying the classical (non-fuzzy) Choquet expected utility model to solve this problem. But as this model cannot take into account NL-described information about utilities, states, probabilities etc., we had to use only numerical information. Assume that the manager assigns numeric subjective probabilities and numerical utilities. Suppose that the manager assigned the following numerical values:

$u(f_1(S_1)) = 0.6$; $u(f_1(S_2)) = -0.15$; $u(f_2(S_1)) = -0.86$; $u(f_2(S_2)) = -0.038$ $u(f_3(S_1)) = 0.6$; $u(f_3(S_2)) = -0.15$; $u(f_4(S_1)) = -0.86$; $u(f_4(S_2)) = -0.038$; $u(f_5(S_1)) = 0.9$; $u(f_5(S_2)) = -0.08$; $P(S_1) = 0.35$, $P(b_1 / S_1) = 0.8$; $P(b_2 / S_2) = 0.7$; $P(b_2 / S_1) = 0.2$; $P(b_1 / S_2) = 0.3$.

To find the best alternative we used Choquet expected utility with possibility measure and obtained the following results for utilities of actions:

$U(f_1) = 0.2775$; $U(f_2) = -0.51$; $U(f_3) = -0.05$; $U(f_4) = -0.05$; $U(f_5) = 0.2825$.

The best action is f_5 – "Extract oil without seismic investigation" as one with the highest utility value $U(f_5) = 0.2825$. This result differs from the above one we obtained when applying the suggested model given the NL-described information. "Extract oil without seismic investigation" appeared to be the best alternative despite of the fact that the probability of occurrence of commercial oil deposits is not high: $P(S_1) = 0.35$. The reason for this is that an assignment of subjective numeric values to probabilities and utilities leads to the loss of important partial information. In turn, this loss of information may result in choosing a decision that may not be suitable.

We also solved the considered problem with other initial information provided by the manager. When the information is *"probability of "occurrence of commercial oil deposits" is low"*, where *"low"* is described by $\tilde{P}_1 = (0.3;0.4;0.5)$ the obtained results being approximated by triangular fuzzy numbers are as follows:

$\tilde{U}(\tilde{f}_1) = (-0.11, 0.082857, 0.1134)$; $\tilde{U}(\tilde{f}_2) = (-0.294, -0.168, -0.138)$;
$\tilde{U}(\tilde{f}_3) = (-0.11, -0.07538, -0.0626)$;
$\tilde{U}(\tilde{f}_4) = (-0.1322, -0.0572, -0.0272)$; $\tilde{U}(\tilde{f}_5) = (-0.08, 0.017, 0.036)$.

These fuzzy numbers are shown in Fig. 12.33:

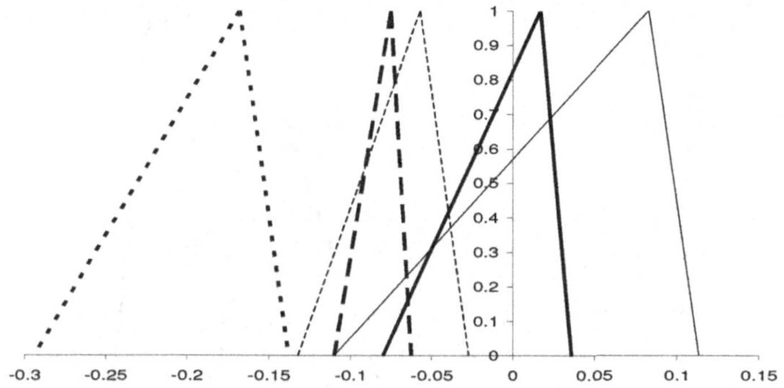

Fig.12.33. Fuzzy values of Choquet integral for possible actions (for $\tilde{f}_1$ - thin solid line, for $\tilde{f}_2$ - thick dotted line, for $\tilde{f}_3$ - thick dashed line, for $\tilde{f}_4$ - thin dashed line, for $\tilde{f}_5$ - thick solid line)

As can be seen, the best actions are $\tilde{f}_1$ and $\tilde{f}_5$. The application of the fuzzy Jaccard compatibility-based ranking method to compare the fuzzy utility values for $\tilde{f}_1$ and $\tilde{f}_5$ resulted in the following:

$\tilde{U}(\tilde{f}_1) \geq \tilde{U}(\tilde{f}_5)$ is satisfied with the degree 0.9902;

$\tilde{U}(\tilde{f}_5) \geq \tilde{U}(\tilde{f}_1)$ is satisfied with the degree 0.4193.

Here the best action is $\tilde{f}_1$ "Conduct seismic investigation and extract oil if seismic investigation shows occurrence of commercial oil deposits" as the one with the highest fuzzy utility value $\tilde{U}(\tilde{f}_1)=(0.1953,0.412,0.4796)$. This is due to the fact that the probability of occurrence of commercial oil deposits is so low that it is better to begin to extract oil only if seismic investigation shows their occurrence.

When the *"probability of "occurrence of commercial oil deposits" is high"* with *"high"* described as $\tilde{P}_1 = (0.8;0.9;1)$ the obtained results approximated by triangular fuzzy numbers are the following (see Fig. 12.34):

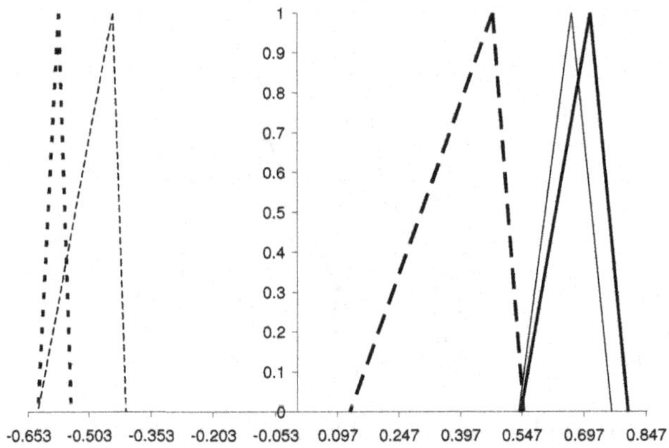

Fig. 12.34. Fuzzy values of Choquet integral for possible actions (for $\tilde{f}_1$ - thin solid line, for $\tilde{f}_2$ - thick dotted line, for $\tilde{f}_3$ - thick dashed line, for $\tilde{f}_4$ - thin dashed line, for $\tilde{f}_5$ - thick solid line)

The fuzzy utilities are as follows:

$$\tilde{U}(\tilde{f}_1) = (0.539,0.668,0.764);$$
$$\tilde{U}(\tilde{f}_2) = (-0.63,-0.5776,-0.5476);$$
$$\tilde{U}(\tilde{f}_3) = (0.127,0.476,0.5508);$$
$$\tilde{U}(\tilde{f}_4) = (-0.63,-0.4432,-0.4132);$$
$$\tilde{U}(\tilde{f}_5) = (0.544,0.713,0.804).$$

Here again the highest fuzzy utilities are those of $\tilde{f}_1$ and $\tilde{f}_5$ alternatives. The use of the fuzzy Jaccard compatibility-based ranking method [368] to compare the fuzzy utility values for $\tilde{f}_1$ and $\tilde{f}_5$ produced the following results:

$\tilde{U}(\tilde{f}_1) \geq \tilde{U}(\tilde{f}_5)$ is satisfied with the degree 0.6164;

$\tilde{U}(\tilde{f}_5) \geq \tilde{U}(\tilde{f}_1)$ is satisfied with the degree 0.9912.

The best action is $\tilde{f}_5$ "Extract oil without seismic investigation" as one with the highest fuzzy utility value $\tilde{U}(\tilde{f}_5) = (0.544,0.713,0.804)$. This is due to the fact that the probability of occurrence of commercial oil deposits is so high that it is more reasonable not to spend money on seismic investigation and to begin to extract oil.

12.4 Application in Medicine

12.4.1 *Selection of an optimal treatment method for acute periodontitis disease under linguistic relevant information [21]*

In this example we will consider selection of an optimal treatment under imperfect information on stages of the disease and possible results of treatment [21]. In the considered problem, probabilities of the two most expressed stages of the disease are assigned linguistically (imprecisely) by the dentist but for the rest and the least expressed stage the dentist finds difficultly in evaluation of its occurrence probability.

Problem description. Case history N583 – patient Vidadi Cabrayil Cabrayilov is entered with symptoms of the heavy stage of the periodontitis disease to the polyclinic of Medical University. He was examined and it was defined that intoxication indicators are approximately of 10%-20% level and exudative indicators are of 60%-80% level. The problem is to define an optimal treatment for the considered patient.

Such problem is essentially characterized by linguistic relevant information due to vagueness, imprecision and partial truth related to information on the disease. The existing decision theories such as SEU, CEU, CPT and others are inapplicable here as they are developed for precisely constrained information. We will apply fuzzy logic-based decision theory suggested in Chapter 6 which is able to deal with linguistic information of the considered problem.

Formal description of the problem [21]. 1) *States of nature*. States of nature are represented by the stages of the disease. During the patient examination it is very important to properly identify the actual stage of the disease. Without doubts, the "boundaries" of phases are not sharply defined, and one phase slips into another. Taking this into account, it is adequately to describe the phases by using fuzzy sets. The set of the fuzzy states of nature is

$$\mathcal{S}=\{\tilde{S}_1,\tilde{S}_2,\tilde{S}_3\},$$

where $\tilde{S}_1$ -intoxication phase (1st stage of the disease), $\tilde{S}_2$ -exudative stage (2nd stage of the disease), $\tilde{S}_3$ -heavy phase (3rd stage of the disease). Membership functions for $\tilde{S}_1, \tilde{S}_2, \tilde{S}_3$ used to describe intoxication, exudative and heavy phases are shown in Fig.12.35.

During a patient examination the development level of the disease is represented by a dentist's linguistic (imprecise) evaluations of likelihoods of various stages of the disease. We consider these approximate evaluations as linguistic probabilities. So, we have linguistic probability distribution $\tilde{P}^l$ over the fuzzy states of nature:

$$\tilde{P}^l = \tilde{P}_1/\tilde{S}_1 + \tilde{P}_2/\tilde{S}_2 + \tilde{P}_3/\tilde{S}_3 ,$$

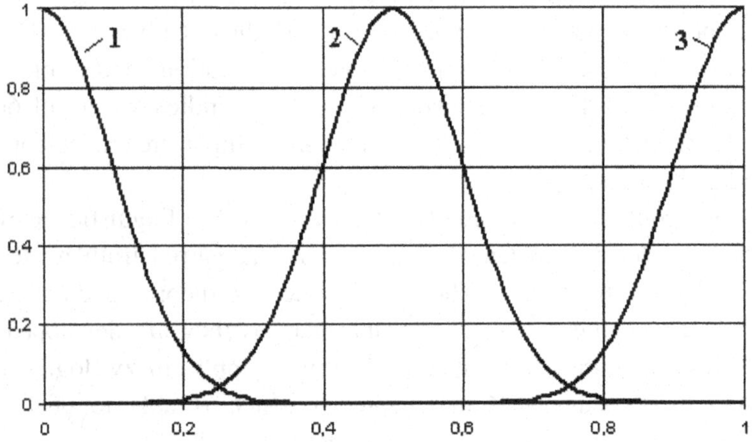

Fig.12.35. Membership functions of $\tilde{S}_1$ (curve 1), $\tilde{S}_2$ (curve 2), $\tilde{S}_3$ (curve 3)

where $\tilde{P}_1$ is the linguistic probability of the intoxication phase occurrence, $\tilde{P}_2$ is the linguistic probability of the exudative phase occurrence and $\tilde{P}_3$ is unknown imprecise probability of the heavy phase occurrence. The membership functions of the linguistic probabilities $\tilde{P}_1$, $\tilde{P}_2$ are shown in the Fig.12.36.

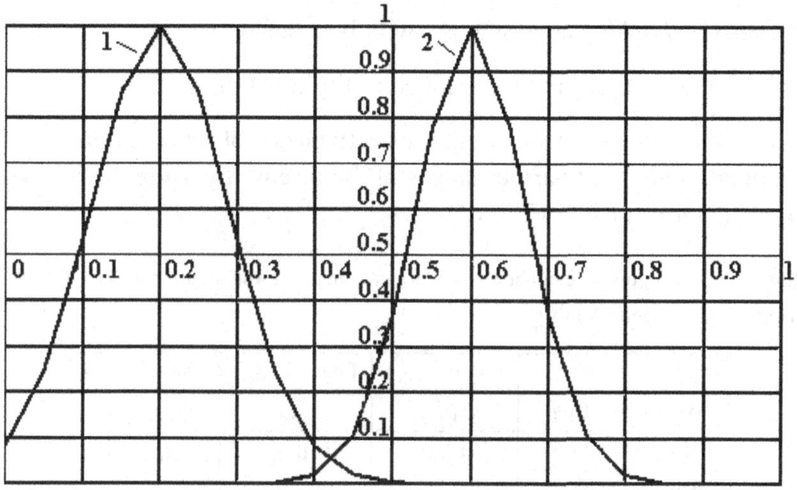

Fig. 12.36. Membership functions of linguistic probabilities $\tilde{P}_1$ (curve 1), $\tilde{P}_2$ (curve 2)

2) *Alternatives.* Alternatives are represented by the available treatment methods. The effectiveness of application of the available treatment methods at the various phases of the disease can be adequately determined in terms of dentist's linguistic (imprecise) evaluations. In view of this, the alternatives should be considered as fuzzy functions [129]. The set of the fuzzy alternatives:

$$\mathcal{A}=\left\{\tilde{f}_1,\tilde{f}_2,\tilde{f}_3\right\},$$

where $\tilde{f}_1$ - closed treatment method, $\tilde{f}_2$ - open treatment method, $\tilde{f}_3$ - surgical entrance and tooth removal.

3) *Utilities.* Utility of an alternative $\tilde{f}_j$ taken at a state $\tilde{S}_i$ is considered as an effectiveness of a corresponding treatment method applied at a corresponding phase of the disease. Without doubts, due to uncertainty involved, effectiveness of application of a considered treatment method at a considered phase of disease can be adequately described by a dentist only in terms of linguistic (imprecise) evaluations. So, utility of an

alternative $\tilde{f}_j$ taken at a state $\tilde{S}_i$ will be considered as a fuzzy value $\tilde{u}\left(\tilde{f}_j\left(\tilde{S}_i\right)\right)$ of a fuzzy number-valued utility function $\tilde{u}$.

Let the dentist evaluate the effectiveness of applications of the treatment methods at various stages of the disease by using the following linguistic terms (Table 12.41):

Table 12.41. Linguistic evaluations of effectiveness of the treatment methods at the various stages of periodontitis

	Phase 1 ($\tilde{S}_1$)	Phase 2 ($\tilde{S}_2$)	Phase 3 ($\tilde{S}_3$)
Alternative 1 ($\tilde{f}_1$)	High	Low	Very Low
Alternative 2 ($\tilde{f}_2$)	Low	High	Medium
Alternative 3 ($\tilde{f}_3$)	Very Low	Medium	High

These linguistic evaluations reflect dentist's subjective opinion expressed in NL. For example, linguistic term "high" expresses the dentist's subjective opinion concerning utility of application of the closed treatment method (alternative $\tilde{f}_1$) in intoxication phase (state $\tilde{S}_1$). As a mathematical description for these linguistic evaluations we use fuzzy numbers shown in Figs.12.37, 12.38 and 12.39 [21].

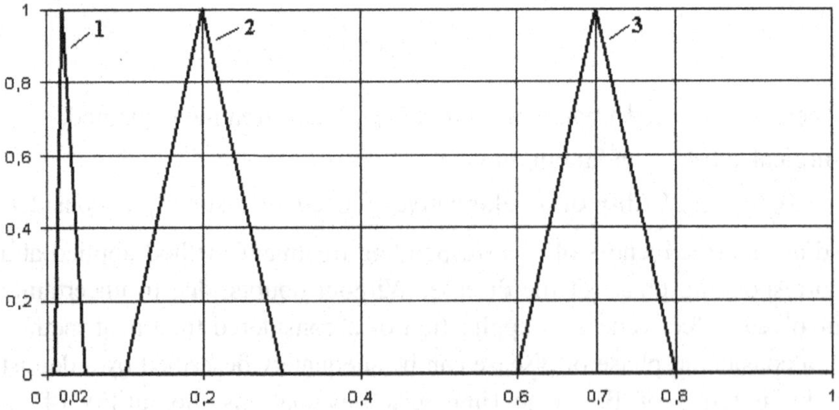

Fig. 12.37. Membership functions of linguistic utilities of the treatment methods application at the intoxication phase: Very Low (curve 1), Low (curve 2), High (curve 3)

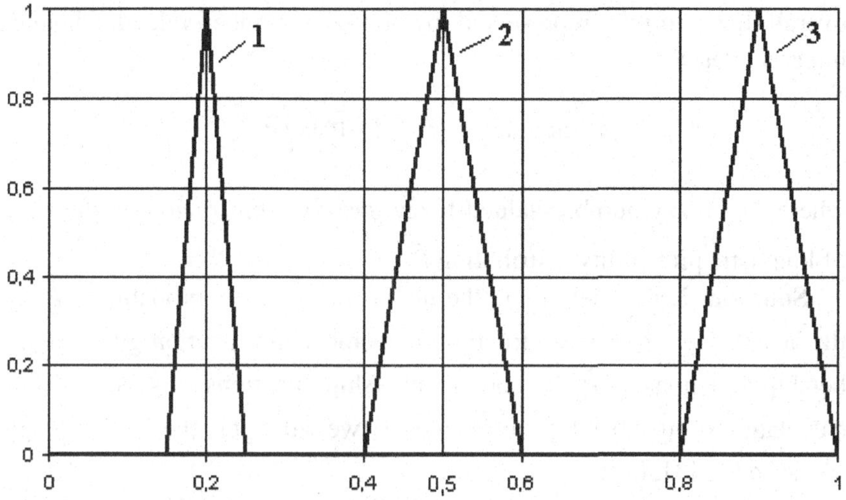

Fig. 12.38. Membership functions of linguistic utilities of the treatment methods application at the exudative phase: Low (curve 1), Medium (curve 2), High (curve 3)

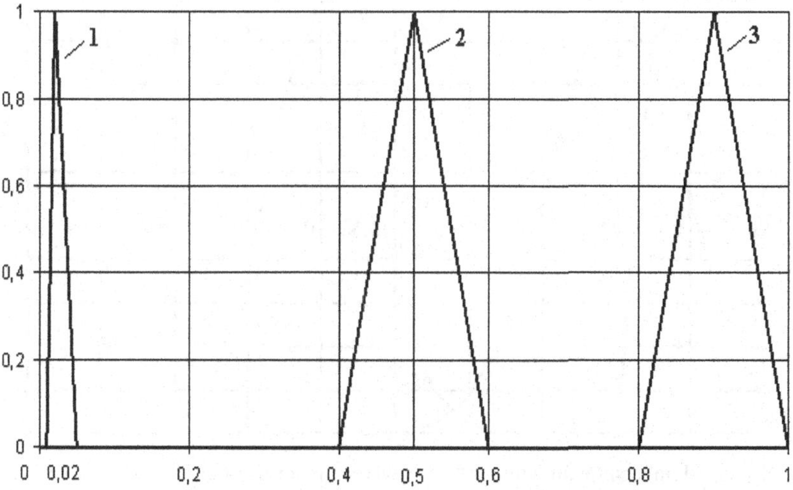

Fig.12.39. Membership functions of linguistic utilities of the treatment methods application at the heavy phase: Very Low (curve 1), Medium (curve 2), High (curve 3)

So, on the base of the theory, suggested in Chapter 6 we will formulate the selection of the optimal treatment method of the periodontitis as a determination of a treatment method with the highest overall fuzzy utility represented by a fuzzy number-valued Choquet integral over $\mathcal{S}$:

$$\text{Find } \tilde{f}^* \in \mathcal{A} \text{ such that } \tilde{U}(\tilde{f}^*) = \max_{f_j \in \mathcal{A}} \int_{S} \tilde{u}(\tilde{f}_j(\tilde{S}_i)) d\tilde{\eta}_{\tilde{P}^l},$$

where $\tilde{\eta}_{\tilde{P}^l}$ - fuzzy number-valued fuzzy measure constructed on the base of linguistic probability distribution $\tilde{P}^l$.

Solution. Let us determine the unknown linguistic probability $\tilde{P}_3$ of the heavy stage $\tilde{S}_3$ by constructing its membership function given membership functions of $\tilde{P}_1, \tilde{P}_2$ and membership functions of $\tilde{S}_1, \tilde{S}_2, \tilde{S}_3$. For calculation of membership function of $\tilde{P}_3$ we will apply the methodology suggested in [31,458].

Membership functions for the given linguistic probabilities $\tilde{P}_1$ and $\tilde{P}_2$ and the obtained linguistic probability $\tilde{P}_3$ are shown in Fig. 12.40 [21].

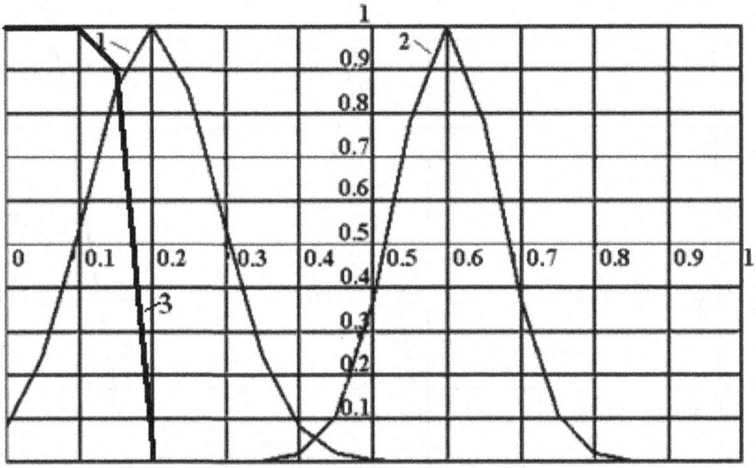

Fig. 12.40. Membership functions of the given imprecise probabilities $\tilde{P}_1$ (curve 1), $\tilde{P}_2$ (curve 2) and computed $\tilde{P}_3$ (curve 3)

So, we have fuzzy probabilities for all the phases of the disease. To calculate the overall fuzzy utility for each alternative we will adopt the suggested fuzzy utility model. According to this model an overall fuzzy utility of a considered alternative (treatment method) will be represented by fuzzy number-valued Choquet integral with the respect to fuzzy number-valued fuzzy measure as follows:

$$\tilde{U}(\tilde{f}_j)=\sum_{i=1}^{3}\left(\tilde{u}(\tilde{f}_j(\tilde{S}_{(i)}))-_h\tilde{u}(\tilde{f}_j(\tilde{S}_{(i+1)}))\right)\cdot\tilde{\eta}_{\tilde{P}^l}(\mathcal{H}_{(i)}),$$

where (i) means that utilities are ranked such that $\tilde{u}(\tilde{f}_j(\tilde{S}_{(1)}))\geq\cdots\geq\tilde{u}(\tilde{f}_j(\tilde{S}_{(n)}))$, $\mathcal{H}_{(i)}=\left\{\tilde{S}_{(1)},...,\tilde{S}_{(i)}\right\},\tilde{u}(\tilde{f}_j(\tilde{S}_{(n+1)}))=0$.

At first it is needed to rank $\tilde{u}(\tilde{f}_j(\tilde{S}_i))=\tilde{u}_{ji}$ for each alternative $\tilde{f}_j$. For each alternative we have:

Alternative $\tilde{f}_1$: $\tilde{u}_{11}=high>\tilde{u}_{12}=low>\tilde{u}_{13}=very\,low$

Alternative $\tilde{f}_2$: $\tilde{u}_{22}=high>\tilde{u}_{23}=medium>\tilde{u}_{21}=low$

Alternative $\tilde{f}_3$: $\tilde{u}_{33}=high>\tilde{u}_{32}=medium>\tilde{u}_{31}=very\,low$

So, fuzzy utilities are ranked as it is shown below.

Alternative $\tilde{f}_1$ (closed treatment method):

$$\tilde{u}_{1(1)}=\tilde{u}_{11}=high\,;\tilde{u}_{1(2)}=\tilde{u}_{12}=low\,;\tilde{u}_{1(3)}=\tilde{u}_{13}=very\ low$$

Alternative $\tilde{f}_2$ (open treatment method):

$$\tilde{u}_{2(1)}=\tilde{u}_{22}=high;\ \tilde{u}_{2(2)}=\tilde{u}_{23}=medium;\ \tilde{u}_{2(3)}=\tilde{u}_{21}=low$$

Alternative $\tilde{f}_3$ (Surgical entrance or tooth removal method):

$$\tilde{u}_{3(1)}=\tilde{u}_{33}=high;\ \tilde{u}_{3(2)}=\tilde{u}_{32}=medium;\ \tilde{u}_{3(3)}=\tilde{u}_{31}=very\ low$$

So, overall fuzzy utilities for alternatives $\tilde{f}_1,\tilde{f}_2,\tilde{f}_3$ will be described as follows:

$$U(\tilde{f}_1)=(\tilde{u}_{11}-_h\tilde{u}_{12})\tilde{\eta}_{\tilde{P}^l}(\{\tilde{S}_1\})+(\tilde{u}_{12}-_h\tilde{u}_{13})\tilde{\eta}_{\tilde{P}^l}(\{\tilde{S}_1,\tilde{S}_2\})$$
$$+\tilde{u}_{13}\tilde{\eta}_{\tilde{P}^l}(\{\tilde{S}_1,\tilde{S}_2,\tilde{S}_3\});$$

$$U(\tilde{f}_2)=(\tilde{u}_{22} -_h \tilde{u}_{23})\tilde{\eta}_{\tilde{P}^l}(\{\tilde{S}_2\})+(\tilde{u}_{23} -_h \tilde{u}_{21})\tilde{\eta}_{\tilde{P}^l}(\{\tilde{S}_2,\tilde{S}_3\})$$
$$+\tilde{u}_{21}\tilde{\eta}_{\tilde{P}^l}(\{\tilde{S}_1,\tilde{S}_2,\tilde{S}_3\});$$

$$U(\tilde{f}_3)=(\tilde{u}_{33} -_h \tilde{u}_{32})\tilde{\eta}_{\tilde{P}^l}(\{\tilde{S}_3\})+(\tilde{u}_{32} -_h \tilde{u}_{31})\tilde{\eta}_{\tilde{P}^l}(\{\tilde{S}_2,\tilde{S}_3\})$$
$$+\tilde{u}_{31}\tilde{\eta}_{\tilde{P}^l}(\{\tilde{S}_1,\tilde{S}_2,\tilde{S}_3\}).$$

We have constructed fuzzy number-valued fuzzy measure from linguistic probability distribution P^l as its lower prevision on the base of the methodology suggested in [31,458]. Finally, we calculated overall fuzzy utility for each alternative and the obtained values approximated as triangular fuzzy numbers are the following:

$$\tilde{U}(\tilde{f}_1)=(0.16;\,0.2;\,0.24)\,;\tilde{U}(\tilde{f}_2)=(0.37;\,0.38;\,0.39)\,;$$
$$\tilde{U}(\tilde{f}_3)=(0.21;\,0.27;\,0.33).$$

Membership functions of these fuzzy utilities are shown in Fig. 12.41.

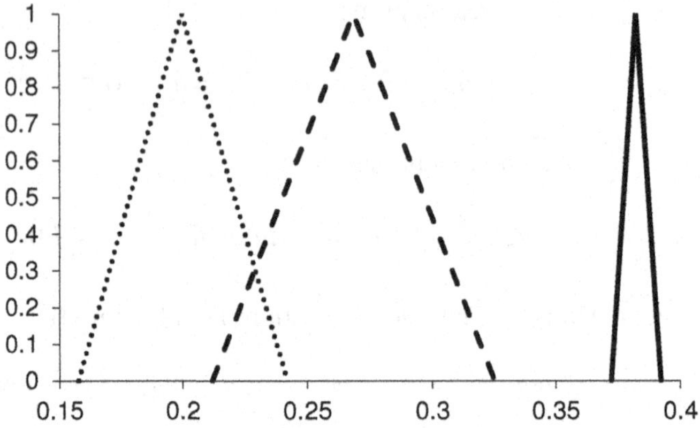

Fig. 12.41. Membership functions of $\tilde{U}(\tilde{f}_1)$ (dotted curve), $\tilde{U}(\tilde{f}_2)$ (solid curve), $\tilde{U}(\tilde{f}_3)$ (dashed curve)

Now it is necessary to compare $\tilde{U}(\tilde{f}_j),\ j=\overline{1,3}$ and determine the optimal treatment method as one with the highest overall fuzzy utility. Comparing fuzzy utilities $\tilde{U}(\tilde{f}_j),\ j=\overline{1,3}$ we found out that the best alternative is $\tilde{f}_2$ as one with the highest overall fuzzy utility. This means that the optimal treatment method for considered patient is an open treatment method. Below we present experimental results of applying the suggested approach to determine an optimal treatment method for patients.

Experimental results. We examined 62 patients suffering from acute periodontitis at the age of 17-65. There were 38 men and 24 women from among them. In order to differentiate chronic periodontitis and to define diagnosis for the patients we held radiological examinations. To differentiate 3 phases of acute periodontitis one from another and to define the diagnosis of each phase together with radiological examinations we evaluated clinical situations on the base of acute periodontitis symptoms (such as pain, hiperemia, palpation, percussion and others) and defined clinical situations.

In oder to define the effectiveness of treatment during 3 different phases of acute periodontitis, together with conduction of the methods of radiological examination we observed the dynamics of changes of some clinical symptoms (pain, hiperemia, palpation, percussion and others) and evaluated the improvements of clinical evidence during the mentioned stages.

The results of our research on cure rates of the given treatment methods depending on 3 different phases of acute periodontitis are given in Table 12.42.

Using various methods of treatment during 3 phases of acute periodontitis, we have got different findings. The comparative results of our research show that in different stages of acute periodontitis "open" and "close" methods were the most effective. So, "open" treatment method proved to be more effective and superior for 21 patients. "close" treatment method was effective for 16 patients, 6 patients used "open" treatment method as it positively effected on their treatment. The tooth of one patient was removed.

Table 12.42. Results of experimental investigation

Different phases of acute periodontitis development	The number of treated patients	Cure rate for the given methods (in number of patients)		
		"closed " treatment method	"open" treatment method	Surgical operation and the tooth removal
Intoxication phase	23	16	6	1
Exudative phase	23	-	21	2
Heavy phase	16	-	3	13

As to the treatment during heavy phase, it's necessary to note that at this phase periodontitis processes are irreversible as it reached the highest level and conservative treatment is less effective(3 patients); most teeth (13 patients), mainly multirooted teeth, were removed by surgical method. During the exudative phase the surgical method was unsatisfactory for 2 patients among the 23. During the intoxication phase for 21 of 23 and during the heavy phase 13 of 16 patients the offered method was satisfactory.

Bibliography

1. Agüero, J. R. and Vargas, A. (2007). Calculating functions of interval type-2 fuzzy numbers for fault current analysis, *IEEE T. Fuzzy Syst.,* no.1, vol. 15, pp. 31-40.
2. Aguilo, I., Suner, J. and Torrens, J. (2010). A characterization of residual implications derived from left-continuous uninorms, *Inform. Sciences,* 180, pp. 3992-4005.
3. Akerlof, G. A. and Shiller, R. J. (2009) *Animal Spirits. How Human Psychology Drives the Economy, and Why it Matters for Global Capitalism.* (Princeton University Press, USA).
4. Alexeyev, A. V., Borisov, A. N., Glushkov, V. I., Krumberg, O.A., Merkuryeva, G.V., Popov, V.A., and Slyadz, N.N. (1987). A linguistic approach to decision-making problems, *Fuzzy Set. Syst.,* 22, pp. 25-41.
5. Aliev, R. A. (1995) *Fuzzy Knowledge based Intelligent Robots.* (Radio i Svyaz, Moscow) (in Russian).
6. Aliev, R. A. (2010). Theory of decision making under second-order uncertainty and combined states, *Proc. 9th Int. Conf. on Appl. of Fuzzy Syst. and Soft Comp.,* ICAFS, pp. 5-6.
7. Aliev, R. A. (2011). Decision making with combined states under imperfect information, *Proc. 6th Int. Conf. on Soft Comp. and Comp. with Words in Syst. Anal., Decis. and Control,* ICSCCW, pp. 3-4.
8. Aliev, R. A. (2013) *Fundamentals of the Fuzzy Logic-Based Generalized Theory of Decisions*. (Springer, New York, Berlin).
9. Aliev, R. A. (2013). Toward a general theory of decisions, *Proc. 7th Int. Conf. on Soft Comp. and Comp. with Words in Syst. Anal., Decis. and Control,* ICSCCW, pp. 13-16.
10. Aliev, R. A. and Aliev, R. R. (1997-1998) *Soft Computing* I, II, III. (ASOA Press, Baku) (in Russian).
11. Aliev, R. A. and Aliev, R. R. (2001) *Soft Computing and Its Application.* (World Scientific, New Jersey, London, Singapore, Hong Kong).
12. Aliev, R. A. and Huseynov, O. H. (2010). Decision making under imperfect information with combined states, *Proc. 9th Int. Conf. on Appl. of Fuzzy Syst. and Soft Comp.,* ICAFS, pp. 400-406.

13. Aliev, R. A. and Huseynov, O. H. (2011). A new approach to behavioral decision making with imperfect information, *Proc. 6th Int. Conf. on Soft Comp. and Comp. with Words in Syst. Anal., Decis. and Control,* ICSCCW, pp. 227-237.
14. Aliev, R. A. and Huseynov, O. H. (2013). Fuzzy geometry-based decision making with unprecisiated visual information, *Int. J. Inf. Tech. Decis.*, accepted, 2014.
15. Aliev, R. A. and Liberzon, M. I. (1987) *Coordination Methods and Algorithms for Integrated Manufacturing Systems*. (Radio i Svyaz, Moscow) (in Russian).
16. Aliev, R. A. and Pedrycz, W. (2009). Fundamentals of a fuzzy-logic-based generalized theory of stability, *IEEE T. Syst. Man CY. B.,* 39(4), pp. 971 - 988.
17. Aliev, R. A. and Tserkovny, A. E. (1988). "Smart" manufacturing systems, *News of Academy of Sciences of USSR, Tech. Cybernetics*, 6, pp.99-108, (in English and Russian).
18. Aliev, R. A. and Tserkovny, A. E. (1988). The knowledge representation in intelligent robots based on fuzzy sets, *Soviet Math. Doklady*, 37, pp. 541-544.
19. Aliev, R. A. and Tserkovny, A. E. (2011). Systemic approach to fuzzy logic formalization for approximate reasoning, *Inform. Sciences,*181, pp. 1045-1059.
20. Aliev, R. A., Aliev, F. T. and Babaev, M. D. (1991) *Fuzzy Process Control and Knowledge Engineering.* (Verlag TUV Rheinland, Koln).
21. Aliev, R. A., Aliyev, B. F., Gardashova, L. A. and Huseynov, O. H. (2012) Selection of an optimal treatment method for acute periodontitis disease, *J. Med. Syst.*, 36(2), pp. 639-646.
22. Aliev, R. A., Alizadeh, A. V. and Guirimov, B. G. (2010). Unprecisiated information-based approach to decision making with imperfect information, *Proc. 9th Int. Conf. on Appl. of Fuzzy Syst. and Soft Comp.,* ICAFS, pp. 387-397.
23. Aliev, R. A., Alizadeh, A. V., Guirimov, B. G. and Huseynov, O. H. (2010). Precisiated information-based approach to decision making with imperfect information, *Proc. 9th Int. Conf. on Appl. of Fuzzy Syst. and Soft Comp.*, ICAFS, pp. 91-103.
24. Aliev, R. A., Bonfig, K. W. and Aliev, F .T. (1993) *Messen, Steuern und Regelnmit Fuzzy- Logik.* (Franzis-Verlag, München) (in German).
25. Aliev, R. A., Fazlollahi, B. and Aliev, R. R. (2004) *Soft Computing and its Application in Business and Economics*. (Springer-Verlag, Berlin, Heidelberg).
26. Aliev, R. A., Fazlollahi, B. and Vahidov, R. M. (2000). Soft computing based multi-agent marketing decision support systems, *J. Intell. Fuzzy Syst.*, 9, pp. 1-9.
27. Aliev, R. A., Huseynov, O. H. and Aliev, R. R. (2009). Decision making with imprecise probabilities and its application, *Proc. 5th Int. Conf. on Soft Comp. and Comp. with Words in Syst. Anal., Decis. and Control*, ICSCCW, pp. 282-286.
28. Aliev, R. A., Krivosheev, V. P. and Liberzon, M. I. (1982). Optimal decision coordination in hierarchical systems, *News of Academy of Sciences of USSR, Tech. Cybernetics,* 2, pp. 72-79 (in English and Russian).
29. Aliev, R. A., Mamedova, G. A. and Aliev, R. R. (1993) *Fuzzy Sets Theory and its Application.* (Tabriz University Press, Iran).
30. Aliev, R. A., Mamedova, G. A. and Tserkovny, A. E. (1991) *Fuzzy Control Systems*. (Energoatomizdat, Moscow).
31. Aliev, R. A., Pedrycz, W. and Huseynov, O. H. (2012). Decision theory with imprecise probabilities, *Int. J. Inf. Tech. Decis.*, 11(2), pp. 271-306.

32. Aliev, R. A., Pedrycz, W. and Huseynov, O. H. (2013). Behavioral decision making with combined states under imperfect information, *Int. J. Inf. Tech. Decis.*, 12(3), pp. 619-645.
33. Aliev, R. A., Pedrycz, W., Alizadeh, A. V. and Huseynov, O. H. (2013). Fuzzy optimality based decision making under imperfect information without utility, *Fuzzy Optim. Decis. Ma.*, vol. 12, issue 4, pp. 357-372.
34. Aliev, R. A., Pedrycz, W., Fazlollahi B., Huseynov O. H., Alizadeh A. V. and Guirimov, B. G. (2012). Fuzzy logic-based generalized decision theory with imperfect information, *Inform. Sciences,* 189, pp. 18-42.
35. Aliev, R. A., Pedrycz, W., Zeinalova, L. M. and Huseynov, O. H. (2014). Decision making with second-order imprecise probabilities, *Int. J. Intell. Syst.*, Volume 29, Issue 2, pp. 137-160.
36. Allais, M. and Hagen, O. (1979) *Expected Utility Hypotheses and the Allais Paradox: Contemporary Discussions of the Decisions under Uncertainty with Allais' Rejoinder.* (D. Reidel Publishing Co., Dordrecht).
37. Alo, R., de Korvin, A. and Modave, F. (2002). Using fuzzy functions to select an optimal action in decision theory, *Proc. of the North American Fuzzy Information Processing Society,* NAFIPS, pp. 348-353.
38. Aminzadeh, F. and Jamshidi, M. (1994) *Soft Computing: Fuzzy Logic, Neural Networks and Distributed Artificial Intelligence*, eds. Aliev, R. A., Chapter 4 "Fuzzy Expert Systems," (PTR Prentice Hal, New Jersey) pp. 99-108.
39. Andreoni, J. and Miller, J. (2002). Giving according to garp: an experimental test of the consistency of preferences for altruism, *Econometrica,* 70, pp.737-753.
40. Anscombe, F. J. and Aumann, R. J. (1963). A definition of subjective probability, *Ann. Math. Stat.*, Vol. 34, No. 1., pp. 199-205.
41. Asto Buditjahjanto, I.G.P. and Miyauchi, H. (2011). An intelligent decision support based on a subtractive clustering and fuzzy inference system for multiobjective optimization problem in serious game, *Int. J. Inf. Tech. Decis.,* 10(5), pp. 793-810.
42. Augustin, T. (2002). Expected utility within a generalized concept of probability – a comprehensive framework for decision-making under ambiguity, *Stat. Pap.*, 43, pp. 5-22.
43. Augustin, T., Miranda, E. and Vejnarova, J. (2009). Imprecise probability models and their applications, *Int. J. Approx. Reason.*, 50(4), pp. 581-582.
44. Aumann, R. (1962). Utility Theory without the Completeness Axiom, *Econometrica*, 30, pp. 445-462.
45. Aven, T. (2003) *Foundations of Risk Analysis: A Knowledge and Decision-Oriented Perspective.* (Wiley, England).
46. Averkin, A. N., Batyrshin, I. Z., Blishun, A. F., Silov, V. B. and Tarasov, V. B. (1986) *Fuzzy Sets in Models of Control and Artificial Intelligence* (Nauka, Moscow) (in Russian).
47. Azadeh, I., Fam, I. M., Khoshnoud, M. and Nikafrouz, M. (2008). Design and implementation of a fuzzy expert system for performance assessment of an integrated health, safety, environment (HSE) and ergonomics system: the case of a gas refinery, *Inform. Sciences,* 178(22), pp. 4280-4300.
48. Baldwin, J. F. and Pilsworth, B. W. (1979). A model of fuzzy reasoning through multivalued logic and set theory, *Int. J. Man-Machines Studies,* 11, pp. 351-380.

49. Baltussen, G., Thierry, P. and van Vliet, P. (2006). Violations of cumulative prospect theory in mixed gambles with moderate probabilities, *Manage. Sci.*, 52(8), pp. 1288-1290.
50. Ban, A. I. and Gal, S. G. (2002). *Defects of Properties in Mathematics: Quantitative Characterizations*. (World Scientific, Singapore).
51. Bandemer, H. and Gottwald, S. (1995) *Fuzzy Sets, Fuzzy Logic, Fuzzy Methods with Applications*. (Wiley, England).
52. Bandemer, H. and Nather, W. (1992). *Fuzzy Data Analysis*. (Kluwer Academic Publishers, Boston).
53. Bandler, W. and Kohout, L. (1980). Fuzzy power sets and fuzzy implications operators, *Fuzzy Set. Syst.,* 1, pp. 13-30.
54. Bandler, W. and Kohout, L. J. (1980). Semantics of fuzzy implication operators and relational products, *Int. J. Man Mach. Stud.,* 12(1), pp. 89-116.
55. Bandler, W. and Kohout, L. J. (1980). The identification of hierarchies in symptoms and patients through computation of fuzzy relational products, *Proc. of the Conf. of British Computer Society: Information Technology for the Eighties,* BCS, pp. 191-194.
56. Bandler, W. and Kohout, L.J. (1984). The four modes of inference in fuzzy expert systems, *Proc. of the 7th European Meeting on Cybernetics and Systems Research*, EMCSR, pp. 581-586.
57. Banerjee, S. and Roy, T.K. (2012). Arithmetic operations on generalized trapezoidal fuzzy number and its applications, *Turkish Journal of Fuzzy Systems*, Vol.3, No.1, pp. 16-44.
58. Bargiela, A. and Pedrycz, W. (2003) *Granular Computing: An Introduction.* (Kluwer Academic Publishers, Amsterdam).
59. Baudrit, C. and Dubois, D. (2006). Practical representations of incomplete probabilistic knowledge, *Comput. Stat. Data An.*, 51, pp. 86-108.
60. Baumfield V. M., Conroy, J. C., Davis R. A. and Lundie, D. C. (2012). The Delphi method: gathering expert opinion in religious education, *British Journal of Religious Education*, Volume 34, Issue 1, pp. 5-19
61. Becker, J. and Sarin, R. (1990) *Economics of ambiguity in probability*, Working paper, (UCLA Graduate School of Management).
62. Bede, B. and Gal, S.G. (2005). Generalizations of the differentiability of fuzzy-number-valued functions with applications to fuzzy differential equations, Fuzzy. Set. Syst., 151, 581-599.
63. Bedregal, B. C., Dimuro, G. P., Santiago, R. H. N. and Reiser, R. H. S. (2010). On interval fuzzy S-implications, *Inform. Sciences,* 180, pp. 1373-1389.
64. Beg, I. (2012). Fuzzy multivalued functions. Centre for Advanced Studies in Mathematics, and Department of Mathematics, Lahore University of Management, Sciences (LUMS), 54792-Lahore, PAKISTAN http://wenku.baidu.com/view/71a84c136c175f0e7cd1372d.html
65. Belman, R. E. and Zadeh, L.A. (1970). Decision making in a fuzzy environment, *Manage Sci.*, 17, pp. 141-164.
66. Belohlavek, R., Sigmund, E. and Zacpal, J. (2011). Evaluation of IPAQ questionnaires supported by formal concept analysis, *Inform. Sciences,*181(10), pp. 1774-1786
67. Ben-Akiva, M. and Lerman, S. R. (1985) *Discrete Choice Analysis: Theory and Application to Travel Demand.* (MIT Press, MA, Cambridge).

68. Berg, J., Dickhaut J. and McCabe K. (1995). Trust, reciprocity, and social history, *Game Econ. Behav.,* 10, pp. 122-142.
69. Berger, J. O. (1985) *Statistical Decision Theory and Bayesian Analysis,* (Springer-Verlag, New York).
70. Bernard, J. M. (2001). Non-parametric inference about an unknown mean using the imprecise Dirichlet model, *Proc. of the 2nd Int. Symposium,* ISIPTA, pp. 40-50.
71. Bernard, J. M. (2002). Implicative analysis for multivariate binary data using an imprecise Dirichlet model, *J. Stat. Plan. Infer.,*105(1), pp. 83-104.
72. Bernardo, J. M., Bayarri, M. J., Berger, J. O. Dawid, A. P., Heckerman, D. Smith, A. F. M. and West, M. (1988). *Bayesian Statistics* **3**, eds. West, M., "Modeling Expert Opinion," (Oxford University Press, UK) pp. 493-508.
73. Bertin, J. (2010) *Semiology of Graphics: Diagrams, Networks, Maps* (ESRI Press, USA).
74. Biglarbegian, M., Melek, W. and Mendel, J. (2010). Robustness of interval type-2 fuzzy logic systems, *Proc. of Annual Meeting of the North American Fuzzy Information Processing Society*, NAFIPS, pp. 1-6.
75. Bilal, M. A. (2001) *Elicitation of Expert Opinions for Uncertainty and Risks.* (CRC Press LLC, Boca Raton, Florida).
76. Billot, A. (1995). An existence theorem for fuzzy utility functions: a new elementary proof, *Fuzzy Set. Syst.,* 74, pp. 271-276.
77. Birnbaum, M. H. (2008). New tests of cumulative prospect theory and the priority heuristic: probability-outcome tradeoff with branch splitting, *Judgm. Decis. Mak.*, Vol. 3, No. 4, pp. 304-316.
78. Birnbaum, M. H., Johnson, K. and Longbottom, J.L. (2008). Tests of cumulative prospect theory with graphical displays of probability, *Judgm. Decis. Mak.*, 3(7), pp. 528-546
79. Blin, J. M. and Whinston, A. B. (1973). Fuzzy sets and social choice, *J. Cybern*, 3 (4), pp. 17-22.
80. Bloch, I. (2011). Lattices of fuzzy sets and bipolar fuzzy sets, and mathematical morphology, *Inform. Sciences,*181(10), pp. 2002-2015.
81. Bobillo, F. and Straccia, U. (2011). Reasoning with the finitely many-valued Łukasiewicz fuzzy Description Logic SROIQ, *Inform. Sciences,*181(4), pp. 758-778
82. Borisov, A. N., Alekseyev, A. V., Merkuryeva, G. V., Slyadz, N. N., and Gluschkov, V. I. (1989) *Fuzzy Information Processing in Decision Making Systems,* (Radio i Svyaz, Moscow) (in Russian).
83. Borisov, A. N., Ujga-Rebrov, O. I., Savchenko, K. I. (2002) *Probabilistic Inference in Intelligent Systems*. (Riga Technical University, Riga) (in Russian).
84. Bouchon-Meunier, B., Marsala, C., Rifqi, M. and Yager, R. R. (2008) *Uncertainty and Intelligent Information Systems*, eds. Ohnishi, S., Dubois, D., Prade, H. and Yamanoi, T., Chapter 16 "A Fuzzy Constraint-Based Approach to the Analytic Hierarchy Process," (World Scientific, Singapore) pp. 217-228.
85. Brafman, R. I. and Tennenholz, M. (1997). Modeling agents as qualitative decision makers, *Artif. Intell.*, 94(1-2), pp.217-268.
86. Braithwaite, R. B. (1931) The Foundations of Mathematics and other Logical Essays, eds. Ramsey, F.P. (1926) "Truth and Probability", in Ramsey, 1931, Chapter 7, (Kegan, Paul, Trench, Trubner & Co., London; Harcourt, Brace and

Company, New York) pp. 156-198.

87. Buckley, J. J. (2003). *Fuzzy Probability and Statistics.* (Springer-Verlag, Heidelberg, Berlin).

88. Buckley, J. J. and Eslami, E. (1997). Fuzzy plane geometry I: Points and lines, *Fuzzy Set. Syst.,* 86(2), pp. 179-187.

89. Bustince, H. and Pagola, M. (2010). Ignorance functions. An application to the calculation of the threshold in prostate ultrasound images, *Fuzzy Set. Syst.,* 161, pp.20-36.

90. Bustince, H., Barrenechea, E., Fernandez, J., Pagola, M., Montero, J. and Guerra, C. (2010). Contrast of a fuzzy relation, *Inform. Sciences,* 180, pp. 1326-1344.

91. Camerer, C. and Weber, M. (1992). Recent developments in modeling preferences, *J. Risk Uncertainty*, 5, pp. 325-370.

92. Cao L. B. and Dai R. W. (2003). Agent-oriented metasynthetic engineering for decision making, *Int. J. Inf. Tech. Decis.,* 2(2), pp. 197-215.

93. Casadesus-Masanell, R., Klibanoff, P. and Ozdenoren, E. (2000). Maxmin expected utility through statewise combinations, *Econ. Lett.,* 66, pp. 49-54.

94. Castillo, O. (2011) *Type-2 Fuzzy Logic in Intelligent Control Applications,* (Springer, USA).

95. Castillo, O. and Melin, P. (2008). *Type-2 Fuzzy Logic: Theory and Applications.* (Springer, Berlin).

96. Castillo, O. and Melin, P. (2008). *Type-2 Fuzzy Logic: Theory and Applications. Studies in Fuzziness and Soft Computing*, eds. Castillo, O. and Melin, P., Chapter 1 "Introduction to Type-2 Fuzzy Logic," (Springer, Berlin) pp. 1-4.

97. Chajda, I., Halas, R. and Rosenberg, I. G. (2010). On the role of logical connectives for primality and functional completeness of algebras of logics, *Inform. Sciences,* 180(8), pp. 1345-1353.

98. Charles, M., Grinstead, J. and Snell, L. (1997) *Introduction to Probability.* (American Mathematical Society, USA).

99. Chateauneuf, A. and Faro, J. (2009). Ambiguity through confidence functions, *J. Math. Econ.,* 45(9-10), pp. 535-558.

100. Chateauneuf, A. and Wakker, P. (1999). An axiomatization of cumulative prospect theory for decision under risk, *J. Risk Uncertainty*, 18(2), pp. 137-145.

101. Chaudhuri, B. B. and Rosenfeld, A. (1999). A modified Hausdorff distance between fuzzy sets, *Inform. Sciences*, 118, pp. 159-171.

102. Chen, S.H. (1985). Operations on fuzzy numbers with function principle, *Tamkang Journal of Management Sciences*, 6, pp. 13-25.

103. Chen, T. (2010). Optimistic and pessimistic decision making with dissonance reduction using interval-valued fuzzy sets, *Inform. Sciences,*181(3), pp. 479-502.

104. Chen, T.-Y. (2011). Signed distanced-based TOPSIS method for multiple criteria decision analysis based on generalized interval-valued fuzzy numbers, *Int. J. Inf. Tech. Decis.*, 10(6), pp. 1131-1159.

105. Chen, T.-Y., Wang, J.-C. and Tzeng, G.-H. (2000). Identification of general fuzzy measures by genetic algorithms based on partial information, *IEEE T. Syst. Man CY. B., Cybernetics,* 30(4), pp. 517-528.

106. Chen, Z. and Epstein, L. G. (2002). Ambiguity, risk, and asset returns in continuous time, *Econometrica*, 70, pp. 1403-1443.

107. Chew, S. H., Karni, E. and Safra, Z. (1987). Risk aversion in the theory of expected utility with rank-dependent probabilities, *J. Econ. Theory,* 42, pp. 370-381.

108. Chiclana, F., Herrera, F., Herrera-Viedma, E. and Martinez, L. (2003). A note on the reciprocity in the aggregation of fuzzy preference relations using OWA operators, *Fuzzy Set. Syst.,* 137, pp. 71-83.
109. Choquet, G. (1953). Theory of capacities, *Ann. I. Fourier*, 5, pp. 131-295.
110. Clementini, E. (2005). A model for uncertain lines, *J. Visual Lang. Comput.*, 16, pp. 271-288.
111. Cobb, L. and Thrall, R. M. (1981). *Mathematical Frontiers of the Social and Policy Sciences,* eds. Zadeh, L. A. "Possibility Theory and Soft Data Analysis," (Westview Press, Boulder, Colorado) pp. 69-129.
112. Compte, O. and Postlewaite, A. (2009) *Mental processes and decision making,* Working paper, (Yale University, New Haven, USA). http://econ.as.nyu.edu/docs/IO/19118/Postlewaite_2011Mar22.pdf
113. Cover, T. and Hellman, M. (1970). Learning with finite memory, *Ann. Math. Stat.,* 41, pp.765-782.
114. Cox, J. C. (2004). How to identify trust and reciprocity, *Game Econ. Behav.,* 46, pp. 260-281.
115. Cox, J. C., Friedman, D. and Sadiraj, V. (2008). Revealed altruism, *Econometrica,* 76(1), pp. 31-69.
116. Cutello, V. and Montero, J. (1994). Fuzzy rationality measures, *Fuzzy Set. Syst.*, 62, pp. 39-54.
117. Da Silva, F. S. C. and Agustí-Cullell, J. (2006). *Capturing Intelligence* **1**, eds. Yager, R. R., Chapter 11 "Using Knowledge Trees for Semantic Web Querying," (Elsevier, Amsterdam) pp. 231-246.
118. Davvaz, B., Zhan, J. and Shum, K. P. (2008). Generalized fuzzy Hv-submodules endowed with interval valued membership functions, *Inform. Sciences, 178,* pp. 3147-3159.
119. De Baets, B. and De Meyer H. (2005). Transitivity frameworks for reciprocal relations: cycle transitivity versus FG-transitivity, *Fuzzy Sets Syst.*, 152, pp. 249-270.
120. De Baets, B. and Fodor, J. (2003) *Principles of Fuzzy Preference Modelling and Decision Making,* eds. Chiclana, F., Herrera, F. and Herrera-Viedma, E., "Reciprocity and Consistency of Fuzzy Preference Relations," (Academic Press, Ghent) pp. 23-142.
121. De Baets, B., De Meyer, H., De Schuymer, B. and Jenei, S. (2006). Cyclic evaluation of transitivity of reciprocal relations, *Soc. Choice Welfare*, 26, pp. 217-238.
122. De Cooman, G. (1998). Possibilistic previsions, *Proc. of 7th Conf. on Information Processing and Management of Uncertainty in Knowledge-based Systems,* IPMU, pp. 2-9.
123. De Cooman, G. (2000). Precision-imprecision equivalence in a broad class of imprecise hierarchical uncertainty models, *J. Stat. Plan. Infer.,*105(1), pp. 175-198.
124. De Cooman, G. and Walley, P. (2002). A possibilistic hierarchical model for behavior under uncertainty, *Theor. Decis.*, vol. 52(4), pp. 327-374.
125. De Finetti, B. (1974) *Theory of Probability,* **1**. (Wiley, New York).
126. De Wilde, P. (2004). Fuzzy utility and equilibria, *IEEE T. Syst. Man CY. B.,* 34(4) 1774-1785.

127. Degtiarev, K. Y. (2013). Visual representation of fuzzy categories based on extended geometric objects, *Proc. of the 7th Int. Conf. on Soft Comp. and Comp. with Words in Syst. Anal., Decis. and Control*, ICSCCW, pp. 49-60.
128. Dempster, A. P. (1967). Upper and lower probabilities induced by a multivalued mapping, *Ann. Math. Stat.*, 38, pp. 325-339.
129. Diamond, P. and Kloeden, P. (1994) *Metric Spaces of Fuzzy Sets, Theory and Applications*. (World Scientific, Singapore).
130. Dian, J. (2010). A meaning based information theory – inform logical space: Basic concepts and convergence of information sequences, *Inform. Sciences, 180, Special Issue on Modeling Uncertainty*, 15, pp. 984-994.
131. Dinagar, S. D. and Latha, K. (2013). Some types of type–2 triangular fuzzy matrices, *International Journal of Pure and Applied Mathematics*, no.1, vol.82, pp. 21-32.
132. Dowling, J. M. and Chin-Fang, Y. (2007) *Modern Developments in Behavioral Economics. Social Science Perspectives on Choice and Decision making.* (World Scientific, Singapore).
133. Dubois, D. (2011). The role of fuzzy sets in decision sciences: Old techniques and new directions, *Fuzzy Set. Syst.,* 184, pp. 3-28.
134. Dubois, D. and Prade, H. (1980) *Fuzzy Sets and Systems: Theory and Applications.* (Academic Press, New York).
135. Dubois, D. and Prade, H. (1985). A review of fuzzy sets aggregation connectives, *Inform. Sciences*, 36, pp. 85-121.
136. Dubois, D. and Prade, H. (1992). When upper probabilities are possibility measures, *Fuzzy Set. Syst.*, 49, pp. 65-74.
137. Dubra, J., Maccheroni, F. and Ok, E. (2004). Expected utility theory without the completeness axiom, *J. Econom. Theory,* 115, pp. 118-133.
138. Dutta, S.(1990). Qualitative spatial reasoning: a semi-quantitative approach using fuzzy logic, *Lect. Notes Comput. Sc.*, 409, pp. 345-364.
139. Eichberger, J. and Kelsey, D. (1999). E-Capacities and the Ellsberg paradox, *Theor. Decis.*, 46, pp. 107-138.
140. Eichberger, J., Grant, S. and Kelsey, D. (2007). Updating Choquet beliefs, *J. Math. Econ.,* 43(7-8), pp. 888-899.
141. Einhorn, H. and Hogarth, R. (1985). Ambiguity and uncertainty in probabilistic inference, *Psychol. Rev.,* 92, pp. 433-461.
142. Ekenberg, L. and Thorbiornson, J. (2001). Second-order decision analysis, *Int. J. Uncertain Fuzz.,* 9(1), pp. 13-37.
143. Eliaz, K. and Ok, E. A. (2006). Indifference or indecisiveness? Choice-theoretic foundations of incomplete preferences, *Game. Econ. Behav.*, 56, pp. 61-86.
144. Ellsberg, D. (1961). Risk, ambiguity and the Savage axioms, *Q. J. Econ.*, 75, pp. 643-669.
145. Enea, M. and Piazza, T. (2004). Project selection by constrained fuzzy AHP, *Fuzzy Optim. Decis. Ma.*, 3(1), pp. 39-62.
146. Epstein, L. G. (1999). A definition of uncertainty aversion, *Rev. Econ. Stud.*, 66, pp. 579-608.
147. Epstein, L. G. and Schneider M. (2008). Ambiguity, information quality and asset pricing, *J. Financ.,* 63(1), pp. 197-228.
148. Epstein, L. G. and Wang, T. (1994). Intertemporal asset pricing under Knightian uncertainty, *Econometrica,* 62, pp. 283-322.

149. Epstein, L. G. and Zhang, J. (2001). Subjective probabilities on subjectively unambiguous events, *Econometrica*, 69, pp. 265-306.
150. Falk, A., and Fischbacher, U. (2006). A theory of reciprocity, *Game Econ. Behav.*, 54, pp. 293-315.
151. Fan, Z-P. and Feng, B. (2009). A multiple attributes decision making method using individual and collaborative attribute data in a fuzzy environment, *Inform. Sciences,* 179, pp. 3603-3618.
152. Farina, M., and Amato, P. (2004). A fuzzy definition of "optimality" for many-criteria optimization problems, *IEEE T. Syst. Man Cy. A: Systems and Humans*, 34(3), pp. 315-326.
153. Fazlollahi, B., Vahidov, R. M. and Aliev, R. A. (2000). Multi-Agent distributed intelligent systems based on fuzzy decision-making, *Int. J. Intell. Syst.*, 15, pp. 849-858.
154. Fedrizzi, M. and Fuller, R. (1992). Stability in possibilistic linear programming problems with continuous fuzzy number parameters, *Fuzzy Set. Syst.*, 47, pp. 187-191.
155. Fedrizzi, M., Kacprzyk, J. and Nurmi, H. (1993). Consensus degrees under fuzzy majorities and fuzzy preferences using OWA (ordered weighted average) operators, *Control Cybern.*, 22, pp. 71-80.
156. Ferson, S., Ginzburg, L., Kreinovich, V., Nguyen, H.T. and Starks, S.A. (2002). Uncertainty in risk analysis: towards a general second-order approach combining interval, probabilistic, and fuzzy techniques, *Proc. of IEEE International Conference on Fuzzy Systems, vol. 2,* FUZZ-IEEE, pp. 1342-1347.
157. Fodor, J. and Roubens, M. (1994) *Fuzzy Preference Modeling and Multicriteria Decision Support.* (Kluwer Academic Publishers, Dordrecht).
158. Franke, G. (1978). Expected utility with ambiguous probabilities and "Irrational Parameters", *Theor. Decis.,* 9, pp. 267-283.
159. Fudenberg, D. (2006). Advancing Beyond "Advances in Behavioral Economics", *J. Econ. Literature*, 44, pp. 694-711.
160. Fukami, S., Mizumoto, M. and Tanaka, K. (1980). Some considerations of fuzzy conditional inference, *Fuzzy Set. Syst.*, 4, pp. 243-273.
161. Fumika, O. (2004). A literature review on the use of expert opinion in probabilistic risk analysis, World Bank Policy Research Working Paper, no. 3201. http://www-wds.worldbank.org
162. Gajdos, T., Tallon, J. M. and Vergnaud, J.C. (2004). Decision making with imprecise probabilistic information, *J. Math. Econ.,* 40(6), pp. 647-681.
163. Gerhke, M., Walker, C. L. and Walker, E. A. (2003). Normal forms and truth tables for fuzzy logics, *Fuzzy Set. Syst.*, 138, pp. 25-51.
164. Ghirardato, P. (2001) Coping with ignorance: unforeseen contingencies and non-additive uncertainty, *Econ. Theory*, 17, pp.247-276.
165. Ghirardato, P. and Marinacci, M. (2001). Range convexity and ambiguity averse preferences, *Econ. Theory,* 17, pp. 599-617.
166. Ghirardato, P. and Marinacci, M. (2002). Ambiguity made precise: a comparative foundation, *J. Econ. Theory,* 102, pp. 251-289.
167. Ghirardato, P., Klibanoff, P. and Marinacci, M. (1998). Additivity with multiple priors, *J. Math. Econ.,* 30, pp. 405-420.
168. Ghirardato, P., Maccheroni F., and Marinacci M. (2004). Differentiating ambiguity and ambiguity attitude, *J. Econ. Theory,* 118, pp. 133-173.

169. Gil, M. A. and Jain, P. (1992). Comparison of experiments in statistical decision problems with fuzzy utilities, *IEEE T. Syst. Man Cyb.*, 22(4) pp. 662-670.
170. Gilboa, I. (2009) *Theory of Decision under Uncertainty*. (Cambridge University Press, Cambridge).
171. Gilboa, I. and Schmeidler, D. (1989). Maximin expected utility with a non-unique prior, *J. Math. Econ.*, 18, pp. 141-153.
172. Gilboa, I., Maccheroni, F., Marinacci, M. and Schmeidler, D. (2010). Objective and subjective rationality in a multiple prior model, *Econometrica,* 78(2), pp. 755-770.
173. Giraud, R. (2005). Objective imprecise probabilistic information, second order beliefs and ambiguity aversion: an axiomatization, *Proc. 4th Fourth International Symposium on Imprecise Probabilities and Their Applications*, ISIPTA, pp. 183-192.
174. Good, I. J. (1962). Subjective probability at the measure of non-measurable set, *Proc. 1st Congress of Logic, Methodology and Philosophy of Science,* CLMPS, pp. 319-329.
175. Grabisch, M. and Roubens, M. (2000) *Fuzzy Measures and Integrals: Theory and Applications,* eds. Grabisch, M., Murofushi, T., and Sugeno, M., Chapter 17 "Application of the Choquet Integral in Multicriteria Decision Making," (Physica-Verlag, Berlin) pp. 348-374.
176. Grabisch, M., Marichal, J., Mesiar, R. and Pap, E. (2011). Aggregation functions: Construction methods, conjunctive, disjunctive and mixed classes, *Inform. Sciences,* 181, 23 p.
177. Grzegorzewski, P. (2011). On possible and necessary inclusion of intuitionistic fuzzy sets, *Inform. Sciences,* 181, pp. 342-350.
178. Grzegorzewski, P., Hryniewicz, O. and Gil, M. A. (2002). *Soft Methods in Probability, Statistics and Data Analysis,* eds. Utkin, L. V., Chapter 14 "A Hierarchical Uncertainty Model Under Essentially Incomplete Information," (Physica-Verlag, New York) pp. 156-163.
179. Guirimov, B. G., Gurbanov R. S. and Aliev R. A. (2011). Application of fuzzy geometry in decision making. *Proc. 6th Int. Conf. on Soft Comp. and Comp. with Words in Syst. Anal., Decis. and Control,* ICSCCW, pp. 308-316.
180. Guo, P. (2011). One-Shot decision theory, *IEEE T. Syst. Man Cy. A,* 41(5), pp. 917-926.
181. Guo, P. and Pedrycz, W. (2013) *Human-Centric Decision-Making Models for Social Sciences*, eds. Aliev, R. A. and Zeinalova, L. M., Chapter 10 "Decision making under Z-information," (Springer) pp. 233-252.
182. Guo, P. and Tanaka, H. (2003). Decision analysis based on fused double exponential possibility distributions, *Eur. J. Oper. Res.,* 148, pp. 467-479.
183. Guo, P. and Tanaka, H. (2010). Decision making with interval probabilities. *Eur. J. Oper. Res.*, 203, pp. 444-454.
184. Gupta, M. M., Ragade, R. K. and Yager, R. R. (1979) *Advances in Fuzzy Set Theory Applications*, eds. Mizumoto, M., Fukami, S. and Tanaka, K. "Some Methods of Fuzzy Reasoning," (Elsevier, Amsterdam) pp. 117-136.
185. Hable, R. (2009). Data-based decisions under imprecise probability and least favorable models, *Int. J. Approx. Reason.*, 50(4), pp. 642-654.
186. Hable, R. (2009). Finite approximations of data-based decision problems under imprecise probabilities, *Int. J. Approx. Reason.,* 50(7), pp. 1115-1128.

187. Hajek, P. (1995). Fuzzy logic from the logical point of view, *Proc. 22nd Seminar on Current Trends in Theory and Practice of Informatics*, SOFSEM, pp. 31-49.
188. Hajek, P. (1998) *Metamathematics of Fuzzy Logic. Trends in Logic.* (Kluwer Academic Publishers, Dodrecht).
189. Halpern, J. Y. (2003) *Reasoning about Uncertainty.* (The MIT Press, Massachusetts).
190. Halpern, J. Y. and Fagin, R. (1992). Two views of belief: belief as generalized probability and belief as evidence, *Artif. Intell.*, 54, pp. 275-317.
191. Halpern, J. Y., and Moses, Y.(1990). Knowledge and common knowledge in a distributed environment, *J. Assoc. Comput. Mach.*, 37(3), pp. 549-587.
192. Hansen, L. and Sargent, T. (2001). Robust control and model uncertainty, *Am. Econ. Rev.*, 91, pp. 60-66.
193. Harris, J. (2006). *Fuzzy Logic Applications in Engineering Science* **29**, eds. Tzafestas, S. G., Chen, C. S., Fokuda, T., Harashima, F., Schmidt, G., Sinha, N. K., Tabak, D. and Valavanis, K., Chapter 2 "Fuzzy Geometry," (Springer, Netherlands) pp. 11-30.
194. Havens, T. C., Anderson, D. T. and Keller, J. M. (2010). A fuzzy Choquet integral with an interval type-2 fuzzy number-valued integrand, *Proc. IEEE International Conference on Fuzzy Systems,* FUZZ, pp. 1-8.
195. Hayes-Roth, B. (1995). An architecture for adaptive intelligent systems, *Artif. Intell.*, 72, pp. 329-365.
196. Herrera, F. and Herrera-Viedma, E. (1997). Aggregation operators for linguistic weighted information, *IEEE T. Syst. Man. Cy. A.*, 27, pp. 646-656.
197. Herrera, F. and Herrera-Viedma, E. (2000). Choice functions and mechanisms for linguistic preference relations. *Eur. J. Oper. Res.*,120, pp. 144-161.
198. Herrera, F. and Herrera-Viedma, E. (2000). Linguistic decision analysis: steps for solving decision problems under linguistic information, *Fuzzy Set. Syst.*, 115, pp. 67-82.
199. Herrera, F., Herrera-Viedma, E. and Verdegay, J. L. (1996). Direct approach processes in group decision making using linguistic OWA operators, *Fuzzy Set. Syst.*, 79, pp. 175-190.
200. Herrera-Viedma, E., Herrera, F., Chiclana, F. (2001). Multiperson decision-making based on multiplicative preference relations, *Eur. J. Oper. Res.,* 129(2), pp. 372-385.
201. Herrera-Viedma, E., Herrera, F., Chiclana, F. and Luque, M. (2004). Some issues on consistency of fuzzy preference relations, *Eur. J. Oper. Res.*, vol. 154, no. 1, pp. 98-109.
202. Hey, J. D., Lotito, G. and Maffioletti, A. (2007). Choquet OK? Discussion Papers from Department of Economics, University of York, York, UK http://eprints.luiss.it/771/1/0712_HEY_2007.pdf
203. Ho, J. L. Y., Keller, P. L. and Keltyka, P. (2002). Effects of outcome and probabilistic ambiguity on managerial choices, *J. Risk Uncertainty*, 24(1), pp. 47-74.
204. Hodges, J. L., and Lehmann, E. (1952). The use of previous experience in reaching statistical decisions, *The Ann. Math. Stat.*, 23, pp 396-407.
205. Hsu, M., Bhatt, M., Adolphs, R., Tranel, D. and Camerer, C. F. (2005) Neural systems responding to degrees of uncertainty in human decision-making, *Science*, 310(5754), 1680-1683.

206. Hu, Q., Yu, D. and Guo, M. (2010). Fuzzy preference based rough sets, *Inform. Sciences, 180*, pp. 2003-2022.
207. Huangm, W.-C. and Chen, C.-H. (2005). Using the ELECTRE II method to apply and analyze the differentiation theory, *Proc. of the Eastern Asia Society for Transportation Studies, Vol. 5,* EASTS, pp. 2237-2249.
208. Huettel, S. A., Stowe, C. J., Gordon, E. M., Warner, B. T., and Platt, M. L. (2006). Neural signatures of economic preferences for risk and ambiguity, *Neuron*, 49, pp. 765-775.
209. Hwang, C. L. (1981) *Multiple Attribute Decision Making.* (Springer-Verlag, Berlin).
210. Insua, D. R. (1990) *Sensitivity Analysis in Multiobjective Decision Making.* (Springer, New York).
211. Insua, D. R. (1992). On the foundations of decision making under partial information, *Theor. Decis.,* 33, pp. 83-100.
212. Insua, D. R. and Ruggeri, F. (2000) *Robust Bayesian Analysis*, eds. (Springer, New York).
213. Jaffal, H. and Tao, C. (2011). *Multiple Attributes Group Decision Making by Type-2 Fuzzy Sets and Systems*. Blekinge Institute of Technology, Master Degree Thesis no: 2011:1.
214. Jaffray, J. Y. (1999). Rational decision making with imprecise probabilities, *Proc. 1st International Symposium on Imprecise Probabilities and their Applications,* ISIPTA, pp. 324-332.
215. Jahanshahloo, G. R., Lotfi. F, and Hosseinzadeh, I. M. (2006). An algorithmic method to extend TOPSIS for decision-making problems with interval data, *Appl. Math. Comput.*, 175(2), pp. 1375-1384.
216. Jamshidi, M., Titli, M., Zadeh, L., and Boverie, S. (1997) *Application of Fuzzy Logic Towards High Machine Intelligence Quotient Systems*, eds. Aliev, R. A. and Aliev R. R., Chapter 15 "Fuzzy Distributed Intelligent Systems for Continuous Production," (Prentice Hall PTR, Upper Saddle River, New Jersey, USA) pp. 301-320.
217. Jantzen, J. (1995). Array approach to fuzzy logic, *Fuzzy Set. Syst.*, 70, pp. 359-370.
218. Jayaram, B. and Mesiar, R. (2009). I-Fuzzy equivalence relations and I-fuzzy partitions, *Inform. Sciences,* 179, pp. 1278-1297.
219. Jenei, S. (1999). Continuity in Zadeh's compositional rule of inference, *Fuzzy Set. Syst.*, 104, pp. 333-339.
220. Jong, Y., Liang, W. and Reza, L. (1997). Multiple fuzzy systems for function approximation, *Proc. of Annual Meeting of the North American Fuzzy Information Processing Society*, NAFIPS, pp. 154-159.
221. Kacprzyk, J. and Roubens, M. (1988). *Non-Conventional Preference Relations in Decision Making*, eds. Tanino, T. "Fuzzy Preference Relations in Group Decision Making," (Springer-Verlag, Berlin), pp. 54-71.
222. Kahneman, D. and Tversky, A. (1979). Prospect theory: an analysis of decision under uncertainty, *Econometrica,* 47, pp. 263-291.
223. Kahneman, D., Slovic, P. and Tversky, A. (1982). *Judgment and Decision Making Under Uncertainty: Heuristics and Biases.* (Cambridge University Press) 544 p.
224. Kallala, M. and Kohout, L. J. (1984). The use of fuzzy implication operators in clinical evaluation of neurological movement disorders, *International Symposium on Fuzzy Information Processing in Artificial Intelligence and Operational*

Research (Christchurch College, Cambridge University).

225. Kallala, M. and Kohout, L. J. (1986), A 2-stage method for automatic handwriting classification by means of norms and fuzzy relational inference, *Annual Meeting of the North American Fuzzy Information Processing Society*, NAFIPS.
226. Kandel, A. and Last, M. (2007). Special issue on advances in fuzzy logic, *Inform. Sciences,* 177, pp. 329-331.
227. Kang, B., Wei, D., Li, Y., Deng, Y. (2012). Decision making using Z-numbers under uncertain environment, *Journal of Information and Computational Science,* 8(7), pp. 2807-2814.
228. Kapoor, V. and Tak, S. S. (2005). Fuzzy application to the analytic hierarchy process for robot selection, *Fuzzy Optim. Decis. Ma.*, 4(3), pp. 209-234.
229. Karni, E. (1985) *Decision Making under Uncertainty: The Case of State Dependent Preferences*. (Harvard University Press, Cambridge).
230. Karnik, N. N. and Mendel, J. M. (2001). Operations on Type–2 Fuzzy Sets. *Fuzzy Set. Syst.,* 122, pp. 327-348.
231. Karnik, N. N., Mendel, J. M. and Liang, Q. (1999). Type–2 Fuzzy Logic Systems, *IEEE T. Fuzzy Syst.*, No. 6, vol. 7, pp. 643-658.
232. Kaufman, A. (1973) *Introduction to Theory of Fuzzy Sets*. (Academic Press, Orlando).
233. Kehagias, A. (2010). Some remarks on the lattice of fuzzy intervals, *Inform. Sciences,* 181(10), pp. 1863-1873.
234. Kenneth, E. T. (2007) *Discrete Choice Models with Simulation.* (Cambridge University Press, New York).
235. Khan, N. A. and Jain, R. (1985). Uncertainty management in a distributed knowledge base system, *Proc. 9th International Joint Conference on Artificial Intelligence*, IJCAI, pp. 318-320.
236. Kiszka, J. B., Kochanska, M. E. and Sliwinska, D. S. (1985). The influence of some fuzzy implication operators on the accuracy of a fuzzy model, *Fuzzy. Set. Syst.*, 15, (Part1) pp. 111-128; (Part2) pp. 223-240.
237. Klibanoff, P. (2000). Maxmin expected utility over Savage acts with a set of priors, *J. Econ. Theory,* 92, pp.35-65.
238. Klibanoff, P. (2001). Characterizing uncertainty aversion through preference for mixtures, *Soc. Choice Welfare*, 18, pp. 289-301.
239. Klibanoff, P., Marinacci, M. and Mukerji, S. (2005). A smooth model of decision making under ambiguity, *Econometrica,* 73(6), pp. 1849-1892.
240. Klir, G. J. and Yuan, B. (1995) *Fuzzy sets and fuzzy logic, Theory and Applications* (NJ: PRT Prentice Hall).
241. Klir, G. J. and Yuan, B. (1996). *Advances in Fuzzy Set Theory and Applications. Fuzzy Sets, Fuzzy Logic and Fuzzy Systems. Selected Papers by Lotfi A. Zadeh* **6**, eds. Zadeh, L. A. "Fuzzy Sets and Information Granularity," (World Scientific,) pp. 433-448.
242. Klir, G. J., Clair, U. S. and Yuan, B. (1997) *Fuzzy Set Theory, Foundations and Applications*, (PTR Prentice Hall, New Jersey).
243. Klir, G., Yuan, B. (1996) *Fuzzy Sets, Fuzzy Logic, and Fuzzy Systems: Selected Papers by Lotfi Asker Zadeh.* (World Scientific, Singapore).
244. Kohout, L. J. (1986) *A Perspective on Intelligent Systems: A Framework for Analysis and Design.* (Chapman & Hall, UK).

245. Kohout, L. J. and Bandler, W. (1985). Relational-product architecture for information processing, *Inform. Science*, 37, pp. 25-37.
246. Kojadinovic, I. (2006). Multi-attribute utility theory based on the Choquet integral: A theoretical and practical overview, *7th Int. Conf. on Multi-Objective Programming and Goal Programming.*
247. Kolesarova, A. and Mesiar, R. (2010). Lipschitzian De Morgan triplets of fuzzy connectives, *Inform. Sciences,* 180, pp.3488-3496.
248. Kolmogorov, A.N. (1936) *Foundations of the Theory of Probability.* (Chelsea Publishing Company, New York).
249. Kuznetsov, V.P. (1991) *Interval Statistical Models.* (Radio I Svyaz Publ., Moscow) (in Russian).
250. Labreuche, C. and Grabisch, M. (2006). Generalized Choquet-like aggregation functions for handling bipolar scales, *Eur. J. of Oper. Res.*, 172, pp. 931-955.
251. Lai, J. and Xu, Y. (2010). Linguistic truth-valued lattice-valued propositional logic system *lP(X)* based on linguistic truth-valued lattice implication algebra, *Inform. Sciences, 180, Special Issue on Intelligent Distributed Information Systems,* pp. 1990-2002.
252. Lakemeyer, G. and Nebel, B. (1994). *Foundations of Knowledge Representation and Reasoning,* eds. Shoham, Y. and Cousins, S. B., "Logics of Mental Attitudes in AI: A Very Preliminary Survey," (Springer-Verlag, Berlin), pp. 296-309.
253. Lakshmikantham, V. and Mohapatra, R. (2003) *Theory of Fuzzy Differential Equations and Inclusions.* (Taylor and Francis, London, New York).
254. Landeta, J. (2006). Current validity of the Delphi method in social sciences, *Technological Forecasting and Social Change*, Vol. 73, No. 5, pp. 467-82.
255. Levy, P. (2010). From social computing to reflexive collective intelligence: The IEML research program, *Inform. Sciences, 180, Special Issue on Collective Intelligence*, pp. 71-94.
256. Li, D.-F. (2007). A fuzzy closeness approach to fuzzy multi-attribute decision making, *Fuzzy Optim. Decis. Ma.*, 6(3), pp. 237-254.
257. Li, D-F., Chen, G-H. and Huang, Z-G. (2010). Linear programming method for multiattribute group decision making using IF sets, *Inform. Sciences,* 180, pp. 1591-1609.
258. Lin, T. S., Yao, Y. Y. and Zadeh, L. A. (2002) *Data Mining, Rough Sets and Granular Computing.* (Physica-Verlag, Heidelberg).
259. Liu, P. and Wang, M. (2011). An extended VIKOR method for multiple attribute group decision making based on generalized interval-valued trapezoidal fuzzy numbers, *Sci. Res. Essays*, 6(4), pp. 766-776.
260. Liu, W. J., and Zeng, L. (2008). A new TOPSIS method for fuzzy multiple attribute group decision making problem, *J. Guilin Univ. Electron. Technol.*, 28(1), pp. 59-62.
261. Loia, V. (2002) *Soft Computing Agents: A New Perspective for Dynamic Information Systems*, eds. (IOS Press, Netherlands).
262. Long, Z., Liang, X. and Yang, L. (2010). Some approximation properties of adaptive fuzzy systems with variable universe of discourse, *Inform. Sciences,* 180, pp. 2991-3005.
263. Lowen, R. and Roubens, M. (1993) *Fuzzy Logic: State of the Art, Theory and Decision Library* **12**, eds. Fuller, R. and Zimmermann, H.-J., Chapter 19 "On Zadeh's compositional rule of inference," (Kluwer Academic Publisher,

Dordrecht), pp. 193-200.

264. Lü, E.-L. and Zhong, Y. M. (2003). Random variable with fuzzy probability. *Appl. Math. Mech.*, 24(4), pp. 491-498.
265. Lu, J., Zhang, G., Ruan, D. and Wu, F. (2007) *Multi-Objective Group Decision Making: Methods, Software and Applications with Fuzzy Set Techniques*. (Imperial College Press, London).
266. Luce, R. D., Bush, R. R. and Galanter, E. H. (1965) *Handbook of Mathematical Psychology*, eds. Luce, R. D. and Suppes, P. "Preferences, Utility and Subjective Probability," vol. III (Wiley, New York) pp. 249-410.
267. Luck, M. and d'Inverno, M. (1995). A formal framework for agency and autonomy, *Proc. 1st Int. Conf. on Multi-Agent Systems*, ICMAS, pp. 254-260.
268. Luck, M. and d'Inverno, M. (1996). Engagement and cooperation in motivated agent modeling, *Proc. 1st Australian Workshop on Distributed Artificial Intelligence*, pp. 70-84.
269. Ma, H. (2010). An analysis of the equilibrium of migration models for biogeography-based optimization, *Inform. Sciences,* 180, pp. 3444-3464.
270. Maccheroni, F., Marinacci, M. and Rustichini, A. (2005). Ambiguity aversion, robustness, and the variational representation of preferences, *Econometrica*, 74, pp. 1447-1498.
271. MacEachren, A. M. (1992). Visualizing uncertain information, *Cartographic Perspective*, 13 pp. 10-19.
272. Magni C. A., Malagoli S., and Mastroleo, G. (2006). An alternative approach to firms' evaluation: expert systems and fuzzy logic, *Int. J. Inf. Tech. Decis.,* 6, pp. 195-225.
273. Mamdani, E. H. (1977). Application of fuzzy logic to approximate reasoning using linguistic syntheses, *IEEE T. Comput.,* C-26(12), pp. 1182-1191.
274. Manski, C. F. (2001). Daniel McFadden and the econometric analysis of discrete choice, *Scand. J. Econ.*, vol. 103, No.2, pp. 217-229.
275. Mas, M., Monserrat, M. and Torrens, J. (2009). The law of importation for discrete implications, *Inform. Sciences,* 179, pp. 4208-4218.
276. Mas, M., Monserrat, M., Torrens, J. and Trillas, E. (2007). A survey on fuzzy implication functions, *IEEE T. Fuzzy Syst.*, 15(6), pp. 1107-1121.
277. Mathieu-Nicot, B. (1986). Fuzzy expected utility, *Fuzzy Set. Syst.*, 20(2), pp. 163-173.
278. Mayburov, S. (2004). Fuzzy geometry of space–time and quantum dynamics, *P. Steklov Inst. Math.*, 245, pp. 154-159.
279. Mayburov, S. (2008). Fuzzy geometry of phase space and quantization of massive fields, *J. Phys. A-Math. Theor.*, 41, pp. 1-10.
280. McCarthy, J. and Lifschitz, V. (1990) *Formalizing Common Sense: Papers.* (Ablex Publishing Group, New Jersey).
281. McFadden, D. and Train, K. (2000). Mixed MNL models of discrete response, *J. Appl. Econometr.*, 15, pp. 447-470.
282. McFadden, D.L. (2000) *Economic Choices. Nobel Prize Lecture.* http://www.nobelprize.org/nobel_prizes/economic-sciences/laureates/2000/mcfadden-lecture.pdf
283. Medina, J. and Ojeda-Aciego, M. (2010). Multi-adjoint t-concept lattices, *Inform. Sciences,* 180, pp. 712-725.

284. Melin, P. (2012). *Modular Neural Networks and Type-2 Fuzzy Systems for Pattern Recognition*. (Springer, Berlin).
285. Mendel, J. (2014) *Type-2 Fuzzy Logic Control: Introduction to Theory and Application,* (Wiley-IEEE Press, New-Jersey).
286. Mendel, J. and Dongrui, Wu. (2010) *Perceptual Computing: Aiding People in Making Subjective Judgments,* (Wiley-IEEE Press, New-Jersey).
287. Mendel, J. M. (2001). *Uncertain Rule-Based Fuzzy Logic Systems: Introduction and New Directions*, (Prentice-Hall, New Jersey).
288. Mendel, J. M. (2003). Fuzzy Sets for Words: a New Beginning, *Proc. 12th IEEE International Conference on Fuzzy Systems,* FUZZ, pp. 37-42.
289. Mendel, J. M. (2007). Advances in type-2 fuzzy sets and systems, *Inform. Sciences*, 177, pp. 84-110.
290. Mendel, J. M. (2007). Computing with words and its relationships with fuzzistics, *Inform. Sciences,* 179(8), pp. 988-1006.
291. Mendel, J. M. (2007). Type–2 fuzzy sets and systems, *IEEE Comput. Intell. M.*, vol. 2, no.1, pp. 20-29.
292. Mendel, J. M. (2009). On answering the question ''Where do I start in order to solve a new problem involving interval type-2 fuzzy sets?", *Inform. Sciences,* 179, pp. 3418-3431.
293. Mendel, J. M. and John, R. I. (2002). Type–2 fuzzy sets made simple, *IEEE T. Fuzzy Syst.*, no.2, vol. 10, pp. 117-127.
294. Mendel, J. M., Jhon, R. I. and Liu, F. (2006). Interval type–2 fuzzy logic systems made simple, *IEEE T. Fuzzy Syst.*, no. 6, vol. 14, pp. 808-821.
295. Meredith, J., Shafer, S. and Turban, E. (2002) *Quantitative Business Modeling.* (Thomson Learning, South-Western, USA).
296. Mesarovic, M. D., Macko, D. and Takahara, Y. (1972) *Theory of Hierarchical Multilevel Systems.* (Academic Press, New York, London).
297. Meyer, R. A. (2009). *Encyclopedia of Complexity and Systems Science,* eds. Zadeh, L. A. "Fuzzy Logic," (Springer, Berlin) pp. 3985-4009.
298. Mikhailov L., Didehkhani, H. and Sadi-Nezhad, S. (2011). Weighted prioritization models in the fuzzy analytic hierarchy process, *Int. J. Inf. Tech. Decis.*, 10(4), pp. 681-694.
299. Miyamoto, J. M. and Wakker, P. (1996). Multiattribute utility theory without expected utility foundations, *Oper. Res.*, Vol. 44, No. 2, pp. 313-326.
300. Mizumoto, M. (1982). Fuzzy conditional inference under max-composition, *Inform. Sciences,*27, pp. 183-209.
301. Mizumoto, M. and Zimmermann, H.-J. (1982). Comparison of fuzzy reasoning methods, *Fuzzy Set. Syst.*, 8, pp. 253-283.
302. Modave, F., Grabisch, M., Dubois, D. and Prade, H. (1997). A Choquet integral representation in multicriteria decision making, *Technical Report of the Fall Symposium of Association for the Advancement of Artificial Intelligence,* AAAI, pp. 22-29.
303. Molai, A. A. and Khorram, E. (2008). An algorithm for solving fuzzy relation equations with max-T composition operator, *Inform. Sciences,* 178, pp. 1293-1308.
304. Mordeson, J. N. and Nair, P. S. (2001) *Fuzzy Mathematics: an Introduction for Engineers and Scientists* (Springer Physica-Verlag, Heidelberg).
305. Mueller, E. (2006) *Commonsense Reasoning.* (Morgan Kaufmann, San Francisco, CA).

306. Muller, J. P., Wooldridge, M. J. and Jennings, N.R. (1997). Is it an agent, or just a program?: A taxonomy for autonomous agents, *Proc. Intelligent Agents III: Agent Theories, Architectures, and Languages,* ECAI, (Springer-Verlag, Berlin, Germany) pp. 21-35.
307. Munoz-Hernandez, S., Pablos-Ceruelo, V. and Strass, H. (2011). RFuzzy: Syntax, semantics and implementation details of a simple and expressive fuzzy tool over Prolog, *Inform. Sciences,* 181(10), pp. 1951-1970.
308. Murofushi, T. (2005). Semiatoms in Choquet integral models of multiattribute decision making, *J. Adv. Comput. Intell. Intell. Informat.*, 9(5), pp. 477-483.
309. Musayev, A. F., Alizadeh, A. V., Guirimov, B. G. and Huseynov, O. H. (2009). Computational framework for the method of decision making with imprecise probabilities, *Proc. 5th Int. Conf. on Soft Comp. and Comp. with Words in Syst. Anal., Decis. and Control,* ICSCCW, pp. 287-290.
310. Nachtegael, M., Sussner, P., Melange, T. and Kerre, E. E. (2011). On the role of complete lattices in mathematical morphology: From tool to uncertainty model, *Inform. Sciences,*181(10), pp. 1971-1988.
311. Nanda, S. (1991). Fuzzy linear spaces over valued fields, *Fuzzy Set. Syst.*, 42(3), pp. 351-354.
312. Nau, R. (2006). The shape of incomplete preferences, *Ann. Stat.*, 34, pp. 2430-2448.
313. Nau, R. F. (1992). Indeterminate probabilities on finite sets, *Ann. Stat.,* 20, pp. 1737-1767.
314. Nazari-Shirkouhi, S., Ansarinejad, A., Miri-Nargesi, SS., Majazi Dalfard, V. and Rezaie, K. (2011). Information systems outsourcing decisions under fuzzy group decision making approach, *Int. J. Inf. Tech. Decis.,* 10(6), pp. 989-1022.
315. Neilson, W. and Stowe, J. (2002). A further examination of cumulative prospect theory parameterizations, *The J. Risk Uncertainty*, 24(1), pp. 31-46.
316. Newell, A. (1981). The knowledge level, *AI Mag.,* 2(2), pp. 1-20.
317. Nguyen, H. T. and Walker, E. A. (1996). *A First Course in Fuzzy Logic,* (CRC Press, Boca Raton).
318. Nobre, F. S., Tobias A. M., and Walker, D. S. (2009). The impact of cognitive machines on complex decisions and organizational change, *AI & Society*, 24, pp. 365-381.
319. Noguera, C., Esteva, F. and Godo, L. (2010). Generalized continuous and left-continuous t-norms arising from algebraic semantics for fuzzy logics, *Inform. Sciences,* 180, pp. 1354-1372.
320. Nwana, H. S. and Azarmi, N. (1997) *Software Agents and Soft Computing*, eds. Nwana, H. S. and Ndumu, D. T., Chapter 1 "An Introduction to Agent Technology," (Springer-Verlag, Berlin, Germany) pp. 3-26.
321. O, Y-L, Toet, A., Foster, D. H., Heijmans, H.J.A.M. and Meer, P. (1994). *Shape in Picture. Mathematical Description of Shape in Grey-level Images* **126**, eds. Ferraro, M. and Foster, D. H., Elements of a fuzzy geometry for visual space. (Springer-Verlag, Berlin), pp. 333-342.
322. Oh, K.-W. and Bandler, W. (1987). Properties of fuzzy implication operators, *Int. J. Approx. Reason.*, 1(3), pp. 273-285.
323. O'Hagan, A., Caitlin, E. B., Daneshkhah, A., Eiser, J. R., Garthwaite, P. H., Jenkinson, D. J., Oakley, J. E. and Rakow, T. (2006) *Uncertain Judgments: Eliciting Experts' Probabilities* (Wiley).

324. Ok, E. A. (2002). Utility representation of an incomplete preference relation, *J. Econ. Theory*, 104, pp. 429-449.
325. Opricovic, S. and Tzeng, G. H. (2004). Compromise solution by MCDM methods: a comparative analysis of VIKOR and TOPSIS, *Eur. J. Operat. Res.*, 156(2), pp. 445-455.
326. Opricovic, S. and Tzeng, G. H. (2007). Extended VIKOR method in comparison with outranking methods, *Eur. J. Operat. Res.*, 178(2), pp. 514-529.
327. Ouyang, Y., Wang, Z. and Zhang, H. (2010). On fuzzy rough sets based on tolerance relations, *Inform. Sciences,* 180, pp. 532.
328. Ovchinnikov, S. (1991). On fuzzy preference relations, *Int. J. Intell. Syst.*, 6, pp. 225-234.
329. Paolo, P. *Cumulative prospect theory and second order stochastic dominance criteria: an application to mutual funds performance,* Working paper. http://caronte.dma.unive.it/~pianca/sigi/dispense/ncwdomina.pdf
330. Park, J. H., Cho, H. J. and Kwun, Y. C. (2011). Extension of the VIKOR method for group decision making with interval-valued intuitionistic fuzzy information, *Fuzzy Optim. Decis. Ma.*, 10(3), pp. 233-253.
331. Pavelka, J. (1979). On fuzzy logic I, II, III, *Z. Math. Logik*, 25, pp. 45-52, 119-134, 447-464.
332. Pedrycz, W. and Chen S.-M. (2011). *Granular Computing and Intelligent Systems*, eds. Aliev, R. A., Pedrycz, W., Huseynov, O. H. and Zeinalova, L. M., Chapter 7 "Decision Making with Second Order Information Granules," (Springer-Verlag, Berlin, Heidelberg) pp. 117-153.
333. Pedrycz, W. and Gomide, F. (2007) *Fuzzy Systems Engineering: Toward Human-Centric Computing,* (John Wiley & Sons, Hoboken).
334. Pedrycz, W. and Peters, J. F. (1998) *Computational Intelligence in Software Engineering*, (World Scientific, Singapore).
335. Pedrycz, W., Skowron, A. and Kreinovich, V., (2008) *Handbook of Granular Computing,* eds. Mendel, J. M., Chapter 25 "On Type–2 Fuzzy Sets as Granular Models for Words," (Wiley, England) pp. 553-574.
336. Pei, D. (2008), Unified full implication algorithms of fuzzy reasoning, *Inform. Sciences,* 178, 520 p.
337. Pena, J. P-P. and Piggins, A. (2007). Strategy-proof fuzzy aggregation rules, *J. Math. Econ.,* 43, pp. 564-580.
338. Piasecki, K. (1986). On the Bayes formula for fuzzy probability measures, *Fuzzy Set. Syst.*, 18(2), pp. 183-185.
339. Poston, T.(1971). *Fuzzy Geometry*. Ph.D. Thesis, University of Warwick.
340. Pytyev, Y. P. (2000) *Possibility. Elements of Theory and Practice.* (Editorial URSS Moscow) (in Russian).
341. Quiggin, J. (1982). A theory of anticipated utility, *J. Econ. Behav. Organ.*, 3, pp. 323-343.
342. Ramík, J., and Korviny, P. (2010). Inconsistency of pair-wise comparison matrix with fuzzy elements based on geometric mean, *Fuzzy Set. Syst.,* 161, pp. 1604-1613.
343. Rao, A. S. and Georgeff, M. P. (2010). Trader species with different decision strategies and price dynamics in financial markets: an agent-based modeling perspective, *Int. J. Inf. Tech. Decis.,* 9(2), pp. 327-344.
344. Rescher, N. (1969) *Many-Valued Logic*. (McGraw-Hill, New York).

345. Riera, J. V. and Torrens, J. (2013). Residual implications on the set of discrete fuzzy numbers, *Inform. Sciences*, 247, pp. 131-143.
346. Rigotti, R. and Shannon, C. (2005). Uncertainty and risk in financial markets, *Econometrica,* 73, pp. 203-243.
347. Roe, J. (1996). Index theory, coarse geometry, and topology of manifolds, *Proc. Regional Conf. Ser. in Mathematics, the American Mathematical Society,* CBMS.
348. Roger, M. (1991) *Cooke Experts in Uncertainty: Opinion and Subjective Probability in Science* (Oxford University Press, New York).
349. Rosenfeld, A. (1984). The diameter of a fuzzy set, *Fuzzy Set. Syst.,* 13, pp. 241-246.
350. Rosenfeld, A. (1985). Distances between fuzzy sets, *Pattern Recogn. Lett.,* 3(4), pp. 229-233.
351. Rosenfeld, A. (1990). Fuzzy rectangles, *Pattern Recogn. Lett.,* 11(10), pp. 677-679.
352. Rosenfeld, A. (1994). Fuzzy plane geometry: triangles, *Pattern Recogn. Lett.,* 15, pp. 1261-1264.
353. Rosenfeld, A. (1998). Fuzzy geometry: an updated overview, *Inform. Science,* 110 (3-4), pp. 127-133.
354. Roy, B. (1996) *Multicriteria Methodology for Decision Aiding.* (Kluwer Academic Publishers, Dordrecht).
355. Roy, B. and Berlier, B. (1972). La Metode ELECTRE II. *Sixieme Conf. Internationale de rechearche operationelle.*
356. Ruan, Da. (2010). *Computational Intelligence in Complex Decision Systems,* (Atlantis Press, World Scientific, Amsterdam-Paris).
357. Rutkowski, L. and Cpalka, K. (2003). Flexible neuro-fuzzy systems, *IEEE T. Neural Networ.,* 14(3), pp. 554-573.
358. Sadeghian, A., Mendel, J. M. and Tahayori, H. (2013). *Advances in Type–2 Fuzzy Sets and Systems. Theory and Applications*. (Springer, New York).
359. Sankar, K. P. and Ghosh, A. (1992). Fuzzy geometry in image analysis, *Fuzzy Set. Syst.,* 48, pp. 23-40.
360. Savage, L. J. (1954) *The Foundations of Statistics*, (Wiley, New York).
361. Schmeidler, D. (1986). Integral representation without additivity, *P. Am. Math. Soc.*, 97(2), pp. 255-261.
362. Schmeidler, D. (1989). Subjective probability and expected utility without additivity, *Econometrita,* 57(3), pp. 571-587.
363. Schockaert, S., De Cock, M. and Kerre, E. (2008). Modeling nearness and cardinal directions between fuzzy regions, *Proc. of the IEEE World Congress on Computational Intelligence,* FUZZ-IEEE, pp. 1548-1555.
364. Segal, U. (1987). The Ellsberg paradox and risk aversion: An anticipated utility approach, *Int. Econ. Rev.*, 28, 175-202.
365. Seizing, R. and Gonzalez, V. S. (2012) *Soft Computing and Humanities in Social Sciences* **273**, eds. Casasnovas, J. and Riera, J.V., Chapter 18 "Weighted means of subjective evaluations," STUDFUZZ, (Springer, Berlin, Heidelberg), pp. 323-345.
366. Seo, K. (2009) Ambiguity and second-order belief, *Econometrica*, 77(5), pp. 1575-1605.
367. Serruier, M., Dubois, D., Prade, H. and Sudkamp, T. (2007). Learning fuzzy rules with their implication operator, *Data Knowl. Eng.*, 60, pp. 71-89.

368. Setnes, M. (1997). Compatibility-based ranking of fuzzy numbers, *Annual Meeting of the North American Fuzzy Information Processing Society,* NAFIPS, pp. 305-310.
369. Shafer, G. A. (1976) *Mathematical Theory of Evidence.* (Princeton University Press, New Jersey).
370. Shieh, B.-S. (2008). Infinite fuzzy relation equations with continuous t-norms, *Inform. Sciences,* 178, pp. 1961-1967.
371. Shoham, Y. (2006). BSV investors versus rational investors: an agent-based computational finance model, *Int. J. Inf. Tech. Decis.,* 5(3), pp. 455-466.
372. Shortliffe, E. H. (1976) *Computer-Based Medical Consultations*: *MYCIN*, eds. (American Elsevier, New York).
373. Simon, H. (1997) *Models of Bounded Rationality: Empirically Grounded Economic Reason* (MIT Press, MA, Cambridge).
374. Small, K. A. and Rosen, H. S. (1981). Applied welfare economics with discrete choice models, *Econometrica*, vol. 49, no. 1, pp. 105-130.
375. Smets, P. Imperfect information: Imprecision – Uncertainty. http://sites.poli.usp.br/d/pmr5406/Download/papers/Imperfect_Data.pdf
376. Stigler, G. (1965) *Essays in the History of Economics.* (University of Chicago Press, Chicago).
377. Su, Z.-X. (2011). A hybrid fuzzy approach to fuzzy multi-attribute group decision-making, *Int. J. Inf. Tech. Decis.,* 10(4), pp. 695-711.
378. Tadayon, S. and Tadayon, B. (2012). Approximate Z-number evaluation based on categorical sets of probability distributions, *Proc. 2nd World Conf. on Soft Computing*, WConSC.
379. Talasova, J. and Pavlacka, O. (2006), Fuzzy probability spaces and their applications in decision making, *Aujstat*, 35(2 and 3), pp. 347-356.
380. Thomaidis, N. S., Nikitakos, N. and Dounias, G. D. (2006). The evaluation of information technology projects: a fuzzy multicriteria decision-making approach, *J. Adv. Comput. Intell. Intell. Informat.,* 5(1) pp. 89-122.
381. Thorani, Y. L. P., Rao, P.P.B. and Shankar, N. R. (2012). Ordering generalized trapezoidal fuzzy numbers using orthocentre of centroids, *Int. J. Algebra*, no.22, vol.6, pp. 1069-1085.
382. Toulmin, S. (2003) *The Uses of Argument.* (Cambridge University Press, UK).
383. Troffaes, M. C. M. (2003). Uncertainty and conflict: A behavioral approach to the aggregation of expert opinions, *Proc. 6th Workshop on Uncertainty Processing*, WUPES, pp. 263-277.
384. Troffaes, M. C. M. (2007). Decision making under uncertainty using imprecise probabilities, *Int. J. Approx. Reason.*, 45(1), pp 17-29.
385. Tsuji, T., Jazidie, A. and Kaneko, M. (1997). Distributed trajectory generation for cooperative multi-arm robots via virtual force interactions, *IEEE T. Syst. Man. CY. B.: Cybernetics*, 27(5), pp.862-867.
386. Tsukamoto, Y. (1972). Identification of preference measure by means of fuzzy integrals. *Ann. Conf. of JORS*, pp. 131-135.
387. Tversky, A. and Kahneman, D. (1992). Advances in Prospect theory: Cumulative Representation of Uncertainty, *J. Risk Uncertainty,*5(4), pp. 297-323.
388. Utkin, L. V. (2003). A second-order uncertainty model for the calculation of the interval reliability, *Reliab. Eng. Syst. Safe.*, 79(3), pp. 341-351.

389. Utkin, L. V. (2003). A second-order uncertainty model of independent random variables: An example of the stress-strength reliability, *Proc. 3rd Int. Symposium on Imprecise Probabilities and Their Applications*, ISIPTA, pp. 530-544.
390. Utkin, L. V. (2003). Imprecise second-order hierarchical uncertainty model, *Int. J. Uncertain Fuzz.*, 11(3), pp. 301-317.
391. Utkin, L. V. (2004). Belief function and the imprecise Dirichlet model, *Proc. of the Int. Conf. on Fuzzy Sets and Soft Computing in Economics and Finance*, pp. 178-185.
392. Utkin, L. V. (2005). Imprecise second-order uncertainty model for a system of independent random variables, *Int. J. Uncertain Fuzz.*, 13(2) pp. 177-194.
393. Utkin, L. V. (2007) *Risk Analysis and Decision Making under Incomplete Information* (Nauka, St. Petersburg) (in Russian).
394. Vahdani, B. and Zandieh, M. (2010). Selecting suppliers using a new fuzzy multiple criteria decision model: the fuzzy balancing and ranking method, *Int. J. Prod. Res.*, 48(18), pp. 5307-5326.
395. Valle, M. E. (2010). Permutation-based finite implicative fuzzy associative memories, *Inform. Sciences,* 180, pp. 4136-4152.
396. Valverde-Albacete, F. J. and Pelaez-Moreno, C. (2011). Extending conceptualization modes for generalized formal concept analysis, *Inform. Sciences,*181(10), pp. 1888-1909.
397. von Neumann, J. and Morgenstern, O. (1944) *Theory of Games and Economic Behaviour* (Princeton University Press, USA).
398. Wakker, P. P., and Zank, H. (1999). State dependent expected utility for Savage's state space, *Math. Oper. Res.*, 24(1), pp. 8-34.
399. Walley, P. (1991). *Statistical Reasoning with Imprecise Probabilities* (Chapman and Hall, London).
400. Walley, P. (1996). Measures of uncertainty in expert systems, *Artif. Intell.,* 83(1) pp. 1-58.
401. Walley, P. (1997). Statistical inferences based on a second-order possibility distribution, *Int. J. Gen. Syst.*, 9, pp. 337-383.
402. Walley, P. (2000). Towards a unified theory of imprecise probability, *Int. J. Approx. Reason.*, 24, pp. 125-148.
403. Walley, P. and De Cooman, G. (2001). A behavioral model for linguistic uncertainty, *Inform. Sciences,* 134(1-4), pp. 1-37.
404. Wang, G. and Li, X. (1999) On the convergence of the fuzzy valued functional defined by μ-integrable fuzzy valued functions, *Fuzzy Set. Syst.*, 107(2), pp. 219-226.
405. Wang, P. P. and Chang, S. K. (1980). *Fuzzy Sets: Theory and Applications to Policy Analysis and Information Systems*, eds. Bandler, W., and Kohout, L. J. Chapter 5 "Fuzzy Relational Products as a Tool for Analysis of Complex Artificial and Natural Systems," (Plenum Press, New York) pp. 341-367.
406. Wang, T. (2003). A class of multi-prior preferences, Discussion paper, Mimeo, *University British Columbia.* *http://citeseerx.ist.psu.edu/viewdoc/download?doi=10.1.1.197.9509&rep=rep1&type=pdf*
407. Wang, T.-C. and Chen, Y.-H. (2008). Applying fuzzy linguistic preference relations to the improvement of consistency of fuzzy AHP, *Inform. Sciences,* 78(19), pp. 3755-3765.

408. Wang, Y. M. and Elhag, T. M. S. (2006). Fuzzy TOPSIS method based on alpha level sets with an application to bridge risk assessment, *Expert Syst. Appl.*, 31(2), pp. 309-319.
409. Wang, Z. and Wang, W. (1995). Extension of lower probabilities and coherence of belief measures, *Lect. Notes Comput. Sc.*, 945, pp. 62-69.
410. Weichselberger, K. (2000) The theory of interval probability as a unifying concept for uncertainty, *Int. J. Approx. Reason.*, 24, pp. 149-170.
411. Weirich, P. (2004) *Realistic Decision Theory: Rules for Nonideal Agents in Nonideal Circumstances,* (Oxford University Press, New York).
412. Wenstøp, F. (1980). Quantitative analysis with linguistic values, *Fuzzy Set. Syst.*, 4(2), pp. 99-115.
413. Werthner, H. (1994) *Qualitative Reasoning, Modeling and the Generation of Behavior* (Springer-Verlag, Wien, New York).
414. Whinston, A. (1997). Intelligent agents as a basis for decision support systems, *Decis. Support. Syst.*, 20(1), pp. 1-2.
415. Wilke, G. (2009). Approximate geometric reasoning with extended geographic objects, *Proc. of the Workshop on Quality, Scale and Analysis Aspects of City Models* http://www.isprs.org/Proc./XXXVIII/2W11/Wilke.pdf
416. Wilke, G. and Frank, A.U. (2010). On equality of lines with positional uncertainty (Ext. Abstract), *Proc. 6th Int. Conference on Geographic Information Science*, GIScience, http://www.giscience2010.org/pdfs/paper_180.pdf
417. Williamson, R. C. (1989). *Probabilistic Arithmetic.* Ph.D. dissertation, University of Queensland, Australia, http://theorem.anu.edu.au/~williams/papers/thesis 300
418. Wilson, A.(2004). Bounded memory and biases in information processing, *NAJ Economics,* 5.
419. Wise, B.P. and Henrion, M. (1985) A framework for comparing uncertain inference systems to probability, *Proc. 1st Annual Conf. on Uncertainty in Artificial Intelligence*, UAI, pp. 69-83.
420. Wooldridge, M. and Jennings, N. R. (1995). Agents theories, architectures, and languages: a survey, *Proc. of the Workshop on Agent Theories, Architectures, and Languages*, ECAI, pp. 1-39.
421. Wu, G. and Markle, A. B. (2008). An empirical test of gain-loss separability in prospect theory, *Manage. Sci.,* vol. 54, no. 7, pp. 1322-1335.
422. Xie, A. and Qin, F. (2012). Solutions to the functional equation I(x, y) = I(x, I(x, y)) for three types of fuzzy implications derived from uninorms, *Inform. Sciences,* 186(1), pp. 209-221.
423. Xu, Y., Liu, J., Ruan, D. and Li, X. (2010). Determination of [alpha]-resolution in lattice-valued first-order logic LF(X), *Inform. Sciences,*181(10), pp. 1836-1862.
424. Yaari, M. E. (1987). The dual theory of choice under risk. *Econometrica,*Vol. 55, No. 1, pp. 95-115.
425. Yager, R. R. (1998). On measures of specificity, *Proc. Computational Intelligence: Soft Computing and Fuzzy-Neuro Integration with Applications*, pp. 94-113.
426. Yager, R. R. (1999). Decision making with fuzzy probability assessments, *IEEE T. Fuzzy Syst.*, vol.7, no.4, pp. 462-467.
427. Yager, R. R. (1999). On global requirements for implication operators in fuzzy modus ponens, *Fuzzy Set. Syst.*, 106, pp. 3-10.

428. Yager, R. R. (2008). Human behavioral modeling using fuzzy and Dempster–Shafer theory, *Proc. 1st International Workshop on Social Computing, Behavioral Modeling, and Prediction*, SBP, pp. 89-99.
429. Yager, R. R. (2010). A framework for reasoning with soft information, *Inform. Sciences,* vol. 180, Issue 8, pp. 1390-1406.
430. Yager, R. R. (2012). On a view of Zadeh's Z-numbers, *J. Adv. Comput. Intell. Informat.*, 299, pp. 90-101.
431. Yager, R. R. (2012). On Z-valuations using Zadeh's Z-numbers, *Int. J. Intell. Syst.*, 27, pp. 259-278.
432. Yager, R. R. and Filev, D. P. (1994) *Essentials of Fuzzy Modeling and Control*, (John Wiley & Sons, New York).
433. Yang, R., Wang, Z., Heng, P.-A. and Leung, K.-S. (2005). Fuzzy numbers and fuzzification of the Choquet integral, *Fuzzy Set. Syst.* 153(1), pp. 95-113.
434. Yoon, K. (1987). A reconciliation among discrete compromise solutions, *J. of Operat. Res. Soc.*, 38(3), pp. 272-286.
435. Zadeh, L. A. (1965). Fuzzy Sets, *Inform. Control,* 8, pp. 338-353.
436. Zadeh, L. A. (1968). Probability measures of fuzzy events, *J. Math. Anal. Appl.*, 23(2), pp. 421-427.
437. Zadeh, L. A. (1971). Fuzzy orderings, *Inform. Sciences,* 3, pp. 117-200.
438. Zadeh, L. A. (1971). Similarity relations and fuzzy orderings, *Inform. Sciences,* 3, pp. 177-200.
439. Zadeh, L. A. (1973). Outline of a new approach to the analysis of complex system and decision processes, *IEEE T. Syst. Man. Cyb.*3, pp. 28-44.
440. Zadeh, L. A. (1975). The concept of a linguistic variable and its applications in approximate reasoning, *Inform. Sciences,* 8, pp.43-80, pp. 301-357; 9, pp. 199-251.
441. Zadeh, L. A. (1978). Fuzzy sets as a basis for a theory of possibility, *Fuzzy Set. Syst.*, 1, pp. 3-28.
442. Zadeh, L. A. (1988). Fuzzy logic, *IEEE Computer*, 21 (4), pp. 83-93.
443. Zadeh, L. A. (1996). Fuzzy logic = computing with words, *IEEE T. Fuzzy Syst.*, 4(2), pp. 103-111.
444. Zadeh, L. A. (1997). Toward a theory of fuzzy information granulation and its centrality in human reasoning and fuzzy logic, *Fuzzy Set. Syst.*, 90(2), pp. 111-127.
445. Zadeh, L. A. (1999). From computing with numbers to computing with words – from manipulation of measurements to manipulation with perceptions, *IEEE T. Circuits-I*, 45(1), pp. 105-119.
446. Zadeh, L. A. (2001). A new direction in AI — toward a computational theory of perceptions, *AI Mag.*, 22(1), pp. 73-84.
447. Zadeh, L. A. (2004). A note on web intelligence, world knowledge and fuzzy logic, *Data Knowl. Eng.*, 50, pp. 291-304.
448. Zadeh, L. A. (2005). Toward a generalized theory of uncertainty — an outline, *Inform. Sciences,* 172, pp. 1-40.
449. Zadeh, L. A. (2006). Generalized theory of uncertainty (GTU) – principal concepts and ideas, *Comput. Stat. Data An.,* 51, pp. 15-46.
450. Zadeh, L. A. (2008). Computation with imprecise probabilities, *Proc. of the 8th Int. Conf. on Appl. of Fuzzy Syst. and Soft Comp.,* ICAFS, pp. 1-3.
451. Zadeh, L. A. (2008). Is there a need for fuzzy logic? *Inform. Sciences,* 178, pp. 2751-2779.

452. Zadeh, L. A. (2009). Computing with words and perceptions—a paradigm shift. *Proc. of the IEEE International Conf. on Information Reuse and Integration,* pp. 450-452.
453. Zadeh, L. A. (2009). Toward extended fuzzy logic. A first step, *Fuzzy Set. Syst.*, 160, pp. 3175-3181.
454. Zadeh, L. A. (2010). A note on Z-numbers, *Inform. Sciences,* 181, pp. 2923-2932.
455. Zadeh, L. A. (2011). The concept of a Z-number - A new direction in uncertain computation, *Proc. of the IEEE International Conference on Information Reuse and Integration*, IRI, pp. xxii-xxiii.
456. Zadeh, L. A. (2012). *Methods and Systems for Applications with Z-Numbers,* United States Patent, Patent No.: US 8,311,973 B1, Date of Patent: Nov. 13, 2012
457. Zadeh, L. A. (2013). Toward a restriction-centered theory of truth and meaning (RCT), *Inform. Sciences*, Vol. 248, 1, pp. 1-14.
458. Zadeh, L. A., Aliev, R. A., Fazlollahi, B., Alizadeh, A. V., Guirimov, B. G., and Huseynov, O. H. (2009). Decision Theory with Imprecise Probabilities, *Contract on, Application of Fuzzy Logic and Soft Computing to Communications, Planning and Management of Uncertainty. Berkeley, Baku,* 95 p., www.raliev.com/report.pdf
459. Zadeh, L. A., Fu, K. S. and Shimura, M. A. (1975) *Fuzzy Sets and Their Applications to cognitive and Decision Processes*, eds. Yeh, R. T. and Bang, S. Y., "Fuzzy Relations, Fuzzy Graphs, and Their Applications to Clustering Analysis," (Academic Press, New York) pp. 125-149.
460. Zahedi, F. (1986). Group consensus function estimation when preferences are uncertain, *Oper. Res.*, Vol. 34, Issue 6, pp. 883-894.
461. Zamri, N., Abdullah, L., Hitam, M.S., Noor, M., Maizura, N. and Jusoh, A. (2013). A novel hybrid fuzzy weighted average for MCDM with interval triangular type-2 fuzzy sets, *WSEAS Transactions on Systems*, Issue 4, vol.12, pp. 212-228.
462. Zeleny, M. (1982) *Multiple Criteria Decision Making.* (McGraw-Hill, New York).
463. Zhai, D. and Mendel, J. (2011). Uncertainty measures for general type-2 fuzzy sets, *Inform. Sciences*, 181(3), pp. 503-518.
464. Zhang, C. (1992). Cooperation under uncertainty in distributed expert systems, *Artif. Intell.*, 56, pp. 21-69.
465. Zhang, G-Q. (1992). Fuzzy number-valued fuzzy measure and fuzzy number-valued fuzzy integral on the fuzzy set, *Fuzzy Set. Syst.*, 49, pp. 357-376.
466. Zhang, J. and Yang, X. (2010). Some properties of fuzzy reasoning in propositional fuzzy logic systems, *Inform. Sciences,* 180, pp. 4661-4671.
467. Zhang, X., Yao, Y. and Yu, H. (2010). Rough implication operator based on strong topological rough algebras, *Inform. Sciences,* 180, pp. 3764-3780.
468. Zhao, S. and Tsang, E. C. C. (2008). On fuzzy approximation operators in attribute reduction with fuzzy rough sets, *Inform. Sciences,* 178, pp. 3163-3176.
469. Zhu, H. P., Zhang, G. J., and Shao, X. Y. (2007). Study on the application of fuzzy TOPSIS to multiple criteria group decision making problem, *Ind. Eng. Manage.*, 1, pp. 99-102.
470. Zimmermann, H. J. (1996) *Fuzzy Set Theory and Its Applications*, 3rd Ed. (Kluwer Academic Publishers, USA).

Index

F

G

H

I

Printed in the United States
By Bookmasters